RR AMERICAN INDIANS

AMERICAN INDIANS

Volume II
Headdresses – Pueblo tribes, Eastern

A Magill Book
from the **Editors of Salem Press**

Consulting Editor
Harvey Markowitz
**D'Arcy McNickle Center for the History
of the American Indian, Newberry Library**

Salem Press, Inc.
Pasadena, California   Englewood Cliffs, New Jersey

Editor in Chief: Dawn P. Dawson   *Senior Editor:* Chris Moose
Consulting Editor: Harvey Markowitz   *Project Editor:* McCrea Adams
Research Supervisor: Jeff Jensen   *Photograph Editor:* Valerie Krein
Proofreading Supervisor: Yasmine A. Cordoba   *Production Editor:* Janet Long
Layout: James Hutson   *Illustrations:* Craig Attebery
Maps: Moritz Design

Library of Congress Cataloging-in-Publication Data
American Indians / consulting editor, Harvey Markowitz
   p. cm. — (Ready reference)
"A Magill Book"
Includes bibliographical references and index.
ISBN 0-89356-757-4 (set : alk. paper) — ISBN 0-89356-759-0 (vol 2 : alk. paper)
  1. Indians of North America—Encyclopedias. 2. Indians of Mexico—Encyclopedias. I. Markowitz, Harvey.
II. Series.
E76.2.A45   1995
970.004'97—dc20

94-47633
CIP

Second Printing

PRINTED IN THE UNITED STATES OF AMERICA

CONTENTS

ALPHABETICAL LIST OF ENTRIES

Volume I

Volume II

Volume III

RR American Indians

Headdresses

TRIBES AFFECTED: Pantribal

SIGNIFICANCE: A symbol of tribal or clan affiliation and of connection to specific spiritual powers, the headdress indicated status and wealth of the wearer and suggested the response appropriate from others

Headdresses were worn as the spirits guided or as honors were bestowed. Everyday head coverings were artfully made, but practical. For ceremonial headdresses, however, there were no limits. All available materials were used: fur, fabric, leather, wood, metal, and bone. Decorations and adornments included feathers, beads, quills, stones, shells, and various metals. The simplest headdress was a single eagle feather, a symbol of status among the Plains people. The brave became a warrior after his first killing of an enemy and was permitted to wear the feather. The familiar fillet headband of fabric, fur, or leather was often beaded or quilled. It also took the form of braids of sweetgrass or crowns of cottonwood leaves or sage.

Eastern Woodlands. A bear claw on a headband held power for dancers; others might dance in a whole bearskin, head and all. The ceremonial crowns of Algonquian men had dozens of turkey feathers fastened only at the quill-tips so that they were kept in motion as the wearer moved. The Seneca used a deerskin cap lined with woven willow twigs for protection in battle. For ceremonies a silver headband was worn with a large bunch of feathers on top. In the Ojibwa Midewiwin (Grand Medicine Society), a headband with upright eagle feathers was used in healing rites.

Southeast. Fur or deerskin headdresses trimmed with heron feathers were favored in the Southeast. At the Green Corn Ceremony the Creek chief wore a duckskin headdress. Warriors and chiefs had wampum or quill-decorated fillets with crane or heron feathers fastened at center front. The Hopewell shaman performed a burial ceremony in a hood made of a human skull trimmed with deer hide fringe and human hair tassels. Shamans-in-training often had a stuffed owl perched on their heads.

Plains. The ceremonial war bonnet of the Plains chiefs had a beaded headband, ermine tails, many eagle feathers slanted back, and more eagle feathers forming a trailer. At times one or two eagle feathers designated warriors or chiefs, such as Sitting Bull and Red Cloud, who had also earned the right to wear the full war bonnet.

The majestic buffalo horn headdress had a cap of buffalo fur, beaded headband, ermine tails, buffalo horns, and a trailer of eagle feathers. Four Bears, a Mandan chief, had a buffalo-horn and eagle-feather bonnet. A red wooden knife fastened through the cap indicated that he had killed with such a weapon.

Men of the Hidatsa Dog Society wore a headdress with a huge spray of magpie feathers, a fan of large upright turkey feathers at the back of the head, and one eagle plume at the crown. Cheyenne and Oto men wore wide headbands of fur decorated with feathers, beaded medallions, or small mirrors. Some Crow warriors perched a full stuffed crow at the back of their heads.

The Pawnee warrior made a striking image with his partly shaved head painted red and topped with a red roach of deer-tail hairs and an upright eagle feather. Sometimes on the Plains a full grizzly bearskin was used with the bear's head as a helmet or with the snout upright.

Southwest. Apache men wore braids of yucca fibers or a folded bandanna. The mountain spirits (Gans) danced in black hoods with turquoise or shell ornaments. Red scarves covered their faces. They wore long horns of yucca or a 2-foot-high wooden slat frame, decorated with powerful symbols. Women in the Corn Dance wore the spectacular "tablita," a large, brightly painted wooden headdress, while men danced with a bunch of small red-dyed feathers on top of their heads.

The Pueblo Deer Dance headdress was made of spruce boughs and deer antlers trimmed with feathers. Hopi men tied their headbands of red cloth, leaving the ends hanging down. For ceremonies, the Snake priest wore a large spray of feathers. In the Southwest Yaqui Deer Dance, the headdress was an actual deer head with red scarves wrapped around its antlers. It was tied upright on the dancer's head over a white scarf.

California. The woodpecker's bright red feathers were prized by the Hupa. Their men's Jumping Dance headdress had more than fifty red woodpecker scalps on a white fur band. The Pomo used orange and black flicker feathers to decorate similar headbands. An elder in the Hupa Jumping Dance had a crown of sea lion teeth. The finely woven basket hat of Hupa women was decorated with painted images. The California Kuksu Cult dancers wore enormous headdresses of feathers and long willow sticks. A trailer of yellow woodpecker feathers swayed as they danced.

Northwest. The young Northwest Coast bride proclaimed her family's wealth with a headdress of thousands of slender dentalium shells, glass beads, and Chinese coins, so long it touched the ground. Kwakiutl people wove basket hats with wide brims and conical tops, trimmed with copper and disk-shaped shells. The Nootka conical hat was waterproof, woven of spruce roots, and painted with stylized animal images. A headdress of long upright feathers was the symbol of power for the Nootka female shaman. Impressive Haida dance headdresses featured the clan animal crest of carved wood trimmed with ermine tails, feathers, and sea lion whiskers. The Kwakiutl dance crest was surrounded by swansdown and feathers and topped with long splints of whalebone.

Tlingit people carved a full-head battle helmet of wood. Their shaman's spirit mask worn on the forehead held a small carved wood face trimmed with feathers and white down. The Tlingit chief's woven hat had a tall cone with rings declaring the number of potlatches he had sponsored.

Arctic. The Aleut men of northwestern Alaska used long whiskers of the sea lion, beads, and paint to decorate their extended-visor caps made of steamed and shaped wood. Aleut women's headbands were beaded with a stylized floral pattern.

Post-contact Influence on Headdresses. Styles and new fabrics from Europe and England led to changes in clothing and headdresses. To replace his deerskin cap, Cherokee chief

Sequoyah adopted the silk turban. Seminole leader Osceola topped his turban with three ostrich plumes. When Shawnee warrior Tecumseh joined the British as a general during the War of 1812, his uniform included a red cap with an eagle feather. The famous Apache Geronimo wore the rolled scarf headband. After his surrender to General Miles in 1886, he was photographed wearing a wide-brimmed European hat.

When a delegation of Osage leaders visited Washington, D.C., President Thomas Jefferson presented them with dark blue U.S. military tunics and top hats trimmed with red and white ostrich feathers. These became traditional wedding outfits for the Osage bride and groom.

Never overshadowed by European styles, the distinctive Plains headdress has been, rather stereotypically, the one considered American Indian. In 1990, the United States Postal Service issued a set of commemorative stamps featuring several eagle-feather war bonnets.   —*Gale Thompson*

See also Beads and beadwork; Dances and dancing; Dress and adornment; Feathers and featherwork; Masks; Pow-wows and contemporary celebrations; Quillwork.

BIBLIOGRAPHY

Billard, Jules B., et al. *The World of the American Indian.* Washington, D.C.: National Geographic Society, 1974.

Brown, Joseph Epes. *The North American Indians: A Selection of Photographs by Edward S. Curtis.* New York: Aperture, 1972.

Gattuso, John, et al. *Insight Guide: Native America.* Reprint. Boston: Houghton Mifflin, 1993.

Mails, Thomas E. *Mystic Warriors of the Plains.* Garden City, N.Y.: Doubleday, 1972.

Sturtevant, William, gen. ed. *Handbook of North American Indians.* 9 vols. by 1995. Washington, D.C.: Smithsonian Institution Press, 1978-   .

Heat-Moon, William Least (b. Aug. 27, 1939, Kansas City, Mo.): Writer

ALSO KNOWN AS: William Trogdon

TRIBAL AFFILIATION: Osage

SIGNIFICANCE: Heat-Moon is a veteran reporter and an astute chronicler of ordinary events whose works provide intimate journeys to self-discovery for all Americans

William Least Heat-Moon, best-selling author and noted lecturer, was born on August 27, 1939, in Kansas City, Missouri, to Ralph G. Trogdon and Maurine Davis Trogdon. His surname, Trogdon, comes from Irish and English ancestors. His pen name, Least Heat-Moon, comes from an Osage Indian ancestor who was born in July—the Moon of Heat. His father is known as Heat-Moon. His older brother is called Little Heat-Moon. Because William is the youngest and last, he took the name Least Heat-Moon. Heat-Moon credits his Osage ancestry as being the influential force in inspiring and shaping his works.

Heat-Moon received his degrees from the University of Missouri at Columbia: a B.A. in literature in 1961, an M.A. in literature in 1962, and a Ph.D. in literature in 1973. He also earned a B.A. in photojournalism in 1978. He taught literature

at Stephen's College in Columbia, Missouri, from 1965 to 1978. Heat-Moon was also a lecturer at the University of Missouri School of Journalism from 1985 to 1987. Since the late 1980's, his main occupation has been that of writer and lecturer.

Although Heat-Moon contributes articles to a variety of prestigious magazines, such as *Esquire*, *Time*, and *The Atlantic Monthly*, he is best known for his nonfiction bestsellers, *Blue Highways* (1983) and *PrairyErth* (1991).

Blue Highways, his first book, is the culmination of a 13,000-mile automobile trek along the backroads of thirty-eight states. Acclaimed by critics nationwide as the greatest travel memoir since John Steinbeck's *Travels with Charley*, *Blue Highways* became an immediate success. In 1983, *The New York Times* named it a notable book, and *Time* listed it as one of the five best nonfiction books of the year. In 1984, it received both the Christopher Award and the Books-Across-the-Sea Award for literary excellence.

Hailed with the same critical acclaim as *Blue Highways*, *PrairyErth*, an old geologic term for the soils of the central grasslands, was published in 1991. Heat-Moon's exploration of 774 square miles of the tall grass prairies and grasslands of Chase County, Kansas, culminated in a meticulous, poetic narrative that celebrates the beauty and richness of the ordinary in America's heartland. The book combines natural history, social history, and ecology with life-affirming vignettes of common people who live in the heart of the Kansas Flint Hills. Valuable information is provided on the Kaw (Kansa) tribe and numerous plants Native Americans once used for food.

Hewitt, John N. B. (Dec. 16, 1859, Lewiston, N.Y.— Oct. 14, 1937, Washington, D.C.): Anthropologist

TRIBAL AFFILIATION: Tuscarora

SIGNIFICANCE: Hewitt, who was perhaps as much as one-quarter Tuscarora, was a leading authority on the Iroquois League and the ceremonials and customs of the Six Nations

John Napoleon Brinton Hewitt was born in Lewiston, Niagara County, New York, in 1859. He was of French, English, Tuscarora, and Scottish heritage. Hewitt hoped to become a physician, but poor health prevented him from completing preparatory schooling. He continued his scholarly pursuits, however, and in 1880 was employed to collect Iroquoian Indian myths from residents of the Grand River and Onondaga reservations. In 1886, the Bureau of American Ethnology began sponsoring his work, and he continued with the same institution and line of research to the end of his life. Hewitt was fluent in Tuscarora, Mohawk, and Onondaga; he also became well versed in several Algonquian dialects and successfully established the connection of the Cherokee language to the Iroquoian family. After 1896, although Hewitt gathered information on Chippewa, Ottawa, and Delaware languages, he concentrated primarily upon Iroquoian. He was painstakingly thorough and slow; thus only a small part of his research was printed before his death. In the bureau's archives there are 250 entries under his name, consisting of 8,000 manuscript pages, 10,000 note-cards, more than 100 articles submitted to the *Handbook of American Indians*, and 25 submissions to *American Anthropologist*.

See also Iroquois Confederacy; Tuscarora.

Hiawatha (c. 1525, Mohawk River valley, N.Y.—c. 1575, Mohawk River valley, N.Y.): Tribal leader, diplomat, orator

ALSO KNOWN AS: Hienwentha, Ayonwartha (He Who Combs)

TRIBAL AFFILIATION: Mohawk

SIGNIFICANCE: Hiawatha translated the concepts and principles of the "Great Peace" into political action, and thus he is credited with organizing the League of the Iroquois or Five Nation Confederacy

Hiawatha is a sixteenth century historical figure, but the reality of his life and the legends surrounding him and the events with which he is connected are inextricably intertwined. Two people, Deganawida and Hiawatha, are credited with founding the Iroquois Confederacy (or League). This event occurred during a time of chronic warfare in the Northeast. Deganawida (the Peacemaker), a Huron, began to present the message of the Great Peace. Traveling eastward, he met a Mohawk leader named Hiawatha, and the two began to work together. Hiawatha, a skilled diplomat and orator, became the principal spokesman for the message of peace (it is often said that Deganawida had some type of speech impediment).

Seneca leader Atotarho had apparently been responsible for the deaths of Hiawatha's wife and several of his daughters. He later was the last holdout to the formation of the league, possibly consenting to it around 1570. Among the inducements presumably offered by Hiawatha was the promise that the league's central fire would be kept by the Onondaga and that meetings would occur in their main village. A number of stories credit Hiawatha with overcoming Atotarho's resistance through the use of magical powers. The three principles of the Great Peace were *Skenno* (including health of body and sanity of mind), *Gaiiwiyo* (righteousness in conduct, thought, and deed), and *Gashedenza* (knowledge of, and faith in, the spiritual power connected to governing and maintaining self-defense).

It should be noted that Henry Wadsworth Longfellow muddied the historical waters considerably with his 1855 epic poem, *Hiawatha*. His story was based mostly on Chippewa legend, although he borrowed the name Hiawatha for his hero. Among the Iroquois tribes today, both Hiawatha and Deganawida are highly esteemed figures.

See also Atotarho; Deganawida; Iroquois Confederacy.

BIBLIOGRAPHY

Burland, *North American Indian Mythology*. New York: Tudor Publishing, 1965.

Henry, Thomas R. *Wilderness Messiah, the Story of Hiawatha and the Iroquois*. New York: Bonanza Books, 1955.

Morgan, Lewis H. *League of the Ho-de-no-sau-nee, or Iroquois*. Rochester, N.Y.: Sage and Brothers, 1851.

Parker, Arthur C. *Seneca Myths and Legends*. Lincoln: University of Nebraska Press, 1989.

Wilson, Edmund. *Apologies to the Iroquois*. New York: Farrar, Strauss and Cudahy, 1960.

Hidatsa: Tribe

CULTURE AREA: Plains

LANGUAGE GROUPS: Siouan

PRIMARY LOCATION: North Dakota

POPULATION SIZE: 1,571 (1990 U.S. Census)

The Hidatsa were a Siouan-speaking people who lived along the middle Missouri River. Like their neighbors the Arikaras and the Mandans, the Hidatsa dwelled in villages of earthen mounds and practiced both agriculture and hunting. Their palisaded villages were near the Knife River, a branch of the Missouri in North Dakota, north of modern Bismarck.

Historically, the Hidatsa had been one with the Crow before they separated in the eighteenth century. One legend has it that the split resulted from a dispute over a certain buffalo that had been killed during a hunting party. The nation at that time was governed by two factions, each with a separate chief. The wives of each of these leaders began arguing over the stomach of the dead buffalo. When one of the women killed the other, a battle began between the two factions. Several people were killed on both sides of the struggle. This resulted in the migration to the Rocky Mountains of about one-half of those remaining. These migrants became the Crow, while those left behind constituted the Hidatsa. Linguistic similarities remained after the separation.

This powerful tribe began to acquire horses in the 1730's and 1740's from nomadic Plains tribes, with whom they traded. The acquisition of these swift animals made the hunting of buffalo easier and faster. The tribe used the products of the buffalo for food, tipi covers, robes, and utensils. To aid in their hunting and to demonstrate their bravery and daring, Hidatsa warriors raided other tribes for horses and loot. War dances often preceded these raids. Occasionally the Hidatsa were raided by members of the Dakota tribe, who called the Hidatsa "Minitari."

The tribe's farming efforts yielded corn, beans, and squash. The men sometimes raised tobacco, which was considered a sacred plant. Clothing was elaborate. Made from animal skins, it was usually decorated with quills and, after the white traders arrived, with beads. The spreading eagle-feather headdress probably originated with either the Hidatsa or the neighboring Mandan.

Clans and societies were important elements of Hidatsa life. Members of these groups often had certain functions and performed particular ceremonies. The supernatural played an important role. Men often sought visions, and shamans with particularly strong visions were consulted for advice. It was believed that they were able to read the future, diagnose sickness, and perform acts of magic.

Many similarities existed between the Hidatsa and their geographical neighbors, specifically the Mandan and the Arikara. They were all semi-nomadic tribes. That is, part of the year was spent in the cultivating and harvesting of crops, while the remainder was spent on the hunt, especially for buffalo. They were also all subject to problems associated with the arrival of whites such as fewer buffalo to hunt and diseases

A Hidatsa mother and child, photographed around 1908. (Library of Congress)

which ravaged their populations. Smallpox epidemics occurred repeatedly through the years. In 1837, the Hidatsa were joined by about one hundred Mandan survivors of the disease. The two tribes lived together from that point.

See also Arikara; Crow; Mandan; Plains; Siouan language family.

Hides and hidework

TRIBES AFFECTED: Pantribal

SIGNIFICANCE: Hide was used by virtually all native groups for a variety of utilitarian purposes

Hide, either tanned or untanned (rawhide), was used by nearly all Native American groups for clothing, hats, burden cases, pouches, shields, masks, snowshoes, moccasins, strapping, hafting of wood and stone tools, stone-boiling, slings, quivers, rattles, weapons, saddles, shelters, fishing floats, survival food, kayak and umiak coverings, and a variety of other utilitarian articles. Though land mammal hide was most commonly used, there were instances of bird, reptile, and even salmon skin being utilized for various purposes.

Hide tanning was laborious and sometimes labor intensive, particularly in the late summer or early fall when land mammal hides were prime. Consequently, a high division of labor existed for procuring and processing hides. Usually men were responsible for acquiring hides through hunting, trapping or snares, and, depending upon circumstances, skinning was accomplished by either gender. Once the animal's skin was removed (usually intact), women were responsible for processing the hide. In fact, a woman could gain considerable status through her proficiency with hides, particularly if the hide was to be decorated with porcupine quills, shells, feathers, or teeth.

A hide, if not to be used as rawhide, was processed in one of two ways: fur dressing, in which the hair was left on the hide, or complete hair removal. Fur dressing was a less complete method of tanning because the hide was not split, and limitations were imposed while tanning so as not to loosen the hair, which meant the hide frequently stiffened when wet. This type of tanning method was usually for clothing.

Tanning a hide required basically four major steps. Regardless of the method of tanning, the skin was first washed and pounded with a stone maul to remove blood, fat, and excess flesh. The pounding broke down and softened the grain of fibers, making the hide more adherent to the tanning chemicals. Next the hide was dehaired, a process which varied among Native American groups. One procedure was to bury the stretched hide in hardwood ashes several inches underground for several days. Another procedure for hair removal was to "sweat" the hide in controlled conditions of humidity or warmth. Some groups would soak the hide in urine to facilitate hair removal.

The next process was "beaming," which removed any remaining hair, subcutaneous fat, and blood. The hide was pegged with wooden stakes or horn to the ground, or stretched onto a nearly vertical frame, or placed sectionally over a smooth log. The beaming was done with either a large mammal rib, scapula, or tibiae to which was hafted a flat, dull, ovid stone. Scraping stones were frequently lunette-shaped to prevent piercing the hide, and often were not hafted, but handheld. Further washing of the hide completed this difficult process. Ideally, the hide was then soft and flexible, ready for tanning.

Among Native Americans there were essentially four methods of tanning, ones that required using either brains, urine, oil, or vegetables. Brain tanning, the most common method, required the brains of the animal to be kneaded into both sides of the pegged or loose hide. Any residue was later scraped away. The brains contained fat and an emulsifier. They were often mixed with animal liver, then kneaded with lichens to form small pads that were stored for future use. Sometimes this method of tanning was supplemented with washes from various deciduous tree barks, which actually was a combination of vegetable and brain tanning.

Urine tanning was common in the Arctic region; it required submersion and manipulation of the hide in human urine, sometimes stored in ice troughs. Both urine- and brain-tanned hides become stiff when dry after being wet, and to maintain suppleness, hides were smoked with punk wood in small tipi-like structures. Oil tanning, though restricted in use, was a method that required working the animal's fat and oil into the hide. In the Arctic and Subarctic, reindeer liver could supplement oil tanning. Vegetable tanning was accomplished with solutions from deciduous tree barks that contain tannin, such as oak, chestnut, and sumac trees. This procedure commonly required enclosing the hide in a bag containing the tanning solution until tanning was complete. Oils were sometimes used in addition to the tannic acids.   —*John Alan Ross*

See also Buffalo; Hunting and gathering; Tanning.

Hitchiti: Tribe

CULTURE AREA: Southeast

LANGUAGE GROUP: Muskogean

PRIMARY LOCATION: Florida, Oklahoma

POPULATION SIZE: 257 (1990 U.S. Census)

At the time of contact with Europeans in the 1540's, the Hitchitis lived on the lower Ocmulgee River in present-day Georgia. Seeing themselves as the original inhabitants of the area, the Hitchitis regarded the other tribes who came into the Creek Nation as newcomers. (Hitchiti tradition located the founding of the Creek confederacy at Ocmulgee Old Field, the site of present-day Macon, Georgia.) Culturally, the Hitchitis were similar to other Creeks, though their language was not intelligible to speakers of pure Muskogee.

Some Hitchitis moved into Florida during the eighteenth century to get away from white settlers and the dominance of the Muskogees within the Creek confederacy. They became an important component of the evolving Seminole nation. Hitchiti-speaking Seminoles were often called Miccosukees, after a town they settled near lake Miccosukee in northern Florida. With other Seminoles and Creeks, many Hitchitis were removed to Indian Territory (modern Oklahoma) in the 1830's and 1840's. The majority of the two hundred or so

Seminoles left behind in Florida were Hitchiti-speakers. In 1961, some of their descendants organized as the Miccosukee tribe of Indians of Florida and received federal recognition.

See also Creek; Muskogean language family; Seminole.

Hogan

Tribe affected: Navajo

Significance: Hogans are unique housing structures suited to the pastoral lifeways of the Navajo

The typical Navajo hogan is a large, comfortable, one-family dwelling place. The usual construction method starts with four support poles, which may represent the four sacred directions or the four sacred mountains that anchor the Navajo universe. The entryway, facing east, represents the union of sun and earth, as in Navajo creation myths. Around the foundation supports, a six-sided structure is built of logs, which are laid against lateral braces and then chinked with clay and rock. The roof curves in to form a low dome with a smoke hole in the center. The smoke hole and an entrance, covered with a blanket or sheepskin in winter, are the only openings.

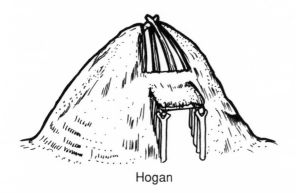

Hogan

The hogan is ideally suited to the high mesas of the Southwest with their dry winds and temperature extremes. From snowy winters to hot dry summers, the log and clay exterior of the hogan provides efficient insulation, while its rounded shape conserves heat in winter. The roomy hogan may also provide a temporary home to newborn lambs or pups, as well as a living space for their owners. Often, a brush shelter is built near the hogan. This allows for outdoor cooking and dining during the summer. In places where wood is scarce, hogans may be constructed of stone.

See also Architecture—Southwest; Navajo.

Hogan, Linda (b. July 16, 1947, Denver, Colo.): Poet, novelist

Tribal affiliation: Chickasaw

Significance: Through her fiction and poetry, Linda Hogan develops unique perspectives on Indian history, nature, and feminism

Born of a working-class Chickasaw father and a white mother of an immigrant family, Linda Hogan learned the history and legends of her people through oral narrative. She received a B.A. and an M.A. from the University of Colorado and was associate professor of American Indian and American studies at the University of Minnesota before turning to full-time writing. In 1989, she began teaching creative writing and American Indian studies at the University of Colorado.

Hogan's first novel, *Mean Spirit* (1990), set in an Oklahoma Indian community during the oil boom of the 1920's, describes the devastation that results from the greed and corruption of non-Indians. *That Horse* (1985) contains several of her short stories.

Hogan has published several volumes of poetry. Her first, *Calling Myself Home* (1978), includes many poems about family and Indian identity; as she has said, "A lot of my poems come from family stories." *Daughters, I Love You* (1981), reprinted in *Eclipse* (1983), is a protest against destruction of the land. Both *Seeing Through the Sun* (1985) and *Savings* (1988) include numerous poems about a kinship with nature and a speaker's (Indian's) interaction with it. Like her novel, which describes especially the plight of Indian women during the oil boom, Hogan's poetry often includes feminist perspectives.

BIBLIOGRAPHY

Balassi, William, et al., eds. *This Is About Vision: Interviews with Southwestern Writers*. Albuquerque: University of New Mexico Press, 1990.

Bruchac, Joseph. *Survival This Way: Interview with American Indian Poets*. Tucson: University of Arizona Press, 1987.

Hogan, Linda. "The Two Lives." In *I Tell You Now*, edited by Brian Swann and Arnold Krupat. Lincoln: University of Nebraska Press, 1987.

Hohokam: Prehistoric tradition

Date: 600-1450

Location: Central and southern Arizona, northern Mexico

Cultures affected: Hohokam, perhaps Pima, Tohono O'odham

The Hohokam were a Classic-period southwestern culture whose heartland was centered on the Gila River and Salt River basins and whose largest site was Snaketown. Hohokam (in the Pima language, "those who have gone") shared many aspects of Classic-period southwestern culture such as maize-based horticulture, relatively dense settlements, and public, ceremonial architecture. Hohokam culture was distinctive in the presence of exotic trade goods and in its ball courts. Because of these unique characteristics, early archaeologists believed that Hohokam culture was derived from Mesoamerica. Most archaeologists now believe Hohokam origins to be indigenous to the Southwest, with roots stretching back to the hunter-gatherer societies of the Archaic period.

Although in the Classic period most Southwest societies continued to live in small, dispersed, unranked agricultural villages, new, more elaborate developments occurred in certain regions. The Hohokam represent one of these new developments, called "systems of regional integration," as their dominance grew to cover a wide region rather than remaining localized. Archaeological evidence suggests that accompanying this growth, social inequality grew among the Hohokam. Evidence pointing to inequality includes differing residential pit house dimensions and locations, public labor projects (such as platform mounds, ball courts, and extensive irrigation canals), craft specialization (especially shell jewelry), long-distance trade of exotic raw materials, and differential treatment of the dead, in that only certain burials held valuable grave goods.

Hohokam subsistence was diverse and included hunting and gathering, although maize, beans, and squash were primary staples. A complex network of irrigation canals was built near rivers. Settlement sizes ranged from communities the size of Snaketown (with about a thousand individuals) to small, dispersed farmsteads. Cremation was characteristic among the Hohokam, although other burial treatments also existed.

Although most archaeologists no longer point primarily to Mesoamerican inspirations to explain Hohokam's rise to cultural complexity, Mesoamerican contacts may have been important in Hohokam society. Well-developed trade networks with quite distant communities existed throughout the Hohokam region. A variety of luxury goods—many from Mexican sources—passed along well-established routes: copper bells; macaw birds and feathers; finely painted, geometric-motif pottery; stone paint palettes; onyx and argillite ornaments; serpentine; obsidian; turquoise; jet; and a variety of shell objects including conch trumpets, decorated bracelets, and beads. Participants within the Hohokam trade network may have shared a common religious and belief system originating in part with Mesoamerican societies, but it was integrated and adapted by the Hohokam as a means of legitimizing the emergence of social inequality.

Apart from prestige goods that remained mostly in the hands of Hohokam leaders, communities were largely self-sufficient. Although ball courts and luxury trade goods are common in larger Hohokam sites, their presence may reflect only superficial similarity with the Hohokam heartland, as regional cultures maintained their autonomy and distinctiveness within the broader region archaeologists have defined as sharing Hohokam culture.

For reasons still under debate, Hohokam culture went into decline; by the arrival of the Spanish, the Hohokam were gone. The modern-day Pima and Tohono O'odham (Papago) may be descendants of the Hohokam.

See also Anasazi; Ball game and courts; Mogollon; Pima; Prehistory—Southwest; Snaketown; Tohono O'odham.

Hokan language family

CULTURE AREA: California, Southwest

TRIBES AFFECTED: Achumawi (Pit River), Atsugewi, Chimariko, Chumash, Esselen, Karok, Pomo, Salinan, Seri, Shasta, Tequistlatec, Washoe, Yana, Yuman

There is an extraordinary amount of controversy regarding the Hokan language classification, including whether it should even exist. Unlike closely related families such as Algonquian or Iroquoian, Hokan comprises several subfamilies whose relationships are not recognized by all linguists.

The Hokan classification was first proposed in *New Linguistic Families in California* (1913) by Alfred Kroeber and R. B. Dixon, who saw a relationship among Karok, Chimariko, Shastan, Yuman, Esselen, Pomo, and Yanan; they named this new family Hokan. Kroeber and Dixon also linked Salinan and Chumash as a new family, called Iskoman. J. P. Harrington (in *American Anthropologist*, vol. 15, 1913) suggested a link between Chumash and Yuman, effectively joining the Hokan and Iskoman families. In 1917 Edward Sapir, in *The Position of Yana in the Hokan Stock*, confirmed Hokan's relationships and added Seri and Chontal to the grouping. In *Linguistic Families of California* (1919), Kroeber and Dixon added Washoe to the list.

A more recent grouping of Hokan divides the family into eight groups: Northern (which includes Karok, Shasta, Chimariko, Palahnihan, Yanan, and Pomo), Washoe, Salinan-Chumash, Seri-Yuman (which includes Seri, Hualapai, Havasupai, Yavapai, Paipai, Mojave, Maricopa, Quechan, Diegueño, Cocopa, and Kiliwa), Waicuri-Quiniqua, Coahuiltecan, Tequistlatecan, and Southern (which includes Tlapanecan, Jicaque, and Jurimaugui). This is the grouping favored by Joseph H. Greenberg in *Language in the Americas* (1987).

A more conservative approach is advised in *The Languages of North America* by Lyle Campbell and Marianne Mithun (1979). These groupings are Northern (as described above), Essalen-Yuman, Salinan-Seri (including Chumash, Salinan, and Seri), Washoe, and Tequistlatec. Following the more conservative grouping, there were approximately fifteen thousand speakers of Hokan languages in the 1970's. The largest number of these speakers (approximately ten thousand) were speakers of Tequistlatec in Mexico, and the majority of them were bilingual in Spanish.

Hokeah, Jack (c. 1900, Caddo County, Okla.—Dec. 14, 1969, Fort Cobb, Okla.): Visual artist

TRIBAL AFFILIATION: Kiowa

SIGNIFICANCE: Hokeah was one of the original members of the Kiowa Five, a group of painters who instituted a style of painting based on traditional cultural scenes

Hokeah was orphaned as a young child; he was reared by his grandparents. His grandfather, White Horse, was known as a warrior. Starting in 1926, Hokeah attended the special non-credit courses for the Kiowa Five at the University of Oklahoma. By 1930, he and other Kiowa painters were attending the Gallup Inter-Tribal Ceremonials in New Mexico to sell their work and compete for prizes. During these visits to New Mexico, Hokeah met Julián and María Martínez, the famous potters of San Ildefonso Pueblo. They became close friends, and he stayed there a number of years. In 1932, he worked on murals for the buildings of the Santa Fe Indian School.

Hokeah was a champion dancer; he also led dance groups. His painting is most known for strong images of dancers in motion. He portrayed details of designs in the costumes and caught the dramatic quality of the dancing. He worked with flat colors, and the dancers were presented against a plain background. After considerable initial success he ended his art career. He experimented with acting for a period in New York and was later employed by the Bureau of Indian Affairs. His work is in the collections of the National Museum of the American Indian, Mabee-Gerrer Museum of Art, Denver Art Museum, Museum of New Mexico, and others.

See also Art and artists, contemporary; Asah, Spencer; Auchiah, James; Mopope, Stephen; Paints and painting; Tsatoke, Monroe.

Hole-in-the-Day (1825—June 27, 1868, Crow Wing, Minn.): Tribal leader

ALSO KNOWN AS: Bugonegijig
TRIBAL AFFILIATION: Ojibwa (Chippewa)
SIGNIFICANCE: A controversial figure, Hole-in-the-Day made a number of agreements for his people that brought him considerable personal gain

There were two Chippewa (Ojibwa) leaders named Hole-in-the-Day; they were father and son. The elder Hole-in-the-Day (a more accurate translation of the Indian name is "Opening in the Sky") was a war leader who waged war against the Sioux, playing a major role in pushing them westward. He also fought with the Americans against the British in the War of 1812. He died in 1846.

The younger Hole-in-the-Day, born in 1825, became head chief of the Chippewa Bear Clan after his father died. He visited Washington, D.C., several times, and at one point he married a white newspaper reporter there. He was known as a bargainer and a person who would take a percentage of any agreement made on behalf of his people. Many Chippewas complained that Hole-in-the-Day was aggrandizing himself at the expense of his people, and in fact he became quite rich. He was politically prudent, however, and distributed benefits to enough people to gain popular support from "progressive" Chippewas. When his people were compelled to move to the White Earth Reservation in Montana, Hole-in-the-Day at first refused to go. He relented, however, just before being murdered by his own people at Crow Wing, Minnesota.

See also Indian-white relations—U.S., 1831-1870; Ojibwa.

Hollow Horn Bear (1850, Sheridan County, Nebr.—Mar. 15, 1913, Washington, D.C.): War chief

ALSO KNOWN AS: Matihehlogego
TRIBAL AFFILIATION: Brule Sioux
SIGNIFICANCE: Hollow Horn Bear favored peace with whites, and he became something of a celebrity; he appeared on a U.S. postage stamp and on a five-dollar bill

Hollow Horn Bear fought with the leading chiefs of the Plains against subjugation until the 1870's; after that, he favored peace with the whites and became something of a celebrity along the East Coast. His likeness appeared on a fourteen-cent stamp as well as on a United States five-dollar bill.

Chippewa leader Hole-in-the-Day was a controversial figure among the Chippewa people. (Library of Congress)

Born in Sheridan County, Nebraska, a son of the chief Iron Shell, Hollow Horn Bear earned his early fame as a warrior. He raided the Pawnees at first, then aided other Sioux leaders in harassing forts along the Bozeman Trail between 1866 and 1868, when the Treaty of Fort Laramie was signed. During this time, he gained fame as the chief who defeated Lieutenant William Fetterman (who had bragged that he would cut through Sioux country with a handful of troops). Hollow Horn Bear also led raids on Union Pacific railroad workers' camps.

In 1905, Hollow Horn Bear was invited to take part in the inauguration of Theodore Roosevelt. In 1913, he led a group of Indians in the presidential inauguration parade for Woodrow Wilson. On that visit, Hollow Horn Bear caught pneumonia and died.

See also Bozeman Trail wars; Fort Laramie Treaty of 1868; Railroads; Sioux.

Brule Sioux leader Hollow Horn Bear defeated William Fetterman during the Bozeman Trail wars. (Library of Congress)

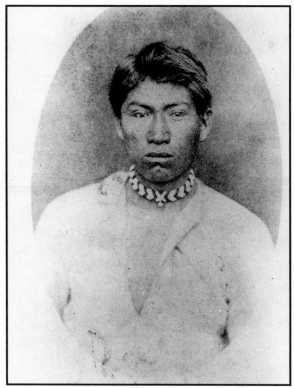

Hooker Jim, a leader of the Modoc War, betrayed fellow leader Captain Jack to white soldiers. (National Archives)

Hooker Jim (c. 1825, Calif.—1879, Quapaw Agency, Indian Territory): Chief

ALSO KNOWN AS: Hakar Jim

TRIBAL AFFILIATION: Modoc

SIGNIFICANCE: As a leader of the Modoc War, Hooker Jim resisted relocation to an Oregon reservation

After relocating to the Klamath Reservation in Oregon, several Modocs returned to California requesting their own reservation. In November, 1872, while resisting army efforts to return them to Oregon, several Modoc men, a woman, and a child were killed. In retaliation, Hooker Jim raided a white ranch, killing twelve settlers. Thereafter he retreated to the California lava fields seeking the protection of the leader of the rebellion, Captain Jack, who refused to surrender him to white authorities. Hooker Jim convinced Captain Jack to assassinate General Edward Canby, commander of the U.S. forces seeking to roust the Modocs. Although mobilizing for war, Canby was also a member of a peace commission. In the midst of negotiations, Captain Jack murdered Canby; there was substantial white retaliation.

After arguing over strategy, Hooker Jim led U.S. forces to Captain Jack's hideout. Bargaining to spare his own life, Hooker Jim testified against his past protector, who was subsequently hanged. Thereafter, Hooker Jim and his followers relocated to a reservation in Indian Territory.

See also Captain Jack; Modoc; Modoc War.

Hopewell: Prehistoric tradition

DATE: 200 B.C.E.-700 C.E.

LOCATION: Eastern United States

CULTURE AFFECTED: Hopewell

The Hopewell cultural tradition is associated with a major florescence of complex village societies in the eastern portion of North America between 200 B.C.E. and 700 C.E. The cultural system that connected societies of the Hopewell tradition is known as the Hopewell Interaction Sphere. Centered at sites in the Scioto Valley of southern Ohio, this network was marked by trade in a wide variety of exotic raw materials used in the manufacture of special craft items. These included goods such as copper from sources in Michigan and Georgia, obsidian and grizzly bear teeth from Wyoming, fine-grained stone from Minnesota and North Dakota, marine shell and shark teeth from the Gulf of Mexico, silver from Ontario, mica and quartz crystals from the southern Appalachians, and galena from Illinois and Wisconsin.

Among the most characteristic features of Hopewell sites are burial mounds and monumental earthworks. The Hopewell site near Chillicothe, Ohio, for which the tradition is named, covered an area of 110 acres and had thirty-eight burial mounds. The largest of these was 33 feet high and 500 feet long, and it contained the burials of more than 250 individuals. One of these wore an elaborate headdress of wooden deer antlers sheathed in copper. Another was buried with a copper axe weighing 38 pounds. The central portion of this site was surrounded by a ditch and low embankment. Mound City, Ohio, has at least twenty-eight burial mounds, also within an earthwork enclosure. Elite burials here were lined with massive quantities of mica. At Newark, Ohio, the state's most extensive complex of geometric earthworks includes a circle, an octagon, and other features that have been preserved as part of a municipal golf course.

Burials in Hopewell mounds have been found to contain a wide variety of exotic artifacts. Heavy breastplates, ear spools, beads, animal cutouts, and musical instruments were made from hammered copper sheets, often decorated with embossed designs. Lumps of native copper were worked into celts, axes, adzes, and punches. Thick sheets of translucent mica were cut into the shapes of human heads and hands, bird talons, snakes, and swastikas. Obsidian and fine chert were flaked into beautiful ceremonial knives, some measuring 18 inches long. Crystals of quartz and galena were used for pendants or included in medicine bags. Among the most spectacular manufactured items, also widely traded, were carved stone platform pipes bearing appealing carvings of birds, bears, beavers, frogs, felines, and humans. Ceramic technology flourished, with a wide variety of vessel shapes decorated primarily through plastic manipulation of the surface.

Sites of the Hopewell tradition have been found over a wide geographical region, ranging from the Great Lakes in the north to the lower Mississippi Valley and the central Gulf Coast. To the east, they are known from West Virginia and western Pennsylvania, while their westernmost extent is in the vicinity of Kansas City, Missouri.

Despite its apparent complexity, Hopewell culture appears to have been based on the intensive exploitation of wild resources of woodland regions, supplemented by some cultivation of sunflowers, squash, and marsh elder. Maize was probably cultivated by late Hopewell peoples, but it remained a minor part of the diet until later periods.

The Hopewell tradition does not represent a single society, but rather a broad phenomenon characterized by extensive networks for the exchange of raw materials and worked goods, the sharing of common notions about artifact manufacture and decoration, the use of mounds for burial grounds, and the emergence of social differentiation as indicated by fine craft objects and individual variation in the quality of grave goods. The apparent decline of the Hopewell tradition after 400 C.E. remains poorly understood, although it has been linked to the consequences of increased competition for farmland as maize became a more important component of the diet. These consequences included a higher frequency of intercommunity conflicts, which may have led to the disruption of existing networks for the exchange of raw materials and ideas.

See also Adena; Mississippian; Mounds and mound builders; Prehistory—Northeast; Prehistory—Southeast.

Hopi. *See* **Pueblo tribes, Western**

Hopocan (c. 1725, Pa.—1794, Captain Pipe's Village, Upper Sandusky, Ohio): Orator, chief
ALSO KNOWN AS: Captain Pipe, Konieschguanokee
TRIBAL AFFILIATION: Lenni Lenape (Delaware)
SIGNIFICANCE: A hereditary war chief, Hopocan battled Americans during the French and Indian War, Pontiac's Rebellion, and the American Revolution

Allied with the French during the French and Indian War, Hopocan led the war faction of his tribe against Gelelemend's peace faction. He participated in Pontiac's Rebellion in 1763 and was captured at Fort Pitt. With the cessation of hostilities, Hopocan settled on the Muskingum River in Ohio.

During the American Revolution, Hopocan led several raids on American settlers. After Colonel William Crawford's forces were defeated by Indians at Sandusky, Ohio, in 1782, Crawford was captured and relinquished to Hopocan. In retaliation for his troops' massacre of peaceful Moravian Delawares at Gnaddenhutten, Pennsylvania, Crawford, a friend of General George Washington, was tortured and executed. His murder was avenged through escalating warfare on the western frontier.

As an orator and diplomat, Hopocan participated in several councils, signing treaties at Fort Pitt (1778), Fort McIntosh, Ohio (1785), and Fort Harmer (1787). After relocating several times during the revolution, Hopocan and his band settled on the upper Sandusky River at what became known as Captain Pipe's village.

See also French and Indian Wars; Indian-white relations—English colonial; Indian-white relations—French colonial; Indian-white relations—U.S., 1775-1830; Pontiac's Conspiracy.

Horses

TRIBES AFFECTED: Pantribal
SIGNIFICANCE: From the seventeenth century onward, the horse was an important aspect of many, if not most, North American Indian societies; it was most dominant in the lives of the Plains Indians

On his second voyage to the New World in 1493, Christopher Columbus imported the first horses to America. The settlement of Santo Domingo in Hispaniola became the horse-breeding center of the Caribbean islands. Subsequently, horse *rancherías*, both royal and private, were established in Cuba, Jamaica and other islands. When Hernán Cortés left Havana for the expedition to New Spain (Mexico) in 1519, he took with him sixteen horses, one of which foaled on board during the trip. After the fall of the Aztec empire, the Spaniards moved quickly to consolidate their gains. Antonio de Mendoza, the first viceroy of New Spain, faced the first serious challenge to Spanish rule since the conquest when natives rebelled in the northwestern province of Nueva Galicia, now the states of Jalisco and Nayarit. The rebellion, known as the Mixtón War of 1541-1542, caused the viceroy, for the first time, to send allied chieftains on horseback and use Spanish weapons to quell the uprising. It was with the Mixtón War that Native Americans started their long relationship with the horse.

Dispersion of Horses. From New Spain, horses moved northward when Francisco Vásquez de Coronado, in his expedition of 1540-1542, took fifteen hundred horses with him to New Mexico (only a few of these animals survived). The first important breeding and distribution center of horses in what is now the United States was established in 1598 by Juan de Oñate in the San Juan Pueblo settlement on the east bank of the Rio Grande River, about 30 miles north of present-day Santa Fe, New Mexico. From this location, the horse was farther dispersed in an ever-northward and northwestward direction, arriving in the following areas in approximately these years: Colorado, 1659; Wyoming/Idaho, 1690-1700; Montana/Oregon/Washington, 1720-1730; Canada, 1730-1750; California, 1769-1775. In an eastern and northeastern direction, the horse was dispersed to the following areas: Texas/Oklahoma, 1600-1690; Nebraska/Kansas/South and North Dakota, 1720-1750.

Except for the Mixtón incident and reports that, in 1567, tribes were observed riding horses in the Sonora Valley of Mexico, there is nothing to suggest that Southwest natives were on horseback before the seventeenth century. When Native Americans acquired horses they did so by stealing them from the Spaniards. By early 1700, horses with Spanish brands had reached the northern Plains, transforming every aspect of life for the people in the region. Before the advent of the horse, people in the Plains area used dogs to help transport personal possessions on travois tied to the dog's back. The newly acquired horse became a "new superior dog" that was harnessed to a larger travois and was capable of transporting greater volumes of material. Dog names were given to horses, honoring their function; the Assiniboine had two names for horses:

Sho-a-thin-ga and *Thongatch-shonga*, both signifying "great dog"; the Blackfoot had *Ponokamita*, "elk dog"; the Gros Ventre, *It-shouma-shunga*, "red dog." The Sioux word was *Shonk-a-Wakan*, "medicine dog"; and the Cree was *Mistamin*, "big dog."

Plains Horse Culture. Inevitably, horseback riding quickly followed the harnessed "big dogs," and with the acquisition of firearms, mounted hunting parties enjoyed easier access to the vast buffalo herds roaming the Plains. Greater meat supplies raised many tribes above subsistence levels, providing time to pursue warlike activities such as raids for the acquisition of horses owned by other tribes. Individual horse ownership became an integral part of social transactions, and standards of wealth were measured in number of horses owned. Spiritual and religious customs incorporated the horse as powerful medicine, and members of horse cults believed they received their powers from horses.

Horse breeding became commonplace among many tribes. The Flathead and Piegan acquired vast herds of horses (said to have numbered in the thousands), while the Nez Perce developed the outstanding, well-conformed, and spotted Appaloosa, which was known throughout the region as the hardiest and most reliable horse. The Blackfoot were the consummate horse keepers and trainers, and they practiced superior husbandry procedures. The Crow developed an honored horse "trading" tradition throughout the northern Plains and mountains. The Cheyenne attempted to steal horses without killing the members of the raided tribe, and the Comanche became the most dreaded and splendid horsemen of the Plains. The extermination of the buffalo, the sheer power of the western movement of European Americans, and the placement of the tribes on reservations ended the Native American horse culture.

—*Moises Roizen*

See also Buffalo; Dogs; Plains.

Horseshoe Bend, Treaty of

DATE: August 9, 1814
PLACE: Alabama
TRIBE AFFECTED: Creek
SIGNIFICANCE: This agreement eliminated any possibility of an effective Creek alliance against U.S. expansion and thus facilitated the removal of the Creek people to the Trans-Mississippi during Andrew Jackson's presidency

After his defeat of the Red Stick faction of the Creeks at Horseshoe Bend, General Andrew Jackson took full advantage of his authorization to secure a peace agreement. His purpose was twofold: to secure large tracts of land as compensation for the cost of his campaign and to eliminate Creek political power by isolating them. In the Treaty of Horseshoe Bend, also known as the Treaty of Fort Jackson, signed on August 9, 1814, Jackson received, on behalf of the United States, 22 million acres in south Georgia and central Alabama, or half of the Creek domain.

Cessions in the west isolated the Creeks from the Choctaws and Chickasaws, while those in the south created a buffer against the Seminoles and the Spanish. Ironically, only one Red Stick signed the treaty; the remaining signatories were Creek allies of Jackson, who lost much of their own land. Each Creek ally was allowed to keep a square mile of land as long as they or their family used it, but the United States reserved the right to build forts, trading posts, and roads on Creek lands.

See also Creek; Creek War.

Howe, Oscar (May 13, 1915, Joe Creek, S.Dak.—Oct. 7, 1983, Vermillion, S.Dak.): Painter

ALSO KNOWN AS: Nazuha Hoksina (Trader Boy)
TRIBAL AFFILIATION: Yanktonai Sioux
SIGNIFICANCE: Howe successfully eschewed the prevailing Native American style with his modernist canvases, initiating the modern Indian art movement

Oscar Howe has been called "the father of the new Native American art." His painting career began under Dorothy Dunn at the Santa Fe Indian School and continued under Oscar Jacobson at the University of Oklahoma. In Howe's career he was a Works Progress Administration commissioner, five-time winner of the Philbrook's Grand Award, professor at the University of South Dakota, 1966 Waite Phillip's Award recipient, Artist Laureate of South Dakota, and holder of several honorary doctorates. Howe's life was a tapestry of difficulties. Health problems included an ugly facial skin disease, trachoma, and tuberculosis. Social problems included ostracism, loneliness, slow advancement through schools (he started high school at age twenty), joblessness, and shyness.

His artistic subjects were Sioux stories, hunts, and myths—images shaped by his use of line and color. Before World War II, he painted in the Santa Fe style, using pastels and shapes bounded by lines. After the war, he moved away from pastels to use bold reds, and he painted straight lines between points in addition to sinuous lines. His stylized postwar art has been called cubist, which Howe denied, explaining that his influence was, instead, Plains Indian hide painting. Howe also painted a number of murals.

See also Art and artists, contemporary; Arts and crafts—Plains; Scholder, Fritz.

Howling Wolf (c. 1850, present-day Okla.—July 2, 1927, Waurika, Okla.): Artist, chief

ALSO KNOWN AS: Honanisto
TRIBAL AFFILIATION: Cheyenne
SIGNIFICANCE: Howling Wolf was a warrior, war chief, and artist

The son of Eagle Head, principal Cheyenne chief, Howling Wolf as a young man proved himself an able warrior, eventually becoming a war chief during the wars for the Plains. Following the Red River War of 1874-1975, Howling Wolf surrendered and was sent to Fort Marion, a military prison in St. Augustine, Florida. While imprisoned, Howling Wolf and fellow prisoners Bear's Heart, Cohoe, and Zotom, were encouraged by Lieutenant Richard Henry Pratt to become artists. The artistic Indians became known as the Florida Boys.

After being released in 1878, Howling Wolf returned to Indian Territory, where he labored as a school janitor, converted to Christianity, and became a farmer. Although initially supporting peace, he quickly abandoned his white sympathies after witnessing recurrent treaty violations.

In 1884, he became chief of the Dog Soldiers, a self-styled Cheyenne reservation police force. He opposed the 1887 General Allotment Act, which provided for the redistribution of tribal lands to individual Indians. Howling Wolf died in 1927, the victim of a car accident.

See also Bear's Heart, James; Red River War; Black Hills.

Huchnom: Tribe
CULTURE AREA: California
LANGUAGE GROUP: Yuki
PRIMARY LOCATION: South Eel River, northwestern California

Huchnom culture was a synthesis of Pomoan and Yuki traits and beliefs. The Huchnom village was the basic socioeconomic and political unit, usually with its own resources and territorial concerns. The Huchnom fished, hunted, trapped, and gathered acorns, seeds, and roots. Their material culture was also similar to the Yuki and Coastal Yuki, as were many of their rituals and ceremonies. They lived in thirty permanent riverine villages. The Huchnom participated with the Pomo and Cahto in rites of intensification as well as in the exchange of differential trade goods, and they served as intermediaries between the Yuki and Pomoan. They cremated their dead.

As with neighboring groups, the Huchnom were greatly affected in the 1850's when lumbermen, miners, and settlers entered their lands. Most Huchnom were forcibly removed by soldiers to the Round Valley Reservation in 1869, where they were known as Redwoods. Their population in 1850 was estimated to be twenty-one hundred, but by 1910 there were only fifteen remaining. By the early 1970's the tribe was no longer considered a distinct group.

See also Coast Yuki; Pomo; Yuki.

Hudson's Bay Company
DATE: Established 1670
TRIBES AFFECTED: Some fifty tribes in the Canadian West, Northwest Territories, Pacific Coast, and Plains, especially the Assiniboine, Ahtna, Blackfoot, Cayuse, Chinook, Chipewyan, Cowichan, Cree, Gros Ventre, Kwakiutl, Nazko, Nootka, Ojibwa, Piegan, Salish, Sioux
SIGNIFICANCE: The Hudson's Bay Company explored and opened western Canada and the northwestern United States, in the process contributing to the ruination of western Indian tribes through the introduction of vices and disease

In 1670 King Charles II of England gave his cousin, Prince Rupert, a royal charter granting Rupert a monopoly in trade and commerce over all lands draining into the Pacific and Arctic oceans and the Mississippi River. The Territory encompassed more than 1.5 million square miles, stretching from Labrador to the Pacific Ocean, southward almost to the Great Lakes and far south into the American West.

The company's formal name was "The Governor and Company of Adventurers of England Trading into Hudson's Bay." European demand for beaver fur stimulated intense competition from the Northwest Fur Trading Company and the development of inland trade in the latter 1700's. In their efforts to acquire furs from the Indians the trading companies catered to their wants, and in the process they debauched, corrupted, and cheated them. Firearms, traps, European clothing, and liquor were readily available on easy credit terms. The Indians developed appetites for these goods and often entered a state of dependency and servitude in order to obtain them.

The Treaty of Ghent, which ended the War of 1812, opened the Pacific Coast region to Americans. American companies vigorously competed against the Canadians. The United States eventually wrested control of the Oregon Country, and the American presence threatened both the Hudson's Bay and Northwest companies with bankruptcy. In 1821 the two companies merged. George Simpson, who served the Hudson's Bay Company in the western Athapaskan region, became governor of the merged companies.

In 1856 gold was discovered in far western Canada, in the area of the Hudson's Bay Company's fur preserve in New Caledonia. The gold business became so profitable that the British Crown intervened and took over the entire coastal mainland as a Crown Colony. New Caledonia became British Columbia. The company retained only the fur-trading monopoly, which had drastically declined because of gold fever. The death of Simpson in 1860 weakened the company's rule even more. In 1863 the International Financial Society bought controlling interest, and the company's focus shifted to real estate speculation and economic development in the West. Rupert's land was sold to Canada in 1870, but the company retained title to the lands where it built trading posts. The company is the largest retailer in Canada, operating about six hundred department stores, and remains one of the world's largest fur-trade companies. Its official headquarters are in Winnipeg.

See also Beaver; Indian-white relations—Canadian; Trade.

Humor
TRIBES AFFECTED: Pantribal
SIGNIFICANCE: North American Indian humor, in various forms, pervades various native traditions and serves important social functions

Playfulness, practical jokes, and other forms of humor were—and are—widespread among North American Indians. Lightheartedness might be used as a way of dealing with traditional restraints on expressing emotions. In the controlled setting of a village or family unit, arguments deriving from inevitable tensions could be very disruptive of common order. Conveying one's point of view through humor rather than contention allowed for a socially acceptable release of emotions which might otherwise lead to socially harmful conflict.

Humor also served as a way of keeping interpersonal aggressions under control, conveying a desired message of rebuke without the likelihood of physical retribution. An example is the tradition of "joking relations," often cousins, who might use sarcasm to suggest corrections in undesirable behaviors. These cousins monitored each other's actions, making pointed comments about a young man's aptitude as a warrior, a young woman's resistance to getting married, or an inappropriate choice of potential mate. In this way humor served as a way of discouraging deviant behavior and encouraging group norms while keeping the rebuke at a safe distance from the harmony of the immediate family.

Similarly, a pejorative nickname based on undesirable physical attributes or lack of appropriate manly or womanly behavior might serve as an incentive to overcome limitations and conform to group norms. An unflattering name suggesting immaturity, unattractiveness, or unworthiness might follow someone through life or might later be replaced with a more desirable name. For example, the Shawnee Prophet was once known as Lalawethika (the Drum or Rattle) because of his boastfulness. After his spiritual awakening, however, he became known as Tenskwatawa—the Open Door.

Indian cultures frowned on sarcasm or ridicule directed from parents toward their children in the interest of preserving family unity and protecting budding egos. At the same time, children—in the tolerant upbringing common to many native people—were often allowed to use humor and practical jokes, even against family members. Humor allowed important messages about behavior to be communicated in nonthreatening ways and thereby served as an important reinforcement of the community.

See also Joking relations; Names and naming; Social control, traditional.

Hump (c. 1848—Dec., 1908, Cherry Creek, S.Dak.): Chief
ALSO KNOWN AS: Etokeah
TRIBAL AFFILIATION: Miniconjou Sioux
SIGNIFICANCE: An important leader in the Sioux Wars of the 1860's and 1870's, Hump later became a Ghost Dancer; in 1890, he went to Washington, D.C., on behalf of his people

Little is known about Hump's parentage, date of birth, or early life. He gained prominence in 1866 leading the attack that killed Captain William Fetterman and eighty soldiers outside Fort Kearney in Wyoming. Refusing to sign the Treaty of Fort Laramie, he joined Crazy Horse, Red Cloud, and other Sioux war chiefs. A distinguished warrior, he was present at Little Bighorn in 1876.

Forced to surrender in 1877, he left to join Sitting Bull in Canada but eventually returned to the Cheyenne River Reservation in South Dakota, In 1890, he participated with fellow Miniconjou, Big Foot, in the Ghost Dance movement. Warned of danger, he led his followers to the safety of the Pine Ridge Agency. Shortly thereafter, Big Foot and the remaining Ghost Dancers were massacred by the U.S. Army at Wounded Knee Creek. Hump and other Sioux chiefs then went to Washington,

D.C., to negotiate for better treatment of the Sioux people. He returned to reservation life and died in 1908 at Cherry Creek, South Dakota.

See also Big Foot; Crazy Horse; Fort Laramie Treaty of 1868; Ghost Dance; Little Bighorn, Battle of the; Red Cloud; Sioux; Sioux uprisings; Sitting Bull; Wounded Knee Massacre.

Hunt, George (c. 1854, Fort Rupert, British Columbia, Canada—Sept. 5, 1933, Fort Rupert, British Columbia, Canada): Ethnologist
TRIBAL AFFILIATION: Kwakiutl
SIGNIFICANCE: Hunt, who worked with anthropologist Franz Boas, recorded Kwakiutl traditions and lifeways

As an ethnologist, George Hunt had a major impact on the study of the Kwakiutls. He was a major contributor to the work of Franz Boas, the pioneer ethnologist of the Northwest Coast. During his lifetime, Hunt supplied Boas with more than six thousand pages of ethnographic material. He also appeared as coauthor with Boas on *Kwakiutl Tears* (1905) and *Ethnology of the Kwakiutl* (1921).

Born in 1854 at Fort Rupert, British Columbia, Hunt was a son of Robert Hunt, a Scotsman who worked for the Hudson's Bay Company in British Columbia. Hunt's mother was Mary Ebbetts, a Tlingit or Tsimshian. Hunt was reared in the traditional Indian manner and had little contact with white immigrants until he was in his twenties. Hunt is famous for acting as a guide and interpreter for the Adrian Jacobsen expedition along the North Pacific Coast between 1881 and 1883.

Hunt first met Franz Boas in 1886, after which he assumed a major role in recording Kwakiutl history and customs in English. Boas taught Hunt to write the native language in a phonetic script which could be precisely translated into English. To support himself while he did scholarly work (which began in earnest about the turn of the century), Hunt worked in canneries and as an expedition guide. As he became an elder, Hunt also became a political leader among his people. He was one of few native informants who maintained the respect of both academicians and his own people. Hunt also worked as a consultant to the American Museum of Natural History. He died at Fort Rupert in 1933.

See also Hamatsa; Kwakiutl.

Hunting and gathering
TRIBES AFFECTED: Many tribes and prehistoric cultures
SIGNIFICANCE: Hunting and gathering societies could not amass surplus food supplies, but they generally met their needs adequately and had significant leisure time

"Hunting and gathering" refers to the economic activities of the simplest and historically earliest form of human society. Hunters and gatherers were migrant people possessing only rudimentary technology who traveled a fixed territory in pursuit of seasonal produce and game animals. Because they were usually ignorant of techniques of food preservation, hunters and gatherers did not collect surplus, thereby making them susceptible to occasional food shortages. Usually, however, tribes were so well adapted that even in the most marginal areas they easily supplied their continuing caloric needs by utilizing a wide range of food sources. Indeed, hunters and gatherers maintained the most leisurely lifestyle of any human societies, often devoting a scant two or three hours per day to subsistence activities.

Hunting and gathering tribes contained several small bands of less than fifty members, all related by kinship or marriage. Occasionally kinship was fictive. Within bands the nuclear family was the primary economic and social unit. Bands usually maintained a central camp, and food sharing was a principal feature of life. Occasionally bands met on ceremonial occasions or for the exchange, through marriage, of men or women.

Of all human societies, hunting and gathering bands were the most egalitarian. Although bands usually acknowledged a headman, his role was merely advisory, and his status was in recognition of unusual prowess in a vital skill such as hunting. Likewise, there was greater sexual equality than among other types of societies. Among the Ute of the Great Basin, for example, instruction of women in abortion techniques and enforced sexual abstinence for more than a year after childbirth freed women from overly burdensome maternal responsibilities. Trial marriages were common, and divorce could be accomplished simply by returning to the parental camp.

Division of labor was by sex, with men hunting and women gathering food. Warfare and political functions were male responsibilities, as were religious and ceremonial leadership; elaborate rituals often surrounded a hunt. Child rearing and domestic activities such as cooking, basketmaking, sewing, and tanning hides were female duties. Hunting was awarded the highest social significance, which resulted in male dominance. Yet fully two-thirds or more of caloric needs were met by women's gathering activities.

Lacking higher authorities, discipline was usually performed within families. Ostracism and gossip within the band were also effective deterrents of crime. Tensions were often diffused by elaborate and ritualized methods such as insult singing.

Because they were limited by their nomadic lifestyles, material possessions among hunters and gatherers were usually few. Oral traditions, including storytelling and historical renditions, however, were often elaborate. Unusual storytelling ability was valued, often conferring high status. Likewise, decorative arts could also be elaborate. The greatest precontact concentration of hunting and gathering tribes in North America was in the semi-arid Great Basin of Nevada, California, Oregon, Idaho, and Utah. By the mid-twentieth century, all American Indian hunting and gathering tribes had abandoned their traditional lifestyles.

See also California; Great Basin; Paleo-Indian; Subsistence.

Hupa: Tribe
CULTURE AREA: California
LANGUAGE GROUP: Athapaskan
PRIMARY LOCATION: Northwestern California
POPULATION SIZE: 2,451 (1990 U.S. Census)

Little is known of Hupa prehistory, but their language indicates that they came from the north about thirteen hundred years ago. Living along the Trinity River in twelve villages, in an area of dense vegetation, their primary subsistence orientation was toward acorns and fish, particularly salmon, which they caught during spring and fall migratory runs with a specialized fishing technology. Hupa religious life was centered on two world-renewal and wealth-display ceremonies, the Jumping Dance and White Deerskin Dance, rituals to ward off famine and natural disaster and to ensure an abundance of resources. The autumn Acorn Feast and spring First Salmon ceremonies were also important.

Woodworking and basketweaving were important status skills. Possession of traditional forms of wealth such as dentalium shell money, scarlet-feathered woodpecker scalp capes, obsidian blades, and albino deerskins were used for a number of purposes. These included the paying of a bride price, resolving conflicts, and paying a shaman's fee. Social control was by achieved through consensus, threat of witchcraft or sorcery, and complex dietary and behavioral taboos.

First European American contact was with fur trappers in the 1840's. Contact became sustained in the 1850's when Chinese and white gold miners prospected the Hoopa Valley, some taking up permanent residence. An estimated aboriginal population of eighteen hundred was reduced in half by 1870, mostly from introduced diseases. Fort Gaston was established in 1858, and by 1864 Congress had authorized nearly the entire Hupa territory for a reservation (87,000 acres). Gradually, the Hupa took to agriculture and lumbering. Though they knew of the 1870 Ghost Dance, they never participated in the messianic movement as did their neighbors the Karok and Yurok. A government boarding school and hospital were established on the reservation.

By the 1990's, much Hupa income was from employment in numerous mills, owned mostly by whites. The wage economy adopted after World War II virtually ended all stock raising and farming. The Hupa enjoy a relatively high standard of living, and they maintain their ethnic identity through native language and self-management of internal affairs.

See also California; Karok; White Deerskin Dance; Yurok.

Huron: Tribe
CULTURE AREA: Northeast
LANGUAGE GROUP: Iroquoian
PRIMARY LOCATION: Oklahoma, Quebec
POPULATION SIZE: 1,947 in U.S. (1990 U.S. Census); 1,450 in Canada (Statistics Canada, based on 1991 census)

The Hurons were a confederacy of four highly organized matrilineal and matrilocal tribes, the Attignaouantan (Bear People), Attigneenongnhac (Cord People), Arendahronon (Rock People), and Tohontaernrat (Deer People). Their historic homeland, Huronia, was in south central Ontario near Lake Simcoe, east of Lake Huron. In the early 1600's, they probably numbered about thirty thousand. The Hurons were horticultural, with women producing the staple crops: corn, beans, squash, and sunflowers. These were supplemented by game hunting, fishing, and berry picking, as well as by trade with other tribes for less common food commodities and other products. The Hurons traveled widely in the 1600's to pursue trade. They had successfully kept tribes to their west and north from trading directly with the French in New France (Quebec) so that they enjoyed a "middleman" role in the burgeoning fur trade of the seventeenth century. All of this came to a crashing halt in 1649-1651 when Iroquois tribes ventured northwest into Huronia and completely dispersed the four Huron tribes along with neighboring tribes. The Hurons had already been plagued with disease and had their culture disrupted by French Jesuit missionaries, who introduced a foreign belief system.

The few Huron people who were not captured by the Iroquois tribes and absorbed as adoptees into those communities moved, with fellow refugees of the Tobacco Nation, north and west of Lake Huron. One group of these refugees subsequently occupied areas around Michilmackinac (Mackinac, Michigan), Green Bay (Wisconsin), the Ohio Valley, Detroit, Sandusky (Ohio), eastern Kansas, and eventually, Oklahoma. The group that eventually settled in Oklahoma took the name Wyandot (Wyandotte). The name originated as "Wendat," their name for themselves in the (nearly extinct) Huron language, meaning "islanders" or "peninsula dwellers." The word "Huron" was French and derogatorily referred to these people as "boarlike" or "unkempt."

The other group of refugees (those not eventually finding a home in Oklahoma) traveled with Jesuit missionaries to the St. Lawrence Valley in the seventeenth century, establishing a village called Lorette, near present-day Quebec City. Like their Oklahoma relatives, the Lorette Hurons are somewhat assimilated into the surrounding culture but still maintain some traditional cultural practices and beliefs.

See also Beaver Wars; Indian-white relations—French colonial; Iroquois Confederacy; Neutral; Petun; Pontiac's Conspiracy; Tecumseh's Rebellion.

Husk Face Society

TRIBES AFFECTED: Iroquois tribes
SIGNIFICANCE: Also called the Bushy Heads, the Husk Faces are an Iroquoian medicine society ministering to specific illnesses and conducting certain ritual functions

Husk Faces wear masks braided or woven from cornhusks. Paraphernalia also includes wooden hoes, shovels, and paddles for spreading or combing ashes. Membership in the Husk Face Society includes both men and women and comes as the result of dreaming of, or visioning, agricultural spirits, which ranking members of the society recognize. Husk Faces function in the Midwinter Ceremony in a key role as clowns. The female members dress as men and the men as women. They also reverse dance roles in the Midwinter Ceremony, and before departing they usually prophesy an abundant corn harvest for the coming year. Husk Faces herald the arrival of False Face Society members during the autumnal Thanksgiving Ceremony. Public appearances at Green Corn and other ceremonies include functioning to dispel disease. During False Face ceremonies, the Husk Faces act as "doorkeepers." Husk Face masks include protruded mouth holes from which healers expel a curative blow on hot coals. Husk Face Society members seem to handle hot coals with ease.

See also Clowns; False Face Ceremony; Midwinter Ceremony.

BIBLIOGRAPHY
Fenton, William N. *The False Faces of the Iroquois*. Norman: University of Oklahoma Press, 1987.

Igloo

TRIBES AFFECTED: Primarily Inuit (Eskimo) groups in the Arctic culture area

SIGNIFICANCE: Igloos were the main dwelling structures of central Arctic tribes

Igloos, found mostly in the central Arctic, were hemispherical structures of varying size made of wind-compacted snow. Blocks were cut with bone or baleen knives. When placed one atop another in an inclined plane, each course of snow blocks decreased in circumference until the very top, which was completed with a capblock. Additional insulation was provided by shoveling loose snow atop the completed structure. A window for light was made of ice. It normally took two men three hours to build such a structure.

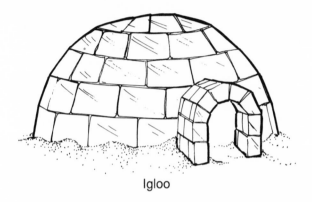

Igloo

The domoid igloo was divided into a living/cooking area and raised sleeping platform. The entrance tunnel sump was always lowest, so that entering cold air was warmed and then exited through a small opening over the sleeping area. It was important that the insulation effect not be reduced by the interior becoming too warm and the ice melting. Igloo size varied from accommodation for an extended family to a large ceremonial structure. On occasion, individual igloos situated at productive resource areas, particularly ice-sealing sites, were joined by tunnels.

See also Architecture—Arctic; Arctic; Inuit.

Ignacio (1828, San Juan, Colo.—Dec. 9, 1913, Ute Mountain Reservation, Colo.): Tribal chief, Ute negotiator

ALSO KNOWN AS: John Lyon

TRIBAL AFFILIATION: Wiminuche Ute

SIGNIFICANCE: Ignacio was leader of the Southern Ute during negotiations with the U.S. government for a Ute reservation

The Southern Ute, comprising the Wiminuche, Muache, and Capote bands, occupied land in the San Juan Mountains of southwestern Colorado. A seminomadic tribe, they ventured into New Mexico, Utah, and the San Luis Valley of Colorado on hunting and trading forays. In 1849, they signed a treaty recognizing the authority of the United States government. In the 1860's, mining discoveries attracted white prospectors to the Colorado mountains; in 1863 the Capote, Wiminuche, and

Tabeguache Utes agreed to accept a large reservation in western Colorado. Pressure from white settlers and miners resulted in reductions of the Ute reservation in 1868 and 1873. In 1878 the Southern Utes accepted a smaller reservation in southwestern Colorado and received their own agency in the San Juan basin.

Ignacio, a member of the Wiminuche band of the Southern Ute, was born in the San Juan mountains in 1828. His father, also a medicine man, was killed by a dying man's family after he failed to cure him. Ignacio exacted revenge by killing all twelve members of the family of the dead man. He grew to be a peace-loving man, however, and a chief of the Wiminuche. He counseled cooperation with whites and abided by all treaties between his people and the United States. Although Ouray of the Tabeguache (or Uncompaghre) band was considered the chief of all the Utes by the U.S. government, the Southern Ute recognized Ignacio, Kaniache, and Ankatosh as their major chiefs. Ignacio would have little to do with Ouray because the Tabeguache chief received a stipend from the U.S. government for his services. Ouray deferred to Ignacio on matters having to do with the land of the Southern Utes, especially the 1878 land settlement. After the death of Ouray in 1880, Ignacio was recognized as the chief of all the Southern Utes. He died at the Ute Mountain Reservation on December 9, 1913. The town of Ignacio, Colorado, was named for him.

See also Ouray, Ute.

Illinois: Tribe

CULTURE AREA: Northeast

LANGUAGE GROUP: Algonquian

PRIMARY LOCATION: Oklahoma

POPULATION SIZE: 1,365 (1990 U.S. Census)

When they first encountered Europeans in the 1670's, the Illinois Indians occupied an area roughly equivalent to the present state of Illinois, though there is evidence that they had previously lived in present-day Michigan. They were among the largest tribes in the region, with an estimated population of thirteen thousand in the 1650's. The size of the tribe may explain its division into at least six subtribes: the Cahokia, Kaskaskia, Michigamea, Moingwena, Peoria, and Tamaroa. Though each of the subtribes had its own chief, all spoke the same language and acknowledged a single chief for the whole tribe.

The traditional economy of the tribe followed a yearly cycle of agriculture, hunting, and gathering. Crops were planted around summer villages; then whole villages would embark on hunting expeditions before returning for the harvest. In winter, smaller groups would scatter to winter villages where hunting continued on a reduced scale.

The Illinois were often involved in warfare with other tribes, a pattern that continued after European contact. Several major wars were fought with the Iroquois in the seventeenth century, at times causing the Illinois to move west of the Mississippi River. The Sioux were also frequent enemies.

The decisive event in the Illinois's history came in 1673 when they established contact with the French. They subsequently became an independent ally of the French and heavily involved in the fur trade. In the process they became increasingly dependent on the French and experienced disruption of their traditional way of life. The Illinois were involved in almost constant warfare with pro-British and pro-Spanish tribes, while disease, especially smallpox and malaria, periodically ravaged the tribe. French success in converting the Illinois to Christianity curtailed what had been a widespread practice of polygamy, with a depressing effect on the tribe's birthrate. By 1700 the number of Illinois had fallen to six thousand.

In the eighteenth and early nineteenth centuries, the tribe experienced significant fragmentation as subtribes often became divided in attitudes toward European powers or other tribes. The attempt to cultivate good relations with the new United States continued to expose the Illinois to attacks from pro-British Indians. All of these factors further weakened the Illinois until by 1800 the tribe's population had fallen to an estimated five hundred. By this time they had ceased to be a significant force in the region.

In 1832 the Illinois signed a treaty with the United States in which they gave up all their lands in Illinois except a small area around Kaskaskia (which was shortly abandoned). After several stops west of the Mississippi, the Illinois were assigned a reservation in the Indian Territory in 1867 in what is now northeastern Oklahoma. There the tribe came to be known as the Peorias and intermarried frequently with other tribes, especially the Sauk, Fox, and Kickapoo. Tribal numbers continued to decline before bottoming out in 1910, when only 130 Peorias were counted. The tribe was terminated by Congress in 1959 but was subsequently restored in 1978.

See also Algonquian language family; Diseases, postcontact; French and Indian Wars; Indian-white relations—French colonial.

Incest taboo

TRIBES AFFECTED: Pantribal
SIGNIFICANCE: This proscription was and continues to be taken very seriously by American Indian cultures

The "incest taboo" refers to the near-universal prohibition against marrying close biological relatives. Incest was condemned in very grave terms by American Indian cultures, even to the extent of being associated with witchcraft and sorcery. The practice of incest was sometimes blamed for reduced success in hunting and other misfortunes which befell communities. The ban on incest involved not only marriage but also any sexual intercourse with forbidden classes of relatives. Such classes included, but were not limited to, biological parents and siblings.

Prohibited relatives also often included parallel cousins (that is, a man marrying his father's brother's daughter or his mother's sister's daughter). In some cultures the same denotation was applied to such cousins as was applied to siblings, as if to reinforce the prohibition on any marital or sexual relationship. One way of examining the likely acceptability of a match between relatives is thus by examining the terms used for the relationships between them.

No such widespread ban, however, existed on relationships between cross cousins (a man marrying his father's sister's daughter or his mother's brother's daughter). In some cultures these marriages were not only permitted but also encouraged, and an alternative partner was wed only when no acceptable cross cousin was available. In such communities, kinship terms for in-laws are often not present, since there is a biological relationship between both parties and their parents. A man was also usually allowed to marry his brother's widow.

Related to the prohibition of incest is the practice of exogamy. Exogamy refers to certain traditional restrictions on marriage that are not based on such close biological ties. One example is the requirement that one marry outside one's clan. Another, local exogamy, dictates bans on marriage within a geographical community, requiring suitors to take a spouse from another location. Exogamy within families may be patrilineal, restricting marriage and sexual bonds with a greater number of relatives of the father; matrilineal, restricting a greater number of relatives of the mother; or bilateral, restricting equal numbers of relatives of both parents.

See also Clans; Kinship and social organization; Marriage and divorce.

Indian

This term is based on one of the greatest mistakes in history. In the late fifteenth century, there was some disagreement over the size of the earth, although it had been accurately determined by the ancient Greeks many centuries earlier. Christopher Columbus and explorers who followed him believed the earth's circumference to be roughly half what we know it to be today.

The purpose of the early explorations of the Americas was to find a pathway to India by sailing west instead of east from Europe, primarily to avoid trouble with the Muslim nations that controlled the territory between Europe and India. Apparently, Columbus thought he had reached India when he landed on the island of Hispaniola (present-day Haiti and the Dominican Republic), named the area the West Indies, and referred to the natives as "Indios" (Spanish for Indians).

While the later British and French explorers who landed in North America did not believe that Massachusetts and Quebec were India, the term was still used, translated into the appropriate languages. The term is still in wide use essentially because no better collective term has been widely accepted. Some native people find the term "Indian" deeply offensive, whereas others find it and "American Indian" acceptable and even preferable to such well-intentioned revisions as "Native American" or the less widely used "Amerind." The most accurate—and most widely accepted—way to identify a person or tradition is simply to refer to the specific tribe or group to which the person or tradition belongs.

See also American Indian; Amerind; Native American; Tribe.

Indian Act of 1876 (Canada)

DATE: 1876

TRIBES AFFECTED: Native Canadians, including status and non-status Indians, Metis, Inuit

SIGNIFICANCE: This act of Parliament was the first comprehensive post-Confederation legislation dealing with Indians, forming the basis for all subsequent Canadian legal policy toward Native Canadians

Not surprisingly, Parliament's first major piece of legislation setting forth the federal government's role and responsibilities with respect to the Indians continued nearly all of the policies established during British colonial rule. As with the British policy, the dual features of the legislation were the protection of the Indians and their eventual assimilation into Canadian society. Ironically, these goals worked at cross purposes. Paternalistic efforts to protect the Indians emphasized the distinctions between Indians and Euro-Canadians and therefore actually discouraged assimilation. This legislation first applied only to Canadians of Indian descent. It was later extended to include Inuit as well.

The act, as it was written, established a series of reserved lands which were to be laboratories for training the Indians in the ways of whites and established elected band councils whose powers were minimal. The reserves, administered by a government agent, were exempt from taxation, and those living on a reserve had access to food and supplies in the form of disaster rations. While the reserves were intended to protect the supposedly naïve Indians from the unscrupulous practices of outsiders, they isolated Indians from most Euro-Canadians and subjected them to the sometimes unscrupulous practices of the all-powerful Indian agents. These agents had control over social, political, and economic activities on the reserves. They also had the ability to withhold rations from those who did not adhere to their dictatorial policies. Numerous abuses occurred. For several decades Indians on the prairies were forbidden to leave their reserve without a pass from the agent. They were further prohibited from staying overnight on a reserve other than their own, and in many cases non-Indians (including non-status Indians) were forbidden from residing on reserves. Subsequent amendments to the Indian Act banned native religious activities such as the Sun Dance and potlatch and made it illegal for Indians to solicit contributions in order to pursue land claims.

The act codified the category "Indian" as a legal rather than racial or cultural designation and gave the government the legal power to determine who qualified as an Indian. It further provided for the enfranchisement of individuals, wherein a man could surrender Indian status for himself, his wife, and his children in exchange for Canadian citizenship and a plot of land. Women who married non-Indians, including non-status Indians, lost their own Indian status and benefits. Their children were also precluded from claiming Indian status. Non-Indian women who married status Indians became status Indians themselves. Enfranchisement could also be imposed upon Indians who earned a college degree or entered a profession such as minister, teacher, lawyer, or doctor.

Though amended many times, the Indian Act was not significantly revised until 1951.

See also Indian Act of 1951 (Canada); Indian Act of 1989 (Canada); Indian-white relations—Canadian; Reserve system of Canada; Treaties and agreements in Canada; Voting rights—Canada.

Indian Act of 1951 (Canada)

DATE: 1951

TRIBES AFFECTED: Native Canadians, including status and non-status Indians, Metis, Inuit

SIGNIFICANCE: The first major revision of the Indian Act in seventy-five years softened, but did not eliminate, the blatant discrimination against native peoples institutionalized by earlier legislation

Although the Indian Act of 1951 was the first comprehensive revision of Canada's 1876 Indian Act, it did little to undo the paternalism of its predecessor. Like the previous law, it gave nearly absolute control of Indian activities to the Department of Indian Affairs and Northern Development (DIAND). This included the development of Indian lands and resources as well as oversight of band councils. The new act also retained the enfranchisement provisions of the earlier legislation, including those that denied Indian status to women who married non-Indians. In a well-known sex discrimination suit brought by Jeannette Lavell, an Ojibwa who was denied Indian status as a result of her marriage, the Supreme Court in 1973 upheld those provisions of the act. A Maliceet woman, Sandra Lovelace, took a similar case before the United Nations in 1981. Although Canada was found to have violated international human rights covenants, the enfranchisement provisions of the Indian Act were not repealed until 1985.

The new act did, however, repeal the most blatant discrimination inherent in the Indian Act of 1876. It no longer prohibited Indian religious ceremonies, political fund raising, or consumption of alcohol off reserve lands. Later amendments permitted the consumption of alcohol on reserves and gave Indians the right to vote in Canadian elections.

The 1951 act continued a number of benefits of the earlier legislation including the exemption of Indian lands from property and estate taxes and exemption of income earned on reserves from taxation. Although these provisions have protected Indian property from seizure, they have also hindered economic development on the reserves. Because Indians have been unable to mortgage their lands, it has often been difficult for them to raise capital for development projects.

Despite the restrictions imposed by the 1951 Indian Act, natives have fought efforts to discard it altogether. Fearing that the federal government would abandon its responsibilities to native welfare, many natives fought the 1969 white paper proposal to repeal the Indian Act. The Indian Act was rewritten in 1985, but other than the repeal of enfranchisement provisions, it remained virtually unchanged.

See also Department of Indian Affairs and Northern Development (DIAND); Indian Act of 1876 (Canada); Indian Act of

1989 (Canada); Indian-white relations—Canadian; Reserve system of Canada; Treaties and agreements in Canada; Voting rights—Canada.

Indian Act of 1989 (Canada)

DATE: 1989

TRIBES AFFECTED: Native Canadians, including status and non-status Indians, Metis, Inuit

SIGNIFICANCE: The Indian Act of 1989 updated and standardized Indian and government rights and responsibilities in Canada

Because of the confusion created by a diversity of local laws in different provinces under the federal government in Canada, legislators have created certain acts that cannot vary according to locality. Such is the case of the Indian Act of 1989. In effect a compendium of earlier acts (of 1927 and 1951), it also added new laws more in keeping with contemporary conditions.

The main divisions of the act provide for the designation of reserves (land vested in Her Majesty's Crown, but "reserved for Indian use"), establishment of band councils and election of band leaders, and a comprehensive Indian Register. By the act, the sole authority of the band council to assign possession of specific reserve lands to individuals is recognized for the first time. This right of possession must be recognized by the Superintendent General of Indian Affairs, who issues a Certificate of Possession. Possessors may transfer their land rights, but only to other members within their band, or back to the band council itself.

Provisions respecting the security of reserves against government expropriation ended misunderstandings that had developed over many years. With the right of security went defined areas of band responsibility (to maintain roads, bridges, and so on) which, if unfulfilled, could lead to government charges against band councils. Common responsibility between councils and government for revenues accruing to bands (through royalties or sale of Indian produced goods) is spelled out, including the government right to use such funds to assure proper sanitary facilities and disease control.

One use of government funds on reserves reflects benevolent subsidies under the 1989 act. Schools are to be provided to all bands on an equal basis, and attendance up to a minimum age is required of all Indian children. Provisions for tax-exempt status (lands, personal property, or salaries earned in reserve areas) and taxable income earned from contacts beyond the reserves are meant to protect both Indian and government interests.

The act contains brief mention of individual rights. There is a right of testamentary wills for family security. Otherwise, where individual Indian rights might be jeopardized owing to band council inaction, government intervention is allowed (mainly to aid orphans or the mentally handicapped).

See also Department of Indian Affairs and Northern Development (DIAND); Indian Act of 1876 (Canada); Indian Act of 1951 (Canada); Indian-white relations—Canadian; Reserve system of Canada; Treaties and agreements in Canada; Voting rights—Canada.

Indian Arts and Crafts Board (IACB)

DATE: Established 1935

TRIBES AFFECTED: Pantribal

SIGNIFICANCE: Activities of the IACB from 1935 through 1944 did much to open American and European markets for Indian arts and crafts

The Indian Arts and Crafts Board (IACB) was founded by an act of Congress in 1935, explicitly to aid the development of arts and crafts markets and to stem the flow of fake "Indian-made" objects which siphoned off much of the potential income. The goal of stimulating markets has been diligently pursued since then, while efforts to create trademarks for authentic works by Indians have waned. In the early 1990's the board was charged with writing the regulations for the 1990 Indian Arts and Crafts Law.

John Collier, commissioner of Indian affairs from 1933 to 1945, appointed a board with René d'Harnoncourt as general manager (1936-1944) and chairman after 1943. D'Harnoncourt's philosophy was that only through personal contact and cooperation with local Indian leaders, background research, and consideration of conditions for each tribe could craftspeople be helped by the board. Work began with a survey of art instruction in government schools. The board then established trademarks for authentic handcrafted Navajo, Pueblo, and Hopi silver products, Navajo wool and rugs, and Alaskan crafts. The board convinced the Great Northern Railway to carry Dakota and Montana tribal crafts in its stores and organized production and merchandising groups in Alaska, Nevada, Oklahoma, and Arizona. It set up an experimental laboratory for tanners, weavers, and silversmiths in New Mexico. The best market potential was predicted for objects deemed both high-quality and useful. Three field assistants were hired in 1938, Gladys Tantaquidgeon (Mohegan) to develop crafts among the Sioux, Alice Marriott to revive arts groups and establish cooperatives, research beading, pottery, and leather work among southern Oklahoma tribes, and Gwyneth Harrington to revive basketry in southern Arizona tribes, particularly the Papago (Tohono O'odham). Of perhaps even greater significance to the mission of the IACB were the exhibits of Indian crafts and working artisans at the 1939 Golden Gate International Exposition at San Francisco, which utilized fifteen galleries, and the 1941 show at the Museum of Modern Art in New York City. Traveling exhibits were launched in other U.S. cities and in Europe. During World War II the board got exemptions from wool and silver rationing for artists and established crafts stores near military bases.

In the 1960's the IACB assumed the administration of three Bureau of Indian Affairs museums—the Southern Plains Indian Museum (Anadarko, Oklahoma), the Northern Plains Indian Museum (Browning, Montana), and the Sioux Indian Museum (Rapid City, South Dakota). It also championed and became adviser to the Institute of American Indian Arts. It began publishing a list of authentic native craftspeople and businesses, which is updated periodically, and developed a seal to certify an authentic Indian business.

Randolph McCurtain was the first Indian (Choctaw) appointed to the five-person board (1945). In 1994 four of the five positions were occupied by Indians. There are four staff positions in the Washington office and others involved in operating the museums.

See also Art and artists, contemporary; Institute of American Indian Arts (IAIA).

Indian Child Welfare Act

DATE: November 8, 1978

TRIBES AFFECTED: Pantribal

SIGNIFICANCE: This act established minimum standards for placement of Indian children in foster or adoptive homes to prevent the breakup of Indian families

The Indian Child Welfare Act, passed into law in 1978, establishes minimum federal standards for the removal of Indian children from their families and the placement of these children in foster or adoptive homes. In essence, the act restricts the placement of Indian children in non-Indian homes and gives jurisdiction to tribal courts in deciding matters of child welfare involving adoptive or foster placement. The law removes state jurisdiction in most Indian child welfare cases, even when problems occur off the reservation.

The law affirms the continued existence and the integrity of Indian tribes and was specifically designed to end discriminatory practices of state and county welfare agencies which disregarded Indian extended family arrangements and placed large numbers of Indian children in non-Indian homes. Senate hearings conducted in 1974 documented evidence that as many as 25 percent of Indian children were being systematically removed from their natural families. This in turn was causing the breakup of the Indian family and a high degree of social disruption in Indian communities.

The law provides that when foster care or adoption is necessary, the child's extended family has first priority to assume custody. If no extended family member is available, a member of the child's tribe or an Indian from another tribe has priority over non-Indians. The law also requires that before removal occurs, there must be documented efforts to provide services necessary to solve the family's problem.

The Indian Child Welfare Act strongly supports tribal sovereignty and affirms the value of tribal courts and the importance of Indian tribes in controlling the fate of their children. Historically, though, full implementation of this law has been hampered by lack of adequate appropriations and lack of administrative cooperation between federal, state, and tribal governments.

The Indian Child Welfare Act of 1978 was intended to help prevent the needless breakup of Indian families through the removal of children by government agencies. (James L. Shaffer)

See also Adoption; Children; Indian Self-Determination and Education Assistance Act.

Indian Citizenship Act

DATE: June 2, 1924

TRIBES AFFECTED: Pantribal

SIGNIFICANCE: This act conferred U.S. citizenship on all American Indians born within the territorial limits of the United States, permitting dual U.S. and tribal citizenship, but did little to secure or improve Native Americans' rights

American Indians hold a unique position in American society and law, so the acquisition of citizenship took special congressional action. Several factors made citizenship difficult to obtain. As long as Indians were members of tribes or nations which negotiated treaties with the United States government as independent political units, they could not be considered American citizens. Two significant rulings made it clear that a specific act of Congress would eventually be required to grant Indians citizenship. An 1870 Senate committee on the judiciary ruled that tribal Indians were not granted citizenship under the Fourteenth Amendment (1868), which gave citizenship to recently emancipated slaves, because Indians were not subject to the jurisdiction of the United States. In 1884, *Elk v. Wilkins*, an Indian who had severed tribal relations and lived among whites was ruled ineligible to be a United States citizen because he had been born a tribal member.

By the 1880's many in the United States sought to end tribal sovereignty, to individualize Indians, and to make them citizens. The General Allotment Act (1887) therefore carried provisions for citizenship as a reward for adopting "the habits of civilized life." In 1901 a congressional act granted every Indian in Oklahoma Territory citizenship, and by 1917, through a variety of federal statutes, more than two-thirds of all Native Americans were United States citizens. It was World War I that reopened the debate about citizenship for all Indians.

American Indians actively supported the war effort through increased food production and contributions to the Red Cross. Most dramatically, six to ten thousand Indians, many of whom were not citizens, enlisted for military service. In return, through the act of November 6, 1919, Congress provided any Indian who received an honorable discharge from military service during World War I the right to apply for citizenship with no restriction on their right to tribal property. Still, by 1920, 125,000 Indians were not citizens, so in 1923 a citizenship bill for all Indians was introduced in Congress. Political maneuverings began at once.

Many mainstream Americans favored citizenship as a way to sever the legal relationship between Indian tribes and the federal government. Full-bloods in many tribes were fearful that citizenship would end tribal sovereignty, bring them under state jurisdiction, and ultimately destroy tribal values. These conflicting views led to a compromise. In January, 1924, Congressman Homer P. Snyder of New York introduced House Resolution 6355, authorizing the secretary of the interior to grant citizenship to all Indians yet stating that "the granting of such citizenship shall not in any manner impair or otherwise affect the right of any Indian to tribal or other property." The American Indian Citizenship Act, signed into law on June 2, 1924, by President Calvin Coolidge, made Indians both citizens of the United States and persons with tribal relations. Ultimately citizenship changed little for Indians; the Bureau of Indian Affairs continued to treat Indians as wards of the government and to administer affairs for Indian citizens, and many Indians were denied the right to vote until the 1960's.

See also American Indian Civil Rights Act; American Indian Religious Freedom Act; Civil rights and citizenship; Reserve system of Canada; Voting rights—United States.

Indian Claims Commission (ICC)

DATE: Established 1946; expired 1978

TRIBES AFFECTED: Pantribal

SIGNIFICANCE: The ICC purported to resolve all pending Indian land claims in the United States

The Indian Claims Commission was established by act of Congress in 1946. Its mandate was to review all pending territorial claims by native peoples within the forty-eight contiguous states and, where these were found to be valid, to retire them through payment of appropriate compensation.

Although the life of the commission was originally expected to be ten years, the sheer volume of the cases it encountered caused its duration to be repeatedly extended. When it was finally suspended on September 30, 1978, the ICC still had a docket of sixty-eight cases remaining to be heard (these were reassigned to the U.S. Court of Claims). In the interim, it had considered several hundred separate claims which, in aggregate, led it to reach some rather striking conclusions in its final report.

As Russel Barsh has summarized the ICC's general findings, "about half a country was purchased by treaty or agreement at an average price of less than a dollar an acre; another third of a [billion] acres, mainly in the west, were confiscated without compensation; another two-thirds of a [billion] acres were claimed by the United States without presence of a unilateral action extinguishing title."

Since the ICC was specifically precluded under its authorizing legislation from effecting transfers of land title where none had previously occurred, the clear implication of the last finding was that legal ownership of the land in question remained vested in American Indians. In effect, then, the United States was engaged in the illegal occupation of approximately one-third of its claimed "domestic" territoriality. There was, however, little the ICC could do to rectify the situation, even if it had been so inclined, because its authorizing legislation also prevented it from actually restoring property to its rightful owners.

For this reason Lakota scholar Vine Deloria, Jr., has observed:

American Indian leaders with President Harry Truman at the signing of the Indian Claims Commission bill in 1946. (Library of Congress)

[T]he Claims Commission ultimately resolved nothing. Rather, it served the useful purpose of clearing away the underbrush of confusion about who really owns what in the United States and thereby paved the way for the resolution of property rights issues at some future point. In the meantime, it assigned some degree of compensation to Indians for the historic loss of use of land to which they never relinquished title.

See also Allotment system; Indian Reorganization Act; Land claims; Sovereignty.

BIBLIOGRAPHY

Barsh, Russel. "Indian Land Claims Policy in the United States." *North Dakota Law Review* 58 (1982): 1-82.

U.S. Indian Claims Commission. *Indian Claims Commission, August 13, 1946-September 30, 1978: Final Report.* Washington, D.C.: Government Printing Office, 1978.

Vance, John T. "The Congressional Mandate and the Indian Claims Commission." *North Dakota Law Review* 45 (1969): 325-336.

Indian Education Acts

DATE: 1972, 1978
TRIBES AFFECTED: Pantribal

SIGNIFICANCE: These acts represent the first legislative victories for Native American peoples under the policy of Indian self-determination, announced by President Richard Nixon in 1970

The Indian Education Act of 1972, Public Law 92-318, was an attempt to remedy some of the problems in Indian education identified in the National Study of American Indian Education (carried out from 1967 to 1971) and in the hearings of the Special Senate Subcommittee on Indian Education that summarized its findings in 1969 under the title *Indian Education: A National Tragedy, a National Challenge* (also known as the Kennedy Report). Both studies found that Indian people wanted a better education for their children, wanted schools to pay more attention to Indian heritage, and wanted more to say in how their children's schools were run.

The 1972 act pertained to public schools on and off reservations and provided supplemental funding for schools with ten or more Indian students in order to meet their special needs. All public schools with Indian students could get this quasi-entitlement funding and were required to involve Indian parents and communities in designing the supplemental programs. Grant money was also provided.

Part A of the act required parental and community participation in impact-aid programs (programs that provided federal money to local school districts to make up for tax-exempt federal lands such as Indian reservations). Part B authorized a series of grant programs to stress culturally relevant and bilingual curriculum materials. Part C provided money for adult-education projects. Part D established an Office of Indian Education within the U.S. Office of Education (now the Department of Education). Part E provided funds for training teachers for Bureau of Indian Affairs (BIA) schools, with preference to be given to Indians. The act also established the National Advisory Council on Indian Education.

The Indian Education Amendments of 1978 (P.L. 95-561) established standards for BIA schools, institutionalized BIA school boards, required formula funding of BIA schools, and provided for increased Indian involvement in the spending of impact-aid funds.

See also American Indian Higher Education Consortium (AIHEC); Bureau of Indian Affairs (BIA); Civil rights and citizenship; Education, post-contact; Indian Citizenship Act.

Indian police and judges

TRIBES AFFECTED: Pantribal
SIGNIFICANCE: In 1878, a native police force and judicial system were created to administer justice on reservations

In 1817, the United States Supreme Court ruled that federal courts had jurisdiction over all cases, criminal and civil, in "Indian country." The army served as the police force for Native Americans, and trials were held in federal courts. That policy remained in effect until 1878, when Secretary of the Interior Carl Schurz recommended to Congress the creation of the United States Indian Police. Schurz received warnings from army officers in the West that starving Indians on reservations were becoming desperate and that a rebellion could break out at any time. Since the army did not have enough troops available to react quickly to such an alarming possibility, it was suggested that Indians themselves be trained to handle such problems. Congress approved the creation of a native police force under the control of Office of Indian Affairs agents. Within three years, 162 officers and 653 privates, all Native Americans, were working at forty agencies in the West.

Congress gave the Indian police the authority to guard reservations against trespassers, find and return "truants" from the reservation, arrest people for drunkenness, and provide other police services. The officers and their men generally received high praise from Indians and white agents for their conduct. Indians respected their own police much more than they did white military personnel.

In 1883, the Department of the Interior authorized creation of Courts of Indian Offenses. The police were to serve as judges in these courts. Policemen serving as both judges and arresting officers created conflicts in many trials, so Congress approved hiring new Native American judges, even though it meant spending a little more money. Some whites in Congress

and in white areas surrounding reservations, however, feared giving Native Americans full control of their criminal justice system. In 1885, the secretary of the interior acted to limit the types of crimes heard in the Indian courts. Indian judges could no longer hear cases concerning murder, manslaughter, rape, assault, arson, burglary, or larceny. These crimes were returned to the jurisdiction of United States marshals and federal district courts. Indian judges could try cases involving only petty criminal offenses. Despite these limits, the Indian police and courts proved a successful reform in treatment of Native Americans by allowing for more self-government on reservations.

See also American Indian Civil Rights Act; Civil rights and citizenship; Indian Citizenship Act; Sovereignty.

Indian Removal Act

DATE: May 28, 1830
TRIBES AFFECTED: All tribes east of the Mississippi River
SIGNIFICANCE: This act resulted in the resettlement, both voluntary and involuntary, of nearly sixty thousand eastern Indians to lands west of the Mississippi River

The federal policy of Indian removal, formalized by the Indian Removal Act of 1830, was advocated by humanitarian reformers seeking to protect Indians from white encroachment, by white settlers who coveted Indian lands, and by state and federal officials who were challenging the vaguely defined constitutional status of Indians living within states' borders. Removal was accomplished by President Andrew Jackson, who was seeking to meliorate conflicts between states and the federal government over issues of state sovereignty.

By the 1820's, efforts to assimilate Indians through education and Christianization appeared unacceptably slow to land-hungry settlers and state officials. Because of disease, wars, treaties, illegal encroachments, and land speculations most regions of the eastern United States already had been virtually cleared of Indians. Several tribes remained, however, including the Five Civilized Tribes—Cherokee, Creek, Choctaw, Chickasaw, and Seminole—of the South and the Iroquois of the North.

With the Louisiana Purchase of 1803 proving a vast new tract of land, President Thomas Jefferson suggested removal—the exchange of eastern for western lands—as a humanitarian measure designed to protect Indians from demoralization and corruption attending their contact with whites. After President James Monroe in 1824 recommended to Congress that all Indians be moved west of the Mississippi, some tribes and groups of individuals accepted subsequent congressional offers for relocation. Others, notably the Five Civilized tribes, refused to vacate their ancestral lands.

When Andrew Jackson assumed the presidency in 1828, Georgia was exerting force on the federal government to meet the terms of an 1802 agreement by which Georgia had ceded claims to western lands in exchange for federal promises to extinguish Indian land claims within Georgia. The ineluctable spread of cotton agriculture and the discovery of gold on

Cherokee lands in 1829 intensified Georgia's impatience. Accordingly, in 1828 and 1829, Georgia enacted laws nullifying Cherokee land claims and extended state law over the Cherokee Nation. The Cherokees, in turn, lodged a congressional protest. Jackson, however, sympathized with Georgia and in 1830 secured passage of the Indian Removal Act, providing for the removal of all eastern Indians to lands west of the Mississippi. Furthermore, in 1831 and 1832, he refused to enforce Supreme Court decisions promising Cherokees federal protection.

Theoretically, removal was to have been voluntarily negotiated between the United States government and Indian tribes. Those Indians choosing to remain in the east as individuals were offered allotments of land and the right to become United States citizens. In practice, however, those who remained were victimized by land speculators and squatters, while those who rejected removal or allotment were moved westward involuntarily. The plight of the Cherokees, as they embarked on a forced march known as the Trail of Tears, symbolized the inexorable and historical dispossession of American Indians facilitated by the Indian Removal Act.

See also Cherokee; Chickasaw; Choctaw; Creek; Removal; Seminole; Trail of Tears.

Indian Reorganization Act

DATE: 1934

TRIBES AFFECTED: Pantribal

SIGNIFICANCE: This act was the central piece of John Collier's Indian New Deal, shifting federal policy away from assimilating Indians and toward preserving and strengthening Indian tribes and cultures

The Great Depression caused considerable rethinking about whether the United States was progressing toward a future of wealth and plenty. Some people, including Franklin D. Roosevelt's commissioner of Indian affairs John Collier, in their doubts looked to the close-knit, nonmaterialistic world of the American Indians for an alternative to what they saw was wrong with modern society. Through the Indian Reorganization Act (IRA), Collier sought to preserve Indian cultures and to implement the recommendations of the 1928 Meriam Report, which was very critical of how the Bureau of Indian Affairs (BIA) had dealt with Indians.

Collier's original version of the Indian Reorganization Act (IRA) was rewritten and toned down in the legislative process, but the act was still radical for the time. The IRA ended further allotment of Indian lands and provided for Indian religious freedom, a measure of tribal self-government, a revolving loan fund for economic development, and Indian preference in hiring within the BIA. Collier hoped to revitalize Indian tribes, but many legislators, while voting in favor of the IRA in the fervor of the first years of Roosevelt's "New Deal," did not really support Collier's goal.

Through 1935, 172 tribes and communities held referendums and agreed to come under the Indian Reorganization Act; another 63 refused. Most tribes were deeply suspicious of any government efforts no matter how beneficial the government said they were. Some tribes were influenced by missionaries and Christianized Indians who saw Collier's admiration of Indian traditional religions as anti-Christian and antiprogressive.

While Collier's efforts received a setback during the termination period after World War II, the IRA continued to provide a legal framework for tribal governments, whose powers greatly expanded when the federal termination policies of the 1950's and 1960's gave way to self-determination policies in the 1970's and 1980's.

The Johnson-O'Malley (JOM) Act authorized the secretary of the interior to enter into contracts with states to pay them for providing services to Indians, including paying them for educating Indians in public schools. Since 1891, the BIA had dealt with each school district individually. Putting Indian children in public schools was problematic. Rural teachers tended to conform to local prejudices against Indians. In addition, public schools in the 1930's were in financial crisis because of the Depression and were dropping health, physical education, shop, and other courses that Collier and others thought were basic for Indian students.

Originally, JOM funding went into the general operating fund of the school districts and could be used to support the education of non-Indian students (as pointed out by a study, *An Even Chance*, done by the National Association for the Advancement of Colored People in 1971). Such reports led to JOM funding being targeted for special programs that required Indian parent committee approval and that were only for Indian students.

See also Allotment system; General Allotment Act; Meriam Report; Oklahoma Indian Welfare Act; Termination policy.

Indian Rights Association

DATE: Since 1882

TRIBES AFFECTED: Pantribal

SIGNIFICANCE: The Indian Rights Association was the most prominent of the humanitarian Christian reform groups, known as "friends of the Indian," which were active in influencing federal Indian policy in the latter part of the nineteenth century

The Indian Rights Association was founded in Philadelphia in 1882 by Henry Panacoast and Herbert Welsh, and it became the most important of the humanitarian groups which formed in the last two decades of the nineteenth century and sought the assimilation of Indians into mainstream American society. Welsh and Panacoast viewed the federal reservation system as a cultural and economic failure and asserted that reservations were obstacles to the civilization of Indians.

The Indian Rights Association diligently pursued its agenda to break up tribalism and bring Christian civilization to Indians by pressing for abolition of the reservation system through allotment of tribal lands, by supporting industrial education for Indians in order to encourage self-sufficiency, and by pressing for immediate citizenship for Indians so they would come under constitutional and state laws. The organization's political goals were inextricably bound to a belief in the superiority of Christian civilization. In 1886 Welsh asserted that the organization was doing God's will by guiding Indians "from the night of barbarism into the dawn of civilization."

The Indian Rights Association was successful because it was well organized and had dedicated members who pushed its agenda. The association hired a lobbyist in order to exert constant pressure on congressional committees, legislators, and Indian affairs officials. The organization also influenced public opinion by publishing pamphlets, news articles, and speeches that advanced its views. The association got much public and congressional support for its programs because it regularly sent representatives into Indian country to gather facts that gave such programs credibility. Additionally, the organization mirrored American society of the day by combining religious sentiment with patriotism in its proposals for reforming Indian policy. The association's goal was to acculturate and assimilate Indians fully into American society, and it viewed Indian culture and traditions as being un-American and pagan.

The Indian Rights Association declined in power and influence after Welsh resigned as secretary in 1902 and as federal Indian policy gradually began to support tribalism in the 1920's. The association continues to exist, although it now supports Indian self-determination and Indian groups seeking federal recognition.

See also Friends of the Indian organizations; General Allotment Act; Indian Citizenship Act.

Indian Self-Determination and Education Assistance Act

DATE: 1975

TRIBES AFFECTED: Pantribal

SIGNIFICANCE: This act marked a significant swing away from the overt assimilationist policies of the federal government and supported the basic concepts of tribalism and Native American sovereignty

The 1970's were marked by support of federal officials for broadening Indian participation in programs that affected them and to lessen the paternalism that had guided federal Indian policy for so long. The Indian Self-Determination and Education Assistance Act of 1975 marked a radical change in federal policy—the assimilationist philosophy of the federal government was replaced by policies favoring tribalism and Native American sovereignty. This law enabled and encouraged tribes to take over and run their own programs.

The act clearly endorsed Indian decision making, and the preamble declared that the United States recognized its obligation "to respond to the strong expression of the Indian people for self-determination by assuring maximum participation in the direction of educational as well as other federal services to Indian communities so as to render such services more responsive to the needs and desires of those communities." It also stated that Congress confirms its commitment to maintain "the Federal Government's unique and continuing relationship with and responsibility to the Indian people through the establishment of a meaningful Indian self-determination policy."

The Self-Determination and Education Assistance Act consists of three major sections. In the first part, Congress outlines the basic federal policy toward native people, denounces federal paternalism, and affirms tribal rights to control their own affairs. Second, Congress asserts it will work for Indian self-determination particularly in education, while maintaining and preserving the trust relationship. Third, Indians will receive hiring preference in all federal government contracts affecting Indian tribes.

The most significant drawback to the act is that, even though decision-making and administrative authority seemed to pass to tribal councils, the Bureau of Indian Affairs maintained the power to decide which tribal contracts it would accept. This reserved power included determining budget allocations provided to tribes who seek to run their own programs. Yet despite limitations placed on tribal authority, many tribes throughout the United States contract and run many programs that were formerly run by the Bureau of Indian Affairs. The most dramatic impact of the act has been in the area of education. A majority of former Bureau of Indian Affairs schools are now run by tribes, and many higher education scholarship programs are tribally run. The act is important in that it supports the basic concept of tribal self-determination.

See also American Indian studies programs and archives; Councils, tribal; Education, post-contact; Indian Education Acts.

Indian Territory

TRIBES AFFECTED: Arapaho, Cherokee, Cheyenne, Chickasaw, Choctaw, Comanche, Creek, Huron, Kickapoo, Kiowa, Lenni Lenape, Osage, Pawnee, Quapaw, Seminole, Seneca, Shawnee, Wichita

SIGNIFICANCE: The removal of eastern tribes to the lands west of the Mississippi River known as Indian Territory (centered in present-day Oklahoma) had devastating and profound effects on tribal populations and cultures

Terms such as "Indian country" and "Indian territory" had different meanings at different times in the history of relations between the United States and various Indian nations. The concept of a defined Indian territory developed alongside the policy of removal—removing eastern tribes to lands west of the Mississippi River—created by the Jackson Administration in the late 1820's and early 1830's. It was first proposed as a large area west of the Mississippi that would include present-day Kansas and Oklahoma as well as parts of Nebraska, Colorado, and Wyoming. The land area considered Indian Territory soon shrank, however, as the government gave large parts of it away to white settlers, until it assumed the size it maintained until Oklahoma became a state in 1907. It is this area, essentially modern-day Oklahoma, that is most often meant by Indian Territory.

In 1828, President Andrew Jackson recommended Indian removal legislation to Congress, and the Indian Removal Act

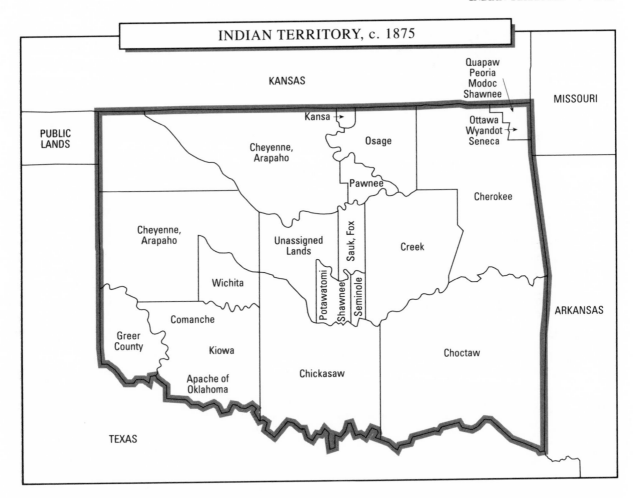

INDIAN TERRITORY, c. 1875

KANSAS

PUBLIC
LANDS

Quapaw
Peoria
Modoc
Shawnee

MISSOURI

Kansa

Osage

Ottawa
Wyandot
Seneca

Cheyenne,
Arapaho

Pawnee

Cherokee

Cheyenne,
Arapaho

Unassigned
Lands

Sauk, Fox

Creek

Wichita

Potawatomi
Shawnee
Seminole

ARKANSAS

Comanche

Greer
County

Kiowa

Choctaw

Apache of
Oklahoma

Chickasaw

TEXAS

was passed May 28, 1830. The Choctaws were the first tribe to cede their homeland and consent to removal to Indian Territory. The main body of the tribe moved between 1830 and 1833. The Creeks were moved second, as a military measure. In 1836, 2,495 Creeks were transported to Indian Territory and left to live or die without clothes, weapons, or cooking utensils. The Cherokees started removal around 1834, and the main tribe was forcibly removed during the bitter winter of 1838-1839. So many died that they finally agreed to manage their own removal. The Chickasaws' removal proceeded without resistance during the winter of 1837-1838. They paid the Choctaws for the right to settle on Choctaw land. The Seminoles resisted removal, were hunted down by the army and navy, and were taken to Indian Territory in chains. In 1856, the United States purchased land from the Creeks for the Seminoles and provided school funds. The Cherokees, Choctaws, and Chickasaws established governments, school systems, and churches as quickly as possible. The Creeks did also, but more slowly. The Seminoles took steps to develop a government and a school system, but progress was interrupted by the Civil War.

The Osages received a large tract along the border of southern Kansas. The Quapaws were removed from Arkansas and

acquired a small reservation northeast of the Cherokees. The Senecas and the Shawnees were also moved into Indian Territory. By the end of the 1830's the Indians owned land in Nebraska, a solid block of reservations along the eastern and most of the southern boundary of Kansas, and all of Oklahoma except the panhandle. This whole region was known as Indian Territory, although a territorial government was never established. Also seeking refuge in Indian Territory were bands of Shawnees, Delawares (Lenni Lenapes), and fragments of other tribes from the Old Northwest. Around 1839, more Shawnees and Delawares and some Kickapoos fled Texas and came to Indian Territory. In 1846, a peace treaty was made with the Caddos, the Tonkawas, and the Penateka (or Southern) Comanches; two reservations in Indian Territory were set aside for them in 1854. When the Kansas-Nebraska Act (1854) created Kansas and Nebraska, the Indians were moved southward and the term Indian Territory became restricted to Oklahoma.

The Civil War created great divisions among and within the tribes in Indian Territory. In 1866, the Five Civilized Tribes signed treaties, forced on them by the United States government for having allied with the Confederacy, that relinquished

An 1879 advertisement for white settlement on land bought by the U.S. government from the Creek, Chickasaw, Choctaw, and Seminole in 1866 (the government's original intent was that the land be settled by other Indians and former slaves). (Library of Congress)

a large part of their western land, thus dividing Indian Territory into two parts. The eastern half belonged to the Five Civilized Tribes, and the remainder became part of the Oklahoma Territory. This western land was to be used as homes for western tribes to be settled on reservations as part of the consolidation policy. In 1907, the remaining Indian Territory, along with Oklahoma Territory, became the new state of Oklahoma.

See also Indian Removal Act; Removal; Trail of Tears.

Indian-white relations—Canadian

TRIBES AFFECTED: Pantribal
SIGNIFICANCE: Canadian Indian-white relations, while less confrontational than relations in the United States, have focused on the same issues of land and self-determination

Whereas American Indian-white relations frequently focused on confrontation and hostility, Canadian relations focused predominantly on trade and legal cession of land. Though both countries followed policies of assimilation and cultural extermination at different points, Canada progressed further in its attempts to treat its native population as participants in the political process.

1500's-1700's. When French and English explorers first "discovered" Canada, they remarked upon the settled natives they encountered. The tribes along the Hudson River lived in large villages around which they farmed and fished. When French sailors were deposited on the shores of Hudson Bay to start a colony in 1542, they found the Indians to be quite helpful. English sailors and explorers felt equally welcomed by the Indians.

By the early 1600's, as the French began to develop permanent outposts, a trading relationship had been established between the Indians and the French. The French placed their forts in places unwanted by the Indians and relied on the Indians for agricultural support as well as trade. They built their trading posts at traditional Indian trading spots. The French generally respected traditional trading patterns. They used tribes that had always been intermediaries for trade and did not attempt to replace them with Frenchmen. This inspired trust and confidence in the French; the English in the American colonies and the Spanish refused to honor such traditional patterns. In short, the French recognized the importance of the Indians within the region.

The fur trade represented the most important aspect of European relations with the Indians. Originally based on beaver, the fur trade tied the French and English traders to the Indians, who not only trapped and killed the beaver but also treated it to be pelted. The French and English traded goods such as hatchets, cloth, and liquor for these treated pelts, while the Dutch traded muskets. These goods dramatically altered Indian life, changing everything from hunting and warfare to cooking.

The Indians also introduced new technology to the English and French. The canoe helped the French and English establish themselves in Canada. The canoe provided them with the means to transport goods through the river and lake systems. Indians also taught white traders how to survive in the wilds of Canada, which increased the interaction and interdependence between the groups.

Additionally, relations between Canadian Indians and the French remained friendly despite the arrival of Catholic missionaries in 1625. Though the French traders transported missionaries, the state did not support priests. Unlike the Spanish Catholic missionaries, they had no support from the military. While the acceptance of priests into an Indian community might be a condition for trade, the acceptance of Christianity was not a requirement for trade with the French.

The French, unlike their English and Spanish counterparts, tended to allow intermarriage. Many traders discovered that intermarriage strengthened the trading ties between the French and an Indian tribe, increasing profit. Many early French trappers married Indian women, creating a Metis population.

The French also encouraged alliances and peace between different tribes. They acted as intermediaries for settling disputes, which worked to their advantage. If the Iroquois refused to trade with the French because the Abenaki did, the French arranged for some sort of settlement so that both would trade with them.

When the English began to establish a foothold in Canada in the early 1700's, the calm relations between the French and the Indians forced the English to adopt similar methods. Unlike in the American colonies, where traders were almost forbidden to marry Indian women, the Hudson's Bay Company, founded in 1670, encouraged such relationships in the name of trade. An Indian or Metis wife offered a certain cachet to the rising trader.

The Hudson's Bay Company became an important definer of Indian-white relations in Canada. Built on the fur trade, it relied heavily on cordial relations with the Indians. Until the French were forced out in 1760, it was necessary to encourage friendly relations with the Indians lest they switch trade to the French. The Hudson's Bay Company also established forts at traditional trading points.

Contact between the whites and the Indians during this period was not always peaceful. Whites in Canada spread disease just as they had in Mexico and the United States. Some groups, such as the Micmacs and the Hurons, suffered greatly from epidemics which destroyed their cultures. Additionally, international tensions spilled over into Canada. The Anglo-French War (French and Indian War) and the American Revolution brought European wars onto Indian soil. Indians had to choose sides, sometimes between enemies and sometimes between trading partners. Often Indian women and children from one tribe were mistaken for those from another by the Europeans and killed for wrongly assumed alliances.

Period of Transition: 1800's. The nineteenth century radically changed the path of Indian-white relations in Canada. The British now controlled Canada and ruled it as a colony. The Hudson's Bay Company controlled the western regions of

A Chipewyan family watches a Hudson's Bay Company steamer on the Great Slave Lake in the Northwest Territories. (National Museum of the American Indian, Smithsonian Institution)

Manitoba, Saskatchewan, Calgary, and British Columbia as well as the Northwest Territories and the Yukon. Protestant and Catholic missionaries began to spread across the country to previously "undiscovered" groups of Indians. Within a hundred short years, the missionaries would alter daily life for most Indians, the Hudson's Bay Company would be gone, Canada would become an independent nation, treaties would cede much Indian land, and settlers would take much of the rest.

In the early 1800's, much remained the same in Canada as it had been for the previous three hundred years. The fur trade remained the main relation between Indians and whites. The Hudson's Bay Company controlled Indian-white relations in the west as well as trade. Intermarriage and interdependence between the whites and Indians still remained.

The nineteenth century, however, soon brought many changes to Indian-white relations. The first big alteration came with an influx of Catholic and Protestant missionaries at the beginning of the century. By the 1830's, missionaries had worked their way into western Ontario and into contact with Plains groups in Manitoba. These missionaries sought to change the Indians into white people through assimilation, agrarianism, and cultural extermination. They built churches and schools. They translated Indian languages and produced Bibles in these languages. The Protestants tried to re-create English villages, while the Catholics absorbed parts of Indian religions into Catholicism to make it more acceptable. Both Protestants and Catholics were disappointed by the conversion rates. Canadian Indian societies tended to remain closed to Christianity; many Indian groups found it interesting but not inspiring. Tensions rose between Indians and white missionaries as missionaries pushed for total acceptance of Christianity and white "civilization."

In 1837 a report presented to the British Parliament stated that frontier development was harmful to the Indians. Parliament reacted by passing the Crown Lands Protection Acts, which placed Indian lands in Crown trust. This accomplished two things. It prevented whites from squatting on Crown lands. It also, however, denied Indians any political rights based on land ownership. This set the pattern for policy after confederation in 1867.

In 1842, the Bagot Commission began to review the Indian Affairs office. It produced three recommendations for British policy regarding the Indians: first, the Indian Affairs office should develop an agricultural program for the Indians; second, schools should be created to assimilate Indian youths into Canadian society; finally, the state should help support religious instruction to the Indians to aid in assimilation. In 1850, the British government continued to encourage assimilation by offering citizenship to any Indians who abandoned their Indian status. Additional legislation blurred the lines between Indians and Canadian citizens. The government offered enfranchisement to any male Indian who was literate (meaning he possessed an understanding of the English language), over twenty-one, free of debt, and possessing a "good character." Though the British/Canadian government did not actually re-move Indians from their land in this period, they did attempt to remove land, status, and culture from the Indians.

By the mid-1800's, the railroads had expanded into western Ontario, bringing more whites to the area. The Hudson's Bay Company remained firm in disallowing settlers within its territories. In 1867, confederation came to Canada. The Hudson's Bay Company released the western territories to Canada, changing Indian-white relations. Indians were no longer protected by their trading relationship, and white settlers and developers wanted Indian land for farms and gold. The white Canadian-born population grew from three million to almost five million between confederation and the end of the century, placing new demands on land and natural resources. During the same period, the number of acres under production rose from eighteen million to thirty million, representing the treaties that removed promising farmland from the Indians.

The newly formed Canadian government followed many of the same policies as the American government, emphasizing assimilation, agrarianism, and cultural extermination. With confederation, the government pushed for land settlements with the Indians, the creation of schools to teach them English and make them Canadian, and the introduction of farming as a means of survival. The reserve system demanded that Indians abandon traditional methods of survival and adopt "peasant" farming. Farming tied native groups to one area of land, making them available for conversion, assimilation, and government control while freeing the land for white farmers. The Canadian government did not seek to create large or profitable farms for the Indians. Instead, they sought to provide them with minimal survival with rudimentary tools and small plots.

The new Canadian government also sought to remove Indian status from the Indians. In 1868 and 1869, the government passed the Indian Act and the Enfranchisement Acts, which created a legal division between "uncivilized Indians" and "civilized whites." The Canadian government promised the same legal and political rights that whites had to any Indian who relinquished his status as an Indian. The Canadian government simply adopted the policies of the British government in erasing the Indian population, politically and legally.

Most Indian groups were not happy with the transfer of power from the Hudson's Bay Company to the Canadian government. Many did not want to surrender their land and adopt farming. One group in particular felt slighted by the arrangements made by the government: the Metis. In 1870, alarmed by government surveyors, a group of Cree Indians and Metis banded together to fight the encroachment on their land. While defending their land, they executed a man from Ontario, which hardened white Canadians against them. The government ended this first rebellion, with leader Louis Riel escaping to the United States. He returned in 1884 to begin the Northwest Rebellion, which stalled the Canadian government for several months. Riel demanded that Metis also receive land settlements. Though they eventually received these rights through the Manitoba Act, Riel was executed for treason and murder in 1885, making him a hero of the Metis and many Indians.

The Cree man on horseback took part in the 1885 Riel Rebellion; the photograph was taken on the Poundmaker Reserve.
(National Museum of the American Indian, Smithsonian Institution)

Between confederation and the end of the century, whites infiltrated the rest of Canada. Miners arrived in the Yukon Territory, bringing missionaries and government officials as well as disease with them. Canadians began to "settle" British Columbia from the Pacific Coast inward. The railroad began to crisscross the country, dividing traditional lands and limiting movement. By 1885, all the major land treaties had been signed. The Plains Indians, who had resisted the longest, relinquished their land as the buffalo disappeared. Only the Indians of British Columbia avoided signing treaties, though whites usurped much of their land without the treaties.

The nineteenth century ended with two notable incidents. First, the Canadian government outlawed the potlatch among the Northwest Pacific coast tribes. This law represented the last act in a war of attrition against Indian cultures. It became a battle cry in the first part of the twentieth century as Indian groups battled for political and legal rights. Second, a smallpox epidemic among the same tribes decimated them. Hundreds of lives were lost, breeding anger, distrust, and discontent among the survivors.

Twentieth Century. The twentieth century did not begin auspiciously for the Indians of Canada. Most resided on reserves, their children sent to boarding schools run by missionaries, their cultures stripped from them, and their movement restricted by laws and pass systems. Many struggled to survive on farming plots that were too small to support families, with outdated tools and equipment. Change, however, eventually came.

Beginning with World War II, Indians began to take back control of their lives. Many Canadian Indians served in World War II, gaining citizenship and political rights without losing their Indian status. This allowed them to challenge certain laws and stereotypes. Though many reserves remained mired in poverty, Indian leaders began to fight for the right to a proper education, for medical reform and access, and for representation. Indians also took control of their natural resources, including timber, oil, and other resources. Inspired by the actions of the American Indian Movement in the United States, several groups formed in Canada in the 1960's and 1970's. The most powerful of these today is the Assembly of First Nations, a coalition of recognized and unrecognized tribal groups.

The Assembly of First Nations has focused on several things since the 1970's. First, it provides political action and a political voice to various groups. Instead of every group fighting the same political and legal battles separately, the assembly helps unify and streamline these battles. Second, it supplies social support in health, business, and education. It organizes arts cooperatives, learning cooperatives and centers, and business cooperatives, centralizing these activities and making them more powerful than small individual groups could be. Finally, its leaders have sought to put Indian concerns firmly on the agenda of the Canadian government. Some of the issues they have focused on in the past are the Great Whale Project on Cree land in Northern Quebec, the lack of treaties in British Columbia, the development of Indian land as tourist attractions, and access to education for Indian men and women.

The Assembly of First Nations has been instrumental in helping make Indian rights an issue for the Canadian government. Indians today represent 5 percent of the Canadian population and are the fastest-growing segment of the population. Yet, until the 1990's, they were not represented in the government. As Canada struggled to maintain its unity and keep Quebec in the Confederation, the Assembly of First Nations and Indian leaders sought to have their concerns included. In 1989, the Canadian government sought ratification of the Meech Lake Accord, which would have allowed Quebec to remain a "distinct society." It made no mention of Indian rights as "distinct societies" or of self-determination. When the accord reached Manitoba for ratification, Elijah Harper, a Cree, stalled the vote in a traditional manner by raising one white feather and refusing comment. He effectively ended the Meech Lake Accord. By 1992, the Canadian government included the Assembly of First Nations in negotiations between provincial governors, finally allowing Indians a voice in their own destiny.

Ironically, 1992 became the unofficial "year of the Indian" in Canada. As well as the assembly being included in the council of governors, the Canadian government returned a large land mass to the Indians of Northern Quebec. An area called Nunavut became available for Indian control, allowing them to regulate hunting, fishing, and development of the land. The area represents almost a complete province in Canada.

Indian-white relations during the twentieth century remain tense. Many contemporary Canadians see Indians as freeloaders on the government. Stereotypes of drunken Indians, Indians wealthy from annuities, and freeloading Indians abound still in Canada. Despite the more peaceful Canadian policy toward Indians, Canada and its Indian population still suffer from the same tensions as those in American society.

—*C. L. Higham*

See also Department of Indian Affairs and Northern Development (DIAND); Fifteen Principles; Indian Act of 1876 (Canada); Indian Act of 1951 (Canada); Indian Act of 1989 (Canada); Indian-white relations—English colonial; Indian-white relations—French colonial; Meech Lake Accord; Reserve system of Canada; Riel Rebellions; Treaties and agreements in Canada; Voting rights—Canada.

BIBLIOGRAPHY

Carter, Sarah. *Lost Harvest: Prairies Indian Reserve Farmers and Government Policy*. Montreal: McGill-Queen's University Press, 1990. Critically exposes the agricultural policies of the Canadian government.

Dickason, Olive. *Canada's First Nations: A History of Founding Peoples from Earliest Times*. Norman: University of Oklahoma Press, 1992. An unparalleled legal, political, and social history of Canadian Indians.

Getty, Ian, and Antoine Lussier, eds. *As Long as the Sun Shines and Water Flows: A Reader in Canadian Native Studies*. Vancouver: University of British Columbia Press, 1983. Includes essays on issues of self-determination, treaty negotiation, and use of natural resources.

Grant, John Webster. *Moon of Wintertime: Missionaries and the Indians of Canada in Encounter Since 1543*. Toronto: University of Toronto Press, 1984. Examines Indian-white contact through the eyes of missionaries and through their cultural legacy.

Miller, J. R. *Skyscrapers Hide the Heavens: A History of Indian-White Relations in Canada*. Toronto: University of Toronto Press, 1989. An excellent study of Indians as politicians and cultural survivors.

Van Kirk, Sylvia. *Many Tender Ties: Women in Fur-Trade Society, 1670-1870*. Norman: University of Oklahoma Press, 1983. Examines relations between white traders and Indian/Metis women.

Indian-white relations—Dutch colonial

TRIBES AFFECTED: Lenni Lenape, Mahican, Mohawk
SIGNIFICANCE: Dutch control of the Hudson Valley (1609-1664) paved the way for the takeover of the southern half of New York by European colonists

The creation of a Dutch colonial claim to the Hudson Valley through the exploration of the river by Henry Hudson, sailing under Dutch charter in 1609, laid the foundations for the creation of a Dutch colony, New Netherland, in the Hudson Valley. The arrival of the Dutch, first as traders and then as settlers, had a disastrous effect on the Indians of the area.

The Fur Trade. Initially, the Dutch perceived the Hudson River valley as the ideal approach to the rich fur trade of the interior. In this view, they were seeing things exactly as their rivals to the north, the French, did. Indeed, with the exception of the Pilgrims, all the Europeans of the late sixteenth and early seventeenth centuries viewed the New World as primarily a source of wealth, to be gained by acquiring its resources and selling these on the European market. For the Spaniards to the south, the resource was gold bullion; for the French and the Dutch to the north (and even for some English traders) the resource was furs. These furs were gained by trading European goods—in the contemporary phrase, "trade goods"—to the Indians in return for their fur harvest.

After the news of Henry Hudson's exploration of the river named for him, the earliest Dutch visitors were all seeking furs. In 1614 the New Netherland Company was chartered to exploit the fur trade; it was superseded in 1621 by the West India Company, which dominated affairs in New Netherland until the English conquest in 1664. Throughout the Dutch period, the hope of those who were interested in the area was that it would be a major source of wealth, because its location offered ready access to the Indians of the interior, principally the Mohawks, the easternmost tribe of the Iroquois Confederacy.

Some of what the Dutch brought to trade with the Indians was of benefit to the Indians. From the Europeans the Indians acquired axes, hoes, and iron cooking pots, all of which enabled them more readily to secure their needs from nature. The Indians soon acquired a taste for coarse woven cloaks of a material known as "duffel." These things were positive. At the same time, however, the Dutch readily supplied the Indians with two items that had negative effects on their culture: guns and liquor. Moreover, with the passage of time the Indian taste for trade goods grew to the point where they were essentially dependent on them.

The focal point of the fur trade was Fort Orange, built near the present site of Albany in 1624. There the West India Company established its trading post, buying furs brought in by the Indians to the west. These Indians were the Mohawks; because of their access to large quantities of furs and their warlike reputation, the Dutch were always careful to maintain good relations with them. The guns furnished to them by the Dutch enabled the Mohawks to carry on vigorous warfare with the Hurons to the north and west. The Dutch were agreeable to that outcome, for it diverted to the Hudson River some of the furs that would otherwise have been sold to the French along the St. Lawrence River.

At home in the United Provinces, however, there were others who had different objectives. A group of wealthy merchants, most notably Kiliaen van Rensselaer, succeeded in breaking the monopoly of the West India Company and opening up New Netherland both to other traders in fur and to settlers. As the English settlements to the north and to the south began to fill with colonists, the Dutch saw their position threatened if New Netherland consisted solely of a few trading posts. Under the leadership of van Rensselaer, a policy of encouraging settlement began in the 1630's.

Settlement and Impact. The earliest settlements were at New Amsterdam, on Manhattan Island, purchased from the local Indians by Peter Minuit in 1626. As the number of settlers grew, frictions with the Indians grew too; many settlers allowed their livestock to roam free (fencing their cultivated fields); as the Indians did not fence theirs, the free-roaming livestock often destroyed Indian crops. As more settlers arrived, more land was needed; although the Dutch were always careful to purchase land from the Indians (sometimes the same land more than once), the Indians began to resent the Dutch presence. The Dutch authorities were also not able to control the actions of free traders, who often sought to defraud the Indians of their pelts.

Conflict peaked in the 1640's and 1650's (in the Peach Wars), during which time the Dutch, through military action, effectively dispossessed the various tribal groups living around the lower Hudson. They continued to maintain good relations with the Mohawks, for they would have been unable to match the Mohawks militarily, especially after the latter were armed with European muskets. By the time the Dutch were forced to cede New Netherland to an invading British fleet in 1664, the local Algonquian tribes had been essentially wiped out. —*Nancy M. Gordon*

See also Beaver; Guns; Indian-white relations—Swedish colonial; Lenni Lenape; Manhattan; Peach Wars.

BIBLIOGRAPHY

Bachman, Van Cleaf. *Peltries or Plantations: The Economic Policies of the Dutch West India Company in New Netherland, 1623-1639.* Baltimore: The Johns Hopkins University Press, 1969.

Donck, Adriaen van der. *A Description of the New Netherlands.* Translated by Jeremiah Johnson. 1841. Reprint. Syracuse, N.Y.: Syracuse University Press, 1968.

Merwick, Donna. *Possessing Albany, 1630-1710: The Dutch and English Experiences.* Cambridge, England: Cambridge University Press, 1990.

Rink, Oliver A. *Holland on the Hudson: An Economic and Social History of Dutch New York.* Ithaca, N.Y.: Cornell University Press, 1986.

Trelease, Allen W. *Indian Affairs in Colonial New York: The Seventeenth Century.* Ithaca, N.Y.: Cornell University Press, 1960.

Indian-white relations—English colonial

TRIBES AFFECTED: Northeast and Southeast polities

SIGNIFICANCE: Indian-English relations developed over the span of two centuries and were dominated by issues of trade, land, and religion; both sides borrowed from their adversary's culture throughout the colonial period

Indian-English relations predate English attempts to colonize the American continent. In the Chesapeake Bay region, for example, groups such as the Powhatans had contact with Europeans in the 1580's. The experience of Don Luis (a *mamanatowick*, or paramount chief, of the Algonquian confederacy) with the Spanish provided a model for his successor, Powhatan, to draw upon when the English established their Jamestown colony in 1607. The English encountered the confederacy further when they began colonizing the Chesapeake Bay region. In New England, Squanto's ability to communicate with the Pilgrims illustrates that there was a familiarity with the English before actual colonization began.

Policies and Preconceptions. When English colonists began establishing colonies on the North American continent, they hoped to coexist with their Indian neighbors. The English assumed that their indigenous neighbors would recognize the superiority of English civilization and would try to emulate the colonists. Unfortunately for the colonists, the Indians were unwilling to accommodate these hopes. Equally distressing to the colonists, more than a few of their own found Indian culture preferable to English society. This phenomenon frightened colonial leaders, and all colonies worked to prevent their citizens from adopting Indian lifestyles. Even when introduced to Indian culture unwillingly, as prisoners of war or other captives, English colonists often preferred to stay with their Indian captors.

The treaty minutes between Native Americans and English delegates illustrate this problem. In these documents, colonial officials demand the return of English captives from the Indians. Inevitably, some of the captured colonists refused to return to colonial society. Their unwillingness to return challenged colonial attitudes of superiority throughout the colonial period. Complicating the relationship was Indian custom. Within the eastern woodlands, when two adversaries agreed to peace, they often exchanged community members, who served as visible reminders of good will. Once the colonists realized this, they demanded that Indian hostages remain with them until the articles of peace were implemented. Some colonial officials proposed placing English orphans among the Indians. Archibald Kennedy, a member of New York's Governor's Council, argued that placing orphans among the Indians would help bind Anglo-Indian alliances.

Indian-English relations went through various phases in the colonial period. Native Americans initially worked to establish peaceful and beneficial relations with the English colonists. Only when Native Americans had reasons to fear the colonists did relations become inhospitable. Each Indian polity welcomed English colonists for different reasons. Over the course of time, each side grew more familiar with the other; familiarity did not produce harmony. Cultural biases on both sides prevented satisfactory resolutions to problems with Anglo-Indian relations. Benjamin Franklin, in his *Remarks Concerning the Savages*, reports how Iroquois leaders rejected an English request to send Iroquoian youths to colonial schools. The Iroquois spokesman declined, stating that schooling made Indian youths unfit for any future work among the Indians.

The second phase of the Anglo-Indian relationship was one of distrust and conflict. The English made it clear that they were not willing to play by traditional tribal rules. The timing of this second period of Anglo-Indian relations depended on local circumstance. In the Chesapeake and New England regions, hostilities broke out within a decade of colonial settlement. Both sides fought these wars within their traditional understandings of war. Colonists saw women and children as legitimate targets and often fought in formations better suited to European plains than American forests. Native Americans ambushed, fought skirmishes, raided, and captured women and children. As both sides learned about the other they adopted various strategies from their opponents. (From this cultural borrowing has emerged the polemical debate about which culture "invented" scalping.)

Many architects of England's early relationships with the Indians based their policy on their experiences in Ireland. Two of the first colonizers, Gilbert Humphreys and Walter Raleigh, fit this generalization. They and their families, like other Devon families, had gained their position in English society through their participation in the Irish wars. Later colonizers, such as John Winthrop and Roger Williams, brought with them the legacy of the struggles of the English Reformation. These sixteenth and seventeenth century settlers brought with them certain convictions that contact with North America's indigenous inhabitants could not alter. English settlers viewed Algonquian society from a European perspective. Algonquian males were "lazy and indolent." Females were immodest and lived a life of drudgery. English settlers believed the Indians "uncivilized." They were convinced that the Algonquian religion was an alliance with Satan. These attitudes provided the theoretical underpinnings of Anglo-Indian relations.

Anglo-Indian relations had two specific spheres. The first sphere concerned official relations. This realm includes treaties, policy decisions, and trade negotiations. The second domain involved informal relations. This area included marriages, cultural borrowing, and cultural critiques. In addition to these spheres, four specific rubrics shaped Indian-English relations. These four areas were disease, trade, land, and religion. Although these areas are interrelated, each requires a separate examination.

Disease. The role of disease in Anglo-Indian relations has, until recently, been a little understood aspect of interaction. Scholars now think that disease was the greatest killer of Native Americans in the colonial period. A series of epidemics known as "virgin soil epidemics" were particularly devastating to Indian communities because these epidemics killed people aged fifteen to forty. This age group was most responsible for the societal tasks of food gathering, making military decisions, and procreation. Native American social practices exacerbated the disease problem, since communities did not isolate the sick originally. Disease often predated significant Anglo-Indian contact and set the parameters for the Anglo-Indian relations that followed. On at least one occasion Englishmen used disease as a weapon of war: Sir Jeffery Amherst, commander of British forces in North America, ordered that blankets infected with smallpox be given to some Delaware Indians during Pontiac's Rebellion.

Disease transformed the Anglo-Indian relationship. For Native Americans, disease meant a declining population base from which to meet European aggression. The most lethal disease that Native Americans encountered was smallpox. Other diseases that swept eastern North America in the colonial period were measles, influenza, diphtheria, typhus, and perhaps bubonic plague. The presence of a devastating disease often called for a reassessment of traditional assumptions about the world. Sometimes this reassessment provided European missionaries with the opportunity necessary to gain a foothold in native communities. Most of the time the missionaries followed the trade routes west.

Trade. From the beginning of contact, Indians and Englishmen traded. Arthur Barlow wrote of trading when he met with the Algonquians around Roanoke in 1584, and European fishermen exchanged items with Native Americans during the seasonal voyages to fishing banks off Newfoundland. From the Indians' perspective, this trade reinforced a traditional manner of integrating foreigners into an existing worldview. While the English saw trade as a simple economic exchange, it was something more complex for the Indians. They based trade on their notion of reciprocity, and reciprocity implied obligation. Both Powhatan and Squanto based their initial relationships with the colonists on the notion of reciprocity. Very quickly this reciprocal relationship became an interdependent one. Initially it was the colonists who depended on

Indian trade items for survival. By the end of the colonial period, however, the Native Americans were dependent on the trade for survival.

Trade flourished partly because it initially required little adjustment for either side. English and Indian traders tapped existing trade networks. In the early colonial period Indian expectations shaped the trade; they determined which goods were traded and at what price. English traders discovered the importance of adhering to Indian cultural expectations when doing business. Some traders found marriage with a native woman a beneficial custom. It opened doors previously closed within the native community. For many native polities, a trader's marriage transformed the trader from a stranger to a family member. The trader now had special obligations to fulfill. As the colonial period progressed, English traders tried to transform such relationships to fit English expectations. They were never truly successful.

One reason that trade predated colonization is that the items both sides exchanged required little change within each cultural tradition. Algonquian males traditionally hunted for bea-ver in the winter, and winter pelts were what Europeans wanted when they began trading. Native peoples had processed deerskins for internal consumption before the arrival of Europeans. For their part, the Englishmen who did the trading did so at first in conjunction with their fishing expeditions. The furs were tangential to the primary purpose. Nevertheless, the trade in pelts and goods produced change.

For some Native American groups, trade with the English stimulated the process of political centralization. Even if trade did not produce political changes for Native Americans, it forced fundamental changes in labor. For the Cherokees, the processing of such large numbers of skins produced a cottage industry. This industry required more labor from the women of the community, which placed strains on Cherokee communities. Other groups experienced increased conflict as neighboring Indian polities attempted to obtain access to the English market. Interior polities sought their own relationships with the English. Various groups tried to force their way onto rivals' territories—the Beaver Wars are perhaps the most famous example of this—in the quest for more pelts and skins. Other

Depiction of a meeting between Ottawa leader Pontiac and a British military leader in the 1760's. (Library of Congress)

polities positioned themselves as intermediaries within the growing trade. Whatever the reason, the fur trade produced an increasing level of violence, which made peaceful Anglo-Indian relations even more difficult. For the Indians, the increasing violence made any attempt to unite against the English difficult. As a result, most Indian polities stood alone against the English when colonists sought Indian land for their own occupation.

Land. Perhaps the greatest strain on Native American-English relations concerned land. English colonists had an insatiable appetite for Indian lands. To justify their taking of Indian land, English officials and colonists relied on three specific arguments. First, they claimed land by right of discovery. Second, they claimed land by right of conquest. Third, they asserted their right to the land because they could better utilize the land than the Indians. Land was probably the single most important irritant to Anglo-Indian relations in the colonial period.

In some areas, however, disputes over land were not a major factor. A smallpox epidemic had wiped out large numbers of Massachusetts Indians on the eve of Boston's founding by the English, for example; it was only when the colonists sought more than the original land ceded them by the Indians that land became an issue. Within two decades of colonization, land was the source of Anglo-Indian conflict. The Pequot War (1636-1637), Metacom's (King Philip's) War (1675-1676), Bacon's Rebellion (1675-1676), Pontiac's Rebellion (1763-1764), and Lord Dunmore's War (1774) were some of the wars that involved, at least tangentially, English-Indian disagreements about land. So important were land issues to Indian-English relations that various attempts to restrict colonial encroachments on Indian land were tried; none of them worked. Nevertheless, the Albany Congress (1754), the creation of the Indian superintendent system, the Proclamation of 1763, and the Treaty of Fort Stanwix (1768) illustrate attempts to alleviate the problems that land created in Anglo-Indian relations.

Religion. English missionaries found their greatest success among Native American polities that had reached the nadir of their cultural existence. In New England, those Indian polities decimated by disease often turned to Christianity because traditional religion no longer explained what was happening to them. Other groups turned to Christianity after they could no longer defend themselves culturally because of lost territory. The "praying Indians" of New England processed the missionaries' message within an Algonquian framework. The songs and rituals associated with Christianity, not the message, were what primarily drew the Algonquians' attention. By the end of the colonial period, Christian Indians acted as missionaries to other Indian groups. Samson Occom, for example, a Mohegan Indian, became a missionary to the Brothertown Indians living among the Iroquois.

The missionaries and their message often divided Indian communities. The result was an increasing level of factionalism within native politics. This factionalism further hindered the Indians' ability to withstand English pressures. The Iroquois Confederacy offers an example of how this factionalism influenced Indian-English relations. Initial Christian factions emerged in Iroquoia with the arrival of French Jesuit missionaries. They arrived at a time when the Iroquois were on the defensive in their struggles against the French and their western Indian allies. In the following years, pro-Christian Iroquois came to dominate confederacy councils. When the Iroquois turned the tables on the French, new traditionalist leaders emerged to lead the confederacy until new troubles appeared and the tide turned once again. This factional ebb and flow continued until the end of the colonial period, when Samuel Kirkland and his Oneida followers challenged the leadership position of Sir William Johnson and the Mohawks. Kirkland had converted a number of Oneida warriors to his New Light Congregationalism. Johnson was a supporter of Anglican attempts to Christianize the Indians. This religious struggle had political overtones because it became part of the colonial-imperial struggles of the 1760's and 1770's. When the American Revolution broke out, the league extinguished its council fire at Onondaga and let each nation determine which side to support: Christianity had helped splinter the Six Nations Confederacy.

Gift-Giving. One area of English-Indian interaction that has received extensive coverage is gift-giving. The use of gifts in Indian society was well established before English colonization. When the English arrived, they found they had to adapt to Indian protocol if they hoped to establish peaceful relations with their Indian neighbors. Indian gifts involved large expenditures on the part of colonial governments. New governors to New York were often presented an allowance of six hundred pounds for the purchase of gifts. Officials in South Carolina spent more than twenty-six thousand pounds on Indian affairs between 1732 and 1755, when the Crown officially took control of Indian relations. A significant portion of South Carolina's Indian expenses went to Indian gifts. These expenditures suggest that colonial and imperial officials understood the importance of gifts to Anglo-Indian relations.

Intermarriage. One area often overlooked in discussions of Indian-English relations is gender. While all European nations were concerned with blood purity, the English were perhaps the most prudish on the matter. Nevertheless, there were many cross-cultural relationships. In 1615 John Rolfe married Pocahontas. In Algonquian terms this marriage served to cement the peace. In the eighteenth century the British Indian superintendent for the northern colonies, Sir William Johnson, married an Iroquoian woman, Molly Brant. Johnson's marriage to Brant gave him an opportunity to operate within Iroquoia that he would not have had otherwise. In the southern colonies the trader Lachland McGillivray married a Creek woman, and his son Alexander became a leading figure in the Anglo-Indian dialogue. Johnson's and McGillivray's marriages provided each man with entry into his wife's community in a manner no outsider could hope to achieve. Equally important, these men were now obligated to meet certain familial and kinship expectations on the part of their wives' families.

In examining Indian-English relations it is important to remember that neither side spoke with a single voice. While scholars have repeatedly mentioned the problems Native Americans had in uniting to oppose English objectives, there has been a tendency to downplay the difficulties the colonists also had in presenting a united front to the Indians. The ramifications of the lack of unity on both sides give the study of Indian-English relations its unique character. The diversity of opinion and actions among British colonial and Indian leaders made that relationship a complex one.   —*Michael J. Mullin*

See also Articles of Agreement; Bacon's Rebellion; Cherokee War; French and Indian Wars; Indian-white relations—French colonial; King Philip's War; Lord Dunmore's War; Massasoit; Pequot War; Pontiac's Conspiracy; Powhatan Wars; Proclamation of 1763.

BIBLIOGRAPHY

Axtell, James. *The European and the Indian: Essays in the Ethnohistory of Colonial North America.* Oxford, England: Oxford University Press, 1981. Many of the essays in this book were previously published; together they provide a good introduction to the study of ethnohistory and Anglo-Indian relations in the colonial period.

Crosby, Alfred W. "Virgin Soil Epidemics as a Factor in the Aboriginal Depopulation in America." *William and Mary Quarterly* 3d ser., 33 (1976): 289-299. This essay is considered a classic examination of the effect of disease on Indian populations in North America.

Jacobs, Wilbur R. "British Indian Policies to 1783." In *History of Indian-White Relations*, edited by Wilcomb E. Washburn. Vol. 4 in *Handbook of North American Indians*, edited by William C. Sturtevant. Washington, D.C.: Smithsonian Institution Press, 1988. As the title indicates, this essay details British policy toward the Indians. It covers the formal relations between Indians and colonists and is particularly good at examining the role of land in the Indian-English experience.

Richter, Daniel K. *The Ordeal of the Longhouse: The Peoples of the Iroquois League in the Era of European Colonization.* Chapel Hill: University of North Carolina Press, 1992. Published for the Institute of Early American History and Culture, this study of the Iroquois League demonstrates the influence of factionalism on an Indian people as they dealt with the Europeans. It synthesizes much scholarship on the Six Nations and their relationship with the French, Dutch, and English. It is particularly strong on seventeenth century relations.

Rountree, Helen C., ed. *Powhatan Foreign Relations, 1500-1722.* Charlottesville: University Press of Virginia, 1993. A series of articles written by leading scholars. The book details Powhatan relations not only with the English but also with other Indian groups in the region. The articles emphasize the complexity and difficulty of thinking about Native Americans as single-culture polities.

Indian-white relations—French colonial

TRIBES AFFECTED: Pantribal

SIGNIFICANCE: French colonial relations with Indian tribes displayed mutual interest in trading, useful political and military alliances, missionary schooling, and protection

France's colonial claim on major portions of North America dates from the reign of the Valois king François I. It was François who protested the assumptions of the 1494 Treaty of Tordesillas, which claimed to divide the newly discovered Western Hemisphere between Spain and Portugal solely. Soon France would be engaged, well before the Pilgrims landed at Plymouth Rock in 1620, in exploring North American lands that were inhabited only by Indian tribes. The French labeled this new territory *Gallia Nova*, or New France.

Early Contacts. Historians date the earliest trading contact between French explorers and American Indians to Jacques Cartier's entry into the Gulf of St. Lawrence in 1534. The French exchanged knives and trinkets for furs offered by Micmac tribesmen. The next year Cartier sailed farther up the St. Lawrence, first encountering Iroquois at the point where Quebec would later be established, and then penetrating as far as the Indian village of Hochelaga (later Montreal).

The sequel to these earliest encounters in the area that would become known as New France was not promising for future relations. After Cartier captured Indians and transported them to France (where they died from exposure to European diseases), returning French parties were not welcome in the St. Lawrence area. Attempts by Cartier's successor, Sieur de Roberval, to found a colony failed after only three years.

The contributions made by Samuel de Champlain, founder of Quebec City in 1608, were more lasting. Champlain was very curious to know more about the origins of the St. Lawrence River, questioning Hurons who came to trade at Quebec concerning their homelands. The Hurons spoke of great interlocking expanses of water—the yet to be discovered Great Lakes. Champlain tried in vain in 1613 to journey to the Great Lakes by ascending the Ottawa River, the most direct path being blocked by hostile Iroquois tribesmen.

It was only several years later, after Champlain became a direct lieutenant of the French Viceroy and founder of what was known as Champlain's Company (composed of traders from Normandie), that a real French colony would develop. Champlain's Company was granted a monopoly of trade with the Indians of the St. Lawrence as far westward as they could succeed. Built into the organization of the chartered trading company was a mandate to support the work of French missionary friars called the Recollects, who represented a reformed branch of the Franciscan Order. The Recollects claimed that they were the first to hold a formal ceremony of the Mass in Canada in June, 1615. It was a Recollect missionary, not the explorer Champlain himself, who first set foot on the easternmost shores of the Great Lakes.

Not much success was registered by the French in the Great Lakes area in this early period, partially because a decision was made to choose Huron peace and trade offers rather than

A somewhat fanciful French drawing of Indians attacking early French explorers. (Library of Congress)

to struggle to win over Iroquois friendship. This meant that the Champlain Company based in Quebec carried on more trade in the rather bleak areas to the north, rather than penetrating the more fertile regions of what would become New York and Pennsylvania, eventually areas where British colonial claims, together with complex relations with the Iroquois, would expand.

During the second half of the sixteenth century a few other French expeditions came into contact with Indian groupings, but in general they decided not to insist on fixed colonization, which inevitably involved a need for military defense and possibly sustained warfare. French expeditions preferred to develop mobile trading networks instead. The lucrative attractions of the fur trade would leave a characteristic stamp on the actions of the *coureurs de bois* ("woods runners," or trappers), who would cover vast inland areas and develop particular relations with several tribes. The nature of traders' alliances with Indians would change significantly in the eighteenth century colonial period, when military considerations in dealing with British enemies in colonial North American came to the forefront.

From Exploration to Conquest. One of the most famous *coureurs* was Nicholas Perrot, who, after beginning but then abandoning training to enter the Jesuit Order and work among tribes as a missionary, began his career at twenty-six as the interpreter for the 1670 Daumont de St. Lusson (copper exploration) expedition into the Miami tribal area around Green Bay

(now Wisconsin). Eventually Perrot mastered not only Algonquian but also a dozen other Indian dialects. The most far-seeing governors-general in Quebec, most notably Louis de Baude, count of Frontenac, tended to place great confidence in the judgment of *coureurs* such as Perrot and sometimes even countered instructions from Paris in favor of "commonsense" counsel offered to them by those who knew the Indians best.

When French colonial policy toward the Indians came under the influence of aggressive governors-general such as the Marquis de Denonville, however, relations could worsen overnight. By the mid-1680's de Denonville was convinced that his British colonial neighbors in New York (then under the governorate of Thomas Dongan) were stirring up Iroquois hostility against the French. When clumsy efforts to deal with the problem through hostage-taking and physical duress failed, de Denonville resorted to massive armed action in 1687, mainly against the Senecas near the present site of Rochester, New York. His force of French soldiers, accompanied by Indian Christian converts and tribesmen who had more interest in fighting Seneca enemies than in Christianity, numbered almost three thousand—nearly ten times the size of any previous military expedition.

Although de Denonville's battle tactics were not strikingly successful, his remarks revealed the psychological distance already growing between official colonizers of his ilk and the commonsense "forest runner" emissaries of New France who knew the manners and customs of the Indians and how to use them to obtain desired ends without violence. When his Indian allies fell ill from overeating (booty and animals taken from the Senecas), de Denonville observed with disgust that "it is a miserable business to command savages who, as soon as they have knocked the enemy on the head, ask for nothing but to go home and carry . . . scalps they have taken off like a skullcap" (quoted in Joseph Rutledge, *Century of Conflict*, New York, 1956, p. 58).

Contributions by French Christian Missionaries. The second main thrust of French influence into American Indian homelands before 1700 was religiously motivated. Among the earliest French Jesuit missions to establish relations with the broad tribal area they called Huronia was Father Bressani. The so-called Black Robes took on special status in dealing with the Hurons not with guns (and not even by formal conversion to Christianity) but by taking on the honorific function of tribal medicine men. Tensions mounted among various factions of Indians, however, when "converts" only, not those who rejected missionary overtures, received firearms from French suppliers (not from the missionaries themselves). By 1649, deteriorating conditions between Hurons and the Five Nations of the Iroquois led to defeat of the former by Seneca and Mohawk nations of the latter. Within five years of their Huron ally's loss, however, the French Jesuits received a request from the Onondaga middle tribe of the Iroquois for the establishment of a trading and missionary post to teach converts in their midst. This new French-Indian alliance was accompanied by arms supplies to aid the Onondagas not only in their war with the Eries but also in defending themselves against hostile attacks from their fellow Iroquois, the Mohawks. The policy would prove a failure when Mohawks destroyed the Onondaga mission in 1658. This act brought a special military force from France under the Marquis de Tracy, who, after burning many villages, forced the Mohawks to accept the presence of missionaries in their midst.

Thereafter, Black Robe policy toward Indian converts in the region changed. To avoid intertribal warfare, the French sent individual converts away from their tribal homelands to mission reservations near the emergent French colonial center at Montreal. Descendants of these mixed Indian Christian communities, who came to form the most reliable allies of French colonists, were called Caughnawaga Mohawks (still identifiable in late twentieth century Canada as "Kahnawake" people, who live on a reservation bearing the same name).

Missionary-Explorers. Some seventeenth century French missionaries combined two callings—that of explorer and that of bearer of Christianity for people who were often considered outright savages—when they entered Indian territories beyond established colonies. One of the best-known French missionaries was Gabriel Sagard, a lay brother (not an ordained priest) in the Recollect Order. Sagard's famous 1632 account of his journey into Huronia contained numerous suggestions that the "savage" life of the Indians contained many positive elements that could benefit European society, including simplicity of relations and rejection of selfish hoarding of material goods.

Sagard's 1632 account of the minute details of Indian habits, including their modes of preparing various foods, their dress, and their recreations, became the first widely read popular treatise on *Gallia Nova*. It would be greatly expanded in a second printing only four years after it first appeared. A second widely read account of French and Indian missionary encounters would appear exactly fifty years after Sagard's famous volume. The later work, by another Recollect, Louis Hennepin, was called "Description of Louisiana," a title which suggests how far westward and southward the French had explored since Sagard's experience among the Hurons.

Much credit for this wider exploration went to the Recollects' missionary "rivals," the French Jesuits. Jesuit Father Jacques Marquette, for example, together with Louis Jolliet, a former seminarian turned fur trader, were among the first white people to explore the Mississippi River valley in the 1670's. It was they who opened the way for the extension of New France into the vast area that would be known as Louisiana (named for King Louis XIV). Jolliet's initial interest in proceeding farther west and south of the territory under Quebec's administrative control was to establish a settlement on the Illinois River. Unsuccessful in getting support for this, Jolliet took on the commissioned task of discovering the upper Mississippi itself. A wealth of information tracing Jolliet's progress is preserved in Father Marquette's journals, which begin when the party received aid from the Mascoutin Indian people, whose territory in the Fox River valley and the Meskousing (later "Wisconsin") River zone held the key to rapid canoe transit toward confluents of the Mississippi. One of these, then called the Pekitonoui River, passed through the territory of the Illinois tribes. There Marquette would later found, on his return north after their long journey down the Mississippi to the point where it is joined by the Arkansas River, the Mission of the Conception in the tiny Indian village of Kaskaskia. He died there in 1675, only to be succeeded by generations of French missionaries and fur traders who would open the Mississippi to extensive exploration and settlement far beyond the new "capital" of St. Louis. By 1700, when Father Jacques Gravier took charge of Marquette's Indian mission program among the Kaskaskia of Illinois, he decided to establish a network of communications to link the Illinois mission to new French settlements as far south as Biloxi (the future state of Mississippi, settled from the New Orleans delta northward). Gravier's 1700 contacts with the Akansa (Quapaw) Indians (who had seen Marquette in 1674) were already tinged with hints of possible hostile reactions by Mississippi Valley Indians to what they feared would be increased takeover of their lands by French settlements.

By 1711 and 1712, all the way back north in the Fox River valley, where Marquette had begun among friends in the 1670's, the hostilities later known as the Fox Wars began, and the safety of the French in a great number of previously peaceful areas would be placed in jeopardy.

The French fur traders, called *voyageurs* ("travelers") as well as *coureurs de bois*, in order to survive in relative isolation among the Indians far from colonial military forts or missionary zones, consciously chose to develop close personal ties with the tribes. They often established networks of what amounted to political as well as trading relationships with different groups by marrying Indian women and adopting many aspects of the Indian way of life. Fur trader knowledge of Indian customs, as well as the configurations of tribal alliances, would serve the needs of more official political policies of administrative authorities of New France when the latter faced military challenges from their main colonial rivals, the British.

Relations During the Seven Years' War. Historians often refer to the North American phase of the Seven Years' War (1756-1763) as the "French and Indian War" because of the importance of English and French alliances with Indian tribes in Canada and several of the thirteen American colonies. For the French, many of these alliances predated the formal period of war by more than half a century. One of France's long-established goals in what would become the United States was to hold the limit of British colonization east of the Appalachian Mountains. Because so few actual French fighting units were present in the vast territories it wished to defend against British occupation, French emissaries in essence "recruited" Indian groups to fight for them against the British. The appointment in 1752 of Marquis Ange Duquesne de Menneville as France's governor-general in Quebec came with instructions to block all British attempts to penetrate the Ohio Territory, a move that could cut off north-south contact between France's Canadian and "Louisianan" colonies. As the much more serious declaration of war in Europe approached, Duquesne soon followed the example of one of his agents, Charles Langlade, who had led Ottawa, Potawatomi, and Ojibwa Indian allies in attacks against other Indians who had joined the Iroquois Covenant Chain (including the Delawares) and were being courted as potential allies of the British cause. When it came to struggles over control of the famous Fort Duquesne, the French attempted to rely on support from so-called Three Fires Indians, who came from points far to the west, where Indian sensitivity to threats of seizure of their lands was not yet as highly developed as it was in the Ohio Territory.

As the terms of war became even more serious, the French strategy of allying with Indians who thought they might regain lands lost to British colonizers seemed to be succeeding. Not only the Lenni Lenapes (Delawares) but also the Shawnees and even some Iroquois broke away from British support to help the French in their attempts to expel English colonizers from Iroquoia (New York). British General John Forbes and a Quaker colonist leader named Israel Pemberton finally succeeded in turning the tide of French and Indian superiority in 1758, when a treaty with the Delawares signed at Easton, Pennsylvania, promised to establish a firm boundary between British and Indian territory after the war. When the struggle finally ended in 1763, the French essentially lost their entire Canadian and Northeast North American colonial empire. For many of their former Indian allies, this defeat meant an unclear future. At Fort Niagara, for example, Seneca Indians were expelled from a stronghold they had held for the French. British control, although it would only last another twenty years in the thirteen colonies, rapidly brought quite different conditions for the Indian people of North America.

—*Byron D. Cannon*

See also Beaver Wars; French and Indian Wars; Huron; Indian-white relations—Canadian; Indian-white relations—English colonial; Iroquois Confederacy; Missions and missionaries.

BIBLIOGRAPHY

Douville, Raymond, and Jacques Casanova. *Daily Life in Early Canada*. New York: Macmillan, 1967. Although this carefully documented study concentrates on various conditions affecting French colonial life in Gallia Nova (transportation, religious life, trapping, and trading), each chapter includes useful information on relations with Indian populations.

Hamilton, Raphael N. *Marquette's Explorations: The Narratives Reexamined*. Madison: University of Wisconsin Press, 1970. This scholarly monograph not only describes the experiences of Father Marquette before and during his famous exploration of the 1670's but also provides a critical analysis of the authenticity of manuscript sources ascribed to Marquette.

Jennings, Francis. *The Founders of America*. New York: W. W. Norton, 1993. An excellent general history of the Indian population of all regions of North America from precolonial to contemporary times. The colonial section contains essential facts of French and Indian relations.

Rutledge, Joseph Lister. *Century of Conflict*. Garden City, N.Y.: Doubleday, 1956. A comprehensive account of American Indian relations with both French and British colonial regimes from the early to the late eighteenth century, including the key Seven Years' War period.

Sagard, Gabriel. *The Long Journey to the Country of the Hurons*. Translated by Hugh H. Langton. Toronto: Champlain Society, 1939. This is a translation of the French explorer's original travel logs, published in 1632.

Indian-white relations—Norse

TRIBES AFFECTED: Algonquin, Inugsuk, Iroquois, possibly Mandan, Thule, others

SIGNIFICANCE: For five hundred years before Columbus' voyage to the Caribbean islands in 1492, people from Scandinavia interacted with the indigenous population of North America; the Norse traded with, influenced, and were influenced by American Indians

Until relatively recently, most historians considered the enduring folktales concerning pre-Columbian Norse colonization of North America and contacts with its aboriginal population to be nothing more than romantic fiction. The few scholars who did take seriously the Icelandic sagas on which the folktales were based assumed that the alleged Norse-Indian contacts had little or no historical significance.

Despite the disinterest of the academic community, many amateur historians and archaeologists pursued the story of the pre-Columbian Norse in North America with an enthusiasm often bordering on fanaticism. Since at least the seventeenth century, sincere but often ignorant proponents of the Norse presence in North America before Christopher Columbus have put forth evidence for their claims in the form of maps, runestones, and purportedly Norse-made artifacts. Some of this supposed evidence proved to be the product of hoaxes, which cast doubt on the entire thesis of an early Norse presence in North America.

Archaeological discoveries during the last third of the twentieth century, however, show conclusively that the Norse established permanent colonies on the North American continent. At L'Anse aux Meadows in Newfoundland, archaeologists have excavated an entire Norse village, dated by radiocarbon methods to around 1000 C.E. or a little earlier. Other archaeologists have recovered indisputably Norse artifacts from dozens of Eskimos (Inuit) sites throughout northern Canada. These discoveries have caused historians to begin reexamining the original Icelandic sources that told of the Norse movement into the area west of Greenland and other evidence of Norse-Indian interaction.

Background. Three Icelandic sagas, probably composed in the twelfth and thirteenth centuries (*Eirik's Saga, Karlsefni Saga,* and the *Graenlendinga Saga*), constitute the primary historical source material for a pre-Columbian Norse presence in North America. Other sagas contain numerous references to the subject but give little detail. The Icelandic sagas began as oral history—stories about people and events passed along orally from generation to generation. Icelandic scribes probably wrote down the stories dealing with what the Greenland Norse called "Vinland the Good" (which many scholars today believe was the coast of New England) in the late fourteenth century.

These sagas tell first of the Norse colonization of Greenland in 985-986 C.E. by Eric the Red. Shortly afterward, according to the sagas, Bjarni Herjolfsson accidentally sighted what must have been the coast of North America when a storm blew his ship off course. After hearing Herjolfsson's story, Leif the Lucky, Eric's son, bought Herjolfsson's ship some years later (around the year 1000) and sailed west from Greenland searching for the land his predecessor had seen. He found several islands or promontories and gave them names during this voyage: Helluland (which many historians now believe was Baffin Island), Markland (often identified with Labrador), and finally Vinland. The sagas relate that Vinland abounded with wild grape vines (thus the name), game of all types, and fertile soil; the rivers teemed with fish. Leif and the thirty-five men who sailed with him built permanent dwellings and explored the surrounding area for almost a year. The next spring, Leif sailed back to Greenland with a cargo of timber, grapes, and grape vines.

The Norse and the Indians. Eric the Red died during the winter following Leif's return from Vinland. Leif became too engrossed in his duties as chieftain of the Greenland colony to follow up his voyage of discovery. The sagas record three more expeditions from the Greenland colony to Vinland during subsequent years. According to the sagas, the Norse encountered aborigines they called Skraelings (literally "wretches") in Vinland and interacted with them on several occasions. If the sagas are correct, the Norse both exploited the Skraelings in trade and killed them in battle and by treachery.

The sagas give no details about any subsequent Norse exploits in Vinland. Despite the anecdotal and undoubtedly embellished nature of the sagas, they have a ring of truth about them. After the archaeological discoveries at L'Anse aux Meadows, many historians have come to regard the sagas as valuable sources (although ones to be used with caution) about the first European contacts with American Indians. From the accounts in the sagas it must be concluded that the Norse exploited the Indians in trade as callously as did the Spanish, Dutch, English, and French after Columbus. The Norse of the sagas had no more compunction about killing the Indians than did the later European explorers.

Other evidence, however, suggests that contacts between the Norse and the Indians were not always as hostile, or trade so one-sided, as portrayed in the sagas. Since 1960, archaeologists have discovered numerous artifacts in Eskimo sites throughout northern and central Canada of undoubted Norse manufacture. These objects include wrought-iron axes, iron spearheads, and carved figurines. Such finds suggest extensive trade between the Norse and American Indians. The game of lacrosse, taught by the Algonquin Indians to French and British colonists, resembles an ancient Norse game so closely that several historians are convinced it is the same game. The Norse introduced it in Vinland, they argue, and from there it spread throughout the pre-Columbian American northeast. If this theory is correct, it suggests amiable relations between the Norse and Indians over a considerable period of time.

One linguist has compiled a large collection of Northeast Indian (especially Iroquois) words that are pronounced similarly and have similar meanings to words in the old Norse language. The language similarity again suggests long and continued contact between the two peoples. Many anthropologists also believe that the Norse left their genes among American Indians, especially several groups of Eskimos and tribes of the interior such as the Mandans. These groups display or displayed a number of European characteristics when first encountered by post-Columbian colonists, including fair hair, light-colored eyes, exceptionally tall stature, and luxuriant beards. If this assessment is accurate, the Norse did not launch a war of extermination against the Indians as did later waves of colonists but rather merged their culture with those of the aborigines.
—*Paul Madden*

See also Dorset; Iroquoian language family; Lacrosse; Old Copper culture; Prehistory—Arctic; Thule.

BIBLIOGRAPHY

Enterline, James Robert. *Viking America: The Norse Crossings and Their Legacy.* Epilogue by Thor Heyerdahl. Garden City, N.Y.: Doubleday, 1972.

Magnusson, Magnus, and Hermann Palsson, eds. and trans. *The Vinland Sagas: The Norse Discovery of America.* New York: Penguin Books, 1980.

Mowat, Farley. *Westviking: The Ancient Norse in Greenland and North America.* Boston: Little, Brown, 1965.

Reman, Edward. *The Norse Discoveries and Explorations in America.* Berkeley: University of California Press, 1949.

Wahlgren, Erik. *The Vikings and America.* London: Thames & Hudson, 1986.

Indian-white relations—Russian colonial

TRIBES AFFECTED: Aleut, Inuit, Yupik, other western Subarctic and Northwest Coast tribes

SIGNIFICANCE: Russia first encountered New World indigenous people while trading furs and missionizing in the area of present-day Alaska

Russian traders made contact with many Indian tribes along the western Canadian and northwestern American coasts, from Alaska south to northern California. Their strongest influence, however, was felt in the Arctic and Subarctic areas by the Eskimos and Aleuts. There were very few early contacts between Eskimos and Europeans because of the remoteness of the Arctic region. Soon after the first encounters, which began with the Russians, the fur trade drew most European powers into the area. This led to a radical change in the nature of indigenous Arctic culture.

Historical Background. Cossacks first heard of the Aleuts when they arrived in Siberia in 1650. The Russians were continuing a policy of eastward expansion and exploration in search of pelts. The indigenous people in Siberia told of their trading with groups in the Aleutian Islands. The desire for sea otter furs, a maritime product, pushed the Russian traders farther to the east into the "Great Land." Knowledge of Europeans and their culture, therefore, reached the Aleuts more than a century before actual European contact.

Alaskan Eskimos first came into contact with Europeans in 1741, at the time of Vitus Bering's expedition on behalf of Russia. Bering was a Danish explorer whose task was to extend the fur trade that had started in Siberia. Sea otter fur obtained on the second Bering expedition precipitated the arrival of many traders in the Aleutian Islands, as they left Siberia for this lucrative fur trade. Eskimos were very hospitable to the Russian explorers, providing their guests with music, dancing, and feasting. They were also, however, skillful traders who drove hard bargains for pelts in order to obtain metal and enamel buttons, Siberian sabers, blue glass beads, and knives. In exchange, the Russians received skins of river otter, red fox, marten, and wolverine.

Traders moving from island to island through the Aleutian chain had reached the Alaska peninsula by 1762. The Aleuts were often brutalized in the process. Aleut laborers were required to pay a tax (*yasak*). In an effort to help stem the cruel treatment by traders, the Russian government made the Aleuts Russian subjects in 1766. The yasak payment was revoked in 1788. Between 1743 and 1797, dozens of Russian companies made numerous voyages along the Aleutians. These companies obtained almost 200,000 pelts worth almost eight million rubles.

Colonization. In Southern Alaska, Grigory Shelekhov and Ivan Golikov founded the first colony at Three Saints Bay, Kodiak Island. Shelekhov was granted a charter in 1799 to form the Russian-American Company as a twenty-year monopoly, although the Imperial Navy undertook an independent expedition in search of a northern path to the Atlantic. More charters were made in 1821 and 1844. The first company chief decreed that the natives must labor for the company. Natives hunted sea otter under dangerous conditions including the possibility of attack by the Tlingit Indians and the threat of bad weather. Official government policy sought to treat the Eskimos and Aleuts fairly, but local exploitation of laborers by traders was common. Each year, sea otter pelts and seal skins were shipped through Siberia to Moscow and then on to China.

There was much intermarriage between Russian hunters and native women. The children of these unions were recognized by a charter of 1821 as Russian subjects. Neither they nor their mothers could leave the colony. Intermarriage was a key factor in the radical cultural changes that took place among the natives of the Arctic region.

With the establishment of St. Michael in 1833, commercial trade became of major importance. A few years later, however, the first of a series of devastating epidemics attacked the area of Norton Sound and southern Alaska. In some parts of the south, up to 50 percent of the population perished. The Aleut population dropped from about seven thousand in 1836 to about four thousand in 1840, the year the epidemic ended. The Russians were able to contain the epidemic through a rigorous vaccination program which began in 1838.

Russian Orthodox Church. The missionaries of the Russian Orthodox church altered Aleut culture as much as the commercialization process. Virtually all Aleuts were converted to Christianity, but the more numerous Tlingits resisted missionization and commercialization. The Russian-American Company and the Russian Orthodox church were often at odds with each other over the control of the region. Father Ivan Veniaminov was the first priest concerned with indigenous people in the northern areas; he arrived in 1829. From a mission on the Yukon River, established in 1844, priests visited the surrounding villages. After the American purchase of Alaska in 1867, most clergy personnel were withdrawn, but a school in St. Michael remained active.

Much of the Aleut culture underwent radical transformation. The new form of religion was markedly different from the former traditional practice. Both the new modes of labor and the amount of intermarriage with Russians had profound effects on social organization. Disease, resettlement, and other effects of contact followed the well-known destructive pattern experienced by the indigenous peoples of the New World.

—*William H. Green*

See also Aleut; Inuit; Tlingit.

BIBLIOGRAPHY

Chevigny, Hector. *Russian America: The Great Alaskan Venture, 1741-1867.* New York: Viking Press, 1965.

Gibson, James R. *Imperial Russia in Frontier America: The Changing Geography of Supply of Russian America, 1784-1867*. New York: Oxford University Press, 1976.

Mangusso, Mary Childers, and Stephen W. Haycox, eds. *Interpreting Alaska's History: An Anthology*. Anchorage: Alaska Pacific University Press, 1989.

Oswalt, Wendell H. *Mission of Change in Alaska*. San Marino, Calif.: Huntington Library, 1963.

Ray, Dorothy Jean. *The Eskimos of Bering Strait, 1650-1898*. Seattle: University of Washington Press, 1975.

Sherwood, Morgan B., ed. *Alaska and Its History*. Seattle: University of Washington Press, 1967.

_____. *Exploration of Alaska, 1865-1900*. New Haven, Conn.: Yale University Press, 1965.

Indian-white relations—Spanish colonial

TRIBES AFFECTED: Apache, Apalachee, Chumash, Pueblo, Timucua, Yuma

SIGNIFICANCE: The Spanish Empire imposed a heavy cost on the Indian peoples of North America from the 1570's until its collapse in the 1820's, in spite of Native Americans' valiant efforts to deal with its demands peacefully

The Indians of North America escaped the violence and disruption of the early Spanish conquest only to encounter later imperial thrusts that contained the seeds of conflict. From the arrival of Christopher Columbus in 1492 to Hernán Cortés' victory over the Aztecs in 1521, the Spanish established their control of the Caribbean area. The riches of the Aztecs inspired expeditions southward to conquer the Inca Empire, but probings into North America failed to locate concentrations of gold or large urban centers. Yet the 3,000-mile stretch of territory from Florida to California became a vital but vulnerable frontier for the Spanish. They wanted to defend the lifeline of their New World empire, which stretched from Mexico to Hispaniola and on to Spain, by the establishment of settlements along the southern fringe of what is now the United States. Relations between the Indians of North America and the colonists and institutions of the empire were characterized by periods of tentative harmony under Spanish domination followed by the growth of tension and distrust among the natives, which often resulted in alienation, rejection, and, in a few cases, open rebellion.

Before the arrival of the Spanish, the Native American peoples along the southern rim of North America had evolved a large variety of languages and cultures that, while lacking the urbanization and centralization of the Aztecs, had internal strengths of their own. From the Apalachees of what is now northern Florida to the Chumash along the California coast, life usually centered on the extended family and villages with various combinations of hunting, gathering, and small-scale agriculture to supply material needs. All was not harmony in pre-conquest North America, however, as the strained relationship between the Pueblos and Apaches revealed. The Pueblos of the upper Rio Grande Valley lived a sedentary existence in their multistory stone and adobe houses. Their agricultural practices gave them a fairly stable source of food in contrast to their neighbors, the Apaches, who were wandering hunter-gatherers. When the Apaches' supplies ran short, they would sometimes raid the villages of the more prosperous Pueblos.

Spanish Institutions. These Apache-Pueblo conflicts were of limited duration, but the arrival of the Spanish brought major disruptions that would permanently change the lives of the Indians. The Spanish transplanted institutions previously established in Mexico, Peru, and other imperial centers. The *encomienda*, a type of land grant, was for many years their chief method of commanding Indian labor. The *encomendero* (holder of the encomienda) controlled Indian workers in exchange for a commitment to protect and to provide for them. A second system of labor supervision was the *repartimiento*, in which colonial officials assigned native workers to a particular settler for a certain amount of time. Although in theory these situations were regulated by colonial officials, in practice encomenderos and settlers took advantage of their Indian charges by requiring them to work beyond the original agreements. In addition to the encomienda and repartimiento, the Spanish enslaved natives as personal servants or as laborers in their agricultural or trading enterprises.

These labor practices, often harsh and exploitative, drew the protests of Catholic missionaries. The priests assigned to frontier areas from Florida to California brought with them an awareness of the ideals of Bartolomé de las Casas, who, from the 1520's until his death in 1566, campaigned against the mistreatment of Native Americans. These missionaries, usually members of the Franciscan order along the North American frontier, attempted to convert the Indians to Christianity. Their missions often served the natives as havens from the demands of encomenderos, settlers, and even government officials.

The presidio, a small fort manned by a detachment of soldiers, generally accompanied the mission. The original purpose of these frontier forts was to protect the missionaries, settlers, and friendly natives from attacks by European rivals such as the British and the French and their Indian allies. As internal institutional and political disputes arose, however, these soldiers were sometimes deployed against the mission Indians to serve the demands of settlers and officials for additional land or native laborers.

Historical records of the interaction of the Indians and the Spanish tend to emphasize institutions such as the mission and the presidio, but the native response to the arrival of the Spanish was much more subtle than early studies limited to archives reveal. Spanish friars reported massive conversions of Indians to Christianity in remarkably short periods of time, but these apparent conversions may have been simply the natives' way of attempting to develop good relations with the Europeans rather than the profoundly religious experiences often described in the reports. The Indians did not passively accept Spanish dominance but rather found ways to accommodate demands for conversion and for labor while, at the same time, preserving much of their own autonomy and tradition.

Florida. The Franciscans began their work in Florida in 1573 and within eighty years had erected more than thirty missions extending northward and westward in two chains from their base in St. Augustine. The Franciscans used music, paintings, and colorful ceremonies to attract the natives' attention. They claimed that twenty-six thousand converts had accepted Christianity by 1655 (this claim is disputed by many historians). The Apalachees, Timucuas, and other nearby tribes were receptive to the missionaries in the early years in part as a response to the Franciscan appeals; however, the Indians also saw strategic advantages in an alliance with the missionaries for protection against Spanish settlers and soldiers. The natives' selective acceptance of Catholicism was indicated by their placement of Christian images among their traditional religious symbols.

The tensions in the Indian-Spanish relationships exploded in the early 1700's under additional pressures from British settlements to the north. The British founded Charleston in 1670 and began to push to the interior, thereby posing a threat to the mission-presidio system stretching out from St. Augustine. The Charlestonians recruited nonmission Indians and welcomed the alienated natives who left the Spanish. The Indians, caught in the struggle between the two European powers, found it necessary to take sides or abandon the area. One Apalachee chief, Patricio de Hinachuba, urged Spanish officials to end their abusive policies in order to hold the support of his people and other nearby tribes. Patricio, a perceptive leader, attempted to represent the interests of the Apalachee while remaining within the Spanish orbit. Through personal diplomacy with the British in 1706, he managed to spare his village from attack and then led his followers toward St. Augustine for sanctuary. His hopes were dashed, however, when a group of pro-British Indians attacked his band just outside the large stone fortifications of St. Augustine. Patricio de Hinachuba perished along with his Apalachee community.

The defeat of the Spanish in the early 1700's was a symptom of the decline of the missions. The British military attacks were important factors in the Spanish loss, but the defection of many of the mission Indians in this time of crisis was also important. As Patricio de Hinachuba attempted to explain to the Spanish, the onerous burdens of repartimiento and slavery weighed heavily on many Native American communities. Apparently many Indians joined the British as an act of rebellion against the Spanish. Only a few Indians remained with the missions at the stronghold of St. Augustine and a handful of sites scattered across the northern part of Florida. These defections, however, brought few if any improvements for the Indians: The British also resorted to enslavement of the able-bodied natives and proved as aggressive as the Spanish in usurping land.

New Mexico. While different in many details, the Spanish colonial effort along the upper Rio Grande in what is now New Mexico and western Texas bore a resemblance to the rise and fall of the mission-presidio system in Florida. Although the New Mexico project may appear to have been a logical exten-

sion of Spanish settlements in northern Mexico, the expedition of explorer of Juan de Oñate in 1598 marked a significant leap for the Spanish across rugged deserts and through hostile Indian territory. New Mexico, like Florida, was isolated from the core areas of the empire and constituted not only an effort to bring Christianity and European civilization to the Native Americans but also a barrier to the occupation of the region by European rivals.

Oñate's settlements took hold, and by the 1620's New Mexico seemed to be a healthy and prosperous colony; particularly impressive was the work of the Franciscan missionaries. By 1629 they had established fifty missions that on a map formed the pattern of a cross running northward up the Rio Grande to the settlement in Taos; the arms of the cross extended westward to the Zuni and Hopi pueblos and eastward to Pecos. Father Alonso de Benavides' report that the Franciscans had baptized eighty-six thousand Indians circulated not only in Mexico City but also in Madrid and Rome.

The actual relationship between the Pueblo Indians and the Franciscans was less dramatic than these early reports indicated. The Pueblos probably turned to the missionaries and the accompanying Spanish soldiers for security against their long-time neighbors and periodic adversaries, the Apaches. The Pueblos were impressed by the church's religious ceremonies, the support that the clerics received from military and government officials, and the Franciscans' presentation of Christian doctrine. The Pueblos, however, much like the Apalachees and Timucuas of Florida, accepted portions of the missionaries' messages while retaining significant components of their own beliefs and customs.

Inevitably, the arrival of the Spanish took a toll on the natives. The initial excitement gave way to the more practical problems of work, food, and clothing. Oñate secured imperial approval for encomiendas for himself and a few of the prominent early settlers. These grants placed certain Indian villages under a legal obligation to pay tribute (a tax) to the encomenderos. Soon colonial officials established the repartimiento as a means of supplying young Indians to work for settlers. Colonial governors of New Mexico often used the repartimiento—and even illegal slave labor—in agricultural and commercial enterprises to augment their salaries. Pueblo communities, with this loss of the labor of many of their vigorous males and females, experienced not only an indignity but also a growing difficulty in feeding themselves.

The natives' frustrations with these conditions erupted in small rebellions as early as 1632 at Zuni and 1639-1640 at Taos, but the Spanish seemed to ignore these ominous signs. Crop losses from bad weather in the 1660's and 1670's and intensified Apache raids added to the Pueblos' difficulties. A leader capable of unifying Indian resistance appeared in the person of Popé, a Pueblo religious mystic punished by the Spanish for alleged sorcery. In August and September of 1680, Popé led a large portion of the seventeen thousand Pueblos in an uprising that killed more than four hundred of New Mexico's twenty-five hundred Spanish settlers and sent the survivors fleeing down the Rio Grande to El Paso. After the expulsion of the Spanish, the native leadership openly rejected Christianity and discouraged the use of the Spanish language. Although the Spanish returned to New Mexico in the early 1690's, the growth of the colony was slow, and its reputation as a center for peaceful conversion was discredited.

Frontier Struggles of the Eighteenth Century. The Indians' defections and rebellions in Florida and New Mexico did not force the Spanish to abandon the northern edge of their American empire, but these events dramatized the need for new approaches in their relations with American Indians. Also, the 1763 acquisition of the vast territory of Louisiana placed new pressures on Indian-Spanish relations. Imperial defense policy called for control of the Apaches and other mobile tribes of Texas because they threatened access to Louisiana by land from northern Mexico.

The Apaches roamed the large area between New Mexico and the small group of missions precariously planted around San Antonio in eastern Texas. The basic unit of Apache social organization was the extended family, and for their material existence, they relied on hunting and gathering, limited agriculture, and, when shortages developed, raids on nearby sedentary Pueblos. In their small, migratory groups, the Apaches confused the confounded Spanish officials, who, in spite of the efforts of missionaries and soldiers, found it impossible to bring them into the colonial system.

The most intensive effort to deal with the Apaches came in the initiatives of José de Galvéz, a powerful colonial official in the 1770's and 1780's. Galvéz continued military actions against the Apaches but also incorporated the French and British strategies of stimulating trade with the natives along the northern frontier to undermine tribal autonomy. Galvéz authorized the sale of alcohol and poorly made firearms to the Apaches. The alcohol was intended to create a dependency among the natives on their merchant-suppliers, and the firearms would require frequent repair and replacement. Historian David J. Weber summarized the new policies as the adoption of "tried and true English and French practices to destroy the basis of native culture" in order to achieve with "the iron fist and the velvet glove what missionaries had been unable to do through less violent and cynical means." Galvéz' changes came too late for the Spanish Empire, however; within a generation, the expansion of the United States and the independence of Mexico would remove Spanish control from the borderlands area.

California. Galvéz also pushed Spanish settlements into Alta California (the present state of California) in response to the rumored encroachments of the Russians moving down the Pacific coast from Alaska. Galvéz did not like the flawed mission-presidio system, but financial problems forced him to implant a variation of this approach in California in 1769. Franciscans led by Junípero Serra recaptured some of the enthusiasm of the first generations of missionaries in Florida and New Mexico. Within five years they had nearly five thousand Indians living on their missions. Mission life for the Chumash and other tribes, while pleasant at first, became another disastrous encounter with Europeans. Epidemic diseases and crowded living quarters brought high infant mortality rates and a rapid decline in the Indian population of California, from about 300,000 in 1769 to perhaps 200,000 in 1821. Many natives eventually fled the missions, but except for the Yumas' attack on the settlements along the California side of the lower Colorado River in 1781, Indian violence against the Spanish was rare. Although these desertions and the decline of the native population strained the Indian-Spanish relationship, the missions enjoyed some prosperity and were among Spain's most viable settlements in California in 1821 when Mexican independence brought an end to the empire in the borderlands.

While Indian-Spanish relations were generally dominated by the Europeans, the natives were resourceful in many of their earlier efforts to limit foreign influences. They had their greatest successes with subtle, diplomatic adjustments to the peaceful methods of the missionaries. The influence of these missionaries, however, survived for only a few decades. Eventually the trauma of epidemic diseases and the burdens of forced labor, tribute payment, and cultural-religious impositions kindled hostile reactions among many native groups. In the borderlands areas, the Spanish were often motivated by strategic factors in response to the expansive actions of their European rivals. These strategic concerns frequently placed military policies at the forefront in Indian-Spanish relations, especially in response to native unrest and rebellion. The ultimate outcome of the clash between Native Americans and the Spanish favored the latter; Native Americans paid an immense price in terms of life, culture, and property. —*John A. Britton*

See also Aztec; Cíbola, Seven Cities of; Horses; Maya; Missions and missionaries; Navajo; Pueblo (Popé's) Revolt; Pueblo tribes, Eastern; Pueblo tribes, Western.

BIBLIOGRAPHY

Hanke, Lewis. *The Spanish Struggle for Justice in the Conquest of America.* Boston: Little, Brown, 1965. Historical study of the Spanish debate concerning the treatment of Indians, with emphasis on the work of Bartolomé de Las Casas.

Hann, John. *Apalachee: The Land Between the Rivers.* Gainesville: University Presses of Florida, 1988. An in-depth synthesis of a crucial area in Indian-Spanish relations based on thorough research and thoughtful analysis.

John, Elizabeth A. H. *Storms Brewed in Other Men's Worlds: The Confrontation of the Indians, Spanish, and French in the Southwest, 1540-1795.* College Station: Texas A&M University Press, 1975. Readable overview of the confrontations involving the Indians, Spanish, and French in the America Southwest from 1540 to 1795. Heavy emphasis on the Native Americans' responses.

McAlister, Lyle. *Spain and Portugal in the New World, 1492-1700.* Minneapolis: University of Minnesota Press, 1984. Includes a clearly written account of Spain's general imperial policies such as the encomienda and the repartimiento.

Sandos, James. "Junípero Serra's Canonization and the Historical Record." *American Historical Review* 93 (December, 1988): 1253-1269. An important article on the controversies surrounding the early California missions.

Spicer, Edward H. *Cycles of Conquest: The Impact of Spain, Mexico, and the United States on the Indians of the Southwest, 1553-1960.* Tucson: University of Arizona Press, 1962. Broad study of the impact of several generations of outside cultural, economic, and military invasions on the Indian peoples. Somewhat dated by more recent research but contains much useful material.

Weber, David J. *The Spanish Frontier in North America.* New Haven, Conn.: Yale University Press, 1992. Excellent detailed synthesis of Spanish imperial efforts from Florida to California based on a comprehensive survey of the research in the field. Includes historical, ethnographic, and archaeological sources to provide a balance of European and Native American points of view. Extensive footnotes and lengthy bibliography provide the reader with valuable citations for further research.

Indian-white relations—Swedish colonial

TRIBES AFFECTED: Asseteque, Lenni Lenape, Mingo, Nanticoke

SIGNIFICANCE: Swedish colonial ventures to the Delaware River valley during the seventeenth century had a lasting impact on the American Indians who inhabited the region, particularly the Lenni Lenape and the Mingo; Swedish occupation, although relatively peaceful, caused the Indians' removal from the area

Contact between American Indians and Europeans in North America during the seventeenth century embodied a wide range of experiences. One component often overlooked is the Swedish venture into the Middle Atlantic region. Although their official occupation was relatively brief—1638 to 1655—they had a lasting impact on the area and the Indians that they encountered. Their officials set the stage for later English negotiations with the Indians of the area, and their colonists contributed to the ethnic diversity of the region. The Swedes and their Dutch allies concentrated their colonial ventures in the region south of the Susquehanna River and north of the Potomac. These endeavors stretched from 1638 through the middle of the century and established the pattern of colonial contact in the area.

Prehistoric Background. Prior to European contact in the late 1630's, the Indians of the Delaware Valley represented two major linguistic and ethnographic groups. The first, the Lenni Lenape, were Algonquian speakers and were closely related to the Asseteque and the Nanticoke that surrounded them. This group, whom the English later referred to as the Delaware, were subdivided into three contingents: the Munsi, the Unami, and the Unalachtigo. According to the oral tradition of the Lenni Lenape, the *Walam Olum*, this tribe migrated into the region from the northwest to cross the Mississippi River and then east over the Appalachian Mountains. The other component consisted of Iroquoian speakers, the Mingo (or Minqua), who were loosely affiliated with the Iroquois Confederacy. The Mingo were later arrivals to the region and were an invasive force aligned with the powerful Iroquois tribes to the north and the west. Both groups were fairly typical of the Northeast Woodlands culture zone which they inhabited. They tended toward political decentralization, with the greatest emphasis placed on tribal integrity. Leadership generally resided with a chief or *sachem*. Economically these peoples depended on agriculture, supplemented by hunting and gathering. They also engaged in extensive trade networking.

Colonial Contact. Swedish colonial enterprise resulted from the monarchy's interest and trade in The Netherlands during the early seventeenth century. Swedish settlement in the Delaware Valley during the 1630's occurred as an extension of the already established Dutch interests in the New Netherlands to the north. In March, 1638, with the aid of the Dutch envoy, Peter Minuit, the Swedish negotiated with local natives for the land that became the Swedish settlement Christina (present-day Wilmington). These settlements then expanded to Passayung (Philadelphia) in the north and to Fort Casmir (New Castle). The Swedes, some three to four hundred strong, concentrated their settlement on the west side of the Delaware River and lived on individual farms in log houses of the sort they inhabited in Sweden. This association focused primarily on the trade of European manufactured goods for animal pelts obtained by Indians and was conducted by representatives of the Swedish government. In the 1640's the Swedish power and influence in the region reached its peak, and the relationships between the settlers and their native counterparts remained relatively peaceful. Officials suggested that the colonists learned from the Indians methods of adapting to their "primitive existences" in New Sweden. By 1650, when the Dutch attempted to reassert their control over the region, approximately one thousand Swedes and ethnic Finns resided under the protection of the Swedish crown in the Delaware Valley. During that decade, the interests of the Swedish monarchy and the Dutch traders in the region faded, and support for the venture declined. The colonists found themselves in increasingly marginal situations; their abilities to trade and to defend themselves waned.

Indian Relations. When the Swedes entered the region in 1638 they approached peoples, the Lenni Lenape and the Mingo, already at odds with each other. The Swedish presence exaggerated each group's concerns about the access to land and the local balance of power. Initial negotiations treated the various tribes generically. Later Swedish discussions, however, resulted in a trade alliance that favored the Mingo, whom the Swedes described as "special friends." According to Johan Rising, Swedish governor, by 1655 the situation in the colony had grown ominous, with the "Renappi [sic] threatening not only to kill our people in the land . . . but also to destroy even trade with the Minques [sic] and the other savage nations." The trade with the Mingo persisted until Swedish trade goods ran out and the beaver trapped by the Indians disappeared. By the end of the 1660's the official Dutch and Swedish presences

Nineteenth century depiction of Peter Minuit helping Swedish colonists buy Indian land for New Sweden in 1638. (Library of Congress)

in the region disappeared, and the English replaced them. The Lenni Lenape had begun a forced retreat to the west. The combination of encroachment on the land by the Swedes, the impact of European disease, and the predations of the hostile Mingo forced them from the valley. The Mingo survived the Swedish occupation but not that of the English who succeeded them.   —*Martha I. Pallante*

See also Indian-white relations—Dutch colonial; Lenni Lenape; Walam Olum.

BIBLIOGRAPHY

Acrelius, Israel. *A History of New Sweden*, 1759. Reprint. Translated by William M. Reynolds. Philadelphia: The Historical Society of Pennsylvania, 1874.

Cochran, Thomas C. *Pennsylvania: A Bicentennial History.* New York: W. W. Norton, 1978.

Munroe, John A. *History of Delaware.* 2d ed. Newark: University of Delaware Press, 1984.

Sachese, Julius F. *History of the German Role in the Discovery, Exploration, and Settlement of the New World.* Reprint. *Germany and America, 1450-1700.* Edited by Don H. Tolzman. New York: Heritage Books, 1991.

Weslager, C. A. *Delaware's Buried Past: A Study of Archaeological Adventure.* Rev. ed. New Brunswick, N.J.: Rutgers University Press, 1968.

Wuorinen, John H. *The Finns on the Delaware, 1638-1655: An Essay in Colonial American History.* Philadelphia: University of Pennsylvania Press, 1938.

Indian-white relations—U.S., 1775-1830

TRIBES AFFECTED: Pantribal

SIGNIFICANCE: Following the Declaration of Independence, the fledgling United States was confronted with designing an Indian policy that combined two contradictory objectives: protecting Indians while aiding westward movement of white settlers

During the two centuries of colonization prior to American independence, Indians had been ineffectual in halting the encroachment of white settlers on tribal lands. Disease, demoralization, alcohol addiction, and wars had tragically diminished native populations. Moreover, Indians lost their principal ally as the French suffered defeat in the French and Indian War (1754-1763), thereafter subjecting Indians to their British enemies as well as to the virtually unchecked and seemingly relentless land hunger of English settlers.

American Revolution. Both the Americans and the British initially sought to ensure Indian neutrality during the American Revolution, for both sides claimed to fear Indian "savagery" in battle. Their policies of neutrality were quickly abandoned, however, as both the Americans and the British sought aid from the powerful Indians still remaining on their eastern tribal lands. The turning point occurred in 1776 as the Cherokees, angered by incessant American intrusions, launched a series of raids on American settlements. Believing them to have been armed by the British, Congress accordingly authorized General Griffith Rutherford to undertake a retaliatory strike against the Cherokees. Rutherford and his troops subsequently rampaged through Cherokee land, razing thirty-six Indian villages, including their crops and stores. The Cherokee War served as a deterrent against further southern Indian involvement in the revolution, as other tribes feared similar retribution would be visited upon them should they elect to participate.

A similar fate befell the powerful Iroquois of New York, whose alliance was courted by both the Americans and the British. A majority of the Iroquois Confederacy joined the British, who sponsored a series of Iroquois attacks intending to sever American supply lines through New York's Mohawk Valley. In response, American commander-in-chief George Washington authorized General John Sullivan to lead a sizable punitive expedition against the Iroquois in 1779. Sullivan's troops mercilessly burned and pillaged, destroying twenty-eight Iroquois villages, along with their stores and crops. Economically the Iroquois never recovered from the Sullivan campaign. In addition, the centuries-old Iroquois Confederacy was destroyed when some Tuscaroras and Oneidas, encouraged by the influential missionaries Eleazar Wheelock and Samuel Kirkland, joined the Patriot cause against the British.

During the revolution most Indians ultimately allied themselves with the British, and at war's end they were once again at the mercy of their enemies; this time, however, their enemies were the Americans.

Indian Rebellions. From the initial Powhatan rebellion in Virginia in 1622 through the pantribal alliance of Pontiac in 1763, Indian tribes had endeavored to safeguard their land rights as the white population advanced at an alarming rate. After the American Revolution, aided by government policy which treated Indian lands as forfeit because of the Indian and British alliance, Americans viewed their victory as license for uninhibited westward expansion. In the north, Americans made no distinction between Patriot and Loyalist Indians; all Indian land was subject to confiscation. Thus, during the Confederation period (in which the U.S. government was operating under the Articles of Confederation), Indians were forced to sign treaties which forfeited their land titles. The Confederation government proved incapable of enforcing treaties that failed when challenged by Indian resistance. In the south, federal treaties were negotiated for Indian protection. Those treaties were not upheld either. One problem was that some southern states, notably Georgia, repudiated Confederation authority. As American settlers vigorously resumed their unremitting westward drive, Indians responded with rebellions.

With British defeat in 1783, steadily increasing numbers of settlers moved into the Old Northwest territory (around the Great Lakes). United by a war chief, Little Turtle, Indians of

that region participated in numerous raids on white settlers between 1783 and 1790. Although President George Washington in 1790 ordered armed resistance, Indian raids continued nearly unimpeded. In 1794, a force of three thousand rigorously drilled and highly disciplined troops under the command of General "Mad Anthony" Wayne earned a decisive victory against Little Turtle at the Battle of Fallen Timbers. The following year, Indians signed the Treaty of Fort Greenville, ceding virtually all of their lands in the Northwest Territory.

The spirit of rebellion persisted, however; in the early 1800's, the visionary Shawnee leader Tecumseh organized a pan-Indian alliance and sought to create a united Indian confederation. He traveled from north to south (from New York to Florida) and westward to present-day Iowa seeking allies among Indian tribes. His resistance was aborted, however, when his brother, spiritual leader Tenskwatawa (the Shawnee Prophet), led a premature, ill-fated attack on November 11, 1811, against the forces of William Henry Harrison at Tippecanoe. His warriors were defeated, resulting in disillusionment and then defections from the alliance. Many tribes pursued rebellions in their own territories, but Tecumseh was thereafter unable to organize a united Indian front. During the War of 1812, he joined forces with the British, proving himself a capable ally. Several other tribes that Tecumseh had courted, however, chose to ally with the Americans.

In the south, Indians invoked Spanish aid against American encroachments. With General Andrew Jackson's victory against the Creeks at the Battle of Horseshoe Bend, March 27, 1814, however, expectations of an ultimate Indian victory were extinguished.

Trade. In the aftermath of Little Turtle's War, President Washington and his secretary of war, Henry Knox, both principled men, sought a policy to ensure peace between Indians and the federal government. To that end, on April 18, 1796, Congress established the "factory system" for the regulation of Indian trade. It was designed to make peace rather than to generate profit. Government trading posts, known as factories, were designated across the frontier as centers for Indian trade. At the government-regulated factories, Indians were assured equitable trade. The factory system persisted until 1822 but failed to withstand the machinations of independent and frequently dishonest American and British Canadian traders.

After the War of 1812, additional measures known as the Trade and Intercourse Acts were enacted to regulate trade and establish a licensing system. These laws were designed to safeguard Indian lands and to provide for the extradition of criminals and the punishment of crimes committed by whites on Indian land. They formed the basis for the Trade and Intercourse Act of 1834.

Civilization. By 1819, through the efforts of the humanitarian reformer Thomas L. McKenney, aided by missionaries' lobbying of the federal government, a new federal Indian policy was initiated. The goal, which was to be accomplished through education, was the assimilation of Indians through Christianization and introduction to white agricultural techniques. Under the Civilization Act, passed in 1819, which allocated ten thousand dollars for establishing schools on Indian tribal lands, Indians were to be taught American culture. Theoretically, civilization would result in the assimilation of Indians into white America, thereby eliminating threats of violence as well as freeing Indian land for white usage. Most Indians, however, continued to resist white culture, preferring to retain their tribal traditions. The minority who were indoctrinated as youths faced racial prejudice if they attempted to live as members of white society.

In the 1820's American encroachment on Indian lands was virtually uninhibited, and regulation of Indian trade, despite the best intentions embodied in the factory system and the Trade and Intercourse Acts, was largely ineffectual. Furthermore, many, including state officials, found assimilation through acculturation intolerably slow. Consequently, federal Indian policy evolved toward a final resolution to the "Indian problem" in the form of relocation of Indians to the newly created Indian Territory (present-day Oklahoma).

Removal. Indian removal, or the exchange by treaty of eastern land for lands west of the Mississippi, had several proponents, including humanitarian reformers concerned with safeguarding Indian culture through resettlement beyond the pale of white America, thereby relieving pressures on Indian tribal lands. Others were motivated by the base expectation of settlement on rich Indian lands. Georgia, coveting the sizable territory of the Cherokee Nation, eventually forced the issue to resolution. Ironically, the Cherokee Nation had become the most "civilized" of the Indian tribes, having adopted sedentary agriculture, a Cherokee syllabary, a written constitution, and a legal system patterned after that of the United States.

The spread of cotton agriculture and the discovery of gold on Cherokee lands, as well as the specter of a foreign nation within the state's boundaries, lent impetus to Georgia's eagerness to annex Indian lands. After the passage of Georgia's statutes extending the state's laws to the Cherokee Nation and disallowing Cherokee land claims, the Cherokee Nation appealed to the United States Congress. Meantime, President Andrew Jackson, elected in 1828, proved unsympathetic to Indian protests. He initiated, and saw to fruition, plans for Indian removal.

On May 28, 1830, Jackson signed into law the Indian Removal Act, by which all eastern Indians were to exchange their ancestral lands for land in the new trans-Mississippi Indian territory. Land exchanges were intended to be peaceably negotiated with Indian tribes. In practice, however, removal was frequently enforced against protesting Indians through both legal and illegal methods. Although 90 percent of the Cherokees resisted removal, for example, the intractable Jackson negotiated a removal treaty with a friendly minority faction. The Cherokee Nation, although disavowing this patently spurious document, was nevertheless bound to it and forced to move westward.

Indian removal eliminated the last obstacles to white expansion east of the Mississippi River. While the benefits to the states were obvious, removal for the eastern Indians was disastrous. Their new lands, often marginal and geographically dissimilar to their homelands, rendered their hunting and agricultural practices obsolete. A number of tribes were moved several times before their final settlement; others were located on land already inhabited by hostile tribes. Moreover, relentless white pressures for Indian lands continued as American settlers pushed their settlements ever farther westward. The process of dispossession begun early in the seventeenth century continued unabated until the end of the nineteenth century.   —*Mary E. Virginia*

See also Dancing Rabbit Creek, Treaty of; Fallen Timbers, Battle of; Fort Greenville, Treaty of; Fort Stanwix, Treaty of; Horseshoe Bend, Treaty of; Indian Removal Act; Northwest Ordinance; Tecumseh's Rebellion; Trade and Intercourse Acts.

BIBLIOGRAPHY

Graymont, Barbara. *The Iroquois in the American Revolution.* Syracuse, N.Y.: Syracuse University Press, 1972. An excellent, highly detailed account of the Iroquois during the American Revolution.

O'Donnell, James H. *Southern Indians in the American Revolution.* Knoxville: University of Tennessee Press, 1973. Focusing on the Cherokees, Chickasaws, Creeks, and Choctaws, O'Donnell describes the attitudes of both the British and the Americans toward their Indian allies and Indian enemies. Indexed, annotated, and bibliography.

Prucha, Francis Paul. "Andrew Jackson's Indian Policy: A Reassessment." *Journal of American History* 56, no. 3 (1969): 527-539. A discussion of Jackson's Indian policy from a sympathetic viewpoint, describing the pressures leading to Indian removal.

_____. *The Great Father: The United States Government and the American Indians.* 2 vols. Lincoln: University of Nebraska Press, 1984. An extensive, fully annotated, indexed, and illustrated history of Indian-white relations from the founding of the United States to the 1980's by one of the premier authorities on Indian-white relations.

Satz, Ronald N. *American Indian Policy in the Jacksonian Era.* Lincoln: University of Nebraska Press, 1975. A thorough treatment of Andrew Jackson and Indian removal. Annotated, indexed with bibliography.

Tyler, S. Lyman. *A History of Indian Policy.* Washington, D.C.: Government Printing Office, 1973. A brief chronological guide to Indian policy. Illustrated, containing maps, time lines, and bibliography.

Viola, Herman J. *Thomas L. McKenney: Architect of America's Early Indian Policy, 1816-1830.* Chicago: Sage Books, 1974. Informative biography of McKenney, superintendent of Indian trade and the first director of the Bureau of Indian Affairs, and description of his Indian policy under the administrations of presidents James Madison, James Monroe, John Quincy Adams, and Andrew Jackson. Illustrated and indexed. Bibliography.

Washburn, Wilcomb E., ed. *History of Indian-White Relations.* Vol. 4 in *Handbook of North American Indians.* Washington, D.C.: Smithsonian Institution Press, 1988. An invaluable reference source containing articles on all aspects of Indian-white relations. Includes biographical dictionary. Fully annotated. Bibliography and illustrations.

Indian-white relations—U.S., 1831-1870

TRIBES AFFECTED: Pantribal

SIGNIFICANCE: In the 1830's, U.S. policy toward Native Americans changed from treating tribes as "separate nations" to forcing integration into white society; European Americans began to view Indians as threatening rather than annoying

The nineteenth century represents a pivotal point in Indian-white relations. Indian tribes went from being independent nations to being treated as wards of the United States. The U.S. government reduced Indian rights and freedoms until they almost disappeared.

1830's. During the 1830's, the U.S. government and its citizens generally viewed Indians as a disposable nuisance. Despite the acculturation of the Five Civilized Tribes, many whites viewed them as dispensable "savages" who failed to utilize "properly" the land under their control. Many Indian groups suffered from white misconceptions. Where whites once searched for the "noble savage" or the Indian with whom they could discuss politics and religion, now whites viewed Indians as "wretched" and as an annoyance.

U.S. policy reflected these changes in attitudes. Beginning in the 1830's, when the U.S. government forcibly removed the Five Civilized Tribes of the southeast (Cherokee, Chickasaw, Creek, Choctaw, and Seminole), the government no longer treated tribes as independent foreign nations. They became "domestic, dependent nations." This meant that treaties could be made with them but that the government treated the land as being held in escrow for the Indians. The Five Civilized Tribes were moved to Oklahoma (then known as Indian Territory) and forced to live in a different climate from the one they knew. Forced to leave behind their farms, tools, and buildings, they faced death and disease in their new homes.

The U.S. government considered removal the best policy for settling disputes between whites and Indians. During the 1830's, the U.S. government removed the Winnebagos from Wisconsin, the Potawatomi from Indiana, and the Sauk and Fox from Wisconsin, as well as removing the Five Civilized Tribes from the Southeast. Removed Indians lost their land, their ways of life, and their political freedoms. Tribal factions erupted over whether to accept removal. Tensions arose again after removal over how to cope with the change. Removal attacked Indian autonomy.

Removal also increased intertribal tensions. Tribes from the east were moved into lands already occupied by western tribes. This meant that more tribes vied for the same resources. Removal upset the tribal balance of power that had existed in the Plains. Eventually, whites joined the fray over the land in the west.

Americans aggressively pursued the policy of Manifest Destiny, taking the Oregon territory from the British in the

1830's. Missionary Marcus Whitman, his wife Narcissa, and the H. H. Spauldings accomplished this by leading settlers into Oregon territory with congressional approval. Though originally sent to Christianize the Cayuse Indians, they focused instead on populating the region so that it could be claimed by the United States. The Cayuse and other groups in the area resented this intrusion of settlers. The British had simply traded with the Indians; they had not brought settlers. Clashes over land and animals erupted constantly as the two groups tried to live together. The Whitmans and the Spauldings ignored warning signs that Indian discontent was rising. Tensions rose steadily throughout the 1830's.

1840's and 1850's. Attitudes toward the Indians changed dramatically during the 1840's. Indians were considered a threat and an impediment to American development of the west. Two incidents particularly influenced this change in attitude: the Whitman Massacre and the Mexican-American War.

By 1845, five thousand settlers a year were moving into the Oregon Territory. The Indians in this region watched as whites subdivided the land with fences and houses. In 1847, frustrated with the tide of white settlers and disease, the Cayuse rose up and massacred the Whitmans and several other whites. Spaulding, who missed the attack, became an opponent of the Indians. The massacre shocked and horrified Americans in the East. It brought back colonial period images of the Indians as bloodthirsty savages. All Indians west of the Mississippi suffered from this characterization.

After the Mexican-American War (1846-1848), according to the Treaty of Guadalupe Hidalgo, the western border of the United States jumped from the Mississippi to the Pacific coast. It destroyed what the government considered the "Indian barrier" of the Mississippi, opening the western half of the U.S. to white "civilization" and settlement. This altered Indian-white relations on the Plains, in the Southwest, and on the Pacific coast. Until the end of the Mexican-American War, most of the Indian groups west of the Mississippi had avoided subjugation to the Spanish and had traded with the French. They did not expect to be subjugated by the Americans. The introduction of whites interested in settlement into western territory increased tensions between Indians and whites.

During the 1840's and 1850's, the Bureau of Indian Affairs (BIA) shared the responsibility of defining policy with the military. The BIA represented one of the most mismanaged of government offices. It was a favorite spot for placing beneficiaries of the spoils system—newly elected senators and congressman placed their political allies in the BIA as a reward for service. Graft and corruption existed at every level, from the agents in the field to the commissioners in Washington. Additionally, these administrators turned over with every new election. Yet the U.S. government placed the BIA in charge of defining long-term Indian policy.

To aid westward expansion, the BIA sought to extinguish Indian land titles during this period. As whites took over more and more western land, it became apparent that removing

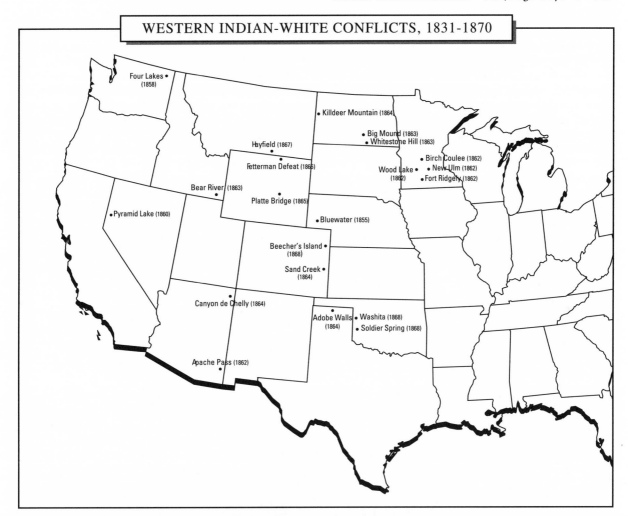

WESTERN INDIAN-WHITE CONFLICTS, 1831-1870

Four Lakes (1858)

Killdeer Mountain (1864)

Big Mound (1863)
Whitestone Hill (1863)

Hayfield (1867)
Fetterman Defeat (1866)

Birch Coulee (1862)
New Ulm (1862)
Wood Lake (1862)
Fort Ridgely (1862)

Bear River (1863)

Platte Bridge (1865)

Pyramid Lake (1860)

Bluewater (1855)

Beecher's Island (1868)

Sand Creek (1864)

Canyon de Chelly (1864)

Adobe Walls (1864)
Washita (1868)
Soldier Spring (1868)

Apache Pass (1862)

Indians to unoccupied land would no longer be feasible. The BIA considered treaties and annuity payments to be the fastest and most efficient way to end titles. Often BIA negotiators lied to Indian representatives to get them to sign the treaties. They withheld annuities from previous treaties to force Indian leaders to sign new treaties. In addition, Congress changed the treaties before ratifying them. Such deceptions led to poor relations between whites and Indians.

The paying of annuities for relinquished land created more tension. Many agents embezzled parts of the annuity payments. Moreover, there was often confusion about who was to receive the payments, a specific chief or each individual Indian in that tribe. Agents also sometimes acted as traders, overcharging for goods so that the goods always equaled the annuity payments. These policies increased the tension between Indians and whites.

As more whites moved west, the "taming of the Indian" became an integral part of Manifest Destiny. To enforce this concept, the military became the second executor of Indian policy. Military protection had to be provided for white citizens moving west. Despite friendly or indifferent receptions by Indians on most parts of the trail, the few incidents of Indian attack appeared in newspapers and books everywhere. Many westward settlers considered the trail to be full of "bloodthirsty savages" looking for scalps and white women. The settlers demanded protection. The U.S. government established forts across the frontier to be able to control and eliminate the perceived Indian menace.

Civil War. The Civil War changed Indian-white relations. First, the U.S. government withdrew the army regulars from the frontier and replaced them with volunteers who resented serving on the "Indian frontier." President Lincoln kept these troops in the West to protect the gold routes and the whites moving westward. Many tribes saw the Civil War as a sign of weakness in the American government. The Sioux, the Five Civilized Tribes, and others chased missionaries and Indian agents from their territory.

Two incidents during this period damaged Indian-white relations for the next several years: the decision by the Five Civilized Tribes to join the Confederacy and the Sioux Uprising of 1862. The Five Civilized Tribes sided with the Confederacy after being convinced that it would treat them as equals after the war. Some leaders, such as John Ross of the Cherokee, feared Northern reprisals if the South lost. Unfortunately, during battles such as Pea Ridge, the Indian units were accused of committing savage atrocities which reinforced negative attitudes towards them. The Sioux Uprising of 1862 frightened western settlers, as newspapers portrayed it as an unprovoked massacre of innocent women and children. (In reality, BIA politics and poor management ignited the massacre.) The aftermath influenced generations of western settlers who remembered only the women and children murdered by Indians.

Tensions between whites and Indians increased during the Civil War. White settlers distrusted the volunteers who had replaced the army regulars and expected the Indians to take advantage of the lack of men and muscle on the frontier to chase the settlers out. Indians also distrusted the volunteers; they tended to be trigger-happy, undisciplined, and unsure of the nature of their mission. The volunteers were unprepared for conflict on the Plains. They were unused to guerrilla warfare. Between the lack of trust of the army and the reinforced fear of the "savage Indians," tensions increased on the frontier.

Post-Civil War. After the Civil War, the War Department and the military fought to gain control of the BIA in order to exterminate the Indians, but the cost of a military solution deterred Congress from this policy. Reformers, including missionaries, moved in to try to take control of the policy and to pacify the Indians.

In 1867, a Senate report changed policy for one year. The report stated that the Indian population was declining rapidly because of disease, war, and malnutrition. Additionally, it accused the military of starting most conflicts with the Indians, thereby reinforcing the idea that military officers were inadequate as agents of peace. The report suggested that the reservation system was the only humane policy. It would allow the Indians to become integrated into American society by teaching them farming and the rules of white society. It would also protect them from the military and from each other.

As punishment for siding with the Confederacy, the U.S. government forced the Five Civilized Tribes to surrender their

Cheyenne and Arapaho representatives discussing the terms of the Treaty of Medicine Lodge Creek with the Indian Peace Commission in 1867. (Alexander Gardner, Museum of New Mexico)

westernmost lands, abolish slavery, grant the railroads rights-of-way through their territory (which would inevitably bring whites into the territory), establish U.S. military posts, and allow the creation of U.S. territorial governments within their territory. Exhausted after the war, the tribes accepted the terms of surrender.

In 1868, as new battles between Indians and the military raged in the West, the Indian Commission announced that it was no longer necessary to recognize tribes as "domestic dependent nations." This effectively meant the end of treaty negotiations. Additionally, the BIA was transferred back to the War Department, temporarily giving the military more control of policy. These policy changes resulted from the violence that existed on the Plains both during and after the Civil War. The government now considered all tribes untrustworthy and limited their rights accordingly. As the 1870's approached, Indian policy and Indian-white relations entered a new and dangerous phase: war and open extermination.   —*C. L. Higham*

See also Black Hawk War; Bozeman Trail wars; Cayuse War; Fort Atkinson, Treaty of; Fort Laramie Treaty of 1851; Fort Laramie Treaty of 1868; Indian Removal Act; Indian-white relations—Canadian; Long Walk; Minnesota Uprising; Navajo War; Removal; Sand Creek Massacre; Sioux uprisings; Trail of Tears; Walla Walla Council; Washita River, Battle of the.

BIBLIOGRAPHY

Berkhofer, Robert F., Jr. *Salvation and the Savage*. Lexington: University Press of Kentucky, 1965. This work focuses on how missionaries portrayed white culture to the Indians and on the policy behind these presentations.

Brown, Dee. *Bury My Heart at Wounded Knee*. New York: Henry Holt, 1970. This work represents the Indian perception of Indian-white relations in the nineteenth century.

Dippie, Brian. *The Vanishing American*. Middletown, Conn.: Wesleyan University Press, 1982. Dippie examines the concept of the extinction of the Indian in the nineteenth century.

Kelley, Robert. *American Protestantism and United States Indian Policy*. Lincoln: University of Nebraska Press, 1983. Discusses how Protestant reformers influenced Indian policy and Indian-white relations.

Utley, Robert M. *The Indian Frontier*. Albuquerque: University of New Mexico Press, 1984. Examines, through vignettes and traditional narrative, Indian-white relations on the military and political frontiers.

Indian-white relations—U.S., 1871-1933

TRIBES AFFECTED: Pantribal
SIGNIFICANCE: This period saw the last of the Indian wars, significant changes in white attitudes toward Native Americans, and important attempts to regularize the legal status of American Indians by new acts of law

In the period between 1871 and 1933, the last of the tragic Indian wars were fought, and several attempts were made by the federal government to reform Indian policy. The attempts at reform were often wrongheaded, and they ultimately had to be reversed, but they demonstrate the popular perception that the existing policy could not be sustained indefinitely.

Indian Wars. A series of serious Indian wars characterized the period between 1871 and 1890. Some of these were precipitated by the desire of whites for Indian lands or by the desire of white settlers to eliminate the Indians because of prejudice or fears of attack. Others seem primarily to have been the result of the inability of many tribes and tribal leaders to accept confinement on reservations, which were often composed of extremely poor land. Confinement also flew in the face of traditional patterns of Indian life.

In 1871, the Kiowas rose up in Texas under Satanta, Satank, Big Tree, Eagle Heart, and Big Bow, engaging in a campaign that included the ambush of a wagon train on Salt Creek Prairie. In the period 1872-1873, the Modoc War erupted as the Modocs, a Northern California tribe, resisted resettlement in Indian Territory. The war ended with the trial and execution of Captain Jack, the Modoc leader. The years 1874-1875 saw the outbreak of the so-called Red River War, with the U.S. Cavalry under General Philip Sheridan and Nelson A. Miles and the Texas Rangers battling an alliance of Comanche, Cheyenne, and Kiowa warriors under Big Tree, Lone Wolf, and Satanta. The war ended with the surrender of Quanah Parker, the feared Comanche chief.

The famous campaign known as the pursuit of the Nez Perce occurred in 1877. It began when young braves resisting a forced march to reservation land led a substantial group of the tribe in flight, with General O. O. Howard in pursuit. Led by chiefs Joseph the Younger and Looking Glass, the Nez Perce evaded army pursuit across Idaho and Wyoming, fighting battles at White Bird Canyon, Clearwater, Big Hole River, Camas Meadows, Billings, and Bear Paw Mountain. They reached a point only 100 miles from their goal of Canadian sanctuary before surrendering.

In 1878-1879, the campaign of the pursuit of the Northern Cheyenne followed the pattern of the Nez Perce campaign, but in less spectacular form. Chiefs Dull Knife and Little Wolf led three hundred braves off the reservation, pursued by regular army troops and civilian volunteers. Dull Knife's faction surrendered at Camp Robinson but then refused to proceed to the reservation. In a fight with the troops, half of Dull Knife's followers were killed. Little Wolf's band surrendered later.

The Bannock War commenced in 1878. Bannocks, under Chief Buffalo Horn, began raiding in southern Idaho and Oregon. Paiutes under Chief Egan and the medicine man Oytes broke out from the Malheur Reservation and joined the Bannocks, pursued by General Howard. The Indian confederates were defeated at the Battle of Birch Creek, and during their subsequent flight Chief Egan was killed by Umatilla warriors through a trick involving a war council with the Umatillas to discuss an alliance.

The year 1879 contained two complete Indian wars. The Sheepeaters War involved a band of renegade Shoshones and Bannocks who raided throughout Idaho and neighboring areas. The Ute War occurred in Colorado when Indian agent

WESTERN INDIAN-WHITE CONFLICTS, 1871-1890

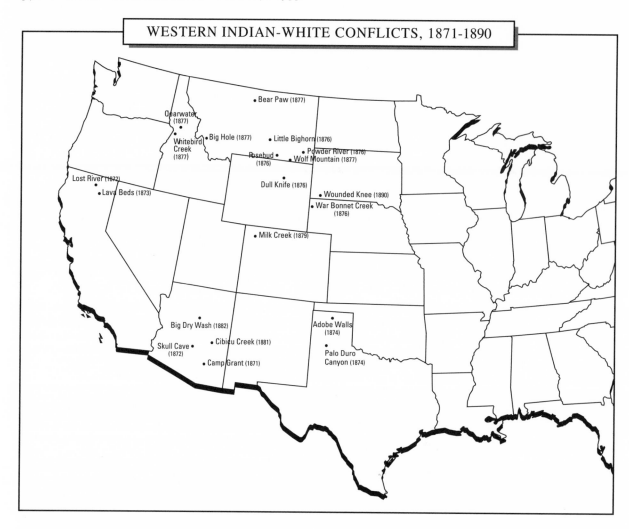

Nathan Meeker telegraphed for aid against restive Utes. Relieving forces were put under siege after the Battle of Milk Creek, and additional forces were required to subdue the Utes.

Less confined in time were the Sioux and Apache wars, which stretched out over many years. In 1872, a band of Yavapais Apaches died at the Battle of Skull Cave in Salt River Canyon; after the subsequent Battle of Turret Peak, many Apaches returned to the reservation. When the Apaches were ordered to the hated San Carlos Reservation in Arizona in 1876, however, the war reignited. There followed several years when Geronimo and Victorio broke from their reservations, raided, and crisscrossed the Mexican border at will. For a decade, until 1886, Geronimo would be a constant problem for the army and for the government.

Finally, in 1876, the Sioux reacted against orders to move from the Black Hills to the San Carlos Reservation in Arizona. Battles included Sitting Bull's attack on General Crook's column at Rosebud Creek, the defeat of Colonel George Armstrong Custer and the Seventh Cavalry at the Battle of the Little Bighorn, the Battle of Slim Buttes, the Battle of Wolf Mountain, and the Battle of Muddy Creek. Sitting Bull fled into Canada with his warriors but returned to surrender to U.S. forces in 1881.

In the latter days of 1890, a sad sequel to the Sioux wars was enacted. The Ghost Dance Uprising and the Battle of Wounded Knee (the Wounded Knee Massacre) ended the era of the Indian wars. The prophet Wovoka preached a vision of Indian resurgence and resurrection based on the use of the magical Ghost Dance. Sitting Bull was killed by reservation police at the Standing Rock Reservation. At the camp of Chief Big Foot at Wounded Knee, three hundred Indians were slaughtered in what has become known as the Wounded Knee Massacre. The surrender of the Sioux the next year at White Clay Creek ended the era of direct warfare between the whites and Indians.

Legal Status and Governmental Policy. When Ulysses S. Grant became president in 1869, a new "peace policy" was adopted in U.S. relations with the Indian tribes. Under the new policy, new appointments of Indians agents would be made from among the religious groups who sent missionaries among the tribes, and extraordinary efforts would be made to get the Indians to adopt white ways—living in houses, practicing agriculture, and so on.

Many other developments in Indian affairs filled the Grant years. In 1870, in the *Cherokee Tobacco* case, the Supreme Court upheld the principle that new acts of Congress supersede prior treaties, including those with the Indian nations, when they contradict. The next year saw the complete abandonment of treaty making in regard to the tribes, with all future agreements replaced by statutes and executive orders. Partly this represented the desire of the House of Representatives to have a say in such agreements, and partly it represented a reaction to the fact that treaties, after the *Cherokee Tobacco* case, offered no enhancement of protection over simple statute. Some reservations were established by treaty, others by statute, but beginning in the 1870's, executive orders were also employed.

In 1874, the Report of the Indian Commissioner proposed major changes in the status of the Indians and their way of life. Citizenship was proposed for any Indian who desired it. It was also proposed that the protection and obligations of white law be extended to Indian Territory and that reservation land be held in individual plots—called "allotments in severalty"—

rather than communally by tribes. This would promote agriculture and the improvement of land.

In 1879, the case *Standing Bear v. Crook*, decided by Judge Elmer S. Dundy of the U.S. Circuit Court, District of Nebraska, declared Indians to be "persons" under the Constitution and extended the writ of habeas corpus to them to protect their liberty.

In 1883, Secretary of the Interior Henry M. Teller instigated "courts of Indian affairs" on reservations to create a rule of law on tribal lands. The drive to bring Indians under white law suffered a major setback in the 1883 Supreme Court case *Ex parte Crow Dog*, wherein the Brule Sioux Chief Crow Dog's conviction and death sentence for the murder of Spotted Tail was overturned on the grounds that there was no federal jurisdiction over the crime of an Indian against another Indian on Indian land. Further separating Indians from white governance was the 1884 Supreme Court case *Elk v. Wilkins*, whereby the Court refused to enforce a franchise right for the plaintiff, who had severed his ties to his tribe and lived among whites.

These moves away from white law began to be reversed in 1885 with Congress's passage of the Major Crimes Act, which placed seven serious felonies under federal law if committed on reservations or other Indian territory in order to avoid

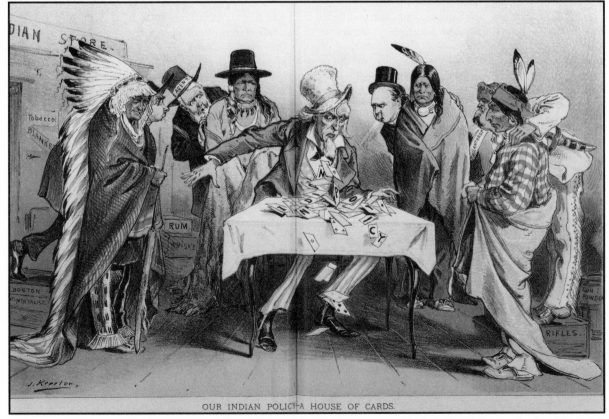

This cartoon in Puck *magazine satirizes the confused and inconsistent nature of U.S. Indian policy in the late nineteenth century; among the problems here are the "Boston sentimentalist," the weapons trader, and the government Indian agent.* (Library of Congress)

situations such as that in the *Crow Dog* decision. In 1886 in *United States v. Kagama*, the high Court upheld the constitutionality of the act.

Assimilation of the Indians into white society became the stated solution to all problems in white-Indian relations, and indeed, to all problems of Indian society. Politicians rushed to embrace this solution, as did many of those who regarded themselves as friends and defenders of the "red man." In 1884, the Lake Mohonk Conference of Friends of the Indian issued a program which called for assimilation by bringing the Indians under territorial law, private individual ownership of land, and other forms of white civilization. Groups such as this were torn between their recognition of the potential loss of Indian culture and the need to prevent further depredations by white society.

In 1887, the General Allotment Act (Dawes Act) provided for allotments in severalty for reservation Indians, providing citizenship for Indians on such allotments. In that year as well, Commissioner J. D. C. Atkins ordered that, in all schools on reservations, all instruction was to be in the English language to aid in assimilation. Two years later, the government moved to establish a system of government-run Indian schools. By 1889, Commissioner Thomas J. Morgan was calling for the conscious destruction of the tribes as the ultimate means of assimilation of the Indians into the dominant culture.

In 1892, Indian courts were authorized to punish as offenses such Indian practices as traditional dances, polygamy, and the practices of medicine men as well as standard criminal offenses such as destruction of property, fornication, and drunkenness. Truancy of children enrolled in government schools was also an offense. The inclusion of several Indian cultural and religious practices as "offenses" struck sharply at the Indian way of life.

In 1898, upon the failure of the Dawes Commission to achieve agreement with the Five Civilized Tribes and the other tribes of the Indian Territory, Congress imposed the Curtis Act, which essentially applied the provisions of the Dawes Act to that territory, destroying tribal government. The Supreme Court upheld the act in *Stephens v. Cherokee Nation* (1899).

Twentieth Century. In *Lone Wolf v. Hitchcock* (1903), the Supreme Court upheld the plenary power of Congress over Indian affairs and established the right of Congress to abrogate treaties. By 1905, however, the government was having second thoughts about its wholesale reforms. Commissioner Francis E. Leupp issued a report to Congress which endorsed attempts to institute Indian self-sufficiency and called for presentation of aspects of Indian culture.

In 1906, the Burke Act provided for discretion in the length of trust periods for allotments and provided that citizenship should come at the end rather than at the beginning of such periods. The Lacey Act (1907) further struck at the tribal system by providing for allotment of tribal funds to individuals under specified conditions.

In 1919, as an acknowledgment of its gratitude for war service, Congress passed an act providing U.S. citizenship to Indian veterans of World War I upon request. In 1928, the Institute for Government Research issued the Meriam Report, which dealt systematically with the general problems facing Indians in the nation and was critical of U.S. government policies. It would lead to milestone legislation in 1934, the Indian Reorganization Act. —*Patrick M. O'Neil*

See also Adobe Walls, Battles of; Allotment system; Burke Act; *Cherokee Tobacco* case; General Allotment Act; Indian Act of 1876 (Canada); Indian Citizenship Act; Indian-white relations—Canadian; Little Bighorn, Battle of the; *Lone Wolf v. Hitchcock*; Meriam Report; Modoc War; Nez Perce War; Wounded Knee Massacre.

BIBLIOGRAPHY

Axelrod, Alan. *Chronicle of the Indian Wars: From Colonial Times to Wounded Knee*. New York: Prentice Hall General Reference, 1993. This work provides a useful and detailed overview of the armed struggles of the Indians and the whites.

Faulk, Odie B. *Crimson Desert: Indian Wars of the American Southwest*. New York: Oxford University Press, 1974. Faulk presents a fine and detailed description of the campaigns of this region.

Jackson, Helen. *A Century of Dishonor: A Sketch of the United States Government's Dealings with Some of the Indian Tribes*. 1880. Reprint. New York: Barnes & Noble, 1993. This volume is a reprint of an 1880 history of Indian-white relations from earliest colonial times through 1871, with many excellent quotations from official documents.

Marshall, Samuel L. A. *Crimsoned Prairie*. New York: Charles Scribner's Sons, 1972. Details the Indian campaigns of the West. The author is an excellent military historian, although slightly biased in the direction of preserving the honor of the military.

Prucha, Francis Paul, ed. *Documents of United States Indian Policy*. 2d ed. Lincoln: University of Nebraska Press, 1990. Reprints major documents in the history of U.S. policy toward native peoples.

Shattuck, Petra T., and Jill Norgren. *Partial Justice: Federal Indian Law in a Liberal Constitutional System*. New York: Berg, 1991. This study carefully analyzes the relationship of U.S. Indian law and policy to the U.S. constitutional order and governmental administrative policy.

Tyler, Lyman S. *A History of Indian Policy*. Washington, D.C.: Government Printing Office, 1973. This work sets out accurately and in great detail the development of the Indian policy of the United States.

Wilkinson, Charles F. *American Indians, Time, and the Law: Native Societies in a Modern Constitutional Democracy*. New Haven, Conn.: Yale University Press, 1987. This treatise traces Indian law and rights through court cases, primarily U.S. Supreme Court cases.

Williams, Robert A., Jr. *The American Indian in Western Legal Thought: The Discourses of Conquest*. New York: Oxford University Press, 1990. This book deals with earlier times in white-Indian relations but is vital reading for anyone who wishes to understand the philosophical and traditional bases of American Indian law.

Indian-white relations—U.S., 1934-1995

TRIBES AFFECTED: Pantribal

SIGNIFICANCE: During the period since 1934, three stages led from open displacement of Indian rights to self-determination policies

The landmark Indian Reorganization Act of 1934, which remained the legislative model for relations between the U.S. government and Indian tribes until the mid-1950's, was based on a massive 1928 report entitled *The Problem of Indian Administration* (also called the Meriam Report). This report had been requested by Secretary of the Interior Hubert Work. It was intended to reexamine the effects of the General Allotment Act of 1887. Briefly stated, the 1887 act had provided for allotment to each Indian family a specific plot of land within their tribe's "traditional" holdings. Under this law, after titles had been held for twenty-five years, families would gain full property rights, including the right to sell their land. Any tribal land that was left after plot allotment to families was to be sold to the government for homesteading. It is estimated that, when the Indian Reorganization Act came into effect in 1934, Indians held legal rights to only one-third of the land they had had before the General Allotment Act. This fact, coupled with a number of other critical factors pointed out in the Meriam Report (including inferior conditions in the areas of health care and education), led to the policy changes embodied in 1934's Indian Reorganization Act. Most of the responsibility for implementing these changes rested with President Franklin D. Roosevelt's appointee to the post of commissioner of Indian affairs, John Collier.

Indian Reorganization Act. In addition to slowing the loss of Indian lands, the 1934 act brought a new philosophy to the Bureau of Indian Affairs (BIA). It proclaimed a need to reverse a long-standing policy of forced assimilation of Indians into "mainstream" America and to build stronger bases for the retention of local Indian cultures. In Collier's words, it aimed at "both the economic and spiritual rehabilitation of the Indian race."

In the first domain, plans were laid to appropriate funds to buy back for the tribes Indian land that had been lost since 1887. The BIA also initiated a program to spread knowledge of land and timber conservation technology to receptive tribes and began steps to provide local development loans. Although the deepening of the Great Depression soon made special appropriations impossible, much surplus government land that had not gone to homesteading was returned. In its bid to encourage a greater sense of local tribal identity, the 1934 act also offered aid for drawing up and implementing tribal constitutions as the basis for their own local government.

World War II. In the period between 1934 and the next major redefinition of BIA policy in 1953, many domestic policy factors intervened to affect what Roosevelt's policy makers had seen as the long-term goals of the BIA. The greatest single factor affecting tens of thousands of Indian lives during the decade of the 1940's, however, was initially set in play by forces far beyond the reservations: This factor was military service in the U.S. forces during World War II. More than twenty-five thousand Indians served between 1941 and 1945. Many thousands more left reservations to work in war-related industrial factories. Indian women were also welcomed as volunteers in the army nurses' corps and the Red Cross.

Whatever their experiences in the ranks of the armed forces, still strictly segregated along racial lines, clear problems confronted thousands of returning Indian veterans at the end of the war. Part of the dilemma stemmed from continuing economic underdevelopment on the reservations they left. Equally debilitating, thousands of returning American Indian veterans felt alienated from their own people after experiencing life off the reservation.

Problems such as these impelled U.S. lawmakers to consider once again whether assimilation, rather than "protected separation," was the best policy to pursue in Indian affairs. Parties supporting the former, including outspoken conservative Republican Senator Arthur Watkins from Utah, introduced what became, in House Concurrent Resolution Number 108, the policy of "termination and relocation."

Termination Act of 1953. When HCR 108 became law in mid-1953, it pledged "to make Indians . . . subject to the same laws and entitled to the same privileges and responsibilities as . . . other citizens . . . and to end their status as wards of the United States." Even as HCR 108 was about to become law, a number of Indian spokesmen for the first tribes scheduled for termination (which meant stopping various forms of federal government "protective" intervention in their affairs) openly questioned Senator Watkins' claims that, since there were multiple sources to develop potential wealth on their reservations, the tribes should be able to "go it better alone."

Menominee leader Gordon Keshena was not alone in expressing worries that, if BIA supervision over local Indian affairs ended, the tribes' lack of experience would produce deterioration of many Indian material interests. Some congressional supporters of the general principles behind HCR 108 also admitted that the government might find itself spending large amounts of money trying to prepare the weakest and poorest Indian groups to know what forms of local self-autonomy might suit them best.

In fact, just as local termination bills began to appear in 1954, President Dwight D. Eisenhower seemed prepared to increase budgetary allocations to encourage the establishment of new industries in or near tribal areas. For example, by 1956, $300,000 of tribal funds formerly held in trust were earmarked to induce industrial plant owners to locate on the fringes of Navaho territory. Two companies constructed factories, one manufacturing baby furniture, the other making electronic equipment, near Flagstaff, Arizona.

In 1957 the Indian Vocational Training Act was intended to provide job skills needed for Indian applicants to be attractive to potential employers, even if such jobs meant relocating off reservations. More than a hundred different occupations were included in the curriculum of free schools located in twenty-six states. This ambitious program continued to expand even as economic recession worsened in 1956 and 1957. Indian policymakers seemed convinced that the overall objectives of the 1953 termination laws would be best served if Indians who could not expect to gain employment on economically backward reservations relocated in off-reservation towns. Ideally, such a movement of families would also ease pressures on the limited economic means of their respective homelands.

Relocation. A separate budget for relocation came by the mid-1950's, to avoid negative consequences for Indians who left the reservations without adequate security. Statistics showed that, of the nearly 100,000 Indians who left reservations between 1945 to 1958, some 75,000 had relocated without federal assistance, sometimes causing familial disasters. Thus, job training and relocation funds expended in 1957 doubled in one year, reaching $3.5 million. In the same year, seven thousand Indians moved from their reservations. Controversy soon developed over shortcomings in the relocation program.

Realistic prospects for employment fell short of demands; moreover, job layoffs left many Indians "stranded" and unemployed in unsympathetic white-dominated environments. At the same time, there were very high dropout rates in BIA-sponsored vocational schools. Nurse's aide programs for women registered the lowest percentage of dropouts (21 percent), while rates for less challenging factory-type programs for men were very high (a 50 percent dropout rate for sawmill workers and a rate as high as 62 percent among furniture factory trainees).

As the 1960's approached, critics of the effects of termination and relocation, including Sophie Aberle, formerly responsible for the United Pueblos Agency, warned Indian Commissioner Glenn Emmons of trouble ahead. Emmons tried to defend his office by reiterating a philosophy that was not accepted by all—that whatever successes were occurring usually stemmed from individual initiative, whereas groups that fell back on the security of "communal lifestyle" tended to accept status quo conditions. Emmons cited gains that were not so easily measured in paychecks, such as advances in tribal health programs and in education. The number of Indians going beyond high school by this date (the 1958-1959 school year) showed an increase of more than 65 percent in only three years.

Toward Self-Determination: 1960's and 1970's. Despite the fact that the Eisenhower Administration's last BIA budget (for fiscal year 1960) was the largest ever ($115,467,000), it was during the 1960 presidential campaign that controversy over Indian policy began to come to public attention. Party platform committees actually heard testimony from tribal leaders such as Frank George, a Nez Perce who asked not for abandonment of termination but for improvement in its procedures for aiding needy tribes. Other claims, such as the Miccosukee Seminole demand for all of Florida to reconstitute their sovereignty, received less sympathy. The new tide that was coming was best expressed by La Verne Madigan of the Association on American Indian Affairs, who stated that Indians should have the right to choose freely between assimilation and "life in cultural communities of their own people."

In general, the Kennedy-Johnson Democratic years (1960-1968) witnessed a continuation of termination actions despite the views of Lyndon Johnson's interior secretary, Stewart Udall. It was Udall's insistence that the BIA should do more to secure better conditions of relocation that led to the replacement of Commissioner Philleo Nash by Wisconsin Oneida Indian Robert Bennett in 1966. Under Bennett's influence, the president began, in the troubled political climate of 1967, to declare the nation's need to end the termination policy. Soon thereafter, Johnson urged passage of the Indian Civil Rights Act (1968).

The 1970's, under Presidents Richard Nixon, Gerald Ford, and Jimmy Carter, brought what has been described as the "self-determination" policy, emphasizing the development of tribal resources on restored reservations. Perhaps the most dramatic example of reversal of what many perceived to be the harmful effects of termination occurred in 1973, when the Menominee tribe was told that (as the tribe had requested) its twenty-year experience of termination was over and that its entire reservation was to be restored to it as "unencumbered Menominee property." Yet despite pronouncements of "better intentions" coming from Washington and the BIA, the cumulative effects of decades of misunderstanding were not to be dispelled easily. In the same year that the Menominees regained tribal control over their own destiny, a breakdown in relations between federal troops and Lakota Indians during a seventy-one-day siege on the Pine Ridge Reservation ended in an assault that the Lakotas call "Wounded Knee II." Similar confrontations with threats of violence came in different regions, pressing government authorities to review its Indian policy yet again.

In May, 1977, the congressional American Indian Policy Review Commission, which included five Indian members for the first time, made more than two hundred recommendations, most of which aimed at confirming all tribes' power to enact laws within the confines of their own reservations. On the heels of this symbol of intended reform, the U.S. Congress passed the 1978 American Indian Religious Freedom Act, which guaranteed freedom for tribes to practice their own traditional religions. This act ended the mixed legacy of several centuries of insistence that missionary conversion and education following Christian principles were vital aspects of Indian-white relations in the United States.

1980's Through 1995. During the Ronald Reagan and George Bush Republican presidencies (1980-1992), budgetary cuts seriously affected the continuity of existing programs of assistance to Indian tribes. In 1981 alone, one-half of the prior budget for health services was cut, while funding for Indian higher education was reduced from 282 million to 200 million dollars. By the mid-1980's, the education budget had been cut further, to 169 million dollars.

Despite alarming cutbacks in BIA funding and looming questions of Indian demands for restoration of their sover-

The 1973 occupation of Wounded Knee, South Dakota, was one of the most dramatic of the 1970's protests against U.S. government treatment of Indians. (AP/Wide World Photos)

eignty, the Republican administration of George Bush made one major contribution by enacting the Native American Languages Act, which allowed tribal use of (formerly banned) traditional languages in BIA schools.

The issue of Indian land claims was prominent throughout the 1980's and early 1990's. In 1980, the U.S. Supreme Court (in *United States v. Sioux Nation*) upheld a $122 million judgment against the United States for having taken the Black Hills from the Sioux illegally. In 1986, a federal court awarded each member of the White Earth Chippewa group compensation for land lost under the 1887 General Allotment Act. A significant piece of legislation regarding land claims was the 1982 Indian Claims Limitation Act, which limited the time period during which land claims could be filed against the U.S. government.

The issue of Indian sovereignty and the related issue of gambling on Indian lands created considerable controversy among Indians and non-Indians in the early 1990's. The 1988 Indian Gaming Regulatory Act legalized certain types of gambling on reservations, and the vast amounts of income that could be generated appealed to many tribes struggling with widespread poverty. Gambling engendered protests by some non-Indians, however, and created tribal divisions that occasionally turned violent; in 1990, violence between gambling and antigambling contingents on the St. Regis Mohawk reservation caused state and federal authorities to intervene. An important court decision involving another aspect of sovereignty was handed down in 1990: The U.S. Supreme Court decided in *Duro v. Reina* that tribes do not have criminal jurisdiction over non-Indians living on reservation lands.

In 1992, a number of American Indian groups protested the celebrations planned for the five-hundredth anniversary of Christopher Columbus' arrival in the Americas. Two events in 1994 symbolized both an increasing respect for, and the continuing problems of, American Indians. The first facility of the National Museum of the American Indian, a new part of the Smithsonian Institution, opened in New York (funding had been approved by Congress in 1989). On the other hand, the National Congress of American Indians and the National Black Caucus announced an alliance, stating that American Indians and African Americans continued to face similar forces of political and economic oppression.

—*Byron D. Cannon*

See also Activism; Alaska Native Claims Settlement Act; Alcatraz Island occupation; American Indian Civil Rights Act; American Indian Religious Freedom Act; Declaration of First Nations; Gambling; Indian Reorganization Act; Indian-white relations—Canadian; Meriam Report; Oklahoma Indian Welfare Act; Relocation; Termination policy; Wounded Knee occupation.

BIBLIOGRAPHY

Falkowski, James E. *Indian Law/Race Law: A Five-Hundred-Year History*. New York: Praeger, 1922. Places the subject of U.S. government policy toward Indians in a wider context both of historical and contemporary international legal models.

Fixico, Donald L. *Termination and Relocation: Federal Policy, 1945-1966*. Albuquerque: University of New Mexico Press, 1986. This is a study of the phase of BIA policy that existed from 1953 to 1960, involving presumed "self-help," including working away from home reservations.

Peroff, Nicholas C. *Menominee Drums*. Norman: University of Oklahoma Press, 1982. A case study of one of the most important examples of tribal termination actions.

Prucha, Francis Paul, ed. *Documents of United States Indian Policy*. Lincoln: University of Nebraska Press, 1975. General policy and issues for specific tribes.

Ingalik: Tribe

CULTURE AREA: Subarctic
LANGUAGE GROUP: Athapaskan
PRIMARY LOCATION: Yukon and lower Innoko rivers, Alaska
POPULATION SIZE: 600-650 (estimate)

The Ingalik were divided into two groups, the Yukon and Kuskokwim; both intermarried with contiguous Eskimo. Their dependence upon fish was reflected in rank, technology, and wealth. The Ingalik had permanent winter villages of semi-subterranean houses, and temporary spring and summer camps for exploiting a diversified food source by fishing, hunting, trapping, and limited gathering. The potlatch was one of seven major ceremonies; rituals involving redistribution of food, change of status, and promoting of group integration.

Russian fur traders and explorers established first European American contact with the Ingalik in 1832, introducing the Russian Orthodox faith and—unfortunately—epidemics of smallpox. Some village populations were reduced by half. The Episcopalians, in 1887, and the Roman Catholics, in 1888, established churches and boarding schools. By 1900, the traditional Ingalik culture had met its demise through intermarriage with non-Ingalik peoples.

Today, little of the traditional culture remains except for some baskets of hide and birchbark and some woodworking. Employment is mostly with local resources, particularly as fishing and hunting guides. Some regional government work is available, and seasonal work is provided by utility companies. In the early 1990's, the Ingalik population was estimated to be between 600 and 650.

See also Athapaskan language family.

Inkpaduta (c. 1815, S.Dak.—c. 1878): Headman

TRIBAL AFFILIATION: Wahpekute Sioux
SIGNIFICANCE: Inkpaduta was the Sioux leader of a bloody outbreak in Iowa in 1856-1857, during a time of increasing settlement by whites

Inkpaduta (Sioux for "scarlet point") was among the Wahpekute Santee Sioux cast out about 1828 after his father, Wamdesapa, killed principal chief Tasagi. Inkpaduta became the leader of the renegades in 1848, after his father's death. In 1849, he led a raid on the Wahpekutes' principal village, killing their leader Wamundeyakapi and seventeen others.

After his brother was murdered by a white liquor dealer, Inkpaduta turned his rage on settlers; during the Spirit Lake (Iowa) Uprising of 1856 and 1857, warriors under Inkpaduta's leadership killed forty-seven colonists and kidnapped four women, only one of whom was later released. Inkpaduta also engaged in skirmishes with other Indians, notably with the Mdewakanton Sioux Little Crow, who killed three of his warriors in a battle at Lake Thompson.

Inkpaduta may have played a minor role in the Sioux Uprising of 1862-1863 in Minnesota, after which reports indicate that he and a few supporters moved westward. Inkpaduta was reported to have allied with the Sioux and Cheyenne at the Battle of the Little Bighorn, after which he fled to Canada with Sitting Bull's people. Various accounts place his death between 1878 and 1882.

See also Sioux.

Institute of American Indian Arts (IAIA)

DATE: Established 1962
TRIBES AFFECTED: Pantribal
SIGNIFICANCE: The training site of most of the leading contemporary Indian artists of the United States

In 1961 Hildegard Thompson, director of Indian education within the Bureau of Indian Affairs, was authorized to start a school for Indian artists. She picked the old Santa Fe Indian School (Santa Fe, New Mexico) as its site. Superintendent George Boyce decided on a co-educational, boarding, college preparatory, and vocational training curriculum. He appointed Lloyd Kiva New as the director of the arts department. Boyce directed the program from 1961 until 1967, stressing that the purpose of the school was to develop the whole individual. Its goal, in fact, was to assimilate the Indian artist into mainstream American culture.

The doors of the IAIA opened on October 1, 1962, to students who were at least one-quarter Indian, aged fifteen to twenty-two years. Offered were grades ten through twelve and two years of postsecondary training. The art areas offered were creative writing, metals, textiles, ceramics, sculpture, painting, and music and performance. Boyce was succeeded as director of the IAIA by Howard Mackey, and he in turn by Lloyd Kiva New, from 1967 to 1978. New redesigned the school into an art school, adding merchandizing courses as well as filmmaking in the early 1970's and a museum training program in 1971. Students were coached in etiquette, required to pass an apartment living course, and visited white homes to speed acculturation.

The 1970's were a troublesome decade for the IAIA. Fiscal problems resulted in program cutbacks, causing a drop in student enrollment which brought more budget cuts. New failed in an attempt to convert the school to a four-year college. In 1975 a charter was granted for operation of the IAIA as a two-year junior college offering the associate of fine arts degree. The secondary education program waned, recovered, and waned. The artistic vitality slipped noticeably. The decade ended with the award of the campus to the All Pueblo Indian Council for a high school, forcing the IAIA to lease facilities from the College of Santa Fe in 1981, where many IAIA graduates completed their college educations. In 1986 the institute was redefined by the federal government as a chartered institution, allowing it to engage in fund-raising as a not-for-profit entity, hire faculty without civil service restrictions, and appoint a national governing board. In 1992 the school opened a museum with gift shop in downtown Santa Fe.

The institute has been credited with revitalizing modern Indian painting. On the staff have been such well-known artists as Allan Houser, Fritz Scholder, Linda Lomahaftewa, Otellie Loloma, and Louis Ballard. Nearly three thousand students have passed through the IAIA, most of them men. Some of them were troubled teenagers for whom art proved no therapy; others, however, have been gifted scholars and artists. For those who sought to become artists, the IAIA experience has been described as "a gift of time."

See also Art and artists, contemporary; Indian Arts and Crafts Board (IACB); Scholder, Fritz.

International Indian Treaty Council (IITC)

DATE: Established 1974
TRIBES AFFECTED: Pantribal
SIGNIFICANCE: Promoted international rights of indigenous peoples; established indigenous presence at the United Nations

The International Indian Treaty Council was founded during a conference convened on the Standing Rock Reservation (North Dakota) during July, 1974. Its initial mandate, conveyed by the Lakota elders, was to "take the 1868 Fort Laramie Treaty and place it before the community of nations." AIM leader Russell Means, asked to assume responsibility for IITC, accepted by agreeing to serve as "Permanent Trustee." Jimmie Durham, a Cherokee AIM member, became IITC's founding director.

By 1975, Means and Durham had established an office in New York and expanded the mission of the "international diplomatic arm of AIM" to include advocacy of the rights of all indigenous peoples, worldwide. Durham then set about organizing the first major forum on indigenous rights in the history of the United Nations.

This resulted in the "Indian Summer in Geneva," an assembly of delegates from ninety-eight indigenous nations throughout the Western Hemisphere at the Palace of Nations in Geneva, Switzerland, during July, 1977. As the coordinating entity, IITC became the first indigenous Non-Governing Organization (NGO; Type-II, Consultative) ever recognized by the United Nations.

The assembly stimulated the U.N. to establish a formal body, the Working Group on Indigenous Populations, under its Economic and Social Council (ECOSOC) for purposes of receiving annual reports on the grievances of the world's native peoples. The Working Group's broader charge was to make the studies necessary to prepare a Draft Declaration on the Rights of Indigenous Peoples by 1992 (later extended to

1994) for ratification by the U.N. General Assembly as international law.

With this established, Durham resigned in 1981 to pursue a career as an artist. He was replaced by Russell Means's younger brother, Bill, who proved a far less appropriate director. Almost immediately, the younger Means initiated a policy of aligning IITC with a range of leftist governments, many of them oppressing indigenous peoples within their borders. The result was a steady erosion of native support for IITC.

By 1986, disputes over IITC's support of Nicaragua's Sandinista regime in its drive to subordinate the Miskito, Sumu, and Rama peoples of the country's Atlantic coast led to a purge. "Indigenists," such as Harvard-trained Shawnee attorney Glenn Morris, were summarily expelled from IITC. The Lakota elders' original mandate was negated, Russell Means displaced from his permanent trusteeship, and IITC structurally separated from AIM by its incorporation under U.S. law.

Thereafter, although Bill Means continued to speak of "representing more than a hundred indigenous nations," IITC's isolation and decline accelerated. By the early 1990's, it was increasingly encumbered by the fund-raising requirements of supporting its staff. Fortunately, many of the peoples whose rights it had once championed had by then learned to represent themselves internationally.

See also Activism; American Indian Movement (AIM); Means, Russell; Pan-Indianism; Sovereignty.

BIBLIOGRAPHY

Deloria, Vine, Jr. *Behind the Trail of Broken Treaties: An Indian Declaration of Independence*. 2d ed. Norman: University of Oklahoma Press, 1987.

Morris, Glenn T., and Ward Churchill. "Between a Rock and a Hard Place: Left-Wing Revolution, Right-Wing Reaction, and the Destruction of Indigenous People." *Cultural Survival Quarterly* 11, no. 3 (1987): 17-24.

Weyler, Rex. *Blood of the Land: The U.S. Government and Corporate War Against the First Nations*. 2d ed. Philadelphia: New Society Publishers, 1992.

Inuit: Tribe

CULTURE AREA: Arctic
LANGUAGE GROUP: Eskimo-Aleut
PRIMARY LOCATION: West Alaska, North Alaska, Arctic Canada (including Labrador), Greenland
POPULATION SIZE: 44,392 in Alaska (1990 U.S. Census); estimated 25,000 in Canada; estimated 46,000 in Greenland

The Inuit are one of the two major branches of the Eskimo family, the other being the Yupik of southwestern Alaska, southern Alaska, St. Lawrence Island, and Siberia. Inuit are distinguished from Yupik on the basis of both culture and language. The Inuit are distributed over the northern tier of the North American continent from Alaska to Greenland and have evolved a lifestyle which allows for efficient adaptation to a cold and harsh habitat.

While the term "Inuit" (meaning "people") is an appropriate designation for all the northern Eskimo groups, there are more specific self-designations for different Inuit subgroups: "Iñupiat" in North Alaska, "Inuvialuit" in the western Canadian Arctic, "Inummaariit" in the eastern Canadian Arctic, and "Kalaallit" for Greenland.

Environment. With a few exceptions, most Inuit groups inhabit Arctic tundra north of the treeline. The climate is harsh and characterized by pronounced seasonality in temperature and light conditions. Those areas north of the Arctic Circle experience varying periods of continuous sunlight in midsummer and continuous darkness in midwinter. For example, in the community of Barrow, located at the northernmost tip of Alaska, the sun does not rise above the horizon for two months from November to January, while there is continuous sunlight from May through July. Because of extreme cold, high winds, and perennially frozen soil (permafrost), trees are unable to thrive in the Arctic. Even in summer, very little sunlight hits the Arctic, resulting in a low level of biological productivity for Arctic tundra, lakes, streams, and oceans. Because of this low level of productivity, most Inuit were forced to be at least seasonally nomadic in their subsistence efforts.

Physical Characteristics. Like the Aleut and Yupik, the Inuit display physical characteristics which indicate their relatively recent Eurasian origins. Eskimo-Aleut populations are more closely related genetically to Siberian groups such as the Chukchee and Koryak than to North American Indians living to the south. Many experts believe that the physical and linguistic evidence suggests that these groups represent a separate and more recent migration into the New World.

Archaeology and History. The Inuit are the direct descendants of Thule whale hunters who moved from Alaska into Arctic Canada and Greenland around the end of the first millennium C.E., a time coinciding with the Medieval Warming Period. The Thule are believed to have replaced the earlier Dorset populations, which had lived in these regions since about 3,000 years before the present. The linguistic and cultural uniformity of contemporary Inuit groups is the direct result of this rapid spread of Thule culture. As the Thule population spread throughout Greenland and northern Canada, different groups adapted to slightly different ecological conditions. During the Little Ice Age (1600-1850 C.E.), the climate once again cooled, resulting in changes in subsistence routines throughout most of the Eskimo region. This period led to the development of historic Inuit culture.

Contacts with Europeans probably first occurred sometime after the establishment of the Norse colonies in Greenland around 985 C.E. From the late sixteenth century onward, numerous naval expeditions set out from Europe in search of the Northwest Passage. These resulted in repeated, if fleeting, contacts with Inuit groups throughout the North. The intensification of whaling in the late nineteenth century had a more substantial impact upon Inuit groups throughout the Arctic. Not only did whalers initiate an active trade in southern manufactured goods, but they also introduced infectious diseases that took a substantial toll in lives in some areas. With

A 1928 photograph of an Inuit mother and child. (Library of Congress)

the collapse of whaling at the beginning of the twentieth century, many Inuit took up trapping as a way to support themselves and obtain valued southern commodities offered by independent traders or large trading companies like the Hudson's Bay Company and the Alaska Commercial Company.

Economy and Subsistence. At contact, the Inuit were highly specialized hunters and fishers, utilizing a subsistence routine based upon the seasonal exploitation of both marine and land resources. For many groups, a summer "land " phase involved hunting and fishing in small, scattered family groups on the tundra, while a winter "maritime" phase involved exploitation of various marine mammals (whales, walrus, seals) either along the coast or on the frozen ocean, often in larger social groupings. Regional variation in subsistence routines was contingent upon ice conditions and the availability of game. In North Alaska, for example, walrus and bowhead whale hunting constituted an important part of subsistence efforts, while in certain regions of the Central Arctic, seals were the primary animal resource. In the interior regions of Alaska and Canada, Inuit groups were heavily dependent upon caribou herds.

Religion and Ritual. The religious practices of the Inuit, like those of all Eskimo groups, were largely oriented toward regulating human relationships with the animal spirit world. Shamanism was highly developed, and illness was usually explained with reference to violations of taboos. It was generally believed throughout the region that animals were not caught by hunters but gave themselves up to the individuals who followed the necessary rituals, maintained their equipment properly, and kept a respectful attitude toward the animals they hunted. Helping spirits and amulets were often important for hunting success. In most regions, ceremonies were followed to appease and thank the spirit of a recently caught animal. In the Central Arctic, it was common for a recently caught seal to be given a drink of fresh water. Considerably more elaborate procedures were followed in North Alaskan whaling communities to greet and thank the whale for giving itself up to a community, culminating at the end of whaling season with the Nalukatok (blanket toss) celebration.

Cold Adaptation. The primary method of adapting to the cold throughout the region was cultural. The preparation of tailored fur parkas, mitts, and boots was an essential survival strategy, especially in those areas with extreme subzero winter temperatures. The snowhouse of the Central Arctic Inuit and the semi-subterranean communal house of the West Greenlanders and North Alaskans were efficient in insulating their human inhabitants from the cold. Cold tolerance was also aided by a highly thermogenic diet based on fat and protein. Such diets were effective in raising the basal metabolic rate of the Inuit so they could withstand long periods of cold exposure. Some evidence also suggests that hereditary factors may be involved, since Inuits are reported to have a very efficient warming response (cold-induced vasodilation) in the extremi-ties. Inuits are also documented to have fewer sweat glands on the body, a phenomenon which aids in keeping clothes dry and warm.

Contemporary Social and Political Status. The Inuit of Alaska, Canada, and Greenland now live in centralized villages and towns that are supported by schools, medical facilities, government offices, retail stores, and other social amenities. Many Inuit continue to be highly involved in subsistence hunting and fishing, often sharing harvested food with a large network of kinsmen. Hunting and fishing are now accomplished with the help of rifles, snowmobiles, all-terrain vehicles, and boats with inboard and outboard motors. In many communities, wage employment and social assistance are the primary means of support. Aside from the government sector, resource extraction industries employ many Inuit, often on a rotational basis. The Inuit arts and crafts industry has also been an important source of income for many communities. A number of regional, national, and international Inuit organizations represent the interests of Inuit to various government agencies. The Inuit Circumpolar Conference, for example, was established in 1977 to bring together the Inuit and Yupik of the circumpolar North to address important social, political, economic, and environmental issues. Land claims settlements in Alaska and Canada have resulted in the creation of regional and village corporations which are active in northern investment and business development. Many of these corporations have a cultural resource component that sponsors archaeological and oral history research. In 1979, a Home Rule government was established in Greenland, effectively releasing the Greenlanders from Danish colonialism. Although living standards and health conditions have improved dramatically for most Inuits, social problems such as suicide, alcohol and drug abuse, unemployment, and underemployment remain significant. —*Richard G. Condon and Pamela R. Stern*

See also Alaska Native Brotherhood and Alaska Native Sisterhood; Alaska Native Claims Settlement Act; Aleut; Architecture—Arctic; Arctic; Arts and crafts—Arctic; Bladder Festival; Dorset; Eskimo-Aleut language family; Prehistory—Arctic; Thule; Whales and whaling.

BIBLIOGRAPHY

Balikci, Asen. *The Netsilik Eskimos*. Garden City, N.Y.: Natural History Press, 1970.

Burch, Ernest S., and Werner Forman. *The Eskimos*. Norman: University of Oklahoma Press, 1988.

Chance, Norman A. *The Iñupiat and Arctic Alaska*. Fort Worth, Tex.: Holt, Rinehart and Winston, 1990.

Condon, Richard. *Inuit Youth: Growth and Change in the Canadian Arctic*. New Brunswick, N.J.: Rutgers University Press, 1987.

Damas, David, ed. *Arctic*. In *Handbook of North American Indians*, edited by William Sturtevant. Washington, D.C.: Smithsonian Institution Press, 1984.

Jacobs, Martina, and James Richardson, eds. *Arctic Life: Challenge to Survive*. Pittsburgh: Carnegie Museum of Natural History, 1983.

Iowa: Tribe
CULTURE AREA: Plains
LANGUAGE GROUP: Siouan
PRIMARY LOCATION: Oklahoma, Nebraska/Kansas
POPULATION SIZE: 1,615 (1990 U.S. Census)

Sharing a common origin in the upper Great Lakes region with the linguistically related Winnebago, Oto, and Missouri tribes, the Iowas moved south and west from the Great Lakes at some point, probably in the early seventeenth century. Following the Mississippi River south from what is now Wisconsin, they settled at the confluence of the Iowa and Mississippi rivers, also migrating west at various times over the next centuries. The Iowas occupied parts of northern Missouri and southern Minnesota as well as much of what is now Iowa.

Reflecting their adaptation from a woodland to a plains environment, the Iowa economy was based on both female-oriented cultivation of crops such as corn, beans, and squash, and male-oriented hunting. The latter brought in deer, buffalo, beaver, raccoon, and otter meat. Iowa farming was known to be productive; a Frenchman who was setting up a trading post in their territory around 1700 persuaded them to move their village nearby because they were "industrious and accustomed to cultivate the earth." The Iowas were also known for their crafting and trade of catlinite pipes or calumets.

Their blending of woodland and plains cultures is evident in traditional Iowa choice of housing styles. At various times, they used four different types: oval or square bark houses (similar to eastern longhouses or wigwams), wattle-and-daub houses (southeastern in origin), the earthlodge, and the skin tipi (more common to the plains).

The Iowas had a complex clan system and were patrilineal (one belonged to the father's clan). Strict rules of marrying outside the clan were maintained. Clans were also the basis of political and religious officeholding, as chiefs and religious leaders were elected hereditarily in each clan. The main religious ceremony of the Iowas was the Medicine Dance, similar to those of Algonquian tribes around the Great Lakes. Mourning and burial practices were highly developed, and in the pre-reservation era especially, scaffold burial was practiced.

Although the name "Iowa" came from the French "*Aiaouez*" ("Ioway") and originally indicated "sleepy ones," the name for the Iowa people in their own Chiwere language, which they shared with the Winnebagos, Otos, and Missouris, was "*Pahoja*," meaning "gray snow," "snow-covered," or "dusty ones." The reason for the name is unclear.

The seventeenth and eighteenth centuries brought increased warfare to the Iowa people; their primary enemies were the Dakota Sioux. Early in this period, they also warred with the Sauk and Mesquakie (Fox), but they later made peace and became closely associated with these people. By 1836, the Iowas had ceded all rights to their lands in Iowa and Missouri and settled along with the Sauk and Mesquakie people on a reservation of 400 square miles along the present Kansas-Nebraska state line. The reservation was reduced several times in the 1850's. By the 1870's, the federal government attempted to move the Iowas to Indian Territory (now Oklahoma). A reservation was established for them there and some moved voluntarily, but others insisted on staying on the original reservation. Many of them had successfully blended into the surrounding farm economy. By 1890, both reservations had been allotted (divided into individual family plots), and the "surplus" land had been sold to non-Indians. When given the chance in the 1930's, both the Oklahoma and the Kansas-Nebraska Iowas set up tribal charters and constitutions, maintaining their political identity as a tribe. Culturally, both groups have outwardly blended with the surrounding non-Indian culture, although they are attempting to recover as much of their cultural heritage as possible.

See also Oto; Plains; Siouan language family; Winnebago.

Irateba (c. 1814, near present-day Needles, Calif.—June 17, 1878): Guide, chief
ALSO KNOWN AS: Arateva, Yaratev, Beautiful Bird
TRIBAL AFFILIATION: Mojave
SIGNIFICANCE: During initial white explorations of the Mojave region of California, Irateba was the principal Indian guide

Irateba, hereditary chief of the Huttoh-pah band, welcomed white explorers into California. In 1849-1850 and again in 1856-1858, he aided Lieutenant Joseph Ives's exploration of the Colorado River. Irateba also guided Lieutenant Lorenzo Sitgreaves's expedition to San Diego, 1854, and Lieutenant Amiel Whipple's trek to Los Angeles.

Dismayed by advancing white settlement, in 1858, militant Mojaves ambushed a wagon train and in 1859 attacked the newly constructed Fort Mojave. When the Mojave chiefs surrendered, Irateba played a key role in negotiations. The chiefs were imprisoned at Fort Yuma and held as hostages to ensure the cooperation of their people. When principal chief Cairook died attempting escape, Irateba assumed leadership of the Mojave. Until the discovery of gold in 1862, Irateba's Mojave enjoyed relative peace.

On a federally sponsored trip in 1862-1863, Irateba traveled to several eastern cities, met with President Abraham Lincoln, and returned with accounts of white wealth and might. Considered exaggerations, his stories were discounted, and Irateba lost influence with the militant chief, Hojmoseah Quahote, who advocated violent resistance. Irateba died in 1878, probably from smallpox.

See also Mojave.

Iroquoian language family
CULTURE AREA: Northeast
TRIBES AFFECTED: Cayuga, Cherokee, Huron, Mohawk, Oneida, Onondaga, Seneca, Tuscarora

The Iroquoian Indians probably organized as the Five Nations some time between 1400 and 1600. About 1722, the Tuscarora joined the league, making it the Six Nations. The term "Iroquois" derived from a nickname used by the French, who supposedly heard the Indians end their speeches with the words *hiro*, "I have spoken" and *koué*, "with joy" or "with sorrow."

The two divisions of the Iroquoian languages are the Northern Iroquoian group, consisting of Mohawk, Oneida, Seneca, Cayuga, Onondaga, Huron (Wyandot), Tuscarora, and possibly Laurentian, and the Southern division, containing only Cherokee. Cherokee is quite different from the Northern languages, perhaps as different as are Russian and English. The Cherokee may have split from the main line of Iroquoian languages significantly more than three thousand years ago.

Six Northern Iroquoian languages were still spoken as of the mid-1970's: Mohawk, Oneida, Onondaga, Cayuga, Seneca, and Tuscarora. Cherokee had about ten thousand speakers at that time as well. Tuscarora is the nearest to extinction, but Onondaga and Cayuga have fewer than one thousand speakers each.

Culture Area. The Mohawk inhabited a number of villages extending roughly from Schenectady to Utica, New York. After the American Revolution, when they sided with the British, many resettled in Canada in two major areas, the Grand River Reserve in Ontario and at Caughnawaga, near Montreal. Since then, smaller groups have lived in Brooklyn and in the extreme northern part of New York, while others live off the reserve in Ontario and at Oka in Quebec.

Some Oneida speakers live on Green Bay, in Wisconsin, and a few live in New York. Others moved to Grand River Reserve in Ontario or settled on the Thamas River in Canada. The Cayuga once lived in central New York, near Cayuga Lake. As of 1990, most lived on the Six Nations Indian Reserve near Brantford, Ontario. Others in Ohio eventually resettled in Oklahoma; they speak a dialect somewhat different from that of the Canadian Cayuga.

A 1990 estimate reports that about seven thousand Seneca-speaking Indians live on one of three reservations in western New York; others are in Oklahoma and Ontario. During the seventeenth century, when two of the Seneca's neighboring tribes were defeated, many Seneca relocated in the area of Lake Erie. A small group living in Pennsylvania on the Cornplanter Grant was displaced in the 1970's when the Kinzua Dam project obliterated the land. A majority of the approximately ten thousand Cherokee speakers are near Tahlequah, Oklahoma, although some still occupy the original land near Cherokee, North Carolina.

The Onondaga group originally lived near Syracuse, New York. Following the American Revolution, some of the Onondaga resettled on the Grand River Reserve in Ontario. Although early New World colonists found Tuscarora living in eastern North Carolina, they later migrated to New York and became the sixth nation of the Iroquois League (Confederacy). As of the mid-1970's, most of the Tuscarora lived near Niagara Falls, in Pennsylvania, and in North Carolina.

Huron (Wyandot) had a few speakers in northeastern Oklahoma until the mid-1970's. This tribe had originally lived in Ontario until they were defeated by the Iroquois; at that time they scattered in various directions.

Writing System. A writing system for the Cherokee language was developed by the Cherokee Indian George Guess, better known as Sequoyah. His unique system was adopted in 1821 and used widely until the early part of the twentieth century. Its indigenous origin as well as the relatively large number of users of the Cherokee language has attracted special interest.

Sequoyah's system had an eighty-six-character syllabary representing every sound in the Cherokee language. Large numbers of Cherokees mastered the system, and within a few years a newspaper was printed in Cherokee, as was a constitution for the Cherokee Nation.

Other Language Research. Laurentian was the first North American language to be recorded by a European. When the explorer Jacques Cartier returned to France with two Indian captives, the "Cartier vocabularies" were elicited. Between the seventeenth and nineteenth centuries, a number of missionaries focused on the language, hoping to be able to preach in it and to translate religious materials.

Jesuit missionaries did intensive work among the Huron. Gabriel Sagard compiled an early dictionary, as did Pierre Potier. Potier's work represents a culmination of the Jesuit work among this group. The first important work in Mohawk was that of Jacques Bruyas in 1863, followed by the work of missionary Jean André Cuoq, who compiled a dictionary. Intensive work has been done more recently by Paul M. Postal.

Possibly the earliest record of the Onondaga language is a dictionary, probably prepared by a Jesuit missionary and published by John G. Shea in 1860. Since then, a number of other scholars, such as David Zeisberger, Albert Gallatin, Henry R. Schoolcraft, Wiliam M. Beauchamp, and Wallace Chafe, have studied various aspects of Onondaga.

Little has been published on Cayuga, but several scholars have studied Seneca, beginning with Asher Wright in the seventeenth century and continuing into the mid-twentieth century with C. F. Voegelin, Nils M. Holmer, and Wallace Chafe.

Cherokee had little systematic study prior to the nineteenth century, when Samuel A. Worcester became to the Cherokee what Asher Wright was to the Seneca. In the twentieth century, William D. Reyburn's work has perhaps been the most significant.

—*Victoria Price*

See also Cayuga; Cherokee; Huron; Iroquois Confederacy; Language families; Mohawk; Northeast; Oneida; Onondaga; Seneca; Sequoyah; Tuscarora.

BIBLIOGRAPHY

Chafe, Wallace L. *Handbook of the Seneca Language*. Albany: University of the State of New York, State Education Dept., 1963.

Katzner, Kenneth. *The Languages of the World*. New York: Funk & Wagnalls, 1975.

Powell, John W. *Indian Linguistic Families of America, North of Mexico*. Washington, D.C.: Bureau of American Ethnology, 1891.

Sebeok, Thomas A., ed. *Native Languages of the Americas*. New York: Plenum Press, 1976.

Wright, Asher. *A Spelling-Book in the Seneca Language.* Buffalo-Creek Reservation: Mission Press, 1842.

Iroquois Confederacy

TRIBES AFFECTED: Cayuga, Mohawk, Onondaga, Oneida, Seneca, Tuscarora

CULTURE AREA: Northeast

LANGUAGE GROUP: Iroquoian

PRIMARY LOCATION: From the Ottawa River, Canada, south to Cumberland, Tennessee; from Maine west to Lake Michigan

POPULATION SIZE: 49,038 in U.S. (1990 U.S. Census); estimated 35,000 in Canada

The word "Iroquois" refers to all the tribes that speak dialects of the Iroquoian language group, including the Saint Lawrence, Mohawk, Cayuga, Onondaga, Oneida, Seneca, Tuscarora, Huron, Erie, Honniasonts or Mingues, and Susquehannock groups. Cherokee is also an Iroquoian language, but it is as different from the northern dialects of Iroquoian as German is from English. The Iroquois Confederacy, or Haudenosaunee (People of the Longhouse), included the Mohawk, Oneida, Onondaga, Cayuga, Seneca, and, after 1722, the Tuscarora. The Longhouse People practiced extensive horticulture (centered on corn, beans, and squash) as well as fishing and hunting. They lived in fortified villages. They were little affected by European contact until after 1760, when the fall of New France in the French and Indian War opened the floodgates to English and American settlers; encroachment on Iroquois land began in earnest.

Three basic understandings were central to Iroquois life. First, all actions of individuals were based on personal decisions, and group action required consensus. Second, everybody shared; generosity and charity were paramount. Third, no one was separate from the web of life. Humankind was not outside nature, and the earth and the woodlands could be neither owned nor exploited.

The Founding of the Confederacy. These central precepts were incorporated into the famous League of the Iroquois, or Iroquois Confederacy. Modern members of the original five tribes of the confederacy, to which was added the Tuscarora band in 1722, still celebrate in ritual and ceremony the founding of the league.

A Huron prophet, the Peacemaker (Deganawida), had a vision of a white pine which reached through the sky to communicate with the Master of Life. An eagle perched atop the white pine was present to keep the peace and watch for intruders. This icon is now at the center of understanding of the Iroquois Confederacy, just as the tree of life is at the center of their cosmology. The tree's roots were the original Five Nations, Seneca (The Great Hill People), Cayuga (People at the Mucky Land), Onondaga (People on the Hills), Oneida (People of the Standing Stone), and Kenienghagas (Keepers of the Flint). "Mohawk," as the Kenienghagas are also known, is an Algonquian term meaning "cannibal." The soil around the tree was three principles: *skenno*, health of body and sanity of mind and peace between individuals and groups; *gaiiwiyo*, righteousness in conduct, thought, and deed, and equity in human rights; and *gashedenza*, faith and knowledge that spiritual power (*orenda*) is connected to governing and the maintenance of self-defense.

The league was probably founded between 1400 and 1600 (some scholars say between 1550 and 1600) in response to constant warfare among the tribes in the Northeast. Its purpose was to unify and pacify the infighting Iroquois and gain strength in numbers to resist the implacable opposition of both the Iroquois-speaking Huron tribe and the Algonquian-speaking people of the area.

The Haudenosaunee created a carefully constructed "constitution" that was transmitted from generation to generation orally from variously colored symbolic cues or mnemonics woven into belts of shells called wampum. (That "wampum" came to be translated as "money" or as valuable in commodity exchanges is an example of the different mindsets of Europeans and American Indians.) Originally, wampum belts passed on ritual, ceremonial, and mythological knowledge as well as political and social instructions.

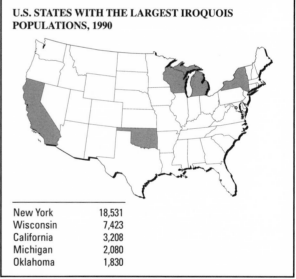

U.S. STATES WITH THE LARGEST IROQUOIS POPULATIONS, 1990

New York	18,531
Wisconsin	7,423
California	3,208
Michigan	2,080
Oklahoma	1,830

Source: 1990 U.S. Census.

Iroquois are known as great orators. Oral communication of the symbols on the wampum belts allowed speakers to become definers. The Great Law of Peace, with its social requirements and legal relationships, can take many hours, even days, to communicate.

At the onset the Onondaga were given the responsibility of keeping the central fire and sacred wampum belts. The Faithkeeper (central religious leader), always an Onondaga, calls a yearly council for the purposes of rehearing the constitution and laws and resolving differences. The council retains

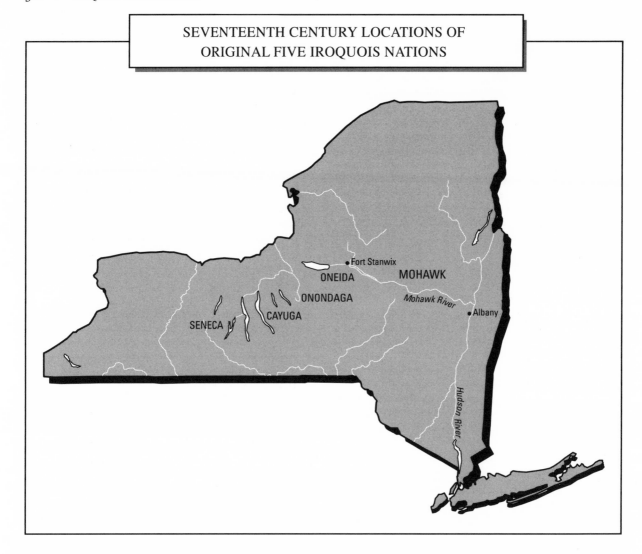

SEVENTEENTH CENTURY LOCATIONS OF ORIGINAL FIVE IROQUOIS NATIONS

tribal relationships. Clan system relationships from ancient times define roles within the council. The traditional clan system was matrilineal; the oldest sensible woman of each clan of each tribe was designated in council with other tribal clan women to select a proportion of the fifty chiefs who made up the council. Chiefs served for life, but the clan mothers could remove chiefs from office for immoral or unethical behavior. Since clan mothers usually selected chiefs from their own lineage, each member of the council was answerable to the women of his maternal family. The power wielded by women had its roots in the early subsistence patterns of the five tribes, since they were dependent on agriculture.

The Confederacy in the Seventeenth Century. The Great Peace was spread by warfare. Warfare was visited on any tribe who did not accept the wampum belts of peace. In one week in March, 1649, as French Jesuit priests attested, the Five Nations essentially wiped out the Huron. Nine months later, the Petun people of western Michigan suffered the same fate. The

Erie tribe, who outnumbered the Iroquois in population, were the next to fall. Those who were not killed were adopted; the Erie tribe ceased to exist. By 1700 the Five Nations, numbering fewer than thirty thousand people, were the political masters of an area from the Ottawa River in Canada south to the Cumberland in Tennessee and from Maine west to Lake Michigan. This hegemony remained in force for another 150 years.

The Five Nations of the Iroquois wrote a crucial chapter in American history. In the year 1609 Samuel de Champlain, a French fur trader and explorer, accompanied a war party of Huron and Algonquin on an expedition to the lake that now bears his name. Met by a war party of Mohawk who had never before encountered a musket, Champlain single-handedly killed three Mohawks with his firearms, scaring the others away in bewilderment and fear. This humiliation made the Mohawk doggedly hate the French from that time on. Within a few years, Five Nation Iroquois were purchasing guns from

Dutch and English traders. The Hudson and Mohawk river valleys were opened to the English; the French were locked out. The subsequent British dominance in the New World was made easier by the political and military power of the Iroquois Confederacy and their hatred of the French. The opening of the frontier moved with the Iroquois and their conquering ways, not with the English or French. The Iroquois stood at a pivotal point and controlled the keys to the interior of the continent.

Following the year 1690, the Iroquois Confederacy developed a level of unity and cooperation that allowed them to capitalize on their pivotal position. They learned to play the various European traders one against the other in ways most beneficial to the Iroquois, and they followed a policy of independent neutrality with diplomatic artistry.

Colonial delegates from the Americas traveled to Albany to learn from the Iroquois. The longhouse sachems urged the colonists to form assemblies and meet to discuss common interests. In 1749 Benjamin Franklin asked, If Iroquois savages could govern themselves with such skill, how much better could the civilized English colonists do? In 1754 the first great intercolonial conference was held at Albany, and Iroquois delegates were in attendance.

Iroquois power in the eighteenth century reached the highest point of any Indian nation in North America. Yet the great orator chiefs who held the respect of all who negotiated with them had no personal wealth to display in the manner of the Europeans. "The chiefs are generally the poorest among them," wrote a Dutch pastor in Albany in 1640, "for instead of their receiving from the common people, they are obliged to give."

Origins, Warfare, and Religious Life. The Iroquois are a prime example of a group whose culture has a well-established pedigree. Archaeological evidence suggests a long period of occupancy in New York State in a cultural continuum of a thousand to fifteen hundred years. A subsistence model culture called Owasco preceded the Iroquois, and its influences are reflected in Iroquois legends and in the design of Iroquois personal clay pipes. The Iroquois carried the highly distinctive Owasco clay pipe designs to another step with more skillful carving and more elaboration in bowl shape. Owasco was preceded by the mound-building cultures of the Hopewell era (Hopewell burial attitudes were reflected in later Huron attitudes toward the dead). By 1400 C.E., proto-Iroquois villages existed, and by 1600 the culture was distinctive to the level that the people referred to themselves as Haudenosaunee.

The Iroquoian speakers of the Eastern Woodlands seemed always to be in a state of war. Before the establishment of the League of Five Nations, war was a ritual, a means of advancing individual or group prestige. Wars were fought primarily for revenge, and such warfare had degenerated into unavoidable ongoing feuds by the time of the emergence of the principles of the Peacemaker (perhaps around 1570). After the establishment of the confederacy, which ended intertribal blood feuds and instead established a spiritual reason for warrior

societies, wars became conquests to expand hunting grounds and dominate neighbors—to "make women of them" if they did not accept participation in the confederacy.

The foundation of the Iroquois confederacy was the fireplace, composed of a mother and her children. Each hearth was a part of a larger *owachira*, a related or extended family traced through the mother. Two or more owachiras made a clan, and eight clans made a tribe.

Religious life was highly organized and included a priesthood of three men and three women who supervised the keeping of the faith. Even though the Iroquois are most noted for their strongly defined and impressive governing organization in which politics dovetailed with complex matrilineal associations, the Five Nations are also well known for their elaborate religious practices. Their cosmology was well defined, and their mythology was more detailed then the origin stories in the Bible. Anthropomorphic deities and complex ceremonies as well as a highly developed theology using impersonal spiritual power have not, even to this day, entirely disappeared. As with all the religious practices indigenous to North America, curing was a central part of the religious life day to day. The Iroquois also had a profound sense of the psychology of the soul and used dreams to communicate with the spirits. The mythological base of the league organization and curing societies formed a stable and traditional charter which has resulted in continuity among the Iroquois to this day despite the overwhelming influx of the Europeans.

The American Revolution to the Present. Iroquois power and strength as a confederacy grew until the American Revolution, when the tribes were divided in their allegiances to the British and the Americans. The westernmost tribes of the league were assaulted, burned out, and chased into Canada by General Sullivan's campaign of 1777. George Washington ordered the invasion of Iroquois land in order to seize land with which to pay both his troops and the Dutch bankers who were financing the revolution at that time. The effects of the American Revolution ended the military power of the Iroquois Confederacy.

The Iroquois, despite conflict and contact with European influences from the earliest times, have retained their social being and many of their cultural practices, including kinship and ceremonial ties. Midwinter ceremonies are still practiced, along with green corn and harvest thanksgiving ceremonies. Condolence songs are still sung when the maple sap flows. The firm base of the People of the Longhouse persists to this day and is still a viable model for the future.

—Glenn J. Schiffman

See also Beaver Wars; Cayuga; Deganawida; French and Indian Wars; Hiawatha; Indian-white relations—English colonial; Indian-white relations—French colonial; Iroquoian language family; Longhouse; Longhouse religion; Midwinter Ceremony; Mohawk, Oneida; Onondaga; Seneca; Tuscarora.

BIBLIOGRAPHY

Henry, Thomas R. *Wilderness Messiah: The Story of Hiawatha and the Iroquois.* New York: Bonanza Books, 1955.

Josephy, Alvin M., Jr., ed. *The American Heritage Book of Indians*. New York: Simon & Schuster, 1961.

_____. *The Indian Heritage of America*. New York: Alfred A. Knopf, 1968.

Spencer, Robert F., Jess D. Jennings, et al. *The Native Americans*. 2d ed. New York: Harper & Row, 1977.

Taylor, Colin F., ed. *The Native Americans: The Indigenous People of North America*. New York: Smithmark, 1991.

Irrigation

TRIBES AFFECTED: Southwestern tribes

SIGNIFICANCE: Irrigation permitted some tribes of the Southwest, particularly in prehistoric times, to practice effective agriculture in arid lands

Irrigation, the bringing of water to agricultural fields, was practiced widely in pre-Columbian Mexico and Peru, but it was used relatively little by prehistoric North American Indians. Most of eastern North America had adequate rainfall for agriculture, and much of western North America was so dry that agriculture was impractical. As a result, irrigation in pre-Columbian North America was restricted to the Southwest. There, the earliest known irrigation was practiced by people of the Hohokam archaeological tradition, beginning around 100 C.E.

The earliest canals were modest in scope, unlined, and without sophisticated water control features. By 700, they had been expanded to a massive network, including one main canal at least 17 miles long; in addition, control features such as trash gates, head gates, and plunge pools had been added to the system. A few centuries later, the canals were lined to reduce loss from seepage. By 1400, however, Hohokam irrigation had diminished to small-scale ditches with far less engineering sophistication than the earlier systems, and this sort of irrigation was continued by the Pima. Other historic tribes using irrigation include the Pueblo peoples and the Colorado River tribes (Mojave and Yuma), who probably adopted their irrigation practices from the Spanish.

See also Agriculture; Technology.

Isatai (c. 1850, northwest Tex.—c. 1900, northwest Tex.): Medicine man

TRIBAL AFFILIATION: Comanche

SIGNIFICANCE: When Isatai was a young warrior, his claims of supernatural power at first brought hope to his discouraged people

A Quahadi Comanche, Isatai was born in Texas about 1850. In 1873, with the Comanche on a reservation, Isatai claimed to have communed with the Great Spirit, who revealed to him how the Comanche could return to their past ways. Isatai reportedly demonstrated his supernatural power by belching a wagonload of cartridges and then swallowing them.

In early 1874, Isatai announced that only a Sun Dance could produce the medicine needed to preserve the buffalo and traditional Comanche life. Although the Sun Dance was not common to the Comanche, they often witnessed it performed by neighboring tribes. In June, the dance was performed. For the only time in their history, the scattered bands of Comanche were united.

Using the medicine that Isatai said would protect them in battle, and joined by Kiowa, Cheyenne, and Arapaho warriors, the Comanche were ready to reclaim their heritage. Led by war chief Quanah Parker and the other war chiefs, on June 24, 1874, the united force attacked Adobe Walls, an old trading post then occupied by white buffalo hunters. Isatai's medicine proved useless against the high-powered buffalo rifles of the hunters. After twelve men had been killed, nine of them Indians, the united force terminated the attack. With his supernatural power discredited, Isatai all but disappeared into historical obscurity.

Quanah Parker and other Comanche leaders never again trusted the power of medicine men. Even the Ghost Dance movement of the late 1880's, which involved many of the Plains tribes, could not restore that confidence.

See also Adobe Walls, Battles of; Comanche; Parker, Quanah.

Ishi (c. 1862, near Deer Creek, Northern Calif.—Mar. 25, 1916, San Francisco, Calif.): Refugee

TRIBAL AFFILIATION: Yahi

SIGNIFICANCE: After all other Yahi people had been annihilated by settlers, Ishi became known throughout America as the "last wild Indian"

In 1911, when the man known as Ishi appeared in the corral of a slaughterhouse near Oroville, in Northern California, the Yahi were all thought to have been annihilated many years before. After resisting the invasion of their territory, the Yahi were hunted down and massacred by settlers in the latter part of the nineteenth century. In the 1890's, Ishi and the few remaining members of his community concealed themselves along Deer Creek and successfully hid any trace of their existence from their European American neighbors. After his last remaining relatives died in 1908, Ishi lived alone until his appearance at the Oroville slaughterhouse.

Ishi immediately became a media sensation and an object of scientific inquiry. To the popular press, he was "the last wild Indian." To anthropologists, Ishi was an important source of scientific knowledge. From Oroville, anthropologists Alfred Kroeber and Thomas Waterman took Ishi to live at the Museum of Anthropology at the University of California, Berkeley. When Ishi, in keeping with Yahi etiquette, would not reveal his name to probing journalists, Kroeber bestowed the name "Ishi"—a Yana term for "man."

In the years before his death from tuberculosis in 1916, Ishi made a home for himself at the museum, patiently educating anthropologists about Yahi life and language, demonstrating skills such as fire-making and stone-tool-making for museum visitors (sometimes as many as several thousand in the course of an afternoon) and working as a janitor.

Although Ishi won the respect and sincere affection of anthropologists such as Kroeber, in many ways he was treated more as a scientific specimen and object of curiosity than as a

Ishi, the last survivor of the Yahi tribe of California, in 1913. (Museum of Natural History)

friend, fellow human being, and refugee of war. Many scholars, therefore, have come to see that Ishi's story holds important lessons about the relationship between science and tribal peoples. Since the 1960's, Ishi has been the subject of a biography by Theodora Kroeber, documentary and feature films, and essays by native studies scholar Gerald Vizenor.

See also California; Yahi.

Isparhecher (1829, Ala.—Dec. 22, 1902, Creek Nation, present-day Okla.): Tribal chief

ALSO KNOWN AS: Spahecha (Whooping While Taking Off Scalp)

TRIBAL AFFILIATION: Creek

SIGNIFICANCE: Leader of the traditionalist faction in the Creek Nation, Isparhecher led an attempt to overthrow the tribal government in 1882

Born in Alabama, Isparhecher (pronounced "Spi-e-che") moved as a child to Indian Territory, losing both parents on the "Trail of Tears." A full-blooded Creek, he grew up steeped in tribal tradition and never learned English. Enlisting in the Confederate Army at the outbreak of the Civil War, he later switched sides and joined the Union forces. After the war, he became active in tribal politics as a follower of the traditionalist Oktarharsars Harjo (Sands). He served in the Creek legislature and was elected a district judge in 1872.

Less acculturated Creeks, many of them full-bloods such as Isparhecher, distrusted the tribal leadership. Not only had it disastrously allied the tribe with the Confederacy, but also traditionalists regarded a centralized tribal government as yet another imported white practice, one inconsistent with the Creek tradition of local autonomy.

Isparhecher became the leader of the conservative opposition in the 1880's. Violence erupted in 1882, when two Creek Light Horsemen (tribal police) arrested a traditionalist leader. Other full-bloods rescued him, killing the two troopers. Soon a rebellion was under way, with Isparhecher leading a rival government. Known as Isparhecher's War, or the Green Peach War, the uprising was eventually put down after Principal Chief Samuel Checote called out the Creek militia. Isparhecher fled to the Cherokee Nation, eventually returning under an amnesty.

Isparhecher continued to be the leader of tribal conservatives and enjoyed some political success. He served as chief justice and was elected principal chief in 1895. He was widely respected by Creeks of all factions for his honesty and dignified personal presence. At the time of his death, he was working to prevent the individual allotment of tribal lands and the opening of the Creek Nation to white settlement.

See also Crazy Snake; Creek; Opothleyaholo; Trail of Tears.

Johnson, Emily Pauline (Mar. 10, 1861, Six Nations Reserve, near Brantford, Ontario, Canada—Mar. 7, 1913, Vancouver, B.C., Canada): Poet, writer

ALSO KNOWN AS: Tekahionwake

TRIBAL AFFILIATION: Mohawk

SIGNIFICANCE: One of Canada's leading poets of the late nineteenth century, Johnson is notable because she celebrated her Mohawk heritage at a time when it was not fashionable; she wrote about the Canadian landscape from a native perspective

Emily Pauline Johnson grew up in a bicultural environment, the youngest of four children of George Henry Martin Johnson, a Mohawk leader of his Six Nations Iroquois community, and Emily Howells, originally from Bristol, England. Her father was an influential leader of the Iroquois community, receiving guests from England and other countries at his home on the Six Nations reserve. Her mother encouraged her to read widely and to become interested in literature. Johnson attended the Brantford Model School and, as a teenager, sent her written verses to periodicals in Canada, the United States, and England. Many of these were published. She also spent much of her time while still living at Six Nations canoeing on the Grand River, which she thoroughly enjoyed and at which she excelled.

In 1892, Johnson began reciting her works in public before an audience of literary highbrows at the Young Men's Liberal Club of Toronto. After success with this event, she became a frequent platform entertainer before both fashionable Toronto audiences and audiences in bars in small-town Ontario. She traveled to England, where she received many invitations to recite her poetry and other written works and became a minor celebrity. This was in part because of her warmth and attractive personality and in part because of her Mohawk ancestry, which she highlighted in her work and in her appearance. She usually wore buckskin clothing, a bear-claw necklace, traditional Iroquois trade silver brooches, and beaded moccasins for her performances. English audiences particularly found this intriguing.

Johnson soon became well known in Canada as well as in England, and high-level politicians and Canadian officials sponsored her work. She found it difficult, however, to be a traveling writer at the turn of the twentieth century because of the vagaries of train and ship travel, and it was particularly difficult for women because of sexism. In fact, Johnson's own sister disapproved of her career and lifestyle, causing a rift between the two. Most family members, however, supported her.

Johnson's first published volume of verse was *The White Wampum*, published in 1895 and followed by *Canadian Born* (1903). She also published prose: *Legends of Vancouver* (1911), *The Moccasin Maker* (1913), and *The Shagganappi* (1913). Her most famous poem, "The Song My Paddle Sings," which generations of Canadian schoolchildren have learned, earned her only three dollars. Her collected poems have been published, with a biographical sketch, under the title *Flint and Feather* (Toronto, no date).

In 1909, Emily Pauline Johnson settled in Vancouver after years of travel had taken their toll on her health. She was tired from her years of touring but had also contracted cancer. Her last years were spent in much physical pain, and she died on March 7, 1913. At her request, her ashes were interred in Vancouver's spectacular Stanley Park. Succeeding generations of British Columbians have revered her with memorials.

Johnson successfully blended two cultures artfully and fearlessly when no one else was doing so. She is also remembered as one of Canada's and Native North America's leading female voices in poetry.

See also Iroquois Confederacy; Mohawk.

Joking relations

TRIBES AFFECTED: Widespread but not pantribal

SIGNIFICANCE: Joking relations refer to the humorous and informal relations between certain relatives in many Indian tribes

A feature of many North American kinship systems is joking relations. Joking relations are almost always paired with, and given definition by, a corresponding set of avoidance relations. In avoidance relations, kin are to act in a reserved, formal fashion with each other; in some cases, kin in avoidance relations are actually to avoid each other physically. In joking relations, by contrast, certain kin engage in free and easy bantering and talk with each other. The kin with whom one may joke are typically a person's grandparents and cross cousins. (A cross cousin is a relative related to a person through that person's father's sister or mother's brother.) Avoidance relations are typically with one's parents, siblings of the opposite sex, and parallel cousins. (Parallel cousins are related through the father's brother or the mother's sister.) North American Indians typically also practiced a strong avoidance relationship between sons- and mothers-in-law; for example, among the Crow, if a man's mother-in-law entered an area, a son-in-law would excuse himself and leave.

Kin with whom a person has avoidance relations are people with whom a person may not have sexual intercourse; if sex between such individuals did occur, it would be judged incest, a crime North American Indians strongly proscribed. To avoid even the appearance of the possibility of incestuous relationships with some relatives, Indians did not joke about or even talk about any topic even remotely related to sex with those kin. Avoidance relations were formal, and behavior around avoidance kin was carefully controlled.

By comparison, joking relations were very informal and often bawdy. With these kin, people were relaxed; mock aggression and sexual allusion were common. Joking kin often tried to outdo one another in the obscenity of references to one another's sexual exploits or attributes. Children were taught from infancy to delight in considering some joking kin in sexual and conjugal terms, and sexual intercourse was permitted between cross cousins. A nonsexual relationship of mutual indulgence existed between grandparents and grandchildren. While a person's interactions with parents were formal, informality, personal warmth, and easygoing bantering marked interactions between grandparents and grandchildren.

In some cultures, such as the Hidatsa, joking relations served an additional function: creating conformity through teasing. A Hidatsa man would tease a joking relative who had achieved few war honors or would tease a member of the Black Mouth secret society, which served as a kind of police force among the Hidatsa, who was thought to be unjust. Once again, the informality of the situation made the circumstances humorous and acceptable, but an important social message was delivered at the same time. Generally, however, joking relations were primarily a source of recreation and entertainment for those involved.

See also Children; Humor; Incest taboo; Kinship and social organization.

Jones, Peter (Jan. 1, 1802, Burlington Heights, Ontario— June 29, 1856, Brantford, Ontario): Missionary

ALSO KNOWN AS: Kahkewaquonaby, Kahkewagwonnaby
TRIBAL AFFILIATION: Ojibwa
SIGNIFICANCE: As missionary, author, and political activist, Jones worked tirelessly on behalf of his people in southern Ontario and New York State

Jones's father, Augustus Jones, was a Welshman and a Canadian government surveyor who married Tuhbenahneeguay, daughter of Wahbanosay, a Missisauga chief. The influential Mohawk Joseph Brant was Augustus Jones's close friend.

Although reared in traditional Indian fashion, Jones was baptized an Episcopalian and given the English name Peter at age sixteen. In 1823, he was converted at a Methodist mission. Serving initially as a church deacon, Jones was later sent on missionary tours. After being ordained in 1830, he lived the remainder of his life working tirelessly as an itinerant minister. As a missionary and also as a political lobbyist, Jones traveled extensively throughout Ontario and New York State.

He also wrote numerous religious tracts and hymnbooks and translated Ojibwa texts into English. Two of his most important works are *The Life and Journals of Kah-ke-wa-quona-by* (1860) and *A History of the Ojebway Indians* (1861), which remains a source for information on Ojibwa customs.

One of Peter Jones's sons by his English wife—his son was also known as Peter Jones—continued his father's missionary work after the elder Peter Jones died.

See also Brant, Joseph; Copway, George; Missions and missionaries; Ojibwa.

Joseph the Younger (c. 1832, Wallowa Valley, Wash.— Sept. 21, 1904): Chief

ALSO KNOWN AS: Hinmaton Yalatkit (Thunder in the Mountains)
TRIBAL AFFILIATION: Nez Perce
SIGNIFICANCE: Chief Joseph the Younger led the Nez Perce in war and a brilliant tactical retreat before surrendering and vowing to "fight no more forever"

Chief Joseph the Younger, son of Chief Joseph the Elder of the Nez Perce tribe of the American Northwest, was a generally peaceful man who ironically became known as one of the great nineteenth century Indian military leaders. Chief Joseph was a tall man, heavyset and dignified, and he was by all accounts a fine orator. In the course of his long life he had four wives and nine children (five girls and four boys), although all but two of the girls died in infancy. Sarah Moses, one of his daughters, lived to maturity and married.

The Nez Perce lived in parts of what is now Washington, Oregon, and Idaho and practiced salmon fishing and hunting. After obtaining horses in the 1700's, they became skilled horsemen and often hunted buffalo outside their normal range. They did not make pottery but were expert weavers of baskets that could be used for every purpose, including cooking.

The Nez Perce had always enjoyed the best of relations with whites since the Lewis and Clark expedition crossed their territory and encountered them in friendship. It was said that the Nez Perce could boast that they had never killed a white man. This would change during the chieftainship of Joseph the Younger, though he always regarded himself as a friend to the whites and to their government. In 1846, a treaty between Britain and the United States divided the Oregon Territory over which both nations had exercised a condominium, and the Nez Perce territory was placed entirely within the borders of the United States.

In the Walla Walla Council of 1855, many tribal leaders in the Pacific Northwest, including the Nez Perce, agreed to cede much land to the whites in exchange for the guarantee of their remaining land as well as schools, money, livestock, and tools. The whites broke their agreement, however, and in the so-called Yakima War of 1856, many tribes rose up in the Northwest, including some of the Nez Perce. In 1863, agents of the government convinced many of the bands of the Nez Perce to endorse the new Treaty of Fort Lapwai. Old Joseph was reliably reported to have refused to sign either the 1855 or 1863 treaty.

In 1871, the chieftainship passed to Joseph the Younger upon the death of his father, putting Joseph in a key position as land negotiations with Washington were intensifying.

The Wallowa Valley, an area especially beloved of the Nez Perce, had been included in the public domain of the United States. As such, it was liable to sale, to mining and timbering, and to homesteading under the decade-old Homestead Act. In 1873, the Nez Perce, with Joseph as their chief diplomat, succeeded in convincing President Ulysses S. Grant to remove the Wallowa Valley from the public domain by executive order. Governor L. F. Grover of Oregon lobbied the federal authorities to alter their position on this matter, claiming in a letter that the Nez Perce never had enjoyed an ownership interest in the valley and that, in addition, several corporations had begun improving the site.

In 1877, the crisis came, for the valley had been reassigned to the public domain, and public officials ordered the Nez Perce to the reservation at Lapwai in Idaho Territory. Facing a

Joseph the Younger was chief of the Nez Perce during the turbulent 1870's and attempted to lead the tribe to Canada to avoid confinement on a reservation. (National Archives)

thirty-day deadline for the move, the Indians resisted, and violence broke out when a group of whites who were harassing the Indians were killed by White Bird and some young warriors.

Chief Joseph now joined the rebellion. All the resisting Indians fled to White Bird Canyon to avoid the forced relocation planned by the government. Some atrocities had been perpetrated by White Bird's band, but with Chief Joseph in charge, the code of warfare was strictly observed. In the Battle of White Bird Creek, which followed, a group of Nez Perce under a flag of truce were fired upon by whites, but in the ensuing fight, thirty-four troopers were killed without a single Indian casualty.

In the subsequent Nez Perce War, the tribe was pursued by three armies over a distance of 1,700 miles through Idaho, Wyoming, and Montana, ending 30 miles from their goal of sanctuary in Canada. In the course of this incredible flight, the Nez Perce crossed mountains, including the Bitterroot, Absaroka, and Bear Paw ranges of the Rocky Mountains, and forded rivers, including the Bitterroot, Yellowstone, Musselshell, and Missouri.

During the flight, the Nez Perce were compelled to fight many battles, including Clearwater Creek (Idaho), Big Hole Valley (Montana), Camas Creek (Idaho), Canyon Creek (Montana), Cow Island (Montana), and Bear Paw (Montana). Despite the numerous battles, however, the Nez Perce strategy relied primarily upon outflanking the U.S. forces.

After six days of fighting at Snake Creek in the Bear Paw Mountains, the Nez Perce surrendered. Many, including Chief Joseph, were transported to reservations in Kansas, then to Indian Territory, and finally to the Colville Reservation (Washington). The conclusion of Chief Joseph's surrender speech is probably the best-known statement by a Native American: "From where the sun now stands, I shall fight no more forever."

The brilliant campaign of the Nez Perce flight helped enormously to build the legend of Chief Joseph, whom some historians and journalists have called the Indian Napoleon and whose exploits some have compared to Xenophon's march of the ten thousand recorded in the *Anabasis*.

Analysis has proved difficult in regard to Joseph's role in military planning because the Nez Perce tended to develop strategy in council together. Other chiefs, such as Joseph's younger brother Ollikut, White Bird, Looking Glass, Red Echo, Rainbow, Five Wounds, and Toohoolhoolzote, as well as Lean Elk (called Poker Joe by the whites), also played important roles.

Despite Joseph's friendliness toward whites, he never abandoned his Indian culture and never converted to Christianity. To his native beliefs he combined the preaching of the prophet Shanoquala (The Dreamer), whose millenialistic doctrines saw divine revelation coming primarily in dreams.

General Oliver Howard, Joseph's chief military opponent, called him the most remarkable Indian who ever lived. Chief Joseph's wisdom, courage, justice, and lack of rancor make him a noble and tragic figure from the last days of the white-Indian wars. —*Patrick M. O'Neil*

See also Looking Glass; Nez Perce; Nez Perce War; Walla Walla Council; White Bird; Yakima War.

BIBLIOGRAPHY

Axelrod, Alan. *Chronicle of the Indian Wars: From Colonial Times to Wounded Knee*. New York: Prentice Hall, 1993.

Beal, Merrill D. *"I Will Fight No More Forever": Chief Joseph and the Nez Perce War*. Seattle: University of Washington Press, 1963.

Gay, E. Jane. *With the Nez Perces: Alice Fletcher in the Field, 1889-92*. Edited by Frederick E. Hoxie and Joan T. Mark. Lincoln: University of Nebraska Press, 1981.

Howard, Helen Addison. *Saga of Chief Joseph*. Caldwell, Idaho: Caxton Printers, 1965.

Josephy, Alvin M., Jr. *The Nez Perce Indians and the Opening of the Northwest*. New Haven, Conn.: Yale University Press, 1965.

Lavender, David S. *Let Me Be Free: The Nez Perce Tragedy*. New York: HarperCollins, 1992.

Journalism

TRIBES AFFECTED: Pantribal
SIGNIFICANCE: American Indian journalism has existed since 1828 and has been faced with such issues as funding and journalistic freedom versus tribal control

After Sequoyah, a mixed-blood Cherokee with no formal education, became the only person in human history known to have created a written language single-handedly, Cherokee leaders founded the first Native American newspaper, the *Cherokee Phoenix*, in 1828 at New Echota, Georgia. Cherokee leaders started the paper to resist Georgia's attempts to take civil rights and land away from the Five Civilized Nations of the American Southeast.

Cherokee Phoenix. Elias Boudinot, a college-educated Cherokee schoolteacher, served as the first *Cherokee Phoenix* editor. Boudinot and others struggled for Cherokee rights, for a separate Cherokee state, and against forced removal to the West. Like the white press (protected by the First Amendment), the Indian press was to be free from prior restraint (censorship prior to the publication of a news story). In 1829, however, the Georgia legislature stripped all Indians of all their legal rights. Subsequently, the *Cherokee Phoenix* reported harassment, arrest, and threats to staff members. Because the newspaper also protested the postmaster's sale of liquor to Indians, the postmaster retaliated by cutting off its mail.

Threats to Boudinot's freedom came from another direction as well. The tribal governing council, which subsidized the newspaper, became deeply divided on the issue of removal, especially after President Andrew Jackson refused to enforce a U.S. Supreme Court decision supporting the Cherokees. Some Cherokee supporters came to see removal as self-preservation. Yet Principal Chief John Ross told Boudinot not to publish dissension within the Cherokee National Council; he told the editor to report a united front of Cherokee resistance against white encroachment. In a published letter of resignation in 1832, Boudinot said he could not manage the paper without a free discussion of such important issues. Ross appointed his brother-in-law Elijah Hicks editor, but Hicks lacked the rhetorical power exhibited by his predecessor. Meanwhile, pressure from the outside continued. Publication became erratic, and Hicks suspended publication in 1834.

Although Boudinot had campaigned against removal, he gave up the fight and signed the Treaty of Echota in 1835, agreeing to removal. Three years later, the U.S. Cavalry forced Cherokee people from their Georgia homes and forced them to walk to Indian Territory (now Oklahoma). Cherokees, who had agreed to removal as self-preservation, saw four thousand men, women, and children die along this winter "Trail of Tears." For his involvement with the treaty faction, Boudinot was killed by Ross supporters in 1839. (Ross himself was not involved.) Although the Cherokee Nation was delayed in starting another paper, the Reverend Samuel Worster, who had been jailed in Georgia for helping Cherokees, moved to Indian Territory and began the *Cherokee Almanac*, published more or less annually beginning in 1835.

Other Nineteenth Century Newspapers. The second Native American newspaper, the *Shawnee Sun* (*Siwinowe Kesibi*), began in 1835 under the editorship of Johnston Lykins, with assistance from a missionary who had taken the first printing press to Kansas for the Baptist mission. The Shawnee mission newspaper used the Shawnee language in the English alphabet. The monthly newspaper was suspended in 1839 but revived from 1841 to 1844. It was apparently the first newspaper published entirely in a native language. It was put out of business, at least temporarily, by the removal of the Shawnee south to Indian Territory.

The *Cherokee Advocate*, like the *Cherokee Phoenix* before it, was established with missionary help as the official newspaper of the Cherokee Nation. Founded in 1844 in the new Cherokee capital of Tahlequah, the *Cherokee Advocate*'s editors were selected by the National Council. The first editor was William Potter Ross, nephew of Principal Chief Ross. Like the *Cherokee Phoenix*, the *Cherokee Advocate* worked to assimilate Cherokees, to provide news, and to defend Indian rights. Except for a suspension during the Civil War, the paper continued as an official mouthpiece of whatever party was in power. The paper ended with tribal government in 1906.

Nontribal newspapers occasionally started near reservations to oppose the parties in power. These Indian-owned publications often operated as for-profit businesses, and commercial imperatives required non-Indian support. Like other newspaper rivalries in the West, arguments between native editors often became personal. During the 1887 tribal campaign Elias Cornelius Boudinot, Jr., engaged in a virulent exchange with opposition editors, especially B. H. Stone of *The Telephone*. In October, Boudinot went to Stone's office, confronted him, and fatally shot him.

Churches and government-sponsored Indian schools have run newspapers over the years. Some have been in native languages, others in English. Still others, such as the *Cherokee Phoenix*, contained articles in both languages. Many of these papers began as part of assimilation programs.

Contemporary Journalism. Most Native American newspapers and radio stations continue to struggle with the issue of tribal support. One of the largest and most successful Native American newspapers, the *Navajo Times*, began in 1959 as a newsletter for a tribal council education committee; it continues as a tribal newspaper.

Intertribal and regional newspapers and press associations have existed since the nineteenth century, but many were short-lived. Indian editors in Oklahoma formed a short-lived press association in the late 1880's. Nearly a century later, the American Indian Press Association lasted from 1970 to 1975. The Native American Press Association began in 1984 and became the Native American Journalists Association in 1989. In 1994, the group claimed four hundred members, about one-fourth from broadcasting. In the early 1990's, Native American writers in Washington, D.C., formed the National Indian Media Association to build a sense of community among native writers in the nation's capital. The group had about forty-five members from native and mainstream media and federal agencies; it also included filmmakers.

Native media have often depended upon federal grants and corporate underwriting, the kind of support received by "National Native News," a daily news and feature program produced with the help of Alaska Public Radio. The program began in 1987 and had reached all twenty-five tribally owned radio stations and 170 other U.S. stations by 1994.

A major urban nontribal newspaper has been *The Circle*, a monthly begun at the American Indian Center in Minneapolis in 1979. Many other regional publications also cover intertribal issues.

National Publications. A few Native American newspapers have sought national audiences. *Akwesasne Notes*, for example, began in 1969 as an official 48-page publication of the Mohawk nation five times a year. Its circulation peaked at more than eighty-one thousand in the 1970's, when it was emphasizing treaty rights. Publication was suspended in 1992 but was revived with a twenty-fifth anniversary issue in 1994.

Computers and color have played major roles in the two major national commercial Native American newspapers, *News from Indian Country*, published near Hayward, Wisconsin, and *Indian Country Today*, published at Rapid City, South Dakota. The Rapid City weekly began its life on the Pine Ridge Reservation as *Lakota Times*, first published in 1981 by Tim Giago. A boost in outside support and the name change reflected the push for a national audience in the early 1990's. *News from Indian Country*, a biweekly begun in 1987, originated on the Lac Courte Oreilles reservation. Managing editor Paul DeMain saw the publication as part of the national networking necessary for native peoples.

Most native journalists continue to work for low pay and high ideals against a system that forces them to keep a wary eye on their financial support. Links to the past were honored when a plaque honoring Elias Boudinot was placed at the restoration of New Echota in 1994.   —*William E. Huntzicker*

See also Activism; Boudinot, Elias; Sequoyah; Syllabaries.

BIBLIOGRAPHY

Giago, Tim, ed. *The American Indian and the Media*. Minneapolis: National Conference of Christians and Jews, 1991.

Journalism History 6, no. 2 (Summer, 1979). Special issue on Native American journalism.

Littlefield, Daniel F., Jr. *Alex Posey: Creek Poet, Journalist, and Humorist*. Lincoln: University of Nebraska Press, 1992.

Littlefield, Daniel F., Jr., and James W. Parins. *American Indian and Alaska Native Newspapers and Periodicals, 1826-1924*. Westport, Conn.: Greenwood Press, 1986.

_____. *American Indian and Alaska Native Newspapers and Periodicals, 1925-1970*. Westport, Conn.: Greenwood Press, 1986.

_____. *American Indian and Alaska Native Newspapers and Periodicals, 1971-1985*. Westport, Conn.: Greenwood Press, 1986.

_____. *A Biobibliography of Native American Writers, 1772-1924*. Metuchen, N.J.: Scarecrow Press, 1981.

Littlefield, Mary Wood. "Cherokee Publishing in Arkansas, 1859-1880." *Native Press Research Journal* 3 (Fall, 1986): 11-20.

McMurtrie, Douglas C. "The *Shawnee Sun*: The First Indian-Language Periodical Published in the United States." *Kansas Historical Quarterly* 2 (November, 1933): 339-342.

Murphy, James E., and Sharon M. Murphy. *Let My People Know: American Indian Journalism*. Norman: University of Oklahoma Press, 1981.

Parins, James W. *John Rollin Ridge: His Life and Work*. Lincoln: University of Nebraska Press, 1991.

Perdue, Theda, ed. *Cherokee Editor: The Writings of Elias Boudinot*. Knoxville: University of Tennessee Press, 1983.

Posey, Alexander. *The Fus Fixico Letters*. Edited by Daniel F. Littlefield, Jr., and Carol A. Petty Hunter. Lincoln: University of Nebraska Press, 1993.

Riley, Sam G. "The *Cherokee Phoenix*: The Short, Unhappy Life of the First American Indian Newspaper." *Journalism Quarterly* 59 (1982): 46-51, 183.

Schramm, Erika. "Pressing the Issues: Native American Journalism Associations." *Wisconsin Journalism Review* (Spring, 1993): 54-57.

Journeycake, Charles (Dec. 16, 1817, Ohio—Jan. 3, 1894, Indian Territory): Chief and preacher

ALSO KNOWN AS: Neshapanasumin

TRIBAL AFFILIATION: Lenni Lenape

SIGNIFICANCE: Journeycake fought for the rights of his people during a number of relocations

Charles Journeycake was one of the founders of Bacone College, an Indian school in Oklahoma. Born in the Upper Sandusky region of Ohio to the Lenni Lenape (Delaware) chief Solomon Journeycake and a French-Indian mother, Charles Journeycake was baptized in 1833 at the age of sixteen. He learned English as a young man and moved with ease between the white and Indian worlds. He served simultaneously as a preacher and as head of the Wolf Clan. He strenuously opposed liquor sales to Indians.

Journeycake led his people during a number of relocations—first to Kansas, then to land formerly allocated to the Cherokees in northeastern Oklahoma. He was also a principal figure in the Indian Defense Association.

See also Lenni Lenape.

Juaneño: Tribe

CULTURE AREA: California

LANGUAGE GROUP: Takic

PRIMARY LOCATION: San Juan and San Mateo river drainages, California

POPULATION SIZE: 1,565 (1990 U.S. Census)

The Juaneño were river-oriented bands or tribelets living in sedentary, self-sufficient, autonomous villages of conical subterranean houses thatched with bark or tules. They exercised control over territorial rights and resources, living northwest of the Luiseño. Their subsistence was based on hunting, trapping, gathering, collecting, and fishing, with acorns and seeds constituting more than half of their food.

The first European contact with the Juaneño was by the Gaspar de Portolá expedition in 1769. In 1776, the San Juan Capistrano Mission was established among the Juaneño. In 1834, the missions were secularized, causing revolts against Mexican rancheros by Indians who were treated like serfs. Indian groups became dispersed and, despite continuing strife, many individuals became wage-earners. When Anglo-Americans entered California, even more Indians lost control of their land. Reservations at La Jolla, Pala, Potrero, and Yapiche were established in 1875.

By the 1960's, many Juaneño had been graduated from college and begun to work as professionals and in skilled labor. Numerous religions are currently practiced, and only a few elders speak the tribe's language or follow traditional beliefs.

See also Luiseño.

Kachinas

TRIBES AFFECTED: Pueblo tribes

SIGNIFICANCE: The kachina cult, concerned with the growth of crops and the fertility of all life, is found among all the Puebloans in the Southwest

The term "kachina" has three distinct meanings: a spirit being, a dancer wearing a mask who impersonates one of the spirits in ceremonial dances, and a wooden figurine or doll made to resemble one of the spirits. These kachina dolls, the best examples of woodcarving found among the Puebloans, are made primarily by the Hopi and to a lesser extent by the Zuni, although belief in the kachina spirits is common to all the groups.

Kachinas are spirits of the dead who act as intermediaries between humankind and the gods and who bring the clouds and the rain. Some Puebloans, the Hopi among them, believe that the kachinas live on mountaintops, while others, such as the Zuni, believe that they live under the lakes. The Hopi kachinas leave their mountain home to live in the villages for six months each year, arriving in late February for an initiation ceremony called the Powamu and returning after the Niman Ceremony, or Home Dance, in July. While they are in the villages, the kachinas are represented in various dances and ceremonies by men wearing masks. There are two major categories of masks: those representing the greater, or most sacred, spirits, which are simple and unchanging, and those representing the lesser spirits, which have more spectacular, and changeable, features such as ears, noses, or beaks.

Masked figures very similar to modern kachina masks have been found in ancient kiva murals at Hopi and in the Rio Grande Valley, as well as in pictographs located throughout the Southwest. Additionally, a small wooden effigy with the face painted to resemble a mask, found at the prehistoric site of Double Butte Cave in Arizona, bears a similarity to Hopi "cradle dolls," the simple flat kachina dolls tied to a baby's cradle. All these suggest a prehistoric origin for the kachina cult.

It is not certain when the Puebloans began to carve modern versions of kachina dolls, although there are no examples

Hopi kachina makers around 1935; kachinas are often carved from cottonwood root. (Museum of New Mexico)

dating earlier than about 1850, nor are there any references to them in the literature of the period. Kachina dolls are carved from cottonwood root and painted by the men of the pueblo to be given to their daughters or nieces in order to teach them the mask, costume, and body markings of each kachina spirit. Therefore, the doll must be accurate and detailed, especially the mask features. The dolls, although referring to religious spirits, are not religious objects themselves and are not worshiped as idols.

The commercialization of the kachina doll began sometime in the 1880's, when the traders who came into the Southwest began to sell the dolls to collectors. This resulted in a greater naturalism in the modeling of the figures as well as the addition of pieces of cloth, fur, and feathers to replace features earlier represented by carving and painting. "Action dolls"—those carved in more active positions—have also been developed to appeal to the collector.

See also Arts and crafts—Southwest; Masks; Pueblo tribes, Eastern; Pueblo tribes, Western; Religion; Sculpture.

Kalapuya: Tribe

CULTURE AREA: Northwest Coast
LANGUAGE GROUP: Kalapuyan
PRIMARY LOCATION: Willamette River, Oregon
POPULATION SIZE: 50 (1990 U.S. Census)

The patrilineal, socially stratified Kalapuya (or Calapooya) people comprised approximately thirteen autonomous tribes, each with dialectic differences. Subsistence was mainly from camas and other seeds, nuts, roots, and tubers, supplemented by hunting and trapping. The Kalapuya occupied multifamily dwellings in permanent villages during the winter, and temporary shelters in spring, summer, and fall. Chieftainship was probably passed on from father to son.

First contact with European Americans occurred in 1812 with Donald McKenzie of the Pacific Fur Company and continued until the 1840's with fur traders, missionaries, and settlers, who introduced various debilitating diseases, including malaria. In 1855 treaties embracing all the Kalapuya were enacted; most of the Kalapuya were resettled on the Grande Ronde Reservation, where many Kalapuya intermarried with other groups.

In 1956 the Grande Ronde Reservation was terminated by the federal government. Indians living there reorganized themselves as the Confederated Tribes of Grande Ronde in 1974; in 1975, they incorporated as a nonprofit organization.

See also Northwest Coast.

Kalispel: Tribe

CULTURE AREA: Plateau
LANGUAGE GROUP: Salishan
PRIMARY LOCATION: Idaho, Montana
POPULATION SIZE: 210 (1990 U.S. Census)

The Kalispel, also known as the Pend d'Oreille, belong to the Plateau tribes, with their land base covering part of the Columbia River basin. Their location in northern Idaho and western

A Kalispel girl named Dusty Dress in an early twentieth century photograph. (Library of Congress)

Montana placed them on the eastern boundaries of the Plateau tribes. As European American contact pushed the Plains Indians farther west, the Kalispel were also affected; they were pushed farther west by tribes such as the Blackfoot.

The Kalispel comprised two groups: the Upper Pend d'Oreille, or Upper Kalispel, who lived below Flathead Lake in northwestern Montana, and the Lower Pend d'Oreille, or Lower Kalispel, who occupied areas along the Clark Fork River and Pend Oreille Lake in northern Idaho. The Kalispel had contact with other tribes throughout the area, including the Spokane, Kutenai, and Flathead. Their economy depended on gathering roots and berries and on fishing. Unlike tribes such as the Nez Perce, whose culture greatly changed with use of horses and firearms (they began to hunt buffalo), the Kalispel continued to rely on traditional food sources and live a traditional Plateau lifestyle.

Initial Kalispel contact with European Americans began with fur traders. In the early 1820's, Alexander Ross of the Hudson's Bay Company managed the Flathead House (near present-day Missoula, Montana) and traded with the Kalispel, Flathead, Kutenai, and Nez Perce. Further contact with European Americans occurred with the arrival of Jesuit missionaries. Similar to the Flathead, who welcomed the arrival of the "Black Robes," the Kalispel (both Upper and Lower) also gave a kind reception to the Jesuits. According to legend, by the time a missionary arrived at the Lower Kalispel camp in 1842, the people already were well-versed in Christianity, having sent one of their members the previous year to the Flathead tribe to learn the faith. Many of the Upper Kalispel were later baptized. In 1844, St. Ignatius Mission was established among the Kalispel.

Traffic across their area increased, and by 1845 settlers had begun moving into the territory. In July, 1855, Washington Territorial Governor and Territorial Superintendent of Indian Affairs Isaac I. Stevens met with the Flathead, Kalispel, and Kutenai on the Hell Gate River to negotiate a treaty. In the final Hell Gate Treaty, the tribes ceded 25,000 acres to the federal government, and the Flathead chief, Victor, became head of the combined tribes. The three tribes were to be removed to the Jocko or Flathead Reservation, which covered 1,280,000 acres, near Flathead Lake. Two problems ensued. First, of the Kalispel tribe, only the Upper Kalispel signed the treaty; the Lower Kalispel were unable to travel to the negotiations because of the Yakima War. Later, most would not move to the Flathead Reservation. Second, the Flathead tribe split over the issue of removal, and many of its members remained in the Bitterroot Valley for almost forty years before accepting removal.

For the Upper Kalispel who conceded their claims and consented to removal, life during the first years on the Flathead Reservation was very poor and very difficult; there was little federal support. In more recent times, the situation has improved; the reservation now derives income from tourist activities, timber, grazing leases, and a hydropower lease. The tribes have also been successful with several claims filed with the Indian Claims Commission. Under the Indian Reorganization Act, the tribes organized in 1935 and today are known as the Confederated Salish and Kootenai Tribes of the Flathead Reservation.

The Lower Kalispel who refused to move to the Flathead Reservation continued to live in the area surrounding Lake Pend Oreille and the Pend Oreille River. White settlement in the area persisted. Finally, in 1914, the remaining members of the Lower Kalispel were granted a reservation of almost 5,000 acres on the Pend Oreille River. The tribe organized in 1939 and is known as the Kalispel Indian Community, Kalispel Reservation. Their numbers are very small, and the economy is limited. Income is derived from grazing leases and some industry. The tribe has been successful in its claims with the Indian Claims Commission for lost territory.

See also Flathead; Plateau.

Kamia: Tribe

CULTURE AREA: California
LANGUAGE GROUP: Yuman
PRIMARY LOCATION: Coastal area of the west Baja and California border
POPULATION: 1,640 (1990 U.S. Census)

The Kamia include the Tipai and Ipai. The Ipai spoke a northern dialect and the Tipai a southern dialect—both being autonomous, seminomadic bands with thirty exogamous, localized patrilineal clans. Though bands controlled communal land, springs were always available to anyone.

The Kamia were greatly influenced from 1769 to 1821 by Spanish Franciscan and Dominican missionaries. Initially, the Tipai-Ipai resisted conversion and missionization. By 1779, however, many had adapted to mission life. In 1834, Mexico secularized all Spanish missions, with half the land going to Indians. This policy failed, however, as the Indians were treated as serfs. In 1875, the first Tipai-Ipai reservation was established. Many Indians continued to labor in mines and on ranches, and to relocate to urban settings.

By 1968, the Tipai-Ipai had twelve reservations, sharing the Pala Reservation with Takic speakers. Despite religious factionalism, Roman Catholicism is the dominant faith. Some aspects of traditional life are still followed.

Kamiakin (c. 1800, near present-day Yakima, Wash.— 1877, Rock Lake, Wash.): Chief

ALSO KNOWN AS: Camaekin (He Will Not Go)
TRIBAL AFFILIATION: Yakima
SIGNIFICANCE: Chief Kamiakin led the Yakima Nation during the Yakima War of 1855-1856

Chief Kamiakin was the most famous leader of the Yakima tribe in south-central Washington. He led the Yakimas at a time in history when they were being overrun by European American settlers, who flocked into the region in search of gold and a better life. Kamiakan was extremely concerned about false accusations against his people and even dictated a letter to Father Pandosy of the St. Joseph's Mission. In the letter he protested hangings without even "knowing if we were right or wrong." He offered to grant European Americans a parcel of land if they would agree not to "force us to be exiled from our native country" onto reservations.

During the summer of 1853, Chief Kamiakin coordinated a meeting of tribal groups in the central and western portion of Washington to make plans for dealing with the white settlers. During June, 1855, Kamiakin and several other tribes and bands attended a grand treaty council in the Walla Walla area. Eventually, treaties were signed by five area tribes, including the Cayuse, Walla Wallas, Nez Perces, and Umatillas. The treaty with the Yakimas was signed by Chief Kamiakin, Owhi, Skloom, and eleven other delegates. After being persuaded to sign the treaty, Chief Kamiakin said, "Don't offer me any presents. I have not yet accepted one from a white man. When the government sends the pay for these lands, I will take my share."

After the treaty was signed, an Indian agent was killed by an unidentified band of Indians in Yakima territory. The murdered agent, Andrew J. Bolon, was on his way to confer with Kamiakin about an ambush of miners in Yakima territory. Major Granville O. Haller led an expedition against Chief Kamiakin and the Yakimas to avenge Bolon's death. Haller was defeated at Toppenish Creek, and Major General Gabriel Rains went to Yakima territory to settle the score with

Kamiakin. Rains burned a Catholic mission at Ahtanum Creek after a skirmish with the Yakimas. Colonel George Wright wanted a meeting with Kamiakin. The Yakima chief had decided that further conflict was futile.

Chief Kamiakin lived a quieter life after the termination of the Yakima War. He moved north to Rock Lake, Washington, where he and his family farmed until his death in 1877.

See also Walla Walla Council; Yakima; Yakima War.

Kansa: Tribe

CULTURE AREA: Plains
LANGUAGE GROUP: Siouan
PRIMARY LOCATION: Oklahoma
POPULATION SIZE: 1,073 (1990 U.S. Census)

The Kansa, or Kaw, tribe, along with the Osage, Quapaw, Omaha, and Ponca, form the Dhegiha branch of the Siouan language family. The Kansa language was most similar to the Osage tongue. A relatively small tribe, the Kansa people numbered about 1,500 in 1700; they were reduced to around 200 people in 1905, of whom only about 90 were full-bloods. Their population has rebounded considerably since then.

Tribal Name and Origin. In the sixteenth century, the Kansas were living in western Missouri and eastern Kansas, at the confluence of the Missouri and Kaw (Kansas) rivers. The origin of the name Kansa is not clear, but it was probably first used by the Spanish and then by the French, as they came in contact with this group. When Juan de Oñate traveled northeast from what is now New Mexico in 1601, he encountered a group which he called the *Escanseques*, meaning "those who stir up trouble." Indeed, the Kansa Nation developed a reputation for belligerence in subsequent centuries. Yet the word *Escanjaques* was spoken by these Indians themselves as they made a sign of peace with their hands on their breasts. In the late seventeenth century, Father Jacques Marquette and other French explorers were using the spellings "Kansa(s)" and "Kanse(s)." There is also a tradition that this root word designates "wind people" or "people of the south wind," stressing their geographic location in the sixteenth century and after in a region known for powerful winds.

The Kansa people called themselves Hutanga, meaning "by the edge of the shore," relating to their possible origins well before the sixteenth century near the Atlantic Ocean. Kansa legends support this history. From that origin well east of the Mississippi some time before 1600, the Kansa people moved west along with others of the Dhegiha linguistic group. A major separation of these Dhegiha relatives occurred at the mouth of the Ohio River, with the Quapaws (meaning "the downstream people") journeying down the Mississippi River and the Omahas ("those going against the wind or current") ascending the river. The remaining groups (Kansa, Ponca, and Osage) followed the Mississippi to the mouth of the Missouri near present-day St. Louis. The Osages remained in the lower Missouri Valley in and around the river valley which bears their name, while the Poncas traveled farther north along the Missouri. The Kansas settled around the confluence of the Kansas (or Kaw) and Missouri rivers. They were in the lower Kansas Valley when the Spanish and French made their first contacts with them.

Contact with Europeans and Americans. Spanish contact was slight, but French relations with the Kansa tribe were significant, lasting more than a century. By the late seventeenth century, French traders had established a fairly regularized trading relationship with the Kansas, bringing them into the fur trade. Hence, they were exposed regularly to French trade goods as well as French people and culture for some time before the Kansas and Missouri valley areas became American territory. Up to the 1850's, French fur trading families maintained a presence in Kansa territory to pursue the lucrative trade with this industrious tribe. French missionaries also attempted to leave their mark on these people starting in the 1720's at Forts Bourgmont and Cavagnial, established by the French in the early 1700's to pursue the fur trade with the Kansa and Osage tribes.

By the 1820's, there was a significant métis (French for "mixed-blood") community living in the lower Kansas (Kaw) Valley, a product of intermarriage between the Kansas and the French. This group spoke French as well as the Kansa language and practiced Catholicism. They were accepted by neither Kansa society nor the emerging Anglo-American community encroaching on Kansa territory by that time. The U.S. government arranged differential land grants to the two groups in an 1825 treaty, the outcome of which was the pitting of the "half-bloods" and "full-bloods" against each other. Another outcome of this 1825 treaty was that the Kansa tribe ceded all of their lands in Missouri in exchange for the land grants (2 million acres) in eastern Kansas. By 1846, another treaty ceded all those two million acres and sent both groups of Kansa descendants to a 265,000-acre reservation on the Neosho River farther southwest in Kansas. With very little success, Baptist, Methodist, and Presbyterian missionaries attempted to Christianize the Kansa people at a mission on the Neosho and later in Indian Territory (now Oklahoma), where the Kansa people moved in 1873. From that point on, the metis and full-blood Kansas were undifferentiated by the U.S. government. The Kansa reservation in Oklahoma was allotted in severalty (parceled out to individual families) in 1902, and consequently the tribe was no longer recognized by the U.S. government as a legal entity. By the late twentieth century, however, there was a movement to revive cultural awareness and preserve the Kansa tribal heritage.

Traditional Culture. The Kansa Nation was divided culturally into sixteen clans. Each clan included several extended families, some reckoned matrilineally, some patrilineally. Villages chose leaders who represented them in tribal-level council meetings, and war "chiefs" were chosen on an ad hoc basis. Kansa villages consisted of anywhere from 80 to 130 earthlodges, each holding an extended family and arranged according to clans. The Kansas were traditionally matrilocal, in that a married couple would live with the wife's family and the oldest woman of an extended family was the head of each household. Women owned the round or oval wood-framed earthlodges, which were anywhere from 30 to 60 feet in diameter, depending on the size of the family. Women also controlled crop lands, as they were the farmers. Cultivating corn, beans, pumpkins, and other crops, women also gathered prairie potatoes and made much of the clothing. Men hunted a variety of game, but as time went on, buffalo became the primary concern, not only for their plentiful meat but also for hides used in making clothing and for trade with the French (and later the Americans). When French forts were in operation along the Missouri River, these Europeans traded with the Kansa people not only for buffalo hides and beaver furs but also for agricultural produce. The Kansas were industrious and successful hunters and farmers. Many of their descendants still farm in eastern Oklahoma, although more in the European American fashion than in the pattern of the Kansas of centuries ago.   —Gretchen L. Green

See also Omaha; Osage; Plains; Quapaw; Siouan language family.

BIBLIOGRAPHY

Bushnell, David I. *Villages of the Algonquian, Siouan, and Caddoan Tribes West of the Mississippi.* Bulletin 83. Washington, D.C.: Bureau of American Ethnology, 1927.

Hoffhaus, Charles E. *Chez les Canses.* Kansas City, Mo.: Lowell Press, 1984.

Miner, Craig, and William E. Unrau. *The End of Indian Kansas, A Study of Cultural Revolution, 1854-1871.* Lawrence: Regents Press of Kansas, 1978.

Unrau, William E. *The Kansa Indians: A History of the Wind People, 1673-1873.* Norman: University of Oklahoma Press, 1971.

_____. *The Kaw People.* Phoenix, Ariz.: Indian Tribal Series, 1975.

Karankawa: Tribe

CULTURE AREA: Southeast

LANGUAGE GROUP: Karankawa

PRIMARY LOCATION: East coast of Mexico north of Tamaulipas, south Texas coast

Over the centuries the Karankawa people developed a lifeway measured by the land and the gulf upon which they depended. They lived amid riches in terms of game and fish, and they cultivated foodstuffs. They moved in dugouts or skiffs on seasonal rotation from the river valleys to the bay inlets along the coast, ranging from West Galveston Bay on the north to the Laguna Madre south of the Rio Grande. The Karankawa never exceeded ten thousand people.

Over thousands of years they nurtured a knowledge of the animals, the plants, the earth, and the sea, upon all of which their existence depended. Karankawa knowledge was passed carefully from one generation to the next. The Karankawa fished the bays and inlets from their dugout canoes, exploiting redfish, snapper, flounder, and green sea turtle; they gathered sea bird eggs and shellfish. They hunted buffalo and deer as well as smaller game, and they cultivated blackberry bushes, arrowroot, and potatoes as well as collected pecans, acorns, and prickly pear.

The Karankawa were spiritually centered people. People paused no matter what they were doing as the sun disappeared behind the horizon. They stood observing the sunset as a system of beauty of which they were a part. Formal celebrations were held at the time of the full moon, and they involved the use of "black drink" or yaupon tea. Music was made with song and instruments—gourd rattles, carved wooden rasps, and cedar flutes. Their sense of being included the marshes, bays, salt flats, brush, and dunes as they established patterns of sustainable behavior in the ecosystem. Karankawa people understood the changes that form the design of the coastal land and the borders of the gulf. They had the foresight and knowledge to protect these lands and waters for centuries.

The site of their villages was always close to the shore or bluff. They bathed every day in the salt water, and they used shark's oil as protection against mosquitoes. The people were tall, and most were in excellent physical condition. They lived in structures made of woven mats of cane, tanned skins, and hides that covered a structurally sound framework of willow and oak resting on foundations of oyster shell. These structures sheltered the Karankawa from the winds and the rains of fall and winter. They had few possessions, as they lived amid the wealth of the coastal environment.

In the late seventeenth and early eighteenth centuries, the Karankawa maneuvered diplomatically between the French and the Spanish. The mission Espiritu Santa de Zuniga was founded in 1722 specifically to influence the Karankawa, but this effort failed within a few years. Some Karankawa people did seek the protection of other missions in the late eighteenth century. Early in the nineteenth century, the Karankawa began to face the Anglo-Americans who moved into the region. Pressure increased until they migrated from Texas south of the Rio Grande into the state of Tamaulipas, Mexico, where they sought sanctuary.

See also Karankawa language; Southeast.

Karankawa language

CULTURE AREA: Southeast

TRIBE AFFECTED: Karankawa

The Karankawan language is thought to be an isolated one. There is revisionist thought put forward by Herbet Landar, however, that Karankawa should be classified as a Cariban language. The language's area in the early modern era (1500 through 1840) was the extreme western coast of the Gulf of Mexico, reaching from West Galveston Bay south to Laguna Madre in the Mexican state of Tamaulipas. Spanish missions were sent to the region to minister to the Karankawa. These included the mission of Espiritu Santa de Zuniga and the Nuestra Señora del Refugio, as well as a number of Franciscan missions south of the Rio Grande or Rio Bravo del Norte. After the Austin Colony of Anglo-Americans settled in the valley of the Brazos, the remaining Karankawa were driven south into Tamaulipas, where they lived in association with the missions along with the remaining speakers of Coahuiltecan, Tamaulipecan, and Janambrian.

Knowledge of the language stems from materials collected by Albert S. Gatschet from Old Simon and Sally Washington, both Tonkawa, and Alice W. Oliver in the late nineteenth century. Word lists were also collected by a few French observers in the late seventeenth and eighteenth centuries.

An adequate comparison of the languages that existed along the western coast of the Gulf of Mexico between Galveston Bay and the Laguna Madre is extremely difficult. Reasons for this difficulty include divergent methods of recording the languages by the various collectors and investigators as well as their different nationalities and the fragmented character of the materials. Nevertheless, it is plain to see that Karankawa differs widely from the other languages of the region in forms of speech and vocabulary. Inspection of the languages indicates that Karankawa is rightly assigned to an independent family. Yet it should be understood that the categories of Coahuiltecan, Tamaulipecan, Janambrian, and possibly Karankawan could also be considered widely separated dialects of a single stock. As the dialects of a single stock may vary widely, the lexical resemblances are more divergent than the resemblances exhibited by the verb complex, the affixes, and the structural codes. The material collected tends to exaggerate differences and conceal the more fundamental resemblances. It is also possible that a greater degree of relationship may be found to extend to Tonkawa, spoken northeast of the Coahuiltecan and Karankawan territories.

Examples from the various word lists provide a sense of the character of the language. For example: *hama'la* is used as a translation for "pretty" or "handsome" in the Oliver list. This is used in the sense of *Ta'l a'kwini hama'la* ("This tree is pretty") or *hama'la kwa'n ko'do* ("pretty little sparrow"). Another example from the Oliver list is *ka'hawan* for "to make," "to produce," or "to manufacture." A complete idea is *Na'-i demo'a ka'hawan*, or "I make arrows." The Talon brothers recorded *tecoyu* as "man," *kahamkeami* as the Spanish, or literally "people of the earth" because they reached them overland, and *kalbasska* as the French or "people who come from the sea."

See also Karankawa.

Karok: Tribe

CULTURE AREA: California
LANGUAGE GROUP: Karok
PRIMARY LOCATION: Northwestern California
POPULATION SIZE: 2,978 (1990 U.S. Census)

The Karok Indians occupied the northwestern corner of California. They subsisted by fishing, hunting, and gathering; tobacco was the only plant cultivated. The Karok used nets, harpoons, and clubs to catch salmon and other fish. Tribesmen used dogs, decoys, bows and arrows, and snares to hunt large animals such as deer and elk. Surplus meat was dried on scaffolds for winter use. Acorns, bulbs, seeds, and nuts were gathered and ground into flour.

A Karok woman preparing food in a traditional mush basket. (Library of Congress)

Rectangular, semi-subterranean, single-family homes were constructed with cedar planks; they had small low doorways and stone porches. Men wore buckskin breechclouts or went naked; women wore deerskin skirts. Both wore fur capes and snowshoes during the winter.

The Karok placed great importance on acquiring and retaining wealth. Riches were in the form of shells, obsidian blades, and woodpecker scalps. The wealthiest person in the group also held the most respect and prestige. Dances were performed to ensure good fishing and hunting, as well as to cure sick children. These ceremonies included displays of wealth and religious rites performed by priests. Everyday life was filled with taboos, and rituals were performed regularly to fend off illness and bad luck. Shamans were usually women, who used herbal medicines or orally sucked out the "pain" that was causing the illness.

In the early 1800's, Hudson's Bay Company traders were the first white people to make contact with the Karok. These early meetings had little effect on tribal life. Then, in the 1850's, gold miners flooded into Karok territory and violent clashes ensued. Whites burned most of the Indian towns, and the Karok fled to the mountains.

In the late nineteenth century, mining prospects died out and many whites left. A number of half-white children were left behind. In the 1870's, many Karoks participated in the Ghost

Dance religion. Ghost Dancers believed that the dances and rituals they performed would bring back dead Indians and a more traditional way of life. No reservations were set aside for Karok Indians, but several moved to Scott Valley, a Shasta reservation.

See also Baskets and basketry; California.

Kaska: Tribe

CULTURE AREA: Subarctic
LANGUAGE GROUP: Athapaskan
PRIMARY LOCATION: North-central British Columbia, southern Yukon Territory
POPULATION SIZE: 705 (Statistics Canada, based on 1991 census)

The Kaska were territorially divided into two bands, the Upper Laird and the Dease River. They had matriarchal moieties (Wolf and Crow). The household was the main socioeconomic unit, relying mostly upon fishing, supplemented with hunting, trapping, and late-summer gathering. Trade goods were transported, according to season and terrain, by toboggans, snowshoes, dugouts, bark canoes, and mooseskin boats.

European American contact with the Kaska was established in the 1820's by the Hudson's Bay Company, primarily for fur trading—which, with the introduction of disease, brought numerous cultural changes. In 1873, gold miners first encroached upon Kaska territory. In 1897-1898, the route to the Klondike crossed their land. Roman Catholic and Protestant missionaries also brought about significant cultural changes, and by 1945 all Kaska were nominally Catholic. The greatest sustained change came in 1942 with construction of the Alaskan Highway. The Kaska now have essentially a cash economy, supported by seasonal employment with fishing and guiding services that cater to hunting parties.

See also Athapaskan language family.

Katlian (late 1700's—mid-1800's): War chief

TRIBAL AFFILIATION: Tlingit
SIGNIFICANCE: Katlian led Tlingit resistance to the Russians in Alaska

Katlian led his people in a sporadic war with Russian freebooters and colonists in the present-day Alaska panhandle. The Russians arrived in the Aleutian chain after the exploratory voyage of Vitus Bering (1741), where they forced the Aleuts to trap furs for export.

Born in Sitka, Katlian led a native raid there in 1799 that destroyed the first Russian fort in America. The Tlingits held the fort with great tenacity for two years until the Russians retook it with a force of 120 Russians and about 1,000 Aleuts. The Tlingets retreated from the fort in the face of cannon fire and armed assault, but they attacked the Russian fort at Yakutat in 1805. Raids continued after that; by 1818, a Russian warship was delegated to patrol Sitka harbor, after traders there appealed for protection.

See also Aleut; Indian-white relations—Russian colonial; Tlingit.

Kawaiisu: Tribe

CULTURE AREA: Great Basin
LANGUAGE GROUP: Kawaiisu
PRIMARY LOCATION: Sierra Nevada, Piute, and Tehachapi mountains, California

As hunters and gatherers, the Kawaiisu were omnivorous in their diet, though deer meat was a favored food. They collected and stored a wide variety of roots, tubers, nuts, berries, and seeds. Acorns were stored in granaries; before eating, the tannic acid was removed by leaching. Most animals were hunted or trapped, and fishing, though minimal, supplemented their diet.

In 1776, Francisco Garcé became the first European to record contact with the Kawaiisu; John Frémont traversed their region in 1844. By the early 1850's, farmers, trappers, and stockmen occupied Kawaiisu territory, along with prospectors—all of which led to ongoing conflict. In 1863, after reports of an intertribal grouping of Indians, a contingent of soldiers under Captain Moses McLaughlin killed thirty-five unarmed Indians. The introduction of disease also reduced the Kawaiisu population, from an estimated 500 to about 150 by 1910. Anthropologists believe that, by 1960, all aspects of tribal life were gone. In the 1990 U.S. Census, only two people identified themselves as Kawaiisu.

Keeler Commission

DATE: Established 1961
TRIBES AFFECTED: Pantribal
SIGNIFICANCE: This commission's report helped end the termination policy that began in 1953

The intent of federal Indian policy from 1953 to 1962 was to dissolve government obligations and responsibilities toward Native Americans in order to bring about assimilation. This disastrous program was called "termination." It undermined tribal governments and resources, eroded ethnic identities, and impoverished groups such as the Klamath of Oregon and Menominee of Wisconsin. By the end of the decade, so much criticism had been generated by these developments that a new political consciousness concerning Indian problems began to emerge.

John F. Kennedy, elected president in 1960, affirmed that Indian land would be protected, that self-determination would be promoted, and that steps would be taken to avoid undermining the cultural heritage of any group. Secretary of the Interior Stewart Udall appointed a special task force on Indian affairs in February of 1961 with an eye toward reorganizing the Bureau of Indian Affairs (BIA) in order to carry out this mandate.

William Wayne Keeler, a top-level executive with Phillips Petroleum Company and principal chief of the Cherokee Nation, was appointed chairman of the task force. Other members included Philleo Nash, an anthropologist and former lieutenant governor of Wisconsin who had participated in the Menominee termination plans; James Officer, a University of Arizona anthropologist; William Zimmerman, Jr., assistant commissioner of the BIA from 1933 to 1950; and consultant John Crow. After hearings and field trips to western reservations, the commission filed its seventy-seven-page report on July 10, 1961. Nash also included a summary of the report in the Annual Report of the Commissioner of Indian Affairs for 1961.

The commission's main finding was that future BIA policy should emphasize development rather than termination. Recommendations included the attraction of industries to reservations, along with job training and placement services. Loan programs were encouraged, rapid settlement of Indian Claims Commission cases was urged, and increased efforts to educate the general public about Indian culture were promoted. The commission report also stressed the need for Indian participation in government programs.

In the 1960's, Congress granted authorization for Indian loans, tribal resources increased, and development of reservation resources replaced the focus on assimilating Indians through relocation to the cities. The Keeler Commission played a small but noticeable role in the shift away from the termination policy.

See also Indian Claims Commission (ICC); Relocation; Reservation system of the United States; Termination policy.

Keetoowah Society

DATE: Established 1859
TRIBE AFFECTED: Cherokee
SIGNIFICANCE: The Keetoowah Society was founded in an effort to advance the interests of full-blooded Cherokees

The Keetoowah Society was founded by two white clergymen in 1859. The men were abolitionists, and their goal, ostensibly, was to organize Cherokee opposition to slavery. Members of the order were full-bloods, and some called themselves "Pin Indians," wearing crossed pins on their left lapels. The Keetoowah Society evolved from simple support of abolition to a group whose purpose was the protection of Cherokee interests. Society goals were taken from the ancient Anti-Kutani, designed to oppose adoption of European American ways. "Pin Indians" were Christians who wished to syncretize their religion with ancient tribal rites.

The Keetoowah Society was popular and at one time had a membership of more than two thousand men. It was fiercely loyal to the Union during the Civil War. That fact threatened the Confederacy, which impressed society members into military service. Stories abound of men who were forced to serve the South and deserted at the first opportunity.

Following the Civil War, the Keetoowah Society remained active in Cherokee political and social life. It opposed the Dawes Commission in the 1890's, insisting on the observance of treaty obligations, a guarantee of self-government, and freedom from territorial organization. When the Cherokee delegation reached agreement with the Dawes Commission in 1900, the full-blood Keetoowah Society urged its members to boycott the agreement. In 1906, the Dawes Commission agreement prevailed. The society then functioned as a political party

(the Union Party) and fraternal lodge. The Keetoowah Society is viable to this day and is the only fraternal lodge in the United States whose principal emblem is the United States flag.

See also Cherokee; General Allotment Act; Indian-white relations—U.S., 1831-1870; Slavery.

Kennekuk (c. 1785, along Osage River in Ill.—1852, along Missouri River in present-day Kans.): Shaman, tribal leader

ALSO KNOWN AS: Kickapoo Prophet
TRIBAL AFFILIATION: Kickapoo
SIGNIFICANCE: As the leader of the peaceful Northern Kickapoo, Kennekuk delayed his tribe's relocation for several years

Influenced by prior spiritual leaders, particularly the Shawnee Tenskwatawa, Kennekuk advocated a return to traditional ways and abstention from alcohol. With the aid of meditation, fasting, and wooden prayer sticks, he urged his tribe to reach a state of holiness and thereby achieve an earthly paradise. He also advocated sedentary agriculture and peaceful relations with whites. For a time, peace prevailed. As the white population increased, however, fertile Indian farm lands were coveted. In the Treaty of Edwardsville, 1819, all Kickapoo, both Kennekuk's peaceful band and the warring southerners, were forced to cede their Illinois lands in exchange for lands in Missouri. Some Kickapoo became militant in their resistance, while Kennekuk's followers passively resisted removal. On several occasions Kennekuk negotiated with white officials, particularly William Clark in St. Louis. After being forced to sign the Treaty of Castor Hill in 1832, Kennekuk's band moved in 1833 to land along the Missouri River in Kansas, where they re-created their farming village. There, he continued his preaching.

See also Black Hawk; Indian Removal Act; Kickapoo; Removal.

Keokuk (c. 1783, Saukenuk, modern Rock Island, Ill.—Apr., 1848, Franklin County near Pomona, Kans.): Chief

TRIBAL AFFILIATION: Sauk
SIGNIFICANCE: Keokuk led the peace band of Sauk Indians in the Rock River Valley of Illinois; often in active opposition to Black Hawk, he proved willing to exchange Sauk and Fox land for personal gain

Keokuk was born into the Fox clan at Saukenuk. His blue eyes and flat cheeks reveal evidence of European ancestry. Keokuk gained a degree of notoriety because of his ability as a horseman. He had a striking physical appearance and demonstrated great oratorical skills.

Keokuk took advantage of the crisis caused within the Sauk Nation by the War of 1812. The Sauk and Fox were divided in their response to the conflict. Many Sauk and Fox migrated across the Mississippi River to Missouri in order to seek the protection of the U.S. government. Others, led by Black Hawk, joined the British. Those who remained behind in the villages along the Rock River felt pressure from both sides.

Keokuk became the dominant Sauk leader in the 1830's. (Library of Congress)

When rumors circulated that an American army was approaching Saukenuk, the village council prepared to abandon their homes. Keokuk was invited to speak, and he advocated organizing a defense before making plans to flee. The council chose him as war chief, but the much-feared American army never arrived.

In June, 1821, Keokuk was instrumental in the apprehension of two warriors accused of murder. From that time forward, U.S. Indian agents Thomas Forsyth and William Clark promoted the ambitions of Keokuk for prestige among his people. His growing influence with the Americans allowed him to speak in councils with great authority. In 1825, the Americans sponsored a great peace council at Prairie du Chien, Wisconsin. Keokuk served as the spokesman for the Sauk and Fox nations.

In May, 1828, Forsyth informed the Rock River Sauk that they would have to abandon their lands east of the Mississippi in order to comply with earlier treaties. Keokuk led the peace band that advocated cooperation with the American demand. Black Hawk and his followers refused to acquiesce. Keokuk's peace band established new homes along the Iowa River in 1829 while Black Hawk's band continued their struggle to occupy Saukenuk.

When open warfare erupted in 1832 between Black Hawk's warriors and the American army, Keokuk offered his services to the Americans. They refused his offer, but, following the destruction of Black Hawk's band during the course of the Black Hawk War, Keokuk emerged as the dominant figure among the Sauk. At the conclusion of the conflict, Keokuk obliged the Americans by negotiating a treaty in which the Sauk, Fox, and Winnebago sold much of their land west of the Mississippi. The Sauk and Fox nations were left with a small reservation along the Iowa River. Keokuk was empowered to distribute an annuity among his people.

Keokuk accompanied Black Hawk on grand tours of the eastern United States in 1833 and 1837. During his 1837 trip, Keokuk participated in negotiations in Washington, D.C., in which 26,500,000 acres of Indian land were ceded to the United States.

In 1845, Keokuk sold the remaining Sauk lands in Iowa, and the Sauks were forced to relocate in Kansas. Keokuk died at the Sauk Agency in Kansas. A bronze bust of Keokuk was placed in the U.S. capitol.

See also Black Hawk; Black Hawk War; Fox; Removal; Sauk.

Keresan language family

CULTURE AREA: Southwest
TRIBES AFFECTED: Acoma, Cochiti, Laguna, Santa Ana, Santo Domingo, Zia

The Keresan language family consists of a group of languages spoken in the northwestern portion of New Mexico and is generally considered to fall into two subfamilies: Western Keresan, consisting of Acoma and Laguna, and Eastern Keresan, comprising the rest of the languages. The varieties of Keresan are so closely related that they can be regarded as dialects of a single language rather than as separate languages. The Keresan dialects form a chain in which geographically contiguous varieties are mutually intelligible. The Summer Institute of Linguistics estimated that in 1977 there were forty-five hundred speakers of the Western Keresan dialects and four thousand speakers of the Eastern Keresan dialects.

Keresan has no known linguistic relatives, although several relationships have been proposed. John Powell and Morris Swadesh both unsuccessfully attempted to relate Keresan to Zuni, while John Harrington put forth some evidence that Keresan is part of the Aztec-Tanoan stock (which is itself not unequivocally accepted). Edward Sapir placed Keresan in the now-defunct Hokan-Siouan phylum. Swadesh also suggested the relationship of Keresan to Caddoan. There is insufficient evidence to demonstrate any of these long-distance relationships.

Franz Boas was the first to record Keresan in the 1920's. In later years, Robert Spencer, J. R. Fox, Irvine Davis, and Wick Miller (among others) also carried out research on the various dialects. Keresan is an "SOV language" (the order of the constituents of the sentence is subject-object-verb) with a complex sound system that includes glottalized consonants and tones. Other traits include voiceless vowels and nasals, reduplication, noun incorporation (in which the object is incorporated into the verb), and a dual versus plural number distinction.

Cultural diffusion was common among the Pueblo tribes, and there is some evidence of linguistic diffusion from other Pueblo languages into Keresan (notably from Zuni). In the more recent past, Keresan speakers were often bilingual in Spanish, leading to the introduction of Spanish loan words into Keresan. The vitality of these languages varies from community to community. For example, the use of the Eastern Keresan dialects is still strong among adults and children; as most children in the Western pueblos prefer English, however, those dialects are in danger of extinction.

See also Prehistory—Southwest; Pueblo tribes, Eastern; Pueblo tribes, Western; Southwest.

Key Marco: Archaeological site

DATE: c. 750-1500
LOCATION: West coast of Florida
CULTURES AFFECTED: Calusa, Glades

Key Marco (also called Marco Island) is the largest of the group of islands off the southwest coast of Florida called the Ten Thousand Islands; it lies a few miles south of the mainland city of Naples. Beginning in 1895, a site at the north end of the island—a sort of courtyard surrounded by shell mounds—was excavated by Frank Hamilton Cushing and others, and a variety of artifacts were uncovered. Their method was to strain the acidic, tannin-filled muck of the courtyard, which had preserved the organic materials of the tools and ceremonial objects. This was fortunate, as only wood, fiber, bone, and shell (no stone or metal) were available to the Key Marco dwellers, and the first two would not have survived if exposed to the Florida climate.

The culture reconstructed from the finds at Key Marco was sophisticated and technologically advanced. The artistic and ceremonial items are executed with a sure hand and a sensitive stylization. Probably the best-known of these items is a wooden statuette of a feline figure now in the Smithsonian Institution in Washington, but there are other animal effigies, wooden face masks (possibly ceremonial), wooden tablets with both incised and painted decorations, and a variety of personal ornaments of wood and shell, most of them strikingly beautiful. The tools that produced these objects are technologically ingenious, with adzes using shark teeth as cutting edges, rasps made of barracuda jaws, and various cutting and shaping tools of wood, bone, and shell. Spear handles are present; apparently the spear thrower, or atlatl, was used. Cordage was well constructed and ranged in thickness from thread up to one-inch rope. Fishing nets with wood or gourd floats and shell sinkers confirm that one of the dietary staples was the mullet of the surrounding waters. Also eaten were shellfish, turtle, alligator, and a variety of roots and berries.

Radiocarbon dating suggests that the Key Marco site was occupied from about 750 until just before Spanish exploration of the area, about 1500. The Indians of Key Marco were probably part of the Calusa empire that covered south Florida.

See also Calusa; Middens; Prehistory—Southeast.

Kichai: Tribe

CULTURE AREA: Plains
LANGUAGE GROUP: Caddoan
PRIMARY LOCATION: Oklahoma

The Kichai (also spelled Kitsei), a branch of the Caddoan family, lived in what is now Texas, Oklahoma, and Kansas. The Caddo tribes had inhabited the southern Great Plains for thousands of years. "Caddo" is a shortened form of *Kadohadacho* ("real chiefs"). The Caddo, the most culturally advanced peoples of the southern Plains, lived in round thatched houses in permanent villages. They were skilled agriculturalists as well as expert hunters, and they were known for their beautiful pottery and weaving. *Kitsash*, the name the Kichai had for themselves, means "going in wet sand"; the Pawnee called them "water turtles." Their first recorded contact with whites was in 1701, when they encountered the French in eastern Louisiana. They remained friendly with the French from that time. Throughout the eighteenth and early nineteenth centuries, their population decreased as they fell victim to new diseases carried by the Spanish, French, and British and as they fought with European and Mexican invaders. In 1855, they were assigned by the United States to a small reservation on the Brazos River. Three years later, they were pushed aside and killed in large numbers by Texans who wanted their land. The Kichai fled north to Oklahoma and merged with the Wichita; they were absorbed by that tribe and lost their own identity. The last speaker of the Kichai language died in the 1930's.

See also Caddo; Wichita.

Kickapoo: Tribe

CULTURE AREA: Northeast
LANGUAGE GROUP: Algonquian
PRIMARY LOCATION: Kansas, Mexico, Oklahoma
POPULATION SIZE: 3,577 in U.S. (1990 U.S. Census); estimated 400-500 in Mexico

Kickapoo comes from the Indian *Kiwegapaw*, meaning "He stands about," or "He moves about, standing now here, now there."

The Kickapoo lived originally in eastern Michigan with the Sauk and Fox, with whom they were most closely related culturally, ethnically, and linguistically, out of the twenty-some Algonquian tribes living in this geographic area. The Kickapoo first appear in historical accounts in the late 1660's, at which time their population was about three thousand.

The Kickapoo lived in fixed villages during the spring and summer, when their economy was primarily agricultural. They grew crops of corn, beans, and squash and gathered roots and berries. During the autumn and winter they were nomadic, hunting animals, especially buffalo, across the Mississippi River. The Kickapoo lived in oval-shaped houses with frameworks made from green saplings and covered with bark or cattail mats. The houses were built with a smoke hole in the roof, and the door always faced east. The Kickapoos' principal crafts were woodworking and pottery. They were known for their wood cradleboards, ladles, and bowls.

The Kickapoo were organized into clans, or *gens*. Marriage was always outside one's gen, and children belonged to the gen of their father. The Kickapoo had a rich mythology, centering on their belief in a cosmic substance that pervaded nature and was given special reverence. Their supreme being was Kicihiata, who lived in the sky and created earth and everything on it. Other spirits existed in earthly objects, as well as throughout the universe. Dogs were given particular significance and were sacrificed to the spirits. Their cultural hero was Wisaka, and their great cosmic myth focused on the death of Wisaka's younger brother. To him were credited all of life's good things and the hope of life in the spirit world after death, which was presided over by the younger brother. The dead were buried in village graveyards with their feet pointed west, toward the land of the dead. Priests conducted the religious life of the Kickapoo. The most important ceremony and feast was a week-long event in spring that centered on opening and restoring sacred bundles.

Although originating in eastern Michigan, the Kickapoo had been driven by the Iroquois and Sioux west into Wisconsin by the mid-1600's, where they had their first contacts with whites, the French. Unlike other Algonquian tribes, the Kickapoo were extremely conservative and independent in their attitudes toward they French and later toward the British and Americans. Their history is one of resistance to any attempts by whites to acculturate them politically, economically, or religiously.

After being driven out of their native home by the Iroquois and Sioux, the Kickapoo formed a powerful confederacy with the Fox and Mascouten tribes and waged effective warfare against the French, Iroquois, and Sioux. Around 1716, the Kickapoo turned on the Illinois Confederacy to their south, and by 1765 they occupied Illinois lands. Through the late 1700's and early 1800's, their history was characterized by a series of shifting alliances with the French, British, Spanish, Americans, and other Indian tribes.

The inexorable European American movement westward resulted in government pressure on the Kickapoo to leave their lands and move farther west, to Kansas and Missouri, which they did by 1834. Over the next thirty years, difficulties with squatters and questionable appropriation of their land by government treaties resulted in a small band of disaffected Kickapoo migrating to Mexico in 1838, where they were joined by another band in 1863, becoming known as the Mexican Kickapoo. Because of their depredations against Texans in cross-border raids, however, the U.S. government attempted to persuade these Kickapoo through warfare and negotiation to return to the United States. A number did, settling in Kansas and Oklahoma. The Kickapoo in Missouri eventually settled in Kansas, so that today the Kickapoo reside on reservations in Kansas, Oklahoma, and Mexico.

The Kickapoo gave up their warlike ways and became successful farmers. All along, however, the chiefs and headmen worked hard to resist the cultural, social, and religious influences of the white culture. The pride and spirit of being a Kickapoo was instilled in the tribe. A course of conciliation with whites only when it was necessary to do so in order to survive was adopted. The Kickapoo have been remarkably successful in adhering to their old ways. As a result, the Kickapoo have retained their proud and fierce independence. Among contemporary Indian tribes, the Kickapoo culture is perhaps the purest of all Indian cultures.   —*Laurence Miller*

See also Kickapoo Resistance; Kickapoo uprisings.

Kickapoo Resistance

DATE: 1819-1834
PLACE: Illinois
TRIBE AFFECTED: Kickapoo
SIGNIFICANCE: Two separate bands of Kickapoo repudiated treaties of 1819 calling for all Kickapoo to move west; not until 1834 did the last band finally do so

The 1819 Treaties of Edwardsville and Fort Harrison required the Kickapoo to vacate their lands in Illinois and move west. Two renegade bands of about 250 Indians each repudiated the treaties and remained, but by very different means.

The band led by Chief Mecina resisted by looting, rustling, shooting livestock, and terrorizing settlers. William Clark, area superintendent of Indian affairs, used persuasion rather than force, and in 1829 Mecina and about 150 tribal members left. About a hundred members joined Black Hawk's band of Sauk and Fox Indians in their ultimately unsuccessful efforts to recover tribal lands by force. Black Hawk was defeated in 1832, after which his supporters also moved west.

The band led by the warrior Kennekuk enjoyed friendly and peaceful relations with whites. Consequently, Kennekuk was able to resist passively and delay leaving. In 1833, however, Clark lost patience and gave Kennekuk an ultimatum to leave or be considered an enemy. In spring of 1834 Kennekuk finally left, leaving the Kickapoo wholly removed from their original lands.

See also Black Hawk; Black Hawk War; Kennekuk; Kickapoo.

Kickapoo uprisings

DATE: 1865-1873
PLACE: Southern Texas
TRIBE AFFECTED: Southern (Mexican) Kickapoo
SIGNIFICANCE: This war of retribution against southern Texans wreaked havoc, caused bitter controversy with Mexico over the sanctity of borders, and marked the beginning of reservation life for some Southern Kickapoos

During a migration of seven hundred Southern Kickapoos from Kansas to Mexico, the Indians were attacked by four hundred soldiers of the Texas Confederate Army on January 1, 1865. The Kickapoos won a decisive victory at the Battle of Dove Creek, but they lost fifteen dead and numerous supplies.

Enraged by this unwarranted attack and considering it an act of war, the Kickapoos unleashed a relentless, merciless, and highly effective campaign of terror, vengeance, and destruction against Texans and their property along the Rio Grande over the next decade.

Unable to persuade the Southern Kickapoos to cease hostilities and return to the United States, the government resorted to force and crossed the border into Mexico without permission in 1873. On May 18, the U.S. Fourth Cavalry killed and captured many women and children at Nacimiento. Desiring to be reunited with their families, 317 Kickapoos agreed to return to Indian Territory in the United States in 1873, with the rest (about 280) remaining in Mexico.

See also Kickapoo; Kickapoo Resistance.

Kicking Bear (fl. latter 1800's): Chief, medicine man

TRIBAL AFFILIATION: Oglala, Miniconjou Sioux
SIGNIFICANCE: Kicking Bear became an apostle of Wovoka and claimed that wearing Ghost Dance shirts would protect the wearers from bullets shot by white men

Born an Oglala, Kicking Bear married into the Miniconjou band and became a chief. He fought in the battles of the Little Bighorn and Rosebud, and in the Black Hills War of 1876-1877. He was a medicine man and is best known as an apostle of Wovoka's Ghost Dance religion. The message of this messianic religion included the idea that God made earth and all people on it; He sent Christ to teach, but white men treated him badly, so He returned to Heaven. Christ, now an Indian (Wovoka), reappeared to let all living and dead Indians inherit the earth. The earth would be filled with grasses, game, and buffalo herds; Indians would live in harmony, avoiding alcohol and the ways of whites. Preparatory rituals included meditation, prayers, chanting, and dancing the Ghost Dance, which would levitate the Indians into space while a great flood drowned all the whites.

Anticipating negative reactions by whites to the Ghost Dance, Kicking Bear claimed that wearing special ghost shirts would stop bullets. Throughout the Plains, Indians wearing ghost shirts danced, the whites attacked, and the shirts did not stop the bullets. The Ghost Dance religion essentially died on December 29, 1890, with the massacre at Wounded Knee.

See also Ghost Dance; Wovoka.

Kicking Bird (c. 1835, Central Plains—May 3, 1875, Cache Creek, Okla.): Chief

ALSO KNOWN AS: Tene-angop'te, Watohkonk, Eagle Striking with Talons

TRIBAL AFFILIATION: Kiowa

SIGNIFICANCE: Kicking Bird led a peace faction during the 1870's Indian wars on the central Plains

Kicking Bird's grandfather was a Crow adopted by the Kiowas. Little else is known of his ancestry. He earned his early reputation as a warrior but soon emerged as a leader of the Kiowa peace faction, envisioning peace with whites as the best opportunity for tribal survival. To that end, he signed the Treaty of Little Arkansas River (1865), by which Kiowas were granted reservations in the Indian Territory and Texas. He likewise signed the Treaty of Medicine Lodge (1867), establishing reservations in Kansas.

With his warrior's reputation challenged by the war faction, Kicking Bird participated in a raid against Texas Rangers in

Kiowa leader Kicking Bird led a peace faction in the 1860's and 1870's. (National Archives)

1870 during which he killed a soldier. Nevertheless, he continued to support peace. In 1872, with his cousin Stumbling Bear, he acted as spokesman for the Kiowa delegation to Washington, D.C. With Indian agent Thomas C. Battey, Kicking Bird developed an educational program and school for Kiowas. His death was probably caused by strychnine administered by a militant Indian. He was buried at Fort Sill, Oklahoma.

See also Big Bow; Kiowa; Lone Wolf; Medicine Lodge, Treaties of; Stumbling Bear.

King Philip's War

DATE: 1675-1676

PLACE: New England

TRIBES AFFECTED: Mohawk, Mohegan, Narragansett, Nipmuck, Pocomtuck, Wampanoag

SIGNIFICANCE: This general Indian uprising resulted in the crushing forever of Indian power in New England, except along the far northern New England frontier

The Algonquian tribes of New England lived in relative peace with the English settlers for a half century (with the exception of the Pequot War in southern New England, 1636-1637). Trouble brewed, however, between the Plymouth colony and the Wampanoags, who dwelled in the southern part of the colony, principally on Mount Hope Neck in Narragansett Bay. The total white population of New England in 1675 numbered about eighty thousand; the Indian population was between ten and twenty thousand, of whom about a thousand were Wampanoags.

The uprising of the Wampanoags in 1675 engulfed all New England in an Indian war. Several groups supported the English cause—the Mohegans, the small remnant band of Pequots called "Praying Indians" (so named because they had been Christianized), and, beyond the western New England border, the Mohawks. The Indian hostilities erupted spontaneously, although the Wampanoags and several other tribes had been planning to join in combined resistance to the English settlers. Causes of the war derived from pressures of white expansion into Indian territory and the insistence of the Plymouth colony on exercising sovereignty over the Wampanoags.

King Philip (also known as Philip, Metacom, and Metacomet), son of Massasoit, the early friend of the Pilgrims, became sachem (chief) of the Wampanoags upon the death of his brother, Alexander, in 1662. For nine years King Philip and his tribe managed to have good relations with the authorities of the Plymouth colony. Beginning in 1671, however, it was suspected that King Philip was plotting war with the English settlers. On September 29, 1671, King Philip signed a treaty with the Plymouth colony stating that his tribe should pay a fine of one hundred pounds (to be paid in goods) for having collected firearms and stating that the Wampanoags acknowledged Plymouth's right to direct the Indians in matters of war and disposal of land. (King Philip did not live up to a pledge to surrender all firearms.) The Wampanoags were to recognize the sovereignty of the British crown and to abide by English laws. The execution by colonists in June, 1675, of three Wampanoags for having killed Sassamon, a Christian Indian and informant to the Plymouth government, was the incident that sparked the rebellion.

The First Months of the War. Apparently without any tribal assault plan having been formulated, young Wampanoag warriors, in June, 1675, destroyed houses and killed eleven settlers near Swansea. Plymouth and Massachusetts troops, under Majors James Cudworth and William Bradford, respectively, quickly responded by attacking King Philip's stronghold on the Taunton River. King Philip showed great military skill. He struck at the towns of Dartmouth, Taunton, and Middleborough and, after hiding for a time in a swamp, escaped and took his band to the Nipmuck country in central Massachusetts. Throughout the late summer and early fall, Wampanoags, Nipmucks, and Pocomtucks raided the towns of Mendon, Brookfield, Lancaster, Deerfield, Hadley, and Northfield. At "Bloody Brook," just south of Deerfield, on September 18, 1675, Captain Thomas Lothrop and eighty Massachusetts soldiers, who were escorting a wagon train of provisions, were ambushed; all but eight were killed.

In order to coordinate their war effort, the Puritan colonies of Massachusetts, Connecticut, and Plymouth revived the New England Confederation (officially titled the United Colonies of New England), which had been formed in 1643 primarily for mutual defense. Two commissioners from each colony held sessions to determine intercolonial policy. The commissioners arranged for two armies to take to the field—one for the western theater of operations (commanded first by Major John Pynchon and then by Major Samuel Appleton) and another, led by the governor of Plymouth colony, Josiah Winslow, for a punitive expedition against the Narragansetts, who resided in the Rhode Island colony. This tribe was deemed by the English authorities to have violated their pledge of fidelity to the colonial governments and neutrality during the war. The Narragansetts refused to surrender Wampanoag refugees as they had promised to do. It was rationalized that the Narrangansetts inevitably would join in the Indian rebellion. An attack upon the Narragansetts, therefore, was justifiable in the Puritan way of thinking as "defensive" rather than "offensive" war.

Attacks and Counterattacks. On December 18, 1675, the Winslow expedition, consisting of troops from Connecticut, Massachusetts, and Plymouth and 150 Mohegan Indians, assembled at Pettaquamscat and marched eastward to a palisaded fort of the Narragansetts (at the present site of West Kingston, Rhode Island). The Indians had gathered for the winter within the 5-acre fort, located in the "Great Swamp" on a tract of upland. Although the Indians thought that they were secure against attack, their safety was imperiled both by the swampwater being frozen and by an unfinished section of the palisade. The Englishmen, aided by an Indian guide, found the defect in the fort's construction, and troops poured through the gap. The Narragansetts ran out of ammunition. During the battle of the afternoon of December 19, the invading army burned all the Indian dwellings and slaughtered three hundred men and a like number of women and children. Total English losses at the "Great Swamp Fight" were twenty killed and two hundred wounded—one-fifth of the English troops. Canonchet, the Narragansett sachem, and a large number of warriors escaped and soon were fighting alongside other Indians in the Connecticut River valley in Massachusetts.

From February through May, 1676, Indians attacked a score of English towns in the Plymouth and Massachusetts colonies. Canonchet led a force of Nipmucks, Narragansetts, and Pocomtucks. Canonchet, however, visiting his people in the Narragansett country, was captured near the Patuxet River and immediately executed. Other setbacks soon doomed the Indian cause. King Philip sought aid from the Mohawks along the western New England frontier; the tribe declined and, moreover, made it clearly known that they sided with the English. The decisive blow to the Indians occurred on May 19, 1676, when Captain William Turner attacked a large encampment of Pocomtucks and other Indians at Peskecompsuct, located at falls of the Connecticut River (near Deerfield). Several hundred Indians were killed, with English losses being only one killed and a few wounded. Major John Talcott, with 250 Connecticut soldiers and a similar number of Indian allies, defeated an Indian force at Hadley on June 12. English troops began to conduct a war of attrition, denying the Indians provisions. Combined Connecticut and Massachusetts troops chased their enemy up the Connecticut River and into New Hampshire (not a separate colony at this time). Throughout the summer of 1676, Indians surrendered en masse. Fighting, however, spread to coastal Maine, with refugee Indians joining with the Saco and Abenaki tribes. Englishmen had to abandon the region between Casco and Penobscot bays. Sir Edmund Andros, governor of New York, constructed a fort at Pemaquid and negotiated a peace with the northeastern "hostiles" on April 12, 1676.

The Final Days. King Philip, with nowhere else to turn, returned to his native territory. On August 12, he was discovered in a swamp near Mount Hope and killed by an Indian auxiliary serving in a detachment led by Captain Benjamin Church. King Philip's body was quartered and left to rot; the hands were sent to Boston, and his head went to the town of Plymouth, where it graced a pike on top of a watchtower for twenty years, the skull often containing a nest of wrens.

Many Indian captives were shot or hanged. Indeed, King Philip's War had degenerated into a race war. Christian Indians were interned in concentration camps. Hundreds of Indians were sold into slavery at Cadiz, Spain, Tangier in North Africa, and the West Indies. King Philip's son and wife met such a fate. Many young Indians were forced into servitude until age twenty-four. Indians not otherwise punished were forced into residence on small reservations.

The war cost the lives of about a thousand Englishmen, equally divided between soldiers and civilians. The three Puritan colonies found themselves with a total indebtedness of about ninety thousand pounds because of war expenditures.

One-tenth of Massachusetts males of military age had been captured or killed. Several dozen English towns had been attacked, and some of these had to be rebuilt completely.

Indian lands were seized and sold, with funds used to pay war debts, provide pensions for invalided war veterans, and provide support for those impoverished by the war. During the war the English colonists had the double task of defending their villages and engaging the enemy in the field. Much of the war resembled modern guerrilla fighting, and the English learned the skills of Indian warriors. The war posed a challenge to the British crown. For example, during the early part of the war, the royal governor of New York, Sir Edmund Andros, had tried to aid the New Englanders, but the assistance was rejected; Connecticut and New York both claimed jurisdiction over the Narragansett country. The three Puritan colonies engaged in cooperation, though with some rivalry and jealousy. Rhode Island did not participate in the war. The experience was instructive for the British crown, which ten years later attempted to combine all the New England colonies, New York, and New Jersey under one consolidated government.

—Harry M. Ward

See also Canonchet; Indian-white relations—English colonial; Massasoit; Metacomet; Wampanoag.

BIBLIOGRAPHY

Bourne, Russell. *The Red King's Rebellion: Racial Politics in New England, 1675-1678*. New York: Atheneum, 1990.

Church, Benjamin. *Diary of King Philip's War, 1675-76*. Tercentary ed. Chester, Conn.: Pequot Press, 1975.

Leach, Douglas Edward. *Flintlock and Tomahawk: New England in King Philip's War*. New York: Macmillan, 1958.

Lincoln, Charles M., ed. *Narratives of the Indian Wars, 1675-1699*. New York: Charles Scribner's Sons, 1913.

Vaughan, Alden T. *New England Frontier: Puritans and Indians, 1620-1675*. Boston: Little, Brown, 1965.

Webb, Stephen S. *1676: The End of American Independence*. New York: Alfred A. Knopf, 1984.

Kinnikinnick

TRIBES AFFECTED: Pantribal
SIGNIFICANCE: This plant was used by Native Americans in many ways

Kinnikinnick, a member of the heather family, is a low, trailing, evergreen shrub that forms dense mats in well-drained sandy soils throughout much of North America. Wherever the plant was found, the leaves and berries were utilized by Native Americans in a variety of ways.

Some groups believed the plant was placed on earth primarily for use as a tobacco. Most commonly, the leaves were picked, dried, and smoked as a substitute for tobacco or used as a mixture with other plants, including wild tobacco, huckleberry leaves, "Indian marijuana," dwarf wild rose, and red osier dogwood. After the plant had flowered, the leaf was dried, toasted, and often greased. The smoke has a sweet smell, and it can make the uninitiated smoker dizzy. The Lillooet sometimes made temporary pipe stems from the dried roots.

The berries were eaten raw or after cooking, which made them more palatable, particularly when cooked slowly in bear, salmon, moose, deer, mountain goat, seal, or sturgeon grease. Kinnikinnick berries were used in meat and soups and, after the introduction of flour, were made into dumplings. The leaf was used commonly for making tea by boiling the dried leaves; the tea was drunk medicinally as a diuretic or tonic.

See also Lillooet; Medicine and modes of curing, precontact; Tobacco.

Kinship and social organization

TRIBES AFFECTED: Pantribal
SIGNIFICANCE: Kinship relationships of various types have often formed the basis for political and social customs among native North Americans, including systems both much like and vastly different from those of Europeans

Like almost all cultures around the world, traditional American Indian cultures considered family relationships to be of paramount importance. Family relationships could be quite complex, as could the larger units of social organization. Therefore, a number of terms must be noted before American Indian social organization can be examined.

The largest societal group was the tribe, or nation. The precise number of tribes that have existed in North America is difficult to ascertain, since many were virtually exterminated by the European invaders, but they certainly numbered in the hundreds. Within some tribes were moieties, two subgroups within the tribe, often identified with particular animals. The next group was the clan, identified by close familial relationship. Finally there was the family group, extended or immediate. Among various Indian tribes, these groups were of varying importance.

The term "matrilineal" describes a society in which lineage, property, and various powers are passed down from mother to daughter. Patrilineal societies pass property and power from father to son. Patrilocal societies are those in which wives move into their husbands' households; in matrilocal societies, men move into their wives' households.

Finally, before further discussion of social organization, it should be noted that some traditions and customs have survived to the present day, whereas others have not. Almost all of those that have continued have been changed—some dramatically—by contact with the dominant European American culture. A prime example of such changes is the fact that most Indians today are at least nominally Christian, and all live within the American legal system. Polygamy used to be common among Indian tribes; today, at least legally, it is nonexistent. Tribal chiefs still exist, but they are ultimately under the control of the United States government. While there will be a brief discussion of modern conditions, all the following will be referred to in the past tense as an indication that times have changed since first contact between Europeans and Indians.

Lineage Patterns. Unlike European traditions, in which the male line is almost always considered predominant, there are a number of different traditions among Indians. Matrilineage

PATTERNS OF DESCENT

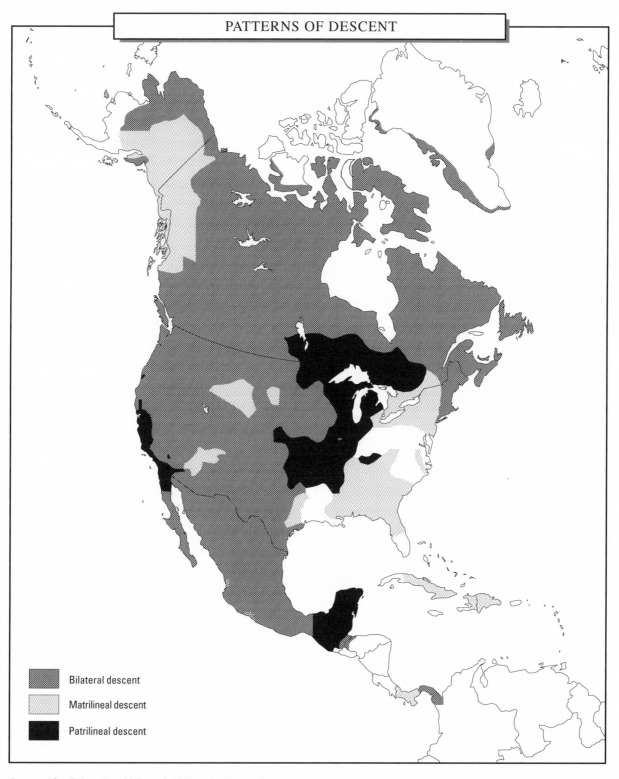

Bilateral descent

Matrilineal descent

Patrilineal descent

Source: After Driver, Harold E., and William C. Massey, *Comparative Studies of North American Indians*, 1957.

was quite common. In many Indian cultures, the men spent most of their time outside, hunting and fishing or conducting warfare. The women were in charge of the household and often tended crops. In some cases, such as certain Inuit groups, the men customarily lived in "men's houses," while the regular households were composed entirely of women and children.

In the Southwest, patrilineal descent was more common. Power and property were passed from father to son or from brother to brother. Wives often moved into their husbands' households at marriage.

In a few cases there was bilateral lineage, and the naming and meaning of various relatives were complex indeed. Some tribes described fathers and fathers' brothers by the same term, while differentiating between mothers and mothers' sisters. Many variations took place. Unfortunately, since many of these customs had already been altered before they were seriously studied, the situations can be confusing.

Marriage within a clan was almost always forbidden. In some cases, the marriage had to be outside the moiety. In some cultures, notably the Subarctic tribes, marriage between cousins was encouraged, but incest was almost a universal taboo. While it is impossible to determine how ancient taboos originated, as they are usually assigned to the dictates of gods and spirits, these rules are remarkably logical in terms of modern genetics, which also discourages marriage between close relatives.

The one common custom among many Indian tribes that was totally abolished (at least legally) by U.S. law was polygamy. In many Indian cultures it was customary for a man, especially a man of power and influence, to have several wives. In some tribes, the number of wives a man married was an important sign of prestige.

Political Power. The common stereotype of the old chief sitting on his blanket and decreeing orders for the tribe was actually a very uncommon system of government among American Indians. There were some such chiefs, certainly; the Natchez of Alabama and Louisiana, for example, were ruled by a chief called the Great Sun, who was practically considered a god, was bowed to regardless of what he said, and was carried on a litter. Lesser men left his presence by walking backward. He was an absolute dictator.

Much more common, however, was a chief who was chosen by election, inherited his title but could be deposed by common opinion, or simply became chief because he proved himself in battle or had great wealth.

The Athapaskan peoples of the Subarctic, whose political system is probably the best understood because they were among the last Indians to be significantly influenced by white culture, elected their chief. This chief was far from dictatorial, and he was answerable to a village council. Chosen for his abilities, he was not necessarily an old man or significantly involved in religious ceremonies.

In many cases, religious leaders were also political leaders. The shamans among the Eskimos (Inuits) were probably the most powerful people in their tribes, but the political structure

there was very loose, and occasionally great warriors achieved political power for a time. The Crow of the northwestern Plains had a chief with widespread power, but he became chief by agreement of the tribal members.

Gender Roles. Gender roles among American Indians, including the division of labor between men and women and the amounts of social and political power held by each, were first observed and studied by European men who applied their own strong cultural biases and perceptions to what they observed. As a consequence, gender roles in American Indian societies represent an area of study that has been subject to some debate and reinterpretation. As a general rule, men were hunters, warriors, and the (official) leaders, while women kept up the homes and often tended crops. Such division is not surprising for societies that were largely agrarian or were oriented toward hunting or fishing; preindustrial European societies functioned in much the same way.

Yet there were a number of exceptions. While men almost always were officially in charge, women sometimes held considerable power. Among the Hopi, for example, the individual households were the most important unit, and they were run by women. The household had a sacred bundle (fetish), which was owned by the oldest woman in the household and passed down from mother to daughter. The ceremonies involving these fetishes were held by the brother or son of this woman. The village chief was a man, and the chief generally was more a mediator than a ruler. This post was handed down from father to son. There was also a war chief, who had dictatorial powers in time of war but was chosen on the basis of his ability rather than lineage.

Social Organization. The degree of social organization within and among groups varied widely among tribes, from loosely knit groups of small families to huge nations with complex political structures.

Probably the most highly organized group of North American Indians were the Iroquois. This was a league of six nations, the Mohawk, Seneca, Oneida, Tuscarora, Cayuga, and Onondaga. While these groups spoke a common language family and had many customs in common, their uniting was mainly a result of their warfare with the Algonquians, the other major group in New York and southeastern Quebec. The union was strengthened when the French, the first European settlers in the area, sided with the Algonquians. In the French and Indian War, the Iroquois Confederacy sided with the English.

The prehistoric traditions of the Iroquois are hard to determine, because they had very early contact with Europeans, and this contact was usually violent. It is known, however, that Iroquois society was probably the closest to a genuinely matriarchal society in North America.

Among the Iroquois, the women owned the property, arranged the marriages, and ruled the extended families, who lived in large numbers in longhouses—log cabins that could hold a great number of people of several generations. The original rulers were called sachems, but they were more mediators in tribal disagreements than rulers or dictators. Early

European reports suggested that the real power was held by the women.

At the opposite extreme were the tribes of the Subarctic and Arctic, including the Athapaskans, Eskimos (Inuits), and Aleuts. These people had an extremely loose political structure. Where there were chiefs at all, they were generally either elected or simply assumed to be in charge because they had proved themselves. These people were not particularly warlike; they were often nomadic, moving in search of game.

Generally, the family unit was the most important social structure. The family unit varied from a small, nuclear family consisting of a husband, one or more wives, and any number of children, to large, extended families spanning several generations. A group of families constituted a clan, with common historical ancestors, often supposedly descended from a spirit or even an animal. Beyond the clan was the moiety. Paramount in most cases was the tribe, although even here there were great differences. In the Northeast, the tribe tended to be highly powerful, with a complex political structure. In the Northwest, small clans tended to be most powerful. In the Southwest, larger clans prevailed, and disputes among clans were settled by councils of chiefs.

Contemporary Conditions. As stated previously, American Indian societies today—although some traditions continue and others are being rediscovered and reintroduced—reflect the disruption and cultural adaptation brought about by centuries of contact with European-derived culture. In addition to the wide variety of traditional lifeways of American Indians, which continue to provide differences among tribes, the structures of contemporary Indian societies are strongly affected by where Indians live today. Broadly speaking, three categories may be delineated: those who live in urban areas or large towns, those who live on reservations, and those who live in very remote areas (as in the Subarctic).

American Indians in cities and towns, although still facing certain biases and prejudices, have generally acculturated to the dominant white culture. Moreover, because there has been considerable intermarriage, it is not always obvious that an individual is of Indian descent. Reservation Indians, on the other hand, are more likely to have preserved the old rituals, and reservation villages often still have chiefs and shamans. (It might be noted, however, that income from tourism has sometimes also played a part in the maintenance or reestablishment of certain ceremonies or customs.)

There are still some Indians, mostly in very remote areas, who have been little affected by white culture. Probably the most widespread group still holding to ancient customs in many ways are the Athapaskans of Alaska, the Yukon, and the Northwest Territories. They live in log cabins in tiny villages, usually with no more than eighty or ninety residents. White residents, or even visitors, are rare apart from a few government officials and schoolteachers. English is the working language, but the native languages are used for traditional ceremonies. Typically, at a major event such as a birth, marriage, or death, two ceremonies will be held. One is in the ancient language (complete with dances and songs) and is usually barred to whites; the other is a Christian ceremony similar to one that might be held in any city or town in North America.

—*Marc Goldstein*

See also Clans; Gender relations and roles; Marriage and divorce; Political organization and leadership; Social control, traditional; Societies, non-kin-based.

BIBLIOGRAPHY

Bandi, Hans-George. *Eskimo Prehistory*. College: University of Alaska Press, 1979. An archaeological study of early Eskimos, including illustrations, diagrams, and maps, discussing their culture from arrival upon the American continent.

Hamilton, Charles. *Cry of the Thunderbird: The American Indian's Own Story*. New ed. Norman: University of Oklahoma Press, 1972. A compilation of articles by American Indians about their culture, including memories of childhood, historical beginnings, and contemporary conditions.

Oswalt, Wendell H. *This Land Was Theirs: A Study of North American Indians*. 4th ed. Mountain View, Calif.: Mayfield, 1988. Description of representative tribes in various regions; includes photographs and maps showing tribal areas.

Spencer, Robert F., Jesse D. Jennings, et al. *The Native Americans*. 2d ed. New York: Harper & Row, 1977. An encyclopedic discussion of American Indian culture, from prehistory to contemporary times.

Viola, Herman J. *After Columbus: The Smithsonian Chronicles of the American Indians*. Washington, D.C.: Smithsonian Institution Press, 1990. A history of North American Indian cultures, with a particular emphasis on the changes in those cultures as a result of European influence.

Kiowa: Tribe

CULTURE AREA: Plains
LANGUAGE GROUP: Kiowa-Tanoan (Uto-Aztecan)
PRIMARY LOCATION: Oklahoma
POPULATION SIZE: 9,421 (1990 U.S. Census)

The Kiowas, whose language is related to the Rio Grande Pueblo Indians, originally lived in western Montana. The earliest Kiowa villages in this area date to the early 1600's. The Kiowas (Kiowa means "main people") moved a century later to the Yellowstone River region in eastern Montana and eventually settled in the Black Hills of South Dakota. Here they traded with the Mandans, learned how to use horses, and began hunting buffalo. They also became noted for their military exploits and organized their tribe into military societies. As nomadic hunters they followed buffalo herds, lived in tipis, worshiped a sun god (Taimay), and performed the Sun Dance. Unlike other Plains tribes, however, Kiowas did not allow violence or self-torture during performance of the eight-day Sun Dance ceremony. Kiowa warriors fasted, prayed, exchanged sacred medicine bundles, and did penance but did not mutilate their bodies with knives or spears as did the Mandans.

Kiowas frequently fought wars against Caddos, Utes, Apaches, Arapahos, Cheyennes, and other Plains tribes. Among the Kiowa, membership in the warrior society called the "Principal Dogs," or "Ten Bravest," was highly sought after and esteemed. Only the ten warriors who had repeatedly demonstrated greatest bravery in battle could belong. The leader of the Principal Dogs wore a long sash over his shoulder when going into battle. When the fighting began he got off his horse, anchored his sash to the ground with his spear, and stood at that spot, shouting encouragement to his comrades. He could not leave his post until another Principal Dog pulled his sash from the ground.

In the 1780's the Sioux drove the Kiowas from the Black Hills, and they moved farther south into Nebraska, Kansas, and northern Oklahoma. The American explorers Meriwether Lewis and William Clark reported meeting Kiowas along the North Platte River in 1805. Comanche Indians living in the areas originally fought off the Kiowas, but the two eventually formed an alliance that lasted into the twentieth century. In their new homeland, the Kiowas continued to hunt buffalo and raid their enemies, chiefly the Apaches and Cheyennes, taking horses and territory. Peace accords were reached in the 1830's when new enemies appeared: American pioneers and traders on the Santa Fe and Butterfield trails. In the "Kiowa Wars" of the 1830's and 1840's, Plains Indians fought together against whites moving through the region on wagon trains or cattle drives. The Great Plains were not yet the destination of these migrants, because many saw the region as too empty, hot, and dry to support any type of agriculture, and called it the Great American Desert. They simply moved through the Plains heading for California and Oregon, which had more hospitable climates.

These views changed after the Civil War, however, when the Plains were considered ready for settlement because of the introduction of railroads. This postwar movement of white settlers into the center of Indian country led to another series of wars in the 1870's. The Kiowas debated how to deal with this new intrusion. Kicking Bird and Little Mountain, two principal chiefs, wanted peace, but Satank (Sitting Bear) and Satanta (White Bear), leader of the Principal Dogs, called for war. Satanta led several raids into Texas, and the Red River War of 1874-1875 began. The war faction killed Kicking Bird when he continued to oppose violent conflict. Satanta became chief but was captured by General George Armstrong Custer's forces and sentenced to prison. In 1878 he took his own life, jumping from a prison hospital window in Huntsville, Texas. Other Kiowa leaders suffered similar violent deaths, Satank being shot while trying to escape from the Fort Sill, Oklahoma, prison, and Sky Walker, the Kiowa religious leader, dying in a Florida prison. Most of these Kiowa warriors were buried at Fort Sill in a cemetery referred to as the "Indian Arlington."

By 1878 most of the Kiowas had submitted to living on a reservation in southeastern Oklahoma. Today the tribe has its headquarters in Caddo County and survives by raising cattle, farming, and leasing oil rights to their land. Kiowa artworks are on display at the Southern Plains Indian Museum and Craft Center in Anadarko. Perhaps the most famous living Kiowa is

N. Scott Momaday, a novelist and professor of comparative literature, who won a Pulitzer Prize in 1969 for his novel *House Made of Dawn* (1968), a sensitive portrayal of a Native American's conflict between traditional ways of life and modern culture.

—*Leslie V. Tischauser*

See also Kicking Bird; Kiowa-Tanoan language family; Military societies; Momaday, N. Scott; Plains; Satanta; Uto-Aztecan language family.

Kiowa Apache. *See* Apache Tribe of Oklahoma

Kiowa-Tanoan language family

CULTURE AREAS: Plains, Southwest
TRIBES AFFECTED: Hano, Isleta, Jemez, Kiowa, Nambe, Pojoaque, Pecos, Picuris, Sandia, San Juan, San Ildefonso, Santa Clara, Taos, Tesuque

The Kiowa-Tanoan language family consists of four languages: Kiowa, Tiwa, Tewa, and Towa. The Kiowa people are a Plains tribe, currently living in southwestern Oklahoma. The Tanoan languages, which include Tiwa (Isleta, Picuris, Sandia, Taos), Tewa (Hano, Nambe, San Juan, San Ildefonso, Santa Clara, Pojoaque, Tesuque), and Towa (Jemez), are spoken primarily in New Mexico, with the exception of Arizona Tewa, which is spoken on the First Mesa of the Hopi Reservation, in the village of Hano.

John Harrington first proposed the relationship of Kiowa to Tanoan in 1910. Wick Miller and George and Edith Trager later published evidence to support this relationship, and in the 1960's Kenneth Hale provided sound correspondences and reconstructions which demonstrated that Kiowa and Tanoan indeed form a closely related language family. The internal subgrouping of Tanoan is more problematic. Some researchers have considered the Tanoan languages to form a subgroup, viewing Kiowa as the most divergent member of the family. Others place Kiowa on the same level as Tiwa, Tewa, and Towa, suggesting that Kiowa-Tanoan split directly into four branches. Dialectal variation exists among the Tiwa and Tewa. Tiwa is generally divided into Northern and Southern Tiwa, while Arizona Tewa (Hano) exhibits several differences from the Rio Grande Tewa dialects. Towa is represented solely by Jemez, although the language of the Pecos Pueblo, which was abandoned in 1838, may have been Towa as well.

In 1929 Edward Sapir posited a relationship between Kiowa-Tanoan and Uto-Aztecan. Benjamin Whorf and George Trager later published a list of 102 proposed cognates in support of the Aztec-Tanoan hypothesis; however, this relationship is controversial, and evidence to date is insufficient to support the proposal.

The languages of the Kiowa-Tanoan family vary widely in their viability. In the early 1980's, Kiowa was spoken by only a few hundred adults, making it an endangered language. The Summer Institute of Linguistics estimated that in 1977 there were about 1,800 speakers of Northern Tiwa, 2,500 speakers of Southern Tiwa, 4,500 speakers of Tewa, and 1,800 speakers of Jemez. The use of native languages is strong in some pueblos (Jemez, Isleta, Taos), while in others the population speaking native languages is composed mainly of older adults.

See also Kiowa; Prehistory—Southwest; Pueblo tribes, Eastern; Uto-Aztecan language family.

Kivas

TRIBES AFFECTED: Pueblo tribes (prehistoric to modern)

SIGNIFICANCE: The kiva is a circular, semi-subterranean structure used for ceremonial purposes; each tribal clan or society, usually exclusively male, has its own kiva, where members meet to commune with the spirits and with one another

The kiva first appeared in the Southwest among the prehistoric Mogollon, Hohokam, and Anasazi cultures. The Mogollon were the first to begin building permanent houses; it is likely that they conceived and developed their architecture themselves, without outside influence. By circa 100 C.E., the Mogollon circular pit house consisted of a hole several feet deep that was lined with poles and brush to create low sidewalls; a single center post supported a conical roof. A short, sloping ramp on one side served as an entryway, and a hole in the center of the roof provided a vent for the fire pit. As the Mogollon constructed their pit house villages, they always built one extra structure, usually deeper and larger, which served as the kiva—their ceremonial center.

The Hohokam were also pit house builders, but their structures differed from those of the Mogollon both in design and in construction techniques. Starting with a large rectangular hole 20 to 30 feet in length, the Hohokam then built an entire "wattle-and-daub" structure within the pit. This method, consisting of small posts interlaced with brush and packed with mud and clay, offered better protection from the elements. The roof now had a double pitch, but entry was still gained through a sloping ramp on one side. Like the Mogollon, they designated one large pit house as a ceremonial kiva.

About 500 C.E., the Modified Basketmaker Anasazi developed a circular pit house, about 5 feet deep and up to 25 feet in diameter. The walls of the pit were plastered with clay, and entrance was by ladder through the smoke hole. In the packed earthen floor, a small hole near the central fire pit represented *sipapu*, the opening through which humankind emerged onto the face of the earth, according to Puebloan legends of creation. Originally, the Anasazi pit house served as both home and ceremonial center; low stone walls were eventually used to divide the pit house into two separate spaces, one for daily living and one for ceremonial functions.

The Pueblo Anasazi refined the earlier pit house into a more formal ceremonial structure which was deeper in the ground; it had stone-lined walls and floor, a stone bench around the inside, and stone pilasters to support the roof. When the Anasazi built their stone pueblos consisting of long, slightly curved rows of contiguous rooms, they placed their kivas in the center.

From ancient times to the present, the kiva has served as the center of Puebloan ceremonial life. Every pueblo has several kivas, one for each of the clans or societies that play roles in influencing the spirits on behalf of all the people. Clan membership and access to the kivas are reserved for men only. Thus, the kiva also serves as a clubhouse for the men, giving them a place to work and socialize that is exclusively their own—an important function in a matrilineal society.

See also Architecture—Southwest; Pit house; Prehistory—Southwest; Pueblo; Religion; Sacred, the.

Klah, Hosteen

Klah, Hosteen (Oct., 1867, Bear Mountain, N.Mex. Territory—Feb. 27, 1937, near Gallup, N.Mex.): Medicine man, weaver

ALSO KNOWN AS: Left Handed

TRIBAL AFFILIATION: Navajo

SIGNIFICANCE: Klah was an influential Navajo medicine man; as a weaver, he represented his people at two world's fairs

Hosteen Klah was born in October, 1867, at Bear Mountain, near Fort Wingate, as his family returned home from captivity at Bosque Redondo. As was Navajo tradition, he was called *Away Eskay* (Baby Boy) until some characteristic suggested a nickname—"Klah" (Left Handed). The ceremonial name given to babies at their naming rites is considered personal property and is seldom known outside the immediate family.

Navajo custom dictates that one studies chants and ceremonies only with teachers belonging to the clans of one's mother, father, or grandmother. In Klah's case, many of his kinsmen were shamans and he began studying at an early age. By age ten, he knew the full ceremony of the Hail Chant; then he learned the Wind Chant and the Bear Chant, which lasts for nine days and includes hundreds of chants, prayers, and several elaborate sand paintings.

When not studying, Klah tended sheep and helped his mother and sister with their weaving. He became an accomplished weaver himself and, in 1892, exhibited his weaving at the World's Columbian Exposition in Chicago as a representative of the New Mexico Territory.

As a youth, Klah began learning the Yeibichai Ceremony from its leading chanter, Hathile Nah-Cloie (Laughing Chanter). There were seven forms of this long and complicated ceremony and Klah eventually knew five of them. Altogether, Klah studied for twenty-six years before holding his first Yeibichai Ceremony as principal chanter. He sent invitations to this nine-day ceremony throughout the Navajo Reservation and, at its conclusion, was acknowledged as the greatest Yeibichai chanter.

In 1916, Klah wove a rug illustrating several Yeibichai dancers. Other medicine men objected, demanding that the rug be destroyed, but the furor died out once the rug was sold and off the reservation. In 1919-1920, Klah wove the first rug based on a sand painting; it was called "The Whirling Log," from the Yeibichai Ceremony. Again, other Navajos protested, thinking that an accurate and permanent representation of a sand painting would bring disaster to the tribe. Klah's status as a medicine man allowed him to do as he pleased, however, and he exhibited the rug at the Gallup Ceremonial, where it won a blue ribbon. The rug was sold to a tourist, who asked Klah to weave two more to complete the set of Yeibichai sand paintings. This was the beginning of Klah's career as a weaver of ceremonial rugs, and between 1919 and 1937, he wove twenty-five sand-painting tapestries.

In 1934, Klah again represented the Navajos in the New Mexico exhibit at the Century of Progress Exposition in Chicago, demonstrating sand painting. He died in February, 1937. The Museum of Navajo Ceremonial Art in Santa Fe was built as a memorial to Hosteen Klah and houses many of his sand paintings and weavings.

See also Chantways; Navajo; Sand painting; Weaving.

Klamath: Tribe

CULTURE AREA: Northwest Coast
LANGUAGE GROUP: Lutuamian
PRIMARY LOCATION: Oregon
POPULATION SIZE: 3,097 (1990 U.S. Census)

Approximately ten thousand years ago, the ancestors of the Klamath and the Modoc moved into an area encircled by the Great Basin to the east, the Cascades to the west, the central Plateau to the north, and the present-day California border. Because of these natural boundaries, the Klamath remained isolated from European Americans longer than many neighboring tribes. Klamath culture remained intact into the 1800's, and when trapper Peter Skene Ogden met the Klamath in 1826, he noted that they owned one horse. Early Klamath population figures are estimated at about a thousand.

Because their food came principally from the water, the Klamath did not require or use the horse as other tribes did for hunting, although by the mid-nineteenth century the Klamath used the horse and gun to raid other tribes. Traditionally Klamath culture followed a seasonal cycle; spring, summer, and fall were devoted to gathering roots and berries and securing a year's catch of fish. One of the staples of the Klamath diet was a pond lily seed, the wokas, which was gathered in the marshes in August. Another staple was fish, including suckers, salmon, and trout, caught in the spring runs. Fishing persisted into the winter, although the winter catch was limited.

By late fall, the Klamath began building their winter settlement, which generally already had some permanent buildings.

This early twentieth century photograph of a Klamath chief shows, in his clothing and headdress, the influence of other Indian cultures. (Library of Congress)

Because the climate could be harsh (with up to several feet of snow), the Klamath built semi-subterranean earthlodges, sometimes up to 4 feet deep. They lived in these for the winter and relied on whatever provisions they had stored.

The clothing of the Klamath differed from that of their neighbors on the Columbia Plateau. Men and women wore skirts made of fibers and wore basketry caps. Buckskin was not worn until the nineteenth century. The Klamath also practiced tattooing, flattening the heads of infants, and the wearing of a dentalium through the nose. The tribe with which they had the most contact before the nineteenth century was the Modoc, who spoke a similar language. The Klamath were more influenced by Pacific Northwest culture than were the Modoc, who were closer to their southern neighbors.

By the mid-nineteenth century, the horse and gun were integrated into Klamath society. Contact with European Americans increased as whites crossed Klamath country on their way to the gold fields in Northern California; some settled in the region. The Klamath tried to sustain peaceful relations with the white settlers, and there were several instances where the Klamath punished their own for committing offenses against whites. The land that the Klamath occupied, however, was wanted for white settlement. In 1864 the Klamath signed a treaty with the federal government; in exchange for their land, they were awarded a reservation of 1,104,847 acres, the Klamath Agency, located in present-day south-central Oregon. The government planned to transform the Klamath into self-sufficient farmers once they were removed to the reservation.

By the twentieth century, their economy included ranching and some business; many incomes were supplemented by or derived from timber revenues. A small number practiced farming. In the early twentieth century, several claims were filed and won regarding boundary disputes. Tribal government consisted of a general council. In the early 1950's a movement for termination gained support. (The tribe had earlier rejected the 1934 Indian Reorganization Act.) By 1954, termination was finalized, and each Klamath enrolled in the tribe was allotted $43,500 in exchange for the sale of reservation land to the federal government. Termination meant the end of tribal status. For many Klamath, termination introduced more problems, as there were no plans for their future. Many were the victims of enterprising and unscrupulous entrepreneurs. After years of effort, tribal status was regained in 1991.

See also Fish and fishing; Modoc; Northwest Coast; Termination policy.

Klikitat: Tribe

CULTURE AREAS: Northwest Coast, Plateau
LANGUAGE GROUP: Sahaptian
PRIMARY LOCATION: Washington State

Before contact with European Americans, the Cayuse had pushed the Klikitats west into south-central Washington, the area with which they have come to be traditionally associated. After the migration west, the Klikitats divided into two groups. The Western Klikitats continued past the Cascade Mountains into southwestern Washington and integrated with the Cowlitzes. The Eastern Klikitats lived on the north side of the Columbia River, along its tributaries, including the Klikitat, Lewis, and White Salmon rivers, in south-central Washington.

The Klikitats followed the nomadic lifestyle common to the Mid-Columbia Indians, and their subsistence patterns were a cycle of rich salmon fishing in the spring followed by the gathering of roots and berries in the summer and fall. The hunting of game supplemented their diet. The narrows at The Dalles on the Columbia River was one of the prized fishing locations. Even before contact, fishing rights were passed down from father to son, with the most powerful families claiming the locations where the salmon could be obtained most easily. Because The Dalles was known for its plentiful catches, the area surrounding it became a popular trading post. Summer berry picking in the foothills of Mount Adams followed, and the Klikitats gathered huckleberries, which were either eaten raw, boiled, dried, or smoked. Roots were another staple, and the Klikitats dug for the camas root with a digging stick as well as digging wild carrots, onions, celery, and parsley. All the food sources—fish, berries, and roots—were preserved for the upcoming winter months. In addition to preserving the food, the women made beautiful baskets and became known for their skill.

Contact with European Americans began in the early 1800's with the Lewis and Clark expedition, followed by fur traders. Because of their location on the Columbia River, the Klikitats undoubtedly interacted with the fur traders considerably, which might explain their subsequent reputation as traders. In 1825 the Hudson's Bay Company established Fort Vancouver on the Columbia River. Company officials asked some of the Klikitats to move to the fort and act as hunters for members living at the fort. By the 1840's, Klikitats had moved into the Willamette Valley, which had been occupied by the Kalapuyas. As more and more settlers moved into the area, pressure mounted for the Klikitats to leave. Not all of their relations with the American settlers were unfriendly, as some of the Klikitats served the Americans in the Rogue Wars of the 1850's.

In 1855, Washington territorial governor Isaac Stevens held the Walla Walla Council with many of the Plateau tribes. The Klikitats were subsumed under the leadership of Kamiakin, the appointed Yakima chief. The Klikitats had always interacted closely with the Yakimas, as was noted by Lieutenant George Gibbs, who participated in a railroad survey in the Columbia Basin. Kamiakin represented fourteen signatory tribes, including the Klikitats, and the Yakima Treaty that he signed (although he claimed that he did not sign the treaty with the intention of relinquishing land) allowed for the creation of the Yakima Reservation, with a land base of 1,250,000 acres. Dissatisfied with the treaty, many Klikitats joined Kamiakin in the Yakima War of 1855 and the Cascade War of 1856. Part of the Klikitat discontent stemmed from the loss of their identity, although one of the first chiefs on the Yakima Reservation was White Swan, a Klikitat.

After 1856, many of the Klikitats moved to the Yakima Reservation and took part in such federal policies as the General Allotment Act of 1887. In 1935, the Confederated Tribes of the Yakima Reservation organized. The government consists of a general council and a Yakima tribal council. A few Klikitats still live near traditional fishing locations on the Klikitat and White Salmon rivers and continue to fish at some twenty sites along the Klikitat River.

See also Cayuse; Kamiakin; Yakima; Yakima War.

Knives

TRIBES AFFECTED: Pantribal
SIGNIFICANCE: Knives have been in use throughout prehistoric and historic times

Knives, which may be defined simply as tools for cutting, doubtless were carried across the Bering Strait land bridge when the ancestors of American Indians entered the Americas tens of thousands of years ago. These early knives would have resembled those in common use throughout the prehistoric period: stone knives flaked on both faces to form a sharp edge. Some knives, mostly for special purposes, were made from other materials or by other techniques in the prehistoric era. These included the cold-hammered copper knives used as grave offerings by Indians around the Great Lakes from 2500 to 500 B.C.E. and the bone snow knives used by Inuits for cutting blocks for igloo construction. Another Inuit knife, the ulu, or "woman's knife," was half-moon-shaped and made from ground slate. With the advent of Europeans, metals became more available for knives, arriving sometimes as trade knives and sometimes as other iron items that were remade into knives by Indian craftspeople. One special type of knife was the crooked knife, used by the Iroquois especially for carving false face masks. The crooked knife was made of trade iron but was based on an earlier native design made of bone.

See also Lances and spears; Projectile points; Tools; Weapons.

Konkapot, John (c. 1700, Housatonic River valley, Mass.—c. 1775, Stockbridge, Mass.): Chief

ALSO KNOWN AS: Captain Konkapot, Captain John
TRIBAL AFFILIATION: Mahican
SIGNIFICANCE: Christianized John Konkapot aided Calvinist missionaries among his band of Mahicans

After the powerful Mohawks forced the Mahicans to abandon their ancestral lands near Albany, New York, in 1664, the band moved to the Housatonic Valley of western Massachusetts. In 1724, tribal chief Konkapot ceded his land to the British. He remained friendly with the British, aiding them during the French and Indian Wars. Konkapot was commissioned a captain in 1734.

In 1736, Yale missionary John Sergeant founded the Stockbridge mission among the Mahicans, who then became known as the Stockbridge. Konkapot was soon Christianized, adopt-

ing the name John, and assisted Sergeant in his mission. When Massachusetts congregational minister Jonathan Edwards succeeded Sergeant in 1750, he befriended Konkapot. Konkapot died on the eve of the American Revolution. His band, under Samson Occom, migrated to Oneida, New York, in 1786, then again, under John W. Quinney, to Wisconsin in 1822, where they merged with the Munsee band of Lenni Lenapes (Delawares).

See also Indian-white relations—French colonial; Mahican; Missions and missionaries; Occom, Samson; Quinney, John W.

Koster: Archaeological site

DATE: 6400 B.C.E.-1200 C.E.
LOCATION: Illinois
CULTURES AFFECTED: Archaic, Mississippian, Riverton, Woodland

Koster is one of the most intensively investigated sites in the midwestern United States. Excavations conducted under the direction of archaeologist Stuart Streuver revealed thirteen sequential strata dating from the Early Archaic through the Mississippian traditions. A seasonally occupied hamlet was established around 6400 B.C.E. Deer, freshwater mussels, and other foods were cooked in hearths, and grinding stones were used to process wild seeds. Stone adzes were used for woodworking, while bone awls and needles were used for basketmaking and leatherworking. Hematite beads, imported from Michigan, indicate long-distance trade.

Between 6000 and 5800 B.C.E., Koster was a seasonal camp for making stone tools. By 5600-5000 B.C.E., there was a permanent village with houses built of large posts on artificial terraces. Tools included gravers and grooved adzes. The longest occupied permanent village at the site was established around 3900 B.C.E. About 100 to 150 people subsisted year-round on wild resources such as fish, ducks, geese, hickory nuts, marsh elder, and goosefoot. Some individuals lived to the age of seventy. Evidence shows that people incapacitated by arthritis were cared for. Copper was traded from Lake Superior.

Koster was reoccupied as a deer-butchering camp around 2000 B.C.E. and as a short-lived village of the Riverton culture around 1500-1200 B.C.E. The earliest pottery was produced by Early Woodland people of the Black Sand culture (200-100 B.C.E.), followed by a Middle Woodland village of the White Hall (400-800 C.E.) culture and a Late Woodland village of the Jersey Bluff (800-1000) culture. The Jersey Bluff occupation, an agricultural village of a thousand people covering more than 25 acres, was the most extensive at the site. The last occupation was a Mississippian village dating from 900 to 1200.

See also Mississippian; Prehistory—Northeast; Woodland.

Koyukon: Tribe

CULTURE AREA: Subarctic
LANGUAGE GROUP: Athapaskan
PRIMARY LOCATION: Central Alaska

The Koyukon tribe is a subgroup of the Athapaskan family, living in small villages along the Yukon and Kuyokuk rivers in central Alaska. Actual population figures are sketchy, because census figures are notoriously inaccurate in these remote areas, but there are probably three or four hundred people who consider themselves Koyukons. The Athapaskans probably migrated from Siberia over the land bridge that existed on what is now the Bering Strait sometime during the last Ice Age, between ten thousand and twenty-five thousand years ago, and may have been the first humans to arrive in North America.

Koyukons were not known by white Americans until the 1890's, when the Klondike gold rush brought many prospectors into the area. Even then, the natives lived in widely separated tiny villages, and there was little intercourse between the two groups. The native culture was largely untouched, and the land was never taken from the Koyukons until the 1980's, when much of it became the Yukon Flats National Monument. Nearing the end of the twentieth century, the villages had few white residents, most of whom were teachers and other government workers.

Koyukons generally live in log cabins heated by wood stoves. Except in the schools, electricity is rare; it is provided by local generators, which are extremely unreliable because of the intensely cold winters. Telephone service is by satellite. There are no roads to any Koyukon villages. English is the working language for most young Koyukons, though some of the older people still speak the native language, and tribal ceremonies are still held in that language.

The villages have a very loose style of government, with an elected chief whose main function is to act as a liaison with the federal and state governments. Children are taught in one-room schoolhouses, with high school available only in Fairbanks or Fort Yukon, neither of which has a significant Koyukon population.

See also Athapaskan language family; Potlatch; Subarctic.

Kuksu rituals and society

TRIBES AFFECTED: Costanoan, Maidu, Miwok, Patwin (Southern Wintu), Pomo, Northern Yokuts

SIGNIFICANCE: The Kuksu ritual and the emergence of the Kuksu society represent a shift from traditional religious beliefs that resulted from contact with European Americans

The "Kuksu complex," as it is sometimes called by anthropologists, refers to an integrated set of rituals or ceremonies originally practiced by the river Patwin of the central Sacramento Valley of California. In its traditional context, Kuksu ritual provided for the initiation of young males into adulthood. Through time, however, as a result of contact with Spanish, Mexican, and Anglo populations and influence from the Native American Ghost Dance, the Kuksu cycle became the domain of a secret society dedicated to revitalizing native culture. As this became more and more the case, the influence of the Kuksu society spread to include a significant number of tribal groups in central-northern California.

The Kuksu Rituals. The Kuksu rituals, as they were traditionally practiced, took place in semi-subterranean houses and involved dancers who impersonated important mythical spirits and deities. For example, the lead dancer typically played the part of Moki, a spirit of great significance in the scheme of Patwin cosmology. Other spirit characters were Tuya ("Big-Headed Dancer") and Chelito—who helped coordinate the movements of Tuya.

Of all the Kuksu ceremonies, Hesi was the most important. This ceremony began the ritual cycle which ran from fall to spring. The Hesi ritual took four days to complete and, as is typical of many Native American ceremonies, was conducted in a highly formal and prescriptive manner. Each dancer had to know the precise set of choreographed movements associated with each of the spirit characters. If a dancer made a mistake, he ran the risk of insulting the spirit and, thus, creating the possibility of bringing bad luck to the village.

Most of the Kuksu rituals involved elaborate use of performance paraphernalia. Masks, veiled headdresses, feathered cloaks, and drums (otherwise rare in California) were all used to enhance the performances of the dancers. Most of these materials actually allowed the dancers to impersonate various spirits, especially those associated with creation myths, and to enhance the status of the dancers as mystics. In the Hesi ritual, for example, young initiates were subjected to a dance that involved the symbolic killing of the initiates. The dancers pretended, through clever manipulation of knives and other sharp objects, to slit the throats of the initiates. After this was done the dancers, most of whom were actual shamans, acted out the revival of their subjects.

Cultural Functions. As mentioned above, the Kuksu ceremonies originally functioned primarily as a means of initiating adolescent males into the status of adults. Anthropologists and historians have also pointed to a number of more subtle functions. For example, most of the religious themes employed in these ceremonies relied to a significant degree on references to mythical characters. This suggests that a major function of these ceremonies involved the reinforcement of mythic stories of cosmogony (origins) and cosmology (the nature of the cosmos). As such, these dances and ceremonies not only had the general effect of telling members of society how the world came into existence but also afforded a way to make these ideas concrete and visible through ritual action.

Anthropologists have also noted that the Kuksu complex defined status differences across both age and gender dimensions. For example, two levels of status based on age were always clearly defined through the structure and carrying out of Kuksu ceremonies: young male initiates and their elders. Furthermore, the ceremonies essentially acted out much of the content of stories and myths, and these stories often carried themes indicating fundamental differences between the roles of males and females. Women, for example, were not allowed to attend Kuksu ceremonies; thus, by way of their exclusion, women were defined as fundamentally different from men. Moreover, many of the stories acted out in the dances pointed to specific tasks associated with men. This had the effect of reinforcing a division of labor into male and female activities.

Another emphasis found throughout the Kuksu cycle centered on the status and role of traditional healers. Among the Pomo, for example, the term "Kuksu" was used to refer to a specific type of healer. This individual was usually responsible for organizing and carrying out those ceremonies connected with the Kuksu cycle. This suggests, at least to some anthropologists, that shamans were extending their roles beyond part-time healing into a different function—that of community organizers. Moreover, some shamans were able to obtain greater overall status by way of elevating their participation in Kuksu rituals.

The Kuksu Society and Cult. As more and more people of European descent began to settle in central-northern California, inevitable problems associated with close and immediate contact with Native American groups arose. During the 1870's, 1880's, and 1890's, the Ghost Dance of the Great Basin and elsewhere in North America extended its influence into California. Kuksu practitioners began to incorporate elements of the Ghost Dance into their rituals. Prior to this time, the Kuksu had been organized into a secret society; with the introduction of Ghost Dance elements, the Kuksu society began to stimulate the formation of a reactionary organization whose primary goal was to invoke dead ancestors who would presumably expel whites from North America. Social scientists have referred to these types of associations as "revitalization" movements, for the underlying purpose of such movements was to revitalize a culture through purging all foreign and hostile elements. By 1900, many of the groups that had been involved with a more traditional approach to Kuksu themes had converted to a Ghost Dance version. This continued into the 1920's, when Kuksu eventually died out.

—*Michael Findlay*

See also California; Costanoan; Patwin; Pomo; Religion.

BIBLIOGRAPHY

Frickeberg, Walter, et al. *Pre-Columbian American Religions*. New York: Holt, Rinehart and Winston, 1968.

Heizer, Robert F., and M. A. Whipple. *The California Indians: A Source Book*. 2d ed. Berkeley: University of California Press, 1971.

Hultkrantz, Ake. *The Religions of the American Indians*. Berkeley: University of California Press, 1979.

Kroeber, Alfred L. *The Patwin and Their Neighbors*. Berkeley: University of California Press, 1932.

Loeb, Edwin Meyer. *The Eastern Kuksu Cult*. Berkeley: University of California Press, 1933.

_____. *The Western Kuksu Cult*. Berkeley: University of California Press, 1932.

Kutchin: Tribe

CULTURE AREAS: Arctic, Subarctic
LANGUAGE GROUP: Athapaskan
LOCATION: Northeastern Alaska, northwestern Yukon
POPULATION SIZE: 1,995 in Canada (Statistics Canada, based on 1991 census); estimated 600 in Alaska

The Kutchin are the largest subgroup of the northern Athapaskan family of tribes. They live mostly in small villages along the major rivers of Alaska and the Yukon, although many have migrated to the cities, principally Fairbanks, in search of a more viable lifestyle.

The largest concentration of Kutchin is in the Alaskan village of Fort Yukon. The rest are scattered around Alaska and the Yukon. Their numbers are impossible to determine accurately, as few fill out the census forms they are sent. Fort Yukon is the only village with a road system, and this system does not extend outside the village. Transportation among the villages is primarily by boat in the summer and dogsled in the winter, although there are airstrips in the villages, and small planes make daily landings, bringing mail and supplies ordered from Fairbanks.

The Kutchin language and lifestyle appear to be losing ground to white culture, though this may change as the movement toward Indian pride in heritage spreads. Fort Yukon has several stores and a reliable electricity supply. Elsewhere, people live in log cabins, trade mostly by barter, and eat a diet largely composed of moose and salmon.

The Kutchins' first major encounters with white people occurred during the Alaskan gold rush of the 1890's, but except in Fort Yukon, which has a significant white population, the effects have been minimal. In the smaller villages, the native culture still survives alongside the white, Christian culture that has been imported.

See also Arctic; Athapaskan language family; Subarctic.

Kutenai: Tribe

CULTURE AREA: Plateau
LANGUAGE GROUP: Kutenai
PRIMARY LOCATION: Washington State, British Columbia
POPULATION SIZE: 643 in U.S. (1990 U.S. Census); 565 in Canada (Statistics Canada, based on 1991 census)

The Kutenai (also spelled "Kootenai" and "Kootenay") lived in southeastern British Columbia and northern Montana and Idaho. Their distinct language places them in a linguistic family of their own. In prehistoric times, they lived east of the Rocky Mountains, but they were driven westward by traditional enemies, the Blackfoot. The tribe was from early times divided into two groups speaking different dialects: the Upper Kutenai, of the upper Kootenay (Kutenai) and Columbia rivers, and the Lower Kutenai, of the Lower Kootenay River. They were a nomadic people, traveling widely in search of buffalo. Known to be unusually tall, they were skilled in canoe building and in raising horses. Because they constantly moved about, there was no central government or chief; rather, each band had its own leader and council of elders. They worshiped the sun and expected their dead to some day meet the living at Pend Oreille Lake. The Kutenai, because of their isolated location, were among the last of the American Indian tribes to be contacted by whites. In fact, the Lower Kutenai were so isolated that they were still using stone tools in the late nineteenth century. Even into the twentieth century, they led relatively peaceful and unhampered lives. By the end of the twentieth century, the Kutenai were no longer nomadic, but lived in wood frame houses and relied mostly on wage labor for their living.

See also Buffalo; Plateau.

Kutenai language

CULTURE AREA: Northwest Coast
TRIBES AFFECTED: Adanekunik, Akamuik, Akeyenik, Akiskemikinik (Upper Kutenai); Lower Kutenai

Kutenai was the language used by tribes from the interior of British Columbia south to Montana and Idaho. It was thought by Edward Sapir in 1914 to be related to Beothukan, Algonquian, Salishan, Wakeshan, Yurok, and Wiyot in the Algonquian-Wakashan family, but this hypothesis has never been proved. There is also speculation of a Kutenai-Blackfoot connection, similarly unproved. In 1987, Joseph H. Greenberg, in *Language in the Americas*, placed Kutenai in the Almosan-Keresiouan family of the Northern Amerind subphylum with, among others, Salishan, Algonquian, and (distantly) Keresan, Siouan, Caddoan, and Iroquoian. Even in this last controversial and unproved grouping, Kutenai is relatively distinct.

The term Kutenai is apparently a Blackfoot word. The Kutenai called themselves San'ka. They were also called Flatbows, Kuspelu, Shalsa ulk, Skelsa-ulk, and Slenderbows. They lived along Kootenay Lake, Kootenay River, Arrow Lake, and the upper course of the Columbia River, and in southeastern British Columbia, northwestern Montana, northeastern Washington, and the northern tip of Idaho.

Kutenai is a tone language, like Chinese or Vietnamese. That is, an identical sequence of sounds will have varying meanings depending on the speaker's rising or falling pitch. Like any living language, it is in a state of flux, adapting to and borrowing freely from English.

The Kutenai have given their name to Kootenay River in British Columbia, Montana, and Idaho; to Kootenay Lake in British Columbia; to the Kootenai Mountains and Kootenai Falls in Montana; to Kootenai County, Idaho; and to a village, Kootenai, in Bonner County, Idaho.

See also Kutenai.

Kwakiutl: Tribe

CULTURE AREA: Northwest Coast
LANGUAGE GROUP: Wakashan
PRIMARY LOCATION: British Columbia
POPULATION SIZE: 4,120 (Statistics Canada, based on 1991 census)

The Kwakiutl Indians inhabited much of the northwestern coast of British Columbia. The tribe was divided into three groups geographically and had a religion that was centered on guardian spirits. They were famous for potlatch festivals in which status was obtained by extravagant gift giving. Kwakiutl villages were composed of wooden multifamily dwellings,

and the main occupation of their inhabitants was fishing. Most modern Kwakiutl are found in various reserves (reservations) throughout British Columbia.

Tribal History. The Kwakiutl Indians, whose name means "beach on the other side of the river," occupied part of Vancouver Island and the British Columbia coast between Bute Inlet and Douglas Channel. They formed three groups called the Haisla, the Heiltsuk, and the Kwakiutl proper (Southern Kwakiutl), and they spoke variants of the Wakashan Indian language. Their known history has large gaps in it; however, it is well known that their primary occupation was fishing and that they depended upon the sea for most needs. Like the other tribes of the region, the Kwakiutl were excellent craftsmen with wood, making beautiful totem poles, elaborate ceremonial masks, and highly sophisticated canoes. After 1780, the year of the first visits by British and American traders, the Kwakiutl obtained steel tools and became even more adept craftsmen.

Traditional Lifeways. The Kwakiutl were organized into a number of autonomous bands whose social organization included chiefs, nobles, commoners, and slaves, interrelated by complex rules. The minimal social unit in a band was an extended family, or *numaym*, wherein descent was patrilineal; the matrilineal Haisla were the exception. Haisla matrilineal descent was patterned after that of the neighboring Tsimshian, who influenced them greatly. Rights, property, dances, and religious position were parceled out to Kwakiutl according to their lines of descent.

The Kwakiutl religion was based on guardian spirits whose aid could be obtained by appropriate prayer and fasting by either men or women. The different guardian spirits divided numaym members into secret societies (such as Cannibals, Warriors, and Grizzlies), each of which had special dances and ceremonies. The most famous of the Kwakiutl ceremonies was the potlatch. These ceremonies of gift giving were common to many tribes of the Northwest Coast region. The Kwakiutl were noted for the elaborate nature of their potlatches, in which the giver might practically beggar himself through the bestowing of gifts. The potlatches were celebrated to commemorate marriages, important births and deaths, the naming of heirs, and the initiation of members into secret societies. At death, Kwakiutl were either cremated or buried. Burial was in caves, in trees, or (in the case of the very rich) in canoes.

Kwakiutl villages were orderly collections of plank houses made from the red cedar tree, whose wood is straight and easy to work with simple tools. The highly decorated Kwakiutl houses looked and were shaped somewhat like barns. Most houses in a village were each occupied by all the members of a given numaym; however, some village houses were used only for religious ceremonies. The Kwakiutl, who were great fishermen, fished and traveled in large, well-designed dugout sailing canoes, also made from red cedar logs. They also used the canoes in warfare with various neighboring tribes.

The Kwakiutl tribal economy was based mostly on fishing for salmon and, to a lesser extent, cod, halibut, herring, and hunting seals. Fishing was carried out with harpoons, nets, weirs, and many other kinds of sophisticated equipment. The Kwakiutl also hunted some deer and moose with bows and arrows. The vegetable foods of the Kwakiutl included seaweed, roots, and berries gathered by the women of the tribe. The Kwakiutl made fine clothing from bark, animal skins, wool, and dog hair.

Contemporary Life. Nineteenth century Christian missionaries attempted to convert the Kwakiutl, who held on to their tribal beliefs strongly. To speed Kwakiutl absorption into mainstream Canadian life, the government outlawed potlatches in the early twentieth century. Today the Kwakiutl live on various reserves throughout British Columbia. Many contemporary Kwakiutl have retained their language and customs, especially in giving elegant funeral potlatches. Contemporary Kwakiutl are often fishermen.   —*Sanford S. Singer*

See also Bella Bella; Haisla; Hamatsa; Northwest Coast; Plank house; Potlatch.

Lacrosse

TRIBES AFFECTED: Pantribal except for the Southwest

SIGNIFICANCE: The most widespread and popular game among Indians in North America, lacrosse often had ceremonial significance; European settlers learned the game, and it became popular in North America and parts of Europe

The actual origins of the game are unknown, but based on its widespread popularity and similarity of rules throughout North America, it is believed to be more than a thousand years old. It was played on fields of varying sizes of up to 2 miles long and 200 yards wide. Teams attempted to score by throwing a hard wooden or sand-filled buckskin ball through a goal. Players carried sticks of 3 to 5 feet in length with a woven leather pouch on the end used to carry, throw, and catch the ball. This feature is emphasized in the French name "lacrosse," meaning "the stick." The game was often part of ceremonial events including healing ceremonies and a regular part of celebrations. While it was usually a man's game, in some areas women also played. Contests were also a means of friendly tribal rivalry and were often the focus for wagering.

European settlers in Canada and the United States learned and adopted the game. Today it remains popular among Indian peoples, most notably the Iroquois. It is also firmly established as a college sport and is growing in popularity at the high school level.

See also Games and contests.

La Flesche, Francis (1857-1932): Author, interpreter

ALSO KNOWN AS: Zhogaxe (Woodworker)

TRIBAL AFFILIATION: Ponca

SIGNIFICANCE: Francis La Flesche struggled to regain the Ponca homeland

Son of Omaha Chief Joseph La Flesche and Elizabeth Esau, Francis La Flesche joined his sister Susette in the Poncas' struggle to regain their homeland in the late 1870's and 1880's.

Francis La Flesche traveled with Ponca Chief Standing Bear and Omaha journalist Thomas H. Tibbles on a tour of several eastern cities to advance the Poncas' cause after they had been given shelter by the Omahas. He worked as an interpreter on the tour. Afterward, he attended National University Law School in Washington, D.C., graduating in 1892. While there, he began working with anthropologist Alice C. Fletcher, and he collaborated with her on *A Study of Omaha Music* (1893). Recordings made under this study are still available. Fletcher and La Flesche also collaborated on *The Omaha Tribe* (1911), published a year after he joined the Bureau of American Ethnology. Francis La Flesche also authored *Middle Five: Indian Boys at School* (1900), *Who Was the Medicine Man?* (1904), *A Dictionary of the Osage Language* (1932), and a play entitled *Da-o-ma* (1912).

See also La Flesche, Susan; La Flesche, Susette or Josette; Ponca.

La Flesche, Susan (June 17, 1865, Omaha, Nebr.—Sept. 18, 1915, Walthill, Nebr.): Physician

ALSO KNOWN AS: Susan La Flesche Picotte

TRIBAL AFFILIATION: Ponca

SIGNIFICANCE: Susan La Flesche practiced medicine, eventually treating almost every member of the Omaha tribe

Daughter of Omaha principal chief Joseph La Flesche, Susan La Flesche became a government doctor on the Omaha reservation during a time when cholera, influenza, tuberculosis, and other diseases were reaching epidemic proportions. She blazed an inspiring career through a number of white schools, and then worked tirelessly serving her people.

By 1892, the intensity of her work was costing La Flesche her health. She was beset by a number of debilitating illnesses for the rest of her life, as she ministered to the everpresent ills of the Omahas. At one point she wearily departed for Washington, D.C., to testify for the Omahas because people had threatened to convey her against her will, so important was her mission to them.

In 1894, her health improving, La Flesche married Henri Picotte, who was part French and part Sioux; she also began a new medical practice for Indians and whites at Bancroft, Nebraska. La Flesche practiced medicine there as long as her own health permitted. After La Flesche's death on September 18, 1915, the Walthill *Times* added an extra page in its September 24 issue filled with warm eulogies to her. Friends recalled that hundreds of people in the area, Indian and European American, owed their lives to her care.

See also La Flesche, Francis; La Flesche, Susette or Josette; Ponca.

La Flesche, Susette or Josette (1854, Omaha reservation, Nebr.—1903, Lincoln, Nebr.): Author, lecturer

ALSO KNOWN AS: Inshtatheumba (Bright Eyes)

TRIBAL AFFILIATION: Ponca

SIGNIFICANCE: Susette La Flesche lectured in support of the Poncas' regaining their ancestral land

Susette La Flesche became a major nineteenth century native-rights advocate through the case of Standing Bear, another Ponca. Like her sister Susan, Susette La Flesche attended the Presbyterian mission school on the Omaha reservation. She also studied art at the University of Nebraska. In the late 1870's, she traveled with her father, Joseph La Flesche, to Indian Territory (later Oklahoma) to render rudimentary medical attention to the Poncas. Standing Bear's people had been forced to move there from their former homeland along the Niobrara in northern Nebraska. When the Poncas attempted to end this forced exile and return to their homeland, they marched for several weeks in midwinter, finally eating their moccasins to survive and arriving at the Omaha reservation with bleeding feet. The Omahas, particularly the La Flesche family, granted them sanctuary and sustenance.

Susette accompanied her brother Francis and Standing Bear on a lecture tour of Eastern cities during 1879 and 1880 to support the Poncas' case for a return of their homeland. Newspaper articles by Omaha journalist Thomas H. Tibbles about the Poncas' forced exile helped ignite a furor in Congress and among the public. In 1882, Susette—who often used the name

"Bright Eyes" in public—married Tibbles. She also coauthored a memoir with Standing Bear, *Ploughed Under: The Story of an Indian Chief* (1832). During ensuing years, La Flesche and Tibbles also toured the British Isles. Later the couple lived in Washington, D.C., but eventually Susette returned to Lincoln, Nebraska, where she died in 1903.

See also La Flesche, Francis; La Flesche, Susan; Ponca.

Laguna. *See* Pueblo tribes, Western

Lake: Tribe

Culture area: Plateau
Language group: Salishan
Primary location: Colville Reservation, Washington State

The Lake, also called Senijextee, were a branch of the Salishan family. They lived along the Columbia, Kettle, and Kootenay rivers in Washington and in the Arrow Lakes area of British Columbia, Canada, which gave them their name. Their dialect was very similar to that of another Salishan tribe, the Okanagan. Evidence suggests they migrated to Washington from Montana and Idaho in prehistoric times. The Lake lived in villages of varying size, in bands or groups of families. They dressed in wool blankets and fur robes. Because they relied on hunting and fishing—salmon was a chief staple of their diet—as well as on gathering roots and berries, they were forced to move throughout the year to find food in different seasons. This prevented the villages from growing and developing as political or social centers. The Lake do not seem to have relied on agriculture. They were skilled in building canoes, but the rapids of the rivers along which they lived were so treacherous that most traveling was done on foot. The introduction of new diseases from Europe and changing economic conditions brought about a great decline in the numbers of surviving Lake. During the twentieth century, most of the remaining Lake Indians in the United States lived on the Colville Reservation in Washington, to which the Lake had been assigned in 1872. By the 1970's, there were no identified Lake in Canada.

See also Colville; Okanagan; Plateau.

Lame Deer (c. 1895, near Pine Ridge, S.Dak.—Dec. 14, 1976, Denver, Colo.): Medicine man, rancher

Also known as: Tahca Ushte, John Fire
Tribal affiliation: Miniconjou Sioux
Significance: Lame Deer is remembered for his autobiography, which recounts his life growing up on a reservation and his protest against the white culture that had robbed the Indians of their land and culture

Named for his grandfather, a Sioux warrior who was killed by the United States cavalry in the 1890's, Lame Deer lived his life between two worlds, that of the reservation and that of white America. After the death of his mother in 1920, Lame Deer inherited horses and cattle from his father, who at that time gave up the old ways. Lame Deer too gave up the old life, as he followed the rodeo circuit. He also received instruction from medicine men. Lame Deer moved between the white world and the world of the Indian on a reservation; he was a rancher, rodeo rider, reservation policeman, and holy man.

With the publication of *Lame Deer: Seeker of Visions* in 1976, written with Richard Erdoes, Lame Deer established himself as a spokesperson and a spiritual leader among American Indians. In the book, he describes his ancestors and treaties that were broken, his upbringing on the reservation, and his forced schooling at government schools (where he had no choice but to repeat the third grade six times because there were no teachers beyond that level). He also recounts his experiences as a medicine man. The book evaluates both white and Indian culture, finding the suburban modern American culture spiritless and sterile. Lame Deer laments the loss of the prairie life.

See also Sioux.

Bibliography

Lame Deer, with Richard Erdoes. *Lame Deer: Seeker of Visions*. New York: Simon and Schuster, 1976.

Lances and spears

Tribes affected: Pantribal
Significance: Lances and spears were widely used since ancient times as weapons of battle and hunting; they were also used as symbols in religious ceremonies

The lance and spear were widely distributed hunting and war weapons, but they were used most extensively by the Inuit and Plains tribes. The Inuit used them primarily for hunting. The

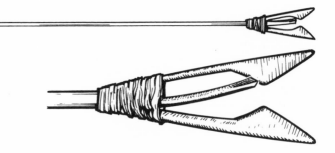

Type of spear used by the Micmac of the Northeast for salmon fishing; the two barbs around the point hold the speared fish in place.

Plains tribes made most extensive use of them in warfare, probably because they were especially well suited to being thrown from horseback.

The lance originated in ancient times as an effective distance weapon, reducing the risk of injury and producing surer results than could be obtained from using close-quarter weapons such as knives. The distance and force with which the lance could be propelled were significantly increased by means of a throwing stick. The spear or lance consisted of a projectile point, similar to an arrowhead, affixed to a long shaft of wood. The specific materials used and the lance's form depended on environmental demands and available materials.

Besides being used as weapons for hunting or combat, lances and spears acquired religious and ceremonial significance. Among some tribes they were housed in elaborately decorated sheaths that signified the society, office, or status of the owner.

See also Atlatl; Bows, arrows, and quivers; Knives; Tools; Weapons.

Land claims

TRIBES AFFECTED: Pantribal
SIGNIFICANCE: American Indians are using a variety of means to repossess land that was taken from them by conquest, treaty, or court decision

Land claims are a key component in conflicts between American Indians and federal, state, and local governments throughout North America. The claims stem from the repeated seizure of Indian lands by non-Indians since the beginning of European contact. American Indians have seen their land taken from them by military conquest, by treaty, by depopulation, and by court action. For example, in the United States, in the 1810 case of *Fletcher v. Peck*, U.S. Supreme Court justice John Marshall ruled that American Indian lands were "effectively vacant" and could be taken from Indians without their consent. Subsequent U.S. court cases in the early nineteenth century ruled that the federal government had precedent rights over American Indians by the fact of discovery; Indian nations were seen as "domestic to and dependent upon" the U.S. government, which could make decisions on their behalf.

Even the reservation land guaranteed to American Indians in the more than three hundred treaties signed between Indians and the U.S. government between 1790 and 1870 was open to non-Indian exploitation. The General Allotment Act of 1887 ended the traditional Indian land tenure system of communal ownership by assigning plots of land as private property to individual Indians on reservations; family heads were assigned 160 acres, for example. Because there were far fewer Indians than land parcels in 1887, the General Allotment Act gave the federal government the right to lease "surplus" reservation land to non-Indians or to incorporate it into national parks or forests. In this way, American Indians lost effective control of two-thirds of the acreage assigned to them by treaty. Individual Indians were also given the right to dispose of their reservation allotment, and many individuals found themselves coerced by poverty or pressure from non-Indians to lease their holdings to non-Indians. On some reservations, such as the Crow Reservation in Montana, non-Indians control nearly half of reservation land.

Many American Indians see land claims as basic to their efforts to improve their economic status and to gain an increased sense of self-worth and autonomy. In the twentieth century, American Indians have used a variety of means, including peaceful demonstrations, violent confrontations, and legal actions against governments or individuals in courts, to gain access to land taken from them. In the United States, Indians have often turned to the federal court system to enforce the terms of treaties or to set aside the effects of the General Allotment Act. The courts have been reluctant, however, to return land leased or owned by non-Indians; in some cases, Indians have instead been awarded restitution or access to former treaty lands for hunting, trapping, or fishing. For example, in 1986, a federal court in Minnesota awarded each individual of the White Earth Chippewa (Ojibwa) compensation for land lost to the General Allotment Act based on the value of the land at the time it was lost plus 5 percent compound interest; an additional six million dollars was granted the tribe for economic development of the reservation. Individuals who did not agree with the court's decision were granted the right to sue for outright return of land within a given time period, but of thirty-nine Chippewa who elected this procedure, none prevailed. Similarly, in 1983, a federal court in Wisconsin gave Indians the right to hunt and fish by traditional methods both on and off their reservations in that state. This led to occasional violent confrontations between Indians and non-Indian sport fishermen when Indians asserted their treaty rights to set their own season and size limit for fishing.

Similar land claim conflicts occur in Canada and Mexico. While the Canadian government has asserted the rights of Indians and Inuits to self-government on native lands since 1989, the actual implementation of those rights has been controversial. For example, in 1991, the Canadian government created a new 770,000-square-mile Arctic territory called Nunavut and assigned 136,000 square miles to the Inuit. In return, however, the Inuit were required to renounce their claims to all ancestral lands, especially those areas rich in oil, gas, and minerals. Many Inuit found that to be too steep a price to pay for land they effectively possessed anyway. In other cases as well, the Canadian government insisted that Indians give up all traditional land claims as part of any agreement on land use and self-government.

In Mexico, Maya Indians in 1992 peacefully marched 1,000 kilometers across Mexico to protest the loss of traditional lands as well as to publicize other grievances; in return, the Mexican government pledged to resolve local land disputes in the state of Chiapas and to finance hundreds of small community development projects. The failure of the Mexican government to fulfill its pledges led to a January, 1994, uprising in Chiapas in which Indians battled with government troops;

nearly one hundred persons were reported to have been killed, and a former governor of Chiapas was kidnapped. Thus, in all sections of the North American continent Indians see land claims as central to their disputes with non-Indians.

See also Allotment system; Indian Act of 1989 (Canada); Indian-white relations—Canadian; Indian-white relations—U.S., 1934-1995; Menominee; Reservation system of the United States; Reserve system of Canada; Termination policy.

Language families

TRIBES AFFECTED: Pantribal
SIGNIFICANCE: A language family's existence indicates that its member languages have descended from a common, ancient source; that fact helps scholars reconstruct the origins and kinship of tribes

Anthropologists believe that humans first reached North America via a land bridge that intermittently connected Alaska and Siberia between twenty thousand and five thousand years ago. They came in a series of migrations, some separated by thousands of years, and (the theory holds) each migrating group spoke a single language. As a group slowly spread through North America and perhaps into Central and South America, it fragmented into subgroups that settled different areas along the way. Many subgroups lost contact with one another. The original language the group spoke changed, because all languages evolve, and it changed at different rates and in different manners among the subgroups as each developed a distinct culture.

Soon subgroups spoke mutually unintelligible versions of the ancestral tongue; in other words, each had its own language. So disparate had the descendant languages become that when Europeans arrived on the American continents in the late fifteenth and early sixteenth centuries, they encountered what seemed to them a bewildering variety of languages radically unlike their own.

Typology and Genetic Classifications. Yet despite the apparent diversity, underlying relationships exist among the languages. There are basically two ways to describe a linguistic relationship. The first, called typology, classifies languages based on structural similarities. Soon after American linguistics began, scholars noted that most Indian languages are polysynthetic (or incorporative), a type that combines major grammatical features into single words. In this sense, New World languages seemed distinct from all other languages then known. Typology, however, does not necessarily prove historical kinship. For example, according to typological criteria, English is more like Japanese than it is like German, to which English has a known historical connection.

The second method, genetic classification, hunts for these historical connections. Historical and comparative linguists analyze languages to discover features that can only have been inherited from the same source. When they find similar pronunciations, words and affixes, and grammatical features among two or more languages that cannot be explained by coincidence or by borrowing, these languages must share a

family relationship—a genealogy—just as organisms descended from the same parent share physical traits. Linguists often use the metaphor of a tree to characterize the relationships: An ancestral language (also called a "proto" language) splits into branches, each branch into sub-branches, and sub-branches into separate languages. The term "family" refers collectively to the descendants of the ancestral language, which lends its name to the family. A grouping of multiple families is called a superfamily or phylum.

Even if the parent language no longer exists, its living offspring reveal much of its nature. By using modern evidence to reconstruct an ancient tongue's sounds, words, and grammar, linguists offer potential evidence of humankind's prehistoric character, evidence parallel to the ruins and middens studied by archaeologists and the skeletal remains studied by paleontologists. Since the early nineteenth century, reapplying linguistic methods developed during the study of the Indo-European languages, scholars have had notable success; many American Indian languages do indeed belong in families. Yet a number of topics—how many families, which languages belong in each, and what the families say about the original settlement of the Americas—have remained controversial from their beginnings.

History of Classifications. In *A Guide to the World's Languages* (1987), Merritt Ruhlen lists 627 Indian and Eskimo languages in the Americas, many of which are extinct and known only from short word lists that European explorers compiled. Although their methods were often crude, these explorers were the first contributors to American linguistics. The first formal studies of individual North American languages appeared in the mid-seventeenth century, John Eliot's Natick grammar in 1666 and Roger Williams' Narragansett phrase book in 1643. As European colonists moved westward and more Indian languages became known, affinities among them led to speculations about their relationships. Thomas Jefferson, for example, wrote in 1789 that a common parentage might become apparent from a study of Indian vocabularies and suggested New World languages may have a kinship to Asian languages, an idea that scholars began exploring seriously in the late twentieth century.

Attempts to define the genetic relationship of American Indian languages began in the mid-nineteenth century. The first comprehensive study came from Albert Gallatin in 1836 (revised and expanded in 1848). Gallatin, a secretary of war, distributed a questionnaire to Indian language experts nationwide, soliciting information on six hundred words and some grammatical features. Gallatin made his classification by systematically comparing the responses. He grouped all North American languages, except those of California, into thirty-two families.

Gallatin's classification remained the standard until 1891, when separate studies by Daniel Brinton and John Wesley Powell appeared. Brinton, who included all the languages in both North and South America about which he could get information, perceived a fundamental unity behind them, although he separated them into about eighty families for each continent in *The American Race*. Powell, as director of the Bureau of American Ethnology and a founder of the American Anthropological Association, had access to much more information than Brinton did; he also had a staff of linguists to help him. His article in the bureau's seventh annual report, however, treated only those languages north of Mexico. Based on comparisons of vocabulary, Powell and his staff distinguished fifty-eight language families and isolates (languages which do not show kinship to other languages). The report served as the basis for subsequent investigations in North American linguistics well into the twentieth century, while Brinton's book did much the same for the languages of South America.

Twentieth century American linguistics has been divided by a dispute over methods, a dispute that gradually arose between Columbia University anthropologist Franz Boas and several former students, principally Edward Sapir. Boas collected and analyzed information on a remarkable number of Indian languages, and early in his career he suggested that structural similarities among some languages bespoke a common origin. Later he changed his mind about the validity of genetic groupings and criticized the findings of his students. Those students, collecting and assessing languages on their own, especially in California, worked to classify them in ever larger families. In an influential 1929 *Encyclopædia Britannica* article, Sapir tentatively proposed six families for all of North America and parts of Mexico and Central America because of similarities in vocabulary and grammar: Eskimo-Aleut, Algonquian-Mosan, Na-Dene, Penutian, Aztec-Tanoan, and Hokan-Siouan. Specialists in individual families denounced Sapir's broad classifications, some claiming that the resemblances he cited were purely fanciful and others faulting him for not distinguishing adequately between coincidental similarities, borrowings, and true cognates when he compared vocabulary items. The controversy persisted through the rest of the century; traditionalist linguists, in the spirit of Boas, resisted large-scale classifications and argued with reductionists, who followed Sapir in proposing families. The two sides were somewhat facetiously known as "splitters" and "lumpers."

Traditionalist Classification. In their introduction to *The Languages of Native America* (1979), Lyle Campbell and Marianne Mithun, rejecting the simple vocabulary comparisons of reductionists, listed three criteria for genetic classifications that would satisfy the traditionalists. First, only purely linguistic evidence is admissible; the findings of cultural anthropologists or archaeologists, for example, are irrelevant. Second, only resemblances between languages that include both sound and meaning are to be considered. If two or more languages have only a similar sound structure (such as the same number and type of consonants) or only employ the same method for constructing words (such as the use of suffixes to turn verbs into nouns), the kinship, Campbell and Mithun argue, should be viewed with skepticism. Basically, in this view, linguists should look for as many cognates as possible. Cognates (from Latin, meaning "born together") are

words in different languages that have similar sounds and meanings because they derive from the same word in an ancestral language. For example, English *yoke*, Latin *iugum*, and German *Joch* are cognates deriving from the hypothetical Indo-European form *jugo*.

Third, comparisons of sounds, words, and grammatical features must not be conducted piecemeal; they must be accompanied by a hypothesis systematically explaining how changes took place. That is, linguists must discover laws of change from a parent language to its offspring languages. Only then will the relation between the offspring languages be proved. Additionally, they warn that not enough attention has been paid to "areal diffusion," or the borrowing of words and (less often) grammatical features between groups living close to one another. Such borrowings prove only physical proximity, not common origins and kinship.

Applying these criteria and cautions, Campbell and Mithun list 62 language families and isolates for North America. Their classifications are pointedly conservative and uncontroversial, intended to summarize contemporary research and serve as a starting point for further work. They recognize that many of the languages they list as isolates and some of the major branches will eventually be proved to belong together, but they refuse to allow lumping based on comparisons of vocabulary alone. Still, they follow Sapir in some cases, notably the universally accepted Eskimo-Aleut and Na-Dene families; however, they completely reject four of his six groupings.

Campbell and Mithun insist that the watchword for linguistics should be "demonstration," not "lumping," in order to give American Indian linguistics a scientific rigor. Yet their call for rigor and their criteria have placed traditionalists in something of a dilemma. Their 62 families for North America and the 117 families posited for South America by the traditionalist Cestmir Loukotka in 1968 amount to considerable linguistic diversity, far more than exists in Europe or Africa—both of which were settled long before the Americas. In general, anthropologists have found that cultural diversity increases with time. That a more recently settled region such as the Americas should show greater linguistic diversity than an older cultural area such as Africa flouts this principle. Furthermore, paleoanthropological evidence fails to support such great diversity, a fact which has made some linguists unhappy with the traditionalist approach.

Reductionist Classification. In 1987 Stanford University's Joseph H. Greenberg published *Language in the Americas*, among the most controversial books about historical linguistics published in the twentieth century. In it he sweeps aside the traditionalists' cautions, which he argues are largely specious. He claims that it is not necessary to reconstruct sound laws in order to show linguistic relationships. If two or more languages contain a sufficient number of cognates, then it is reasonable to assume that those languages descend from a common protolanguage. To ignore cognates because no sound laws exist to explain their varying forms, Greenberg argues, eliminates much valuable evidence.

Greenberg and Ruhlen, his former student, applied their system of "multilateral analysis" to hundreds of languages. For this method, they compiled lists of words for universal concepts and natural phenomena, such as pronouns, terms for family members, names for body parts, and names for water, because such words are seldom borrowed. Then they compared the words for a particular concept all at once, not language by language as traditionalists would have it. Together they discerned the etymologies (historical roots of modern words) of about five hundred words and found 107 grammatical features existing in more than one language. From this evidence, Greenberg concluded that all the languages in the Americas belong to one of three phyla: Eskimo-Aleut, Na-Dene, and Amerind.

Eskimo-Aleut includes ten languages and is spoken by about eighty-five thousand people living on the Aleutian Islands and in a belt of land that extends from western Alaska across the top of Canada to the coasts of Greenland. The Eskimo branches fall into two sub-branches, western (or Yupik) and eastern (or Inuit), which meet at Alaska's Norton Sound. Because it has relatively little diversity, Eskimo-Aleut is thought to be the youngest of the three phyla.

Na-Dene contains three independent languages, Haida, Tlingit, and Eyak, which together have perhaps two thousand speakers, and a large branch, Athapaskan, which has thirty-two languages, most notably Chipewyan, Beaver, Apache, and Navajo. Navajo, with about 149,000 speakers, is the largest single Indian language in North America and the only one with a growing number of speakers. The Na-Dene phylum spreads from central Alaska as far as Hudson Bay in the east and south well into British Columbia. There are also small linguistic islands of Athapaskan in coastal Washington, Oregon, and Northern California and a large island that covers a substantial portion of New Mexico and Arizona.

There has been little controversy about Eskimo-Aleut and Na-Dene, but Amerind, by far the largest group with 583 languages, was immediately denounced by traditionalists, who not only rejected the phylum but many of the branches and sub-branches in it because Greenberg does not distinguish typological similarities from genetic similarities. The large number of etymologies, however, has impressed some scholars. Most telling is the appearance of *n* in first-person pronouns and *m* in second-person pronouns in all Amerind subgroups, while *i-* is a common third-person marker; such widespread features for basic language concepts, Greenberg contends, can only point to a common ancestral language.

Greenberg and Ruhlen divide the Amerind phylum into six major stocks, two of which apply to North America. Northern Amerind contains Almosan-Keresiouan (sixty-nine languages), which in its sub-branches has such famous languages as Blackfoot, Cheyenne, Arapaho, Cree, Ojibwa, Shawnee, Massachusett, Tillamook, Crow, Dakota, Pawnee, Mohawk, and Cherokee; Penutian (sixty-eight languages), with Chinook, Nez Perce, Natchez, Choctaw, Alabama, and Yucatec; and Hokan (twenty-eight languages), with Pomo, Mojave, Yuma, and Washoe. Central Amerind includes Tanoan (forty-nine languages), with Kiowa and Taos; Uto-Aztecan (twenty-five languages), with Hopi, Paiute, Shoshone, Comanche, and Nahuatl (the Aztec language); and Oto-Manguean (seventeen languages). The remaining four major stocks, Chibchan-Paezan (forty-three languages), Andean (eighteen languages), Equatorial-Tucanoan (192 languages), and Ge-Pano-Carib (117 languages), occupy South America and the Caribbean islands. Quechau, an Andean language in Colombia, Ecuador, Peru, and Bolivia, has the largest number of speakers, about eight million.

Greenberg remarks that his broad approach to classification is a beginning, not an end in itself. Detailed reconstructions of languages and sound laws, the scrutiny which traditionalists demand, are still needed to work out the details in his proposal. Although he admits that some features of his groupings may need revising after such examinations, he remains confident that the overall plan is correct. He further proposes that the three American phyla show connections to Old World language groups. Eskimo-Aleut may belong in Eurasiatic, a postulated immense superfamily whose members include English, Turkic, and Japanese; Amerind may also be related to Eurasiatic, but much more distantly. Since *Language in the Americas* appeared, some Russian and American scholars have placed Na-Dene and Caucasian (languages of central Russia) in Dene-Caucasian, with possible affiliation to Sino-Tibetan, a family that includes the Chinese languages. Ultimately, Greenberg suggests, all modern languages may descend from a single stock, which he calls Proto-Sapiens and others have called Proto-World and Proto-Human.

Nonlinguistic Evidence. Despite the debate among linguists, Greenberg's Eskimo-Aleut, Na-Dene, and Amerind categories have found some support from other scientific disciplines. The findings all appear to substantiate the theory that American Indians and Eskimos crossed from Asia in at least three migrations that correspond to the three language phyla. The first, the ancestors of Amerind speakers, came no more recently than twelve thousand years ago and may correspond, in anthropological terms, to the Clovis, or Paleo-Indian, culture. The Na-Dene migration began to arrive sometime between seven and ten thousand years ago and probably became the Paleo-Arctic culture. The Eskimo-Aleuts came last, about four to five thousand years ago, and may have been the Thule culture, although that identification is uncertain. The periods are so vague because the archaeological and linguistic evidence is difficult to date precisely.

Geneticists also have found that American Indians belong in three distinct groups. A team led by L. L. Cavalli-Sforza studied variations in Rh factor, a blood antigen, by population; Cavalli-Sforza claims that Greenberg's language phyla accord with his genetic groups. Studies of variations in mitochondrial deoxyribonucleic acid (DNA) by Douglas C. Wallace also appear to support Greenberg. Finally, analyses of human teeth, immunoglobulin G, and blood serums in modern Indian populations have produced corroborating findings.

A majority of linguists reject, or at least are skeptical of, the multilateral analysis Greenberg and Ruhlen used to reach their conclusions. At the same time, most assume that large-scale relationships do exist among the more than six hundred known Indian languages, which language-by-language comparison and deduction of sound laws will eventually confirm. Thus, scientists largely agree that the Americas were populated by a small number of groups who traveled from Asia and whose languages slowly differentiated as the groups spread throughout the New World.   —*Roger Smith*

See also Algonquian language family; Athapaskan language family; Caddoan language family; Culture areas; Eskimo-Aleut language family; Hokan language family; Iroquoian language family; Keresan language family; Kiowa-Tanoan language family; Migrations; Muskogean language family; Na-Dene language family; Penutian language family; Salishan language family; Siouan language family; Uto-Aztecan language family; Wakashan language family; Yakonan language family; Yuman language family.

BIBLIOGRAPHY

Bright, William, et al., eds. *Linguistics in North America.* Vol. 10 in *Current Trends in Linguistics*, edited by Thomas A. Sebeok. The Hague: Mouton, 1973. Essays devoted to the history of American linguistics, protolanguages, and the mutual influence of languages within regions present summary information on genetic and typological classifications.

Campbell, Lyle, and Marianne Mithun, eds. *The Languages of Native America: Historical and Comparative Assessment.* Austin: University of Texas Press, 1979. The editors propose sixty-two language families and isolates, based on rigorous and systematic classification methods, and contributors summarize research on seventeen of the families.

Greenberg, Joseph H. *Language in the Americas.* Stanford, Calif.: Stanford University Press, 1987. This controversial book classifies all languages in North and South America into three phyla based on correspondences in vocabulary and grammar.

Greenberg, Joseph H., and Merritt Ruhlen. "Linguistic Origins of Native Americans." *Scientific American* 267 (November, 1992): 94-99. Summarizes the authors' classification of American languages into three phyla, discusses their relation to Old World language families, and outlines corroborating evidence from genetics and anthropology.

Ruhlen, Merritt. *Classification.* Vol. 1 in *A Guide to the World's Languages.* Stanford, Calif.: Stanford University Press, 1987. An illuminating chapter on classification methods helps make sense of the long-standing controversy over American Indian languages; another chapter presents major classification proposals for them and repeats Greenberg's conclusions.

La Venta: Archaeological site

DATE: c. 1100-400 B.C.E.
LOCATION: Tabasco, Mexico
CULTURE AFFECTED: Olmec

La Venta is the site of an ancient Olmec city in southeastern Mexico. Begun about 1100 B.C.E., La Venta is not the oldest of the known Olmec cities. San Lorenzo, south and west of La Venta, was settled well before 1300 B.C.E. Nor was the site of La Venta easy to locate, for the city had been demolished several hundred years before the birth of Christ. It was uncovered only in 1925 by the Danish anthropologist Franz Blom. Since then, archaeological excavations have uncovered the ancient Olmec city with its ceremonial center. Archaeologists have learned much about the skills and society of this prehistoric culture from excavating the city.

La Venta exhibited a carefully planned site with many mounds and a large pyramid nearly 100 feet high. This pyramid, when fully uncovered, proved to be conical in shape, unlike the pyramids of other Mesoamerican cultures, which had rectangular bases and flat, sloping sides. La Venta's structures were different from those of other cities because they were built of dried mud instead of stone. Some of these structures served as burial sites for important individuals, and many impressive artifacts, perhaps burial offerings, have been found throughout the city. One pit contained hundreds of polished and decorated stone axes, and there are several large mosaic floors in other pits. These mosaics are indicative of a people with great skill; they consist of hundreds of pieces which formed, in some cases, the shape of a jaguar. Archaeologists have been impressed by the care and skill that went into these artifacts, which were apparently buried immediately after they were made. They were intended for the dead rather than the living. A puzzle for archaeologists is the lack of any human remains in what appear to be burial sites.

Among the greatest accomplishments of the Olmecs were large stone sculptures, several of which have been found at La Venta. Six gigantic stone heads were located at the site, ranging from 5 to 10 feet in height. Also discovered in La Venta were several large stelae, which depict religious symbols.

The achievements of the people at La Venta have given rise to questions about the size of the city and its functions. The site does not contain indications of dwellings, and an early theory suggested that it was a ceremonial center rather than an urban nucleus. Also unresolved is the exact form of administration or government. Was La Venta an administrative center or the capital city of an empire? What was its relationship to other cities throughout the area? Flourishing after the San Lorenzo period, La Venta may have been the center of a large Olmec state. Its chief purpose and the manner of its destruction are still mysteries to the archaeologists who continue to research the site of La Venta.

See also Olmec; Tres Zapotes.

Lawyer (c. 1795—Jan. 3, 1876): Tribal leader

ALSO KNOWN AS: Hallalhotsoot, Hollolsotetote (The Talker)
TRIBAL AFFILIATION: Nez Perce, Flathead
SIGNIFICANCE: Negotiated Nez Perce land rights with the U.S. government

Lawyer negotiated treaties in the name of the Nez Perce that were repudiated by Chief Joseph the Younger before his Long March in 1877. Chief Joseph gave Lawyer that name because

Lawyer, a Nez Perce leader, ceded considerable areas of land to the U.S. government, provoking conflict within the tribe. (Library of Congress)

(as Joseph noted in a speech to Congress in 1879) "he talked too much" and gave away land that did not belong to him.

Lawyer was a son of Twisted Hair, a Nez Perce chief who had greeted Meriwether Lewis and William Clark, and his Flathead wife. Lawyer often worked as a guide and interpreter for missionaries and traders, and became well-known for his oratorical skill in both the English and Nez Perce languages.

Lawyer was designated as a representative of all the Nez Perces by Washington territorial governor Isaac Stevens at a treaty council in 1855. The outcome of that council was bitterly protested by Old Joseph, his son Chief Joseph the Younger, and other antitreaty Nez Perces. During the ensuing Yakima War of 1855-1856, Lawyer's band protected Stevens from attack by warriors seeking revenge for the death of Peopeomoxmox. In 1863, Lawyer signed another treaty and ceded even more land that Old Joseph insisted was not his to give. By 1868, Lawyer himself was upset at the number of treaties that had been broken, and he traveled to Washington, D.C., to protest. He died in 1876, one year before the Long March of the antitreaty Nez Perces under Chief Joseph the Younger.

See also Joseph the Younger; Nez Perce.

Lean Bear (c. 1813—c. 1864): Peace chief

ALSO KNOWN AS: Awoninahku, Starved Bear
TRIBAL AFFILIATION: Southern Cheyenne
SIGNIFICANCE: Lean Bear was one of the principal Plains Indian leaders who strove for peace

Cheyenne leader Lean Bear, the brother of Bull Bear, was part of the 1863 delegation to Washington, D.C., that met with President Abraham Lincoln to negotiate a peace. The delegation included Ten Bears (Comanche) and Lone Wolf (Kiowa).

The following year, a detachment of troops attacked a group of Cheyenne who had stolen three cattle, thus launching a war with the Cheyenne. In May, 1864, Lieutenant George Eayre entered the Nebraska Territory with the intent of attacking Cheyenne on sight. Lean Bear's camp at Ash Creek was friendly, but when Lean Bear (the peace chief) and several other leaders, including Star and Wolf Chief, rode forth to offer peace to the soldiers, the troops moved into battle formation and opened fire. Lean Bear was shot on his horse and then shot again as he lay on the ground.

On his chest was the peace medal given to him in Washington; in his hand were the papers signed by Lincoln saying that he was a friend to the whites and a keeper of peace. This attack, and the Sand Creek Massacre soon afterward, led to the Cheyenne-Arapaho War (or the Colorado War) of 1864-1865 and to later fighting on the southern Plains.

See also Black Kettle; Bull Bear; Lone Wolf; Sand Creek Massacre.

Lean-to

TRIBES AFFECTED: Pantribal
SIGNIFICANCE: Lean-tos were most useful as quickly constructed, temporary shelters

Lean-tos were used as temporary structures throughout North America, mostly for shelter, windbreaks, or privacy when people were in transit or at resource exploitation sites. A lean-to was basically an inclined rectangular or V-shaped side roof that was free-standing using several vertical supporting upright poles. It might also be supported against a tree or large boulder. The main attribute of this simple but effective structure was its ease of construction; natives utilized natural materials available on the site such as tules, cattails, strips of bark, plaited willow,

Lean-to

seaweed, leaves, grass, or even clothing or blankets. The size of the structure was dependent upon materials at hand, number of occupants, and time required to construct the shelter.

A basic lean-to could accommodate four to five persons; in the Great Basin, these structures were relatively large and were used for several weeks or even months by an extended family. Lean-tos were strategically situated so the prevailing wind was at a right angle to the opening, to draft away any smoke or embers from a cooking or warming fire. With more complex lean-tos, the bearing poles were carefully tied and stored in or against a tree for future use.

Left Hand the First (1820's, eastern Colo. or western Nebr. or Kans.—Nov. 29, 1864, Sand Creek, Colo.): Tribal leader

ALSO KNOWN AS: Nawat, Niwot
TRIBAL AFFILIATION: Southern Arapaho
SIGNIFICANCE: The first Left Hand was a leading peace chief during the Plains Indian wars

There were two Left Hands of considerable renown in Southern Arapaho history, a fact which has led to some confusion in the historical record. The first Left Hand learned English from his sister's husband. He became an important translator and leader in Arapaho dealings with whites. He worked with Little Raven, the principal chief of the Southern Arapaho at the time, attempting to keep peace as white Americans moved into the Plains. Despite his known peaceful intentions, he appears to have been killed in the 1864 massacre at Sand Creek, Colorado.

See also Left Hand the Second; Little Raven; Sand Creek Massacre.

Left Hand the Second (c. 1840, eastern Colo. or western Nebr. or Kans.—June 20, 1911, Geary, Okla.): Principal chief

ALSO KNOWN AS: Nawat, Niwot
TRIBAL AFFILIATION: Southern Arapaho
SIGNIFICANCE: The second Left Hand was a principal chief, and he signed an agreement permitting allotment of Arapaho land

The second Left Hand replaced Little Raven as principal chief of the Southern Arapaho in 1889. Although he could not speak English, he was an important intermediary between his people and the whites, visiting Washington, D.C., on a number of occasions. His reasoning ability and his willingness to compromise helped make the transition to reservation life smoother for the Southern Arapaho than it was for many tribes. In 1890, however, he created considerable enmity when he signed an agreement that allowed the allotment of Arapaho lands in Indian Territory in spite of opposition from the Southern Cheyenne, who shared a reservation with the Arapaho.

See also Left Hand the First; Little Raven.

Lehner: Archaeological site
DATE: 10,000-9000 B.C.E.
LOCATION: Southern Arizona
CULTURE AFFECTED: Paleo-Indian

Lehner is one of the best-documented mammoth kill sites of the Llano complex in the southwestern United States, with Clovis projectile points found in direct association with the bones of extinct animals. It is located at an elevation of 4,190 feet on the side of a small arroyo, a tributary of the San Pedro River in southern Arizona. Excavations were undertaken in 1955-1956 under the direction of Emil W. Haury. Lehner's significance lies in the quality of its information about Paleo-Indian times from several different lines of data.

Excavations focused on a bone bed and a hearth area. Remains of two hearths—one a basin-shaped pit—provided evidence for the use of cooking fires. Radiocarbon dates place activities between 11,000 and 12,000 years ago, during which time the climate was somewhat wetter and cooler than it is today. Bones include remains of nine immature mammoths as well as remains of tapir, horse, camel, bear, muskrat, and rabbit.

A wide variety of stone tools was found, including thirteen projectile points made of chert, jasper, chalcedony, and quartz, ranging from 31 to 97 millimeters long. All but three have fine pressure flaking and basal fluting. The majority were found with mammoth bones, indicating that they were embedded in the animals. Other stone tools include unifacial scrapers, both prismatic and flat flake knives, and a simple pebble chopper. The scrapers were thick and heavy, probably for butchering.

Lehner represents a kill site and butchering locality. Animals were trapped at a watering hole by hunters, who took advantage of the steep and slippery sides of the arroyo to isolate and kill young mammoths. Butchering took place on the spot, and the location was subsequently used for trapping other animals.

See also Paleo-Indian; Prehistory—Southwest.

Lenni Lenape: Tribe
CULTURE AREA: Northeast
LANGUAGE GROUP: Algonquian
PRIMARY LOCATION: Oklahoma
POPULATION SIZE: 9,321 in U.S. ("Delaware," 1990 U.S. Census); 590 in Canada (Statistics Canada, based on 1991 census)

The Lenni Lenape were the first tribe encountered by the European explorers who landed in the area of what is now northern Delaware, New Jersey, and southeastern New York.

The name "Lenape" has been ascribed various meanings: "a male of our kind," "our men," "men of the same nation," "common," "ordinary," or "real" people. "Lenni Lenape" is redundant, as if to say, "the common, ordinary people." They are sometimes referred to as the Delawares, which is not an Indian word at all; the early English settlers, who had difficulty pronouncing Indian names, were responsible for this term. In August of 1610, Sir Samuel Argall, captain of the ship *Discovery*, sailed into the bay which he later named De la Warre Bay in honor of Sir Thomas West, third Lord De la Warre, who was governor of the Virginia colony. The Indians who lived along the shore of the bay and the banks of the river which fed into it were called the De la Warres, later shortened to Delawares.

Subtribes. Before the arrival of the Europeans, the Lenape lived in small villages containing only twenty-five or thirty people. Scholars are not sure of the total Lenape population before the coming of the Europeans; the usual estimates range from eight to twelve thousand people.

The early Dutch, Swedish, and English explorers soon realized that the Lenape could not simply be lumped together as one unified group. There were separate groups or bands scattered along the major waterways. One main division was the Minsi ("men of the stony country"), which included the Esophus, Tappan, Haverstraw, Canarsee, and Hackensack, among others, who lived in the area of what is now northern New Jersey, Manhattan Island, and the lower Hudson River valley. The Unami ("fishermen"), which included the Raritan, Navesink, and Mantaes, lived in central New Jersey and along the Atlantic coast. The Unalachtigo ("people living near the ocean") were found along the coast in present-day Delaware and southern New Jersey. Along the upper Delaware River valley lived the Minisinks and other small, unnamed Indian bands. These groups differed greatly in their language, religious beliefs, and culture; in fact, the Unami dialect of the Delaware language was so different from the Minsi that they could barely understand each other.

U.S. STATES WITH THE LARGEST LENNI LENAPE POPULATIONS, 1990

Oklahoma	2,913
New Jersey	1,249
California	889
New York	490
Texas	454

Source: 1990 U.S. Census.

Political Organization. The individual tribes did not form a single Indian nation because the Lenape villages functioned as separate political units. Each village was governed by at least two chiefs, a council, and the residents of the village. One chief, who either inherited or was elected to the position, held authority in times of peace, and his power was limited by the

council and the village at large. His main function was to preside over meetings and ceremonies, direct hunting drives, and mediate disputes. The chief was usually no wealthier than his neighbors, as the Lenape practiced a communal way of life in which all members of the tribe shared equally. The second chief was a war chief, who was appointed because of his skills in war. With a war's end, the peace chief resumed his limited authority. This system of government gave all members of the tribe considerable personal liberty and great equality of wealth.

Methods of Subsistence. The early Lenapes were primarily hunters and fishermen, pursuing bear, elk, deer, beaver, and muskrat. Their weapons consisted of spears made of wood or bone with a stone point. Fish were caught with nets, lines, or spears. Later, as their life became more sedentary, they began to produce articles of clay pottery. The women of the tribe engaged in agriculture and food gathering as villages became more permanent. Corn was the primary crop, which was ground into corn meal. They also grew squash, beans, and tobacco, and learned how to preserve food for future use. Meat was dried and cured, and ground corn and beans were placed in earthen pits and covered with bark or leaves. Fish was either dried in the sun or smoked. Many of the Lenape agricultural practices and food preservation methods were later adopted by European colonists.

Village Life. The largest and most permanent villages were usually located along major rivers or other large bodies of water. They were moved from time to time when the soil was depleted, as the Lenape were unaware of methods of crop rotation. For shelter they built simple, circular structures constructed of curved saplings lashed together with hickory twigs or hemp and covered with strips of bark. A hole was left in the center of the structure to allow smoke from the inside fire to exit. In the northern parts of New Jersey, they built longhouses in which several families would live.

The Lenape wore simple clothing made from deer, elk, beaver, bear, fox, and raccoon skins. Children wore little or no clothing in summer. Both men and women wore jewelry fashioned from shark's teeth, bear claws, or shells, and for warfare and festive occasions they painted their bodies with paints made from minerals, berries, roots, and bark.

On land they traveled on foot, and for water transportation they built dugout canoes fashioned from felled trees. A fire was started in the middle of the log, and the charred pieces were slowly removed with stone axes.

European Contact. Beginning with the arrival of the explorer Giovanni da Verrazano in 1524, the Lenape had increasing contact with the Europeans. With the arrival of the Dutch and English, competition for trading with the settlers among tribes became fierce. The Lenape highly valued the articles brought from Europe, especially textiles, guns, metal tools, and jewelry.

Unfortunately, an unanticipated consequence of contact and trade with the Europeans was the introduction of two deadly commodities: alcohol and disease. The Lenapes had never known any form of alcoholic beverage, and they quickly developed a craving for beer, rum, and brandy. Alcohol was frequently abused, and many European traders took advantage of the Indians' weakness regarding alcohol, offering them strong drink during trading encounters and then cheating them out of their money.

The Europeans also unwittingly transmitted diseases for which the Lenape had no natural immunity: smallpox, typhus, influenza, venereal diseases, and malaria. These sicknesses were so severe among the natives that they sometimes wiped out whole communities. During the colonial period, there were also epidemics of measles, chicken pox, and scarlet fever which dramatically reduced their numbers.

Social Life. The average Lenape family had from four to six children, but infant mortality was very high. Newborn children were wrapped in animal skins, which were fastened to a cradleboard by three braided strips; one went over the baby's forehead, one went over the arms, and one secured the legs. While the mother was working in the fields, the cradleboard and the baby were hung on the branch of a tree. At an early age, boys were instructed in the techniques of hunting, war, and woodcraft, while girls were trained in planting and cultivating crops as well as housekeeping duties.

Because their life expectancy was not very long, boys were considered ready for marriage at seventeen or eighteen, once they had proved that they possessed the necessary hunting skills to provide for a family. Girls were eligible for marriage once they became sexually mature, at around thirteen or fourteen years of age. Marriages were usually arranged by parents, with some consent of the couple allowed. There was little ceremony involved. In some cases, a man would simply ask a woman if she wanted to live with him, and if she agreed the tribe considered them to be married.

Death was considered to be caused by evil spirits. Burial rites were simple, the body being placed in a shallow pit lined with bark. Food, clothing, tobacco pipes, and clay pots were often placed with the corpse for use by the deceased in the next life.

Religious Beliefs. Like most Native Americans, the Lenape were a deeply religious people. Unlike the European settlers, whose Christian beliefs taught them that God favored them over other creatures, the Lenape believed that they were an integral part of the natural world. They also firmly believed in an afterlife. The soul, they thought, left the body at the time of death but remained nearby for several days, consuming the food left at the grave site. Then it departed to the land of the spirits, a pleasant place where one met one's deceased relatives and had plenty of food and good hunting.

The Lenape worshiped many gods, with a supreme being, Manito, at the head. Manito created the earth and everything on it. Lesser gods served as his agents; in addition, almost all plants and animals were considered to contain supernatural spirits. Communication with the gods was through prayers and offerings. Lenape tribes also had a shaman who specialized in curing illnesses or foretelling the future. Since illness was attributed to evil spirits entering the body, it was the job of the

shaman to scare the spirits away. The shaman was considered a special member of the tribe, and his secrets were passed on only to a legal descendant or a close and trusted friend. There is some evidence that a special house was constructed in some villages for the exorcism of disease.

In the early years of contact with Europeans, Lenape religion was relatively unaffected. The settlers considered the Indians to be godless, and some religious groups, most notably the Moravians, attempted to learn the Lenape language and convert them to Christianity. A few did convert, but they often quickly went back to their native beliefs; Christian sermons did not make sense within their worldview, and Christian practices simply did not fit into their way of life. Perhaps the only lasting effect of Christianity upon Lenape religion was the emergence of an annual ceremony celebrating the harvest. A "big house," a bark-covered structure about 40 feet long and 25 feet wide was constructed exclusively for this purpose. For twelve nights in mid-October, sacred fires were maintained at each entrance, and the interior was decorated with twelve posts with faces carved on them to represent the twelve gods who occupied the heavens. A cooking fire burned in the center, and deer meat was hung from a pole or tree, before which prayers were said to aid the hunters. Other prayers gave thanks for a bountiful harvest.

Relocation. The Lenape were the dominant tribe in the East until about 1720. As the white settlers continued to arrive, the Indians were gradually crowded out. The settlers had cleared many of the forests for farming, thus driving away the deer, bear, and wild turkeys. They dammed the rivers to power their mills, disrupting the annual spawning runs of fish. With these drastic changes, the traditional Lenape way of life was destroyed. Those who remained began to sell their remaining lands to the eager colonists and move across the Delaware to the west, never to return.

The Unalachtigo were the first to depart, around 1725, relocating to northern New York State. They were followed by the Minsi around 1742, who settled for a time in southeastern Pennsylvania and later in Ohio and Indiana. Some crossed Lake Erie into Canada, while others went to the area around the Kansas and Missouri rivers. In 1867, many Lenapes moved into the Indian Territory in what is now Oklahoma and were incorporated into the Cherokee tribe. A few went to Green Bay, Wisconsin, where they remained for many years.

—*Raymond Frey*

See also Algonquian language family; Indian-white relations—Dutch colonial; Indian-white relations—English colonial; Northeast; Walam Olum.

BIBLIOGRAPHY

Cross, Dorothy. *New Jersey's Indians*. Trenton: New Jersey State Museum, 1976. A very readable account of Lenape life; sections on Lenape culture are especially informative.

Dowd, Gregory Evans. *The Indians of New Jersey*. Trenton: New Jersey Historical Commission, 1992. A brief but well-researched history of the Lenape, including a useful bibliography of sources for further study.

Kraft, Herbert C. *The Lenape: Archaeology, History, and Ethnography*. Newark: New Jersey Historical Society, 1986. An excellent study of archaeological investigations of the Lenape, written by the foremost scholar of New Jersey Indians.

_____. *The Lenape Indians of New Jersey*. South Orange, N.J.: Seton Hall Museum, 1987. The story of the Lenape, intended for younger readers.

Philhower, Charles A. "The Aboriginal Inhabitants of New Jersey." In *New Jersey: A History*. New York: American Historical Society, 1930. A classic account of the Lenape, with an excellent discussion of their westward movements.

Lillooet: Tribe

CULTURE AREA: Plateau
LANGUAGE GROUP: Salishan
PRIMARY LOCATION: Southwestern British Columbia
POPULATION SIZE: 2,570 (Statistics Canada, based on 1991 census)

The Lillooet, a branch of the Salishan family, lived in the vicinity of the Lillooet and Fraser rivers in southwestern British Columbia. They were divided into the Upper and Lower Lillooet, and each division was composed of several named bands. The name means "wild onion" and was at first applied only to the Lower Lillooet. The Upper Lillooet called themselves *Stla'tlium*, the meaning of which is unknown.

The Lillooet lived in small villages, each representing one clan. Their primary source of food was fish, especially salmon, which they caught with spears, nets, and traps. They also hunted bear, beaver, rabbit, raccoon, squirrel, and mountain goat. Men were the primary hunters, while women worked to preserve the meat and to gather berries and food from the wild. They made good use of the animals they hunted, using the skins for clothing, quills for ornamentation, and wool and hair for weaving cloth. Their homes were often made of logs or wood planks, and housed four to eight families. Other villages had circular earthlodges with warming earth berms for winter and mat houses for summer. In the front of a house there was likely to be a totem pole, featuring the clan's totem. Lillooets had sustained contact with white traders from about 1809, when explorer Simon Fraser and his party first traveled through their land. The Lillooet traded heavily with whites as well as with their tribal neighbors.

After gold was discovered in the area in 1858, they encountered many white miners, maintaining mostly friendly relations with them. They fought at times with their neighbors, especially the Thompsons. In 1863, a great epidemic of smallpox hit the area and killed many people; the Lillooet lost many members to the disease. Shortly afterward, they were afflicted by a famine that further reduced their numbers. Near the end of the twentieth century many still lived on traditional territory, on several small reserves, and were making their living by wood cutting and other forms of wage labor.

See also Diseases, post-contact; Plateau; Salishan language family; Shuswap; Thompson; Totem poles.

Little Bighorn, Battle of the

DATE: June 25-26, 1876
PLACE: Little Bighorn River, Montana
TRIBES AFFECTED: Arapaho, Arikara (army scouts), Crow (army scouts), Northern Cheyenne, Sioux
SIGNIFICANCE: The stunning defeat of the Seventh Cavalry unleashed relentless pursuit of the victorious Indians, culminating in their surrender, their exile to reservation life, and the end of traditional Plains culture

The Treaty of Fort Laramie (1868) guaranteed the Sioux a permanent reservation that encompassed all of present South Dakota west of the Missouri River and from which encroaching white settlers were forbidden. The Sioux were also guaranteed the right to hunt in a larger unceded territory, also closed to whites. About three thousand free-roaming Sioux lived on these lands and despised the thought of reservation life. Crazy Horse and Sitting Bull were the most famous of these Sioux.

Background to the Battle. The terms of the treaty, however, were blatantly violated. From 1871 to 1874, surveying parties with army escort trespassed on both the reservation and unceded territory, charting routes and finding gold in the sacred Black Hills. By mid-1875 hordes of white prospectors and adventurers were poised to invade Sioux territory, held back only by the army.

The government tried through persuasion and threats to induce the Sioux to sell the Black Hills but were unequivocally rebuffed. This led President Ulysses S. Grant to devise a plan to justify a war against the Sioux. Their defeat would remove the free-roaming Sioux from the unceded territory and place them on the reservation. The Black Hills and unceded territory would be opened for settlement and prospecting. The plan began with a decision not to enforce the ban on prospectors entering the Black Hills. Lies about Sioux misdeeds and crimes were publicly circulated. Then in December, 1875, the government gave an ultimatum to the free-roaming Northern Cheyenne and Sioux to surrender at their agencies by January 31, 1876, or be forced there by military action.

The Indians bitterly resented this ultimatum. It violated the 1868 treaty, and the free-roaming groups were determined to maintain their traditional way of life and not go to reservations. Resentment was further fueled by a famine on the reservation caused largely by negligence and graft in the distribution of guaranteed rations. In addition, the sale of firearms to hunt needed food was prohibited. The Platte Sioux had been arbitrarily removed from their reservation to save on freight charges for their rations.

Annihilation of Custer's Forces. The Indians ignored the ultimatum, and the army was ordered to capture or disperse them. On June 24 the Seventh Cavalry, under the command of General George Armstrong Custer, found an Indian camp (predominantly Sioux but including some Northern Cheyenne and Arapaho) on the south bank of the Little Bighorn River. In the mid-afternoon of June 25, 1876, the Battle of the Little Bighorn commenced. Major Marcus Reno and his three companies of 175 soldiers and Indian scouts attacked the southern end of the camp. Reno aborted the attack, however, when he realized the number of Indians he would engage. He took cover in timber along the river but was forced to withdraw to a more defensible hilltop on the bluffs across the river when set upon by an overwhelming force of Indians. The withdrawal turned into a panic and a rout. Seven officers and eighty-four men made it to the hill. Forty were killed, thirteen were wounded, and several were missing.

Custer observed Reno's charge from Weir Point, a high bluff. He searched for an opening that would permit him and his 210 troops to join the battle as soon as possible. Custer made contact with the Indians at around 3:45 P.M., near the river. What then happened is not exactly clear, but Custer moved away from the river and ended up on Custer Hill, about 4 miles from Reno's hill. Almost two thousand Indians attacked Custer's force and completely surrounded it. Within about an hour Custer and all his men were annihilated.

The third unit of Custer's force, five officers and 110 soldiers, was commanded by Captain Frederick Benteen. Benteen was under orders to search for hostiles to the left of Custer's force and then hurry back and join Custer. Benteen, however, contrary to orders, dawdled behind, probably in the belief that there were no Indian warriors in the area. Benteen did not get to the battlefield in time to help Custer. The fourth unit of Custer's force, the pack train carrying supplies, was manned by two officers and 134 soldiers. It languished in the rear and could not be of assistance when Custer was attacked.

When Benteen and the pack train arrived at the Little Bighorn they joined Reno on Reno Hill. This total force of 367 was able to withstand Indian attacks on the morning of June 26, with a loss of seven killed and forty men wounded. The Indians were gone by June 27, and the battle was over. Total army casualties numbered 263 killed and fifty-nine wounded.

The army's defeat was the result of several factors. Inadequate intelligence led Custer to underestimate the strength and temper of his foe: two thousand battle-tested warriors resolved to defend their way of life against 597 cavalry. Custer's troops were divided into four units, only two of which fought, and then at different times and places and against overwhelming odds. Another factor was the strength of the Indians' leadership; Crazy Horse, Gall, and Rain-in-the-Face were all actively involved in the fighting.

The Indians' victory was short-lived. An angry American public, Congress, and military demanded revenge. The Indians were relentlessly pursued in 1877, and by the end of the 1870's nearly all Plains Indians had been killed or confined to reservations; the traditional Plains culture passed into history.

—*Laurence Miller*

See also Black Hills; Crazy Horse; Fort Laramie Treaty of 1868; Rosebud Creek, Battle of; Sioux; Sitting Bull.

BIBLIOGRAPHY

Dillon, Richard H. *North American Indian Wars*. New York: Facts on File, 1983.

Gray, John S. *Centennial Campaign*. Ft. Collins, Colo.: Old Army Press, 1976.

Rosenberg, Bruce A. *Custer and the Epic of Defeat*. University Park: Pennsylvania State University Press, 1974.

Russell, Don. *Custer's Last*. Fort Worth, Tex.: Amon Carter Museum of Western Art, 1968.

Vaughn, Jesse W. *Indian Fights*. Norman: University of Oklahoma Press, 1966.

Little Crow (c. 1820, near South St. Paul, Minn.—July 1863, near Hutchinson, Minn.): Tribal chief

ALSO KNOWN AS: Cetan Wakan Mani, Tahatan Wakan Mini (Hawk That Hunts Walking), Taoyateduta (His Red People)

TRIBAL AFFILIATION: Mdewakanton (Dakota) Sioux

SIGNIFICANCE: Little Crow was a tribal leader during the Sioux Minnesota Uprising of 1862

Little Crow was born at Kapoosa, a Mdewakanton Dakota village on the west bank of the Mississippi River. Little is known of his childhood or youth. By the time he was fully grown he was a big man with a powerful, dominant personality.

Accounts differ, but apparently one of Little Crow's brothers was jealous of the chief and tried to kill him in 1846. Little Crow was badly wounded in both arms and never fully regained the use of his hands. The chief had six wives and produced twenty-two children.

He was one of the signers of the Treaty of Mendota, which ceded most of the Dakota Sioux territories to the whites. In spite of this 1851 pact, Little Crow subsequently spoke out against ceding Indian lands. The chief raised an Indian "posse" against Inkpaduta, a Sioux whose band had killed thirty-four whites at Spirit Lake, Minnesota, in 1857. Though his band was defeated, Inkpaduta escaped.

The Minnesota Sioux lived peacefully for a number of years, but grievances developed. There was white pressure for Indian land, government annuities failed to arrive, and white merchants refused credit, the latter meaning near-starvation for the Sioux. When a group of young warriors killed some whites, it sparked the great Minnesota Sioux uprising in the summer of 1862.

Little Crow became a major leader in Indian resistance to the whites. It is said that he was against war but changed his mind when accused of cowardice. The chief led a large force against Fort Ridgley, but the warriors were repulsed and Little Crow himself wounded. The brief but bloody uprising was ended when the Sioux were defeated at Wood Lake on September 23, 1862. Little Crow managed to escape with some two hundred followers.

He returned to Minnesota, where it is alleged that he continued his raiding. He was shot and killed by a white farmer near Hutchinson, Minnesota, on July 3, 1863. Little Crow's skeleton was given to the Minnesota Historical Society, but the remains were turned over to his descendants in 1971. He was laid to rest in a Sioux cemetery near Flandreau, South Dakota.

See also Minnesota Uprising; Sioux.

Little Priest (d. Sept., 1866): Chief, representative, scout, warrior

ALSO KNOWN AS: Hoonk-hoo-no-kaw, Little Chief

TRIBAL AFFILIATION: Winnebago

SIGNIFICANCE: Little Priest was a Winnebago tribal representative and warrior

Little Priest followed his father in the role of chief of his village in 1840. In that same year, the people of the village had relocated from Wisconsin to Iowa. Then, in 1846, he and other Winnebago leaders signed a treaty trading the reservation land in Iowa for land in Long Prairie, Minnesota. He traveled to Washington, D.C., in 1855 to sign the treaty that exchanged the Long Prairie lands for reservation space south of Mankato, Minnesota.

Little Priest supported the Minnesota Uprising of the Sioux that took place from 1862 to 1863. He may also have participated in the fighting. Most Winnebagos did not fully support the Sioux, and Little Priest was arrested for taking part in the uprising in October, 1862; he was tried and acquitted.

In 1863, the Winnebago were once again relocated, this time to a reservation in South Dakota. There was no food at this reservation, however, so the Winnebago left the reservation and reached Nebraska, where the Omaha granted them some land. Little Priest became a scout and company leader for the Omaha, fighting the Sioux between 1866 and 1868 in a war for the control of the Bozeman Trail. In March, 1866, by the Powder River in Montana, Little Priest single-handedly held off a party of advancing Sioux. He killed three Sioux, being shot various times himself before reinforcements arrived. In September, 1866, he died as a result of the wounds suffered at the engagement.

See also Little Crow; Minnesota Uprising; Winnebago.

Little Raven (c. 1825, on the Platte River, Nebr.—1889, Cantonment, Indian Territory): Chief

ALSO KNOWN AS: Hosa, Little Crow

TRIBAL AFFILIATION: Arapaho

SIGNIFICANCE: As principal Arapaho chief, Little Raven supported accommodation and peace with whites

After earning his warrior's reputation in battle against the Sauk and Fox, Little Raven succeeded his father as hereditary chief in 1855. Little Raven's intelligence, leadership, and oratorical skills were admired by Indians and whites.

As chief, Little Raven signed the Treaty of Fort Wise (1861), establishing a reservation in Arkansas. Retaliating against white encroachment during the Civil War, he led several raids in Kansas and Colorado. Distrusting Colorado governor John Evans and militia commander John Chivington, Little Raven declined their false promises for protection at Sand Creek and led his people farther south.

In 1865 and 1867, Little Raven signed the treaties of Little Arkansas and Medicine Lodge by which Indians were further relegated to reservations. During a trip in 1871 to several eastern cities, he earned a reputation among whites for oratory. Returning convinced of the president's peaceful intentions, he

remained neutral during the Red River War of 1874-1875. At his death in 1889, Little Raven was succeeded as chief by Left Hand.

See also Arapaho; Black Kettle; Medicine Lodge, Treaties of; Red River War; Sand Creek Massacre.

Little Robe (1828-1886): Peace chief

TRIBAL AFFILIATION: Southern Cheyenne

SIGNIFICANCE: Succeeded Black Kettle as leading peace chief of the Southern Cheyenne

As a young man, Little Robe distinguished himself as a warrior against traditional Cheyenne foes including Utes and Pawnees; in 1863 he became a chief. Briefly, following the Sand Creek Massacre, he fought against whites in the Cheyenne-Arapaho War. Thereafter he advocated peace, joining with Black Kettle and George Bent to bring the militant Dog Soldiers to the signing of the Medicine Lodge Treaty of 1867. After Black Kettle's death in 1868 at the Battle of Washita River, Little Robe succeeded him as principal peace chief and surrendered to General Philip Sheridan at Fort Cobb in the Indian Territory. In 1873 he headed the delegation of Southern Cheyenne and Arapaho chiefs who traveled to Washington to negotiate with the commissioner of Indian affairs. During the Red River War of 1874-1875, Little Robe continued to counsel peace.

Following the war, Little Robe lived on the North Canadian River in Indian Territory. Although he desired peace, he did

Southern Cheyenne Little Robe became the tribal leader after Black Kettle's death in 1868. (Library of Congress)

not readily adapt to "white ways," as evidenced by his refusal to send children from his band to white schools and his work to keep white-owned cattle off reservation lands.

See also Black Kettle; Cheyenne; Medicine Lodge, Treaties of; Red River War; Washita River, Battle of the.

Little Turtle (c. 1752, near Fort Wayne, Ind.—July 14, 1812, Fort Wayne, Ind.): Tribal chief

ALSO KNOWN AS: Michikinikwa

TRIBAL AFFILIATION: Miami

SIGNIFICANCE: Little Turtle led a coalition of Indian forces in an attempt to retain the Ohio River as the southern boundary of their land; he inflicted several defeats upon the U.S. Army in the 1790's

Little Turtle was born along the banks of the Eel River in Indiana. His father was a powerful Miami chief; his mother was believed to be a Mahican. Little Turtle actively campaigned against the Americans during the American Revolution. He participated in the routing of a small American force led by Colonel Augustin Mottin de la Balme during the summer of 1780 at the Aboite River.

As American settlers pushed north of the Ohio River after the close of the revolution, conflicts with the Indians intensified. A loose coalition of Miami, Shawnee, Potawatomi, and Ojibwa formed to resist the incursion.

On September 26, 1790, General Arthur St. Clair ordered Brigadier General Josiah Harmar northward from Fort Washington (present-day Cincinnati) on a mission to pacify the hostile Indians. As Harmar moved through the wilderness with an armed force of fifteen hundred men, Little Turtle organized a masterful strategy to lure him forward. The Miami towns around Fort Wayne were intentionally destroyed by the Indians in order to convince Harmar that the Indian coalition was in disarray. On October 18 and 19, 1790, Little Turtle's army defeated Harmar's force in two sharp engagements. The Americans suffered more than two hundred casualties and retreated southward.

A second punitive expedition was organized the following year. On October 3, 1791, General St. Clair left Fort Washington, moving toward the upper Wabash River. On November 4, 1791, Little Turtle's Indian army struck St. Clair's men at dawn. The ferocity of the attack panicked the militia units and delayed the formation of organized battle lines. Desperate fighting allowed a portion of St. Clair's army to escape total annihilation. Of the fourteen hundred American soldiers who participated in the battle, fewer than six hundred survived.

In 1792, General Anthony Wayne was placed in command of the U.S. army in the west. He managed to raise and train an army of three thousand men. As he moved northward, Wayne built a series of forts, including Fort Recovery on the site of St. Clair's defeat. On June 29, 1794, Little Turtle ordered a probe of Fort Recovery's defenses. Finding them too strong, Little Turtle began to advocate negotiating a peace settlement. The other Indian leaders rejected his counsel, and he was replaced by Turkey Foot (some scholars say Blue Jacket) as commander of the Indian army.

Following the defeat of the Indian forces at Fallen Timbers (1794), Little Turtle helped to negotiate the Treaty of Greenville. By the terms of that treaty, the Miami and associated tribes ceded their rights to most of modern Ohio and a large portion of Indiana.

Following the Treaty of Greenville, Little Turtle aided William Henry Harrison in his policy of gaining title to additional Indian lands. His influence prevented the Miami from joining the Indian Confederacy being created by Tenskwatawa and Tecumseh. In later years, he suffered from gout. He died at Fort Wayne while being treated by an army surgeon.

See also Fallen Timbers, Battle of; Fort Greenville, Treaty of; Indian-white relations—U.S., 1775-1830; Miami; Tecumseh; Wabash, Battle of the.

Little Wolf (c. 1820, near the Eel and Blue rivers, Mont.— 1904, Tongue River Reservation, Mont.): Chief

ALSO KNOWN AS: Ohkom Kakit, Two Tails

TRIBAL AFFILIATION: Northern Cheyenne

SIGNIFICANCE: Little Wolf fought alongside such leaders as Crazy Horse and Gall in the 1860's; along with Dull Knife, he led some 350 Cheyennes on a 1,500-mile journey from Indian Territory back to their Montana homeland

Little Wolf first distinguished himself as a warrior in battle against other tribes. In 1864, his generally peaceful attitude toward whites changed when he learned how Black Kettle and his people were killed. Along with fellow Cheyenne Dull Knife, Little Wolf fought in many of the major battles against whites that occurred in the northern Plains. He fought in the Bozeman Trail wars (Red Cloud's War) in 1866-1868 and in the Fetterman fight of December, 1866. Little Wolf was one of the signers of the 1868 Fort Laramie Treaty. He was also one of the most active war chiefs in the war for the Black Hills in 1876 and 1877, under the leadership of Sitting Bull.

The village of Dull Knife and Little Wolf was attacked by eleven hundred cavalry troops under the command of Colonel R. S. Mackenzie on November 25, 1876. Forty Cheyennes were killed in the attack; just as devastating was the destruction of their tipis, clothing, and entire winter food supply. The night of the attack, temperatures dropped below zero and many more died. During the course of the fighting, Little Wolf was erroneously reported to have been shot a number of times. He surrendered the following May and was sent to Indian Territory. About 1,000 of his people were sent to the Darlington Agency in August, 1877, with hundreds becoming ill and 43 dying within the first two months. Little Wolf and Dull Knife failed to convince authorities to allow them to return home to Montana. Nevertheless, about 350 people, under their leadership, left for Montana in September, 1878.

The group divided en route, with some following Dull Knife and others going with Little Wolf. The group following Little Wolf eluded the thousands of troops pursuing them until March, 1879, at which time Little Wolf surrendered to W. P.

Along with Dull Knife, Little Wolf was a major Northern Cheyenne leader in the 1860's and 1870's. (National Archives)

Clark near the mouth of the Powder River. He and his people were returned to Fort Keogh, Montana, with the promise of a reservation in their homeland. Dull Knife's group did not fare as well. Captured in October and imprisoned at Fort Robinson, many lost their lives in a winter attempt to escape.

Little Wolf and many of his warriors enlisted in the army as Indian scouts for General Nelson A. Miles, perhaps because military life seemed more familiar to them than reservation life. Little Wolf lived for almost thirty years on the Tongue River Reservation. Though blind in his old age, he remained mentally astute.

See also Bozeman Trail wars; Crazy Horse; Dull Knife; Fort Laramie Treaty of 1868; Gall; Little Bighorn, Battle of the; Two Moon.

Logan, James (c. 1723, Shamokin, present-day Sunbury, Pa.—1780, near Detroit, Mich.): Military leader

ALSO KNOWN AS: Logan the Mingo, John Logan, Tahgahjute
TRIBAL AFFILIATION: Cayuga
SIGNIFICANCE: A leader in Lord Dunmore's War, Logan on several occasions raided white settlers in the Appalachian region

Logan's mother was a Cayuga and his father, Shikellamy, was probably a Frenchman who was reared by Oneidas. After being elected by the Iroquois council as representative for Iroquois holdings in Pennsylvania, Shikellamy and his family moved to Shamokin, Pennsylvania.

James Logan rose to prominence among the Pennsylvania and Ohio Cayugas, known as Mingos, and was initially friendly toward whites. Indeed, his name was probably adopted from his friend, James Logan, colonial secretary of Pennsylvania. In 1774, Logan and his band moved to the Sciota River in Ohio. There, following an unprovoked attack in which white settlers killed his wife and several children, Logan became militant. Aligning himself with the Shawnee leader Cornstalk in Lord Dunmore's War, Logan conducted retaliatory raids throughout the region. After the Battle of Point Pleasant, 1774, and his refusal to participate in a peace conference, he sustained his raids against white settlers throughout the American Revolution.

He was murdered in Detroit in 1780, probably after a quarrel with a nephew.

See also Cornstalk; Lord Dunmore's War; Shikellamy.

Lone Wolf (c. 1820—c. 1879): Tribal chief

ALSO KNOWN AS: Guipago
TRIBAL AFFILIATION: Kiowa
SIGNIFICANCE: Lone Wolf was principal chief of the Kiowa from 1866 to 1879 and participated in many major battles against whites

Lone Wolf grew to manhood within the ceremonial life and ritual of his tribe, preparing for the warrior's role. After the death of the great leader Dohasan, an 1866 Kiowa council acknowledged Lone Wolf's war leadership and selected him to serve as principal chief, although he never achieved the he-

gemony of his predecessor. He attended the Medicine Lodge council (1867) and toured the nation's capital as a guest of the federal government in 1872. Following the death of his son a year later, he led attacks on hide hunters, teamsters, and the U.S. Cavalry, and participated in the Wichita Agency melee in August, 1874, which set off the Red River War on the southern Plains. He fled pursuing army troops, survived the Palo Duro Canyon disaster, and finally reluctantly surrendered in early 1875. Because of his prominence, Lone Wolf was singled out as the yardstick for antiwhite sentiment, and he was among the resisting Indians exiled to Fort Marion, Florida. He died in 1879, shortly after his release from confinement and his return home. Ethnologist James Mooney noted that Lone Wolf's passing marked "the end of the war history of the Kiowa" and the final tribal surrender to reservation assimilation.

See also Adobe Walls, Battles of; Kiowa; Medicine Lodge, Treaties of; Red River War.

BIBLIOGRAPHY

Boyd, Maurice, ed. *Kiowa Voices*. 2 vols. Fort Worth, Tex.: Texas Christian University, 1981, 1983.

Jones, J. Lee. *Red Raiders Retaliate: The Story of Lone Wolf, The Elder*. Seagraves, Tex.: Pioneer, 1980.

Lone Wolf v. Hitchcock: Legal case

DATE: Argued October 23, 1902; decided January 5, 1903
TRIBES AFFECTED: Apache, Comanche, Kiowa directly; pantribal by implication
SIGNIFICANCE: This case established the precedent that congressional plenary power over tribal property was virtually unlimited and that Indian treaties were subject to unilateral abrogation

In this litigation, Lone Wolf, a principal chief of the Kiowa Nation, sought a perpetual injunction against congressional ratification of a 1900 agreement that allotted tribal lands and led to a direct loss of more than 2 million acres of Indian territory. The tribes contended that the forced allotment of their lands violated Article Twelve of the 1867 Treaty of Medicine Lodge. This article explicitly stated that no cession of tribal lands would be valid without the consent of "three-fourths of all the adult male Indians."

In 1892 the Jerome Commission concluded an allotment agreement with certain representatives of the Kiowa, Comanche, and Apache (KCA) tribes. Although the commissioners secured a number of Indian signatures, the three-fourths provision was unfulfilled. Nevertheless, the agreement was rushed to Washington, D.C., for congressional ratification. Almost immediately upon hearing about the allotment agreement, more than three hundred KCA tribal members urged the Senate to disapprove the 1892 agreement because "misrepresentations, threats, and fraudulent" means had been used by the government's commissioners to secure Indian signatures. Tribal consent, in other words, had not been legitimately secured.

More important, as the 1892 agreement wound its way through the ratification process, Congress substantially revised the agreement. These revisions were never submitted to the KCA tribes for their approval. Nevertheless, on June 6, 1900, and despite the protestations of the tribes concerned, Congress ratified the amended agreement.

Justice Edward D. White wrote the opinion, which was, shortly after its pronouncement in 1903, called the "Dred Scott decision number two" because it inculcated the doctrine that Indian treaty rights, although the "supreme law of the land," could be disregarded with the passage of virtually any federal law. White stated that the 1867 treaty provision had been abrogated by the 1900 agreement even though the later statute contradicted the treaty provision and lacked tribal consent. This, White said, was in keeping with "perfect good faith" toward the Indians.

White inaccurately stated that Congress had exercised plenary authority over tribes "from the beginning" and that such power was "political" and therefore not subject to judicial review. These statements were legal rationalizations, yet they were also in line with the reigning policy view of Indians at the time held by the federal government: Indians were dependent wards, subject to their sovereign guardian—the United States.

Lone Wolf v. Hitchcock was a devastating blow to tribal sovereignty. The Court's brazen refusal to examine congressional acts that abrogated treaty-acknowledged property rights was particularly oppressive because the lion's share of tribal sovereign, political, and property rights was defined by the hundreds of ratified treaties and agreements tribes negotiated with the United States. Indian rights, in short, were not created by or included in the federal Constitution. As a result of this decision, treaties as legal contracts were no longer enforceable if Congress decided to act in a manner that violated their provisions.

See also Allotment system; Indian Rights Association; Land claims; Sovereignty.

Long Walk

Date: August, 1863-September, 1866
Place: New Mexico
Tribes affected: Mescalero Apache, Navajo
Significance: The unsuccessful relocation of Mescalero Apaches and Navajos from their ancestral lands to Bosque Redondo (Fort Sumner), New Mexico, caused the U.S. government to reassess its policy toward southwestern Indian tribes

In early March, 1864, 1,443 Navajos (*Dineh*, meaning "the people," "men," or "earth people" in the Navajo language) began the Long Walk, as they described their journey, of 250 miles from their ancestral homes in northeastern Arizona and northwestern New Mexico to the Bosque Redondo reservation, located on New Mexico's eastern plains at Fort Sumner. Bosque Redondo, named by Spanish explorers for a round grove of cottonwood trees situated on the Pecos River, and adjacent Fort Sumner were viewed by the American military as appropriate locales for the forced assimilation into American life of the 8,354 Navajos and 405 Mescalero Apaches

confined there by December, 1864. Although most Navajos made the journey in 1864, smaller groups had made the journey the year before.

Historical Background. Following the Mexican government's cession of 1.2 million square miles of territory to the United States by the Treaty of Guadalupe Hidalgo, February 2, 1848, relations between Americans and Navajos became increasingly tense as the United States government exerted control over the Southwest, land now under United States sovereignty. This increased tension characterized Colonel James Macrae Washington's expedition into *Dinetah* (Navajo land) in August, 1849, an invasion which resulted in the death of a respected Navajo headman (*naataani*), Narbona, August 31, 1849. Narbona was "shot in four or five places and scalped," according to an eyewitness. Ostensibly undertaken to assure Navajos of American "peaceful" intentions in constructing forts in and settling Navajo land, Washington's expedition had the opposite effect. Angered by Narbona's murder, his son-in-law, Manuelito, vowed to drive all white men from Navajo country. With the aid of another Navajo headman, Barboncito, on the night of April 29, 1860, Manuelito launched an offensive against Fort Defiance, built by Colonel Edwin Vose Sumner in 1851. Fort Defiance and its nearby canyon, Cañoncito Bonito (both adjacent to present-day Window Rock, Arizona, capital of the Navajo Nation), became central staging areas for the Long Walk.

Carleton's War, 1862-1864. Tensions with the Mescalero Apaches, evidenced in the murder of Nodnhi Apache chief Mangas Coloradus in January, 1863, and the incursions of New Mexican raiding parties on Navajo land to purchase Navajo slaves resulted in planned effort to exterminate both Mescalero Apaches and Navajos. Another impetus was Union brigadier general James H. Carleton's view that Apache and Navajo country contained gold and other minerals. Appointed commander of the New Mexico military department, Carleton reasoned that, following his successful 1862 recapture of Tucson for the Union, he could destroy Confederate designs on New Mexico by removing Indians from their ancestral homes and opening their lands to Anglo-American prospectors.

To realize this ambition, General Carleton's Indian policy (approved by Mauhuache Ute agent Christopher "Kit" Carson; James L. Collins, Superintendent of Indian Affairs in New Mexico; and New Mexico territory's new governor, Henry Connelly) called for his fifteen hundred California volunteers to force New Mexico's nonslave Indians to surrender and to relocate at Bosque Redondo, situated on the alkaline Rio Pecos, 175 miles southeast of Santa Fe. There the Mescalero Apaches and Navajos would be taught agriculture and Christianity. Not without his misgivings about Carleton's policy, Kit Carson, now a colonel in the New Mexican territorial militia, waged war against the Mescalero Apaches and their chief, Cadete, during the 1862-1863 winter. By March, 1863, more than four hundred Mescalero Apaches—men, women, and children—were confined to Bosque Redondo in an experiment in agricultural self-sufficiency from which they would flee in

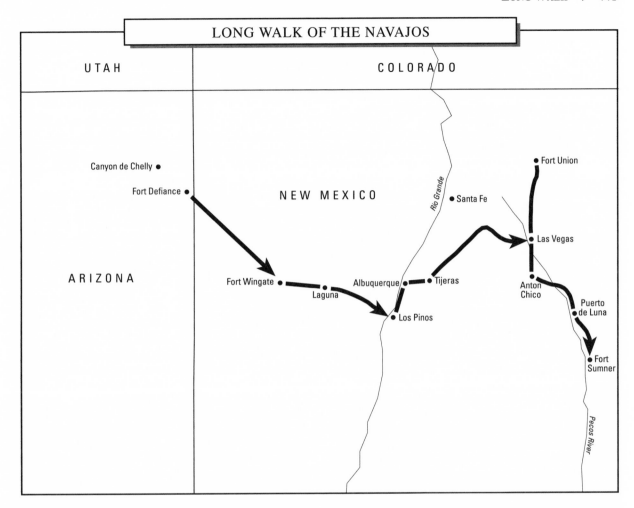

LONG WALK OF THE NAVAJOS

UTAH

COLORADO

Canyon de Chelly ●

Fort Defiance ●

NEW MEXICO

● Fort Union

Rio Grande

● Santa Fe

ARIZONA

Fort Wingate ●
Laguna

Albuquerque ●
● Tijeras

● Las Vegas

Anton
Chico

Puerto
● de Luna

● Los Pinos

● Fort
Sumner

Pecos River

the autumn of 1865. Carson turned the attention of Carleton's California volunteers to the Navajos.

During the summer of 1863, General Carleton ordered a campaign of subjugation against the Navajos, an offensive begun August 5, 1863. From Forts Defiance and Wingate, Colonel Carson and his one thousand volunteers vied with Governor Connelly's companies of civilian volunteers to take Navajo captives. Connelly's civilians assumed that, if the Navajos surrendered to Carson, opportunity to profit from Navajo slavery was impossible. Carson urged his Ute guides to take Navajo captives, thus destroying the "collectiveness" of Navajo tribal interest.

Carson's War, 1863-1864. Navajos eluded capture by Carson's volunteers, headquartered at Fort Defiance (renamed Fort Canby by Carson in July, 1863). General Carleton reported to the federal government at the beginning of September, 1863, that a mere fifty-one Navajos, including children and women, had been rounded up and sent to the Bosque Redondo reservation. Carleton ordered Carson to tell Navajo males: "Go to the Bosque Redondo, or we will pursue and destroy you." In the harsh 1863-1864 winter, Carson's pursuit

of the impoverished Navajos, now scattered in small bands throughout Navajo country, was successful.

Carson's destruction of Navajo crops and livestock between Fort Canby and Canyon de Chelly resulted in the surrender of 188 Navajos and their Long Walk to Bosque Redondo in the autumn of 1863. The captured included Delgadito, a prominent Navajo headman, who agreed to Carleton's request to convince other headmen to relocate to the Bosque Redondo. Repeated American forays into the Navajo stronghold, Canyon de Chelly, resulted in the surrender of twelve hundred Navajos at Fort Canby by mid-February, 1864. Many of this group and the seven hundred Navajos surrendering to Fort Wingate authorities on Delgadito's advice formed the main part of the Long Walk of the Navajos to Fort Sumner and the Bosque Redondo in March, 1864, accompanied by nearly five hundred horses and about three thousand sheep. Of the 1,443 Navajos on this trek, ten died during the Long Walk and three children were kidnapped for use as slaves by New Mexican members of the soldier escort.

The Long Walk. In the mid-1860's approximately nine thousand Navajos were forced to live in imprisonment at

Bosque Redondo. Navajo deaths among Long Walk participants were steep. On March 4, 1864, twenty-four hundred Navajos, their numbers reduced by the deaths of 126 from dysentery the preceding week, left Fort Canby for the Bosque Redondo reservation. On reaching Fort Sumner, 197 remained behind, either dead or dying. The eight hundred Navajos leaving Fort Canby for their new home on March 20, 1864, experienced a four-day snowstorm, the kidnapping of many Navajo children, the loss of twenty-three wagons used to transport the infirm and elderly, and the loss of supplies at Los Pinos (south of Albuquerque). By the time the group reached Fort Sumner and Bosque Redondo on May 11, 1864, 110 had perished. By July, 1864, some fifty-nine hundred Navajos were resettled at Bosque Redondo. General Carleton, guessing that only two thousand Navajos remained in *Dinetah*, advised Kit Carson that Bosque Redondo could feed seventy-five hundred Navajos.

Navajo leaders Barboncito and Ganado Blanco, son of Ganado Mucho, temporarily fled Bosque Redondo in July, 1865. Their later return left two headmen, Ganado Mucho and Manuelito, remaining free in Navajo country. Manuelito had participated in the Long Walk but quickly returned home, informing a delegation of Navajo headmen sent by Carleton from Bosque Redondo that he would not return. On September 1, 1866, however, forty-eight-year-old Manuelito surrendered at Fort Wingate, arriving at Bosque Redondo one month later. In the autumn of 1865, Ganado Mucho and his band surrendered at Fort Wingate, New Mexico. Preceded on their Long Walk to Bosque Redondo by women and children, Ganado Mucho and the men of his band who herded his livestock learned in reaching Fort Sumner that Mucho's two daughters had been kidnapped near the Rio Grande. This tragedy was compounded by the tragedies of Navajo resettlement at Bosque Redondo.

End of the Long Walk. Brigadier General Carleton's plan for the resettlement of Mescalero Apaches and Navajos at the Long Walk's terminus, Bosque Redondo, was not achieved. Indian self-sufficiency in agrarian pursuits was overshadowed by traditional animosity between Mescalero Apaches and Navajos, corn crop failures caused by cutworm invasions, Comanche attacks, smallpox epidemics, and increased criticism of Carleton's policies from a number of quarters. Secretary of War Edwin M. Stanton removed Carleton from his command on September 19, 1866. The 7,304 Navajos living at Bosque Redondo were promised a return to a new 3.5-million-acre reservation on their homeland by the terms of a June 1, 1868, peace treaty signed by United States representatives William T. Sherman and Colonel Samuel F. Tappan and by nine Navajo headmen. The U.S. Congress appropriated $150,000 for Navajo travel expenses from Bosque Redondo. Escorted by four companies of U.S. cavalry, they began their long walk home on June 18, 1868.   —*Malcolm B. Campbell*

See also Apache; Barboncito; Canyon de Chelly; Delgadito; Ganado Mucho; Guadalupe Hidalgo, Treaty of; Mangas Coloradus; Manuelito; Navajo; Navajo War.

BIBLIOGRAPHY

Bender, Norman J. *"New Hope for the Indians" : The Grant Peace Policy and the Navajos in the 1870's*. Albuquerque: University of New Mexico Press, 1989.

Dutton, Bertha P. *American Indians of the Southwest*. Rev. ed. Albuquerque: University of New Mexico Press, 1983.

Iverson, Peter. *The Navajo Nation*. Albuquerque: University of New Mexico Press, 1983.

_____. *The Navajos*. New York: Chelsea House, 1990.

Locke, Raymond Friday. *The Book of the Navajo*. Los Angeles: Mankind Publishing, 1976.

Underhill, Ruth. *The Navajos*. Rev. ed. Norman: University of Oklahoma Press, 1967.

Longest Walk

DATE: February 11-July 15, 1978
PLACE: From San Francisco, California, to Washington, D.C.
TRIBES AFFECTED: Pantribal
SIGNIFICANCE: The Longest Walk, one of the several major Indian protest movements of the 1970's, was an attempt to persuade the U.S. government to recognize and protect Indian treaty rights and Indian sovereignty

The Longest Walk was a five-month cross-country demonstration by Indian people to protest federal bills in Congress that were seen as destructive of the Indians' very existence. About two hundred Native Americans began the walk from the once Indian-occupied Alcatraz Island, in San Francisco Bay. Thousands of Indians participated along the way, ultimately arriving in the nation's capital on July 15, 1978. One of the demonstrators was Russell Means of the American Indian Movement. The protesters set up a camp at the Mall, hoping to convince lawmakers not to pass the bills.

The pending legislation would have weakened Indian rights to land, resources, and self-government. For example, one bill proposed to limit Indian water rights, while others threatened to cancel Indian hunting and fishing rights and terminate all treaties between the United States and Indian tribes.

Congressional supporters and others assured the Indians that the anti-Indian bills would not pass. Nevertheless, they agreed with the Indian demonstrators that Congress and the American public should be aware that such legislation had been proposed. The Longest Walk was a symbolic victory for Indian people. It also demonstrated a solidarity among Indians.

See also Activism; American Indian Movement (AIM); Civil rights and citizenship; Indian-white relations—U.S., 1934-1995; Means, Russell; Pan-Indianism; Sovereignty.

Longhouse

TRIBES AFFECTED: Iroquois, Northwest Coast tribes, others
SIGNIFICANCE: The longhouse is a distinctive architectural structure used by various tribes for housing in traditional times and used as the setting for religious ceremonies today

The longhouse is an architectural form that occurs widely throughout the world, including native North America, Africa,

Participants in the Longest Walk across from the White House in July 1978, five months after the march began. (Library of Congress)

Micronesia, and Scandinavia. The longhouse is, as the name implies, relatively long and narrow, often reaching 50 to 70 feet in length and 12 to 15 feet in width. Longhouses usually have several fires for cooking and heating arrayed along their central axis, each maintained by a nuclear family. The nuclear families within a longhouse usually are closely related and form a matrilineal extended family. In North America, longhouses have been traditional for the Iroquois and various of the Northwest Coast tribes. Among the Iroquois, the longhouse is a symbol of traditional values and, when it was the primary form of housing, was the site of various traditional religious ceremonies. Though the twentieth century Iroquois live mostly in single-family housing, the religious association of the longhouse has been continued. The religion of Handsome Lake, commonly called the "Longhouse religion," holds its ceremonies in a longhouse dedicated to that purpose. Most twentieth century Northwest Coast tribes use longhouses solely for potlatches and other ceremonies.

See also Architecture—Northeast; Architecture—Northwest Coast; Iroquois Confederacy; Longhouse religion.

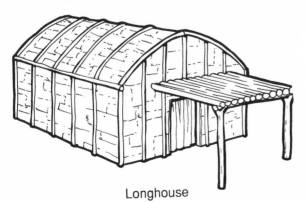

Longhouse

Longhouse religion

TRIBES AFFECTED: Seneca, other Iroquois tribes

SIGNIFICANCE: The Longhouse religion, influential among the Iroquois, particularly the Senecas, stressed the importance of the family and the harmful effects of such "sins" as promiscuity, wife beating, and alcoholism

The Longhouse religion, or the *Gaiwiio*, "the good word," is the modern religious tradition that traces its roots to the Seneca prophet Handsome Lake, who delivered his prophecies in 1810. His first vision occurred in 1799. Handsome Lake was born at the Seneca village Canawaugus, near Avon, New York. He was a recognized Seneca chief, as was his half-brother, Cornplanter. Cornplanter was the better known of the two among non-Indians, having traveled widely on behalf of Seneca, and general Native American, issues.

In June, 1799, Handsome Lake was seriously ill and fell unconscious. He reported having a vision while in this state. In this vision he saw three men holding berry bushes; they offered berries to Handsome Lake. The berries had a healing effect, and as he recovered, he began to talk with the three men. It was understood that there was one man missing, a fourth, whom Handsome Lake later identified with the Great Spirit, who would come again at a later time. During his conversations with the three men, Handsome Lake heard them condemn alcoholism, pronounce a death sentence on a witch, and condemn witchcraft generally. Handsome Lake himself was told not to drink anymore. Furthermore, Handsome Lake was given to understand that his sins were not unforgivable and that he was to teach his people the proper way to live.

Handsome Lake had many such visions after this initial one, and over sixteen years of activity, a "Code" of teachings was gathered and became a part of Seneca oral tradition. The Code sounds very similar to apocalyptic biblical visions, such as those found in the books of Daniel and Revelation, in that it describes visions of heaven and hell and involves a conversation between a mortal and a being who describes what the person is seeing, emphasizing the importance of the message. Among the more significant of the visions of Handsome Lake are his reports of punishments in hell for specific sins, such as stinginess, alcoholism, witchcraft, sexual promiscuity, wife beating, gambling, and quarrelsome family relations. Each of these "sins" was associated with a particularly graphic punishment in hell.

As the Code reads in Arthur C. Parker's 1913 edition (based on oral tradition as it existed in 1910), it is a series of admonitions and bits of advice on preserving personal piety and family life and rejecting alcohol, gambling, and other threats to social existence. The Code is worded in a concerned and compassionate tone, as advice from the Great Spirit.

It is clear that the enumerated "sins" are signs of social breakdown and trouble among the Senecas themselves in times of contact with European American culture. Indeed, the religion of Handsome Lake was to become a significant response to and survival mechanism for the Seneca people. By 1861, traditional religion among the Senecas had been almost entirely replaced by membership in either a Christian missionary church or the Longhouse religion based on the teachings of Handsome Lake. Many Senecas then, as now, saw little conflict in active membership of both movements.

Most of the information about the early development of the Handsome Lake religion, and the visions of Handsome Lake himself, come from two main sources. Arthur C. Parker, working with a descendant of Cornplanter, sponsored a project involving Edward Cornplanter and a Seneca Baptist Christian, who translated into English the oral tradition as recollected by Cornplanter himself in about 1910.

The other main source of information is the journals of Quaker workers who lived with the Senecas at the time of Handsome Lake's visions and were on hand to record many of those visions at the precise time of Handsome Lake's activity. In 1798, the Quakers sponsored the work of Henry Simmons, Jr., Joel Swayne, and Halliday Jackson. They were not so much missionaries as relief workers whose intention was to teach trades and skills such as agriculture and spinning and to teach reading and writing to any young Senecas who were interested in attending regular school sessions, held at first in Cornplanter's home. The journals of these Quaker workers represent eyewitness accounts. The journals have been edited and published by Anthony F. C. Wallace.

The modern practice of the Longhouse religion is largely a private affair, not open to non-Indian investigation. In response to modern questions, respondents generally reply with answers similar to the following: "I do not have the right to exploit this tradition, since it is not mine to give—I am only a follower." Modern practitioners frequently describe the Longhouse religion as "a way of living and feeling that is our way" or say that "the Earth is filled with gifts, and we should give thanks for what is received, according to the Code of Handsome Lake."

From written accounts, it is possible to summarize Longhouse religious practice as highly personal and often emotional; it involves strong encouragement to maintain a pure lifestyle according to the teachings of Handsome Lake and emphasizes such important matters as alcoholism and family unity. Furthermore, regular occasions are set aside for recounting the Code of Handsome Lake, which must be read before noon; this may take from three to five days. Modern estimates of Longhouse religious practice suggest that nearly half of the Seneca-Iroquois are active participants and that adherents stretch from modern New York into southern Canada, and into Oklahoma on Seneca reservations there. Non-Indian students interested in the Longhouse religion should exercise great care in investigating this tradition with Seneca members, keeping in mind the sad history of exploitation that is very much in the minds of most Native American practitioners of native religious traditions, such as the Longhouse religion, the Shaker Church, the use of peyote (as in the Native American Church), and other expressions of religious faith.

—*Daniel L. Smith-Christopher*

See also Cornplanter; Handsome Lake; Iroquois Confederacy; Seneca.

BIBLIOGRAPHY

Handsome Lake. *The Code of Handsome Lake*. Bulletin 163. Edited by Arthur C. Parker. New York: New York State Museum, 1913.

Wallace, Anthony F. C. *Death and Rebirth of the Seneca*. New York: Alfred A. Knopf, 1973.

_____, ed. "Halliday Jackson's Journal to the Seneca Indians, 1798-1800." Part 1. *Pennsylvania History* 19, no. 2 (1952): 117-147.

_____, ed. "Halliday Jackson's Journal to the Seneca Indians, 1798-1800." Part 2. *Pennsylvania History* 19, no. 3 (1952): 325-349.

Looking Glass (c. 1823, near present-day Asotin, Wash.—Oct. 5, 1877, Bear's Paw Battlefield, Bear's Paw Mountains, Mont.): Chief

ALSO KNOWN AS: Allalimya Takanin, Apushwahite

TRIBAL AFFILIATION: Nez Perce

SIGNIFICANCE: Looking Glass, one of the important nontreaty Nez Perce chiefs, served as war leader and guide in the ultimately unsuccessful retreat to Canada in the Nez Perce War of 1877

Looking Glass was the son of Looking Glass the leader (Apah Wyakaikt), an illustrious and respected chief. He was reared to be a warrior, buffalo hunter, and chief. He and his father were of the Nez Perce faction that was never Christianized by missionaries and never signed any land treaties with whites. Their faction represented one-third of the Nez Perce people.

In January of 1863, the elder Looking Glass died and his son became chief. He adopted his father's name and, just as his father had done, hung his father's small, round trade mirror

Nez Perce leader Looking Glass in 1877. (National Archives)

around his neck (hence the name Looking Glass). His village was located on the Clearwater River just above the present town of Kooskia, Idaho. The village of about 40 men and 120 women and children raised livestock, planted crops, and generally prospered. In 1863, however, gold was discovered on Nez Perce lands and Looking Glass was a realist concerning the invading whites. Aware of their strength and numbers, at tribal council in 1873 and 1877 he advised against war. Nevertheless, the Nez Perce War began in 1877.

In the early stages of the war, Looking Glass remained aloof from the hostilities, convinced that nothing was to be gained by war. He was falsely accused of aiding the hostiles, however; an arrest warrant was issued, and a fight broke out. The Indians deserted their village, which was destroyed by the whites. Seething with hatred, Looking Glass joined the other nontreaty Nez Perce in their war.

At a council on July 15, 1877, Looking Glass persuaded the other combatants to cross the Lolo Trail and seek safety with the Crow tribe in Plains country. If necessary they could continue on to join Sitting Bull in Canada and then return to their lands when the trouble had subsided. Looking Glass became war leader of all the bands and was responsible for guiding them. Encountering no resistance from whites along the route, Looking Glass proceeded confidently at a slow and leisurely pace, brushing aside concerns about the pursuing soldiers. The Nez Perce were overtaken on August 9 at Big Hole and suffered significant casualties before they escaped. Looking Glass was held responsible, and—in disgrace—was relieved of his leadership. In September, he again counseled a slower pace because the pursuing soldiers were far behind and his people needed rest. Once more he had his way and was reinstated as leader of the march.

This time, his decision proved fatal. The Indians were overtaken again in the Bear's Paw Mountains, just 30 miles from Canada, and defeated. Looking Glass was the last casualty of the Nez Perce War, fatally shot in the head on October 5, 1877.

See also Joseph the Younger; Nez Perce; Nez Perce War; Yellow Wolf.

Lord Dunmore's War

PLACE: Ohio River valley

DATE: 1774

TRIBES AFFECTED: Huron (Wyandot), Lenni Lenape, Mingo (detached Iroquois in Ohio), Ottawa, Shawnee

SIGNIFICANCE: This Indian-Virginian conflict on the northwest frontier stirred the lasting enmity of Indians in the Ohio country toward white settlers

Various factors contributed to the outbreak of Lord Dunmore's War. John Murray, fourth earl of Dunmore and the royal governor of Virginia, in 1773 declared western Pennsylvania part of the Virginia colony and desired to secure the area from claims of Pennsylvania. Settlers, in violation of the Proclamation of 1763, encroached upon Indian lands. Surveyors, on behalf of claimants of French and Indian War land bounties

and private land companies, entered Indian territory. During the spring of 1774 violence broke out among Indians and Americans along the Ohio River. The precipitating incident for the war came on April 30, when Jacob Greathouse, a frontiersman, and a half dozen others wantonly murdered five Mingo braves and the sister of Chief Logan at Yellow Creek, 50 miles below Fort Pitt on the Ohio River. Logan asserted that all of his relatives (thirteen in all) had been murdered by frontiersmen; he took revenge by killing an equal number of whites. John Connolly, whom Dunmore had appointed commandant at Fort Pitt, issued a fiery proclamation for people in the backcountry to take measures to defend themselves. Terror seized the frontier from western Pennsylvania to the Carolinas.

Lord Dunmore's War directly involved the Shawnees, with Mingos and Ottawas giving only very limited support. Delawares (Lenni Lenapes) and other Ohio country Indians, the Iroquois, and Cherokees, although tempted to join the Shawnees, did not do so. Lord Dunmore decided to punish the Indians by having two columns of Virginia militia converge upon Shawnee towns in present-day southeast Ohio. Dunmore and Colonel Adam Stephen, with eleven hundred men, traveled via Winchester (Virginia) and Pittsburgh. Colonel Andrew Lewis, with thirteen hundred troops from the far western Virginia counties, moved down the Great Kanawha River to its juncture with the Ohio. Lewis made camp at Point Pleasant on the Ohio, and Dunmore established camp (Fort Gower) at the mouth of the Hocking River further down the Ohio.

During the night of October 9, the Shawnee chief, Cornstalk, and a thousand Indians crossed the Ohio to its south bank and at daybreak attacked Lewis' force. Fortunately for Lewis, he had warning from hunters of the approaching Indians. The battle lasted all day; at nightfall the Indians withdrew across the river. Cornstalk and his warriors had been close to a decisive victory. A flanking movement during the battle led by Evan Shelby, however, convinced the Indians that additional Virginia troops under William Christian had arrived (this detachment had been expected but did not arrive at the scene of battle until midnight of October 10). The Battle of Pleasant Point is sometimes regarded as the first battle of the American Revolution. Seventy-seven Americans were killed, and seventy were wounded.

Meanwhile, Dunmore halted about 8 miles from the Shawnee villages at Chillicothe, Ohio. Cornstalk and other Shawnee chiefs, finding themselves virtually alone in the war and fearful for the safety of their women and children, had little choice but to agree to peace terms. The Indians pledged to give up Kentucky as a hunting ground, to stop molesting settlers traveling down the Ohio, to return prisoners, and to accept trade regulations to be determined at a later time. A treaty, however, was not formally ratified (with five Virginia and two continental commissioners) until an Indian conference held at Fort Pitt from September 12 to October 12, 1775. With the American Revolution having started by that time, the Ohio Indians agreed to neutrality, which lasted but two years, with most of the tribes of the Old Northwest then siding with the British. The delay, however, was of great assistance to the American Patriot cause. Lord Dunmore has been accused of starting the 1774 Indian war in order to divert the attention of Virginians from the American-British crisis at the time. Dunmore gained instant popularity from his Indian campaign, but the campaign left him overconfident and negligent in preparing for the defense of the royal government in Virginia.

See also Cornstalk; Indian-white relations—English colonial; Proclamation of 1763; Shawnee.

Luiseño: Tribe
CULTURE AREA: California
LANGUAGE GROUP: Takic
PRIMARY LOCATION: Southern California (southern Los Angeles to Newport Beach and inland)
POPULATION SIZE: 2,694 (1990 U.S. Census)

The Luiseño are among the Takic-speaking tribal groups of the Uto-Aztecan language family in Southern California. Like a number of other California groups (including the Gabrielino, Fernandeño, and Juaneño) the name by which they are known refers to the Spanish mission established in their territory; in their case, it was the San Luis Rey mission.

The Luiseño developed in a different cultural direction from those of their northern neighbors, the Gabrielino and Fernandeño, from about 1400 C.E. One of the most notable additions to the material culture of the Luiseño was pottery, clearly an influence of more southern tribal groups. The Luiseño were a conservative group who generally pursued an isolationist policy in relations with their neighbors. According to Lowell John Bean and Florence Shipek, four major aspects of the Luiseño culture are known: an extensive social class structure that extended into carefully observed property ownership and closely guarded borders, often carefully marked; a ruling family, interrelated among ruling families of the other villages; the use of hallucinogenic plants in religious ceremony; and the use of sand paintings and other religious rituals involved with recognition of Chingichngish, seen by the Luiseño as a vengeful, godlike figure.

Acorns and other seeds were the major food source for the Luiseño, who ground and cooked them in the form of mush. Like other Southern California tribes, the Luiseño also created baskets. The men wore ear and nose ornaments.

Among the Luiseño there was a hereditary chief, who had an assistant; the chief conducted negotiations in peace and war and economic matters. He was advised by a council of religious leaders who were involved in the cult of Chingichngish.

There is no Luiseño reservation, and most modern Luiseño live in southern Los Angeles and Orange counties, California.

See also California.

Lumbee: Tribe
CULTURE AREA: Southeast
LANGUAGE GROUP: Siouan (?)
PRIMARY LOCATION: North Carolina
POPULATION SIZE: 48,444 (1990 U.S. Census)

The origins of the Lumbee Indians are obscure. When they first attracted the serious attention of their white neighbors in the early 1900's, they were already English-speaking small farmers living largely in Robeson County, North Carolina. At one time, it was believed that they descended from Croatan Indians who had absorbed the survivors of Sir Walter Raleigh's "lost colony." Some Lumbees have claimed descent from the Cherokees and Tuscaroras. Most likely, however, they are descendants of Siouan-speaking Cheraw Indians who inhabited southeastern North Carolina in the seventeenth and eighteenth centuries. General use of the name Lumbee (from the Lumber River) dates only from 1953; previously, the Lumbees were referred to as Croatans, Indians of Robeson County, or, derisively, as "Scuffletonians."

Lumbee history has been a struggle to preserve an Indian identity. In 1835, North Carolina classified them as "free people of color." (Many white Carolinians believed them as much African as Indian in background.) When the state attempted to draft Lumbees as laborers during the Civil War, armed resistance led by Henry Berry Lowry resulted. After the war, North Carolina began to recognize the Lumbees as Indians, establishing schools and a college for them. Under the Jim Crow system of racial segregation, North Carolina Indians occupied a third category distinct from whites and blacks.

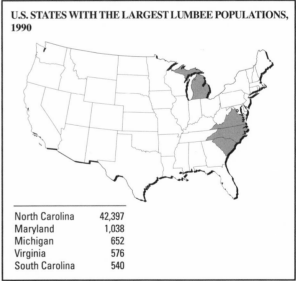

U.S. STATES WITH THE LARGEST LUMBEE POPULATIONS, 1990

North Carolina	42,397
Maryland	1,038
Michigan	652
Virginia	576
South Carolina	540

Source: 1990 U.S. Census.

Lumbee assertion of Indian identity continued into the twentieth century. In 1958, the Lumbees gained national attention when they forcibly broke up a Ku Klux Klan rally. In 1968 the Lumbee Regional Development Association was organized, serving as a tribal government as well as an economic development agency. Rural poverty remained a major tribal problem, prompting many to move to cities, especially Baltimore. Lumbees also became increasingly active in pan-Indian activities. Federal recognition became a goal. (The Lumbees had no treaty relationship with the United States government.) While an act of Congress did take formal notice of the Lumbees as an Indian tribe, an 1987 petition for full federal recognition was not successful.

See also Cape Fear; Cheraw; Pan-Indianism; Siouan language family; Southeast; Waccamaw.

Lummi: Tribe

CULTURE AREA: Northwest Coast
LANGUAGE GROUP: Salishan
PRIMARY LOCATION: Washington State
POPULATION SIZE: 2,956 (1990 U.S. Census)

In their homeland of the San Juan Islands and adjacent mainland in northern Puget Sound, the Lummi people traditionally spoke a dialect of Coast Salish which was also spoken by the Songish people of southern Vancouver Island. Their economy was based on sockeye salmon, caught in nets from canoes, and herring, codfish, dog salmon, humpback salmon, and silver salmon caught with traps, weirs, hooks, dip nets, and spears. Ducks were also caught in underwater nets, and clams and crabs were gathered along the shorelines. In addition, the Lummis occasionally hunted and trapped beaver, otter, muskrat, and bear. Camas bulbs and other roots were dug and cooked in rock-lined pits to add variety to the diet. Plentiful berries also added to the variety of foods.

Cedar was used for many purposes, such as building the large extended family longhouses in which Lummi people lived in their permanent coastline villages. Cedar was also used to make huge dugout canoes, the bark used for clothing, baskets, and other uses. The Lummis traded and intermarried with tribes as far north as the Fraser River and as far south as the White River. Warfare occasionally disrupted peaceful relations, making palisades in front of their villages necessary. In 1827, a Hudson's Bay Company post invaded the region, and by the 1850's, settlers were also intruding on the Lummi homeland. Disease, unscrupulous trading, and alcoholism, as well as the cession of most of Lummi territory to the United States government, took their toll on this proud nation. Nevertheless, the Lummi population was higher in 1980 than it had been in the 1790's. The Lummi Reservation near Bellingham, Washington, was home to about 2,500 Lummi people in the late twentieth century. The Lummis have experienced a cultural renaissance by reviving many traditional cultural and spiritual celebrations. They have also embarked on a pioneering self-government project, giving them independence from the U.S. Bureau of Indian Affairs. In the 1980's, the tribal government set up an ambitious aquaculture project to preserve salmon, oysters, trout, and other marine species.

See also Nooksack; Northwest Coast; Salishan language family; Skagit.

McGillivray, Alexander (c. 1759, Tallassee Village near Elmore County on Coosa River, east central Ala.—Feb. 17, 1793, Pensacola, Fla.): Chief

ALSO KNOWN AS: Hippo Ilk Mico, Isti Atcagagi Thlucco (Great Beloved Man)

TRIBAL AFFILIATION: Creek (Muskogee moiety)

SIGNIFICANCE: A wealthy trader and skilled diplomat, McGillivray sought to unite the Creeks and thwart white incursions into Indian territory; he was party to the first treaty concluded with the U.S. government

Alexander McGillivray was born into the Wind clan of the Creek Indians, the son of Scottish trader and planter Lachlan McGillivray and a French-Creek woman, Sehoy Marchand. At most McGillivray was one-fourth Indian. Until age fourteen, he resided with his mother at his father's trading post on the Tallapoosa River. He was then educated tutorially in Charleston, South Carolina, by the Reverend Farquhar McGillivray, a relative and Presbyterian minister. McGillivray also received business training at a countinghouse in Savannah, Georgia.

At the beginning of the American Revolution, McGillivray became a British agent and commissary to the southern Indians, which involved visits and residences among the various Creek groups. As Loyalists, Lachlan McGillivray and his son fled Georgia, the father returning to Scotland and Alexander, to the area of his birth in Alabama. The younger McGillivray helped to send out war parties to assist British and Loyalist troops during the war. McGillivray himself led raids, plundering Patriot plantations and stealing slaves.

McGillivray assumed leadership of the Creeks in 1783, when he summoned a gathering of representatives from thirty-four Creek towns, resulting in a repudiation of the Treaty of Augusta between Creeks and Georgia. The treaty had ceded lands to Georgia between the Oconee and Tugaloo rivers. McGillivray was elected chief and head warrior of all the Creeks.

McGillivray became a silent partner in the commercial firm of Panton, Leslie, and Company, which, under the protection of the Spaniards in the Floridas, had trade outlets at Pensacola and Mobile. McGillivray engaged extensively in the peltry trade and stock raising. He owned three plantations in the Alabama country and had sixty slaves. He worked diligently to strengthen the National Council of the Creeks. In 1784, McGillivray accepted a Spanish appointment as Indian commissary at $50 a month. He hoped to involve the Spaniards in a frontier war against American settlements along the southern frontier. McGillivray's Creeks raided in western Georgia and along the Cumberland River. In 1787, the Spaniards stopped supplying arms to McGillivray and sought strict neutrality with the American government. McGillivray now decided to play the American and Spanish governments against each other.

In 1790, McGillivray led an Indian delegation of thirty Creeks, accompanied by a detachment of U.S. soldiers, to the federal capital in New York City. On August 7, on an extraordinary occasion, McGillivray and the other Creek chiefs met with the U.S. Senate, and on the spot, the Treaty of New York was signed and ratified. McGillivray and the Creeks agreed to come under the protection of the United States and to cede lands between the Ogeechee and Oconee rivers but not to recognize any other claims by Georgia. In secret clauses, McGillivray received a $1,200 annual salary from the U.S. government and was made a brigadier general in the American army. Abigail Adams, wife of the vice president, at the time commented that McGillivray "dresses in our own fashion, speaks English like a native . . . is not very dark, [and is] much a gentleman." The treaty had little immediate effect because McGillivray prevented surveys of the new boundary. He continued, however, as a pensioner of both the Spanish and U.S. governments.

McGillivray had at least two wives and two children, Alexander and Elizabeth. A very heavy drinker, he died of "gout in the stomach" at the home of William Panton in Pensacola and was buried in the garden of the estate.

See also Creek; Indian-white relations—English colonial; Indian-white relations—U.S., 1775-1830.

McIntosh, William (c. 1775, Coweta, Ga.—May 1, 1825, Acorn Town, Ala.): Tribal chief

ALSO KNOWN AS: Tustennugee Hutkee (White Warrior)

TRIBAL AFFILIATION: Creek

SIGNIFICANCE: McIntosh led the pro-American faction of the Creeks during the early nineteenth century, signing treaties ceding much land to the United States

Son of a Scottish father and Creek mother, William McIntosh was principal chief of the important Lower Creek town of Coweta. He and his followers sought a more centralized tribal government and good relations with the United States, even at the cost of ceding tribal lands. McIntosh adopted the lifestyle of a southern planter and moved easily in both Creek and white culture.

McIntosh was opposed by the Red Stick faction of Creek traditionalists and fought against them in the Creek War (1813-1814). McIntosh signed several treaties ceding Creek land, climaxing in the 1825 Treaty of Indian Springs, which ceded most of the tribe's remaining land east of the Mississippi. This violated a decree of the Creek National Council that prescribed the death penalty for any Creek who ceded tribal land without the council's consent. The council ordered McIntosh's execution. This was duly carried out by a party led by the former Red Stick Menewa. McIntosh's brother and sons subsequently played major roles in Creek politics.

See also Big Warrior; Creek; Creek War; Menewa; Weatherford, William.

McNickle, D'Arcy (Jan. 18, 1904, St. Ignatius, Mont.—Oct. 18, 1977, Albuquerque, N.Mex.): Writer, administrator

TRIBAL AFFILIATION: Salish, Kutenai

SIGNIFICANCE: After writing one of the first novels by an American Indian, McNickle worked as an administrator and political organizer and authored works of anthropology and history

Of Canadian Cree, French, and Irish American ancestry, McNickle grew up in a Salish, or Flathead, community in western Montana. As a child he became an enrolled member of the Confederated Salish and Kutenai Tribes.

Much about McNickle's early life can be learned from his largely autobiographical novel, *The Surrounded* (1936). The novel, now a classic in American Indian literature, describes the difficult homecoming of a "mixed-blood" man educated in mission and federal boarding schools. The novel presents a devastating view of early twentieth century reservation life and recounts a tragic tale of a man struggling between two irreconcilably different worlds.

Despite the bleakness of his first novel, McNickle's own life was an inspiring one. After beginning a career as a novelist, in the 1930's McNickle was hired by John Collier to work for the Bureau of Indian Affairs. In this capacity, McNickle spent many years working to improve relationships between Indian communities and the federal government. McNickle also produced numerous works of anthropology and history; he is widely respected as one of the first scholars who attempted to write histories from an Indian perspective. McNickle served as a founding member of the National Congress of American Indians in 1944 and, from 1972 to 1977, as director of what is now known as the D'Arcy McNickle Center for the History of the American Indian at the Newberry Library in Chicago.

See also American Indian studies programs and archives; National Congress of American Indians (NCAI).

McQueen, Peter (?—1818, Fla.): War leader

ALSO KNOWN AS: Talmuches Harjo
TRIBAL AFFILIATION: Creek, Seminole
SIGNIFICANCE: McQueen's band of Creek Red Sticks touched off the Creek War (1813-1814) by battling Alabama militia at Burnt Corn Creek

Peter McQueen was born in the Upper Creek town of Tallassee, the son of a white father and Creek mother. Though he prospered as a trader, he was drawn to the Red Stick faction that sought to preserve the traditional lifestyle and resist white settlement. As he returned from Pensacola, West Florida, with munitions and supplies on July 27, 1813, McQueen and his party of warriors were attacked by Alabama militia at Burnt Corn Creek. McQueen turned back the militia in what is usually considered to be the first engagement of the Creek War.

The tide turned against the Red Sticks, however, and after 1814 McQueen led his followers into northern Florida, where continued friction led to General Andrew Jackson's invasion (the First Seminole War, 1817-1818). McQueen, now regarded as a Seminole, was defeated but evaded capture. He fled to southern Florida, where he died in 1818. His band survived to become followers of his grandnephew, Osceola.

See also Creek; Creek War; Osceola; Seminole; Seminole Wars; Weatherford, William.

Mahican: Tribe

CULTURE AREA: Northeast
LANGUAGE GROUP: Algonquian
PRIMARY LOCATION: Hudson River valley (New York State), Wisconsin, Saskatchewan, Oklahoma
POPULATION SIZE: 2,069 ("Stockbridge," 1990 U.S. Census)

The Mahican were Algonquian-speaking people closely related to the Delaware or Lenni Lenape and very strongly influenced by the Mohawk. They lived on both sides of the Hudson River and in northern New York nearly to Lake Champlain. When the Iroquois Confederacy became an allied military force after 1650, and Dutch and English settlers began moving into the lower Hudson River valley, the Mahican were pushed first east of the Hudson and then onto settlements in western Massachusetts near present-day Stockbridge.

Mahican, translated as "People of the Wolf," are easily confused with the Mohegan, also of Delaware lineage, who lived in the Connecticut and lower Hudson River area. (It is not certain which tribe James Fenimore Cooper was referring to in his 1826 novel *Last of the Mohicans*.)

White encroachment and the Iroquois alliance forced many Mahican in the early 1800's to migrate south into Pennsylvania and then down the Ohio River. Some migrants continued with other Delaware tribes into Oklahoma, while others went north through the straits of Mackinaw into Canada.

Mahican who stayed behind became associated with the Stockbridge Indians. Educated in white mission schools, many assimilated into white culture. During the revolutionary war, Stockbridge Indian men in high percentages joined the American army, influenced in part by the Iroquois alliance with the British.

History's most famous Mahican was John W. Quinney (Quinequan, 1797-1855). He was instrumental in purchasing Menominee land in Wisconsin to secure the survival of the remnants of the Mahican. Quinney also created a constitution for his people and resisted American citizenship for his tribe, that they might better preserve their heritage. He served as grand sachem from 1852 until his death.

A beaded coat on display in the Milwaukee Museum shows craftsmanship and design patterns closely related to northeast Algonquian-speaking Narragansett people. There is no visible Iroquois influence. The Mahicans had three clans: Bear, Wolf, and Turtle. The office of sachem was hereditary. The sachem was assisted by councillors called Hero, Owl, and Runner, indicating lineage to the Delaware. Mahican lived in longhouses and were matrilineal. Their lifestyle was identical to the way of life of Eastern Woodland natives.

See also Algonquian language family; Mohegan; Quinney, John W.

BIBLIOGRAPHY

Dyer, Louisa A. *The House of Peace*. New York: Longmans, Green, 1955.

LePoer, Barbara Leitch. *A Concise Dictionary of Indian Tribes of North America*. Edited by Kendall T. LePoer. Algonac, Mich.: Reference Publications, 1979.

Skinner, Alanson. "Mahican Ethnology." *Bulletin of the Public Museum of the City of Milwaukee* 2, no. 1 (1912): 87-116.

Maidu: Tribe

CULTURE AREA: California
LANGUAGE GROUP: Maiduan
PRIMARY LOCATION: Northern California
POPULATION SIZE: 2,271 (1990 U.S. Census)

Maidu Indians occupied a large portion of northeastern California. They hunted, gathered, and fished for subsistence. Women and children gathered acorns, grass seed, roots, nuts, and berries. Surplus foodstuffs were dried, ground into flour, and stored in baskets. The Maidu used nets to catch salmon and other fish. Surplus fish were dried whole and ground into a powder that was eaten dry. They hunted deer, bear, elk, rabbit, and geese with bows and arrows, spears, and hunting dogs. Extra meat was dried for winter usage. Fishing and hunting lands were owned by the entire tribe.

Because of the warm climate, the Maidu wore very little clothing. Men might wear deerskin breechclouts or nothing at all; women wore apron skirts decorated with tassels made from the same material. Fur robes and snowshoes were worn in winter. Maidu lived in dome-shaped, semi-subterranean, earth-covered dwellings that housed two to three families. During the summer, flat-roofed shade shelters were constructed with oak branches.

The Maidu believed that mysterious powers and spirits surrounded their world, and superstitions abounded. They depended on their shamans' mysterious powers and ability to speak to the spirit world. Tribal shamans oversaw political meetings, directed ceremonies, and cured the ill.

European explorers originally came through Maidu territory in the first half of the nineteenth century. A few Hudson's Bay Company trappers later worked in the area. Gold miners came in the mid-1850's and hired local Indians at low wages. As soon as white settlers permanently moved onto Maidu lands, food became scarce and the Indians raided local farms for livestock. Violent skirmishes between Maidu and settlers resulted.

In 1863, soldiers forced 461 Indians onto Round Valley Reservation. During the two-week journey, thirty-two Maidu died. Through the twentieth century, Maidu Indians experienced very high unemployment and poor education, housing, health, and sanitary conditions. At the same time, there was renewed interest in traditional values and increased pride in Maidu heritage.

See also California.

Makah: Tribe

CULTURE AREA: Northwest Coast
LANGUAGE GROUP: Chinookan
PRIMARY LOCATION: Washington State
POPULATION SIZE: 1,597 (1990 U.S. Census)

Living on the northwestern tip of the Olympic Peninsula of present-day Washington State, the Makah were one of twenty-eight tribes of Native Americans living along 1,400 miles of coast from Northern California to southeastern Alaska who collectively formed the Northwest Coast Native American culture area. The Makah were bordered on the west by the Pacific Ocean, to the north by the Strait of Juan de Fuca, to the east by the Klallam tribe, and on the south by the Quileute/Hoh. Although Makah origins are unclear, anthropologists believe ancestors of the Makah were living in the same area ten thousand years ago.

About the time of the arrival of Christopher Columbus, the Makah were part of a thriving culture and society. At this time, a Makah village at Ozette was covered in an enormous mudslide. In 1966, Washington State University anthropologists began excavating the site. This natural disaster perfectly preserved thousands of artifacts including several wooden longhouses, harpoons, whale lances, and various wooden artworks such as totem carvings. This find is now preserved at Neah Bay, Washington, at the Makah Cultural and Research Center. Dale Croes and Eric Blinman have written about a more recent find at the Hoko River, believed to be a twenty-five-hundred-year-old fishing camp.

When Europeans arrived after 1775 and docked at Makah settlements, they found a people who were willing trade partners and had an abundance of goods to trade. The Makah had little to no agriculture, but they were probably among the wealthiest tribes in North America. There was such an abundance of food in the Pacific Northwest that the Makah needed to hunt, fish, and gather only from May through September. This provided them with plenty to eat and enough surplus to trade for externally produced goods, both with other tribes and with European merchants.

The region's climate, which is moderate and wet, yielded food in abundance. Salmon, trout, cod, halibut, herring, whales, sea lions, sea otters, clams, mussels, sea urchins, seaweed, berries, bird eggs, deer, elk, bear, wolves, mountain goats, and beavers were some, but not all, of the available resources.

Perhaps the greatest excitement in the Makah cyclical calendar of events involved the whale hunt. When a whale was seen near the coast, the men would jump into cedar or redwood dugout canoes and chase it. On the bow, the chief harpooner (a position passed down from father to son), who held a musselshell-bladed 18-foot harpoon with attached buoys, stood ready to throw. Once the whale tired and died, the canoes would pull the mammal back to shore, where the village would make use of every part of the catch (meat, oil, and bones).

Although anthropologists have generally considered agriculture a prerequisite for a sophisticated civilization, the complexity of the Makah culture emerges when one examines a few of the Makah rituals, beliefs, and ways of life. The Makah believed that the salmon were gods who lived during the winter in houses under the sea but who sacrificed themselves each year to humans. An elaborate ceremony surrounded the year's first catch of salmon, and the Makah were careful to throw the salmon bones back into the water to ensure a return of the fish the following year.

The Makah had a strict social division based on wealth and rank. A combination of material ownership and birth determined one's position in the village. Sometimes, though not

This 1890's photograph of a Makah village on Tatoosh Island shows the contrast between the traditional plank house and adopted European American styles. (National Archives)

often, a lower-class person could wield great influence, perhaps as a shaman (man or woman) who was believed to possess great magical powers.

Several families lived within the long wooden houses which always faced the sea; the highest in rank would receive the premium sleeping and storage space near the back wall of the house. The wealthiest Makah would periodically host potlatches, extended feasts intended to impress neighbors and reinforce the host's status in the society. Often, many guests were invited and gifts were given liberally. At these potlatches, private and exclusive songs might be performed which would signify and reinforce the rank of the performer and his or her family.

The Makah represent the wealth, trade, and social structuring present among Northwest Coast Indians before the arrival of the Europeans and exemplify the efforts of Native American groups today to preserve the heritage of their ancestors.

See also Chinook; Northwest Coast; Potlatch; Whales and whaling.

Maliseet: Tribe

CULTURE AREA: Northeast
LANGUAGE GROUP: Maleseet-Passamaquoddy
PRIMARY LOCATION: New Brunswick, Quebec, Maine
POPULATION SIZE: 1,705 in Canada (Statistics Canada, based on 1991 census); 900 in U.S. (1990 U.S. Census)

The Maliseet (also spelled Malecite) include both the Passamaquoddy and the Natick peoples. The Passamaquoddy settlement patterns were maritime, whereas the Natick were oriented along inland waterways with an emphasis on land-mammal hunting. Both had extended family organization. Chieftainship was patrilineal. Birchbark was utilized for implements, housing, canoes, and other utilitarian products. Hunting and trapping of moose and deer and other animals was supplemented by saltwater and freshwater fishing. Periodic boat excursions were made to neighboring islands for shellfish, lobsters, clams, and seals.

In 1604, Samuel de Champlain visited and described the inhabitants at the mouth of the Saint John River. Relations with the French were friendly; they were less so with the British, who issued land grants to non-Indians. Many Maliseet moved to the Kingsclear and Tobique reservations. Other reservations were established as population increased. By the 1900's, assimilation had increased, and more Indians were living off-reservation. The 1960's and 1970's saw a revitalization of traditional knowledge and language, a reduction of factionalism, nonprofit tribal corporations, and an increase in college graduates.

See also Passamaquoddy.

Manahoac: Tribe

CULTURE AREA: Southeast
LANGUAGE GROUP: Algonquian
PRIMARY LOCATION: Potomac and North Anna rivers, Maryland/Virginia

Little is recorded about the river-oriented Manahoac tribe, who had a diversified subsistence base that included horticulture, hunting, trapping, fishing, and gathering of nuts, seeds, roots, and tubers. They wintered in permanent villages that were part of the Manahoac Confederacy, and there may have been seven tribes. They warred with the Iroquois and Powhatan and maintained an allegiance with the Monacan. Eventually the Manahoac were forced from their territory by the Susquehanna in the mid-seventeenth century.

John Smith was probably the first European American to observe the Manahoac. Thomas Jefferson, in 1801, said that he had found some of the Manahoac living on the Rappahannock River, but he probably had observed the Hassinunga, a tribe of the Manahoac Confederacy. Disease, combined with continual warfare, brought the Manahoac to ethnographic extinction; by the late colonial period, the Manahoac were no longer a distinct tribe.

See also Indian-white relations—English colonial; Southeast.

Mandan: Tribe

CULTURE AREA: Plains
LANGUAGE GROUP: Siouan
PRIMARY LOCATION: North Dakota
POPULATION SIZE: 1,207 (1990 U.S. Census)

The Mandan, a branch of the Siouan-speaking people, migrated from their original homes along the Ohio River to the northern Great Plains in the early 1400's. Since then they lived in the region around the Big Bend of the Missouri River.

Traditional Culture. Mandans were called the "Prairie People" by other Indians. They lived in permanent villages and grew corn, beans, squash, and tobacco. Once a year hunting parties went into the prairies in search of buffalo, which until the introduction of horses in the 1750's, were killed by warriors on foot driving the bison off high cliffs. After learning how to use horses, Mandan warriors went out more frequently on these hunts, but killing methods did not change. Huge graveyards of buffalo bones have been found at the bottom of killing cliffs in North Dakota and eastern Montana. The Mandan depended on the buffalo for food, clothing, and shelter.

Mandan religious beliefs centered on a sun god and the yearly Sun Dance. Warriors performed the dance twice, before and then after the buffalo hunt. The eight-day ceremony included self-torture and mutilation. The event's chief sponsor, the Okipa (or Okeepa) maker, gave away large quantities of his wealth and was required to suffer more extreme tortures than anyone else. The ceremony began with a fast. Then volunteers were brought into a sacred lodge and hung from leather thongs inserted into their arms and chests. The warriors who withstood the most pain without crying out were considered the bravest. After the torture they ran around the lodge with buffalo skulls tied on ropes attached under the skin of their legs. Most men did this only once in their lives as part of an initiation ceremony, but others—holy men and great warriors—underwent this test of endurance many times. Warriors gained power (Hopini) from this torture, and the more often it was endured the mightier they became. Young warriors often fasted and suffered until they had visions of a guardian spirit (manitou), who would become a personal god and guardian. This spirit could be called upon for strength and protection until the day the warrior died.

Power also was gained through being kind to old people, participating in religious rituals (including frequent fasts), learning the ancient language of the gods, being generous, and inviting an older man to have sexual relations with one's wife. The older man's power would be passed on to the wife, who would then pass it on to her husband. (This misunderstood practice caused much confusion among white merchants and fur traders, who accused Mandans of being totally immoral.)

Mandan villages each had a sacred bundle, containing items such as a buffalo skin and pipe that belonged to Good Furred Robe (an important god), a fox skin headdress, some white sage, a pair of moccasins, a clay pot, the heads of several blackbirds and a duck, and various food items grown in village gardens. This bundle was brought out only on certain important religious occasions and was handed down intact from one generation to the next. Individual warriors kept their own bundles, also brought out only on holy days, which contained items considered sacred by them. These bundles were normally transferred to the eldest son upon the death of the father.

Post-contact Life. Mandans first made contact with whites, mainly French fur trappers, in the mid-1700's. It was not until 1837, when the American Fur Company established a trading post along the Missouri River at Fort Clark, that a permanent relationship developed. Only a few months after the building of Fort Clark, a serious smallpox epidemic broke out. This disease, brought in by white merchants, killed thousands of Mandan people. The population, estimated at nine thousand in 1750, fell to less than two hundred after the devastation. The smell of dead bodies became so noxious that Fort Clark had to be abandoned temporarily. Two years later, many of the remaining Mandan villagers were slaughtered during a Sioux attack. After the killing, Sioux warriors burned the entire Mandan camp to the ground.

In 1874 a government census found 241 Mandans living in North Dakota. Most were moved to a reservation, where they lived on land allotments provided by the General Allotment Act (Dawes Severalty Act) of 1887 and tried to survive on corn and beans. Today few full-blood Mandans can be found, as there has been considerable intermarriage with Sioux and Chippewa (Ojibwa) residents of the Fort Berthold Reservation. —*Leslie V. Tischauser*

See also Bundles, sacred; Mato Tope; Okeepa; Plains.

Mangas Coloradus (c. 1791, N.Mex.—Jan. 19, 1863): Chief

Also known as: Red Sleeves, Dasoda-hae (He Just Sits There)

Tribal affiliation: Apache

Significance: Mangas Coloradus was an important war chief during the era of the so-called Apache Wars

Along with his equally famous son-in-law, Cochise, a Chiricahua Apache, Mangas Coloradus was a leader in the guerrilla warfare waged by the Apaches against the Mexicans. Toward

Chiricahua Apache leader Mangas Coloradus fought against both Mexican and American encroachment onto Apache land. (Library of Congress)

the end of his life, Americans replaced Mexicans as his adversaries.

A long peace was disrupted in 1860 when prospectors discovered gold in the Mimbres Mountains, homeland of Mangas Coloradus' people. During a visit to negotiate peace, the great leader was bound to a tree and whipped. He was released to return home with deep wounds.

The decisive event for both Cochise and Mangas Coloradus was probably the "Bascomb affair"—Lieutenant George N. Bascomb's charge that the Chiricahua Apaches had kidnapped a "half-breed" boy. The Chiricahuas blamed the Coyotero Apaches. During the investigation, prisoners were murdered on both sides; retaliation replaced investigation and dialogue.

During the following summer, in July of 1862, Mangas Coloradus and Cochise were besieged by infantry from Star Chief Carleton's command. In the fighting that ensued, Mangas Coloradus was wounded in the chest. Cochise took his father-in-law to a surgeon in the Mexican village of Janos. A strong, broad-shouldered man, still towering over six feet tall in his seventies, Mangas returned to his Mimbres Mountains later that year.

In January of 1863, perhaps reflecting on the "perpetual peace" he had pledged in an 1852 treaty, Mangas Coloradus committed his final days to securing peace for his people. Although accounts vary, historians agree that he went alone and unarmed to discuss peace under a white flag with Captain Edmond Shirland of the California Volunteers. The great leader's body was found in a ditch the next day. His feet and legs had been burned by heated bayonets; his body was pierced by close-range multiple bullet wounds; his head had been removed and defleshed to be sold. From that point, the Apaches went to war in earnest.

See also Apache; Apache Wars; Cochise.

Manhattan

Date: 1626

Place: Manhattan Island

Tribes affected: Canarsee, Manhattan

Significance: Peter Minuit's purchase of Manhattan Island from the Indians for sixty guilders was the first significant land purchase by the Dutch in the New World

Henry Hudson, representing the Dutch East India Company, entered New York Bay in September, 1609. He explored the river he found there and claimed the surrounding land for the United Netherlands.

New Netherland was founded in 1615 by the United New Netherland Company and originally stretched from Eastport, Maine, to Barnegat Bay, New Jersey. It was established to further an expanding European economy, and its main vehicle was fur trading. New Netherland was first settled in 1624. In the summer of 1626, Peter Minuit began a six-year term as the first director-general or governor. New Amsterdam became the central city. Minuit established the newest emigrants at the lower end of Manhattan Island. He constructed a fort at the present location of the Battery for protection from the Indians and from other traders and explorers.

From the very beginning, relations between the Dutch and Indians were given high priority. Minuit was empowered to make treaties and alliances with the Indians that would be advantageous to the company. He was to maintain peaceful relations with the Indians and to treat them fairly. This policy was not developed from respect or love for the Indians; rather, it was seen as the most effective way to further company interests.

The most sensitive issue involved how to take the Indians' land from them. The company had originally viewed commerce rather than colonization as its main purpose. Therefore its charter never gave it any original title to land. Colonization began to assume greater importance, however, and it became apparent that ownership of the land would further the economic pursuits of the company. The charter grant stipulated that the company could acquire land only if the Indians relinquished their ownership of it. The instructions to Minuit, and to all subsequent governors until the end of Dutch rule, was that the relinquishing of land had to be voluntary and not obtained through fraudulent or dishonest means. (The delineators of this policy were probably legitimately unaware that Europeans and American Indians had quite different understandings of land "ownership.")

The first significant land purchase was made by Peter Minuit. In the summer of 1626 he purchased all of Manhattan Island, which abounded in forests, fruits, and animals, from the Canarsee Indians for sixty guilders. The Canarsees had other lands that suited their purposes equally well, and they considered the selling price to be fair recompense. It was later discovered that the Canarsees had no definitive claim to the land, and payments had to be made to the Manhattans, who claimed hunting rights to the island. Peter Minuit later established a Swedish colony near New Netherland and Fort Christina (at present-day Trenton, New Jersey) as a Swedish trading post.

See also Indian-white relations—Dutch colonial; Northeast; Wappinger.

Manibozho

TRIBE AFFECTED: Ojibwa

SIGNIFICANCE: Manibozho—legendary wise man, prophet, and messenger from the Great Spirit—was also a trickster who was sometimes outdone by his own tricks

Tales of Manibozho are told throughout the Great Lakes region, where he is also known as Nanabozho, Nana, Wenebojo, and the Great Hare. Manibozho was a messenger from Gitche Manitou (Great Spirit). His grandmother, Nokomis, was daughter of the Moon; his father was the West Wind. Shortly after Manibozho's magical birth near Gitchee Gumee (Lake Superior), he turned himself into a white rabbit. Manibozho changed his form at will—to a tree, a rock, or any animal.

Manibozho was said to have brought his people the gift of fire. He also invented kinnikinnick (smoking mixture), created the Midewiwin (Grand Medicine Society), and remade the earth after the great flood.

According to one story about Manibozho, one day while he was picking berries, a flock of geese landed on the nearby lake. Determined to catch as many as possible, he wove a rope of cedar bark strips. Swimming quietly under the floating birds, he strung them all together by tying their legs. His greedy task took so long he gasped loudly for air when he came up. The geese took flight, with the middle goose in the lead and the others forming a *V*, with Manibozho dangling at one end. He shouted for them to stop, but they flew on. Letting go, he landed in a swamp. Wild geese have been flying in a *V* ever since.

People listened respectfully when Manibozho sang of flying far and high, but later they sang, "High in the sky, geese are calling. Down from the sky, Nana is falling."

Once a great creator and magician, Manibozho was turned to stone by Gitche Manitou and now lies sleeping as an island in Gitchee Gumee. Tales of Manibozho still abound; they are told in the winter, when spirits of the forest are asleep.

See also Humor; Kinnikinnick; Midewiwin; Ojibwa; Oral literatures; Tricksters.

Mankato (c. 1830, near present-day Minneapolis, Minn.— Sept. 23, 1862, Wood Lake, Minn.): War chief

ALSO KNOWN AS: Mahkato (Blue Earth)

TRIBAL AFFILIATION: Santee Sioux

SIGNIFICANCE: Mankato was a leader of the Minnesota Uprising of 1862, an event which marked the end of the Indian wars in Minnesota

Born on the Minnesota River, Mankato became a village chief in 1853 following the death of his father. With Little Crow, he worked to maintain peace with white settlers, helping to negotiate the Treaty of Washington of 1858. By 1862, the failure of government officials to provide food and supplies as indicated in the treaties caused tensions. Faced with starvation, small groups of warriors attacked isolated settlers. Caught in the accelerating conflict, Mankato joined Little Crow in the Minnesota Uprising. After Little Crow was wounded on August 22, 1862, during the attack on Fort Ridgely, Mankato assumed command. He led attacks on New Ulm and Birch Coulee. He was killed in the Battle of Wood Lake on September 23, struck in the back by a cannonball. He was buried in the bluffs of the Yellow Medicine River so that whites could not find his body.

See also Little Crow; Minnesota Uprising.

Mankiller, Wilma Pearl (b. Nov. 18, 1945, Tahlequah, Okla.): Chief

TRIBAL AFFILIATION: Cherokee

SIGNIFICANCE: After taking part in the Indian civil rights movement of the 1960's and later working to improve conditions among rural Indian communities, Mankiller gained national respect in the 1980's when she became the first woman to head a major Native American tribe

In 1838, many of Wilma Mankiller's ancestors were forcibly removed from their tribal home in Tennessee and brought to

Wilma Mankiller was elected principal chief of the Cherokee Nation in 1985. (AP/Wide World Photos)

Oklahoma along what became known as the Trail of Tears. By the time of Mankiller's birth in 1945, Cherokee communities were firmly rooted in rural Oklahoma. After spending her early childhood at her family home on Mankiller Flats, near Tahlequah, Mankiller and her family moved to California in the 1950's. During that time, they participated in an effort led by the federal government to relocate Indians to urban areas. In the San Francisco Bay area, Mankiller became acquainted with Indian people from many different parts of the country. She first became devoted to revitalizing tribal communities after joining the Indian activist takeover of Alcatraz Island in 1969. Mankiller worked as a community activist among the Pit River tribe before moving back to her childhood home in Oklahoma with her two daughters in 1976.

In Oklahoma, Mankiller worked to improve conditions in rural Cherokee communities. In 1981, she became the found-ing director of the Cherokee Nation Community Development Department and, in 1985, principal chief of the Cherokee Nation of Oklahoma. Her leadership soon gained her widespread admiration, not only among Indian people but also among non-Indians—particularly women—throughout the United States. In 1993, Mankiller published her autobiography, *Mankiller: A Chief and Her People*, which she coauthored with Michael Wallis.

See also Activism; Alcatraz Island occupation; Cherokee; Political organization and leadership.

Manuelito (c. 1818, near Bears Ears Peak, Utah—1894, Navajo Reservation, N.Mex.): Resistance leader

ALSO KNOWN AS: Hastin Ch'ilhajinii (Man of the Black Weeds), Hashkeh Naabah (Angry Warrior), Pistol Bullet

TRIBAL AFFILIATION: Navajo

SIGNIFICANCE: A leader in the Navajo War of 1863-1866, Manuelito was the first commander of the Navajo police, established in 1872

Manuelito, born in southeastern Utah, became a prominent warrior and married the daughter of a well-known leader. When his father-in-law was killed by federal soldiers, Manuelito took his place.

A conflict in 1858 led to greater prominence. Federal soldiers at Fort Defiance in New Mexico demanded the use of pastures that had been reserved for Navajos. When troopers shot Navajo horses, Navajos undertook raids to replace the losses. The Navajo had chosen a leader to negotiate with the Federals; when he resigned, Manuelito was selected in his place.

Manuelito repudiated previous agreements with the United States, so soldiers burned his home. He in turn attacked Fort Defiance in April, 1860, and mauled a pursuing force. The post was abandoned in a treaty signed by Manuelito in February of 1861, but conflict erupted anew at Fort Fauntleroy in September, 1861, after a dispute over a horse race resulted in the slaughter of more than a dozen Navajo by soldiers.

Manuelito led Navajos in their 1860's fight against U.S. forces, and in the 1870's he was a leader on the newly created reservation. (National Archives)

The Navajo War of 1863-1866 was delayed by federal efforts to cope with Confederates, but scorched-earth tactics, including the destruction of Navajo refuges in Canyon de Chelly, soon forced most Navajo leaders to surrender. One of the last was Manuelito, who in September, 1866, led twenty-three starving warriors to join the other Navajo at Bosque Redondo, where many died from disease and lack of food.

Manuelito was one of the delegates who went to Washington in 1868 and secured a reservation of 3.5 million acres. Recognized as a prominent leader by U.S. administrators, in 1872 he became the commander of the new Navajo police. He was ruthless in maintaining order, but he represented the Navajo twice again in Washington and led a rebellion in 1875 against corrupt federal administration.

Manuelito advocated education for the Navajo; ironically, his son died while at school. Depressed, Manuelito resigned as chief and succumbed to alcoholism. He died from measles and pneumonia.

See also Barboncito; Canyon de Chelly; Navajo; Navajo War.

Maple syrup and sugar

TRIBES AFFECTED: Northeast tribes
SIGNIFICANCE: Maple syrup and possibly maple sugar were used by tribes of the Northeast as foodstuffs and occasionally as trade goods

Many indigenous tribal peoples in the Northeastern Woodlands relied on the saps and gums of certain trees for food and gum products. Among these trees were spruces, birches, and maples. The last often supplied the tribes with a sweet, syrupy substance they mixed with other foodstuffs and possibly boiled down to make sugar. Tribes from the Abenaki of northern New England and Quebec to the Chippewa (Ojibwa) of Minnesota and Ontario tapped the abundant maples for these products.

The techniques of gathering the sap varied only slightly. The Abenaki cut a slanting gash and inserted an elderberry twig spile with its pith hollowed out and collected the drips in birchbark containers. The Chippewa used a cedar spile. Later, with the introduction of metal technology by European Americans, the iron or tin spile came into use (the dating for this switch is unclear). Once they had gathered enough syrup, tribal peoples used the sweetener in various ways. The Iroquois mixed it with corn mush. The Chippewa stirred it into wild rice, vegetables, and fish dishes, blended it with water for a beverage, and stuffed sugar into duck bills for portable candy treats for their children. What they could not use immediately, the Chippewa stored in mococks, sewn birchbark packages that often held five pounds of sugar. Tribes in Michigan, such as the Ottawa, apparently distributed the syrup and sugar as a trade good.

There exists some dispute among historians about the sugar-making capacities of the indigenous people. One school of thought holds that tribal peoples did not begin to boil down the syrup until the arrival of reliable iron pots from the Europeans. They point to the absence of description in contemporary travelers' accounts. The other camp believes that sugar making definitely predated European contact, perhaps by centuries. The Abenaki, according to the second theory, employed birch-bark pails and clay pots for the boiling.

Whatever the case, early European American settlers soon adapted the customs themselves eagerly. Many a colonist depended on maple syrup for a nip of sweetness, because it was more plentiful and cheaper than cane products on the frontier. Over the centuries, maple syrup and sugar production became a thriving industry in the Northeast and Canada to the point that states such as Vermont have become stereotypically identified with those products. Demonstrations and images of sap gathering and sugar making, however, rarely point to the indigenous origins of the practice.

See also Northeast.

Marriage and divorce

TRIBES AFFECTED: Pantribal

SIGNIFICANCE: For the American Indian, the integrity of the family was paramount; divorce was possible, but it was not expected

Marriage customs differed from tribe to tribe. In the Northeast and Plains tribes there was usually not a ceremony to celebrate the wedding, but there were very strict arrangements made between the two uniting families before the couple came together. The groom usually contacted the girl discreetly but personally to see whether she would accept him. This encounter might be a formal courting situation, or it might only be a quick look at a public event. Marriage partners had often known each other all their lives; even if not in personal contact with each other, they knew the families involved.

Establishing the Marriage. Once the young man believed that there was a mutual attraction, he would contact the bride's family to arrange the terms of the union. Usually, it was the groom who would provide for the bride's family. The amount of goods brought to the girl's family was in accord with the status of the family and the girl. A virtuous, reserved, industrious girl who would bring honor to a man's home commanded respect. That respect was publicly demonstrated by bringing goods to her family. Among Plains tribes this could include a number of horses, weapons, cooking utensils, tanned hides, clothing decorated with quillwork or beadwork, tanned and painted robes, and food. If accepted, these items were distributed among the girl's relatives. Among most tribes, the bride's family reciprocated with a feast and gifts for the groom's relatives. During these events, many items were also given to the new couple so that when they began their lives together it would be in the manner they were accustomed to. Among the Hopi and Zuni of the Southwest the marriage was less public, with the man moving in with his bride's family. No marriages with members of one's own clan were permitted.

Divorce. It was not unusual for a young man to come to stay at the home of his potential in-laws for a week or more prior to the wedding ceremony. In this way, the couple could decide without any pressure whether they were compatible. Likewise, marriages could be easily terminated by the woman. She had only to put her husband's personal items—his clothing and weapons—outside the door of their abode and the divorce was complete. Divorce was not uncommon, but it was the exception rather than the norm. Most couples lived in harmony according to custom, but if there was disharmony it was thought best to separate. The house, household goods, and any children were to be cared for by the wife. The husband took his things and returned to the house of his mother or another female relative. It was not unheard of for men to remain single for years or not to marry at all. These men added another presence to the households of their female relatives, helpful in supplying food and teaching the children in the households. They often had obligations to their sisters' children. This was the case in most matrilineal tribes. Patrilineal tribes, such as the Ojibwa, differed somewhat because the right to use land was passed from father or uncle to son or nephew. In this case, a divorced woman took her household goods and children and returned to her family's area.

Marriage was considered a lifetime commitment. Infidelity was frowned upon, although a man could take a second wife in the form of a captured woman of another tribe or, more often, a younger sister or cousin of his wife. If the man were able to provide for such a large family, he would choose a wife who was compatible with his first wife to maintain harmony in his home. Sometimes when the second or third wife was especially troublesome, the first wife, who retained primacy, would demand that the husband return her to her family. An unhappy home was rarely chosen over removing the person in question. In some tribes, wives were shared with guests for their pleasure. This did not imply any disrespect for the wife; it was done as a comforting gesture to a man risking his life in travel. Any children that were born belonged to the wife and were an accepted part of the household. Most women practiced birth control with native herbs, so unwanted children were rare.

Sexual Relations. Most tribes considered sexual behavior to be private; within the communal atmosphere of the home, it was practiced discreetly. Girls were warned not to succumb to boys' advances and were usually chaperoned by an older female relative when they became teenagers. Girls were expected to be virgins when they married in most (but not all) tribes, although if they had tried marriage and found it unsuitable, it was not held against them. Because mutual respect between a virtuous woman and a man who was a bountiful provider was the basis for an honorable home, all members of the extended family tried to provide an environment to support good behavior. Unmarried pregnancy was rare. The integrity of the family was foremost. Behavior within marriage was designed to bring esteem to the family and to create a harmonious home.

Elopements were another way of uniting. There was no exchange of goods and no honoring between families, so this alternative was less desired. Still, it was considered a socially acceptable way for a young couple to begin if neither had much social standing and neither could provide goods. Even among those who could, it was an acceptable, though not esteemed, way to come together. Occasionally, women who were not faithful were physically punished. Among some Plains tribes, women had their noses cut off in retribution for their behavior. —*Nancy H. Omaha Boy*

See also Children; Clans; Gender relations and roles; Kinship and social organization; Women.

BIBLIOGRAPHY

Embree, Edwin R. *Indians of the Americas*. Boston: Houghton Mifflin, 1939. Reprint. New York: Collier Books, 1970.

Parsons, Elsie Clews, ed. *American Indian Life*. New York: Dover, 1992.

Powers, Marla N. *Oglala Women: Myth, Ritual, and Reality*. Chicago: University of Chicago Press, 1986.

Reader's Digest. *America's Fascinating Indian Heritage*. Pleasantville, N.Y.: Author, 1978.

Spencer, Robert F., Jesse D. Jennings, et al. *The Native Americans*. 2d ed. New York: Harper & Row, 1977.

Martínez, Crescencio (c. 1890, San Ildefonso, N.Mex.— June 20, 1918, Santa Fe?, N.Mex.): Painter

ALSO KNOWN AS: Ta'e or Te E (Home of the Elk)

TRIBAL AFFILIATION: San Ildefonso Pueblo

SIGNIFICANCE: Crescencio Martínez is considered by many to be the father of watercolor painting among Puebloan Indians, leading to the Southwestern school of Indian painting

Crescencio Martínez began drawing sometime before 1910, using crayons he picked up while working as a janitor at the San Ildefonso Day School. Edgar Hewett, excavating near San Ildefonso in about 1915, hired Crescencio as a laborer and found him drawing on the ends of cardboard boxes. Hewett gave him drawing paper and watercolors, and bought many of his drawings. In 1916, Crescencio began painting the summer and winter dances of his pueblo for a museum commission arranged by Hewett. The ease with which his work sold influenced the men of his pueblo to turn to watercolor painting for income, and it was his style they often followed.

Crescencio married Maximiliana (Anna) Martínez, sister of potter María Martínez and herself an accomplished potter. Crescencio painted Anna's pots, as well as those of his mother, sister, and sister-in-law. Other relatives were painters Alfonso Roybal, Romando Vigil, and Alfredo Montoya.

Anna and Crescencio moved to Santa Fe during World War I, working for the Rocky Mountain Camp Company grooming horses. There they continued potting and painting. Crescencio Martínez died of pneumonia.

See also Art and artists, contemporary; Arts and crafts—Southwest; Martínez, Julián; Martínez, María Antonía; Paints and painting; Pueblo tribes, Eastern.

Martínez, Julián (1897, San Ildefonso, N.Mex.— c. 1943, San Ildefonso, N.Mex.): Painter

TRIBAL AFFILIATION: San Ildefonso Pueblo (Tewa)

SIGNIFICANCE: Julián Martínez collaborated with his wife, María Antonía Martínez, in making pottery prized by museums and collectors worldwide

In 1908, Julián Martínez was one of several men from San Ildefonso hired to help with the excavations at Tyuonyi and Frijoles Canyon, led by Edgar Hewett, director of the Museum of New Mexico. When Hewett wanted a potter who could produce pottery based on fragments of prehistoric vessels found at the sites, Julián suggested that his wife, María, might attempt it. She agreed, on condition that Julián decorate the pots. María was an exceptional potter who, by simply coiling the clay, could make large, thin-walled pots of perfect symmetry. Julián proved to be an equally exceptional painter, decorating the pots with his own intricate and flawlessly executed designs based on his intensive study of both prehistoric and historic sources.

After producing polychrome pottery for several years, María and Julián began to experiment with the firing technique which finally resulted in the black-on-black ware (c. 1918-1920). Julián, by now the leading pottery decorator at San Ildefonso, developed his two most innovative design elements, the *avanyu* (plumed serpent) and his own adaptation of the prehistoric Mimbres feather design, for use on the black pottery.

Although he is best known for his designs on María's pottery, Julián's paintings and graphics do appear in many major collections of American Indian art in museums throughout the United States.

See also Art and artists, contemporary; Arts and crafts—Southwest; Martínez, Crescencio; Martínez, María Antonía; Mimbres; Paints and painting; Popovi Da; Pottery; Symbolism in art.

Martínez, María Antonía (Apr. 5, 1887, San Ildefonso, N.Mex.—July 20, 1980, San Ildefonso, N.Mex.): Potter

ALSO KNOWN AS: Poveka (Pond Lily)

TRIBAL AFFILIATION: San Ildefonso Pueblo

SIGNIFICANCE: María Martínez revitalized the vanishing art of pottery among Pueblo peoples

In 1908, María Martínez was asked by archaeologist Edgar Hewett to reproduce and decorate pottery in the style of that being unearthed near San Ildefonso. Few women in the pueblo made pots. Hewett bought and reordered her simple polychrome reproductions, launching a revival in pottery-making in the pueblo and immeasurably helping its economy. Decorating her pots were Crescencio Martínez, her sister Maximiliana, husband Julián, daughter-in-law Santana, and son Popovi Da.

Her first son was born in 1904, and three other children followed. In 1909, she became the leader of an important women's ceremonial society. María worked all year forming, firing, slipping, and burnishing pottery; by 1915, she had far surpassed all other potters in the pueblo in skill and reputation. In 1921, she and Julián revealed their technique for making black-on-black pottery. In 1923, she initiated the practice of signing pottery—using the name "Marie" until the 1950's because white customers were more familiar with it. She earned about $5,000 from pottery sales in 1931, and $1 an hour for teaching pottery classes. In the course of her seventy-year career, she won hundreds of prizes; showed at three World's Fairs; visited the White House four times; and received the Craftsmanship Medal, Palmes Academiques Medal, Jane Addams Award, and honorary doctoral degrees.

See also Art and artists, contemporary; Arts and crafts—Southwest; Martínez, Crescencio; Martínez, Julián; Popovi Da; Pottery; Pueblo tribes, Eastern.

Maru Cult

TRIBE AFFECTED: Pomo
SIGNIFICANCE: The Maru Cult, a revitalization movement, has beliefs in common with the Ghost Dance movement

The Maru Cult of the California Pomo (surrounding the Clear Lake area in Northern California) is a direct offshoot of the Ghost Dance, which began as a religious ceremony and ideology in the 1870's and resurfaced in the 1890's among Plains Indians. The Ghost Dance involved various ideological aspects, among them a return to Indian ways and a rejection of settler culture. As such, the Ghost Dance, and the many religious movements it inspired, was seen as "revivalist," a religious response to social circumstances of breakdown and change brought about by contact between two alien cultures—and the power difference between them.

The inequality in settler/Indian relations may explain why many tribal members sought supernatural comfort and deliverance, believing that the simple ways of traditional warfare were not effective against the encroaching settler. The main influence of the Ghost Dance movements in California were the "Earthlodge" cults, which arrived in Pomo territory as early as 1872. In its Pomo manifestation, the cult was led by a "Maru," or "dreamer," who was the head functionary of religious ceremonies. Originally, the selecting of lodges for these ceremonies was inspired by the notion that large houses (dome-roofed constructions, of which some pictures are available) were to be a place of refuge from an anticipated destruction. The influence of Christian missionaries can be discerned in the Noah's Ark theme of these longhouse constructions.

A Maru who dreams becomes the individual leader of the ceremonies. He or she (for, since 1920, women have played an increasingly large role in the Maru ceremonies) who dreams and calls the ceremonies dictates the rules of the ceremony itself, and the dream is highly respected as a source of direction from supernatural promptings. The actual ceremony usually involves an opening flag-raising to "purify" the hall where the ceremonies are to take place. Prominent in most observations of the Maru Cult are "Big-Head Dancers" (so named because of their large headdresses), typically four in number, and a number of drummers and singers. There are other dancers who must also observe a number of purity rules throughout the occupation of the ceremony itself. The ceremony may last many days and may vary in the style of dances and songs that are performed, all according to the dreams of the specific Maru.

Although less frequent today, Maru ceremonies are still observed, and it is not unusual for non-Pomo, or part-Pomo, peoples to be recognized as "dreamers" who may call for the ceremonies to begin. The occasion for the ceremonies varies, but is always dependent on the dream instructions of the Maru.

See also Ghost Dance; Kuksu rituals and society; Pomo.

BIBLIOGRAPHY

Meighan, Clement W., and Francis Riddell. The Maru Cult of the Pomo Indians: A California Ghost Dance Survival. Los Angeles: Southwest Museum Papers, 1972.

Masks

TRIBES AFFECTED: Aleut, Bella Coola, Cherokee, Eskimo, Haida, Iroquois tribes, Kwakiutl, Lenni Lenape, Makah, Maya, Naskapi, Navajo, Nootka, Plains tribes, Pueblo tribes, Salish, Seneca, Tlingit, Tsimshian, others
SIGNIFICANCE: Masks have been used by many American Indian tribes since prehistoric times for ceremonial, social, and religious purposes, allowing access to and control of the spiritual world

The making and wearing of masks was an art form that served religious, social, and artistic purposes for American Indians. Putting on a "false face" could provide protection or disguise, be used as a vehicle for contact with supernatural powers, or enhance the role of storytelling.

Types of Masks. The simplest way of wearing a mask was to paint the face. This allowed the wearer to present a different persona easily by changing the color of the face and by emphasizing certain features. By painting the face, a transformation of personality took place, giving the wearer a different outlook and the ability to affect the impression and response of others.

In the prehistoric times, masks were used to control the spiritual world and for magical purposes. By putting on a false face it was believed that one could engage the power of the surrounding spirits, who, being good or evil, had an impact on one's life. Masks were considered holy and sacred objects in themselves as they had the power to transform the wearer into the representative spirit. Very often they were used in ritual dances to exorcise evil or invoke blessing. Masks made the powers visible, and the wearer could become one with the spiritual power. Some Indians believed that the spirits of deceased ancestors returned in a mask.

Ceremonial use included such occasions as initiations, war dances, and fertility rites. Storytelling and dramatization of symbolic legends made use of masks and provided entertainment. In the Southwest masks were used to invoke spirits to help in providing rain, and in the Northwest masks were related to the clan totem, the spirit protector of the clan.

Masks were made of wood, animal hides, and plant fibers in North America and of wood, metals, stone, and clay in Central and South America. Which material was used depended upon the region and its natural resources and the degree of development in the use of masks, which varied from tribe to tribe.

Regional Examples. The Northwest Coast area had perhaps the greatest development in the quality and use of masks. They were used in curing ceremonies and midwinter performances of dramatized myths and legends in song and dance.

A Cowichan masked dancer; the Cowichan are a Northwest Coast tribe. (Library of Congress)

The masks were made by carvers (who were held in high esteem by the community) of wood, generally cedar, and were colorfully and boldly painted, with dark green being a favorite color. The Kwakiutl made highly expressive, complex masks with moveable parts such as beaks. Masks were often in the form of a human face, or the head of a bird, animal, or spirit, all having supernatural power. Clan masks represented the clan totem. A shaman wearing a mask could be transformed into the animal or spirit represented by the mask. Sometimes masks were double-layered, representing the duality of the inner human spiritual form and the outer animal form.

Eskimos (Inuits) used masks in acting out cosmic dramas. Their masks displayed animal features representing a host of beings and phenomena. Some masks were hinged; others were made of fur. They also made large wooden masks to represent and honor the dead; they were left unpainted and bore solemn expressions.

In the Southwest, Pueblo Indians made simple head coverings of animal hides that were painted and decorated with feathers, cloth, herbs, and carved wooden beaks. Rounded heads represented the male, and square heads represented the female; the respective shapes could also represent deities or lesser spirits.

Masks were sacred to the Pueblos, who did not allow exact photographic reproductions of them. The wearer had to be purified before wearing a mask, and masks were ceremonially sanctified with sacred pollen or corn meal before being stored in the kiva. Most Pueblo masks represented spirits, with a few representing animals. The kachina dancer portrayed the spirit of a deceased clan member who lived in the underworld and was called upon for aid in assuring rain and good crops.

In the Eastern Woodlands region, masks were used to drive away evil spirits. Wooden masks were worn only by men, but Husk Faces, made of bands of braided corn husks, were worn by both men and women. The Iroquois made masks for False Face Ceremonies to exorcise demons. These masks had distorted features, long hair, and deeply set eyes, and they were painted in red and/or black. The Iroquois also made buffalo-head masks that were used in the Buffalo Dance. The Cherokee made masks for hunting, as aids to help them get close to game animals. Their masks boldly emphasized the distinctive features of animals, such as the eyes, ears, nose, or antlers. The Living Solid Face mask of the Lenni Lenape (Delaware) was considered a helpful spirit and guide as well as a living mask.

In Mesoamerica, mask making was a complex art form in which masks were used to record the history, religion, and aesthetics of the people. Made of a wide variety of materials, masks were symbolic expressions of beliefs and were worn at ritual dances.

Masks made by American Indians today are still used for ceremonial purposes. Among some tribes, masks are also made for commercial purposes. —*Diane C. Van Noord*

See also Buffalo Dance; Dances and dancing; False Face Ceremony; Husk Face Society; Kachinas; Totems.

BIBLIOGRAPHY

Conn, Richard. *Native American Art in the Denver Art Museum.* Denver: Denver Art Museum, 1979.

Cordry, Donald. *Mexican Masks.* Austin: University of Texas Press, 1980.

Furst, Peter T., and Jill L. Furst. *North American Indian Art.* New York: Rizzoli International, 1982.

LaFarge, Oliver, et al. *Introduction to American Indian Art.* Glorieta, N.Mex.: Rio Grande Press, 1973.

Macgowan, Kenneth, and Herman Rosse. Reprint. 1923. *Masks and Demons.* New York: Kraus Reprint, 1972.

Wherry, Joseph H. *Indian Masks and Myths of the West.* New York: Thomas Y. Crowell, 1974.

Massachusett: Tribe

CULTURE AREA: Northeast
LANGUAGE GROUP: Algonquian
PRIMARY LOCATION: Massachusetts

"Massachusett" meant "at the great hill." The Massachusett tribe (from whom the state gets its name) inhabited a coastal region centered on Massachusetts Bay. To the north, across the Charles River, was the Pawtucket tribe. To the south were the Wampanoag, with the boundary near modern Marshfield. Like other Algonquian-speaking peoples of southern New England, the Massachusett were horticulturists subsisting principally on the corn, beans, and squash raised by the women. Men hunted game to provide meat, and both sexes joined in collecting the rich harvest of fish and shellfish provided by the area's rivers and estuaries.

Captain John Smith reported that in 1614 the Massachusett occupied thirty villages. The villages had several hundred inhabitants who lived in bark-covered wigwams. Each wigwam typically housed two or more nuclear families. A sachem ruled over each village, advised by a small council made up of men who had earned the rank of *pniese* through success in warfare and other deeds. A chief sachem held a tenuous but traditionally defined authority over the entire nation.

The Massachusett were traditionally considered to number three thousand warriors, implying an overall population of twelve thousand to fifteen thousand, but even before European settlement Old World diseases to which the Indians had no immunity began their ravages. From 1617 to 1619 an epidemic of European origin struck, killing more than half the Massachusett. A 1633 outbreak of smallpox destroyed many of the survivors. By 1674, there remained only a tenth of the original number (three hundred warriors). By that date, much of the remnant population, largely Christian converts, lived in several villages of so-called "praying Indians." Natick, near Boston, was the largest and most enduring of these. During King Philip's War of 1675-1676, these villages were dispersed, as both pagan Indians and suspicious Englishmen attacked the Christian Massachusett. Many of the survivors took refuge with other Indians in the region, and by the nineteenth century the Massachusett had ceased to exist as a separate people.

See also Algonquian language family; Indian-white relations—English colonial; King Philip's War; Northeast; Praying Indians; Wampanoag.

Massasoit (c. 1580, near present-day Bristol, R.I.—c. 1662, near Bristol, R.I.): Grand sachem

ALSO KNOWN AS: Ousamequin (Yellow Feather)

TRIBAL AFFILIATION: Wampanoag

SIGNIFICANCE: From the landing of the *Mayflower* in 1620 to his death in 1662, Massasoit worked to preserve a peaceful relationship with the English colonists

Massasoit was born about 1580 in Rhode Island. He became the grand sachem over the Wampanoag towns along the coastal regions of Massachusetts and Rhode Island. Massasoit led the sachems of the individual towns, but he was not an authoritarian ruler.

Massasoit was responsible for the welfare of his people. When the Plymouth Colony was established in 1620, Massasoit determined that his people would be best served by friendly relations with the colonists. In March, 1621, Massasoit went to Plymouth. Soon trade and communication between the Wampanoags and the English were well established.

When the colonists held their first service of thanksgiving in November, 1621, they invited the Wampanoags. Massasoit and about ninety others went, taking with them five deer.

Until his death in 1662, Massasoit was able to maintain peace with the English; however, the increasing number of colonists soon caused the goodwill to dissolve, leading to the bloody King Philip's War (1675-1676), led by Massasoit's son.

See also King Philip's War; Metacomet; Narragansett; Sachem; Wampanoag.

Mathematics

TRIBES AFFECTED: Pantribal

SIGNIFICANCE: The most highly developed mathematical systems in the pre-contact Americas were the Mayan and Aztec calendar systems, but number systems for counting were developed by most tribes

Mathematical skills developed by American Indian tribes included the development of number systems—words and symbols used for calendrical measurement and economic bookkeeping. In the former case, this allowed the passage of days, months, seasons, and years to be independently followed; in the latter case, it simply meant counting objects, people, animals, and so on. Hunting tribes, for example, had little use for

Artist's depiction of Wampanoag sachem Massasoit with the Pilgrims. (Library of Congress)

extensive number systems, since small numbers were sufficient for enumeration in the counting of objects such as spears, knives, fish, and canoes.

Similar to the number systems of most ancient cultures throughout the world, many number systems of North America were based on the decimal system, meaning that their numbers were based on groupings of ten. (The origin of the decimal system, noted by Aristotle long ago, was a result of the fact that humans are born with ten fingers and ten toes.) Almost one-third of American Indian tribes that have been studied used the decimal system. In North America, this included the Algonquian, Iroquois, Salish, and Sioux. In parts of California, number systems were based on groupings of twenty, known as the vigesimal system. Other systems based on two, three, and five (the binary, ternary, and quinary systems, respectively) were also used. To derive numbers, most tribes used additive and multiplicative principles and, to a lesser extent, subtractive and divisive principles. Nine was considered one less than ten, and eleven was one greater than ten. Repeated addition (multiplication) was used for large numbers. The fingers and toes of five men could be used to count one hundred objects. To preserve a record of counted objects a pile of stones could be used, one stone for each object counted. Bundles of sticks were also used to count and keep track of days, one stick being removed from a bundle to represent the passage of a day. A tally of years was kept by scratching notches in sticks.

The complex Mayan and Aztec calendar systems used both the 365-day year and a 260-day cycle tied to the cultures' religious rituals. In the Mayan system, the more accurate of the two, there were 360 "named" days in the years and five unnamed days. The 360-day period of named days was called the *tun* and was composed of eighteen *uinals*, or months, of twenty days each. The 260-day and 365-day cycles overlapped; every fifty-two years the two cycles returned to the same relative positions; scholars refer to this fifty-two-year period as the Calendar Round. Every day—18.980 in all—in the round had a unique combination of day numbers and names and month numbers and names.

See also Aztec; Maya.

Mato Tope (c. 1795—July 30, 1837): Chief

ALSO KNOWN AS: Four Bears
TRIBAL AFFILIATION: Mandan
SIGNIFICANCE: Mato Tope accused whites of genocide when an epidemic of smallpox decimated his tribe

There were two Mandan leaders known as Mato Tope, or Four Bears; they were father and son. Mato Tope the elder was born around 1795 and died in 1837; his son, who became chief after his father's death, died in 1861.

Mato Tope the elder was second chief of the Mandans when George Catlin visited in 1832 and painted his portrait. Catlin said at the time that the elder Mato Tope was one of his favorite artistic subjects and Native American friends. Karl Bodmer also painted the elder Mato Tope when he visited the

Mandans two years after Catlin, and the portraits by the two men were widely reproduced.

The elder Mato Tope was selected head chief in 1837 just as a smallpox epidemic was sweeping in with an influx of transient whites. Smallpox descended on the Mandans with a virulence that ultimately killed all but thirty-one of some sixteen hundred people. Mato Tope succumbed to the disease on July 30, 1837. On the day he died, he is said to have raged against the smallpox epidemic that was killing him and his people and to have called upon his people to rise up and kill all white people. (Whether he actually made this speech has been debated by historians.) After the younger Mato Tope assumed tribal leadership, the Mandans attempted to find a strategy to resist further white encroachment, but they did not launch a major campaign against whites. The younger Mato Tope was a signatory of the 1851 Fort Laramie Treaty.

See also Demography; Diseases, post-contact; Mandan.

Matonabbee (c. 1736, near Fort Prince of Wales, Hudson Bay, Canada—1782, Fort Prince of Wales, Hudson Bay, Canada): Guide

TRIBAL AFFILIATION: Chipewyan
SIGNIFICANCE: As a guide for the Hudson's Bay Company, Matonabbee led the third Coppermine expedition in search of precious metals and the Northwest Passage

Following his father's death, Matonabbee was adopted and educated by the Hudson's Bay Company governor, Richard Norton. With Norton's recall to England, Matonabbee joined relatives in a Chipewyan hunting band roaming regions of present-day northern Manitoba, Saskatchewan, and eastern Northwest Territories.

At age sixteen, Matonabbee returned to Fort Prince of Wales, where he hunted animals for the British and accompanied them during several trading trips. After serving as an interpreter and guide, he rose to the position of chief of his tribe and became a respected ally of the Hudson's Bay Company. In 1770, Matonabbee found and aided the return of the stranded second Coppermine expedition under Samuel Hearne. Afterward, Hearne and Matonabbee made a third expedition, from 1771 to 1772, to search for metals and the Northwest Passage. During the expedition, Matonabbee led his men in a raid against a band of Inuit, their traditional enemies. After smallpox killed many of his people in 1782, Matonabbee committed suicide.

See also Chipewyan; Hudson's Bay Company; Trade; Trading posts.

Mattaponi: Tribe

CULTURE AREA: Northeast
LANGUAGE GROUP: Algonquian
PRIMARY LOCATION: Virginia
POPULATION SIZE: 490 (1990 U.S. Census)

The Mattaponi, a small tribe of the Algonquian family, lived on the river of the same name in Virginia. Along with other tribes, they were members of the Powhatan Confederacy. In 1608, the British explorer John Smith visited their village and found about one hundred members. He included the tribe, which he spelled *Mattapanient*, on his map of the area. In 1781, Thomas Jefferson visited the Mattaponi, recording the visit in his *Notes on Virginia* (1825). They were closely related to the Pamunkey, another Powhatan tribe. By 1900, the Mattaponi and Pamunkey were living side by side on reservations, intermarrying freely but maintaining continuity as tribes, as they had for more than three hundred years.

In the twentieth century, a small number of people—probably all of mixed blood—still claimed the name Mattaponi. They worked at hunting, trapping, and fishing, although state game laws now forbade several traditional methods. The state of Virginia funded a shad hatchery on the Mattaponi Reservation, which was run by the Indians. Women still made honeysuckle-stem baskets in the late twentieth century, and the tribe was run by an elected chief and his council of elders. Most Mattaponi were Baptists and attended the Mattaponi Indian Baptist Church, established in 1931. The reservation school was closed by the state in 1966, causing some concern at the time that traditional ways would not be passed to the next generation.

See also Algonquian language family; Northeast; Powhatan Confederacy.

Mattole: Tribe

CULTURE AREA: California
LANGUAGE GROUP: Athapaskan
PRIMARY LOCATION: West of Trinity River to Pacific Ocean
POPULATION SIZE: 62 (1990 U.S. Census)

Though linguistically and territorially contiguous, the groups referred to collectively as Mattole—consisting of the Nongatl, Lassik, Sinkyone, and Wailaki—were autonomous. They maintained trade of differential resources. Where possible, villages were on a river. Vertical-slab, conical houses were built. The Mattole's main food was acorns and other nuts and seeds, supplemented by hunting, trapping, fishing, and gathering of numerous roots and tubers. The Sinkyone exploited sea mammals. Anadromous fish were important for winter food and trade.

By 1853, these groups had interacted with European Americans. They were assigned to reservations in the Round Valley and to the Smith River reservations. Armed conflict continued between the Indians and settlers, lumbermen, miners, and government agents, which, along with introduced disease, reduced the indigenous populations. This conflict was exacerbated by the settlers' forbidding the Indians to practice controlled burning and by a general misuse of the land and resources by non-Indians. Today many Mattole people live and work off the reservations, and some are involved with traditional lifestyle and religious revitalization.

See also Athapaskan language family.

Maya: Tribe

CULTURE AREA: Mesoamerica
LANGUAGE GROUP: Mayan
PRIMARY LOCATION: Central America, Southern Mexico

Mayas inhabited southern Mexico and most of Central America. The heart of their territory was centered in the present Mexican state of Chiapas and the Yucatán peninsula, and the countries of Belize, Honduras, and Guatemala.

Origins. The origin of the Maya is unknown, although some believe their roots were in the Petén region of Guatemala, where old and relatively crude ceremonial centers have been discovered. Others locate their roots more northerly, in the Olmec region of Mexico, because of traces of Olmec culture seen in the Maya dot-and-bar calendar system and in ceremonial centers with their early round mud pyramids.

One reason that so much mystery surrounds such a relatively advanced civilization as the Maya is that Bishop Diego de Landa, in his fervor to convert these indigenous people, seen as savage pagans, publicly burned almost all hieroglyphic records of Maya history and religion in 1552. Hundreds of idols, inscribed stelae, and altar stones were also destroyed. Ironically, however, Landa is credited with providing the single best source of information about the Maya: His book on the Maya included not only details of their life but also some explanation of their calendar, which contained two main cycles, one of 260 days and the other of 365 days.

Only three Maya hieroglyphic texts are known to have survived. Today they are known by the name of the place where they are preserved. These are the Codex Dresdensis in Dresden, Germany; the Codex Peresianus in Paris, France; and the Codex Cortesianus in Madrid, Spain. In addition to these, a number of stelae also exist; however, not all Maya hieroglyphics have been deciphered. A few later textual records, or books, also exist. The *Popol Vuh* was written by the Quiche Mayas in historical times using letters of Spanish script. It deals primarily with the story of creation. The *Books of Chilam Balam* are mythological histories of the Maya, and the *Annals of the Cakchiquels* presents a genealogical history of the Cakchiquels and relates the events of the Spanish conquest. In all these works, religion and myth are intertwined with factual history.

History. Scholars who study Maya history have divided it into three major periods. The Formative period (1800 B.C.E.-100 B.C.E.) was characterized by the gradual development of complex ceremonial centers, monumental architecture, hieroglyphic writing, calendrics, social stratification, trade networks, and city states. The Classic period (200 C.E.-900 C.E.) saw the maturation of the above, resulting in large, powerful ceremonial centers, ritual and solar calendrical systems, large agricultural bureaucracies, and often violent competition between ceremonial centers. This period is sometimes referred to as the "Old Empire." The Post-Classic period (1000 C.E.-conquest) was a time of renaissance in the northern, or Yucatán, region under Toltec influence. Religious compulsion was largely replaced by military concerns, resulting in secular government gaining ascendance over religious leadership. This period is sometimes referred to as the "New Empire."

In reality, the Maya never formed an empire, since there was no dominant capital city or single ruler. Rather, there was a loose federation of city-centers bound together by similarities of culture and religion under the control of religious leaders. These priest-rulers, who maintained power by virtue of their superior education and knowledge of the supernatural, shared common interests and concerns. Under their leadership Maya civilization witnessed extraordinary achievements in fine arts, architecture, engineering, astronomy, mathematics, and hieroglyphic writing. Two accomplishments deserving special mention were the development of the mathematical concept of zero and a calendar which was more accurate than the Gregorian calendar introduced in Europe in 1582 C.E. These accomplishments enabled Mayas to record the dates of important events accurately on Katun stones, or stelae, every twenty years.

Building was a constant part of Maya life. Ceremonial centers were built, rebuilt, and enlarged. These centers typically included one or more pyramids with a temple on top, a paved courtyard or plaza, and a number of low stone buildings. Often there was a ball court where a game was played utilizing a small hard rubber ball, leather hip pads, and stone rings on the walls. The marketplace was set up, especially on important ceremonial days, near the temple-pyramid. These ceremonial centers were ruled by a largely hereditary class of priest-aristocrats who had almost a total monopoly on education, wealth, and power. The great Maya centers of Tikal, Uaxactun, Palenque, and Copan experienced long dynasties of priest-rulers. Copan, one of the longest-lived dynasties, had sixteen rulers. One, Smoke Imix, ruled for sixty-seven years.

Around 800 C.E., Maya civilization in the southern lowlands began to decline; it had virtually collapsed by 900. Maya civilization continued to flourish in Yucatán. Possible explanations for the demise in the southern area include natural causes, such as disease, soil exhaustion, or change of climate, as well as social causes, such as continued warfare or the loss of control by the priest-aristocracy. Whatever the reasons, the result was the end of the classic indigenous cultures in Mesoamerica.

The conquest of the Maya by the Spanish began around 1524 and ended with the defeat of five thousand Itzás at Lake Petén Itzá in 1697 by Martín de Ursua. During these years some fierce battles took place, but the Maya were unsuccessful in defending their land against the invaders from Spain. Meanwhile, Spanish soldiers under the command of Francisco de Montejo subdued the Maya in Yucatán, where they were aided by a prophecy which had foretold the coming of white men with beards. Because of the efforts of missionaries such as Fray Andres de Avendano y Layola, who learned their history, culture, and language, the Maya were converted to Christianity, thus fulfilling another of their prophecies: "All moons, all years, all days, all winds take their course and pass away."

Religion. Religion was at the heart of Maya life. Religious ceremonies controlled the activities of the seasons and the growth of crops. Religion was also the driving force in the development of science and art. The Maya universe contained an array of divinities who controlled every aspect of nature. Each day of the week was regarded as a god whose behavior could be divined through the use of an intricate calendar system. Mathematics and astronomy were important to the divinations and astrology, which were basic elements of their religious beliefs. At birth, children were taken to priests who predicted the future of the baby with the aid of astrological charts and sacred books. They also identified the specific god to whom the child would owe lifelong devotion based on the exact time and date of birth. A perpetual round of sacrificial ceremonies, prayers, fasting, and incense burning was required to please the gods. The elevated status and power of priests was thus ensured. The gods also required human blood. Accordingly, human sacrifices were offered, as was self-mutilation. Priests and other pious individuals pierced their tongues, earlobes, and genitals in order to draw blood and thereby please the gods.

According to the *Chilam Balam*, one of their sacred books, the earth was flat with four sides, each with its own color: white for north, yellow for south, red for east, and black for west. The color of the center was green. Four gods upheld the sky, and on each side there was a sacred ceiba, or wild cottonwood tree. In the center stood a giant green ceiba with its roots in the underworld and its branches in the upperworld. Surrounding the earth were thirteen heavens and nine hells. The heavens were ordered in six ascending and six descending steps, with the seventh at the top. Similarly, the nine hells were arranged in four descending and four ascending steps, with the fifth at the bottom. This structure of the universe is reflected in the form of the stepped pyramids crowned with temples. They served as the link between heaven and earth, with the priests as mediators.

In another sacred book, the *Popol Vuh*, the story of creation is recorded. The gods inhabited a dark world when they decided to create humankind. First they created men from mud, but they were soft and pliable, without mind or soul. The gods destroyed these men. Men were created a second time from wood, but they were stiff and inflexible without mind or soul, unable to remember their creator. Most of these were destroyed by a flood of fiery rain, while those who survived were changed into monkeys. The gods created men a third time. Four men were formed from the dough of white and yellow corn. They possessed intelligence and wisdom, but these powers were limited so they would be less than gods. Next, four women were created to be wives for the men. After the humans multiplied in the world of darkness the gods created the Morning Star, Icoquih, which precedes the sun. Then the sun arose and humankind rejoiced. Maya tradition locates the birthplace of the gods and man in the Usamacinta Valley in the region near Palenque.

Although the Mayas recognized and served a multitude of gods, not all were of equal rank. Belief in the Feathered Serpent god was shared with other indigenous people of Mesoamerica. This god, commonly known as Quetzalcóatl by the Aztecs, was called Kukulcan by the Mayas, among whom it became one of the most important deities.

Art and Architecture. Mayas have been called the Greeks of the New World not only because of their level of civilization but also because of the development of their art and architecture. Both art and architecture were ancillary to religion. Artists painted murals in bright colors recording selected aspects of Maya life. These paintings, as well as stone carvings and vase decorations, often show priests as they receive offerings, give orders, or pass judgments. Artists also worked in stucco and formed large plaster masks of rulers which symbolized the institution of kingship. Mosaic jade masks and small busts were also made of important individuals.

Works of art which are particularly noteworthy are the sarcophagus lid for the ruler Pacal, which was found in a hidden chamber at Palenque, and the large carved jaguar throne found in a sealed chamber at Chichén Itzá. The lid was carved in bas-relief on a single 12-foot slab of limestone. It depicts the cosmos at the time of Pacal's death, including his image and a large cosmic tree decorated with jewels, mirrors, bloodletting bowls, dragons, bones, and a celestial bird on top. The gaping jaws of the underworld await at the bottom in the form of two huge skeletal dragons joined at the chin. At Chichén Itzá the throne carved in the form of a jaguar was discovered in the Temple of Kukulcan. It was painted bright red, with eyes of jade and fangs of flint. The spots on its coat were made of inlaid jade disks.

Certain symbols or images appear repeatedly in Maya art and architecture. These include the jaguar, earth-dragon or crocodile, screech owl, bat, rattlesnake, snail, and butterfly. These and other animal forms served as guardian spirits and were found in the sacred calendar. Not all art was dedicated to religious purposes, however; common people and daily activities were also represented, especially on pottery and clay figures.

Professional musicians also flourished. A wide array of musical instruments was used, including wooden drums, hollow tortoise-shell drums, reed flutes, bone whistles, clay whistles, long wooden trumpets, conch shell trumpets, and rattles. Music was utilized for battles, celebrations, and funeral processions.

Maya architecture was among the most impressive in the New World. The use of cut stones made their structures strong and durable, able to survive the passage of centuries. They were often monumental in scale. They built pyramids topped with temples which soared more than 200 feet in the air, a ball court the size of a football field, a 320-foot-long building on the top of a hill, a stone arch 20 feet high, a four-story stone tower, and a building with scores of stone columns which supported a vaulted stone roof. They also built celestial observatories, water reservoirs, and irrigation systems.

Common architectural features include majestic temples topped with stone combs, the use of corbeled roof vaults or the "false arch," carvings on the facades and lintels of stone structures, steep-sided pyramids crowned with temples, and paved courtyards. It was customary to cover older structures such as pyramids or courtyards with new ones. At the end of the Classic Period, some architectural changes occurred in Yucatán. Pyramids were smaller, stone combs on the top of temples were smaller, and ornamental figures on facades became more abstract designs.

Although the culture of the Maya gradually disappeared, there are still an estimated 3.2 million people who speak the Mayan language. —*Philip E. Lampe*

See also Ball game and courts; Codices; Copan; Mathematics; Migrations; Palenque; Quetzalcóatl.

BIBLIOGRAPHY

Craine, Eugene R., and Reginald Reindorp, eds. and trans. *The Codex Perez and the Book of Chilam Balam of Mani.* Norman: University of Oklahoma Press, 1979. Collection of documents, including almanacs, prophecies, horoscopes, computations of time, herbal remedies, methods of bleeding, land documents, and history of the Itzas and Xius. Contains drawings and photocopies of documents.

Henderson, John S. *The World of the Ancient Maya.* Ithaca, N.Y.: Cornell University Press, 1981. Examines the Maya cultural tradition from earliest settlements through the period of the Spanish conquest in the sixteenth century. Contains many useful maps, drawings, and photographs.

Hunter, C. Bruce. *A Guide to Ancient Maya Ruins.* Norman: University of Oklahoma Press, 1974. Excellent source for discussion and description of selected major archaeological sites. Contains maps and site plans as well as drawings, illustrations, and photographs.

Landa, Diego de. *Yucatan Before and After the Conquest.* Translated by William Gates. 1937. Reprint. New York: Dover, 1978. Begins with a historical explanation of the manuscript by Landa, which is the source of much of the information available on Maya history and culture. Includes documents, maps, drawings, and photographs.

Thompson, John Eric S. *Maya History and Religion.* Norman: University of Oklahoma Press, 1970. Broad coverage of Maya life with an emphasis on religion. Contains photographs, drawings, and maps. Includes a useful bibliography of earlier sources and references.

Means, Russell (b. Nov. 10, 1939, Pine Ridge Reservation, S.Dak.): Activist

TRIBAL AFFILIATION: Oglala Lakota (Sioux)

SIGNIFICANCE: Means has been a principal leader of the American Indian Movement (AIM)

Russell Charles Means was born on the Pine Ridge Reservation in South Dakota on November 10, 1939, and reared in Oakland, California, where his parents moved during World War II. In 1969, he was asked to join the American Indian Movement (AIM). He soon revealed talent as a media strategist, attracting national attention through actions such as painting Plymouth Rock red on Thanksgiving Day of 1971.

By the time of the Trail of Broken Treaties occupation of the Bureau of Indian Affairs (BIA) headquarters building in Washington, D.C., in November, 1972, Means was one of AIM's primary leaders. He continued this role in subsequent confrontations, notably the armed standoff at Wounded Knee from February to May of 1973.

AIM leader Russell Means speaking in July, 1978, a week before the Longest Walk protest march arrived in Washington, D.C. (AP/Wide World Photos)

After Wounded Knee, Means was charged with forty-seven felonies, most of them dismissed when it was proved that the FBI and federal prosecutors had fabricated evidence with which to "neutralize" him. Meanwhile, he suffered four assassination attempts. He was finally imprisoned in 1978, after South Dakota obtained his conviction on the somewhat arcane charge of "criminal syndicalism." Means later resumed his activism, launching the occupation of Yellow Thunder Camp in the Black Hills (1981 to 1985) as part of an effort to recover Lakota treaty lands. In 1988, he became the first American Indian to pursue the U.S. presidency in an attempt to "inject Indian issues into the consciousness of the American public."

In the years prior to the Columbian quincentenary, Means also led a series of demonstrations in Denver, Colorado—the city in which commemoration of "Columbus Day" originated—to "protest celebration of the genocide of American Indians embodied in the Columbian legacy." He was successful in stopping the events planned for Denver in 1992.

See also Activism; American Indian Movement (AIM); Banks, Dennis; Black Hills; Civil rights and citizenship; International Indian Treaty Council (IITC); Pan-Indianism; Trail of Broken Treaties; Urban Indians; Wounded Knee occupation.

BIBLIOGRAPHY

Matthiessen, Peter. *In the Spirit of Crazy Horse*. 2d ed. New York: Viking Press, 1991.

Weyler, Rex. *Blood of the Land: The U.S. Government and Corporate War Against the First Nation*. 2d ed. Philadelphia: New Society Publishers, 1992.

Medicine and modes of curing, post-contact

TRIBES AFFECTED: Pantribal

SIGNIFICANCE: Meeting the health care needs of contemporary American Indians, especially those living on reservations, is largely the responsibility of the Indian Health Service

By the middle of the nineteenth century, the American Indian population had been decimated by three centuries of contact with Europeans and European Americans. Among the primary factors in this vast depopulation was the devastation caused by infectious European diseases (such as smallpox), against which Indians did not have immunity. Moreover, by the mid- to late nineteenth century, nearly all the native population of the United States had been consigned to reservations. These reservations, found today in thirty-two states, are located primarily in Alaska, Arizona, Minnesota, Montana, New Mexico, South Dakota, Utah, Washington, and Wisconsin.

In various treaties with the federal government, Indians were historically guaranteed health care services. Until the late nineteenth century, such care was under the jurisdiction of the Department of War and was provided by military doctors stationed on or near reservations. Some health care was also provided by religious and social groups. It was not until 1921 that the federal government, in the Snyder Act, officially mandated that health services be provided to American Indians.

By the middle of the twentieth century, Indian health care had come under the jurisdiction of the Indian Health Service of the federal Public Health Service. Central issues such as the rural location of many American Indians, the widespread existence of Indian poverty, and the high incidence of certain health problems among Indians—especially accidental death, diabetes, depression, and many alcohol-related diseases—have complicated the problem of providing adequate health care to Indians.

Early Indian Health Care. In many cases, nineteenth century peace treaties between the federal government and the Indian tribes who agreed to live on reservations included some sort of health care provisions. Initially, the radically underfunded programs aimed at meeting these needs were of two types. First, health funds were combined with funds aimed at general education and were administered by either religious or philanthropic organizations that operated with widely varying degrees of success. Second, the Department of War used the most appropriate—or convenient—personnel at military posts close to the individual reservations to carry out Indian medical care and training in health-related areas such as sanitation. The quality of the health care Indians received varied greatly and depended on the attitudes of the personnel who were involved in it.

Development of the Indian Health Service. In the middle of the nineteenth century, the U.S. Department of the Interior was created. At this time civilians took over Indian health care entirely as this charge passed into the hands of the Bureau of Indian Affairs (BIA). While initially inefficient at providing health care, the BIA began to organize a medical care division in the middle of the 1870's. This division grew slowly; by the 1920's its main efforts were in the treatment of trachoma, tuberculosis, and the other contagious diseases that were endemic among reservation populations. Indians were given the right of American citizenship in 1924. Regrettably, however, the next thirty years saw relatively little overall improvement of their health, despite the efforts of the health care practitioners who worked among them.

In 1955 the Public Health Service took over Indian health care via the Division of Indian Health, which is now called the Indian Health Service. This change was mandated by Public Law 83-568 (the Transfer Act), which stated that "all the functions, responsibilities, authorities, and duties . . . relating to the maintenance and operation of . . . health facilities for Indians, and conservation of Indian health . . . shall be administered by the Surgeon General of the Public Health Service." Three factors enabled the Indian Health Service to operate more efficiently than had previous agencies concerned with American Indian health.

First and foremost of these was the widespread use of antibiotics such as penicillin, which could cure many diseases very quickly and gave Indians more faith in the efficacy of white medicine. Second, federal legislation made it possible for physicians and other health professionals to serve in the Public Health Service Officer Corps instead of performing active military service. This brought a great many more qualified individuals into the Indian Health Service. Third, many of the Indians who had served in the U.S. armed forces during World War II had returned to their reservations. Now familiar with life and medical care off reservations, they became an essential cadre of advocates for the Indian Health Service; they also soon represented many members of its staff.

Another valuable aspect of the Indian Health Service is its efficient hierarchical organization and governance at all of its levels from the national office to its management areas to its service units (often a whole tribe). The hierarchy leads to swifter action and to better communication than was possible under other systems. One problem associated with the Indian Health Service is the lack of choice of individual physicians; reservation inhabitants must accept the care of a reservation's appointed doctors or must purchase their own health care.

Health Service Weaknesses and Solutions. Most weaknesses of the Indian Health Service arise from its relatively inadequate funding, the transience and undersupply of its biomedical staff, and the fact that it is smaller than might be desired (fifty-one hospitals and about 425 outpatient clinics and health centers). These factors are aggravated by the lack of many essential, high-technology medical services at its component hospitals, health centers, and clinics. Nevertheless, these facilities are usually very well run within their limitations, such as the facts that the population being served lives mostly on reservations that are located in isolated rural areas and that transportation difficulties arise when patients must be moved to distant, private-sector health providers for services that are otherwise unavailable to them.

The problems of Indian Health Service health care delivery, as well as some of the solutions, are exemplified by the Navajo reservation, with a population of more than 200,000. This reservation, on which live the members of the largest American Indian tribe, is located on an area about the size of West Virginia and sprawls over parts of Arizona, New Mexico, and Utah. The reservation's Indian Health Service component is divided into eight of the 137 service units found in the United States. It contains hospitals with a total of about five hundred beds as well as numerous clinics and other health centers.

Problems of overcrowding and the already mentioned lack of high-technology health services necessitate the expensive transfer of many Navajo Indian patients to private-sector facilities. A partial solution to this logistics problem is the use of a relatively economical ambulance service operated by the Navajo tribe. Other problems include the high incidence of heart disease, alcohol-related deaths (from cirrhosis of the liver, for example), homicide, suicide, and diabetes that consume much of the resource base of the Navajo reservation service units. Present solutions include using both Medicare and Medicaid revenue obtained for qualifying Indians. In the long run, increased budgets for the Indian Health Service and additional hospital facilities will be required.

Another severe problem is the high turnover and shortage of nurses and other essential health care professionals. Permanent nursing positions in the Indian Health Service, for example, are reported to be only 75 to 80 percent filled. It has been

LEADING CAUSES OF DEATH FOR NATIVE AMERICANS/ALASKA NATIVES AND FOR U.S.

Cause	Percentage of Total Deaths	
	Native Americans and Alaska Natives	U.S. All Races
Diseases of the heart	22.2	35.3
Accidents and adverse effects	16.3	4.5
Malignant neoplasms	13.7	22.4
Cerebrovascular diseases	4.5	6.9
Chronic liver disease and cirrhosis	4.3	(1)
Chronic obstructive pulmonary diseases	(1)	3.8

Source: U.S. Department of Health and Human Services, *Regional Differences in Indian Health, 1993*. Rockville, Md.: Public Health Service, 1993.

Note: Data compare causes of death in all Indian Health Service areas, 1987-1989, with U.S. all races, 1988.

(1) Not listed as a leading cause of death.

noted by upper-level Indian Health Service administrators that increasing staff salaries will only partly solve the problem. Rather, the problem is viewed as being largely attributable to both geographic and professional isolation. Complicating the issue still more are the existing decreases and the expected ending of some federal programs that pay all of the educational costs of physicians and nurses in return for a term of practice in the underserved regions of the United States, including Indian reservations. This is particularly problematic because a large percentage of the Indian Health Service professional staff comes from this source (the National Health Service Corps, NHSC). Even in the best of times, however, only 5 to 10 percent of NHSC physicians have remained in the Indian Health Service for even one year beyond the time required by their scholarship program obligations. A positive change is the increased number of Indians entering and projected to enter the system as professional staff.

Identifying Indians to Be Served. Estimates of the percentage of American Indians who are being treated by the Indian Health Service vary from 60 to about 80 percent, depending upon the source of the estimate of the total U.S. Indian population. One basis for counting the Indian population is self-assessment of being an Indian via the U.S. Census. Another approach is based on the percentage of Indian blood possessed by a person. The Indian Health Service itself is not concerned with quantifying the amount of Indian blood in the people it serves. Rather, service at one of its facilities depends on being recognized as an Indian by a contemporary Indian tribe. Requirements for this recognition vary from tribe to tribe, but they often consist of being of one-fourth Indian blood. Indian Health Service facilities are not limited to reservation-based Indians, although most facilities are located on or near reservations. One reason that the service provides care for both reservation and nonreservation Indians is that many tribes count individuals as members regardless of their formal place of residence.

Special Health Needs. The American Indian population has traditionally exhibited a significantly greater incidence of infant mortality as well as adult deaths from a number of diseases than seen in the general U.S. population. These problems have been attributed to Indian families' generally lower incomes as well as to their poorer nutrition and living conditions. Inroads had been made, however, in most of these areas by the late 1980's.

For example, there has been a drop in infant mortality from 22.2 per 1,000 live births to 11.1, a rate very near that for the "U.S., all races" category. Improvement of both health services and living conditions has also diminished the absolute numbers of deaths from the main diseases that kill modern Indian adults. Contemporary deaths from accident, alcoholism

LEADING CAUSES OF AMERICAN INDIAN OUTPATIENT VISITS, 1991	
Cause	*Total Clinical Visits*
Otitis media	302,496
Upper respiratory infection; common cold	300,637
Diabetes mellitus	278,494
Hypertensive disease	217,157
Prenatal care	214,966
Immunization	205,958
Prescription refills	191,893
Laboratory tests only	177,246
Well child care	141,076
Pharyngitis, tonsilitis, and non-streptococcal infection	127,542

Source: U.S. Department of Health and Human Services, *Trends in Indian Health—1993*. Rockville, Md.: Public Health Service, 1993.

Note: Data represent outpatient visits for Indian Health Service and tribal direct and contract general hospitals, fiscal year 1991.

LEADING CAUSES OF AMERICAN INDIAN HOSPITALIZATION, 1991		
Cause	*Combined Discharges*	*Combined Percentage Distribution*
Obstetric deliveries and complications of puerperium and pregnancy	19,511	21.9
Respiratory system diseases	11,038	12.4
Digestive system diseases	9,353	10.5
Injuries and poisonings	8,951	10.0
Circulatory system diseases	5,951	6.7
Symptoms and ill-defined conditions	5,306	6.0
Genitourinary system diseases	4,807	5.4
Mental disorders	3,812	4.3
Endocrine, nutritional, and metabolic disorders	3,685	4.1
Supplementary conditions	3,016	3.4
All other conditions	13,658	15.3

Source: U.S. Department of Health and Human Services, *Trends in Indian Health—1993*. Rockville, Md.: Public Health Service, 1993.

Note: Data represent hospitalizations for Indian Health Service and tribal direct and contract general hospitals, fiscal year 1991.

and related problems, diabetes, homicide, influenza/pneumonia, suicide, and tuberculosis still exceed those in the "all races" population by 185, 388, 169, 91, 42, 480, and 52 percent, respectively. One yardstick of this relatively at-risk status for the American Indian is the 1981 observation that 37 percent of all Indian deaths occur before age forty-five, compared with 12 percent of "all races" deaths.

The Indian Health Service has attempted to diminish the extent of these health problems in a variety of ways. Among efforts directed toward accident reduction is an injury prevention program that includes motor vehicle aspects such as child passenger protection, the promotion of seat belt use, and the deterrence of drunk driving. Furthermore, educational programs on such topics as smoke detector use and drowning protection are widespread.

Another aspect of disease prevention among Indians is a widespread nutrition and dietetics program in which clinical nutrition counseling and general health aspects are promoted. This aspect of Indian Health Service activity is viewed as possessing a very high potential for success, having had more than 200,000 contacts per year with patients in the early 1990's. Also important is the provision by the Indian Health Service of modern sanitary facilities for many Indian homes. Between 1960 and 1991, almost 200,000 homes were provided with modernized sanitary facilities by the service. This assistance has included water and sewage facilities, solid waste disposal, and the development of local organizations to maintain the new systems. Yet much more help is needed in these ventures.

Shamanic and Modern Health Care. A particularly intriguing aspect of modern medical treatment is the combination of conventional Western treatment with the activities of the traditional tribal shaman. This combination of treatments may be found in many Indian Health Service facilities and elsewhere. Its use is partly attributable to the fact that shamanic treatment is comfortable to many Indians. Many of today's physicians find that the shamanic ceremonies and medicinal treatments are a useful complement to their ministrations. These procedures are deemed to be particularly important in resolving mental health problems, but they have also found wide utility in problems ranging from heart disease to dermatitis to cancer. —*Sanford S. Singer*

See also Alcoholism; Civil rights and citizenship; Diseases, post-contact; Medicine and modes of curing, pre-contact; Religious specialists.

BIBLIOGRAPHY

Gregg, Elinor D. *The Indians and the Nurse*. Norman: University of Oklahoma Press, 1965. Points out problems, shortcomings, strengths, and other interesting aspects of federally funded care of American Indians from 1922 to 1937. Provides much insight into physicians, nurses, and Indian patients.

Hammerschlag, Carl A. *The Dancing Healers: A Doctor's Journey of Healing with Native Americans*. San Francisco: Harper & Row, 1988. Various aspects of a psychiatrist's experience with Indian healing are described. Includes examples of syntheses of Indian and Western medicine that produce useful, interactive processes are carefully explored.

Hultkrantz, Ake. *Shamanic Healing and Ritual Drama: Health and Medicine in Native North American Religious Traditions*. New York: Crossroad, 1992. A detailed survey of Indian practice and belief in health, medicine, and religion. Both the historical and modern aspects of shamanic ritual are covered. Also included is a copious set of valuable references.

Kane, Robert L., and Rosalie A. Kane. *Federal Health Care (with Reservations)*. New York: Springer, 1971. Indian Health Service strengths, problems, and shortcomings are described knowledgeably. Included are the capacity to respond to patient needs and conflicts engendered when health providers and consumers have different cultural backgrounds. Kane was a director of the Indian Health Service Navajo service unit at Shiprock, New Mexico.

Torrey, E. Fuller, E. F. Foulkes, H. C. Hendrie, et al. *Community Health and Mental Health Care Delivery for North American Indians*. New York: MSS Information Corporation, 1974. This interesting multiauthored book covers mental health problems of North American Indians. It includes articles on general problems, cultural conflicts, alcoholism, drugs, suicide, and Indian mental health care needs. Shamanic aspects are also described.

U.S. Department of Health and Human Services. Indian Health Service. Division of Program Statistics. *Trends in Indian Health, 1989-*. This report briefly describes the Indian

Health Service and its history and gives many modern statistics about Indian health care. Included are organizational data, handy health statistics, and statistics on many related issues.

U.S. Office of Technology Assessment. *Indian Health Care*. Washington, D.C.: Government Printing Office, 1986. This substantive book covers, in depth, many aspects of Indian health care. Included are the federal-Indian relationship, a population overview, American Indian health status, the Indian Health Service, selected special health topics, and extensive references.

Medicine and modes of curing, pre-contact

TRIBES AFFECTED: Pantribal

SIGNIFICANCE: Traditional American Indian cultures had a number of explanations of illness and approaches to healing, including medicinal, ritualistic, and supernatural approaches

During the prehistoric period, Native American groups had adequate medical systems for successfully treating illness and disease, consisting of a corpus of time-tried explanations and therapeutic procedures that were inextricably related to the notion of supernatural and natural causes. The cause, diagnosis, and prognosis of all illnesses and diseases were explained by a definite classification that was usually unique to a particular group.

Medical Systems. Most external injuries, such as fractures, dislocations, wounds, bruises, skin irritations, snake and insect bites, and even occupationally related deaths, were considered to have been caused by natural means. Many internal illnesses and psychological afflictions, however, were diagnosed as being the result of sorcerers who were capable of manipulating supernatural malevolent powers, resulting in maladies that could be treated only by medical practitioners, or shamans, who possessed special benevolent religious powers and abilities.

Indigenous medical systems resulted from a group's particular adaptation to a certain environment—its wide variety of medicinal as well as noxious plants. It was not unusual for Native Americans to learn medical procedures from the close observation of certain animals. For example, in the early spring, when deer go from browsing to grazing, they will develop diarrhea, and they consume clay to correct this condition. Similarly, clay eating, or geophagy, was universally utilized by Native Americans for curing diarrhea. Clay was also applied externally for certain dermal eruptions, as clay effectively absorbs liquids.

Hunters and gatherers were more concerned with illness than with the advent of death because of their need to maintain a high degree of mobility in order to exploit the animal and plant foods that were located in different areas, according to elevation and time of year. Consequently, illness could debilitate a group's strategies for obtaining food. Because of this concern, Native Americans developed extensive and successful methods of interpreting and treating different afflictions by the use of medical practitioners.

Shamans. The principal medical practitioner was the shaman, a man or woman who had acquired supernatural curing power through a variety of ritualized procedures, but more often through the vision quest, dreaming, receiving a sign, inheritance from a kinsperson, survival of an illness, and less frequently, resurrection after "death." The supernatural power to cure could be general or specific to certain maladies, and usually one's tutelary spirit was associated with curing a particular illness. For example, bear power was most effective in treating burns, heron power to retrieve a lost soul.

Shamans maintained their power through frequent renewal rituals such as sweating, dreaming, reciting special curing songs, isolation, fasting, and continually revitalizing their medicines and paraphernalia through purification. Usually, during an annual rite, shamans would publicly demonstrate their powers to the congregation; this was an occasion when one's power could be stolen by a more powerful individual. The practitioner's life was further burdened by almost continual stress in observing strict behavioral and dietary taboos, which, if violated, could mean the shaman's loss of power or even illness and possibly death.

The curing knowledge and skills of a shaman were sometimes acquired through serving an apprenticeship to a known shaman or to an established practitioner of one's family who would serve as a sponsor and guide during the often long and arduous training period. Shamans tended to work individually but sometimes required the assistance of herbalists, women who usually had a more complete knowledge of local plants and their medicinal uses and properties than did men. Often esoteric medical knowledge was jealously guarded.

Shamans were respected and even feared, for a person who could cure was also believed capable of sorcery. If a patient died, the attending shaman could be accused of being the sorcerer. Medical practitioners were sometimes physically different because of blindness, minor congenital defects, or permanent injuries. They were also considered psychologically different from others because of their ability to perform shamanistic rites such as soul-flight, physical and spiritual transformation, legerdemain, ventriloquism, glossalalia (non-meaningful speech or "speaking in tongues"), and various prophetic skills.

Causes of Illness. Native Americans were not disease-free. They experienced mostly gastrointestinal problems, arthritis, pneumonia, and some endemic maladies. Therefore, illnesses and injuries attributable to natural causes were well understood and could be treated by an elderly, more knowledgeable kinsperson. Supernatural maladies and death could be caused by moral transgression, unfulfilled dreams, misusing one's power, sorcery (as in soul loss, spirit intrusion, or object intrusion), and, in some cases, poisoning.

In a ceremony that has changed little in hundreds of years, Navajo medicine man Hosteen Tso-Begay treats a four-year-old boy; the boy's body has been annointed with an herb potion. (AP/Wide World Photos)

Spiritual or supernatural illnesses were invariably thought to be caused by a sorcerer who had successfully manipulated an individual's soul or tutelary spirit because the victim had offended or humiliated someone—or simply because the sorcerer was malicious. A person who was greedy, selfish, boisterous, or malicious was subject to being sorcerized. Consequently, the fear of sorcery was an effective means of social control, not only because of the dire consequences but also because one was not always certain who was a sorcerer.

Illness could be self-induced through breaking a taboo or by not informing a person who was to suffer an illness or some misfortune, as revealed in one's dream. If one had such a prophetic dream, and if the person in the dream was not properly warned, it was common for the dreamer to experience that specific misfortune. In fact, many Native Americans, upon awakening in the morning, revealed their dreams to an elderly member of the family who would interpret the dream's significance and prescribe appropriate behavior to prevent misfortune.

It was not unusual for an aged or sick shaman to give up his or her curing power through a special ritual, one that ensured the particular power would be acquired later by another person. It also freed the aged shaman from further responsibilities and possible maladies. Illness or even death could occur if one failed to acknowledge that one possessed curing power and should fulfill the obligations of this responsibility.

Women sometimes became shamans after menopause, when they could receive obstetrical power for assisting as midwives in difficult deliveries, prolapse, uterine hemorrhaging, or cases of malposition. Female shamans were knowledgeable about abortives and contraceptives, and they instructed the new mother about postnatal dietary and behavioral taboos. They often instructed a menarcheal girl about pertinent taboos associated with being a woman. They administered decoctions, roots, powders, and other medicines for dysmenorrhea and other female disorders, even when fecundity was thought to be a problem. Female shamans were, on occasion, sought for empowering courting flutes or providing love incantations or medicines.

Universal to Native Americans was the strict observance of dietary and behavioral taboos that surrounded an individual's death, for if the survivors violated purification rites intended to prevent spiritual contamination, failed to accord the deceased certain respect, mentioned the name of the deceased, or dreamed improperly of the dead person, or if the widow or widower married too soon, then a specific illness would beset the offender, inflicted by the dead person's ghost.

Nor was it unusual for a person who had not accorded proper respect through the strict observance of taboos associated with killing an animal to become ill. For example, a man who killed a bear had to sing the death song of the creature and, for a prescribed period, abstain from sexual relationships and eat a restricted diet. If the hunter was remiss, the dead bear might appear in the man's dream and pull back its scalp, which could result in the hunter losing his mind and being condemned to endless wandering and continual hunger.

Curing Rituals. Treatment of supernatural illnesses depended upon an impressive array of medicines, cures, and ritual therapies that required the intervention of a shaman. These rituals were shamanistic performances that included dancing, singing, drumming, and the use of religious paraphernalia that were personal and power-associated. Medical knowledge was jealously guarded, for it was feared that a shaman could lose his or her power if the knowledge were divulged.

An important aspect of treating supernatural illnesses was the group medical inquest, or therapeutic interview, a collective ceremony in which the patient and shaman were joined by family and friends, and on occasion the entire village. This collective psychodrama functioned to integrate the group and to reinstate a moral order. It was an effective therapeutic session that publicly permitted shamans to demonstrate their power and ability. Shamans were sometimes attended by a medical chorus who chanted curing songs and played percussion and wind instruments which were believed to facilitate a shaman's power flight in seeking a vision or recovering a lost soul.

The group medical inquest also afforded the patient a managerial role, expiated guilt through oral catharsis, facilitated group confession of moral transgressions, and provided an opportunity for others to make confessions of transgressions that would prevent them from becoming ill. These rituals invariably lasted until the patient was completely rehabilitated, which meant that the practitioner and his or her entourage would reside temporarily with the patient, noting reasons for illness and anxiety.

Shamans effectively utilized various prophetic rituals and interpreted signs to ascertain the diagnosis and prognosis of illness, and even the specific cause. The offending sorcerer could be identified and might later participate in removing the malevolent power that was causing the affliction. Often a shaman's prophetic abilities in foreseeing medical problems were enhanced by the use of drugs, tobacco, fasting, spiritual transformation, hypnosis, dreaming, trances, and the use of musical instruments and singing. Some groups had prophetic devices such as special tule mats, sand paintings, smoke, or a container of water, or they had tutelary spirits that would communicate the needed information.

Prior to a curing ceremony, it was not uncommon to tie a shaman's hands and feet securely with rawhide and place him behind a hide screen. Immediately he would throw the loose rawhide over the screen. To demonstrate their power before curing, shamans might also perform different proofs of ordeal, such as withstanding excruciating pain or demonstrating unusual manipulative skills. For example, shamans might dramatically plunge an arm into boiling water or hold a hot stone to show the patient and group they were impervious to pain because of their power.

During curing ritual shamans often had to be protected as their personal powers might be elsewhere seeking the cause of a patient's malady. Temporarily without power, shamans were believed susceptible to danger, since their power could be lost

Plant	Symptom	Preparation	How Used
TRADITIONAL INDIAN MEDICINES OF CANADA STILL USED			
Black spruce	Cough	Soft inner bark	Chewed
Devil's club	Aching muscles	Boiled	Drunk
Fireweed	Swelling	Large infusion steamed	As poultice
Lichen	Ulcers	Mixed with other herbs	Chewed
Sage	Colds	Boiled	Inhaled
Soapberry	Diarrhea	None	Eaten
Spruce needles	Eye infection	Needles boiled	As eye wash
Spruce pitch	Infected wound	Applied directly	As poultice
Strawberry leaf	Ensure safe pregnancy	Dried and boiled	Drunk
Strawberry root	Diarrhea	Boiled	Drunk
Tamarack bark	Stomach trouble	Beaten, tea added	Drunk
Wild rhubarb	Arthritis	Boiled as tea	Drunk
Wild rhubarb	Infected wound	Pounded root	As poultice
Willow leaves	Insect stings	Chewed and applied	As poultice

Source: Duane Champagne, ed., *The Native North Amerian Almanac.* Detroit: Gale Research, 1994. Primary source, Medical Services Branch, Alberta Region, Health and Welfare Canada.

Note: A partial listing of herbal medicines still used today in Canada.

or taken by a more powerful person. On occasion, the shaman may have been required to have a power duel with the malevolent power, a struggle which was evident by the practitioner's unusual behavior when he or she was thrown about or lifted into the air. A shaman of lesser power could be killed by the illness when it was removed from the patient, particularly if the shaman used a sucking tube.

Medicines. Through continual observation and long use, Native Americans developed an extensive materia medica, estimated to have been approximately 54 percent chemically active. It was constituted from geological, floral, and faunal substances. These compounds and simple medicaments were administered to most internal and external afflictions by shamans who were knowledgeable of the intended effect.

Medicines were administered in the form of poultices, salves, expectorants, vermifuges, emetics, cathartics, astringents, febrifuges, poisons, anesthetics, stimulants, narcotics, diuretics, and infusions. Most medicines were acquired locally, but some were obtained through trade.

—*John Alan Ross*

See also Diseases, post-contact; Medicine and modes of curing, post-contact; Religious specialists.

BIBLIOGRAPHY

Corlett, William Thomas. *The Medicine-Man of the American Indian and His Cultural Background.* Springfield, Ill.: Charles C Thomas, 1935. A book that explains the cultural significance of medicines and their ritual application, particularly the role of the shaman.

Radin, Paul. *The Story of the American Indian.* New York: Boni & Liveright, 1927. An early but significant recognition of Native American medical systems that explains the role of ritual in treating psychosomatic illnesses.

Ross, John Alan. "Indian Shamans of the Plateau: Past and Present." *Medical Journal* 62, no. 3 (1989). An article dealing with aboriginal and syncretic medicine in the Plateau, which is representative of many Native American groups.

Stone, Eric. *Medicine Among the American Indians.* Clio Medicia 7. New York: Hafner, 1962. A comprehensive text explaining indigenous Native American medical systems that contains an extensive bibliography.

Vogel, Virgil J. *American Indian Medicine.* Norman: University of Oklahoma Press, 1970. This excellent book is the most definitive study of Native American medicine because of extensive research, references, and readability for the nonspecialist. It is illustrated and stresses the significance of medicinal plants. Contains a comprehensive bibliography.

Medicine bundles

TRIBES AFFECTED: Pantribal

SIGNIFICANCE: A medicine bundle is a physical token of an individual's, clan's, or nation's relationship to the spiritual world and its power

A medicine bundle is a collection of objects that have connection with sacred power. The objects may include artifacts such as the carved stone statue of the Kiowas (known as the Taime), gaming dice, or whittled sticks, as well as natural or found items such as feathers, smooth stones, naturally occurring crystals, and herbs and sweet grasses collected for the bundle. Whatever the contents, the bundle is always carefully arranged, whether bound by string and tied with special knots or rolled into a bark or buckskin container. Sweet grass, sage, and other aromatic herbs are renewed periodically. The bundle may be inherited from clan or family, may be given by a mentor to a disciple, or may be constructed according to directions received in a vision. In any case, the bundle represents and contains great power: It is the physical embodiment of the spiritual power of the owner, whether shaman, warrior, or priest.

See also Bundles, sacred; Clans; Ethnophilosophy and worldview; Medicine and modes of curing, pre-contact; Religion; Religious specialists.

Medicine Lodge, Treaties of

DATE: October, 1867

PLACE: Kansas

TRIBES AFFECTED: Apache of Oklahoma, Arapaho, Cheyenne, Comanche, Kiowa

SIGNIFICANCE: In an attempt to end the hostilities between Indians and white settlers in the southern Plains, the United States negotiated the Treaties of Medicine Lodge with the largest southern Plains tribes; the treaties marked the beginning of the reservation period for the Plains Indians

In 1867, after several years of intermittent war between the southern Plains nomads and the United States, the Congress established the Indian Peace Commission to conclude a peace with the southern Plains tribes. The Peace Commission included Indian Commissioner Nathaniel G. Taylor, Senator John B. Henderson of Missouri, the New England reformer Samuel F. Tappan, and army generals Alfred Terry, William S. Harney, William T. Sherman, and John B. Sanborn. Before the Commission met with the southern Plains tribes in October, 1867, Sherman was recalled to Washington and replaced by General C. C. Augur.

In August, 1867, the Peace Commission requested the southern Plains tribes to assemble at Medicine Lodge Creek in southern Kansas. At first, their entreaties attracted only the bands under "friendly" chiefs: Black Kettle of the Cheyenne, Little Raven of the Arapaho, and Poor Bear of the "Kiowa Apache" (Apache of Oklahoma). By October, however, most of the bands had come to Medicine Lodge Creek. When the commissioners arrived at the council, the camp included 100 Comanche lodges, 150 Kiowa lodges, 85 Kiowa Apache lodges, 171 Arapaho lodges, and 250 lodges of Cheyenne.

The Comanche, Kiowa, and Kiowa Apache agreed to a treaty with the commissioners on October 21. Sitting Bear and Satanta of the Kiowa and Ten Bears of the Comanche were among the signatories. The negotiations with the Cheyenne and Arapaho, however, were less expeditious. Their recent successes against the army made the Cheyenne—particularly the soldier societies—reticent to sign a treaty. Yet on October 28, the Cheyenne agreed to a treaty; among the Cheyenne signatories were Black Kettle and Tall Bull; the Arapaho signatories included Little Raven. Both treaties were ratified by the Senate on July 25, 1868.

The Southern Cheyenne and Arapaho gained a reservation of three million acres between the Arkansas and Cimarron rivers; the Comanche, Kiowa, and Kiowa Apache acquired a reservation of a similar size between the Washita and Red

Nineteenth century artist's rendition of Arapaho and Comanche council at Medicine Lodge Creek. (Library of Congress)

rivers. The treaty forbade the tribes to occupy any territory outside the reservations permanently but stipulated that they retained the right to hunt bison anywhere south of the Arkansas River "so long as the buffalo may range thereon in such numbers as to justify the chase." While the agreements prohibited white settlers from moving into the Indians' hunting territory, they did not expressly forbid European American buffalo hunters from pursuing the herds south of the Arkansas River. In the early 1870's, white buffalo hunters nearly exterminated the bison south of the Arkansas.

See also Black Kettle; Buffalo; Fort Laramie Treaty of 1851; Indian-white relations—U.S., 1831-1870; Little Raven; Sand Creek Massacre; Satanta; Tall Bull; Ten Bears; Washita River, Battle of the.

Medicine wheels

TRIBES AFFECTED: Pantribal
SIGNIFICANCE: A medicine wheel is a circle of iconic stones used as a teaching tool

The medicine wheel is a sacred, powerful teaching circle. There were numerous medicine wheels composed of stones laid out by the indigenous North Americans, some of which are still extant. The most famous, found in the Bighorn Mountains in north central Wyoming, was used by a number of different tribes, including Crow, Cheyenne, Arapaho, and Lakota. It is a circle 80 feet in diameter with twenty-nine spokes of numerous limestone slabs, with three small outer circles, two outer vessel shapes, and one inner vessel shape, all placed at about 8,700 feet in altitude on Medicine Mountain. One of the spokes points to the place on the horizon where the sun rises at summer solstice. Another spoke points to Arcturus rising at spring equinox. The Department of the Interior wishes to turn this site into a tourist attraction and build a visitor center, picnic area, and campground. Tribes have petitioned the government to declare twelve days on both sides of equinoxes and solstices limited to tribal use of the site. The tribes also want the protected area around the medicine wheel enlarged so that the habitat within three miles of the wheel is undisturbed.

See also Religion; Sacred, the.

Meech Lake Accord

DATE: Proposed 1987; defeated June, 1990
TRIBES AFFECTED: Canadian native groups
SIGNIFICANCE: A coalition of native organizations rallied support around an Indian politician and successfully prevented the passage of a constitutional provision that failed to recognize aboriginal rights

Fears that Quebec might break away from the rest of Canada led Canadian prime minister Brian Mulroney and the ten provincial premiers in 1987 to propose a set of amendments to the 1982 Constitution Act. The proposal, known as the Meech Lake Accord after the site of the meeting, recognized French-speaking Quebec as one of the founding nations of Canada and as a distinct society with its own language and culture. The accord, however, granted no such courtesy to the aboriginal peoples of Canada. In order for the accord to become law, it required ratification by all ten provinces before June 23, 1990.

An additional provision of the Meech Lake Accord dealt with admission of a new province to the Confederation. That provision required the unanimous consent of the ten existing provinces in order to establish a new province. Since many of the provinces have territorial desires to extend their borders north, this virtually ensured that the Yukon and Northwest territories, as well as the proposed Nunavut Territory, would be precluded from ever achieving provincial status. Unlike the rest of Canada, the two regions have overwhelmingly native populations.

Native organizations fought bitterly against ratification of the accord. Their leaders insisted that native cultures were no less distinct than Quebec's and that aboriginal rights also deserved formal recognition in the body of the Constitution. Since the courts had held that despite the addition of the Charter of Rights and Freedoms to the Constitution, aboriginal rights were not assured, the natives' concerns were well justified. The leaders further demanded guarantees that they would be given a role in all future First Ministers' conferences affecting natives. George Erasmus, national chief of the Assembly of First Nations, was especially vocal.

Thinking that a looming deadline would help assure passage, Prime Minister Mulroney delayed pushing for ratification of the accord until the very end of the ratification period. That delay proved fatal to the proposal. It allowed Elijah Harper, Manitoba's only native legislator, to prevent consideration of the Meech Lake Accord by the Manitoba Legislative Assembly. Supported by native organizations, Harper exploited a procedural error made by Manitoba Premier Gary Filmon. Manitoba law required unanimous consent of the legislators to begin public hearings on any issue with less than a forty-eight-hour notice. Harper withheld his consent, and the deadline for ratification passed without the Meech Lake Accord ever being considered by the Manitoba Legislative Assembly.

See also Declaration of First Nations; Harper, Elijah; Indian Act of 1876 (Canada); Indian Act of 1951 (Canada); Indian Act of 1989 (Canada); Indian-white relations—Canadian.

Menewa (c. 1765, along the Tallopoosa River, present-day Ala.—1865, Indian Territory, present-day Okla.): Chief

ALSO KNOWN AS: Hothlepoya, Crazy War Hunter
TRIBAL AFFILIATION: Creek
SIGNIFICANCE: As a leader of the Creek war faction, Menewa fought Andrew Jackson at the Battle of Horseshoe Bend

As a young man in Tennessee, Menewa established a warrior's reputation for daring horse raids. He became a leader of the traditional Creek warrior faction, the Red Sticks. When William McIntosh, leader of the White Sticks peace faction, committed a murder, white settlers burned Menewa's village.

Thereafter, Menewa joined the Red Sticks' principal leader, William Weatherford, aiding Tecumseh, leader of a pan-Indian rebellion. Menewa fought General Andrew Jackson during the Creek War and was shot eight times and left for dead at the Battle of Horseshoe Bend in 1814. After recovering from his wounds, he surrendered, forfeiting all of his lands.

Menewa, a leader of the Creek Red Sticks. (Library of Congress)

The Creeks appointed Menewa executioner of McIntosh, who in 1825 had illegally ceded twenty-five million acres of Creek land. Thereafter, Menewa traveled to Washington with Creek leader Opothleyaholo and translator Paddy Carr for negotiations. In exchange for promises of peace, the Creeks were allowed to retain some of their lands. After supporting federal troops during the Seminole War of 1835-1842, Menewa was nevertheless forced to relocate to Indian Territory.

See also Creek; Horseshoe Bend, Treaty of; Opothleyaholo; Seminole Wars; Weatherford, William.

Menominee: Tribe

CULTURE AREA: Northeast
LANGUAGE GROUP: Algonquian
PRIMARY LOCATION: Great Lakes region
POPULATION SIZE: 7,543 (1990 U.S. Census)

The Menominees belong to the large family of indigenous people called the Algonquians. They occupied the Great Lakes region since before recorded history. They were travelers and traders, visiting distant clans in their birchbark canoes. Today there is a Menominee reservation on the Wolf River in northeastern Wisconsin.

Culture. Menominee culture resulted from environmental experience, clan and tribal oral histories, and information gathered via the tribe's network of water and land trails. Intertribal marriage gained acceptance to maintain extended family units, while diminishing the chances for inbreeding among the original clans. The earliest French explorers and trappers reported the Menominees to be "gentle of spirit," although they boasted of their warlike exploits and supernatural adventures. A rigidly defined social system required strict adherence to gender roles and various customs. There were some positions, such as war chief, that could be achieved only by men, but most were open to women. Menominees have traditionally been a matriarchy. The Menominees prized individual rights for all people, including children. This belief precluded punishment for disobeying social rules.

The numeral 4 was considered to be sacred by the tribe; its sacredness may be surmised as having come from the four directions—crucial for navigation on water. Prayers are repeated four times, sometimes to each of the four directions. The Signing of the Cross taught by the French Catholic missionaries, with four points on the body, may have coincidentally created a powerful inducement for religious conversion. Early priests had no initial trouble converting Menominees to Catholicism. The Menominees did not believe in one omnipotent being, but in several levels of gods, encompassing humor and even violence. Menominees who sought to improve their spiritual luck prayed to many different deities and performed many rituals. Tribal members belonged to many societies in a poly-religious blend of science, superstition, and stoicism.

There were once witches and sorcerers among the people, but they were not thought to be evil. Magic as well as medicine was thought to be neutral, but there were inevitably some who wished harm to others. These people would "witch" the target with incantations and a bundle made of herbs and minerals that was referred to as a "witch bag." These animal-hide pouches were reputed to be fed the released human energy occurring upon death and other misery. The Serpent Cult, a secret society which celebrated the commission of evil, was once a potent force within some clans.

Geography. The Menominees trace their beginnings to a village near the mouth of the Menominee River. During the early colonial era, the French documented the tribal range, which was bordered by the Milwaukee River to the south, the Mississippi River to the west, and Lakes Superior, Huron, and Michigan to the north and east. This territory encompassed ten million acres. The predominant geography is small lakes, interconnected with rivers, and large stands of timber. There was surface copper that was considered a source of tribal wealth.

The tribe made four types of snowshoes, each named after a clan, to deal with the heavy snowfalls of the region, but the Menominees were primarily a water people. A significant part of their diet was derived from shallow waters. Living near waterways eased transportation problems and allowed a sense of community. It was proximity to navigable waterways that brought the tribe to European attention as early as 1634.

Tribal History. The birthplace of the tribe can be traced through its oral history. The present city of Menominee, Michigan, was once known as Mini' Kani, the source of the Menominees. According to their legends, the Great Mystery permitted a Giant White Bear with a copper-colored tail to emerge from an underground den as the first man and establish the village. This village established by the White Bear became home to the Bear Clan. Each clan and village had its own chief, but all were subordinate to the Bear Clan. There were several original clans, including the Beaver, the Wolf, and the Eagle. The Menominees spread to other rivers that drain into Lake Michigan. There were reputed to be more than thirty major Menominee villages on the shores of Lakes Michigan, Huron, and Superior, with another center of population near Detroit.

Rivers provided an abundance of sturgeon and wild rice to eat. The dependence on wild rice, in fact, provided the name for the tribe. The Algonquian word for wild rice was *manomin*; hence an eater of wild rice became *Manominee*, now generally spelled Menominee. Rivers provided freshwater mussels, fowl, and other game besides the staple of wild rice. Only war could bring famine.

A trail network maintained by Potawatomis and protected by Menominees existed from present-day Detroit to St. Louis, and from the north around Lake Superior south to Chicago. Both white and Indian groups used the same trade routes and sites for their cities.

European Contact. Menominee involvement in world politics began in 1608. Their list of allies began with the French, the first white people they had seen; then the English, who bought their allegiance with gifts of firearms and alcohol; and finally, the Americans, who were glad to get their military help. Since the first treaty with the Americans, there have been Menominees who served in all U.S. wars.

Menominees inadvertently became enemies of the Iroquois, hence the English, after French interference. In 1608 near the north shore of Lake Superior, the governor general of New France, Samuel de Champlain, and two other white companions, accompanied by an exploratory force of Algonquian people, encountered an Iroquois party. The battle was decided by the French use of matchlock rifles. This united the Iroquois tribes in a war that spread to involve the entire Great Lakes region. Constant fear of attack on the waterways, which were primary trade routes, spread to involve the entire St. Lawrence drainage system. This interrupted the fledgling fur-trading industry. By 1611 the Iroquois, who were well armed, spread war to all waterways except Lakes Superior and Michigan. Menominees provided refuge to fellow Algonquians, a fact which created a population explosion that had dire consequences through the eighteenth century.

The first official meeting between France, represented by Jean Nicolet, and Menominees took place at Mini' Kani in 1634, with a signed pledge of peace. With the hope of profits from the fur trade, the French planned for the exploitation of their New France territory. The Menominees formed an instant market for costly goods. The price for a matchlock rifle from the French was a stack of furs piled alongside the weapon. The low price paid for pelts placed the Great Lakes ecosystem in distress while keeping the growing number of inhabitants virtually unarmed. Thus, France interceded and protected the tribe from the better-armed Iroquois.

There was no further Menominee involvement with the French until 1661, when Me'dort des Grosilliers and Pierre Esprit Radisson entered the main village of Mini' Kani and were amazed at the amount of fish and game in the region. Another Frenchman, Father Jerome Lalemont, explored Lake Superior and found nearly pure lead mines, fist-sized copper nodules, and veins of turquoise and amethyst.

Sometime after this contact of 1661 there occurred a great war, noted by Claude Allouez in 1670. He stated that he found the tribe almost exterminated. When Jacques Marquette visited in 1673 and recorded the use of wild rice by the tribe,

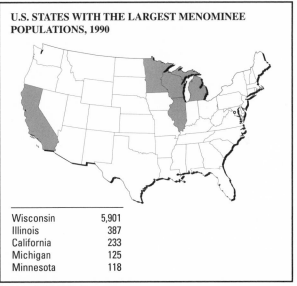

U.S. STATES WITH THE LARGEST MENOMINEE POPULATIONS, 1990

Wisconsin	5,901
Illinois	387
California	233
Michigan	125
Minnesota	118

Source: 1990 U.S. Census.

however, he made no mention of recent war. It is probable that the Sturgeon War occurred in the spring of 1669 or 1670. This large battle took place in a village on the Menominee River after the erection of a dam prevented the sturgeon from moving upriver. The combatants may possibly have been Chippewa, yet they could have been another band of Menominees. Whoever was involved, the reason as remembered by tribal elders was stress on the environment from the swelling population. It was 1682 before a coalition of Algonquians, including many Menominees, decisively thwarted the English and Iroquois in two separate actions at Chicago and near the Illinois River near Utica, Illinois.

The Nineteenth and Twentieth Centuries. The English sought the friendship of the Menominees after the French departure. With gifts, the English were able to maintain an alliance against the Americans. Although not friends with the English, Menominees kept their agreements. In the War of 1812, the tribe victoriously fought the Americans at Prairie du Chien, Wisconsin, and on the island of Mackinac, Michigan.

During the Civil War the tribe responded with many volunteers. At the Battle of Petersburg, Company K, consisting of Wisconsin infantry volunteers, suffered eleven Menominee wounded, nine killed in action, seven dead in prison camp, and two released from prison camp because of illness (they later died). The company was on duty at Washington, D.C., during the trial and execution of the conspirators in the Abraham Lincoln assassination.

After a treaty with the Americans in 1856, the tribe lived on 235,000 acres. The fur trade had finally collapsed, and they were forced to log their beloved forest. The Bureau of Indian Affairs (BIA) built a sawmill in 1908 and managed the resources. The tribe sued the bureau for mismanagement in 1934 and finally won its suit in 1951.

A 1952 report from BIA Commissioner Dillon Myer issued instructions to tribes for a step-by-step withdrawal of the BIA from their affairs. In 1954, President Dwight Eisenhower signed the Menominee Termination Act, effective on May 1, 1961. A 1965 survey reported that there were 2,526 Menominee County residents, 57 percent of whom were under nineteen years of age. Social problems and economic instability were epidemic. The Menominee Restoration Act of December, 1973, returned the tribe to federally recognized status.

Beginning in the late 1980's, the tribe created a new school district, including a community college. Indian gaming in the 1990's provided enough revenue for social programs and investment. In 1992, the reservation comprised 222,552 acres and had a population of 3,182 American Indians. The median age was 21.4 years old; 48.7 percent were high school graduates, and 74 percent of persons sixteen to nineteen years old were enrolled in school. —*Thomas F. Weso*

See also Federally recognized tribes; Guns; Indian-white relations—French colonial; Termination policy; Trade.

BIBLIOGRAPHY

Ourada, Patricia K. *The Menominee Indians: A History.* Norman: University of Oklahoma Press, 1979. A comprehensive history of the tribe, particularly concerned with the pre-1900's.

Peroff, Nicholas C. *Menominee Drums: Tribal Termination and Restoration, 1954-1974.* Norman: University of Oklahoma Press, 1982. A documentation of the political and socioeconomic strife precipitated by termination of federal recognition as a tribe. Gives a personal perspective to the push to gain federal restoration of identity.

Skinner, Alanson. *Social Life and Ceremonial Bundles of the Menomini Indians.* Vol. 13. New York: American Museum of Natural History, 1913. A source for the cultural history and folktales of the Menominee Indians.

Smith, Huron H. *Ethnobotany of the Menomini Indians.* Westport, Conn.: Greenwood Press, 1970. Originally published in 1923 as the *Bulletin of the Public Museum of the City of Milwaukee,* a dated and somewhat biased account of the edible and medicinal plants found among the tribal territory.

Spindler, George, and Louise Spindler. *Dreamers with Power: The Menominee.* Prospect Heights, Ill.: Waveland Press, 1971. A view of the culture of the tribe with particular care given to the religious and belief system.

Menses and menstruation

TRIBES AFFECTED: Pantribal

SIGNIFICANCE: Indigenous tribal peoples have viewed menstruation as an important phenomenon, meriting ritual treatment

Menstruation occasioned widely varied responses and rituals by indigenous tribal peoples. Older women in Mesoamerican groups tried to keep a girl's first menstruation secret from the men in the tribe, but tribes in the intermountain basin, the Yukon, and Canadian Subarctic regions treated the girl as dangerous to the welfare of herself and the group and constructed elaborate rules she had to follow to prevent contaminating others. Other tribes, especially in Northern California and Apache territory, celebrated the onset of a girl's puberty as a milestone of maturation with a great feast. Some groups on the Northwest Coast, to safeguard a young woman's virginity, cloistered her from her first menstruation onward in part of the dwelling until her marriage.

Believing that a menstruating woman possessed supernatural powers that might harm her or her tribe, most tribal peoples required her to go into seclusion, avoid contact with men, and undergo special diets (often abstaining from eating meat) and baths. Often an older woman supervised her, but some customs dictated that the menstruant remain alone. Watchers scrutinized the woman to see how well she adhered to these prohibitions; some groups viewed these as tests that predicted a woman's future behavior. In some practices she could not touch her hair or skin for fear of self-contamination. At the end of the seclusion, usually the woman underwent a ritual bathing and received new clothes.

Even those tribal groups that did not insist on strict cloistering demanded that a menstruating woman keep clear of cooking areas and away from any task necessary to tribal survival. Many tribal groups assumed that a menstruating woman would scare off game animals during the hunt or diminish a warrior's medicine during warfare. After Cheyenne chief Roman Nose was fatally wounded during the Battle of Beecher's Island in 1868, for example, either he or others in the tribe blamed his wound on his having eaten food that a menstruating woman had prepared or touched.

European American settlers and missionaries did not find these indigenous menstruation customs strange. Although most European American groups did not force menstruating women into seclusion or insist they refrain from cooking, menstruation was the subject of certain cultural taboos. Many men thought a menstruating woman unclean morally and physically and sometimes shunned her. She was often treated circumspectly, for fear she possessed special magic or linkage with the Devil.

See also Children; Puberty and initiation rites; Rites of passage.

Meriam Report

DATE: 1928

TRIBES AFFECTED: Pantribal

SIGNIFICANCE: This report documented the failures of the Bureau of Indian Affairs to help Indian people and thus helped lead to the 1930's reforms of John Collier's Indian New Deal

In 1926, Secretary of the Interior Hubert Work asked the Institute for Government Research (Brookings Institution) at The Johns Hopkins University to conduct a nonpolitical investigation of Indian affairs. Work's goal was to counter the harsh criticisms of John Collier and other Indian Office critics. The results of the Brookings study were published in 1928 as *The Problem of Indian Administration*, popularly known as the Meriam Report after Lewis Meriam, who headed the investigation. The report condemned the allotment policy that had been instituted with the passage of the General Allotment Act of 1887, as well as the poor quality of services provided Indian people by the Bureau of Indian Affairs (BIA). It urged protection for Indian property, and recommended Indians be allowed more freedom to manage their own affairs.

The Meriam Report emphasized the BIA's educational role and called for higher academic standards in BIA schools. W. Carson Ryan, Jr., a prominent figure in the progressive education movement, wrote most of the education section of the Meriam Report, with help from Henry Roe Cloud (a Winnebago). The education section was influenced by the teachings of John Dewey and other progressive educators.

In 1921, all Indian schools had their appropriations for food and clothing cut 25 percent. These cuts were a result of government debts from World War I. This underfunding of BIA schools continued through the 1920's. In one extreme case, a Red Cross investigator found students to be subsisting on a diet of bread, black coffee, and syrup for breakfast; bread and boiled potatoes for dinner and supper; and a quarter cup of milk with each meal. In general, the Meriam Report found the food in boarding schools to be "deficient in quantity, quality and variety." The poor food made Indian students more susceptible to tuberculosis and trachoma, which were endemic in Indian communities. Half-day student labor allowed the government to save even more money educating Indians, and the Meriam Report noted that some of the work required of students violated state child labor laws. Among other activities, students raised crops, worked in dairies, made and mended their own clothes, and cleaned their schools.

Flogging and other severe forms of punishment existed at some schools. The Meriam Report found that most BIA schools had locked rooms or isolated buildings used as "jails"; in some schools, children were forced to "maintain a pathetic degree of quietness."

To quell the growing criticism of the government's Indian policy, President Herbert Hoover in 1929 appointed a fellow Quaker and president of the Indian Rights Association, Charles J. Rhoads, to be commissioner of Indian affairs. Rhoads got Ryan to become director of Indian education. Rhoads and Ryan began to implement the recommendations of the Meriam Report, including an end to a uniform BIA curriculum that stressed only white cultural values.

See also Bureau of Indian Affairs (BIA); Cloud, Henry Roe; Education, post-contact; General Allotment Act; Indian Reorganization Act.

Mesa Verde: Archaeological site; prehistoric tradition

DATE: 1150-1450

LOCATION: Four Corners area of southwestern Colorado

CULTURES AFFECTED: Acoma, Anasazi, Hopi, Western Pueblo peoples, Zuni

Between 900 and 1150 C.E., a widespread and sophisticated culture evolved within the San Juan Basin of northern New Mexico and southwestern Colorado. Archaeologists designated it the "Chaco Phenomenon," characterized by at least nine major pueblos, each of several hundred rooms, in addition to several hundred smaller ten-to-twenty-room pueblos. These centered on Anasazi peoples of the Chaco Canyon in northern New Mexico, who created a regional administrative and exchange system linked to outlying pueblos. From 1020 until their decline in the 1150's, this system stretched northward into southwestern Colorado.

Although during the 1100's the Chaco regional system failed, the Mesa Verde Anasazi reoccupied an outlying area in southwestern Colorado familiarly known by its cliff dwellings. Locally, these had been preceded by Anasazi housing located atop mesas, on talus slopes, and in canyon bottoms in the Mogollon Highlands. It was these structures that evolved into the famed Double House, Cliff Palace, and similar dwellings sited in rock shelters between 1150 and their abandonment before 1450. Cliff dwellings continued important elements of Mogollon-Anasazi architectural traditions, namely pueblos, that emerged around 700.

Mesa Verde's cliff habitations were sometimes four stories high; there was considerable variation because of limitations imposed by cliff sites. Its kivas, viewed diagrammatically, were generally keyhole-shaped and lined with rock. Because water supplies were critical to traditional agriculture in a relatively dry environment, these pueblos also included artificial reservoirs and stone check dams, as well as stone fieldhouses. Other cultural characteristics were manifested by common ceramic utility vessels—bowls, mugs, and jars—known to archaeologists as Mesa Verde corrugated and Mesa Verde black-on-white. Perishable items—leather moccasins, yucca baskets, rush mats, and wooden prayer sticks—have also been unearthed on site. Mesa Verde's Anasazi traditions anticipated

Partially restored ruins of the "Cliff Palace" at Mesa Verde, Colorado. (Jesse L. Nussbaum, Museum of New Mexico)

those of Hopi, Zuni, Acoma, and other pueblo peoples of historic times. Why the cliff dwellings were abandoned has never been satisfactorily explained.

See also Anasazi; Chaco Canyon; Mogollon; Plano; Prehistory—Southwest; Pueblo tribes, Western.

Metacomet (c. 1639, Pokanoket, probably present-day Mass.—Aug. 12, 1676, near Bristol, R.I.): Chief

ALSO KNOWN AS: King Philip, Metacom

TRIBAL AFFILIATION: Wampanoag

SIGNIFICANCE: Wampanoag leader Metacomet is primarily known for waging King Philip's War against the English Puritan colonists in seventeenth century New England

Metacomet, or Metacom, also widely known as King Philip, was one of the two sons of the Wampanoag chief Massasoit. Massasoit is supposed to have died about 1662. Before his death he brought his sons, Metacomet (or Pometacom) and Mooanum (or Wamsutta), to a meeting with the English governor of the Massachusetts Bay Colony to renew their treaty of peace about the year 1656.

In order to protect his sons and ensure their survival, he allowed the English governor to stand as godfather to them. The governor, in open court, gave the boys the names Philip and Alexander. Massasoit believed that the colonists could be bargained with and the peace maintained in this way. The

colonists made some honest but misguided attempts to be fair to and to educate and Christianize the native peoples while trying to respect their human rights. Within a few years after the death of Massasoit, however, relations deteriorated rapidly, eventually resulting in hostilities.

Metacomet was suspicious of the Puritans from the start and disliked the fact that they so easily intruded on his territory and attempted to win the support and confidence of his people with gifts of trinkets, tools, and metal implements. At the same time, they destroyed woodlands to create pastures, farmland, and towns and engaged in missionary activity.

He succeeded his brother as sachem (leader) of his people in 1662 and honored his father's peace for nine years. In 1671, however, he was summoned to Taunton, Rhode Island, fined for actions viewed as hostile by the colonists, and ordered to surrender. He refused and continued to resist colonial expansion for four more years.

In 1675, three Wampanoags were executed for the murder of a Christian Wampanoag informer. The colonial government tried to apply its laws to the Indians, but this only served to enrage Metacomet. He allied with the Nipmuck and Narragansett tribes, which were nearly destroyed because of their taking part in the burning of outlying towns, where they killed everyone. Metacomet preferred not to battle in the open and was difficult to engage. He went to the Mohawk and French and asked for their support, but they refused, even though he made a trip to Albany, New York, to negotiate for peace.

Metacomet became an eloquent statesman for his people as he encouraged them to drive the invaders out. His public statements contributed to a growing tension and antagonism between the colonists and the Wampanoags. He was an able and crafty leader.

The tribe engaged in continually escalating conflicts with the colonists, leading to the infamous Swamp Fight, which set off a series of brutal battles. Metacomet led many of the raids, and the ensuing conflict of 1675 was thus called King Philip's War. It was proportionately the bloodiest in early American history. More than six hundred colonists and hundreds more Indians are said to have died in this conflict.'

Connecticut was defensive from the start, but Massachusetts Bay and settlements in Rhode Island were vulnerable to attack. The whites retaliated and destroyed tribal cornfields, captured women and children—including Metacomet's wife and son, who were sold into slavery—and gave pardons to Indian deserters.

Metacomet was finally defeated, and the coastal tribes of New England were destroyed as independent, sovereign powers. He was shot and killed at Mount Hope, Rhode Island, near Bristol, by a party of vigilantes under Benjamin Church, on August 12, 1676.

See also King Philip's War; Wampanoag.

Metalwork

TRIBES AFFECTED: Hopewell prehistoric tradition, Northeast tribes (especially Cayuga, Iroquois, Onondaga, Seneca), Southwest tribes (especially Navajo, Zuni)
SIGNIFICANCE: Copper and, more recently, silver, have been used extensively for Indian ornamentation

The earliest examples of metals being used in North America date to around 4000 B.C.E. In the Great Lakes region, pieces of native copper were gathered and hammered into lance points and decorative or ritual objects. Archaeologists have discovered necklace beads composed of thin copper strips and fish-shaped pieces fashioned from the same metal during this era. These so-called Old Copper culture people did not practice true metallurgy, since the native metal was simply beaten and treated as a malleable stone. Copper ornaments and weapons produced by cold hammering, and some engraved sheets of silver of the Hopewell people, have also been found that date to the Common Era. The use of copper for personal ornamentation is one of the most striking differences between North American tribes and the pre-Columbian cultures of South and Central America, where gold was extensively used. Most North American tribes lacked any effective metalworking skills until after contact with other cultures, whereas the sixteenth century Spanish explorers of the New World found well-developed metalwork skills in Mexico and Central America.

By the seventeenth century, Northeast tribes, such as the Seneca, Cayuga, and Onondaga, hammered, shaped, and cut European silver coins for jewelry. The more intricate techniques of silverworking were introduced to the Southwest Navajo by Mexican silversmiths during the early second half of the nineteenth century. Later, the Zuni (Pueblo) learned the craft from the Navajo. The Navajo style was distinguished by die-stamp designs that showed off the metal itself. Zuni work was more intricate in detail, and die work was rarer.

Indian silversmiths produce work of extraordinary variety and beauty that reflects the unique creativity of Indian art. Bracelets, rings, earrings, necklaces, bow guards, concha belts, and buttons are only a few of the objects that, through the years, have been created from hand-wrought silver. Turquoise, which was frequently used in ornamentation long before the introduction of silversmithing, has also featured prominently in Indian silverwork. Although commercial imitations of Navajo and Zuni work have been mass produced for the tourist market in the twentieth century, they are unable to reproduce the beauty of authentic hand-made pieces.

See also Gold and goldworking; Navajo; Old Copper culture; Ornaments; Pueblo tribes, Western.

Methow: Tribe
CULTURE AREA: Plateau
LANGUAGE GROUP: Salishan
PRIMARY LOCATION: Colville Reservation, Washington State

The Methow, a branch of the Salishan family, lived along the Methow River and Chelan Lake in eastern Washington. A detached band, the Chilowhist, spent the winters on the Okanogan River. The Methow were related to another group called the Moses Columbia band. The name they called themselves is not known. "Methow" (pronounced Met how) was given them by whites, after their location. Evidence suggests they migrated to Washington from Montana and Idaho in prehistoric times. The Methow lived in villages of varying size. Because they relied on hunting and fishing—salmon was a chief staple of their diet—as well as on gathering roots and berries, they were forced to move throughout the year to find food in different seasons. This prevented the villages from growing and developing as political or social centers. The Methow do not seem to have relied on agriculture. They were skilled with horses and used them in their travels after food. Generally, Salishan tribes enjoyed relatively peaceful lives and were involved in no protracted struggles with their neighbors. In the late nineteenth century, the Methow were pushed out by whites who wanted their land. They were resettled on the Colville Reservation in Washington in 1872. By the end of the twentieth century, the Methow lived very much like their non-Indian neighbors and made their living by raising cattle, farming, and logging.

See also Columbia; Colville; Lake; Plateau.

Metis: Mixed Indian-European ethnic group
CULTURE AREA: Canada
LANGUAGE GROUPS: Algonquian, Athapaskan, English, French
PRIMARY LOCATION: The prairie provinces of Canada and as far north as the Mackenzie Delta; Montana
POPULATION SIZE: Unknown

The Metis (or Métis) of Canada are representative of what is known as a "mixed" population, a blend of races and cultures resulting from contact and colonial expansion by Europeans. The name Metis (commonly pronounced mā tē) comes from the French, *métis*, meaning "half-breed" or "half-caste." The Metis perceive themselves, and are perceived to be, members of a distinctive group with a specific heritage and identity that evolved as a culture during the eighteenth century. Their heritage is a combination of European and Indian (either Algonquian or Athapaskan). The Red River Metis, typically Roman Catholic and bilingual in French and Cree, emerged as descendants of French-Canadian workers and their Indian wives. The Northern Metis have descended from Athapaskan women and their unions with Scottish and English recruits of the Hudson's Bay Company. Northern Metis are bilingual in Athapaskan and English and generally follow the Anglican faith. The Metis have been cultural interpreters and intermediaries in several capacities, providing a link between European Canadian and Indian groups.

Metis Identity and Society. At times, identity as a Metis can depend more on sociological conditions than genetics: A person whose known ancestry is exclusively white may be considered Metis, but the majority are mixed. Because the definition of Metis varies, population counts are difficult and can be unreliable. For example, numbers from a 1970's census conducted in the Northwest Territories by four different sources ranged from a high of ten thousand to as low as fifteen hundred people.

Unlike other tribes who have a specific homeland, the Metis reside throughout Canada and into Alaska, living in many communities, for the most part as a minority. The household arrangement of Subarctic Metis is similar to that of a nuclear European family; however, as late as the 1960's, observers noted that the social class ranking and stratification of European society did not exist among the Metis. As a group, Metis have a more favorable chance at employment and success at schooling than do Indians, possibly because their home life has better prepared them to meet the expectations of European institutions.

The majority of Metis share a dozen or so surnames, names that are well known and frequently appear in the histories of the Northwest and the fur trade. Beaulieu, Mandeville, Bouvier, Fabien, Stewart, McKay, and Linkletter are the most common. Marriage was at one time arranged but has now become an unrestricted choice, illustrated by the high proportion of Metis who marry outside their community, creating far-ranging social networks and connections. A long-distance social life is characteristic of the Metis and is preserved through various communication outlets. Visiting, writing letters, sending messages by travelers, radio broadcasting, and storytelling all serve to maintain social ties.

Despite an increase in research concerning Subarctic peoples after 1950, little attention has been given to the Metis, culturally or otherwise. One art that may be called distinctively Metis is the elaborate floral embroidery on pouches, sashes, mittens, and other articles of clothing.

Economy and Politics. Because the Metis emerged after contact, there is no traditional or independent economy. They have engaged in a variety of occupations, such as fur trapping and trading and commercial fishing, mostly as wage earners rather than as entrepreneurs. Currently, they have turned to fire suppression, game patrol, policing, construction labor, and road maintenance as sources for employment. Individual Metis are likely to have several careers over the course of a lifetime, which allows freedom of movement and freedom from repetition.

During most of the twentieth century, the Metis struggled for their rights and against social abuses. They have been the object of bigotry and have been marginalized socially and culturally. Their position among Subarctic peoples is unique: They lack the political power of either Indians or whites, and even though this power heavily favors white interests, most Indians have some control over land and resources. The Metis have no such political or economic leverage and lack the organization necessary to be considered a force requiring, at the very least, acknowledgment by the government. Since the 1960's, Metis associations of the Canadian provinces and territories have developed or expanded to advance the group's political interests.   —*Kimberly Manning*

See also Indian-white relations—Canadian; Riel, Louis, Jr.; Riel Rebellions.

Miami: Tribe

CULTURE AREA: Northeast
LANGUAGE GROUP: Algonquian
PRIMARY LOCATION: Oklahoma, Indiana
POPULATION SIZE: 4,477 (1990 U.S. Census)

The Miami occupied the Green Bay, Wisconsin, region in the seventeenth century but later migrated to the southern end of Lake Michigan. The name "Miami" is most probably derived from the Ojibwa word *oumamik*, "people of the peninsula."

The tribe had a fairly sophisticated political structure, based largely on the clan system. Each Miami belonged to his or her father's clan. Clan chiefs in each village made up a council that ruled the community. Village councils sent delegates to band councils, which in turn sent chiefs to a tribal council.

The Midewiwin, or Grand Medicine Society, was a hallmark of tribal life. It consisted of priests noted for their special curing powers. Other Miami shamans used roots and herbs to combat disease. According to most accounts, the sun was the principal deity for the Miami and was called the "Master of Life."

Miami villages consisted of pole-frame houses covered by rush mats. Each village usually had a large council house for council meetings and ceremonies. The tribe was famed for its superior strains of corn; the Miami also grew melons, squash, beans, and pumpkins. Buffalo was hunted once a year.

Originally, the Miami consisted of six separate bands: Atchatchakangouen, Kilatika, Mengakonkia, Pepicokia, Wea, and Piankashaw. The first three united into the Miami proper, and the Pepicokia were absorbed by the Wea and Piankashaw. The Wea and the Piankashaw were separate entities from the

Miami, and they were politically independent by 1818, the year they set up separate tribal councils.

During the eighteenth century, the Miami in Michigan migrated to the headwaters of the Maumee in Ohio. Similarly, the Wea and Piankashaw moved to the Wabash region of Indiana. In the late eighteenth century, the tribe fought a valiant battle to save their lands from the tide of white settlement.

The Miami war chief Michikinikwa, known to the white people as Little Turtle, led a coalition of Miami, Shawnee, Potawatomi, and others against United States troops. Little Turtle's warriors gained a major victory over General Arthur St. Clair on November 4, 1791. The Americans lost 647 dead and 217 wounded in the battle, one of the worst defeats the United States Army ever suffered at the hands of the Indians.

The Indian triumph was short-lived. Little Turtle and Shawnee leader Blue Jacket were decisively defeated at the Battle of Fallen Timbers in 1794. By the Treaty of Greenville in 1795, the Indians ceded most of Ohio and a slice of Indiana to the United States.

Between 1832 and 1840, the Miami moved to Kansas, where they were given reservations. Following a separate course, the Wea and Piankashaw joined the Peoria. Both the Peoria and the Miami settled in Indian Territory (now Oklahoma) in 1867. Most of their descendants live in Ottawa County, Oklahoma. A few members of the Miami tribe managed to avoid removal to the south and stayed in their original homelands. Their descendants, mostly of mixed ancestry, live around Peru, Indiana.

See also Fallen Timbers, Battle of; Illinois; Little Turtle; Midewiwin; Wabash, Battle of the.

Miantonomo (c. 1600-1643): Principal chief

TRIBAL AFFILIATION: Narragansett
SIGNIFICANCE: Miantonomo attempted to build an anticolonial alliance

A nephew of Chief Canonicus, Miantonomo became the Narragansetts' principal chief about 1632. He maintained alliances with the colonists of Massachusetts Bay and with Roger Williams' new colony at Providence Plantations, later Rhode Island, begun in 1635 with Narragansett aid. Miantonomo even attended church with some of the colonists.

Despite these signs of friendship, Miantonomo was suspected of provoking Indian hostility toward the New England colonies, largely because of statements by Uncas, the founder of the Mohegan tribe who made a specialty of betraying "hostile" Indians to the Puritan authorities. In 1642, Miantonomo was imprisoned briefly by the Puritans, who scolded and then released him. After that incident, Miantonomo attempted to build an anticolonial alliance. When word of the attempt got to Uncas, he turned Miantonomo over to the English, who sentenced him to die at the hands of Uncas' brother Wawequa in September, 1643.

See also Narragansett.

Micanopy (c. 1780, St. Augustine region of Fla.—Jan. 2, 1849, Fort Gibson, Indian Territory): Tribal chief

ALSO KNOWN AS: Sint-Chakkee
TRIBAL AFFILIATION: Seminole
SIGNIFICANCE: As principal chief of the Seminoles, Micanopy resisted removal during the Second Seminole War

Though the Seminoles had no central government, Micanopy was regarded as the tribe's principal chief by virtue of his descent from a line of past chiefs. Micanopy was also one of the wealthiest Seminoles of his day, with considerable holdings of land and slaves. He was a strong opponent of U.S. influence in Florida, and he sought to protect Seminole ways after Florida passed to American control in 1819.

When federal representatives arranged the Treaty of Paynes's Landing in 1832 as a prelude to removing the Seminoles from Florida to Indian Territory (modern Oklahoma), Micanopy refused to sign. The government accepted the treaty even though tribal leaders regarded it as fraudulent, and in 1835 began to prepare to move the Seminoles out of Florida. Micanopy supported the efforts of younger tribal leaders such as Osceola and Wildcat (Micanopy's nephew) to rally resistance. In December of 1835, Seminoles under his and Osceola's leadership attacked Major Francis Dade's column as it moved from Tampa Bay into the interior. Dade was killed—by Micanopy, it was said—and only three of his men survived. The Second Seminole War was under way; it would last until 1842.

The Seminoles proved able warriors, but Micanopy came to doubt their ability to hold off the United States indefinitely. He surrendered to U.S. forces in June, 1837. He was subsequently kidnapped by Osceola, who was intent on continuing the struggle and aware of the chief's symbolic value. Micanopy was recaptured by American forces while under a flag of truce in December of 1837. He agreed to accept removal to the West. After a brief period of imprisonment, he was transported to Indian Territory in 1838. There he found the Seminoles assigned to the Creek Nation, an arrangement that created friction between the two tribes. In 1845, Micanopy negotiated an agreement that allowed the Seminoles to settle as a group within the Creek lands. Ten years later, after his death, the Seminoles formally separated from the Creeks and received their own land.

See also Arpeika; Creek; Creek War; Osceola; Removal; Seminole; Seminole Wars.

Micmac: Tribe

CULTURE AREA: Northeast
LANGUAGE GROUP: Algonquian
PRIMARY LOCATION: Maritime Provinces, Quebec
POPULATION SIZE: 14,625 in Canada (Statistics Canada, based on 1991 census; 2,765 in U.S. (1990 U.S. Census)

The Micmac, a branch of the Algonquian family, lived a migratory life in Nova Scotia, northern New Brunswick, and Prince Edward Island. Their name, from their own language, means "allies." The Micmac were divided into several clans, each with its own chief and identifying symbol. These symbols were tattooed onto members' bodies, painted on canoes and snowshoes, and used as ornaments on clothing and jewelry.

During the winter, the Micmac lived inland in small groups in the forest; they hunted moose, caribou, and porcupine. In warmer weather, they moved in groups of two hundred or more to the seashore and fished, hunted seals, and gathered shellfish. They made cone-shaped wigwams and canoes from birchbark, wooden bowls and bows, and stone or bone weapons and tools. They also made beautiful baskets and porcupine-quill embroidery. They had a rich tradition of impressive rituals—for marriage, death, installation of chiefs, and passage to adulthood. They also enjoyed games, including an indigenous form of football.

The Micmac welcomed white visitors—traders and missionaries—from the first. They accepted Christianity from the Jesuits and traded and intermarried with the French colonists. They were strong allies of the French, and they fought with the French and English to eradicate the Beothuk Indians of Newfoundland in the late eighteenth century. This close association with whites, however, was in many ways costly to the Micmac. A third of their population was killed by typhus in 1746. They lost their traditional religious beliefs; they adopted agriculture as a means of livelihood perhaps more reliable than hunting; they stopped practicing their traditional crafts; and they intermarried so freely that it is doubtful whether any pure-blooded Micmac were left by the mid-twentieth century. By 1970, many men were employed in "high steel," and government scholarships enabled Micmac men and women to learn skilled trades. At the end of the century, the Micmac were poor but generally no poorer than other people in the Maritime Provinces.

See also Algonquian language family; Beothuk; Indianwhite relations—English colonial; Missions and missionaries.

Middens

Date: Since 9600 B.P.

Tribes affected: Tribes living near coasts and rivers

Significance: The accumulation of middens in prehistoric and later native cultures provides an excellent source of information about early North American human activities

A midden is a type of archaeological site in which shell is the most prominent component of the matrix visually. The term "midden" signifies that the shell was discarded after the meat was consumed for food, but the ethnographic record provides many reasons for intentionally accumulating shells in one place. These reasons include industrial waste disposal (for example, from shell button, cameo, porcelain, and lime manufactures) and the building of architectural features (such as bleachers, mounds, and retaining walls).

Humans accumulated notable quantities of marine shells as early as 9,600 years ago in Diablo Canyon, California. The oldest Atlantic Coast shell middens are 7,000 years old. Along some rivers in the eastern United States mounds of shells dating from 8,000 to 2,000 years ago were the loci of burials for hundreds of humans, dogs, and trade goods. The majority of shell-bearing sites in North America, however, appeared in the last 5,000 years, when modern shorelines were established.

The earliest pottery in North American has been found in shell rings on the South Carolina and Georgia coasts and along the Savannah River.

Sites on interior rivers and the Pacific Coast are composed of dozens of species of shellfish, while those on the Atlantic and Gulf of Mexico are usually composed of few species. The calcium in the shell creates an alkaline soil which significantly improves the preservation of bones, plants, and shells, making these sites excellent sources of information about human activities and adaptation.

See also Shells and shellwork.

Midewiwin

Tribes affected: Fox, Iowa, Menominee, Miami, Ojibwa (Chippewa), Ponca, Winnebago

Significance: Midewiwin refers to a secret society and set of rituals that transferred knowledge of healing rites, herbal medicines, and moral codes to succeeding generations

The Midewiwin, also called the Grand Medicine Society, was both a secret society and a series of initiation and healing ceremonies. In tribal myths, this knowledge and power were given by the Great Spirit through an intermediary during a time of trouble and death. A central symbol is the white shell, representative of one which appeared to the Ojibwa from the eastern sea and led them west. Simultaneously with the shell, rules for moral living were given. The songs, rites, and stories of tribal origins are recorded in picture writing on birchbark scrolls. These scrolls are one of the few examples of Indian writing north of Mexico.

To join a society, a man or woman had to be recommended by a member. If accepted, they paid a fee and were assigned a teacher. There were eight degrees of instruction, each of which required separate initiation rites. At the higher levels, persons were taught the use of herbal medicines and poisons. At each level, a Mide bag (medicine bundle) made of bird or animal skin containing the elements associated with that degree was presented.

In the central ceremonies, usually celebrated in the spring and lasting several days, initiates were ritually shot with pieces of white shell from a Mide bag, after which they feigned death. The fragments were then removed by Mide leaders, reviving the initiates to new life, both moral and spiritual.

The Midewiwin powers of healing and code for living were believed to guarantee a long life. The power of the Midewiwin was considered so great that members resisted Christian conversion. Eventually, however, legal and cultural pressures led to a decline of the practice. With the renewal of Indian culture that began in the 1960's, movements such as the Three Fires Society have revived the practice of the Midewiwin. Similar practices are found in the shell society of the Omaha and the Navajo chantway rituals.

See also Chantways; Medicine and modes of curing, precontact; Medicine bundles; Miami; Religious specialists; Secret societies.

Midland: Archaeological site
DATE: 10,000 B.P. and earlier
LOCATION: West central Texas
CULTURE AFFECTED: Paleo-Indian (pre-Folsom)

In the summer of 1953 an amateur archaeologist, Keith Glasscock, was exploring a dune blowout (wind scouring of dune sand down to a resistant geological layer) near the town of Midland, Texas, when he found parts of a human skull and other bones uncovered in the lower layer of sand. He removed these bones and some other artifacts that were already blown free, but did not disturb the sand deposits by further searching. Instead, he called in professional anthropologists. What followed was a triumph of cooperation among scientists of many different disciplines that resulted in the authentication of "Midland Man" as the oldest specimen of human life found in the United States. Geologists were able to certify that the gray sand in which the bones were found was an ancient lake bed now covered by two further layers of sand: the rusty red Judkins, and on top of it the orangy-gray Monahans. Archaeologists determined that the contact zone between the Monahans and the Judkins contained the typical Folsom fluted spear points; hence the skeletal remains must be pre-Folsom—more than eight thousand years old. They also recovered enough additional skull fragments to know the size and shape of the cranium. Paleontologists recovered enough faunal specimens from the lower sands to date them as Pleistocene, during or immediately after the Wisconsin glaciation. Chemical testing gave variable dates by different methods, but they correlated well enough to indicate that the bones are at least ten thousand and perhaps twenty thousand years old. "Midland Man" is actually a female, about thirty years old, with a relatively thin skull and a light, gracile figure. The skull does not display the Mongolian traits that are supposed to have arisen from migration of Asian stock into North America.

See also Clovis; Folsom; Paleo-Indian.

Midwinter Ceremony

TRIBES AFFECTED: Iroquois Confederacy (Six Nations)
SIGNIFICANCE: The Midwinter Ceremony was, and is, the pivotal event of the annual Iroquois ceremonial cycle; eight days of thanksgiving, propitiatory, and curing ceremonies traditionally began five days after the first new moon after the Pleiades were directly overhead at sunset

The Midwinter Ceremony, sometimes called the New Year Ceremony, is the biggest annual ceremony in Iroquois culture. Although the ceremony is still important today, this article will discuss it in the past tense to emphasize that the discussion concerns the ceremony as it existed before it was somewhat modified by contact with European culture. The Midwinter Ceremony began at dawn of the first day with shamans entering the village compounds beating on drums. The ashes of each hearth were swept to find glowing coals, which were brought to the longhouse where the ceremony was held. Here a new fire was kindled. Hearth fires for the new year were kindled from this fire.

The villagers assembled were congratulated for having survived to participate in another Midwinter Ceremony. The Thanksgiving Address, a cosmological statement of profound holistic knowledge, was then offered. Fifty-three songs accompanied the Thanksgiving Prayer.

Next the children born since the Green Corn Ceremony of midsummer were given clan names. Other events included washing with fire; the rite of personal chant; and a dream-guessing festival to initiate new members into the established medicine societies and to purge living souls of bad thoughts and spiritual tortures. The Iroquois put much faith in the sacred quality of dreams.

One fun event of the Midwinter Ceremony was the gambling game. One moiety of four clans played against the other moiety for personal power and certain political and ceremonial rights in the coming year. The game did not end until one moiety controlled all 108 dice. This ritual reflected the game of dice played between Creator and Dead Earth for the right for life to exist on earth. Then the Great Feather Dance was conducted, with its many songs, interspersed with pauses for praying and rejoicing that life continues.

Another key ceremony was the arrival of the Husk Face Society, men who imitated women, acted as clowns, and prophesied an abundant corn harvest in the coming year. The last ceremony of the Midwinter Ceremony was the sacrifice of the white dog. The spirit of the dog served as messenger to the Master of Life, conveying the good wishes and thankfulness of the people.

The Midwinter Ceremony was ordained first by the Peacemaker, and mnemonics for its recitation are found on wampum belts. The prophet Handsome Lake adjusted the Thanksgiving Prayer to fit the needs of the 1800's, and that version is the one in use today.

See also Games and contests; Handsome Lake; Husk Face Society; Iroquois Confederacy.

BIBLIOGRAPHY

Cornelius, Carol. "The Thanksgiving Address: An Expression of the Haudenosaunee Worldview." *Akwe:kon Journal* 9, no. 3 (Fall, 1992).

Henry, Thomas R. *Wilderness Messiah: The Story of Hiawatha and the Iroquois*. New York: Bonanaza Books, 1955.

Josephy, Alvin M., Jr. *The Indian Heritage of America*. New York: Alfred A. Knopf, 1968.

Morgan, Lewis H. *League of the Ho-de-no-sau-nee, or Iroquois*. Rochester, N.Y.: Sage and Brothers, 1851.

Spencer, Robert F., Jesse D. Jennings, et al. *The Native Americans*. 2d ed. New York: Harper & Row, 1977.

Tooker, Elisabeth, ed. *Native North American Spirituality of the Eastern Woodlands*. New York: Paulist Press, 1979.

Migrations

TRIBES AFFECTED: Pantribal
SIGNIFICANCE: Humans probably crossed into North America from Asia between 40,000 and 23,000 B.C.E. and spread

throughout the continent, developing an astonishing variety of cultures which flourished in diverse habitats

The Bering land bridge theory relies upon archaeological and linguistic evidence to explain how the ancestors of American Indians arrived in North America. In this widely accepted theory, glaciation caused sea levels to drop and exposed a somewhat marshy area called Beringia, between Siberia and Alaska. Either on foot or by boat, people crossed this "bridge" and entered Alaska, eventually migrating southward through corridors open between glaciers. By 10,000 B.C.E., glacier melt had closed Beringia to foot travel, although it cannot be argued conclusively that people were unable to negotiate the Bering Strait by boat.

With this theoretical entry point now 300 feet under the sea, scientists have had to rely upon artifacts and linguistic similarities to posit the movements of these peoples southward and eastward from Alaska. Cooperation between American and Russian scientists in the late 1980's revealed similarities between tribal peoples of Siberia and Alaska, indicating a common origin. Nevertheless, the Bering land bridge theory, however widely accepted, remains unprovable, and alternate theories exist. Jeffrey Goodman, for example, has suggested that humans migrated northward and westward from the Americas to Asia.

Populating the Americas. Scientists adhering to the Bering land bridge theory have found indications of three major waves of migration, although smaller groups could have passed without leaving traces. Possibly following migrating animals, these peoples fanned out in different directions. Those of the Thule culture spread eastward in the Arctic regions, maintaining a culture that enabled them to survive in the harsh climate. Other peoples headed southward along the Pacific Coast, gradually developing unique cultures. There was also inland migration, south along the eastern slope of the Sierra Nevada mountains and into the Great Basin. These Pacific Coast and inland groups continued south through Mexico, Central America, and eventually into the South American continent. Some headed east from Mexico, populating the Gulf Coast. A major split occurred near what is now the United States/Canadian border as some groups headed east into the Great Lakes region and others went south through the Mississippi floodplain and then southeast as far as Florida.

These migration patterns seem to indicate steady southward and eastward movement, as people filled an "empty continent." There is also some evidence, however, that migration occurred from South America northward to the Caribbean islands. It is not possible to identify precisely when various movements occurred with available technology and physical evidence.

Thousands of years passed, and the migrating cultures developed separate identities and lifeways. While cultures remained apart from one another, there is evidence of extensive trading networks that brought the artifacts and products of widely separated cultures together. Highly complex cultures developed in Mesoamerica, and they had a profound influence on the peoples of North America. The Mesoamericans had cultivated a grain called teosinte, the ancestor of maize. Maize culture diffused into North America between 200 and 400 C.E., then disappeared. In 900, it was reintroduced by colonizers migrating north from troubled regions of Mesoamerica to found settlements along the Mississippi and east of the Appalachian range. These migrants constructed truncated pyramids, or "platform mounds," similar to ones constructed in Mesoamerica. A tradition of the Natchez Indians clearly states that their ancestors came from far to the south, although their story was ignored until archaeologists began to find evidence that supported it.

Around 1300, the Anasazis, or "old ones," flourished in the Southwest, the Delawares migrated east, and the Apacheans began to differentiate. By 1400, the Athapaskan-speaking tribes, including Apaches and Navajos, had migrated to the Southwest. Migrations continued on a smaller scale as neighboring tribes vied for territory. The acquisition of the horse brought expansion to Plains tribes such as the Comanches, who pushed the Apacheans west, and the Sioux, who alternately drifted east and west again, putting pressure on the tribes they encountered.

Invasion and Forced Migrations. Beginning in the sixteenth century, the arrival of Europeans from a number of directions forced Indians from their homelands. The Spanish invaded from the Caribbean into the Gulf of Mexico and from the west, down the Pacific Coast and into Mexico, enslaving and murdering Indian populations. The French entered as traders in the Northeast and Southeast, changing the economics of hunting for native tribes. Russians came southward from Alaska, affecting Pacific Coast tribes.

The greatest pressure put on tribes to migrate from their traditional territories came from the English, who had no need for Indian labor and traded with tribes mainly to produce an economic dependency that would facilitate the seizure of Indian lands. Through the various wars between these European colonizers, Indians lost more territory; through diseases brought from the Old World, tribal numbers were severely reduced.

American expansionism in the nineteenth century forced Indians westward. By the end of the nineteenth century, most Indians had been resettled on reservations representing a fraction of the lands they had once held. Many tribes had been uprooted repeatedly as their reservation lands became attractive to European American settlers. By the end of the nineteenth century, the American Indian population had reached its lowest point; gradually, numbers began to increase in the twentieth century. The most noticeable migration pattern of the twentieth century was from rural reservation lands to urban areas; in the 1950's, there was a federal "relocation" program to encourage resettlement in cities. Many of these new urbanites, however, unable to find sufficient work to support families, eventually returned to reservations.

—*Patricia Masserman*

See also Anasazi; Beringia; Corn; Dating methods; Demography; Mounds and mound builders; Relocation; Removal;

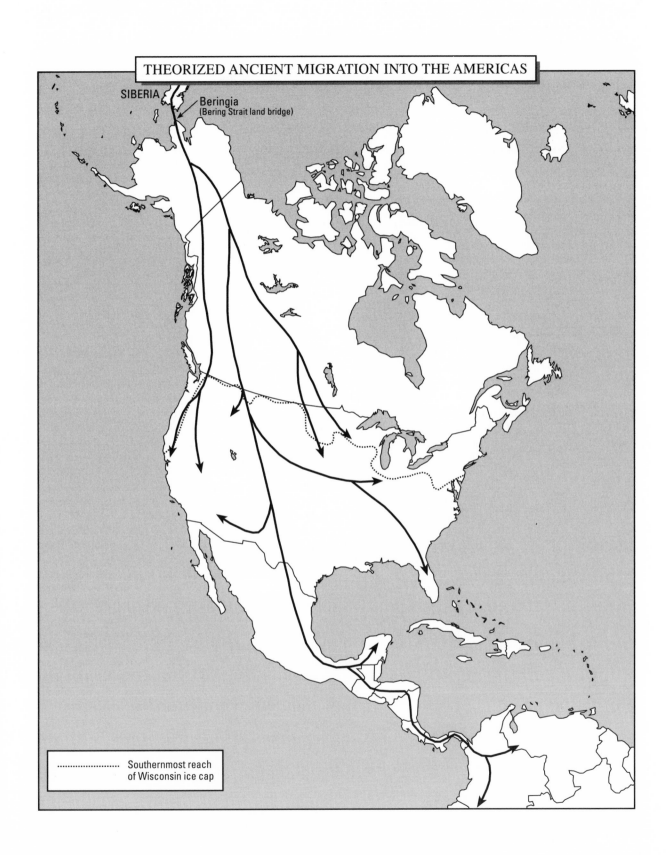

THEORIZED ANCIENT MIGRATION INTO THE AMERICAS

SIBERIA

Beringia
(Bering Strait land bridge)

.... Southernmost reach
of Wisconsin ice cap

Reservation system of the United States; Reserve system of Canada.

BIBLIOGRAPHY

Ceram, C. W. *The First American: A Story of North American Archaeology*. Translated by Richard and Clara Winston. New York: Harcourt Brace Jovanovich, 1971.

Fagan, Brian M. *The Great Journey: The Peopling of Ancient America*. New York: Thames and Hudson, 1987.

Goodman, Jeffrey. *American Genesis*. New York: Summit Books, 1981.

Jennings, Francis. *The Founders of America*. New York: W. W. Norton, 1993.

Stuart, George E., and Gene S. Stuart. *Discovering Man's Past in the Americas*. Washington, D.C.: National Geographic Society, 1969.

Military societies

TRIBES AFFECTED: Primarily Plains tribes
SIGNIFICANCE: The main function of military societies was to enculturate young men into the ways and ethos of warfare

Military societies, or sodalities, were made up of men from different bands within a tribe. They were most common, and highly developed, in the Plains. These voluntary societies were often age-graded, with a person usually gaining greater status with age. Sometimes one could shift membership and allegiance to another society. Some tribes, such as the Blackfeet, had as many as seven military societies. The societies' leaders were the main war chiefs of the tribe, who would have an entourage of subchiefs, messengers, and "ambassadors." There was often competition between the societies in games, physical endurance, and military deeds. Each fraternity, though fundamentally alike in their internal organization, had its own sacred and profane paraphernalia, war and dance songs, power bundles, rattles, pipes, emblems, and dress. Many societies were totemic by name and origin, which was sometimes reflected in dances and in art form upon shields, horses, and even a member's body.

The main functions of these societies were to enculturate young men into the ways and ethos of warfare; to embody the concepts of self-control, bravery, and honor; to exercise social control during communal bison hunting; to police tribal ceremonies; and to accord status to a society's members.

See also Secret societies; Societies, non-kin-based.

Mimbres: Prehistoric tradition

DATE: 1100-1150
LOCATION: Central Arizona
CULTURES AFFECTED: Western Pueblo tribes

The Mimbres culture, especially Classic Mimbres, represents a localized florescence of Mogollon culture in the Mimbres Valley of the central highlands of Arizona between 1000 and 1150 C.E. During this time there was a rapid growth in local population size together with the establishment of several large pueblos that each housed several hundred people. Mimbres is best known for its beautiful black-on-white ceramic bowls, decorated with designs of people and animals. Unfortunately, unscrupulous collectors and illegal looters have practically obliterated existing Mimbres sites in their attempts to recover prehistoric art objects. These activities have silenced the archaeological record with respect to many questions about Mimbres culture.

Most of the known pueblos in the Mimbres Valley, such as the Swarts and Mattocks ruins, are quite large, with 60 to 125 rooms. These were constructed of mud and stone masonry walls that were coated with mud plaster on the interior. Rooms were rectangular and were roofed with wooden beams. They usually contained storage bins, wall niches, fireplaces, and benches. Burials were often made under the floors of pueblo rooms that had been abandoned as living quarters. In some instances, however, graves were covered with stone or clay, and the rooms presumably continued to be used. Grave offerings consisted of tools, precious stones, jewelry, and decorated pottery vessels. The Swarts site was organized into two large house blocks of about sixty rooms each, some built on two levels. Its population is estimated to have been 175 people or thirty-five families during the Mimbres phase.

The Mimbres people were agricultural, with a subsistence system based on the rainfall cultivation of maize, beans, squash, sunflowers, cotton, and other domesticated plants. Wild foods continued to be an important part of the diet. Hunting in upland regions and fishing in rivers supplemented the diet with animal protein, while nuts and seeds were collected during periods of seasonal abundance. Evidence for Mimbres ceremonialism is found on painted vessels from burials. Practices included the use of prayer sticks, elaborate tablita-style headdresses and masks, and shrines. Costumes and ornaments were made with turquoise and exotic feathers, such as those from parrots and macaws.

The most distinctive pottery type of Classic Mimbres is called Mimbres black-on-white. Jar and bowl forms are known. These were decorated with both geometric and highly stylized naturalistic designs. The former include arrangements of hatched and solid triangles, scrolls, zigzags, and frets in black and white. The latter, especially as executed on the interior surfaces of open, hemispherical bowls, are among the most striking of indigenous American art traditions. The center of the bowl was utilized as a visual focal point, in which were painted representational designs. These include depictions of humans and animals in a wide variety of attitudes. Representations of deer, sheep, birds, fish, rabbits, frogs, and even insects were utilized.

A large number of the paintings on Mimbres vessels portray scenes from both daily and ceremonial life. There are depictions of hunting, fishing, and gathering wood. There are also representations of childbirth, dances, game playing, and even human sacrifice. Interestingly, the majority of these painted bowls have been "killed" through the ceremonial puncturing of the vessel bottom. This may have been done in order to release a spiritual essence of the artifact prior to its deposition as a burial offering.

See also Mogollon; Pottery; Prehistory—Southwest.

Minnesota Uprising

DATE: August-December, 1862
PLACE: Minnesota Valley, Minnesota
TRIBE AFFECTED: Eastern (Santee) Sioux
SIGNIFICANCE: The Minnesota Uprising was a result of the reservation policies forced upon the Eastern Sioux by the U.S. government

Deprived of their annual distribution of annuities during the summer of 1862, the Eastern (Santee) Sioux—Mdewakanton, Wahpekute, Wahpeton, and Sisseton—grew angry and indignant. Warehouses were full of food and other supplies, but Thomas Galbraith, the Indian agent, refused to give it to the Indians until the cash annuities arrived. The agent feared he would not receive his customary monetary kickback.

Once an independent, self-sufficient group, the Eastern Sioux had become dependent on annuities for their survival. When Minnesota became a territory, a census indicated that Eastern Sioux outnumbered the six thousand white settlers by more than two to one. When Minnesota became a state in 1858 and the number of white settlers increased, Indians ceded much of their land. The treaties of 1851 and 1858 saw the Sioux cede 28 million acres to the whites in exchange for annuities and reservation life.

Faced with the starvation of his people, Little Crow—an unusually articulate leader—tried to persuade Galbraith to distribute the food to his hungry people. His arguments fell on deaf ears. The attitude of the white trader Andrew Myrick typifies the lack of concern toward the Indians' condition: If the Indians are hungry, let them eat grass or dung.

The Indians' anger over Galbraith's decision, years of mistreatment by white officials, and the threat of starvation came to a head when four young warriors murdered five white settlers on August 17, 1862. As a result of these actions, militant Mdewakanton and Wahpekute chiefs persuaded Little Crow to lead an assault on the whites. On August 18, 1862, they attacked the Redwood Agency, killing twenty men and taking twelve women captive. Among the dead was Andrew Myrick, his body mutilated and his mouth stuffed with grass as an answer to his callous remark. After this attack, the Indians swept throughout the countryside plundering, looting, killing, and raping. The white settlement at New Ulm, for one, suffered staggering losses but repelled the attackers.

The Indians were decisively defeated by General Henry Sibley's troops at the Battle of Wood Lake on September 23. This battle virtually ended Sioux resistance. On December 26 of 1862, 38 out of 303 Sioux were tried and convicted of rape and murder. They were sentenced to death by mass hanging. Little Crow, who fled west, was killed during the summer of 1863 by a Minnesota farmer.

As a result of the uprising, between four hundred and eight hundred whites were killed. In addition, the Eastern Sioux were forced to relocate to reservations in present-day South Dakota.

See also Indian-white relations—U.S., 1831-1870; Little Crow; Sioux; Sioux uprisings.

Missions and missionaries

TRIBES AFFECTED: Pantribal
SIGNIFICANCE: Missionaries and their missions provided American Indians with their first concentrated contact with white culture; missionaries helped implement the policies of assimilation, agrarianism, and cultural extermination

From the 1500's, when Spanish and French explorers brought Roman Catholic priests to North America, until the 1950's, missionaries influenced both American Indians and American policy toward Indians. Missionaries taught English, built schools and churches, and created pantribal connections. They also, however, spread disease and forced assimilation and Christianization on Indians. Most missionaries were well-meaning, but their efforts were often (at best) misguided. They were so convinced of the correctness and superiority of their own culture and belief system that they tried to suppress and destroy those of the Indians. Missionary work supported by various denominations continues today, but since the 1950's, missionaries have been more sensitive than their predecessors about understanding and respecting Indian culture. Missionaries and their missions remain controversial in most American Indian communities today.

Sixteenth Through Eighteenth Century. Missionaries first entered North America through the Spanish Empire in Mexico and through French trading posts in Quebec. The Spanish viewed Christianization as a pillar of conquest and provided state-sponsored Catholic missionaries. These missionaries developed missions in New Mexico, Texas, Arizona, and California. They provided protection, food, and shelter to the weaker tribes, such as the Pueblo Indians, while being constantly threatened by the stronger tribes, such as the Apaches and the Navajos. This system suffered a setback in the 1680 Pueblo Revolt, when tribes rose up and chased the missionaries and the Spanish settlers out of New Mexico. The Spanish reestablished the missions within fifteen years.

The French allowed Catholic missionaries into their territory, but they were not state-sponsored as they were in the Spanish Empire. Jesuits attempted to Christianize the Hurons, but instead they brought smallpox, which decimated the tribe. This upset the tribal balance of power, and the Iroquois attacked and killed off most of the Hurons. The Jesuits retreated and simply kept missions at trading posts until the 1790's.

The English Protestants also saw Christianization of the Indians as part of their role in North America. In the seventeenth century, John Eliot of Massachusetts established praying villages where Indians lived "as white men": They wore English clothes, learned farming techniques, and became Christians. As disease decimated many of the Northern Woodlands tribes, the remaining members joined the praying villages for survival. The villages appeared to be successful at attracting converts. Though many of the Indian residents did convert, most died from diseases spread by the whites within the praying villages.

David Brainerd, an Eliot student, began a mission among the Cherokees in Tennessee. The Cherokees used the mission to learn English and to learn about white culture. The high attendance rate made the school appear to be a success, which inspired other Protestant groups to send missionaries among the Indians. All these early missionaries—Spanish, French, and English—believed in the power of Christianity, the importance of sedentary farming, and the necessity of extinguishing Indian culture.

Nineteenth Century. Mission work exploded with the development of large missionary societies between 1830 and 1850. Presbyterian, Methodist, Baptist, and Catholic societies sponsored hundreds of missionaries, both male and female, to work with Indians. Missionaries built schools and churches to attract Indians to Christianity and white civilization. They expected Indians to convert in large numbers and to support their own missions financially (as the natives of India and Africa had done). Despite these efforts, the Indians showed little interest in converting to Christianity.

In the 1850's, the missionary societies grew impatient with the lack of progress. They accepted money from the American government to help support their missions. In return, the government demanded that the missionaries increase their efforts to Christianize and "civilize" the Indians. Money was supplied to help assimilate all Indian groups to sedentary farming and Christianity. This method was a general failure, perhaps most conspicuously with Plains and Northwest Coast groups.

By the 1870's, missionary societies lost patience with the lack of success and cut off funding for missionaries. Individual missionaries became responsible for their own financial support. Many entered into agreements with the U.S. government that tied them to conversion quotas. The government wanted a certain number of "pacified" Indians in exchange for its invested dollars. Additionally, missionaries wrote pamphlets and books about the "wretched condition" of specific Indian groups. These writings influenced public views of the condition of the American Indian. Many of these missionary works formed the basis for anthropological studies of the Sioux, the Cheyenne, the Navajo, the Salish, and other native groups.

Despite their funding problems, missionaries continued their program of assimilation, agrarianism, and cultural extermination. The height of this policy occurred during the 1870's when the government's "peace policy" allowed missionaries to administrate the Bureau of Indian Affairs (BIA). At this time, residential schools became popular. Missionaries removed Indian children from their parents and sent them away to be acculturated into white society. Missionaries forbade the children to speak their own language, wear their own clothes, or practice any aspect of their own culture. At this point, missionary and government policy coalesced into one united front against Indian culture. By the end of the nineteenth century, missionaries had fallen out of favor with the government, which saw their attempts at fostering assimilation as failures. Few Indians had converted to Christianity; most had developed a resentment of missionaries and saw them as agents of cultural genocide.

Missionaries remained part of Indian policy through the 1950's. They ran schools, wrote reports, and continued to act as agents and intermediaries for the government.

Positive Contributions. Though missionaries generally attempted to destroy Indian cultures and societies in their efforts to help Indians, they made some positive contributions. First, education and acculturation provided Indian groups with a common language—English. Second, the residential school system provided a common experience for native leaders and gave them the opportunity to meet people from different tribal groups. Finally, education created bicultural natives who understood their own culture and white culture. This development helped many tribal groups in their legal battles against white governments. —*C. L. Higham*

See also Carlisle Indian School; Indian Rights Association; Minnesota Uprising; Praying Indians; Pueblo (Popé's) Revolt.

Bibliography

Beaver, Robert Pierce. *Church, State, and the American Indians*. St. Louis: Concordia, 1966.

Berkhofer, Robert F., Jr. *Salvation and the Savage*. Lexington: University Press of Kentucky, 1965.

Devens, Carol. *Countering Colonization: Native American Women and Great Lakes Missions, 1630-1900*. Berkeley: University of California Press, 1992.

Grant, John Webster. *Moon of Wintertime: Missionaries and the Indians of Canada in Encounter Since 1543*. Toronto: University of Toronto Press, 1984.

Kelley, Robert. *American Protestantism and United States Indian Policy*. Lincoln: University of Nebraska Press, 1983.

Mississippian: Prehistoric tradition

Date: 900-1540
Location: Midwestern and southeastern North America
Cultures affected: Caddo, Cherokee, Chickasaw, Choctaw, Creek, Natchez, Pawnee

The Mississippian tradition was a widespread cultural phenomenon that affected peoples of the vast Missouri-Mississippi drainage and neighboring regions of the Midwest and southeastern United States between 900 C.E. and the arrival of the first Spanish expedition by Hernando de Soto in 1539-1540. Also known as the "temple mound" period, the Mississippian tradition was characterized by the presence of sedentary, village societies with marked social ranking whose agricultural economies were characterized by a strong reliance on the cultivation of maize and whose technology included shell-tempered pottery. Large Mississippian settlements, such as Cahokia, Etowah, and Moundville, were dominated by the presence of massive, pyramidal mounds of earth that served as the bases for temples and residences of powerful individuals. The term "Mississippian" has been applied to a wide variety of sites and complexes, and the culture was by no means uniform.

The Mississippian people were accomplished at a variety of crafts. Among them was the manufacture of elaborate ceramic vessels, often bearing symbolic decorations. A distinctive class of vessels are those sculpted to look like trophy heads taken in warfare. Ground stone objects included elaborate pipes and ceremonial axes. From a number of sites, most notably the Spiro Mound in eastern Oklahoma, come beautiful shell gorgets, carved with representations of warriors, snakes, and esoteric symbols. Cold-hammer metallurgy was used to manufacture copper sheet-metal portraits and representations of warriors.

The religious life of the Mississippians included the observation of celestial events, such as the summer and winter solstices, and occasional human sacrifice. Toward the end of the period, a phenomenon called the "Southern Cult" is manifest in the production and trade of ceremonial objects decorated with symbols such as hands with eyes, crosses, and snakes as well as depictions of individuals dressed in bird costumes holding severed human heads. Some archaeologists have suggested that these are related to ceremonial traditions from Mesoamerica.

The Mississippian tradition came to an end as a result of a variety of stresses. The most significant of these was the introduction of European diseases and the subsequent devastation of native populations by fatal epidemics in the sixteenth century. Problems such as malnutrition and internecine warfare were present long before the arrival of the Spanish, however, resulting in the decline and abandonment of large sites such as Cahokia generations before European contact. The legacy of complex Mississippian societies continued into the historic period among tribes such as the Creeks.

See also Cahokia; Etowah; Moundville; Prehistory—Southeast; Southern Cult; Spiro.

Missouri: Tribe

CULTURE AREA: Plains
LANGUAGE GROUP: Siouan
PRIMARY LOCATION: Oklahoma
POPULATION SIZE: 1,840 ("Otoe-Missouria," 1990 U.S. Census)

The Missouri occupied villages on the Missouri River near present-day northwest Saline County, Missouri. They were related linguistically to the Winnebagos, Otos, and Iowas. Their semisedentary lifestyle combined hunting and gathering with horticultural activities. When not hunting large game such as deer and buffalo, they inhabited settlements—especially in the spring and fall—to tend to agricultural duties, woodworking, and pottery. While once a strong tribe, they were gradually weakened with their westward movement because of divisions and wars.

Oral traditions trace the origins of the Missouri to the area of the Great Lakes near Green Bay, Wisconsin. Before the period of European contact in this area, there lived a group of Indians called the Hotonga, or "fish eaters." The Hotonga divided at Green Bay, and the group that remained there became known as the Winnebago. The ones who left went to the confluence of the Mississippi and Iowa rivers. Here a further division took place: The Iowa remained there, and those who continued on to the confluence of the Missouri and Grand rivers became the Missouri. A final split produced the Oto, who traveled farther up the Missouri River. The Missouri, after a war with the Osage, separated again; a part went to live with the Iowa, and another group followed the Oto.

The Missouri were first known to have been in contact with French fur traders in 1673, when they were contacted by Jacques Marquette. Thereafter, they made treaties, traded, and intermarried with the French from Detroit to St. Louis until the 1820's, the time of Missouri statehood. They made a peace treaty with the United States on June 24, 1817. Between the time of contact and statehood, the Missouri suffered devastating tribal attacks by the Sauk and Fox as well as a series of epidemics. The remaining Missouri had combined with the Oto by 1829, forming the Oto-Missouri tribe. All of their lands, except for the reservation at Big Blue River, Nebraska, were ceded to the government by 1855. The descendants of this group continue to exist on reservation land in Oklahoma.

See also Iowa; Osage; Oto.

Mitla: Archaeological site

DATE: 500-1700
LOCATION: Oaxaca, Mexico
CULTURES AFFECTED: Zapotec, Mixtec

Mitla, located in the Valley of Oaxaca southeast of the neighboring center of Monte Albán, was one of the most important center of Zapotec culture during Mesoamerica's Postclassic period. The name of the site is derived from the Nahuatl name *Mictlan*, a legendary "Place of the Dead," which may refer to the presence of royal tombs. The earliest settlement of the area dates to 1200 B.C.E., and some building was undertaken during Monte Albán II (200 B.C.E. to 200 C.E.), but the site's principal occupation probably dates to after 1000 C.E., contemporaneous with the Toltec presence in Central Mexico. Mitla was still in use at the time of the Spanish conquest.

Mitla architecture consists of five clusters of impressive palaces and courtyards, arranged in groups of buildings around central patios. The South Group, located south of the river at Mitla, is a group of four early pyramidal structures that may represent the original ceremonial core of the site, dating to Monte Albán III (200-700 C.E.). The Western Group, on the west side of the site, is similar in layout and may date to the same period. The Church Group, the Group of the Columns, and the Arroyo Group are each composed of arrangements of palaces around three quadrangles. Most buildings are constructed in levels, with walls consisting of cut stone masonry over a rubble fill of mud and stone covered with plaster. Among the most impressive features are massive monoliths of cut stone, some weighing up to 25 tons, used at the site for lintels and columns.

The Church Group is so named because of a colonial Spanish church built in one of the quadrangles. The Group of the Columns is the largest and most ornate. It is named for a colonnade of massive cylindrical monoliths that once supported heavy wood beams and a flat roof. The Arroyo Group, the smallest of the palace compounds, was also constructed with large stone lintels.

The walls of palace structures are decorated with friezes of intricate, three-dimensional geometric patterns. Some of these were executed as relief carvings, but the majority were made by assembling facades of carefully carved stone blocks of soft, volcanic tuff. More than 150 mosaic panels survive. The designs were based on the step-and-fret motif, which was also widely used on pottery from this time period. These walls were painted with colorful pigments. Many of the geometric designs are painted white against a red backdrop. These decorations resembled elements of place-name glyphs found in Mixtec codices, or folding books, and their use on the palaces at Mitla may indicate the political control or affiliations of individual polities.

Painted frescoes on the walls of palaces at Mitla recall the styles of Mixtec codices, and it is likely that some of these were occupied by individuals mentioned in pre-Columbian documents. Spanish accounts from the seventeenth century report that Mitla was once the home of a paramount Zapotec priest and that the buildings there contained the residence of this high priest and his attendants. There were also apartments used by visiting dignitaries. According to the sources, the power of the priest of Mitla was readily acknowledged by a secular king and his court. Subterranean tombs at the site with cruciform plans were probably the burial places of priests and rulers over several generations. Mitla was widely known as a burial ground for the highest-ranking members of Zapotec nobility.

See also Mixtec; Monte Albán; Oaxaca; Zapotec.

Miwok: Tribe

Culture area: California
Language group: Miwok-Costanoan
Primary location: Western central California
Population size: 3,381 (1990 U.S. Census)

Miwok Indians lived in western central California. They are divided into three groups: the Lake, Eastern, and Coast Miwok. Miwok Indians hunted, gathered, fished, and traded for food. Both men and women fished using nets, baskets, spears, and their bare hands. Men used bows and arrows to kill waterfowl and large game such as deer, elk, and bear. Surplus meat and fish were mixed with salt and dried for winter use. Men and women made baskets which were used in ceremonies as well as for gathering, storing, and preparing food. The Miwok harvested numerous types of acorns, nuts, berries, roots, and other vegetation for food, medicine, and basketweaving materials.

The Miwok Indians lived in large, permanent multifamily homes covered with brush, leaves, tule, and dirt. A basket was set over the small doorway opening at night. Women wore deerskin apron skirts and men wore loincloths of the same material. Animal skins were cut into strips and sewn together for winter robes.

The shaman was the tribal doctor as well as a ceremonial and religious leader. There were two kinds of shaman: power (or singing) shamans and sucking shamans. Sucking shamans sucked on the skin to extract foreign bodies that were believed to cause illness. Power shamans danced and prayed to guardian spirits for cures. Many superstitions and taboos were observed to ensure health and good luck.

In 1595, Spanish explorers met the Coast Miwok. In the early 1800's, missions were established and Miwok Indians were forcibly taken there for conversion. Many ran away but were captured and returned by Spanish soldiers. Disease epidemics and warfare with the Spanish decimated and weakened the tribe. When white settlers arrived in California, hostilities were aimed at the ranchers. In 1850, federal troops from Sonoma killed a large number of Miwok. In the early 1900's, the federal government purchased land for a small reservation. Many Miwoks found seasonal work on local ranches.

See also California; Missions and missionaries.

Mixtec: Tribe

Culture area: Mesoamerica
Language group: Oto-Manguean
Primary location: Guerrero, Oaxaca, and Puebla, Mexico

The Mixtec people shared a common language and a distinctive Mesoamerican culture. Unlike many Mesoamerican societies, there was never a Mixtec empire with a capital city. Rather, numerous, small, politically independent kingdoms characterized the Mixtec political landscape. Each kingdom was headed by its own prestigious royal dynasty, centered in its own town boasting public buildings, temples, ball courts, hieroglyphic writing, luxurious royal residences, and elaborate tombs. The mountaintop sites of Monte Negro, Yucuñudahui, and Huamelulpan are examples of such royal centers in the Mixteca Alta.

The social system was one of the most rigidly hierarchical in Mesoamerica, with clear class divisions between nobility and commoners as well as ranked divisions within each of these broad classes. Mixtec royalty were among those in Mesoamerica who claimed (possibly fictional) descent from the Toltec of Central Mexico. A small but professional military helped maintain social order and was sometimes used for territorial expansion at the expense of neighboring Mixtec kingdoms. Agricultural produce (maize, beans, and squash) and crafts were extracted from the commoners as tribute.

The Mixtec were divided into three principal groups. The most northerly group inhabited the Mixteca Baja, a series of hot, humid valleys descending toward the Gulf Lowlands. Kingdoms within the Mixteca Baja flourished from 600 to 900 C.E., after the decline of Teotihuacán and Monte Albán and before the rise of Tula. A second Mixtec group, the Mixteca de la Costa, occupied the Pacific coastal lowlands of Oaxaca state, where cacao (chocolate bean), a valuable trade item, was grown. The third group lived in the Mixteca Alta, the cold, high mountains and upland valleys west of Oaxaca. The Mixteca Alta lies near the Zapotec Valley of Oaxaca, and this group had the closest relationship with the Zapotec kingdoms, especially in the Late Postclassic period (after 1200 C.E.), when the Mixtec expanded and royal intermarriage was common.

The Mixtec were highly skilled craftsworkers. Elaborate luxury goods were produced for the Mixtec nobility and for trade with the elite of other regions. Gold and silver were worked with amber, turquoise, jade, pearl, jet, coral, and shell to produce exquisite necklaces, bracelets, and ear and nose ornaments. Craftsworkers producing such luxury goods and working with such valuable materials may themselves have been part of the nobility.

The Mixtec developed their own unique script. In addition to stone slabs, the Mixtec wrote codices—books with accordion-shaped paper pages with elaborately painted pictures in vivid colors. The codices contain genealogical and historical records as well as religious information related to Mixtec deities and divination. Although the Mixtec script resembles Mesoamerican script symbols in general, it remains only partially deciphered.

Beginning in the late 1400's, most Mixtec kingdoms fell prey to the powerful and expanding Aztec empire. Less than twenty-five years later, the Mixtec kingdoms again fell prey to the Spanish. Today it is estimated that there are about 260,000 people who speak Mixtecan languages.

See also Aztec; Codices; Maya; Monte Albán; Olmec; Teotihuacán; Toltec; Tula; Zapotec.

In addition to their own language, the Mobile spoke a so-called Mobilian lingua franca, or trade language, which actually was a corrupted Choctaw jargon used by most tribes from Florida to Louisiana, and north along the Mississippi.

See also Choctaw.

Moccasins

TRIBES AFFECTED: Pantribal
SIGNIFICANCE: Animal-skin moccasins, comfortable and practical, were the type of American Indian footwear most widely worn in North America

The word "moccasin" is an Anglicization of the Natick term *mohkussin*, which is derived from the Algonquian word *maxkeseni*. Moccasins are soft leather shoes or slippers made of animal hide and worn throughout the Americas in areas where animal skins are used in the making of clothing and footwear.

There are many styles of moccasin. Although this type of footwear is widely used, particulars regarding materials, construction, styles, and decoration are tribe-specific. The hides of deer, elk, moose, buffalo, and other large game are most often used, although in the Arctic sealskin is preferred. On the Northwest Coast, footwear is most often made of cedar and other vegetable fibers.

Three types of moccasins: left to right, Abenaki, Navajo, and Hopi.

Mobile: Tribe

CULTURE AREA: Southeast
LANGUAGE GROUP: Muskogean
PRIMARY LOCATION: Choctaw Bluff on the Alabama River

Despite extensive historical data on the Mobile, there is little prehistoric information. In 1540, Hernando de Soto first fought with the Mobile, who were under the leadership of their chief, Tuscaloosa, who rallied his people and neighboring groups to oppose the Spanish successfully.

Later, many Mobile moved south to Mobile Bay, where the French encountered them in 1700. The Mobile appealed to the French for protection from their traditional enemies, and in 1708 they were settled near Fort Louis, along with the Tohome. French Roman Catholic missionaries were relatively successful in Christianizing the Mobile, who were absorbed into the Choctaw Nation. By 1758 there remained fewer than two hundred Mobile.

Moccasins can be cut low, in the form of a slipper; cut to medium height to make an ankle-high shoe; or made in the form of a boot that can be tied as high as the thigh. Some are slipped on, some use laces, while others are tied with straps. Moccasins are often decorated with beautiful designs using porcupine quills or beads of various kinds.

See also Dress and adornment.

Modoc: Tribe

CULTURE AREA: Plateau (some authorities indicate Great Basin)
LANGUAGE GROUP: Klamath-Modoc
PRIMARY LOCATION: Northern California, southwestern Oregon, Oklahoma
POPULATION SIZE: 574 (1990 U.S. Census)

Modoc, California's northeasternmost county, is named for a Native American tribe whose ancestors arrived in that area not later than 6100 B.C.E. By that date, the Modoc (which means "southerner") also inhabited the nearby Tule Lake region (presently in Siskiyou County, California), as well as south-central Oregon's Klamath Lake and Lower Klamath Lake region. Archaeological discoveries in the Surprise Valley of northeastern California, as well as near Oregon's Klamath lakes, indicate the occupancy of large semi-subterranean lodges (or pit houses), suggesting old, well-established societies that were at least partially sedentary. Around 2500 B.C.E., however, the appearance of brush wickiup housing, denoting adaptations to a less settled life, suggests changes in Klamath-Modoc cultural conditions or a shift in the ranges of the Modoc. Generally, the Klamath-Modoc were hunter-gatherers; that is, they specialized in fishing, fowling, and plant gathering, particularly along lake shores. Their legacy of artifacts consists of leaf-shaped and large side-notched projectile points, which at later dates changed to smaller, notched and barbed arrowheads. Mortars and pestles, knives, scrapers, twined basketry, and sagebrush sandals have also been found in abundance, although the archaeological record for relatively more recent ancient times has been destroyed by modern relic collectors.

Since the Modoc inhabited a relatively isolated region of rich grasslands and lava beds, unlike other Plateau tribes they remained relatively unaffected by extensions of the nineteenth century European mining frontier and the ruthless search for gold and other precious metals that characterized it. Nevertheless, trouble began in the early 1860's when Modoc grasslands began attracting white ranchers who were eager to clear Indians from their path. Under pressure from the ranchers, the federal government negotiated a treaty with the Modoc in 1864 that resulted in the Modocs' movement to a reservation north of Tule Lake. Whatever advantages the treaty brought to white ranchers, it brought little solace to the Modoc, for they were obliged to share the reservation with the Klamath tribe among whom, despite their language affinities, the Modoc were both culturally alien and badly outnumbered.

Faced with these disabilities, Captain Jack (Kintpuash), a Modoc leader, encouraged his people to return to their original homes around Tule Lake, an area that in the meantime had been occupied by white settlers who were panicked by the Indians' reappearance. Initial efforts by whites to persuade Captain Jack to remove his people to the reservation once again failed. The appointment in 1869 of Alfred B. Meacham, a staunch Oregon Republican and a reformer, as superintendent of Oregon's Indian affairs, soon resulted in the Modocs' reluctant return to the reservation. There, faced once again with the hostilities of the Klamath as well as with pressures from other Indian agents, the Modoc for a second time left the reservation and returned to their homeland. By 1872, federal efforts to force the Modoc back to the reservation brought on the Modoc War. For a year, the military campaign against the Modoc proved an embarrassing stalemate to federal troops led by General Edward R. S. Canby, whom Captain Jack

treacherously murdered during peace parleys. Simultaneously, the war deeply divided the Modoc themselves. Confronted in the aftermath of Canby's murder with national outrage and intensified federal military operations, the Modocs swiftly surrendered. Captain Jack and three associates were hanged. The surviving 153 Modocs were exiled under the aegis of the Department of Interior to Oklahoma Indian Territory, where subsequently they farmed peacefully. In 1909, those who remained were given the option of returning to Oregon's Klamath reservation.

The Modocs' contacts with whites proved disastrous. The Bureau of Indian Affairs counted four thousand Modocs in 1873. By 1994, between three hundred and five hundred of their descendants lived near Chiloquin, Oregon, and a few hundred more in Oklahoma (the 1990 U.S. Census gave the Modoc population as 574). In 1986, through the Modoc tribe of Oklahoma, the tribe was restored to direct federal recognition and government-to-government relations with the United States. The Modoc's rich cultural tradition lives on in its myths about Kmukamch, the ancient creator, and Loon Woman.

—Clifton K. Yearley

See also Captain Jack; Klamath; Modoc War; Plateau.

Modoc War

DATE: November 29, 1872—June 1, 1873
PLACE: Boundary of Northern California and southern Oregon
TRIBES AFFECTED: Klamath, Modoc
SIGNIFICANCE: The Modoc War was another example of attempted Indian resistance to the loss of their homelands

In 1864, the Modocs signed a treaty in which they agreed to leave the Lost River valley of Northern California and southern Oregon, and live on a reservation with the Klamaths. By 1872, Kintpuash, called Captain Jack by the whites, and other Modocs found reservation life and policies unacceptable. They missed their homeland and could no longer endure sharing a reservation with the Klamaths, who outnumbered them and made life extremely difficult for them.

Kintpuash and a group of Modocs decided to return south to the ceded lands at Lost River. White settlers, whose numbers had continued to increase, refused to accept them and demanded that the Modocs return to the reservation. Government officials tried in vain to convince the Modocs to do so. On November 29, 1872, troops attacked Kintpuash's camp at Lost River. The Indians fled, crossed Tule Lake, and strategically entrenched themselves in the Lava Beds, a natural fortress on the lake's southern shore. For four months, Kintpuash skillfully defended the area with about sixty men against forces that numbered nearly a thousand.

The government again tried negotiation, creating a peace commission headed by General Edward R. S. Canby, a Civil War hero. Kintpuash favored negotiating for a settlement, but other Modoc leaders such as Hooker Jim and Curley-Headed Doctor forced Kintpuash to accept a plan to kill the peace commissioners at a meeting that was to take place on Good Friday, April 11, 1873. At this meeting, Kintpuash and other

Modocs drew their hidden weapons and attacked. Two of the four commissioners were killed, including General Canby, who thus became the only regular army general killed in the Indian wars.

This rash action provoked a national outcry for revenge. More troops and officers were sent. Meanwhile, factionalism intensified among the Modocs. In May of 1873 the army defeated a Modoc band, and some of the defeated Modocs agreed to help the army catch Kintpuash. He was finally captured on June 1. All the Modoc prisoners were taken to Fort Klamath, Oregon.

Kintpuash and several other Modocs were tried and found guilty of the murders of the two peace commissioners. Kintpuash and three others were hanged on October 3, 1873, with two other Modocs receiving life sentences at Alcatraz. The executed Modocs' heads were severed and sent to the Army Medical Museum in Washington, D.C. The other Modocs were removed to the Quapaw Agency in Oklahoma; in 1909, they were allowed to return to the Klamath Reservation.

The Modoc War lasted seven months and cost more than $500,000. The war seriously weakened the Indian Peace Policy, a program under the Grant administration that attempted to use reservations as a panacea for the "Indian Problem."

See also Captain Jack; Hooker Jim; Klamath; Modoc.

Mogollon: Prehistoric tradition

DATE: 200 B.C.E.-1000 C.E.
LOCATION: Arizona, New Mexico
CULTURES AFFECTED: Western Pueblo tribes

The Mogollon tradition represents the emergence and florescence of agricultural village life in central and eastern Arizona and western New Mexico, especially in mountainous, highland regions. It begins with the appearance of pottery and ends with the transition from pit house villages to a Western Pueblo settlement pattern. Definitions of the Mogollon cultural sequence have become very complex with the proliferation of regionalized phases, and there is a lack of agreement on a generalized nomenclature.

Excavations at Tularosa Cave and Bat Cave (New Mexico) have provided evidence for the local development of the Mogollon tradition from Archaic period Cochise cultures, signaled by

A late nineteenth century sketch of an 1873 skirmish in the Modoc War. (Library of Congress)

the emergence of pottery and increased sedentism. The timing of this transition is still poorly understood, and interpretations of dates for the beginning of ceramics in the Mogollon region range from 600 B.C.E. to 200 C.E., with most scholars favoring the later date. The earliest Mogollon pottery is plain, with a red wash or slip. Red-on-brown and black-on-white styles appear around 650 C.E., with a red-on-white type appearing around 800.

Early Mogollon villages were situated on mesas and high ridges, close to cultivable alluvial valleys, possibly for defensive purposes. The earliest dwellings were pit houses with central posts and circular or D-shaped layouts, entered via sloping ramps. Over time, these became more rectangular in shape. In the final Mogollon phase before the transition to the Western Pueblo tradition (circa 800-1000), pit houses were often lined with stone masonry and occasionally had roof entries instead of inclined ramps. Typical Mogollon villages were small, averaging about six to eight houses, although larger examples may have had as many as fifty dwellings. At larger villages, especially large pit houses were used for ceremonial rather than residential functions, and some scholars have identified these as "great kivas."

Mogollon farming was based on the use of rainfall rather than irrigation, as with the Hohokam tradition. Given the proximity of highland forest regions, hunting remained an important adjunct to Mogollon agriculture. Typical subsistence technology included digging sticks, milling stones, bows and arrows, fine baskets, and pottery.

By the year 1000, the Mogollon tradition had given way to that of the Western Pueblo pattern of aboveground, multiroomed structures with great kivas (subterranean ceremonial structures with circular plans). As population density grew, reaching a peak in the late thirteenth century, populations in the northern Mogollon area coalesced into large pueblos such as Point of Pines, Kinishba, and Grasshopper. To the south, in the Mimbres Valley, the Mogollon tradition evolved into the Mimbres phase (1100-1150), characterized by large pueblos of several hundred inhabitants and beautiful black-on-white Mimbres pottery. This was followed by the Animas phase (1150-1300), during which the southern pueblos had close ties to cultures such as that of Casas Grandes in Chihuahua, Mexico.

Casas Grandes, also known as Paquimé, was a large pueblo occupied between 1060 and 1350 C.E. At its height, the site had a central core of sixteen hundred rooms and an estimated population of twenty-two hundred people. There is abundant evidence at Casas Grandes for craft specialization, especially in the working of marine shell. The people of this site engaged in long-distance trade with Mesoamerican cultures to the south, exchanging painted pottery and turquoise for marine shells, macaws, and exotic bird feathers.

See also Bat Cave; Mimbres; Prehistory—Southwest; Pueblo tribes, Western; Sinagua.

Mohawk: Tribe

CULTURE AREA: Northeast
LANGUAGE GROUP: Iroquoian
PRIMARY LOCATION: Northern New York State, Ontario, Quebec
POPULATION SIZE: 15,490 in U.S. (1990 U.S. Census); 9,305 in Canada (Statistics Canada, based on 1991 census)

The Mohawks, the easternmost tribe of the Iroquois Confederacy, originally called themselves *Kaniengehaga*, the flint people. Among the most warlike of the eastern Indians, the Mohawks in prehistoric times fought with all their neighbors, both fellow Iroquoian Indians and the Algonquians living to the east of them. They, according to legend, were the source of the idea of the Iroquois Confederacy. It vastly reduced the amount of intertribal warfare among the Iroquois of New York State, though not that with their non-Iroquois neighbors.

According to legend, two men of peace, Deganawida and Hiawatha (also spelled "Hayenwatha"), came to the Mohawks and convinced them to spearhead a proposal of peace among the tribes in what is now New York State. It took a considerable amount of persuasive argument, but eventually the Seneca, the Oneida, the Cayuga, and (most reluctantly) the Onondaga agreed to join in a confederacy. The tribes of the confederacy retained total independence in internal affairs, but "foreign relations" were to be conducted by a council composed of the chiefs of all the tribes. The confederacy was probably founded between 1400 and 1600.

Hiawatha, again according to legend, was also responsible for introducing wampum to the Mohawks and, through them, to the other tribes of the confederacy. Hiawatha persuaded the Mohawks to use monetary compensation, to be paid in wampum, instead of the blood feud to compensate the family of the victims of murder. This practice helped materially to reduce the murder rate among the Iroquois.

Iroquois society was matrilineal. The sachems, or tribal leaders, were selected by otianders, the matriarchs of the tribe. The organizational system of the Iroquois was the clan system, each of which had a natural figurehead, such as a wolf or an eagle. The strength of the clans was maintained through the practice of adoption; that is, Indians captured in war were adopted by the captor, becoming an integral member of the adopting clan.

The Mohawks were a very religious people, attributing success in the harvest or in warfare to the invisible spirits of nature. As agriculture spread among them, they began holding feasts to commemorate the harvest of squash, beans, and corn. The Green Corn Festival celebrated the corn harvest.

The Mohawks were the "Keepers of the Eastern Door of the Lodge" of the Iroquois Confederacy. As such, they were the first to become involved with the European settlers. They were allied with the Dutch and the English and were, except for brief intervals (especially during the first half of the eighteenth century), at war with the French in Canada. They aided the British during the American Revolution.

Following the American Revolution, the new American government concluded the Treaty of Fort Stanwix (1784) with the Mohawks. This treaty eliminated almost all Mohawk land claims in New York State, and most of the Mohawks retreated to Canada, where the British offered them a reservation on the Grand River. A few Mohawks remained in New York, many on the St. Regis Reservation along the shores of the St. Lawrence River.

In 1802, under pressure from the U.S. government, the Mohawks agreed to adopt a "democratic" system of government for the tribe, with first three, later twelve, elected "trustees." This system persists to this day, but alongside it has grown a revival of the old system under which tribal leaders are selected by the matriarchs of the tribe. The Mohawks have become known for their skills in high-rise steel construction, and many are employed in building today's skyscrapers.

See also Cayuga; Fort Stanwix, Treaty of; Hiawatha; Iroquois Confederacy; Oneida; Onondaga; Seneca; Tekakwitha, Kateri; Tuscarora.

Mohegan: Tribe
CULTURE AREA: Northeast
LANGUAGE GROUP: Algonquian
PRIMARY LOCATION: Connecticut
POPULATION SIZE: 674 (1990 U.S. Census)

The Mohegans occupied the Thames River valley and its tributaries in Connecticut. Originally, they were part of the Pequot Nation, but they formed their own separate entity in the early seventeenth century. Their original name before the division, "Pequot," means "destroyers," while the name "Mohegan" means "wolf."

The Mohegan lived in palisaded villages, with bark houses clustered around an open area for games and gatherings. Women planted corn and beans, while men hunted deer and other wild game. Their chiefs were called "sachems."

No tribe in the Northeast has been the subject of so much confusion and so many differing interpretations as the Mohegan. Part of the confusion stems from James Fenimore Cooper's famed novel *The Last of the Mohicans*, published in 1826. The author was from New York, and he probably patterned his Indians after the Mahican of that region, an entirely separate tribe. Cooper spelled the name "Mohican," and the Connecticut Mohegan's name was sometimes spelled in that way. Cooper made the confusion worse by naming one of his characters "Uncas," the name of a real-life Mohegan subchief.

It was the sachem Uncas who led the Mohegans in their split with the Pequots. A figure of controversy, Uncas generally remained an ally of the English. In fact, the Mohegans joined the English in the Pequot War of 1637, a conflict that led to the virtual destruction of the Pequot tribe.

There is also some debate over when Uncas finally severed the Mohegan's connection with the Pequot. He married a daughter of Sassacus, a prominent Pequot chief, but a rebellion against Sassacus led to Uncas' defeat and banishment. The Mohegans escaped destruction in King Philip's War of 1675-1677, thanks largely to their alliance with the English. In 1721, the Mohegan still owned 4,000 acres of the Thames Valley, though it had been reduced to 2,300 by 1850.

The tribe entered into a long and steady decline. Some Mohegans left New England and settled in the Oneida region of New York, while others migrated to Wisconsin, where a small reservation was created in 1832.

In 1861, Connecticut took over many unoccupied Mohegan lands. Though descendants have scattered all over the country, the Mohegan never entirely abandoned their ancestral enclaves around Uncasville, Connecticut. The Uncasville region boasts a Mohegan church and the Fort Shantok Point burial grounds, where members of the tribe are interred. The Mohegans could not stand the pressure of the dominant white culture and eventually assimilated. Extensive intermarriage produced a population that is mainly of mixed ancestry.

See also Mahican; Pequot; Sassacus; Uncas.

Mojave: Tribe
CULTURE AREA: Southwest
LANGUAGE GROUP: Yuman
PRIMARY LOCATION: Lower Colorado River
POPULATION SIZE: 1,386 (1990 U.S. Census)

The name Mojave comes from a native word meaning "three mountains." These people have lived along the lower Colorado River since the 1100's. The early people had sprawling encampments scattered throughout the valley near cultivable land, and their mud-covered houses were above the floodplain on low rises. Most of the year the Mojave slept under flat-topped shades (ramadas), using the houses in winter months.

The Mojave considered themselves one nation and one territory, regardless of the location of the residence. They had loosely defined bands and local groups. Warfare was common, and in war they presented a united front. The hereditary tribal chief was expected to look after the welfare of the tribe and exert a moral influence.

Farming was the principal occupation, and maize was the chief crop. Other products included beans, pumpkins, and melons. The diet was supplemented by fishing, hunting, and wild plants, especially the mesquite bean and screwbean. The men cleared the land, planted, and cultivated, while women did most of the harvesting. Soil fertility depended on the silt deposited by yearly flooding of the Colorado River.

Dreams were the most important part of the Mojave religion; it was believed that special skills, talents, and success in life depended on dreams. Ordinary dreams were considered to be omens; the few individuals who had great dreams became the leaders.

The traditional Mojave culture had mostly vanished by the early 1970's as the people became assimilated into American culture. Pride in tribal identity remained, but the old way of life had gone, the language was being forgotten, and much intermarriage had occurred. The last hereditary chief died in 1947.

The Colorado River Reservation, with 225,995 acres, was established in 1865, and Fort Mojave in 1880. In 1940, part of the reservation was taken for Parker Dam and its reservoir. The

Mósa, a Mojave youth, photographed around 1903. (Library of Congress)

acreage in the early 1990's was 22,820. Both reservations are shared with other tribes. The present tribal offices are in Needles, California.

See also Southwest; Yuman language family.

Molala: Tribe

CULTURE AREA: Plateau
LANGUAGE GROUP: Molale (Penutian)
PRIMARY LOCATION: Oregon
POPULATION SIZE: 14 (Molala, 1990 U.S. Census)

The Molala (or Molale), a poorly recorded tribe, lived in the interior of Washington and Oregon. Their language, while related to that of the Cayuse, was quite distinct. Cayuse tradition suggests that the Molala once lived with them on the Deschutes River but that the two tribes were driven apart and to the west by hostile neighbors. "Molala" is the name of a creek in the Willamette Valley, which a Molala band occupied by joining with the Klikitat to drive out its former inhabitants. Other bands settled on the Umpqua and Rogue rivers to the north. The Molala were greatly feared because they raided neighboring tribes to capture people as slaves. In 1855, the Molala joined with a number of other Willamette Valley tribes in two treaties. They agreed to give up their lands and move with other small tribal groups to a reservation. Many moved to the Grande Ronde Reservation in Oregon, where they adopted European American clothing and customs. They intermarried freely with other tribes and were considered by official enumerators to have been absorbed by other tribes. In 1881, as many as twenty Molala were living outside the reservation in the Cascade Mountains. In 1964 the tribes of the reservation formed the Confederated Tribes of Grande Ronde. The 1990 U.S. Census listed the Grande Ronde tribal population as 1,230.

See also Cayuse; Klikitat; Penutian language family; Plateau.

Momaday, N. Scott (b. Feb. 27, 1934, Lawton, Okla.): Writer

ALSO KNOWN AS: Tsaoi-talee (Rock-Tree Boy)
TRIBAL AFFILIATION: Kiowa
SIGNIFICANCE: A professor of literature and Native American studies, N. Scott Momaday is best known for his innovative and extremely influential works of autobiography and fiction

The child of a Kiowa father and a Cherokee mother, N. Scott Momaday (the N. is for Novarre) grew up in several different Indian communities. In the 1930's, he moved with his family from rural Oklahoma to Navajo country in New Mexico and Arizona. Then, in 1946, when Momaday was twelve years old, his parents began teaching at Jemez Pueblo, where Momaday spent his adolescence. Thus, Momaday grew up an Indian child in Indian communities but was never fully integrated into those communities. Such a fragmented experience, common among contemporary Indians, has served as the focus of much of Momaday's writing.

After attending the University of New Mexico, Momaday received a Ph.D. in American literature from Stanford University in 1963 and embarked on a distinguished career as a professor and writer. In 1969, he was awarded a Pulitzer Prize for his novel *House Made of Dawn* (1968). His other publications include an autobiography, *The Names: A Memoir* (1976); a book of poetry, *The Gourd Dancer* (1976), illustrated with Momaday's own sketches; and *Ancient Child* (1989).

Momaday's works have often explored the power of names and the stories that accompany them. Many twentieth century Indian writers have struggled to reconcile written literature with oral storytelling, but Momaday was one of the first Indian authors to express a concern with oral tradition and storytelling by experimenting with the structure of his prose. Momaday's disjointed narratives and his juxtaposition of prose, poetry, photographs, and sketches have exerted a powerful influence on many Indian authors.

See also American Indian studies programs and archives; Kiowa; Oral literatures.

Moneton: Tribe

CULTURE AREA: Northeast
LANGUAGE GROUP: Siouan
PRIMARY LOCATION: West Virginia

The Moneton, a branch of the Siouan family, lived in West Virginia. As is the case for many of the eastern Sioux, there is no information about the Moneton language. Evidence suggests they lived in matrilineal clans and that they conducted harsh initiation ceremonies. They wore long hair and tattoos—decorations which set them clearly apart from their Iroquoian neighbors. Probably the Sioux had been in what is now the southeastern United States for hundreds or even thousands of years before the first Europeans arrived. Scholars have struggled to learn about the prehistoric migrations of the Sioux, but without much success. What is clear from oral tradition and the records of early white settlers is that through the fifteenth, sixteenth, and seventeenth centuries the southeastern Sioux suffered greatly. Constant attack by Iroquoians and the introduction of new diseases by Europeans decimated the tribes. Many people fled and disappeared from record, while others were absorbed into other tribes; many died. In 1671, the Moneton were visited by the trader Thomas Batts. Three years later they were visited again by Gabriel Arthur, who reported finding them living in "a great town." They were not heard of again and are assumed to have united with Siouan groups in the Piedmont region of Virginia.

See also Siouan language family.

Money

TRIBES AFFECTED: Pantribal
SIGNIFICANCE: A variety of monetary systems were developed by American Indians for economic and ceremonial purposes; although these systems differed from European coinage systems, the two shared many features

Money can be defined as a medium of exchange that is used by common consent to pay for goods and services. Money has certain defining criteria: value (worth and desirability), standardization (which may be established by authority or custom), durability, portability, divisibility (it can be separated into parts), stability (its value is relatively constant), and cognizability (it is known or recognized). Barter, on the other hand, need only involve mutual consent involving an exchange between two parties. Money came into being when certain items became desirable and symbolized wealth.

By these criteria, Indians clearly had money, although coinage was entirely unknown. This money assumed many different forms and, unlike European systems of coinage and currency, was often intimately involved with myth and religion. Shells symbolized water (the Haida believed the first people came from a shell; to the Omaha shells embodied the Great Spirit). Shells also symbolized fecundity, birth, good luck, and health. Red ochre, traded by the Apaches and Mojaves, symbolized blood or earth's life substances. Stones were thought to resemble animals and had healing powers. Feathers represented the wind, soul, and rain. With the advent of trade with whites, money became more secularized, as tools, weapons, cloth, and blankets became valued exchange media. For several centuries sacred and secular monies existed side by side and sometimes were combined into a single medium.

In southern and central California, golden orange magnesite cylinder beads were most valued and white clam or snail shell discs less so. These materials were ground and shaped to a uniform size and appearance and polished on deerskin to give them a beautiful shine. At one time a necklace of 160 clam shell beads was worth about one dollar; as it circulated eastward, its value and desirability increased significantly. In contrast, an average two-inch-long piece of finished magnesite was worth about eight hundred clam shells. Woodpecker scalps, the shells of haliots, olivella, abalone, and dentalia, and obsidian blades also had monetary value. These monies were used for a variety of purposes, such as purchase of staples and goods, bride buying, "blood money" indemnification, atonement for religious trespass, and ornamental symbols of wealth and status.

Dentalium, a type of shell, was the exclusive medium on the Northwest Coast. For the Chinook, the *hiaqua* consisted of no more than twenty-five shells to the fathom (six feet). *Kop kop* consisted of smaller shells strung together with broken ones and shells of poorer quality and was used as small change. Dentalium eventually gave way to blankets, which were acquired from whites for beaver fur. The Tlingit used sea otter and caribou skins as money.

See also Blankets; Shells and shellwork; Trade; Wampum.

Montagnais: Tribe

CULTURE AREA: Northeast
LANGUAGE GROUP: Algonquian (Cree)
PRIMARY LOCATION: Labrador Peninsula, Newfoundland, Quebec provinces
POPULATION SIZE: 12,025 (combined Montagnais/Naskapi population, Statistics Canada, based on 1991 census)

The Montagnais have resided north of the St. Lawrence River on the Labrador Peninsula since before Europeans arrived in North America. Living to their southwest is a culturally and linguistically related but distinct group, the Attikamek, who were decimated by smallpox and Iroquois warriors late in the seventeenth century and seem to have been confused with the Tête de Boule until the 1970's, when the Attikamek name was revived concurrent with rising Attikamek political awareness. Both the Montagnais and Attikamek lived by hunting, trapping, and fishing prior to the Europeans' arrival as well as by fur trading afterward. Both were organized in bands loosely tied by marriage and proximity and, in the seventeenth century, by the Iroquois threat. The Labrador Peninsula had abundant game, and the residents were well adapted to it, moving seasonally with what the environment provided. They transported themselves and supplies in canoes during summer and by snowshoes and toboggans in winter. The basic traveling unit was a band of three to four families (fifteen to twenty people), typically led by older men with practical knowledge or religious charisma rather than by a formal or elected chief. Band membership could easily change if a need arose. One effect of the advent of trading posts in the region was an evolution toward bands associating with trading posts and defining band hunting territories. Marriages became opportunities for alliances between families with neighboring hunting territories.

European influences on the Montagnais and Attikamek were limited primarily to the fur trade until the mid-nineteenth century, when the area was invaded by loggers, and the early twentieth century, when there was railroad and dam construction. White hunters and trappers, combined with the construction projects, reduced fur-bearing animals and forced Montagnais into wage employment, which, along with local schools, interrupted seasonal migrations. World War II drew away the loggers, opening jobs for residents of the Weymontachingue reserve. The traditional conical lodges housing fifteen to twenty people were replaced with prefabricated houses. Montagnais religious practices have been influenced by Christianity but still include the shaking tent rite, various feasts, and ceremonial drumming. Religion is very personal, with some individuals gaining considerable power and becoming shamans—men or women with especially close relations with spirits and able to influence people's health or success in hunting. Despite the increasing presence of non-Indians, the Montagnais and the Attikamek retain their identity.

See also Algonquian language family; Cree; Naskapi.

Montauk Confederacy

TRIBES AFFECTED: Corchaug, Manhassett, Massapequa, Matinecock, Merric, Montauk, Nesaquake, Patchogue (Poospatuck), Rockaway, Secatogue, Setauket, Shinnecock, Unquachog
CULTURE AREA: Northeast
LANGUAGE GROUP: Algonquian
PRIMARY LOCATION: Central and eastern Long Island

The Montauk Confederacy was formed as a protective league against mainland tribes, primarily the Pequot and Narragansett. All of its member groups shared essentially the same culture patterns and language. Thus, they may have been loosely connected elements of one group or tribe. The Montauk were the most powerful and controlled the others. Montauk may mean "fortified place."

The Montauk subsisted on plant, land, and sea animals. Food cultivation required a complex and frequent pattern of seasonal shifting of residences, from the summer fields to the deep forests in the winter. A trade network linking regional and adjacent groups was also developed. Trading with Europeans began in the sixteenth century.

The tribes lived in villages of small circular houses holding two families during the temperate seasons. In winter they lived in large longhouses that held forty to fifty people. Villages were relocated when the supply of firewood was depleted.

Each village was presided over by a hereditary chief or sachem. Sachems had limited power and always made decisions in consultation with a council of "great men." Women also held respected positions. Quahawan, the sister of Nowedonah and Paygratasuck, Shinnecock and Manhassett sachems, became a Shinnecock sachem around 1667. The confederacy was presided over by the Montauk sachem, the grand sachem or great chief. Wyandanck (mid-seventeenth century), brother of the above three named sachems, was the most famous leader of the confederacy.

The confederacy population was about six thousand in 1600. Because of white diseases, alcoholism, and raids, numbers rapidly declined. Around 1788 most of the one hundred or so remaining members joined the Brotherton Indians in New York and moved with them to the Oneida reservation in Wisconsin about 1833. The handful of remaining Montauk and Shinnecock, the last representatives of the Long Island tribes, preserved tribal organization into the nineteenth century. Their last hereditary grand sachem, David Pharoah, died about 1875. The old customs and native language were lost soon thereafter.

Limited hunting, fishing, crop cultivation, and sale of craft items on the 400-acre Shinnecock reservation provided subsistence. Limited financial support from New York State and off-reservation low-wage jobs provided additional income. The encroachment of suburbia and tourists wanting to see "real Indians" rekindled an interest in traditional tribal customs and dress, self-respect, and group pride beginning in the 1900's. Renewed interest in tribal incorporation occurred in the 1930's. Intertribal associations, such as the Algonquin Council of Indian Tribes (1926), were formed. The Shinnecock are represented by an elected council in their dealings with New York State.

See also Algonquian language family; Northeast; Poospatuck; Shinnecock.

Monte Albán: Archaeological site
DATE: 500 B.C.E.-900 C.E.
LOCATION: Oaxaca, Mexico
CULTURE AFFECTED: Zapotec

Monte Albán, located on a hilltop in the Oaxaca Valley of southern Mexico, was the center of the Zapotec civilization for more than a thousand years. Founded around 500 B.C.E., it served as a focus of political and ceremonial activity from the Middle Preclassic (1000 to 500 B.C.E.) through the Early Postclassic (1000 to 1200 C.E.) periods of Mesoamerica.

Systematic excavations of the site began in 1931 and included eighteen field seasons under the direction of archaeologist Alfonso Caso. This work focused on the Main Plaza and included the reconstruction of major buildings, stratigraphic excavations, and the exploration of more than 170 tombs. In the 1970's, a detailed program of mapping and settlement pattern surveying directed by Richard Blanton provided additional information about the occupational sequence and changes in subsistence strategies over time.

The first phase of occupation at the site, Monte Albán I (500 to 200 B.C.E.), is represented by more than three hundred relief carvings on irregular stone panels known as Danzantes ("dancers"). These depict naked individuals in states of disarray, many of whom have been clearly wounded, mutilated, or killed. Carved for public display, they bear some of the earliest known hieroglyphic inscriptions in Mesoamerica, which refer to the names and affiliations of individuals. The Danzantes have been interpreted as a sort of war memorial, and archaeologist Richard Blanton has suggested that Monte Albán was founded as a "disembedded capital" built on neutral territory for the purpose of providing centralized political control of Oaxaca Valley populations. That Monte Albán continued military engagements, expanding beyond the Valley of Oaxaca during Monte Albán II (200 B.C.E. to 200 C.E.), is indicated by "conquest slabs" that document the defeat of various communities and the construction of defensive walls.

During the Classic Period, or Monte Albán III (200 to 700 C.E.), the center reached a maximum size of twenty-five thousand to thirty thousand people. Populations were concentrated on artificial terraces constructed on hillslopes around the ceremonial core. Farming of alluvial bottomlands was augmented by the construction of irrigation systems for farming in the piedmont zone. The ritual precinct received its current layout, consisting of a series of stepped masonry palaces and stone-faced pyramids surrounding a rectangular, north-south plaza.

Sculptures at the site attest a variety of ceremonial activities, including contacts with the distant but contemporaneous city of Teotihuacán. Among the most spectacular artifacts of Classic Monte Albán are elaborate ceramic *incensarios*, or funeral urns. These were large vessels on which cut slabs of clay were used to re-create masked costumes of a variety of deities, including Cocijo, the Zapotec god of storms and rain.

The decline of Monte Albán as a demographic and political center occurs after 700, possibly as a result of the collapse of Teotihuacán and consequent ruptures of economic and ceremonial networks. Activities at the hilltop site gradually ceased as rival polities in the Oaxaca Valley sought to extend their power through marriage ties and military engagements. The site continued to be revered as a sacred location, however, and in the Early Postclassic period several Classic period tombs were reused by Mixtec nobility. Among these was Tomb 7, which yielded to archaeologists Mexico's richest assemblage of gold ornaments and fine craft items. These included gold ear spools, rings, armbands, and pendants, necklaces of gold and shell beads, delicately carved jaguar bones, translucent stone bowls, and objects of jade, turquoise, rock crystal, and other precious minerals.

See also Mitla; Mixtec; Teotihuacán; Zapotec.

Montezuma, Carlos (c. 1867, Superstition Mountains of central Ariz.—Jan. 31, 1923, Fort McDowell Reservation, Ariz.): Physician, activist

ALSO KNOWN AS: Wassaja (Signaling or Beckoning)

TRIBAL AFFILIATION: Yavapai

SIGNIFICANCE: Montezuma was one of the first American Indians to earn a physician's degree and practice European American medicine on reservations

In the mid-1860's, Carlos Montezuma was born to Yavapai parents in central or southern Arizona. He received the name "Wassaja," meaning "signaling" or "beckoning." Wassaja's childhood was far from peaceful, as during that decade European Americans were mining and settling the area and indigenous peoples were maintaining warfare with one another. In 1871, Pimas attacked the Yavapai and abducted Wassaja to Mexico. He never saw his natural parents again, but a photographer named Carlos Gentile purchased the boy out of pity. Gentile had the boy christened "Carlos Montezuma" and took him to Chicago.

After schooling in Chicago and Galesburg, Illinois, and a brief stay in Brooklyn, Montezuma found himself back in Urbana, Illinois, as the ward of a Baptist minister, William Steadman. Under such tutelage he prepared for college, matriculated at the University of Illinois, and earned a degree in chemistry. After a brief period of uncertainty, Montezuma enrolled at the Chicago Medical College. By 1889, he had completed his medical training.

Even before finishing his training, Montezuma was in touch with Captain Richard Henry Pratt, the head of the assimilationist Carlisle Indian School. Pratt immediately took an interest in Carlos as living proof of the value of "civilizing" the Indians. Commissioner of Indian Affairs Thomas Jefferson Morgan did the same and in 1889 he appointed Montezuma as a clerk and physician at Fort Stevenson in the Dakota Territory. From there, Montezuma moved on to the Western Shoshone Agency in Nevada and the Colville Agency in Washington. At each place, however, his philosophy of Indian rights clashed with that of government agents, missionaries, and tribal shamans. By 1893, he was in Carlisle, Pennsylvania as the school's physician, a post he kept until 1896 when he ventured into private practice. Montezuma had a happier time at Carlisle, although he suffered a romantic spurning from the prominent Sioux woman Zitkala-Sa (Gertrude Simmons Bonnin).

Once outside the Indian Service, Montezuma began to devote his energies to political activism on behalf of indigenous causes. He helped create the Fort McDowell Yavapai (or Mojave-Apache) Reservation in 1903. By 1905, he was attracting attention as a national Indian leader. Suspicious of the assimilationist agenda of the Bureau of Indian Affairs, Montezuma joined with other like-minded indigenous intellectuals to form a loose front insisting on tribal peoples' control of their destiny. Although he was never completely at ease with the progressivist Society of American Indians that emerged in 1911, Montezuma moved in and out of the organization over the next four years or so. By 1915, however, his political views took him out of the progressivist camp. Convinced that the Bureau of Indian Affairs was a fraud that deprived indigenous people of land and livelihood, Carlos sharpened his attack on the agency, calling for its abolition and ridiculing those indigenous leaders who cooperated with it. To this end, he began publishing a newsletter, *Wassaja*, in 1916. Over the next seven years until his death, Montezuma crusaded for citizenship rights for Indians and economic protection of tribal people, especially in his native Arizona. His was not a call for a nativist resurrection of old tribal ways; instead, he sought political autonomy and the economic empowerment of his people in the context of modern America. When by 1918 the Society of American Indians was beginning to embrace his views, he rejoiced. His elation proved short-lived when the movement began to lose its clout nationally. Personal matters, such as his attempt to enroll as a San Carlos Apache (because some genealogical searching led him to believe his parents had ended up with that tribe), foundered as well.

By the summer of 1922, Montezuma's health had deteriorated significantly. He diagnosed his condition as tuberculosis and headed back to Arizona. There, shunning European American medicine, he lingered in a wickiup until his death on January 31, 1923. Several newspapers and indigenous leaders, as well as the Society of American Indians, eulogized him, but the memory of his passions faded quickly. Not until the late 1960's and early 1970's did scholars and indigenous leaders rediscover Carlos Montezuma and his earlier form of resistance to European American domination.

See also Bonnin, Gertrude Simmons; Medicine and modes of curing, post-contact; Yavapai.

Mopope, Stephen (Aug. 27, 1898, near Red Stone Baptist Mission, Kiowa Reservation, Okla. Territory—Feb. 3, 1974, Fort Cobb, Okla.): Artist

ALSO KNOWN AS: Qued Koi (Painted Robe)

TRIBAL AFFILIATION: Kiowa

SIGNIFICANCE: Mopope was one of the Kiowa Five artists who helped to define and establish the Oklahoma style of Native American painting in the 1930's

Mopope was the son of a distinguished Kiowa family. He was a painter most of his life, though he also worked as a farmer. Two granduncles, Haungooah (Silverhorn) and Hakok, taught him as a youth to paint on tanned skins in the traditional way. He was an expert performer of traditional dances and songs, and later in life built his own dance ground to sponsor dances.

Mopope drew from that background to paint portraits, traditional costumes, and dances. He frequently portrayed dancers doing the same steps that he himself danced. He painted or participated in the making of murals for a number of public buildings, including the chapel of St. Patrick's Mission School in Anadarko, Oklahoma; the University of Oklahoma (with Monroe Tsatoke); Southwestern State University (Oklahoma); U.S. Navy Hospital in Carville, Louisiana; the Federal Buildings in Anadarko and Muskogee, Oklahoma; First National Bank of Anadarko; Fort Sill Indian School; and Northeastern State University (Oklahoma). His work is in the collections of the National Museum of the American Indian, University of Oklahoma Museum of Art, Oklahoma Historical Society Museum, and others.

See also Art and artists, contemporary; Asah, Spencer; Auchiah, James; Hokeah, Jack; Paints and painting; Tsatoke, Monroe.

Morning Star Ceremony

TRIBE AFFECTED: Pawnee

SIGNIFICANCE: The Morning Star Ceremony, a sacred Pawnee ritual, was intended to ensure the abundance of corn and buffalo

The Morning Star Ceremony was one of the most sacred Pawnee rituals. Its central act was the raiding of another village, the capture of a young girl, and her sacrifice at the rising of the Morning Star (Mars or Venus). Tied to a wooden scaffold, she was killed by an arrow through the heart. Her blood was included in a burnt offering of buffalo meat. The many songs sung during the ceremony indicate its purpose was to ensure the growth and abundance of corn and buffalo. The Skidi Pawnee of the central Plains were the last group to practice this ritual.

For the Pawnee, the Morning Star (a young warrior) and the Evening Star (a young woman) were the parents of a daughter who was the mother of the first humans (the son of the Sun and Moon was the father). The stars entrusted humans with sacred bundles that became the focus of Pawnee ceremonies.

The ceremony itself was orchestrated by the caretaker of the Morning Star bundle. It began when a young warrior underwent purification rituals and prepared special materials. He was equipped with objects from the bundle, including an otter-fur collar, a hawk, an ear of corn, and a sacred pipe. After observing the rising of the Morning Star, he undertook the raid and brought back an adolescent girl to sacrifice. Preparations included the procurement of buffalo meat. The sacrifice commenced with sacred songs and dances extending over four days. During this time, the victim was treated well and instructed to eat with a special horn spoon and bowl. She was then dressed in ritual clothing and fixed to a scaffold made of several different kinds of wood. After her death, male members of the village (including children) shot arrows into her body as part of their contributions to the ritual.

See also Pawnee; Petalésharo.

Mosaic and inlay

TRIBES AFFECTED: Aztec, Carib, Chichimec, Maya, Mixtec, Navajo, Olmec, Pueblo, Tlingit, Zapotec, Zuni

SIGNIFICANCE: Mosaic and inlay were used for decorative purposes by Indians prior to European contact and continue to be used by modern Indians

Mosaic is an art form using small pieces of stone, glass, tile, or other materials such as feathers and straw to form a decorative design or picture. Used for such things as masks, jewelry, and architecture, mosaic art was common among the Indians of Mesoamerica, the Southwest, and the Northwest.

In Mesoamerica, mosaic and inlay were used by the Maya Indians for funeral masks—small pieces of turquoise, jade, red and white shells, and mother-of-pearl were glued to a wooden base and buried with the deceased. The Mixtec Indians made ceremonial shields by covering a ceramic base with cut and polished turquoise stones. They also covered the interior and exterior of buildings with precisely patterned tiled mosaics. The Zapotec Indians decorated their cultural center with stone mosaics in zigzag patterns. The Aztecs made feathered mosaic shields for their commanders and chiefs. Ceilings, floors, walls, pavements, and walkways were often covered with tiled mosaics. Some exterior walls had patterns inlaid on them using cut stones that were cemented in the walls like bricks.

In North America, the Tlingit Indians of the Northwest made headdress frontlets and hats carved out of cedar and inlaid with abalone shells. In the Southwest, the ancient Anasazi were known to have made turquoise mosaic pendants. The Pueblo and Zuni made jewelry and pendants with colored shell mosaics. After the Spanish conquest, the Pueblo made crosses with inlays. The Navajo are known for making silver and turquoise jewelry, such as the squash blossom necklaces, bracelets, and small silver boxes, using turquoise stones inlaid in polished silver forms. Twentieth century Zuni jewelry uses mosaic patterns of stones and shells in turquoise and white, red and black.

Turquoise was the most commonly used stone in mosaic design and inlay in the Southwest and Mesoamerica because of its availability and also because of its mystical association with both the sky and water. In the Northwest region, abalone shell was most commonly used for inlay.

See also Feathers and featherwork; Metalwork; Shells and shellwork; Turquoise.

Moses (c. 1829, Wenatchee Flat, central Wash.—Mar. 25, 1899, near Wilbur, Wash.): Chief

ALSO KNOWN AS: Quelatikan (The Blue Horn)

TRIBAL AFFILIATION: Kowachinook

SIGNIFICANCE: A tribal leader and diplomat, Moses was associated with a number of chiefs of the Northwest, including Chief Joseph and Kamiakin, and he provided counsel during the wars of the 1850's

Chief Moses, a member of the Kowachinooks, eventually claimed to be a spokesperson for numerous upper Columbia River groups, particularly the Yakimas, Spokanes, Kowachinooks, Methows, and Okanagans. Quelatikan acquired the biblical name Moses while attending the Spaulding mission school at Lapwai but never became a Christian. It was here that he met and became a lifelong friend of Chief Joseph, the famous Nez Perce warrior. Moses is best known for his leadership and counsel during the wars between Indians and whites in eastern Washington from 1855 to 1858, a time when he was closely associated with Owhi, Kamiakin, and Qualchien, local chiefs who had opposed Colonel George Wright's efforts to force Indians onto local reservations.

After Chief Moses refused to settle on the Yakima Reservation, the Moses-Columbia Reservation was established on April 19, 1879, but on July 7, 1884, the so-called Moses Agreement was ratified in which Moses gave up claim to the area and eventually settled on the Colville Reservation in 1884. Moses was described as a proud, handsome, and physically imposing man, with great intelligence and judgment, who was opposed to war and enjoyed gambling. He died from Bright's disease on March 25, 1899.

Mother Earth

The original people of the Americas viewed Mother Earth as the source of all life. This personification of the regenerative and provident attributes of nature has its roots in animism.

Animists believe that all things are alive and related. Everything that exists is further defined by its relationship to all other things. In many mythopoeic oral traditions throughout the Americas, all things receive their life from the earth itself. Plant and animal life as well as the elements and forces of nature are the source of human life. Human beings are seen as the spiritual guardians and stewards of the natural world. They are the children of Mother Earth and must treat her in ways that show respect and honor.

Numerous ceremonial and ritual means can be used to address Mother Earth—such as the sweatlodge ceremony and prayer—in order to ensure her continued beneficence. It is thought that when people cease to use such means to express their respect and gratitude for her blessings all life will be destroyed and human life on this planet will come to an end.

The spiritual traditions which have their roots in the natural world see all things as part of the sacred web of life. Spiritualism is seen as the highest form of political consciousness. Those who honor Mother Earth live in accordance with traditions that sustain life. Traditional native peoples and their belief in Mother Earth are seen as the primary sources of knowledge that can reverse the destructive materialistic worldview and processes of Western civilization.

See also Ethnophilosophy and worldview; Religion; Sacred, the; Sacred narratives.

Mounds and mound builders

TRIBES AFFECTED: Northeast and Southeast tribes (prehistoric and historic)

SIGNIFICANCE: Various groups of American Indians built earthen mounds at different time periods in different loca-

tions, which served different cultural functions; the American Indian construction of these mounds was not fully accepted until 1894

Earthen mounds are located in the eastern United States from the Gulf of Mexico to the Great Lakes, with concentrations in the Midwest along the Ohio and Mississippi River drainages. These mounds were constructed by a number of different Native American groups during several different time periods, and they were used for a range of functions. In some cases, Indians built conical mounds to inter their dead, while in other locations or time periods, they constructed flat-topped pyramidal mounds to serve as the foundations for important buildings such as temples or chiefly residences. Some of the better-known mound sites are Cahokia, near St. Louis, Missouri (with a florescence between 1050-1250 C.E.), Moundville, Alabama (a dominant center from 1250 to 1500 C.E.), and those associated with the Hopewell culture (circa 200 B.C.E.-400 C.E.), centered in the Ohio Valley.

When these mounds were first noted by Europeans in the late eighteenth century, they stimulated acrimonious debate concerning their origins, namely whether Indians, their ancestors, or others had constructed them. These arguments continued unabated until Cyrus Thomas' *Report on the Mound Explorations of the Bureau of Ethnology* (1894), which demonstrated that Native Americans had built the mounds.

There are several underlying factors that explain why it took scholars so many years to accept the aboriginal origins of the moundbuilders. First, the dispute originated during the early colonial period, when settlers' understanding of Native American culture was based on their interactions with socially disrupted Indian groups no longer continuing all of their pre-Columbian activities. Second, based on these data, and on racist beliefs concerning Native Americans, it seemed unlikely to them that the Indian ancestors of these groups would have possessed the technological skills to construct the mounds. In addition, in some instances, Native American land rights could be denied if it could be demonstrated that earlier, more "civilized" people had once inhabited the area. European Americans also may have desired to construct a heroic past for members of their own cultures, which may explain the proliferation of hypotheses proposing that various early European groups built the earthen monuments. For example, in 1787, it was suggested that the Ohio mound builders were Danes, while an 1812 work opted for the Welsh. Caleb Atwater's article "Description of the Antiquities Discovered in the State of Ohio and Other Western States" (1820) went so far as to propose Hindu builders. Others, such as E. G. Squier and E. H. Davis, in their *Ancient Monuments of the Mississippi Valley* (1848), favored Mayan or Aztec construction, believing them to be of a different, more evolved "race" from the local Indians.

Granted, there were a few dissenters from the prevailing views of the time, but these dissenting voices did not affect general public opinion. By the 1880's, the United States Congress became involved in the controversy, and it provided funds to the Smithsonian Bureau of Ethnology, directed by

A mound in Charleston, West Virginia, built by people of the prehistoric Adena culture. (McCrea Adams)

Major John Wesley Powell, to investigate the mounds. Powell appointed Cyrus Thomas to lead the Division of Mound Exploration. With the publication of Thomas' 1894 report, the "mound builders controversy" was effectively quelled, and a Native American origin for these constructions was accepted.

See also Adena; Effigy mounds; Etowah; Hopewell; Moundville; Serpent mounds; Southern Cult; Spiro; Timucua.

Moundville: Archaeological site

DATE: 1000-1350
LOCATION: Alabama
CULTURES AFFECTED: Mississippian, Creek (Muskogee)
The site of Moundville was one of the most important political and ceremonial centers of the Mississippian tradition, which flourished in the southeastern United States after 1200 C.E. It is the second-largest site of this period after Cahokia (Illinois). Situated on a bluff above the Black Warrior River in Alabama, Moundville is marked by a large number of ramped, pyramidal platform mounds arranged around a central plaza. At one time, these earth-fill mounds were bases for perishable superstructures that served as temples and elite residences.

Excavations at the site were first undertaken by Clarence B. Moore in 1905-1906. Further research was conducted from 1929 to 1941 by staff of the Alabama Museum of Natural History. This early work has been augmented by more recent investigations under the direction of archaeologist Christopher Peebles. Altogether, fieldwork has documented more than seventy-five structures, some three thousand burials, and more than one million artifacts.

Although the earliest occupation of the site dates to 1050 C.E., when the first large mound was built, the principal occupation occurred after 1300. Moundville's florescence took place when Cahokia was in decline, suggesting a shift in political and ceremonial alliances. At its height, the site covered an area of more than 370 acres and is estimated to have had a population of around three thousand. Its central core consisted of a 75-acre plaza with twenty large platform mounds. The two largest mounds were located along the plaza's north-south axis, one on the side nearest the river and the other near the plaza center. The eighteen remaining mounds were arranged around the plaza periphery, roughly arranged in groups of two. These mound pairs consist of a larger and a smaller platform, the latter of which usually contained burials. These may represent platforms for elite residences and accompanying mortuary temples, each pair representing a single kinship group. Other structures near the plaza include a group of elite residences to the northwest, charnel houses, and sweat houses.

Society at Moundville was highly ranked, as evidenced by both settlement patterns and grave goods. Commoners lived in dwellings that decreased in size with distance from the plaza. High-status burials, always located within mounds, included rare and valuable artifacts such as copper axes and objects of engraved shell. Large quantities of shell beads were also included. Lower-status burials have also been found within mounds, but the majority occurred away from the ceremonial core. These contained small quantities of simple ceramic vessels.

The elite at Moundville were able to subsidize and support activities such as craft specialization. Ceramic workshops had large hearths and caches of shell. Shellworking areas had concentrations of shell beads, unworked shell, and tools for making beadwork. A possible leather workshop is indicated by hundreds of bone awls and sharpening stones.

Moundville, together with Etowah (Georgia) and Spiro (Oklahoma), was one of the centers of a phenomenon known as the Southern Cult, also known as the Southeastern Ceremonial Complex. It was characterized by the widespread appearance of distinctive artifacts and art styles, such as embossed copper plates, engraved shell gorgets and cups, copper axes, and polished stone axes at sites from Mississippi to Minnesota and as far west as Oklahoma. Motifs of the Southern Cult include a variety of esoteric designs, including representations of snakes, hands with eyes in the palm, sunbursts, weeping eyes, and warriors holding axes and severed human heads. Among the best known Southern Cult items are ceramic vessels in the forms of trophy heads, often with closed eyes and mouths that have been sewn shut. These have been attributed to an increase in ritual warfare, possibly linked to influence from Mesoamerican cultures. The fact that Southern Cult items have a very wide geographical distribution indicates the presence of extensive long-distance trade networks, most likely managed by members of a wealthy class of elite individuals.

The occupation of Moundville and other sites of late Mississippian culture may have persisted until the sixteenth century, when European expeditions brought epidemic diseases that decimated indigenous population centers. The Creek Indians, who were living in villages with temple mounds and central plazas when encountered by Hernando de Soto in the 1540's, may be descendants of these prehistoric peoples.

See also Mississippian; Mounds and mound builders; Prehistory—Southeast; Southern Cult; Spiro.

Mountain: Tribe

CULTURE AREA: Subarctic
LANGUAGE GROUP: Northeastern Athapaskan
PRIMARY LOCATION: Mackenzie Mountains, Northwest Territories, Canada

The Mountain Indians, commonly associated with the Goat Indians, lived in semi-permanent winter camps in the mountains. They depended on hunting moose, Dall sheep, woodland caribou—and trapping of ground squirrels—for subsistence and utilitarian by-products. Some fishing was done.

Mooseskin boats were essential to river travel and trading, particularly after European Canadian contact. As a composite band, Mountain people had much knowledge of their terrain and good mobility. They sometimes faced starvation, which reduced their number, as did internal feuds and hostilities with the Yukon peoples.

Canadian trappers and traders knew of the Mountain Indians as early as 1789, but it was not until 1822 that they interacted with them. The building of Fort Simpson in 1822, and Fort Norman in 1823, brought sustained European contact and trading with many Mountain Indians. The introduction of influenza and measles reduced their population. The signing of Treaty 11 in 1921 created a chief and council who represented their people at Fort Norman. Today most Mountain employment is local, with some involvement in Canadian government programs. The Mountain population has been estimated to be between 100 and 150.

See also Athapaskan language family.

Mountain Wolf Woman (April, 1884, East Fork River, Wis.—Nov. 9, 1960, Black River Falls, Wis.): Autobiographer

ALSO KNOWN AS: Xehaciwinga, Haksigaxunuminka (Little Fifth Daughter)
TRIBAL AFFILIATION: Winnebago
SIGNIFICANCE: Mountain Wolf Woman's autobiography is a unique account of adaptation of traditional Winnebago lifeways to modern conditions

In 1958, Mountain Wolf Woman spoke into a tape recorder in the presence of her adopted kinswoman, Nancy Oestreich Lurie, who then edited a translation from Winnebago into English to produce Mountain Wolf Woman's autobiography, *Mountain Wolf Woman, Sister of Crashing Thunder* (1961). The youngest of seven children, Mountain Wolf Woman was a member of an extraordinary Winnebago family: She was younger sister of Crashing Thunder (Sam Blowsnake), who worked with anthropologist Paul Radin, supplying Radin with most of the material for the myth cycle called The Trickster (1956), Sam Blowsnake's autobiography *Crashing Thunder* (1926), and the ethnology *The Winnebago Tribe* (1923). Mountain Wolf Woman's life involved her own education in traditional Winnebago culture and her work in preserving and passing on that culture to her descendants. Mountain Wolf Woman was married twice, the first time reluctantly to a husband chosen by her brother, and later to a man named Bad Soldier. She had eleven children and was the caregiver for many of her grandchildren and great-grandchildren. Mountain Wolf Woman embraced three major religious traditions in her life, weaving into an integrated philosophy Winnebago traditional beliefs and practices, Christian theology, and the peyote rituals of the Native American Church.

See also Crashing Thunder; Native American Church; Winnebago.

Mourning Dove (c. 1885, near Bonner's Ferry, Idaho—Aug. 8, 1936, Medical Lake, Wash.): Writer

ALSO KNOWN AS: Humishuma, Christine or Cristal Quintas-ket, Mrs. Fred Galler

TRIBAL AFFILIATION: Okanagan

SIGNIFICANCE: Mourning Dove's *Cogewea* was one of the first novels by an American Indian to be published in the United States

Mourning Dove was one of the first American Indian writers to publish a novel. *Co-Ge-We-A, The Half-Blood: A Depiction of the Great Montana Cattle Range* appeared in 1927. Mourning Dove's novel was extensively edited by her mentor, friend, and agent, Lucullus Virgil McWhorter, who believed that the text provided a good platform to protest the mistreatment suffered by Indians; however, the essential story, which draws upon the romance novel and western genres in order to offer a realistic view of the Montana frontier, is substantially Mourning Dove's work.

Mourning Dove's love for Okanagan culture derived from the education in tradition she received from an elder who lived with the family when she was a young girl. Mourning Dove continued her study of Okanagan traditions as an adult and compiled a collection of tales which was first published under the title *Coyote Stories* (1933); it had been heavily edited, however, by Heister Dean Guie, who omitted important material and rewrote the text to address a juvenile audience.

Mourning Dove left many unpublished manuscripts when she died, and two works have been published posthumously. The collection of traditional tales was reedited by Donald M. Hines as *Tales of the Okanogans* (1976); this edition is more complete and closer to Mourning Dove's own lively style. *Mourning Dove: A Salishan Autobiography* (1990) was edited by Jay Miller from various unpublished manuscripts.

See also Okanagan.

Muckleshoot: Tribe

CULTURE AREA: Northwest Coast

LANGUAGE GROUP: Salishan

PRIMARY LOCATION: White and Green rivers, Washington

POPULATION SIZE: 985 (1990 U.S. Census)

The Muckleshoot comprised four separate territorial groups: Sekamish, Skopamish, Smulkamis, and Dothliuk. They had complex ceremonialism, part of which regulated their yearly pattern of moving to obtain subsistence, which was basically maritime and riverine in orientation. They had guardian-spirit beliefs and used shamans for curing, making predictions, and maintaining social control. Decisions were by group consensus and advice of elders.

The Muckleshoot Reservation was established in 1857 by executive order after a 1855-1856 war, but many did not move to the reservation. In the early 1880's the Indian Shaker Church was established as a reaction against the U.S. government's "peace policy" of 1869, which had favored Roman Catholic missionaries among the Muckleshoot.

Today the Muckleshoot have established their own business enterprises, planning department, tribal government, and school system on the reservation. In the late 1970's the Muckle-shoot sued for damages created by diversion of water from the reservation and its fishery by a hydroelectric plant. There exist several reservation programs for revitalizing myth, art, and language.

See also Northwest Coast; Salishan language family.

Multnomah: Tribe

CULTURE AREA: Northwest Coast

LANGUAGE GROUP: Chinookan

PRIMARY LOCATION: Sauvie Island and Columbia River, Oregon

The Multnomah, living in a densely populated stretch of riverside villages, were composed of ten separate territorial bands, situated between the Clackamas to the south and the Cathlamet to the north. Their stratified society was based on ocean and river harvesting as well as hunting and trapping on land. They had well-developed trading relations within the region. Chinookan jargon was a lingua franca (trade language) on the Northwest Coast and along the Columbia River.

The first European American contact was probably by John Boit and Robert Gray in 1792, but by the time of first contact, the Multnomah population had already been drastically reduced by epidemics, particularly smallpox. Population reduction and the effects of trade created demographic changes for the Multnomah and other groups, causing the merging of certain groups. Some Multnomah lived on the Grand Ronde Reservation along with the Clackamas, and some lived off-reservation in the Willamette Valley.

See also Northwest Coast.

Murie, James (1862, Grand Island, present-day Nebr.—1921): Ethnographer

TRIBAL AFFILIATION: Skidi Pawnee

SIGNIFICANCE: Murie collaborated with anthropologists and later wrote his own anthropological works about the Pawnee

James Murie, a Skidi Pawnee of mixed blood, was born in Nebraska in 1862. At that time, Nebraska was still a scene of Pawnee struggle with their traditional enemies, the Sioux. As a youth, Murie was among the first Native Americans to attend Hampton Institute in Virginia. Originally founded to encourage secondary education for blacks, the institute had only recently been opened to Native Americans.

Murie's advanced training was gained not in school but by association with professional anthropologists who were interested in Pawnee traditions but lacked language training to do field work without a native intermediary. Murie's situation paralleled that of other Native Americans, such as George Hunt (a Kwakiutl), who worked with Franz Boas; George Bushotter (a Sioux), who collaborated with James O. Dorsey; and Cleaver Warden (Arapaho), who, like Murie, worked with George A. Dorsey.

Murie's earliest contribution to anthropological studies was near the beginning of the twentieth century, when he served as an informant to Alice C. Fletcher, who wrote the first major works on the Pawnees, including, in 1904, a detailed description of their unique Hako Ceremony.

Thereafter, Murie became more involved in noting down firsthand data, including ceremonial texts, either on his own or working with other anthropologists. The first product of his collaborative ventures was a typescript entitled, "The Pawnee: Society and Religion of the Skidi Pawnee," written jointly with George A. Dorsey between 1905 and 1907. By this date, Murie and Dorsey had begun a project that was unique for its time. They recorded the autobiography of an elderly Skidi priest on wax cylinders. These were transcribed and translated by Murie and served as a basis for the first systematic study of phonemic distinctions in Pawnee.

When he died in 1921, Murie's name as sole author had appeared on one original work only—three volumes of transcribed Pawnee mythology. After 1912, however, he had written (during a period in which he collaborated with anthropologist Clark Wissler, working at the same time for the U.S. Bureau of American Ethnology) a major monograph entitled *Ceremonies of the Pawnee*. This would be published posthumously by the Smithsonian Institution.

See also Pawnee.

Musgrove, Mary (c. 1700, Coweta, Ala.—c. 1763, St. Catharine's Island, Ga.): Interpreter, trader, political leader

ALSO KNOWN AS: Consaponaheeso, Coosaponakeesa, Creek Mary, Mary Bosomworth

TRIBAL AFFILIATION: Creek

SIGNIFICANCE: Mary Musgrove was instrumental in the founding and development of the colony of Georgia

Mary Musgrove was born in 1700. She was a member of what was known as the Creek Confederacy. Her Creek name was Consaponaheeso, and she was given the significant title of "Beloved Woman" by her people. She was an active leader in the matrifocal spheres that influenced the politics in the traditional Creek society of her day. Her exploits included a march on Savannah over a Creek land dispute, which was a precursor to the "Red Stick Revolt." Her political prowess distinguished her as a "chief" by the Europeans who had to deal with her; they also bestowed on her the name of "Creek Mary" in admiration.

It is often said that Mary had a mistrust of whites because of her Creek nationalism. This apparently did not prevent her from marrying three white men. Her first husband was John Musgrove, Jr., the son of a key British military commander in the Carolinas during the eighteenth century. The two had children while operating a trading post on Yamacraf Bluff in Georgia, but they moved to South Carolina to live near his father. After his death, her second marriage was to another Englishman, Jacob Matthews, but it was short-lived. In 1749, she was married for the third and last time, to the Reverend Thomas Bosomworth, a minister of the Church of England. He was also the chaplain to General James Edward Oglethorpe's Highland Regiment, whose later military reign involved the expropriation of Creek lands in Georgia for the Crown of England. Bosomworth played an active role in assisting his general in obtaining Creek lands. The minister also transferred real estate to himself instead of the Crown.

As Carolyn Thomas Foreman implies in her treatise on Mary Musgrove, she was in a strategic position between her tribespeople, her husband's private interests, and Oglethorpe's competing claims. The plan fell through when Creek leaders denounced the enterprise and Mary and her spouse's duplicitous natures. The enterprising couple were jailed, a situation which did not deter either one from continuing to expropriate Creek lands for the British Crown. On the other hand, it has also been written that she was an advocate for the early "pan-Indianism," an intertribal movement that was espoused by the Shawnee leader Tecumseh and his brother Tenskwatawa, the Prophet.

She was a complex individual with a dual nature, one who engaged in what others have referred to as "sexual politics" through her interracial marital liaisons. It has been asked whether she was a heroine or a pawn, a patriot or a traitor to her Creek Nation. It is most likely that she was a player in the politics of this period, which saw the development of American colonialism at the expense of her Creek homeland. Mary Musgrove has emerged in the historical literature as a symbol of Creek patriotism, despite her marital commitments. She was in the forefront of Creek resistance to European conquest and colonization, and she was an extraordinary role model to many native liberationists.   —*M. A. Jaimes*

See also Creek; Indian-white relations—English colonial.

BIBLIOGRAPHY

Brown, Dee. *Creek Mary's Blood*. New York: Holt, Rinehart and Winston, 1980.

Churchill, Ward. "The Historical Novel and *Creek Mary's Blood*." *Journal of Ethnic Studies* 12, no. 3 (Fall, 1984): 119-128.

Foreman, Carolyn Thomas. *Indian Women Chiefs*. 1954. Reprint. Muskogee, Okla.: Hoffman Printing, 1966.

Green, Michael D. *The Politics of Indian Removal: Creek Government and Society in Crisis*. Lincoln: University of Nebraska Press, 1982.

Holm, Tom. "Indian Removal and Creek Government." *Journal of Ethnic Studies* 12, no. 3 (Fall, 1984): 129-130.

Martin, Joel W. *Sacred Revolt: The Muskogees' Struggle for a New World*. Boston: Beacon Press, 1991.

Music and song

TRIBES AFFECTED: Pantribal

SIGNIFICANCE: Music has always played an important role in American Indian culture; singing, in particular, is essential in many ceremonies, including religious rituals, as well as at social gatherings

When Europeans first encountered the natives of North America, they found a culture vastly different from their own. Because this culture was considered "primitive" and was thus branded inferior, there was little attempt to understand the culture of the "savages" at first. American Indian music was often described as atonal chanting, and it was assumed that Indian songs, like other aspects of their culture, were less advanced than those of the Europeans. This attitude persisted well into the twentieth century. Late in the twentieth century, as American Indians began the attempt to reclaim their cultural heritage and scholars began taking this culture seriously, it was found that American Indian music, song, and dance were complex; moreover, they varied greatly among the assorted cultures of North America.

Indian Concept of Music. One of the major reasons that early settlers and explorers found American Indian music so difficult to comprehend was that the Indians had a completely different concept of music in general, and singing in particular. The Indians use songs for specific purposes, often of a religious nature. There are songs to appease the spirits, songs for success in hunting and fishing, songs in preparation for war, and songs celebrating victory in war. There are also personal songs composed by individuals who have had visions.

Indian cultures have never codified music as European cultures have. Undoubtedly, musical styles changed over the centuries before the Europeans' arrival, but modern researchers are at a loss to trace prehistoric developments of this sort, as none of the American tribes developed written languages or a system of describing specific tunes in a permanent manner.

Possibly the most essential difference between the European and American Indian cultures when it comes to music is that, in Indian cultures, virtually everyone may participate in music and singing. There is no group of professional composers or performers. In this sense, all Indian music is folk music. There has never been a difference between popular or folk songs, religious music, and "serious" music, as there has been in Europe and in the cultures the Europeans brought to North America.

The Indian Scale. As a general rule, Indian singing is accompanied only by percussion instruments or is unaccompanied. For this reason, a song does not have to be "in tune" in the sense that a specific scale must be used at all times. A common scheme is a steady fall in pitch during the song, though this is far from universal. (Some tribes play flutelike instruments made of hollowed wood or reeds, but these have a very limited range in pitch and are not used to accompany songs.) The result of this situation is that many Indian songs sound discordant to people used to European musical traditions. A song may not even come close to the harmonic patterns to which white cultures are accustomed. It is therefore impossible to play American Indian music on an instrument that is limited to the twelve-tone chromatic scale that has played an essential role in European music at least since the time of the ancient Greeks. It is also impossible to use standard musical notation to record tunes accurately.

Religious Songs. To the American Indian, all music has a strong supernatural element. This aspect can also be found in Christian cultures; hymns are an important part of church services, for example, and there is considerable popular music based on religious themes. Yet this element is far more essential to American Indian songs. Music is considered a gift of the gods and is vital to almost all religious ceremonies. The songs involved are not hymns as such; rather, they are specific to a particular spirit or aspect of nature.

One very common type of religious song is essentially a prayer. Many songs in many tribes are named after animals and are intended to appease the spirit controlling the animal, thus giving the hunter or fisherman a greater chance of subduing his prey. The Inuits (Eskimos), for example, are greatly dependent on the sea for their survival. In their boats, they sing specific songs for whales, seals, fish, and other potential food sources. The Plains Indians have songs for buffalo, deer, and other game.

Another type of religious singing is the chanting of spells to cure disease. An Indian with a serious disease is often considered to be possessed by an evil spirit, and the proper chant may drive out this spirit. When other remedies, especially herbal treatments, are used, the songs still play a vital role. The herbs must be sung over to ensure their potency.

There are also songs to control the forces of nature. In arid areas, there are many songs to appease the rain spirits and cause much-needed rain. In areas subject to flooding, there are songs to appease the water gods and lessen the rain. There are songs to ensure crop fertility as well.

Finally, some religious songs are used as a celebration of religious events rather than as an invocation. These songs are usually of an individual nature, composed and sung by a person who has had a vision. These are personal songs, owned by the singers. The Navajo have a strong tradition in this regard. Personal songs are considered a form of wealth.

Secular Songs. American Indians have never separated the religious and secular sides of life to any great extent. Most modern Christians, Jews, and Moslems worship once a week, and may say prayers at other special times. During the rest of the week, they work in secular occupations that have no relation to their worship.

In American Indian cultures, the case is vastly different. Everything on earth is controlled by spirits, and every facet of life has a religious aspect. For this reason, there is really no way of speaking of secular songs in a strict sense of the term. Not all songs are related to specific religious rituals, however, and spirits may not be mentioned in them at all. There are, of course, love songs, sometimes related to courting rituals but often made up simply to express affection. In essence, they are not much different from the love songs that are sung in European cultures. There are also lullabies to put children to sleep and children's songs for pure entertainment.

An unusual aspect of some Indian songs is the use of nonsense syllables (vocables). Often these meaningless syllables are inserted into a song to fill out a necessary rhythm, but sometimes entire songs have no concrete meaning whatsoever. It is difficult to explain this, except that it is not limited to American Indian cultures. From the "tra-la-las" of traditional European songs to the "doo-wahs" of 1950's rock and roll

Singers and drummers at a pow-wow in Springfield, Missouri. (Terry Barner, Unicorn Stock Photos)

songs, other cultures have often used this device. Its use in American Indian songs, however, may have a somewhat deeper meaning.

The very fact that not all Indian songs have literal meaning suggests that the act of singing is enjoyed for its own sake and is not always a prayer or a prelude to war or hunting. A comparison can be made to European culture's development of instrumental music unaccompanied by singing; a Beethoven sonata has no concrete meaning. American Indians have developed very little in the way of instrumental music, apart from percussion accompaniment to singing. The singing of nonsense songs may be an indication that music for music's sake is a universal enjoyment.

Song and Dance. A virtually universal aspect of American Indian song is its relationship to dance. With rare exceptions, songs are accompanied by body movements, often highly ritualized body movements specific to a particular song. One major reason for this is the close ties both singing and dancing have to religious rituals.

This is another great difference between the European and American Indian cultures. There was probably religious dancing at some time in ancient Europe, as it seems to be a nearly universal aspect of cultures around the world. Many centuries ago, however, dancing in Europe became strictly a social event, and most dancers did not sing at the same time. Among American Indians, dance still retains its religious aspect and is often accompanied by songs. Both the dance steps and the songs can be extremely complex and are often performed in elaborate sequences. There are dance/song cycles in many areas, especially among the Navajos and a number of Plains tribes. In some cases, hundreds of songs with their related dance steps must be sung in a specific sequence to fulfill a religious obligation.

Modern Changes. Like virtually all aspects of American Indian society, Indian songs have been somewhat altered by contact with white culture. The traditions are still very much in evidence, but in many cases they have lost their original significance. Many modern American Indians have adopted the Christian religion and no longer sing and dance to appease spirits. At important tribal ceremonies, there may be Christian hymns intermixed with ancient tribal songs.

It is difficult to assess fully the influence of white culture on Indian music, at least partly because the only written records of Indians in the earliest days of contact were written by whites, who did not understand the cultures they were facing. Yet one particular modern development must be considered. In the 1960's, American folk music changed drastically in many ways. There was a movement toward increasing social and political meaning in a genre that was once mostly concerned with romance, religion, and historical events. American Indians were among the many who used this vehicle to express their concerns. Usually these songs were written in English so that they could reach as wide an audience as possible.

The "protest songs" written and sung by American Indians are in some ways fundamentally different from those written by white Americans. They often speak of love of the earth, of ancient traditions and ceremonies, of a return to the land. They rarely have the angry tone that so many songs protesting ill conditions have. Rather, they tend toward a longing for a return to basics, for a recapturing of a lost world. The most common tone is one of sadness.

This development suggests a true resurgence of the ancient uses of song among the Indian cultures. Even if they are sung in English, to the accompaniment of electric guitars or even orchestras, the lyrics often involve some use of a native language and are essentially born of the same thoughts and feelings that inspired the ancient songs.

Musical Accompaniment. Indian songs are almost always accompanied by drums of various sorts. The particular musical instruments involved will be discussed below, but it is essential here to stress that tonal instruments are rarely used while singing is going on. As discussed above, this has meant that Indian song is not necessarily confined to a particular scale.

Drumming, however, is a common accompaniment of singing. It does not provide an exact rhythm for the song. One of the most disturbing aspects of American Indian music for someone used to the European tradition is that the singers may not follow the rhythm of the drums; it is completely acceptable to be "off the beat."

Drums. The musical instrument most often associated with American Indians is the drum. Drums are almost always used to accompany singing and dancing and have also been used as a form of communication, with a sort of "Morse code" utilized to send messages over long distances.

One common type of drum is a hand drum, which can be carried about by an individual and played while dancing. The materials used in construction vary according to the materials available. Most often the body of the drum is made of hollowed wood, but woven baskets are used in some areas, and hollowed gourds are used in the Southwest. The head is generally the hide of an animal, most often a deer.

Another type of drum is a large drum around which several people are seated; they play it together. This may be made by simply planting stakes in the ground and stretching a hide over them, or a large wooden structure may be made. In modern times, wooden or metal washtubs have sometimes been used. Water drums are made from hollowed logs that are partially filled with water. The water greatly increases resonance, and the sound of such a drum can be heard for miles.

Drums are frequently decorated in elaborate fashions. The paintings are often filled with religious symbolism; beads and leather thongs are often added. The proper spirits must be invoked for many ceremonies, and, since drums are so heavily involved, one of the ways to invoke the spirit is by drawing or painting the appropriate pictures on the drum.

Indians place a somewhat greater importance upon drumsticks than European cultures do. Although in many cases the drumsticks are merely twigs, quickly discarded, in other ceremonies, the drumsticks may be decorated, covered with leather, and have particular ceremonial meanings. A decorated drumstick can be a sign of prestige in certain tribes. There are other percussion instruments used in Indian music, including poles or planks around which a number of players are seated, and stretched hides with no drum body attached.

Wind Instruments. Some Indian tribes have used flutes and whistles to produce music. The most common sort of flute is much like a recorder; it has a few holes to vary pitch and is blown through the top end. It may be made of clay, wood, or reeds, again depending upon available materials. Whistles are far simpler and are used more often as signals than for playing music. They are used by men courting women, by shamans invoking spirits, or by war parties passing signals.

Wind instruments are not generally used as an accompaniment to song. While they may have variable pitch, they are made individually from natural materials and are far from standard in their scales. Flutes and whistles are used alone or in concert with percussion instruments.

Rattles. Rattles are nearly universal instruments among North American Indian tribes. The most common type of rattle is a hollow object filled with pebbles, bits of clay, or seeds. This sort of rattle is very important in many tribal ceremonies and is an essential component of many medical treatments.

In many areas, the body of a rattle is a hollowed gourd. In some places, rawhide is shaped into an appropriate receptacle. Like drums, rattles are often painted and decorated. Rattles are also made by suspending small objects so that they clash together.   —*Marc Goldstein*

See also Dances and dancing; Drums; Feasts; Flutes; Medicine and modes of curing, pre-contact; Pow-wows and contemporary celebrations.

BIBLIOGRAPHY

Bancroft-Hunt, Norman. *People of the Totem*. New York: G. P. Putnam's Sons, 1979. A description of the Northwest American Indian culture, including a study of their history, ceremonies, music, and contemporary conditions.

Butree, Julia M. *The Rhythm of the Red Man*. New York: A. S. Barnes, 1930. A descripton of Indian rituals, especially music and dance, including step-by-step instructions for a number of songs, dances, and rituals followed by a variety of tribal groups.

Densmore, Frances. *The American Indians and Their Music*. New York: Woman's Press, 1936. A comprehensive guide to American Indian music, song, and dance. Includes an overview of Indian culture and specific discussions of songs, musical instruments, and dances.

Nettl, Bruno. *Folk Music in the United States*. 3d rev. ed. Detroit: Wayne State University Press, 1976. A general overview of American folk music, from prehistoric times to the 1970's, including a long and comprehensive chapter on American Indian music, both as discussed by the first European settlers and as it exists in contemporary times.

Spencer, Robert F., Jesse D. Jennings, et al. *The Native Americans*. New York: Harper & Row, 1977. An encyclopedic discussion of American Indian culture, from prehistory to modern times.

Muskogean language family

CULTURE AREA: Southeast
TRIBES AFFECTED: Alabama, Creek (Muskogee), Chickasaw, Choctaw, Coushatta, Hitchiti, Mikasuki

Although the available knowledge of the Southeast tribes is somewhat limited, it is certain that the Southeast was an area of great linguistic diversity. Many of the smaller tribes in this area have disappeared, and a number of tribes are identifiable by name only. Often names of lakes, counties, and towns in the southeastern part of the United States suggest that tribes bearing those obviously Indian names must have once inhabited the area.

The Muskogean language family, the only linguistic family lying exclusively in the Southeast, is divided into eastern and western branches. The eastern branch includes Alabama and Coushatta (Koasati), Hitchiti-Miccosukee, and Creek-Seminole. The western branch consists of Choctaw-Chickasaw.

Extant Languages. The Muskogean languages that were extant as of the early 1990's are Choctaw, Chickasaw, Alabama and Coushatta, Hitchiti and Miccosukee, and Creek (Muskogee). The extent to which the languages have developed writing systems is somewhat problematic. As Thomas Barthel points out in an essay on North American Indian writing systems in *Native Languages of the Americas*, volume 2 (1976), native writing systems in the New World have not developed into systems complete enough to reflect all the oral language, so there is a real limitation in this field of research. Nevertheless, there is a relatively extensive body of literature on the known languages, based chiefly on languages of the larger and more powerful tribes such as the Creek and the Choctaw.

The Choctaw Indians trace their national origin to a sacred mound, Nanih Waiya, in what became Winston County, Mississippi. In the 1830's, however, the Choctaw were forced to cede their lands to the United States government and move to what would become the state of Oklahoma in 1907. As of the mid-1970's, there were about seven thousand speakers of Choctaw. Choctaw is most closely related to Chickasaw.

During the early part of the nineteenth century, Cyrus A. Byington, a missionary to the Choctaw, recorded and translated Choctaw extensively. His work included translations of parts of the Bible, as well as a grammar, edited in 1870 by Daniel G. Brinton, and a dictionary, edited by John R. Swanton and Henry S. Halvert in 1915. These works provide the most extensive body of materials available on Choctaw. David I. Bushnell produced a monograph on another Choctaw dialect in 1909.

While Chickasaw is usually listed as a language rather than a dialect, some consider it to be a subvariety of Choctaw. In the mid-1970's, some twenty-five hundred speakers of the language were identifiable, most living in the area of Ardmore, Oklahoma.

William Pulte wrote an essay entitled "The Position of Chickasaw in Western Muskogean" that focused on differences in words and sounds. By the late 1970's, the Chickasaw

Council had completed work on a small dictionary of Chickasaw, emphasizing its distinctness from Choctaw.

Coushatta (and possibly Alabama), unlike other Muskogean languages, has three conjugational classes of verbs. The language also makes clear distinctions between men's and women's speech, as does Hitchiti (Creek also did at one time, as noted by Mary Haas in 1941).

Hitchiti is only dialectally different from Koasati. During the late nineteenth century, Albert S. Gatschet and Buckingham Smith, in particular, published some materials on words and grammar of Hitchiti. William C. Sturtevant and David West have done more recent work.

Creek, also known as Muskogee, has received the most attention of all the Muskogean languages. Since it was the main language of members of the once powerful Creek Confederacy, this is not surprising. The Creek Nation was an alliance of separate and independent tribes that, over a long period of time, gradually became a single political organization. These Indians lived originally in Georgia and Alabama; their forced move in 1870 led to most of them living near the town of Okmulgee, south of Tulsa, Oklahoma. It has been estimated that not more than half still speak the Creek language.

Missionaries to the Creek helped them to develop an alphabet for their language, so that many Creeks were able to read and write not only religious material, but also newspaper articles and their own constitution. In Florida, the Creek dialect is called Seminole, from the Creek word *simaló-ni* or *simanó-li*, a loan word from the Spanish *cimarrón*.

Extinct Languages. At least two-thirds of known Muskogean languages had become extinct by the 1900's. Some of these include Apalachee, which had only fifty speakers in Louisiana in 1814; Pensacola, extinct some time after 1764; Chakchiuma, spoken in Mississippi until extinction around 1722; Chatat, which became extinct during the nineteenth century; Eufaula, a Muskogee division in Alabama; Guale, which is said to have had a grammar written by Domingo Augustin sometime after 1569; Ipitoupa; Napochi, which probably became extinct after they joined the Chickasaw

about 1699; Oconee, no longer spoken after about 1761; Okelousa, also extinct during the eighteenth century; Okmulgee, an Eastern Muskogean language that had no speakers by the end of the seventeenth century; and Pascagoula, with two speakers in 1912. Quinipissa, along with Tangipahoa, became extinct during the seventeenth century. Sawokli and Tamathli had fewer than five hundred speakers in the early nineteenth century. Taposa, Tekesta, and Tohome had fewer than two hundred speakers by the third quarter of the eighteenth century. Tuskegee and Yamasee became extinct during the nineteenth century. In scanning the list, names familiar to areas of Louisiana, Mississippi, Alabama, Georgia, Florida, and Tennessee are evident. —*Victoria Price*

See also Chickasaw; Choctaw; Creek; Hitchiti; Southeast.

BIBLIOGRAPHY

Bright, William, et al., eds. *Linguistics in North America*. Vol. 10 in *Current Trends in Linguistics*, edited by Thomas A. Sebeok. The Hague: Mouton, 1973.

Buckner, Henry F., and Goliah Herrod. *A Grammar of the Masjwke, or Creek Language*. Marion, Ala.: Domestic and Indian Mission Board of the Southern Baptist Convention, 1860.

Byington, Cyrus A. *A Grammar of the Choctaw Language*. Edited by Daniel G. Brinton. Philadelphia: McCalla & Stavely, 1870.

Haas, Mary R. "The Classification of the Muskogean Languages." In *Language, Culture, and Personality*, edited by Leslie Spier, et al. Menasha, Wisc.: Sapir Memorial Publication Fund, 1941.

_____. "A Proto-Muskogean Paradigm." *Language* 22 (1946): 326-332.

Katzner, Kenneth. *The Languages of the World*. New York: Funk & Wagnalls, 1975.

Rand, Earl. "The Structural Phonology of Alabama, a Muskogean Language." *International Journal of American Linguistics* 34 (1968): 94-103.

West, John David. "The Phonology of Mikasuki." *Studies in Linguistics* 16 (1962): 77-91.

Nabedache: Tribe

CULTURE AREA: Southwest
LANGUAGE GROUP: Caddoan
PRIMARY LOCATION: Oklahoma

The Nabedache were the westernmost of the nine tribes of the Hasinai Confederacy in East Texas, linguistically related to the Caddo. Their homeland was west of the Neches River; they lived in scattered rancherias, farming and hunting.

During the two Spanish occupations (1690-1693 and 1716-1821), missions were established for the Nabedache. They refused to Hispanize, however, maintaining good but reserved relations with the Spanish. They retained their own culture and independence. Between the 1750's and 1799 the Nabedache were the dominant tribe among the Hasinai. Leaders Bigotes, or Sauto (to 1778), and Baltasar Bigotes (post-1778) interacted with the Spanish regarding French trade, war with the Apache, and relations with the Comanche and other tribes to the west. In 1800 they were faced with Indian and American encroachment and the effects of disease. Within seven years they were reduced to 120 people.

During the period of the Texas Republic (1836-1845), their fortunes waned further. They were forced into central Texas, where they faced hostile Comanche raiders and Texans. Under U.S. control after 1846, the Nabedache were removed to Oklahoma in 1859. The Nabedache survived the Civil War and, after 1870, entered a period of peace and stability. Today they are listed under Hasinai and Caddo but are governed by their own tribal government.

See also Anadarko; Caddo; Caddoan language family; Texas.

Na-Dene language family

CULTURE AREAS: California, Northwest Coast, Plains, Plateau, Southwest, Subarctic
TRIBES AFFECTED: Ahtna, Apache, Beaver, Carrier, Chipewyan, Dogrib, Eyak, Galice-Applegate, Haida, Hare, Hupa, Ingalik, Kaska, Kolchan, Koyukon, Kutchin, Mountain, Navajo (Dine), Sarcee, Sekani, Slave, Tagish, Tahltan, Tanaina, Tanacross, Tanana, Tlingit, Tolowa, Tutchone, Tututni, Umpqua

Na-Dene, considered to be a language phylum by some comparative linguists, is composed of one large language family (Athapaskan-Eyak) and two possibly related language isolates (Haida and Tlingit). The distribution of Na-Dene languages extends through six culture areas, making it one of the largest linguistic units in North America.

The Western Subarctic is dominated by groups speaking Na-Dene-related languages (all Athapaskan). These include such groups as the Beaver, Carrier, Chipewyan, Dogrib, Hare, Ingalik, Kaska, Koyukon, Kutchin, Mountain, Slave, Tahltan, Tanaina, and Tanana. In the northern Plains, the Sarcee speak a language which has been subsumed under the Na-Dene phylum. In the Southwest, languages closely related to Plains and Subarctic Athapaskan are represented by Navajo (Dine) and Apache (Apachean stock). In the Northwest Coast culture area and extending partially into the Plateau, Na-Dene languages can be found in central Oregon. These are represented by Galice-Applegate, Tututni, and Upper Umpqua. Farther north, in British Columbia and southeastern Alaska, are Haida and Tlingit, both classified as possible relatives of Athapaskan. In California, the Hupa and Tolowa are known to speak Athapaskan languages closely related to those of the Oregonean groups.

The designation of Na-Dene as a linguistic entity has been called into question by many comparative linguists. In 1915, Edward Sapir, a linguist who specialized in classifying and analyzing North American languages, established Na-Dene as a possible phylum composed of, as he saw it, remotely related languages. Problems arose, however, over the supposed relationship of Haida and Tlingit to Athapaskan. Many comparative linguists now believe that Haida and Tlingit are not members of the Athapaskan family; they recognize that Haida and Tlingit share phonological and grammatical structures with Athapaskan but argue that they are significantly different in morphology and lexicon (basic semantics). This controversy has not been adequately resolved.

See also California; Northwest Coast; Plains; Plateau; Southwest; Subarctic.

Naiche (c. 1857-1921, Mescalero, N.Mex.): Chief

ALSO KNOWN AS: Natchez
TRIBAL AFFILIATION: Chiricahua Apache
SIGNIFICANCE: Said to be Geronimo's closest associate in war and captivity, Naiche was a leader of the Apache people during their late nineteenth and early twentieth century interactions with the U.S. government

Reared by his father, Cochise, to be loyal to his older brother Taza (Tahza, Tazi), Naiche was unprepared to assume the leadership role he inherited when Taza died unexpectedly.

Naiche, with Geronimo, led many of the Apache raiding parties in the Southwest in the 1880's. Although photographs reveal the deference with which Geronimo saluted Naiche, invariably placing Naiche on the right, interpreters believed Geronimo dominated. The two leaders were nearly inseparable in battle and in captivity for half a century.

In 1886, Naiche, Geronimo, Chihuahua, and Nana met with Lieutenant Marion Maus in the Sierra Madre to discuss surrender. Nine Apaches were held hostage, including Naiche's oldest wife, Nah-de-yole, and their son, who would be known later as Paul. Naiche's other wives were E-clah-heh and Ha-o-zinne. Naiche and Geronimo fled but were taken prisoner and sent to Florida.

In 1891, Naiche became one of the first soldiers in Company I of the Twelfth Infantry. He would later serve as a scout searching for Apaches still living in the Sierre Madre. In 1893, he was moved to Oklahoma, still as a prisoner of war. He was instrumental in accomplishing the 1912 congressional legislation releasing the Apaches as prisoners of war.

See also Apache; Apache Wars; Cochise; Geronimo; Nana.

Nakaidoklini (c. mid-1800's, Ariz.—Aug. 30, 1881, Cibecue Creek, Ariz.): Shaman

TRIBAL AFFILIATION: Apache

SIGNIFICANCE: Nakaidoklini was an Apache prophet whose murder precipitated the final stage of the Apache Wars

At the San Carlos Reservation in Arizona, Nakaidoklini prophesied the resurrection of dead warriors through the practice of a new dance. The ritual was performed with Nakaidoklini standing in the center of a group of dancing warriors, anointing them with sacred pollen. In June, 1881, he announced his intention of performing a dance designed to resurrect two chiefs who would aid Apaches in their struggles against whites.

After Nakaidoklini reputedly claimed that his resurrection dance would fail because of white presence in the region, Fort Apache's commander, Colonel E. A. Carr, was ordered to arrest or kill him. Failing to lure him to the reservation, on August 30, 1881, Carr led cavalry troops and twenty-three White Mountain Apache scouts to Nakaidoklini's village. Although he surrendered, the White Mountain scouts rebelled; fighting ensued and Nakaidoklini was killed.

In retaliation, Nakaidoklini's followers attacked Fort Apache, precipitating a new phase of Apache Wars.

See also Apache Wars; Ghost Dance; Religious specialists.

Names and naming

TRIBES AFFECTED: Pantribal

SIGNIFICANCE: Indian names were often descriptive of a person's unique trait or of a significant action or event in his or her life

At the time of first contact with Europeans, North American Indians generally used a single name for an individual, rather than attaching a surname as was the European fashion. Indian names were often descriptive of some action or trait or of some occurrence in the life of the bearer. The translations were deemed "colorful" by Europeans, although mistranslations were common, such as the case in which a name meaning "Young Man Whose Very Horses Are Feared" was mistranslated as "Young Man Afraid of His Horses." These names were not static throughout life, but could change many times between birth and late adulthood. Various tribes followed different naming practices. Usually Indians did not name themselves but were given names by parents, shamans, or other members of their tribal group. Some names could be inherited from a dead ancestor, and were bestowed following the prevalent line of descent, either matrilineal or patrilineal. It was considered improper for an Indian to mention his or her own name, and husbands and wives generally did not use their proper names when speaking to each other.

When an Indian child was born, naming might be delayed from a few days to a few months. This often paralleled the intensification of pregnancy taboos surrounding the mother, which were extended after the baby's birth. Baby names were not considered particularly important or anticipatory of an individual's character or performance in later life. When the baby was given the name of a dead ancestor, some tribes believed that the ancestor's spirit entered into the child. (Inuit parents refrained from slapping or verbally abusing their children, fearing that the ancestor's spirit would be offended and depart the child's body, resulting in the child's death.)

Some tribes gave children derogatory or unflattering nicknames, with the intent of encouraging them to seek accomplishments that would bring the bestowal of an appropriate new name. Common occasions for the bestowal of new names included the onset of menses for girls, success in hunting or warfare for boys, or the acquisition of a supernatural power during the vision quest for both genders. For boys, initiation into a sodality (a club or organization for men), also served as an occasion for a new name. When names were inherited from living relatives, such as a father, the boy might be prevented from assuming the name until he had attained a status in warfare or hunting comparable to that of his father.

Older men past the age of active hunting and warfare would often turn their attentions to civil and religious affairs and would assume new names related to their activities. Some names were taboo and were never used, such as the names of certain animals. Many tribes did not speak the name of a deceased member for fear of attracting the departed's spirit back from the other world, but when a living person was given the name, the taboo was lifted.

Belief in the power of a name was strong. The origin of this belief can be traced to ancient tales of the beginnings of the people, when the spoken word could be made manifest within the creation. Among the Apaches, use of a person's name called forth obligations that were almost impossible to ignore. If a warrior was about to be left behind in battle, he could call out the name of a companion, and that warrior was honor-bound to return and attempt to rescue him, even if such action meant his own certain death.

Modern American Indians choose names in many different ways. Surnames are common—often tying the bearer to parents, famous ancestors, or perhaps identifying clan affiliation. Others have adopted or been given names from the mainstream American culture that do not reflect their Indian heritage.

See also Children; Ethnophilosophy and worldview; Puberty and initiation rites; Rites of passage.

Nampeyo (c. 1860, Hano, First Mesa, Ariz. Territory—July 20, 1942, Hano, First Mesa, Ariz.): Potter

TRIBAL AFFILIATION: Hano, Hopi

SIGNIFICANCE: Inspired by prehistoric Sikyatki Polychrome pottery, Nampeyo created her own style, known as Hano Polychrome, which revived the declining pottery tradition in the Hopi pueblos

When the Fewkes Expedition of 1895 excavated Sikyatki, a prehistoric Hopi site, Nampeyo's husband, Lesou, was a member of the team. More than five hundred intact pots and thousands of fragments were recovered, all of which Nampeyo had an opportunity to study. She did not copy the Sik-

Nampeyo's pottery was inspired by prehistoric motifs. (Museum of New Mexico)

yatki patterns in her work but combined many of the elements and motifs, such as spiral bird beaks, wings, and feathers, with her own ideas to re-create the Sikyatki sense of form. She also experimented with different clays until she discovered the one that had been used by the prehistoric Sikyatki potters.

Among modern Hopi potters, the two most popular vessel shapes are the bowl and the jar. It was Nampeyo who revived the jar shape that was characteristic of Sikyatki Polychrome— a shallow jar with a short neck, an in-curing rim, and a low, flattened shoulder that presents an interesting design field. Nampeyo had a highly developed sense of the appropriateness of design to vessel shape, and the placement of her decorative elements always complemented the form of the pot.

In the early 1900's, with the Fred Harvey Company promoting her work, Nampeyo inspired many other Hopi potters to work in the Hano Polychrome style. With her creative ability and technical mastery, she set the standards for a pottery tradition that has continued under the leadership of her daughters, granddaughters, and great-granddaughters.

See also Arts and crafts—Southwest; Pottery; Pueblo tribes, Eastern; Pueblo tribes, Western.

Nana (c. 1810-1895?, Fort Sill, Okla.): Chief

ALSO KNOWN AS: Nané, Nanay
TRIBAL AFFILIATION: Chiricahua Apache

SIGNIFICANCE: Nana was said to have had the longest fighting career of any Apache warrior

Nana, who married Geronimo's sister, Nah-dos-te, was closely allied with Victorio in fighting removal to reservations. Nana was one of only seventeen Apaches to escape the 1880 massacre of Victorio and his people living in the Sierre Madre. The scalps of 62 warriors and 16 women and children earned the Mexican force under Colonel Terrazas $50,000. The Mexican force sold an additional 68 women and children into slavery. Nana, then seventy years old, gathered the survivors and stepped into the leadership role.

From July of 1881 through the next year, Nana terrorized New Mexico. After surrendering to General George Crook's forces in May, 1883, Nana and about 320 Apaches were marched from Sierre Madre to San Carlos. In May, 1885, Nana and about 140 Chiricahuas broke away from the reservation once more. Their flight into Mexico and subsequent raids ended March 25, 1886, when the leaders negotiated with Crook to return to the reservation. The terms of surrender were violated, and Crook resigned. Over the next four months, five thousand men were employed to "capture or destroy" 38 Chiricahuas. Removed as a prisoner to Florida, Nana survived captivity to return to Oklahoma, where he died, probably in 1895 or 1896. He was buried in the Apache cemetery near Fort Sill.

See also Apache; Apache Wars; Cochise; Geronimo; Mangas Coloradus; Victorio.

Nanticoke: Tribe

CULTURE AREA: Northeast
LANGUAGE GROUP: Algonquian
PRIMARY LOCATION: Delaware, New Jersey
POPULATION SIZE: 1,471 (1990 U.S. Census)

The Nanticoke originally inhabited the eastern shore of Chesapeake Bay along the Nanticoke River in Maryland. Culturally, they were closely associated with surrounding Algonquian-speaking groups such as the Conoys. Unfortunately, only a few details survive about traditional lifeways. Men hunted and fished, and women practiced maize horticulture. The Nanticoke were adept at the production of shell beads for peake (wampum) and at the processing of furs. A hereditary chief ruled over several villages and, with elders, formed an upper social stratum. Individuals traced their ancestry through women. The Nanticoke buried their dead in ossuaries (mass graves) after lengthy interment in aboveground mortuary structures.

Sustained contact with white settlers began after 1608. By the early eighteenth century, the Nanticoke had suffered greatly from disease and from harassment by colonists. To lessen conflicts, they agreed to live on two reservations along the Nanticoke, known as Broad Creek and Chicacoan. This greatly reduced their territory and limited their ability to sup-

Chiricahua Apache leader Nana, along with Victorio, fought against confinement to reservations. (Library of Congress)

port themselves. During this period, the Nanticoke became tributaries of the powerful Five Nations of the Iroquois of New York.

By the mid-1700's, because of further interference by colonists, the Nanticoke petitioned the Iroquois for protection. Several hundred migrated to Iroquois territory in Pennsylvania before regrouping at Otsiningo, near present-day Binghamton, New York. By then, they had merged with the Conoys. After the American Revolution they moved west, finally settling in Oklahoma, where they became identified with and absorbed into the Delaware (Lenni Lenape) tribe.

By the 1760's, the Nanticokes who remained in Maryland had abandoned their land. In the succeeding years, they settled with members of local tribes on Indian River Hundred near Millsboro, Delaware. In 1903, after many attempts, they gained official recognition as Nanticoke Indians from the state. The formation of the Nanticoke Indian Association furthered tribal causes during the twentieth century. A separate organization, known as the Nanticoke-Lenni Lenape Indians of New Jersey, developed in 1978 near Bridgeton, New Jersey, where members of the two tribes had settled. Both organizations strive to preserve community history, revive traditional ways, and educate the public through museums and annual pow-wows.

See also Algonquian language family; Northeast.

Narragansett: Tribe

CULTURE AREA: Northeast
LANGUAGE GROUP: Algonquian
PRIMARY LOCATION: Rhode Island
POPULATION SIZE: 2,456 (1990 U.S. Census)

The Narragansett were a powerful tribe of southern New England. They spoke an Algonquian language, and their territory encompassed much of present-day Rhode Island. Recent estimates suggest that there may have been as many as sixteen thousand Narragansetts in 1600. The name "Narragansett" is usually translated "at the narrow point of land."

Narragansett culture and lifeways were similar to those of other tribes in the region. They were adept at agriculture, regularly planting corn, beans, squash, and sunflowers. The diet was supplemented by hunting and trapping. The wigwam, a circular shelter of bent poles covered with bark, was the typical dwelling.

Sachems (chiefs) wielded authority in Narragansett society, aided by councilors, usually warriors of distinction. *Powpows* were also important, healers with great spiritual powers. First white contact came with Giovanni da Verrazano in 1524, though permanent white settlement did not come until a century later.

In 1616-1617, a devastating plague (probably smallpox) decimated neighboring tribes, but the Narragansett were spared. The Narragansett warred with their neighbors and dominated such tribes as the Wampanoags. In 1633 the plague, long delayed, finally struck the Narragansett, killing at least seven hundred.

White-Narragansett relations were cordial at first; Rhode Island founder Roger Williams championed Indian land rights. Yet though the Narragansett helped the English in the Pequot War of 1637, the colonists were suspicious of their allies; they were also hungry for more land.

When King Philip's War broke out in 1675, the Narragansett maintained neutrality, though they sheltered Wampanoag women and children. When the English demanded the surrender of the Wampanoag fugitives, Narragansett sachem Canonchet refused. The English assembled the largest colonial army up to that time—a thousand men—and launched a surprise attack on the Narragansett. On December 19, 1675, the English assaulted a large Narragansett fort near present-day Kingston, Rhode Island. The resulting battle, called the Great Swamp Fight, was one of the bloodiest of the war. At least six hundred Narragansett were killed, and three hundred were taken prisoner. Most of the Indian casualties were women and children.

King Philip's War destroyed the Narragansett as a distinct tribal entity. Some survivors joined the Niantic, and in time the combination was called Narragansett. A reservation was established in Rhode Island. In the eighteenth and nineteenth centuries, assimilation seemed the only alternative to extinction. The last full-blooded Narragansett died in the nineteenth century, and the language died out about that time as well.

In 1880, the Narragansett were detribalized and their reservation sold. Though the remaining people were of mixed Indian-white-black blood, and the culture was virtually dead, some measure of Narragansett identity survived. Beginning in the 1920's, pan-Indianism caused the embers of the Narragansett heritage to flare again.

The culture was revived, and activists such as Ella Thomas Sekatau and Eric Thomas Sekatau managed to secure federal recognition of the tribe in 1983. In 1978, as part of the Rhode Island Indian Claims settlement, the state gave the Narragansett 1,800 acres of wooded public and private land that was once part of tribal territory. Every year, the tribe holds an Annual August Meeting. The two-day festivities bring the Narragansett closer together.

See also Algonquian language family; Canonchet; King Philip's War.

Naskapi: Tribe

Culture area: Subarctic
Language group: Algonquian
Primary location: Labrador Peninsula
Population size: 12,025 (combined Montagnais/Naskapi population, Statistics Canada, based on 1991 census)

The Naskapi, closely associated with the East Cree and Montagnais, lived in semipermanent winter villages in rectangular, split-log lodges. During the rest of the year, temporary hide-covered conical dwellings were used during the subsistence round, which focused upon hunting and trapping caribou, moose, and Dall's sheep. Nearly every species of bird was also hunted. Watercraft were usually made of birchbark, although some moose-skin boats were utilized, mostly for load transportation.

The first sustained European Canadian contact was with the trapper-traders of the Hudson's Bay Company, who introduced considerable change to aboriginal settlement patterns, subsistence orientation, and eventually to the Naskapi religion. The once highly mobile Naskapi developed ties to trading posts and became dependent on the exchange of furs for trade goods.

Today the traditional self-sufficient Naskapi culture no longer exists; Naskapis are dependent on the European Canadian market economy, and most earn a living by wage employment. They are served by government schools and health programs.

See also Cree; Montagnais; Subarctic.

Natawista (c. 1825, Alberta, Canada—c. 1895, Alberta, Canada): Interpreter, diplomat

Also known as: Natawista Iksana, Madame Culbertson
Tribal affiliation: Blood
Significance: After marrying Major Alexander Culbertson, Natawista became an interpreter, diplomat, and trading post hostess

When she was fifteen years old, Natawista accompanied her father, Men-Es-To-Kos, on a trading voyage from their home in Alberta to Fort Union on the Missouri River, near the North Dakota-Montana border. There she married Alexander Culbertson, the fort commander, in an Indian ceremony. Four of their children lived to adulthood; two daughters married white easterners, while two sons remained in the West to work as traders.

During the early years of her marriage, from 1840 to 1845, Natawista resided at Fort Union, acting as hostess and diplomat. In 1845, the Culbertsons moved farther north along the Missouri, establishing Fort Benton in Montana. There, Natawista functioned as an interpreter for several Indian tribes, including the Blackfoot, Blood, and Gros Ventre, while simultaneously acting as hostess to visiting white traders.

After his appointment as special agent to the Blackfoot Confederacy in 1847, Culbertson and Natawista traveled to Indian camps throughout the territory. Natawista again assisted her husband by acting as interpreter and diplomat. On several occasions, she diffused tensions and helped maintain peace.

Retiring to Peoria, Illinois, in 1858, the Culbertsons were married in a Catholic ceremony. In Peoria they lived extravagantly for ten years before losing their fortune through failed investments, thereafter returning to the upper Missouri where Culbertson resumed trading. In the 1870's, Natawista left Culbertson and returned to her native Alberta, where she remained until her death.

See also Missions and missionaries; Trading posts.

Natchez: Tribe

Culture area: Southeast
Language group: Natchez
Primary location: Natchez, Mississippi
Population size: 98 (1990 U.S. Census)

Natchez social complexity fascinated early explorers of the Mississippi River as well as later ethnographers and archaeologists. For this reason, much has been written on these Native Americans.

The Natchez occupied an area east of the Mississippi River, centered at contemporary Natchez, Mississippi. They raised corn, beans, squash, and other crops in addition to hunting, fishing, and gathering wild plants. The agricultural surplus permitted a sedentary lifestyle, and their villages impressed European visitors, as did the lavish material culture, both of which were complemented by an elaborate sociopolitical system. Natchez social organization was hierarchical, with numerous low-level positions overseen by the tribal leader, known as the Great Sun. The Great Sun controlled events during peaceful times; however, he relinquished command to a male relative (brother or uncle) in times of war. These ruling titles were inherited, and visitors remarked upon the elaborate funerary rituals (including human sacrifice and burial in mounds) which accompanied the death of one of the leaders.

European contact was initiated with René-Robert Cavelier, Sieur de La Salle's visit of 1682. By the early 1700's, a French priest was residing in their midst (Jean François Buisson de Saint-Cosme, who was later killed by the Chitimacha), and they received regular visits from Jesuits and other dignitaries, such as Pierre LeMoyne, Sieur d'Iberville in 1700, and Penicaut in 1704, all of whom wrote of their experiences. By 1713, a French trading post was established among the Natchez. After some minor social unrest, Fort Rosalie was constructed in approximately 1716 to demonstrate French dominion.

During the mid 1720's, two minor uprisings occurred among the Natchez. In both cases, the French overpowered them and reinforced their control. The major Natchez Revolt of 1729, however, resulted in many deaths among both the French and the Natchez, and this sealed the fate of the remaining Natchez; the French were determined to quell the insurrection forcefully. By 1731, approximately four hundred Natchez were enslaved and sent to the Caribbean colonies, while the remainder escaped to seek refuge among the Chickasaw, some ultimately joining the Creek or the Cherokee. Ultimately, the remaining Natchez took part in the enforced migrations of 1830-1839 known as the Trail of Tears. The last speakers of the Natchez language died in the 1940's in Oklahoma. In 1990, fewer than one hundred people identified themselves as Natchez.

See also Great Sun; Mounds and mound builders; Natchez Revolt; Prehistory—Southeast; Southeast.

Natchez Revolt

DATE: 1729
PLACE: Natchez, Mississippi
TRIBE AFFECTED: Natchez
SIGNIFICANCE: The Natchez Revolt gave rise to the French policy of encouraging enmities among the different Indian groups in order to forestall future uprisings

The Natchez Revolt occurred on November 28, 1729. The main factor underlying this event was the ineptness of French colonial rule, which controlled this region from the late seventeenth century. The Natchez were first encountered by the French on the eastern shore of the Mississippi River, at the location of the modern town of Natchez, Mississippi. In 1713, the French built a trading post there, evidence of their desire to control the region. Skirmishes between the Natchez and the French resulted in the 1716 construction of Fort Rosalie and in colonial settlement in its vicinity. After the fort was built, there were two additional small Natchez uprisings, although each was swiftly quelled.

Commandant De Chepart, placed in control of Fort Rosalie in 1728, marred his command with drunkenness and other abuses as well as with his insensitivity toward the Natchez. Within a year, De Chepart antagonized the Indian community with his proposal to establish his own plantation on fertile lands of the Natchez White Apple village. He proposed the use of force to assist in the relocation of the aboriginal inhabitants. In response, the Natchez planned war; their ceremonial preparations lasted for several months, culminating in a November attack on the French. They killed more than two hundred settlers, and they captured approximately fifty colonists and three hundred slaves.

On January 27, 1730, Sieur Jean-Paul Le Seur led a five-hundred-strong Choctaw force against the Natchez in retaliation. They managed to rescue most of the surviving women and children, plus approximately a hundred slaves; in the process they killed about the same number of Natchez. A week later, the French force received reinforcements from New Orleans, and they laid siege to the Natchez, who agreed to surrender on February 25.

In punishment, approximately four hundred Natchez were enslaved by the French and shipped to the West Indies. An indeterminate number escaped and sought refuge with the Chickasaw. This ensured Chickasaw animosity toward both the French and their powerful Choctaw allies. The Natchez never recovered, and their culture was soon lost.

See also Great Sun; Indian-white relations—French colonial; Natawista.

National Congress of American Indians (NCAI)

DATE: Established 1944
TRIBES AFFECTED: Pantribal
SIGNIFICANCE: The NCAI was formed to fight for the rights of Native Americans, including education and preservation of traditional values

The National Congress of American Indians (NCAI) is a coalition of sovereign nations recognized by the United States through treaty and executive agreement. Its purpose is to protect the rights of American Indians as citizens of nations and tribes within the boundaries of the United States. It is supported through annual membership dues and special fundraising endeavors. It is organized as a congress, with American Indian governments voting to participate and selecting delegates and alternates to represent them in the NCAI convention and executive council, where they have blocks of votes.

The NCAI was organized in 1944. American Indian delegates representing fifty tribes with homes in twenty-seven western states met in Denver, Colorado. Its initial stated goals included pursuit of American Indian rights within the United States, expansion and improvement of Indian education, preservation of Indian values, and equitable settlement of Indian claims. During the 1950's, it aided in the struggle against termination and relocation. More recently, it has been in the forefront of the struggle for Native American cultural rights legislation, which has brought on more reasonable approaches to repatriation of Indian remains and artifacts.

See also Activism; Civil rights and citizenship.

National Council of American Indians

DATE: Established 1926
TRIBES AFFECTED: Pantribal
SIGNIFICANCE: The National Council of American Indians was important in the 1920's and 1930's as a Red Progressive movement; it was important in developing Indian voting and supporting the Collier "Indian New Deal" reforms

In the early part of the twentieth century, a movement known as the Red Progressive movement called for American Indians to assimilate to the general American lifestyle. It was led by Indians who were well-educated and had achieved success in mainstream American society. Among its leaders were Henry Roe Cloud, Thomas L. Sloan, Arthur C. Parker, physicians Charles Eastman and Carlos Montezuma, and Gertrude Simmons Bonnin, a Sioux writer and musician.

The Red Progressives united at first under the Society of American Indians (SAI), but by the early 1920's that organization had split into several rancorous factions. A number of new organizations appeared, including the National Council of American Indians, founded in 1926 by Gertrude Bonnin and her husband. The organization was closely aligned with the General Federation of Women's Clubs, a mostly white and black organization of successful women. Bonnin had served as secretary of the Society of American Indians and in 1924 had coauthored *Oklahoma's Poor Rich Indians: An Orgy of Graft and Exploitation of the Five Civilized Tribes—Legalized Robbery*, a muckraking expose of graft and greed involving Oklahoma lawyers, judges, and politicians.

The slogan of the National Council of American Indians was "Help the Indians Help Themselves in Protecting their Rights and Properties." Its major early emphasis was promoting voting and participation in politics after the passage of the Indian Citizenship Act in 1924. It was most successful in these efforts in Oklahoma and South Dakota. The organization also advocated banning peyote use and the Native American Church; it took a moderate stance toward the Bureau of Indian Affairs.

In January, 1934, representatives of several organizations were called together in Washington, D.C., to confer with Franklin Roosevelt's commissioner of Indian affairs, John Collier, on reforms needed to ameliorate the living conditions of Indians. The Bonnins represented both the National Council of American Indians and the General Federation of Women's Clubs. They strongly supported the Indian Reorganization Act, which was adopted by Congress the same year. The council successfully pushed for a requirement for majority rule elections for tribal offices.

The National Council of American Indians, like its predecessors, was torn by factionalism; the Bonnins were its major support. With the coming of World War II, the council faded from existence, but it left behind a strong heritage of Indian political participation.

See also American Indian Defense Association (AIDA); Bonnin, Gertrude Simmons; Cloud, Henry Roe; Eastman, Charles Alexander; Indian Citizenship Act; Indian Reorganization Act; Montezuma, Carlos; Society of American Indians (SAI).

National Indian Association

DATE: Established 1879
TRIBES AFFECTED: Pantribal
SIGNIFICANCE: The National Indian Association was one of several organizations that comprised the Friends of the Indian lobbying group, seeking to ameliorate Indian living conditions and help Indians assimilate into American society

After the Civil War, a series of groups devoted to Indian "reform" arose in the eastern United States. The events of 1876-1878, including Custer's defeat in 1876, the Nez Perce escape attempt of 1877, and the Bannock War and the tragic Cheyenne escape attempt in 1878, led to the establishment of several influential organizations. Five of these became the core of the Friends of the Indian movement. One was the U.S. government's Board of Indian Commissioners, founded in 1869 and consisting of private citizens who served without pay. Two others, established in 1879, were the Boston Indian Citizenship Commission and the National Indian Association (also known as the Women's National Indian Association), established by a group of Protestant churchwomen in Philadelphia. The Indian Rights Association and the National Indian Defense Association followed in the early 1880's.

Between 1879 and 1886, the National Indian Association established eighty-three branches in cities across the nation. It published a monthly periodical, *The Indian's Friend*, often presented petitions to Congress and the president protesting the mistreatment of Indians, stridently pushed for reform of the Bureau of Indian Affairs, and—more than any other group—demanded that the U.S. government follow the provisions of its treaties with the Indians with "scrupulous fidelity." Its other major issues included improving delivery of education for Indians (with regard to the number and quality of schools), extending citizenship to all Indians, and dividing Indian lands into private homesteads for each family.

The association participated yearly in the Lake Mohonk Conference of the Friends of the Indian and the annual meeting of the Board of Indian Commissioners. These agencies shared responsibility for helping persuade the government to pass the General Allotment Act (Dawes Severalty Act), enacted in 1887, which subdivided the majority of Indian reservations into individual allotments. This act was ultimately disastrous for Indians, as the National Indian Defense Association had feared. The National Indian Association failed to influence the government's honoring of treaties. The association's other major success was increasing the number of schools available to Indians.

See also Allotment system; Education, post-contact; General Allotment Act; Indian Rights Association.

National Indian Youth Council (NIYC)

DATE: Established 1961

TRIBES AFFECTED: Pantribal

SIGNIFICANCE: Provides Native American youth with knowledge about tribal communities and traditions; develops leadership, employment, and civil liberties

Ten Native American college students gathered to form the National Indian Youth Council (NIYC) in August, 1961, at Gallup, New Mexico. Two months earlier, these students had met at the National Congress of American Indians (NCAI) conference at the University of Chicago. After hearing the discussions encouraging self-determination and denouncing termination, the students decided to start their own group.

The foundation for the NIYC had been laid in 1953 when Herbert Blatchford (Navajo) initiated the first intertribal student group, the Kiva Club, at the University of New Mexico. In expanding his visions for native youth, Blatchford was the founding director of the NIYC. At the August meeting, Mel Thom (Paiute) was elected the chairperson; Clyde Warrior (Ponca), president; Shirley Witt (Mohawk), vice-president. The NIYC's founding group came from different tribes and interests, but they had a common bond: a spirit to recover native rights and respect. Differing from the NCAI, the NIYC focused on the voices of the youth and employed strategies that were more aggressive and activist.

During its first decade, NIYC targeted problems with Native American education and discrimination. Members editorialized their opinions through NIYC's first publication, *American Aborigine*, edited by Blatchford. In 1963 the NIYC began publishing its long-running newspaper, *ABC: Americans Before Columbus*. The following year, the NIYC took its first step of direct action by going to Washington State to hold a series of "fish-ins." Members defied state law by fishing in rivers that had been closed to native fishing even though treaty language had reserved for the tribes permanent fishing rights. During this time of national unrest, other activist groups banded together to assist NIYC's "Washington Project."

With national support, NIYC members stepped into the political arena. Mel Thom encouraged a 1964 Washington, D.C., audience to stand up for self-determination. At a Memphis, Tennessee, poverty conference in 1967, Clyde Warrior delivered his passionate speech, "We Are Not Free." When

Warrior died the following year, the NIYC initiated the education-based Clyde Warrior Institute in American Indian Studies. Another educational project was a 1967 Carnegie Foundation program that researched educational methodology and addressed acculturation. With this growth, the NIYC in 1970 had opened chapters on several college campuses and reservations to serve more than two thousand members.

In expanding its political involvement, the NIYC then undertook lawsuits against irresponsible mining companies on reservation lands and instituted native employment and training programs. Other NIYC projects range from conducting voting surveys to creating an all-native film company, Circle Film. To help preserve native sacred lands and to protect native rituals, the group appealed to the United Nations and was granted recognition as an "official and non-governmental organization."

From its headquarters in Albuquerque, New Mexico, the NIYC hosts international native conferences that create strong networks of indigenous views. With its broadened vision, NIYC's nationwide membership had grown to more than forty-seven thousand in 1994.

See also Activism; Civil rights and citizenship; Education, post-contact.

Natiotish (fl. mid-1800's): War chief

ALSO KNOWN AS: Nantiotish, Nantiatish

TRIBAL AFFILIATION: White Mountain Apache

SIGNIFICANCE: Bitter over the death of the Apache prophet Nakaidoklini, Natiotish led White Mountain Apache warriors in the Battle of Big Dry Wash, 1882

In 1881, fearing the influence of the prophet Nakaidoklini, who preached a religion in which dead warriors would be resurrected to fight in battles against whites, Fort Apache's commander ordered the prophet's arrest. A rebellion of White Mountain Apaches ensued and Nakaidoklini was killed.

Angered by Nakaidoklini's death, Natiotish led his militant band of White Mountain Apaches on a retaliatory raid on the San Carlos Reservation, July 6, 1882. Four policemen, including the chief of police, "Cibecue Charley" Colvig, were killed.

Thereafter, Natiotish's band relentlessly raided the Tonto Basin, pursued by U.S. Cavalry led by Captain Adna Chaffee. Natiotish planned an ambush for Chaffee at a canyon near General Springs on the Mogollon Rim on July 17, 1882. Warned by army scout Albert Sieber and reinforced by troops under Major Andrew Evans, Chaffee's forces outnumbered and outfought Natiotish. The Apaches suffered a major defeat in the battle, during which they had abandoned their typical guerrilla tactics. Twenty-seven Apache warriors, probably including Natiotish, were killed in the skirmish, which became known as the Battle of Big Dry Wash. The survivors returned to the reservation and abandoned further resistance. Only the Chiricahuas and Mimbrenos under Geronimo remained militant.

See also Apache; Apache Wars; Cochise; Geronimo; Nakaidoklini; Victorio.

Native American

The term "Native American" is commonly used to refer to the many peoples of North America whose cultures existed on the continent when Europeans first arrived. It does not eliminate the possibility of foreign origin in an earlier era. It was coined as a collective name for the native peoples of the Americas (primarily North America) that would not carry the obvious falseness and the historically racist overtones of such terms as "American Indian" and "Indian." Yet, as is the case with virtually any collective term suggested, there are problems inherent in the term; for example, literally speaking, anyone of any ethnicity born in the Americas could be considered a "native American."

Beginning in the 1970's, the term Native American lost favor among activist groups and many others concerned with American Indian politics. Nevertheless, the term is still widely used, and some still prefer it to American Indian (although by the 1990's, the latter had become more common). Some American Indians find the offensiveness of all such collective terms to be about the same. All are generalizations that deny the unique, tribal-specific cultural heritage and political legacy of the many original inhabitants of the Americas.

See also American Indian; Amerind; Indian; Tribe.

Native American Church

DATE: Established 1918

TRIBES AFFECTED: Pantribal

SIGNIFICANCE: From its beginnings in the late nineteenth century, the Native American Church has been a unfiying force for scattered Native American peoples

The collection of teachings that became the doctrine of the Native American Church had their beginnings in the 1880's, probably among the Kiowas and Comanches living in Oklahoma. The church emphasizes the brotherhood of all American Indians. Among the main themes of the church's ethical code are mutual aid among members, a strong family, self-reliance, and the avoidance of alcohol.

The Native American Church was chartered as a Christian church in 1918. At that time, American Indians of every tribe were still reeling from the devastating effects of three centuries of contact with European American culture. Indians had been subjected to slaughter, enslavement, forced labor, the destruction of food supplies, the confiscation of land, forced dispersal, catastrophic depopulation, and forced religious conversion. Yet American Indians in the late nineteenth and early twentieth centuries created a monotheistic church with discernible and complex doctrines, ethics, and rituals; a strong sense of morality; a body of symbolically rich origin legends; and an individualistic approach that emphasized profound original spiritual experiences.

The ceremony that was to become central to the Native American Church was first described by anthropologist James Mooney in 1892. Its form was similar to that of present-day meetings. After 1900 the ceremony spread rapidly throughout tribal North America. Opposition to its spread came from tradi-tional tribalists, Christian missionaries, and Indian agencies. Wherever the church entered a tribe, it rejected both significant belief aspects of that tribe and the dominant white culture. In 1918 it was chartered as a legal church. Anthropologists helped write the articles of incorporation and appeared before judicial and legislative bodies in defense of the church, shrewdly aided by insightful Indians who included Christian elements to make the chartering process more amenable to legislatures.

The ingestion of peyote is part of the ritual of the church (the church has sometimes been called the Peyote Church). Peyote produces an altered state of consciousness. To the Native American Church, peyote is both a teacher and a healer. The use of peyote is strictly limited to the church's ceremonies, and other use is vigorously opposed. Nevertheless, the use of peyote has at times made the church controversial among Indian leaders and organizations. Jesus is seen as a deified spirit with whom church members can communicate. Today church members find the universalism of Christian ideology acceptable, but it is rare to find Christian symbols in the ceremony. Some songs still appeal to Jesus for health and help. Christian sin, judgment, and redemption are not found in Native American Church doctrine.

By 1947 the Native American Church was a widely prevalent religion among the Indians of the United States and had assumed the proportions of an intertribal religion. In 1960 the church was believed to have about 200,000 members, or half the population of adult Indians. Since U.S. law classifies peyote as a psychotropic drug and prohibits non-Indian participation, non-Indian participation is minimal. The Native American Church continues to exist as an important pan-Indian movement uniting diverse cultures in common goals.

See also Peyote and peyote religion; Religion.

BIBLIOGRAPHY

LaBarre, Weston. *The Peyote Cult.* 1938. Reprint. Hamden, Conn.: Shoestring Press, 1964.

Laney, John H. *On the Symbolism of the Native American Church of North America.* Zurich, Switzerland: C. G. Jung Institute, 1970.

Shonle, Ruth. "Peyote, the Giver of Visions." *American Anthropologist* 40 (1932): 698-715.

Slotkin, James. *The Peyote Religion.* Glencoe, Ill.: Free Press, 1956

Native American Rights Fund (NARF)

DATE: Established 1970

TRIBES AFFECTED: Pantribal

SIGNIFICANCE: NARF, established to represent Native American legal interests, has become a well-known and respected, if sometimes criticized, organization in the arena of American Indian rights and politics

The Native American Rights Fund (NARF) is a nonprofit, public-interest legal organization that was founded in 1970. It was established to represent tribal clients in litigation in state and federal courts and to strengthen tribal governments. Operations are supported by federal funds as well as by private and corporate contributions. Its attorneys are mostly Native

Americans; the group's headquarters is in Boulder, Colorado, with satellite offices in Washington, D.C., and Anchorage, Alaska. One of the organization's primary activities is to handle cases involving "federally recognized tribes" that cannot afford the full financial burden of litigation in U.S. courts. A staff of sixteen attorneys (in the early 1990's) handles about fifty cases at any given time. NARF also acts as a consultant in the drafting of federal Indian policy.

NARF's objectives include preservation of tribal existence and independence, protection of tribal resources, promotion of human rights such as education and the equitable treatment of Indian prisoners, and development of Indian law to improve tribal legal resources. The Indian Law Support Center and the Carnegie-sponsored National Indian Law Library are components of NARF, working in conjunction with its Legal Services Corporation. The law library houses a collection of more than six hundred tribal codes.

The Native American Rights Fund has taken on a number of well-known cases involving tribal land and water interests. The group gained national notice and respect for its handling of the 1982 land rights case brought by the Penobscot and Passamaquoddy against the state of Maine. The tribes were awarded $27,000 plus the money to purchase 300,000 acres of land. (An important footnote is that, although the case was regarded as a success story, the money did not go very far for some recipients. In addition, many such cases, even when legally successful, become bogged down by governmental bureaucracy.) NARF has been involved in litigation to strengthen aspects of the 1978 American Indian Religious Freedom Act dealing with the repatriation of ancestral bones and archaeological artifacts. NARF also assists non-federally recognized tribes in attempts to gain official tribal recognition, which may involve the restoration of at least some tribal homelands. It has litigated successfully for the Menominee of Wisconsin and the Siletz of Oregon.

NARF has not been without its critics. Some have argued that, because the organization is not self-sufficient and must rely on federal funding, it cannot truly be an effective advocacy group. From this perspective it may appear to be an extension of the federal system. Another criticism leveled against the group is that it has never attempted to challenge the European American legal paradigm by insisting on complete internal sovereignty for a client; rather, its negotiations seek negotiation, consensus, and settlement.

See also Civil rights and citizenship; Federally recognized tribes; Land claims; Menominee; Passamaquoddy; Penobscot.

BIBLIOGRAPHY

Deloria, Vine, Jr., and Clifford M. Lytle. *American Indians, American Justice.* Austin: University of Texas Press, 1983.

_____. *The Nations Within: The Past and Future of American Indian Sovereignty.* New York: Pantheon Books, 1984.

Native American Rights Fund. *Annual Report.* Boulder, Colo.: Author, 1993.

_____. *Legal Review* 19, no. 1 (Winter/Spring, 1994).

Nauset: Tribe
CULTURE AREA: Northeast
LANGUAGE GROUP: Algonquian
PRIMARY LOCATION: Cape Cod, Massachusetts

The Nauset, a branch of the Algonquian family, lived on Cape Cod in Massachusetts. The meaning of their name is not known; they were also commonly known as Cape Indians. They were related to or controlled by the Wampanoag ("eastern people"). Evidence suggests they had lived in the area for thousands of years. Because of their coastal location, they probably came into contact with white traders and navigators very early. In 1614, seven Nauset were kidnapped and sold into slavery by Captain Thomas Hunt of England. They were also visited early in the century by the French explorer Samuel de Champlain. For the most part, the Nauset were friendly with English settlers in the area, and many adopted Christianity. Most stayed friendly even through King Philip's War between the settlers and Indians, and some went so far as to aid the white settlers. The Nauset lived in permanent villages and ate a diet of fish and seafood as well as maize, beans, and pumpkins. They cooked food in clay pots, stirred it with wooden utensils, and created beautiful woven fabrics and leather goods. In 1622, the Nauset shared corn and beans with starving Plymouth colonists. In 1617, they escaped the great pestilence that killed many Indians along the East Coast, but around 1710 they lost many people to fever. By 1802, only two Nauset were still alive.

See also King Philip's War; Wampanoag.

Navajo: Tribe
CULTURE AREA: Southwest
LANGUAGE GROUP: Athapaskan
PRIMARY LOCATION: Northeastern Arizona, northwestern New Mexico, southern Utah
POPULATION SIZE: 219,198 (1990 U.S. Census)

There has been disagreement among scholars regarding when the ancient ancestors of the Navajo (or Navaho) migrated to North America. Some believe that they came in a relatively recent migration across the Bering Strait, about three thousand years ago. The linguistic designation of the main group is Na-Dene. This grouping contains several subgroups, the largest of which is Athapaskan. These hunting and gathering peoples, who once occupied Alaska and northwestern Canada, also began moving south. How and why the Athapaskans migrated into the Southwest is still a matter of discussion among scholars. As they did, they called themselves *Diné* ("the people"). The Navajo and their linguistic cousins, the Apache, reached the Southwest sometime in the mid-fourteenth century, with the Navajo occupying the area of the Gobernador and Largo tributaries of the San Juan River some 75 miles north of Santa Fe. This became the traditional homeland, the *Dinetah*, which means "among the people" in the Navajo language.

Prehistory. Anthropologists have pointed out a major difference between the Puebloans and the Navajo in prehistory. By the time the Navajo arrived in the Southwest, the Puebloans had been there for centuries and were firmly committed to the traditions of their ancestors, one of which was putting the good of the group or village as a whole above that of the individual. The Navajo, on the other hand, considered the individual to be of primary importance. They were also not as resistant to change as the Puebloans were.

The first Navajo in the Southwest were organized into fairly small groups, each with a headman whose duties consisted of leading his people to places where water, game, and wild grains and berries were plentiful. As they tended to move with the seasons, following the game, they built semipermanent circular wooden dwellings called hogans. Excavation of several prehistoric hogan sites has established that the Navajo were in the area at least as early as 1540.

Most scholars agree that the Navajo were greatly influenced by the culture of the Puebloans, which they recognized as more advanced than their own. Many Navajo myths and folk tales portray the Puebloans as sophisticated, rich, and powerful. Apparently, the Navajo were especially impressed by Pueblo religion and the complexity and power of its ceremoni-

als, which surpassed anything in their own culture at the time. Their first rudimentary efforts at agriculture were also inspired by the Puebloans.

The Spanish-Mexican Period. The first Spanish colonists in northern New Mexico, who came with Don Juan de Oñate in 1598, recorded that many raids on their settlements were carried out by "Apache or Apachean" peoples. In 1626, Fray Zárata Salmerón was the first to designate the Navajo as a specific Apachean group. By this time the Navajo had become a large and powerful tribe, whose various bands were led by both war and peace chieftains. They traded with and raided both the Puebloans and the Spanish settlers equally. As the numbers of the Spanish colonists increased, they became more demanding and cruel, especially to the Puebloans, attacking and burning the pueblos and killing or enslaving the people. As a consequence, the Puebloans began to encourage Navajo and Apache raids on the Spanish. By the mid-seventeenth century, the Spanish effort to convert all the Indians to Christianity had driven both the Puebloans and Navajo to conduct their own religious rituals in secret.

Navajo mother and child photographed by Ansel Adams at Canyon de Chelly, Arizona. (National Archives)

Navajo-Pueblo Contact. After the Pueblo Revolt of 1680 and the Spanish reconquest of 1692, many Puebloans fled north to the San Juan River area, which brought about greater contact with the Navajo. It has been established that, as a result of this interaction, the Navajo continued to learn much from the Puebloans: more sophisticated agricultural practices, styles of architecture, manufacturing techniques, and art forms such as weaving and improved pottery-making. Pueblo and Navajo ceremonial articles have been found in the same caches in the upper San Juan, establishing that Navajo religious practices were also greatly influenced by the Puebloans.

In the last decade of the seventeenth century, in the upper reaches of the San Juan, the Navajo and some of the Pueblo refugees built both open clusters of hogans and small masonry pueblos (*pueblitos*) consisting of fewer than six rooms each. Then, moving south into the Gobernador and Largo canyons, they built large masonry compounds and pueblitos, where they lived by hunting and gathering, herding, and dry farming. By the end of the century, they had acquired horses, cattle, sheep, and goats by trading with or raiding the Spaniards. In the next fifty years or so, they moved into Chaco Canyon and the Big Bead Mesa area, and then into Canyon de Chelly in northeastern Arizona.

Although the first bands of Navajo to reach the Southwest had been patrilineal, the close contact with the Puebloans in the late seventeenth century led the Navajo to adopt a matrilineal system of descent, with matrilocal residence, a characteristic they have retained into the modern period. The Navajo also adapted the Puebloan idea of clans into their own cultural pattern.

1700-1845. Throughout the eighteenth century, the Navajo continued their raids on Spanish communities and the Puebloans in the Rio Grande Valley, greatly aided by their acquisition of the horse. As many scholars have pointed out, the Navajo considered these raids to be an economic pursuit rather than war, and they were therefore never as anxious to drive the Spanish out as the Puebloans were. Although the Navajo in the Mount Taylor region rejected the Spanish attempt of 1745 to establish missions among them, for example, they remained friendly to the Spanish. On the other hand, Spanish and Mexican reports on the Navajo in the eighteenth and early nineteenth centuries were contained largely in official government documents and therefore dealt mostly with warfare, describing countless Navajo raids and Spanish or Mexican reprisals.

The fact that the horse gave the Navajo greater mobility, increasing their range for hunting, raiding, and trading, has led some to think that the Navajo reverted to nomadism, which was not the case at all. The horse made the Navajo more mobile, but that mobility was confined, in almost all cases, to specific areas where a family might build one or more houses which would serve as fixed centers of family life. With these centers as a permanent base, some family members might follow the sheep herds from their summer to winter grazing lands or go off to hunt or trade while others remained behind

to tend the crops. The fact that clan names are almost always place names as well also reinforces the fact that Navajo nomadism in the historic period is largely a myth.

Sheep and goats were also important to the growth of the Navajo population, providing not only a more dependable food supply but also a renewable source of trade goods, such as raw wool and woolen textiles, that could be exchanged for other necessities.

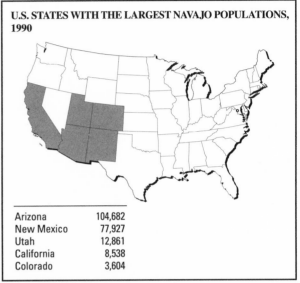

U.S. STATES WITH THE LARGEST NAVAJO POPULATIONS, 1990

Arizona	104,682
New Mexico	77,927
Utah	12,861
California	8,538
Colorado	3,604

Source: 1990 U.S. Census.

The U.S. Period. When the United States took possession of the southwestern territories from Mexico in 1846, General S. W. Kearny, arriving with his armies in August of that year, declared that he would stop all Indian raids. After a military expedition against the Navajo in November, 1846, Colonel A. W. Doniphan signed a treaty with thirteen Navajo leaders, among whom were Zarcillos Largos, Antonio Sandoval, and Narbono. This was only the first of many treaties into which the United States entered with local headmen in the mistaken belief that they were tribal "chiefs" who could speak for the entire Navajo Nation. Thus, when these treaties were broken by Navajo from groups not led by the signers, United States authorities, completely misunderstanding Navajo social and political organization, concluded that the Navajo were without honor and could not be trusted. In an attempt to control the Navajo, the United States mounted numerous campaigns against them and built military posts in their territory.

With the outbreak of the Civil War in 1861 and the resultant decrease in U.S. troop strength in the Southwest, both the Navajo and Apache took advantage of the opportunity to increase their raids on settlers and Puebloans. The government reacted by adopting a merciless policy of resettlement developed by General James Carleton. In June, 1863, Colonel Kit

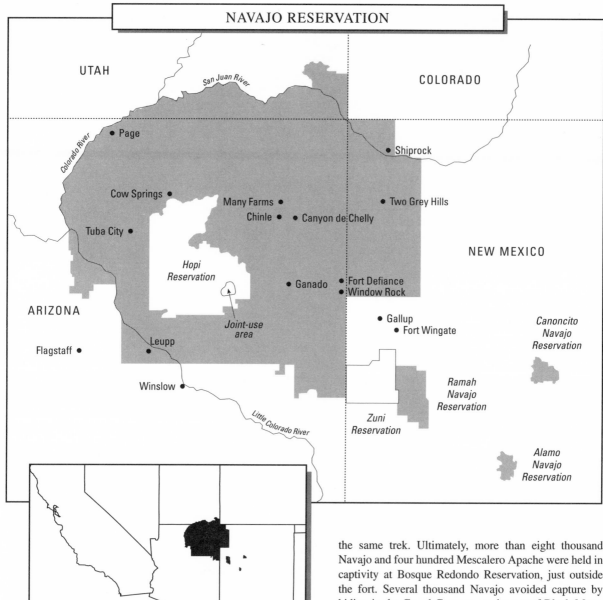

NAVAJO RESERVATION

Carson was sent into Navajo country to order the Navajo to surrender at Fort Defiance in Arizona. Many fled and were pursued and many were killed in the fighting which followed. In the end, however, Carson did not subdue the Navajo by military actions but by destroying their crops and livestock, the economic basis of their lives. Finally, on March 6, 1864, twenty-four hundred people, thirty wagons, four hundred horses, and three thousand sheep and goats began the "Long Walk" of 300 miles to Fort Sumner in eastern New Mexico. In April, thirty-five hundred more Navajo were forced to make

the same trek. Ultimately, more than eight thousand Navajo and four hundred Mescalero Apache were held in captivity at Bosque Redondo Reservation, just outside the fort. Several thousand Navajo avoided capture by hiding in the Grand Canyon, on the top of Black Mesa, north of the San Juan River, and in other inaccessible areas of Navajo country.

The Return Home. Now totally impoverished and not understanding their group captivity and the loss of their freedom to roam where they pleased, the Navajo suffered greatly from humiliation and homesickness, illness from an alien diet and bad water, and new diseases caught from their captors. Many died.

Finally, the United States government admitted that the resettlement had been a horrible mistake, and Carleton's despotic regime was ended in the fall of 1866. Custody of the Navajo was given to the Bureau of Indian Affairs in January of 1867. Late in 1868, after the signing of a treaty which created a 3.5-million-acre reservation for the Navajo within their old territory, they were allowed to return home. Although this was only a small part of their previous holdings, the Navajo were happy to be going back. They soon found that their troubles were far from over, however, as they struggled to make a living in a land that had been devastated by Carleton and Carson. All their homes had been razed, they had no livestock, and their fields had been destroyed. Fort Wingate and Fort Defiance served as distribution centers for the rations which the government eventually agreed to issue to help them, but there were many delays and shortages.

More stable conditions were finally established, however, and the Navajo enjoyed a short period of prosperity and growth. About 1870, the first schools promised in the Treaty of 1868 were established, although with mixed results. Some of these boarding schools were run more like reformatories than schools and produced graduates who were prepared neither for life in white society nor life back on the reservation. In the 1880's, the building of the railroad across New Mexico and Arizona brought new problems to the Navajo in the form of liquor, diseases, and economic exploitation. They were forced to give up much of their best range land and water to the railroads in exchange for less desirable areas. Since 1868, the most persistent factor of Navajo life has been the struggle with whites for land. From time to time, the Navajo reservation has been extended, from the original 3.5 million acres to about 15 million acres located in an area bounded on the northeast by the Continental Divide, on the southeast by the Rio Puerco, on the south by the San Jose and Puerco rivers, on the west by the Little Colorado and Colorado rivers, and on the north by the San Juan River. The area contains more spectacular scenery than good farming and grazing land; thus, increases in land holdings have never kept pace with the needs of the people, who depend upon sheep and cattle as the basis of their economy.

The Twentieth Century. The Navajo population increased from an estimated twelve thousand to thirty-five thousand by 1930, the beginning of the so-called stock reduction period. (The first attempts at stock reduction had actually begun in the 1920's, when the Navajo were told that they would not be given new grazing lands through congressional approval of boundary extensions until they had reduced the number of horses on the reservation.) In 1930, Indian Service foresters reported that the Navajo range was seriously overgrazed and that land erosion was an immediate problem. When the government instituted a stock reduction program, the Navajo equated it with the destruction of their culture because it affected not only their economic life but also their religious life. Sheep were essential to their entire ceremonial process, being used to pay the medicine men and to feed the large crowds who assembled for many days at a time for each ceremonial. Navajo resistance to and governmental insistence upon stock reduction caused additional misunderstanding and bitterness between the Navajo and non-Indians for many years.

The twentieth century has also seen the discovery of oil, uranium, and coal on the Navajo Reservation. It was the discovery of this mineral wealth that prompted the creation of the Navajo Tribal Council in 1938 as a major governing body authorized to decide how these new resources could be put to the best use. Prior to that, the only entity that represented the interest of all the Navajo was the Business Council, which first met in 1923. The Business Council consisted of three influential men, including Henry Chee Dodge. Dodge, an intelligent, well-educated man with great leadership abilities, helped guide the Navajo for more than seventy years.

As many scholars have observed, World War II marked the beginning of the contemporary Navajo world. As thousands of Navajo who served in the armed forces or were recruited to work in defense industries were exposed to life beyond the reservation for the first time, they realized that formal education and more consistent economic development were necessary for their survival. Consequently, they built a system of public schools across the Navajo Nation and, utilizing funds from the Navajo-Hopi Long Range Rehabilitation Program, provided highways and other programs to improve their economic development. Their industrial and commercial enterprises include those involving the arts and crafts; timber, oil, and gas production; power plants, and a parks and recreation department with a corps of Navajo Rangers. The center of their tribal government is housed in an attractive complex of buildings in Window Rock, Arizona.

Until recently, the Navajo did not live in groups large enough to be called villages or towns; they settled in smaller family groups in desirable locations dispersed throughout the reservation. In their matrilineal society, the grandmother is the central person in the family, and the children belong to her clan. Since it is taboo for a Navajo man to look upon or socialize with his mother-in-law, a woman and her husband do not live with the wife's mother but have their home nearby so that mother, daughter, and grandchildren can spend much time together. The typical Navajo dwelling is still the hogan, which is round or hexagonal and built of logs and adobe, with an air vent in the center of the roof.

Among the Navajo, ownership of property is individual, so that wife and husband have their own to do with as they choose. The wife usually owns the house and has her own crops and livestock, which she and the children tend. Additionally, the money she makes from her pottery and weaving is hers to keep. The husband has income from his own livestock and crops, plus whatever money he earns from his jewelry making or any other kinds of employment. It is he who represents the family at ceremonials and other public functions.

Weaving and Silversmithing. Traditionally, it is the women who make the pottery and weave the textiles. The earliest Navajo weavings were woolen wearing blankets, made on an upright loom which was adapted from one used by the Puebloans to weave their own cotton textiles. After the establishment of trading posts on the reservation in the early 1870's, the traders persuaded the Navajo to weave heavier textiles which could serve as rugs, having discovered that there was a market for these in the eastern United States. At the time, Turkish carpets were very popular with eastern buyers but were fairly expensive, so Turkish designs had been reproduced on linoleum—a less costly floor covering. Each trader provided the weavers in his area with samples of different Turkish designs on linoleum, declaring that he would henceforth buy nothing from them but rugs woven in these patterns. The Navajo weavers made their own adaptations from these designs, which have since evolved into the beautiful and exquisite Navajo rug of the present day.

Navajo men have always excelled in silversmithing and have led the way in the overall development of this art in the Southwest. The first smith was Atsidi Sani, who learned to work iron from a Mexican smith around 1850. He made knife blades, bits, and bridles, which he sold to earn his living. During the Bosque Redondo captivity, he taught other Navajo to work with iron, copper, and brass. After returning home, Atsidi Sani learned to work silver from the same Mexican smith and then taught his sons and other Navajo. The forms and the decorative styles originated by the Navajo have been adopted by other tribes, but Navajo silver has remained the most widely known and is the badge of distinction among the Navajo themselves.   —*LouAnn Faris Culley*

See also Arts and crafts—Southwest; Chantways; Hogan; Indian-white relations—Spanish colonial; Long Walk; Navajo-Hopi Land Settlement Act; Navajo Rehabilitation Act; Navajo War; Ranching; Weaving.

BIBLIOGRAPHY

Dutton, Bertha P. *American Indians of the Southwest.* Rev. ed. Albuquerque: University of New Mexico Press, 1983. An authoritative introduction to the subject, this book covers the history, contemporary tribal affairs, cultural and social characteristics, and arts and crafts of each group in the Southwest.

Dyk, Walter. *Son of Old Man Hat: A Navajo Autobiography.* New York: Harcourt, Brace, 1938. The classic autobiography of a Navajo from childhood to maturity in the late 1880's. The narration is chronological and vivid, recording a Navajo's relations with his kinsmen in daily life, his marriage, his accumulation of property in sheep, cattle, and horses, and the importance of religion and ceremonials in his life.

Kluckhohn, Clyde, and Dorothea Leighton. *The Navaho.* Cambridge, Mass.: Harvard University Press, 1974. In a thorough and readable manner, the authors consider four aspects of Navajo life: history, economic situation, cultural heritage, and social structure.

McPherson, Robert S. *The Northern Navajo Frontier, 1860-1900: Expansion Through Adversity.* Albuquerque: University of New Mexico Press, 1988. A well-documented and thorough study of the history of the northern Navajo frontier. This is an aspect of Navajo development which has been passed over by most scholars in their study of the Navajo.

Underhill, Ruth M. *The Navajos.* Norman: University of Oklahoma Press, 1967. Underhill, professor emeritus of anthropology at Denver University, was associated with the United States Indian Service for thirteen years. Her book offers many insights into the history and rich cultural background of the Navajo.

Navajo-Hopi Land Settlement Act

DATE: December 22, 1974

TRIBES AFFECTED: Navajo, Hopi, San Juan Southern Paiute

SIGNIFICANCE: This act was designed to settle land disputes between the Hopi and Navajo; it triggered tremendous controversy surrounding the removal and relocation of several thousand Navajos

The Navajo-Hopi Land Settlement Act was enacted by Congress in 1974 primarily to clarify rights of the Navajo and Hopi tribes in the 1882 "Executive Order Reservation" established by President Chester A. Arthur. This executive order set aside 2,472,095 acres "for the use and occupancy of the Moqui [Hopi] and such other Indians as the Secretary of the Interior may see fit to settle thereon." At the time, both Hopis and Navajos were living in the set-aside area. Disputes increased as the Navajo population in the area expanded.

In 1934 Congress consolidated the boundaries of the Navajo Reservation without altering the 1882 Executive Order Reservation. The Bureau of Indian Affairs then established grazing districts on both reservations. District 6, exclusively for Hopi use, consisted of about 25 percent of the 1882 reservation. The remainder was occupied largely by Navajo stock raisers. Disputes between members of the two tribes continued.

In 1958 Congress authorized a lawsuit to settle conflicting claims to the 1882 reservation. In 1962 a federal court, in *Healing v. Jones*, held that for the area outside District 6, the Hopi and Navajo had "joint, undivided and equal interests." Because the Navajos occupied most of the area, however, they controlled the most surface resources in the Joint Use Area (JUA).

Negotiations between the two tribes concerning management of the JUA were unsuccessful. In the early 1970's the Hopis sought and obtained a court order for livestock reduction in the area. The continuing controversy stimulated congressional interest, and the Navajo-Hopi Land Settlement Act was enacted in 1974.

The act was comprehensive. It directed that a mediator make recommendations to the district court, which would then partition the surface rights of the JUA. In 1977 each tribe received half of the JUA. Money was appropriated for livestock reduction and boundary fencing. The act, and a 1980 amendment, allowed for the transfer of some federal lands to the Navajos to help offset lost JUA land. In 1983 about 370,000 acres of "new lands" along the southern edge of the Navajo Reservation were selected.

The act required the removal of members of one tribe living on lands transferred to the other tribe. This involved a relatively small number of Hopis but thousands of Navajos. An independent commission was created to administer the relocation program, but it was inept, contributing to the hardships of relocatees. The $52,000,000 initial appropriation was inadequate. Congress belatedly responded in the 1980's, amending the act to restructure the commission and authorizing hundreds of millions of additional dollars for relocation.

As a final touch of irony, one section of this legislation, designed to resolve controversy over the 1882 reservation, allowed the tribes the right to sue to settle rights in lands within the 1934 Navajo Reservation. In 1992 a federal district court decided that the Hopis and San Juan Southern Paiutes (who had intervened in the lawsuit) had rights in portions of the Navajo Reservation long used by tribal members.

See also Navajo; Paiute, Southern; Pueblo tribes, Western; Reservation system of the United States.

Navajo Rehabilitation Act

DATE: April 19, 1950
TRIBES AFFECTED: Hopi, Navajo
SIGNIFICANCE: In an attempt to improve conditions in one of the most impoverished areas of the United States, this act funded the construction of roads, schools, and other developments on the Navajo and Hopi reservations

The Navajo-Hopi Long Range Rehabilitation Act of 1950 (Public Law 81-474) was passed by Congress to construct basic facilities on the Navajo and Hopi reservations. Passed in response to more than twenty years of deteriorating economic conditions on the Navajo Reservation, the act authorized funding for school construction, roads, and other projects.

In the 1930's the federal government had initiated a range-management program on the Navajo and Hopi reservations. Central to the program was reducing the amount of livestock on the range. This devastated the Navajo sheep-based pastoral economy. The full effects of stock reduction were partially obscured during World War II, when thousands of Navajos joined the service or worked in war-related industries. When these people returned home, however, livestock regulations and insufficient resources prevented a renewal of the pastoral economy. Unusually harsh winters added to the distress and drew national attention to the impoverished conditions among the more than sixty thousand Navajos residing in Navajo country.

Reservation schools could accommodate only about 25 percent of the student-age population. All-weather roads were practically nonexistent on the reservations. Inadequate roads contributed to health, education, and economic problems. Infant mortality was high and school enrollments low. After passing minor emergency relief measures, Congress considered a more comprehensive approach.

A 1949 bill to fund improvements on the Navajo and Hopi reservations, reflecting a resurgent congressional interest in limiting tribal sovereignty, also included a provision which extended the jurisdiction of state law over the two reservations. Citing this provision, President Harry Truman vetoed the bill.

In 1950 the president signed the Navajo Rehabilitation Act, which emerged from Congress without the offending jurisdictional provision. This version also provided expanded opportunities for Hopi participation in projects. The act appropriated $88,570,000. The largest portion, $25 million, was for school construction, followed by $20 million for roads and $19 mil-

lion for rangelands and irrigation projects. Lesser amounts were appropriated for health and water facilities, industrial development, and other projects. More than $9 million was allocated for relocating and resettling individuals away from the two reservations. There were also provisions for loans and leases. Finally, one provision (ignored for more than thirty years) authorized the Navajo tribe to adopt a tribal constitution.

In 1958, Public Law 85-740 provided an additional $20 million to complete road construction. By 1962, more than 80 percent of the total appropriation had been expended, including nearly all the dollars targeted for roads and schools.

The major benefit of the act was the substantial improvement in roads and schools on the reservation. All-weather roads have provided greater access to job locations and markets. School attendance increased dramatically through the 1950's and 1960's, as did the overall educational attainment of the population.

See also Indian Education Acts; Navajo; Pueblo tribes, Western; Ranching; Reservation system of the United States.

Navajo War

DATE: September, 1863-November, 1866
PLACE: New Mexico
TRIBE AFFECTED: Navajo
SIGNIFICANCE: Disputed grazing lands helped lead to this conflict, which resulted in Navajo relocation to the barren Bosque Redondo

Disputed grazing lands near Fort Defiance were a major factor leading to the 1863-1866 war. The site was favored for rendezvous by Navajo medicine men who collected herbs there. For generations, these lands were also used as pasture for Navajo livestock. Shortly after the establishment of Fort Defiance on September 18, 1851, soldiers who wanted to pasture their horses on these lands shot the Navajo-owned horses. Revenge was swift: Navajos raided army herds to replace their losses.

Through the decade, the raids continued and the army retaliated until, in 1859, army troops attacked and destroyed the home, crops, and livestock of the Navajo clan leader, Manuelito. In 1860, Manuelito—aided by leaders of other clans—assaulted Fort Defiance and nearly captured it, but was driven back. The army pursued the attackers into the Chuska mountains but was demoralized by the hit-and-run tactics of the Navajos. In January of 1861, the Navajos met with army representatives and agreed to work for peace. The uneasy truce was broken when, in September of 1861, a riot broke out over a horse race. Artillery was used to quell the disturbance, killing ten Navajos.

Raids for plunder and revenge increased, and the army responded. On September 6, 1863, Colonel Christopher "Kit" Carson was chosen to lead a campaign of "pacification." In the following months, Carson's scorched-earth offensive burned Navajo corn fields, orchards, and hogans; livestock was confiscated and destroyed. Tribes unfriendly to the Navajos were encouraged to attack and harass them. Navajo tribe members surrendered or were rounded up and relocated to Bosque Redondo (Round Forest) in the barren plains of eastern New Mexico. Some clan leaders and their followers held out as long as possible, but by the end of 1864 about 8,000 half-starving Navajos surrendered and were marched to Bosque Redondo. Some two hundred people died on the grueling three-hundred-mile march known as the Long Walk. Manuelito and twenty-six followers surrendered in September of 1866. When another clan leader, Barboncito, surrendered in November of 1866 with twenty-one followers, the Navajo War of 1863-1866 was over.

See also Barboncito; Long Walk; Manuelito; Navajo.

Neutral: Tribe

CULTURE AREA: Northeast
LANGUAGE GROUP: Iroquoian
PRIMARY LOCATION: West of Lake Ontario

A large sedentary tribe occupying palisaded villages north of Lake Erie and west of Lake Ontario in the early 1600's, the Neutral tribe was closely related to the Huron and other Iroquoian tribes. Like these other tribes, they were organized into matrilineal clans and lived matrilocally in female-headed, extended-family longhouses and had an economy based on tobacco, corn, beans, and squash. These crops were produced by the women; men hunted and fished to round out this healthy diet. There were about fifteen thousand Neutral people by the early 1600's. A major economic boon to these people was their monopoly on a regional supply of flint near Lake Erie. Perhaps because of this singular access to an important trade commodity, they remained neutral in the rivalry between the Hurons and the Iroquois, hence the name given to them by the French. The Hurons called them Attiwandaron, or "people who speak a language slightly different from ours."

Despite their monopoly on an important trade item, the Neutrals were prevented from trading directly with the French by the Hurons, who wanted to preserve their middleman role between tribes to their west and the French. In addition, despite the Neutrals' neutrality in the battle for control of trade between the Hurons and the Iroquois, the Iroquois attacked and destroyed them as a nation along with the Huron, Erie, and Tobacco tribes in 1650-1651. A few Neutrals survived as refugees along with the Hurons in the area around Lake Huron (later migrating to Quebec), but most were absorbed into Iroquois tribes by being adopted into Iroquois families by clan mothers.

See also Erie; Huron; Iroquoian language family; Iroquois Confederacy; Tobacco.

Nez Perce: Tribe

CULTURE AREA: Plateau
LANGUAGE GROUP: Sahaptin (in Sahaptian language family)
PRIMARY LOCATION: Idaho
POPULATION SIZE: 4,113 (1990 U.S. Census)

Nez Perce is the French name (meaning "pierced nose") for one of the Sahaptin tribes located in what is today Idaho. The term seems to be a misnomer, since few if any members of this Native American tribe actually pierced their noses.

The Nez Perce were the largest and most powerful component of the Sahaptin. "Sahaptin" (also spelled Shahaptin) is a collective term for a group of Indian tribes that share linguistic commonalities. All Sahaptian languages are of Penutian stock. The Sahaptin, as a collective group, inhabited an area which today is southwestern Washington, west-central Idaho, and northeastern Oregon. The Sahaptin may be divided into two major groupings, the western tribes (Molala, Tenino, and Yakima), and the eastern tribes (Nez Perce, Palouse, Cayuse, and Umatilla). The eastern and western groups differ culturally. The western Sahaptin constitute a loose tribal confederation and are generally pacifistic. The eastern tribes marry intertribally, share stronger intertribal relations, and tend to be more warlike than their western counterparts.

The Nez Perce themselves originally thrived along the lower Snake River and along its tributaries in what is now central and western Idaho, northwestern Oregon, and southwestern Washington. The staple food of the Nez Perce was dried salmon and other fish, as the Columbia River is the greatest producer of freshwater salmon in the world. In addition, their diet consisted of berries, roots, and small game, as well as deer and elk. Housing consisted of both square houses and long A-frame communal sleeping rooms that could house up to thirty families and were approximately 150 feet in length. This living style, in addition to other customs and conventions of the Nez Perce, was influenced by the Plains Indians; the Nez Perce were one of the easternmost Sahaptin tribes.

During the eighteenth century the Nez Perce became more involved in intertribal affairs, including wars with Plains tribes. This was attributable especially to the introduction of the horse around 1730. As a result, the Nez Perce participated in more distant hunting expeditions and in trade with Plains tribes beyond the Rockies. Frequently, the Nez Perce allied themselves with such groups as other Sahaptin tribes and the Umatilla, Cayuse, Walla Walla, Flathead, Spokane, and Coeur d'Alene. At various times, the enemies of the Nez Perce included the Blackfoot, Shoshone, Bannock, Crow, and Gros Ventre. Along with a greater frequency of warfare there were ushered in subsequent cultural adaptations such as war dances, equine tactics and maneuvers, and the introduction of the tipi.

The Nez Perce are particularly known for their selective breeding of horses to produce better stock. This resulted in raids upon the Nez Perce from Plains tribes so that they could improve their own herds. This selective breeding facilitated more distant intertribal relations of which the Nez Perce became a dominating force.

The first contact with European explorers and settlers in the early nineteenth century evidently affected the Nez Perce. Shortly after the expeditions of Meriwether Lewis and William Clark between 1810-1815, traders and fur trappers flocked to the region of the Nez Perce. Later, missionaries began their influx. During the 1820's and 1830's, the Nez Perce themselves engaged in fur trading. This prolonged con-

Nez Perce man in nineteenth century clothing and headdress. (Library of Congress)

Depiction of Chief Joseph the Younger's surrender (painting by Frederick Remington). (Library of Congress)

tact with foreigners contributed to epidemics among the Nez Perce, whose numbers dropped to under two thousand by 1850. This was a marked reduction in population compared with the early nineteenth century census yielding a population estimate of six thousand for the Nez Perce.

In 1855 the Nez Perce, along with other Sahaptin tribes, were pressured to sign a treaty which entitled them to a reservation consisting of various parts of their former ancestral land. Several reservations were formed for the Sahaptin peoples: Nez Perce Reservation, Colville Reservation, Yakin Reservation, Umatilla Reservation, and Warm Springs Reservation, plus other smaller reservations. Tribes were frequently broken up and collected indiscriminately when placed on reservations. Today it is difficult to distinguish among Sahaptin tribal groups or determine the ancestral traditions that were original to each.

The Nez Perce condition considerably worsened in 1860 with the discovery of gold in the Salmon and Clearwater rivers. This event led to a redrawing of reservation boundaries in 1863 by U.S. commissioners. With the loss of the Walowa and Grande valleys, the acreage of the Nez Perce Reservation was reduced by an estimated three-fourths. There was an enormous influx of miners, settlers, and homesteaders into the area.

A period of increasing hostility and intolerance culminated in the Nez Perce War of 1877. A militant band of Nez Perce—numbering between 250 and 450—led by Chief Joseph and Looking Glass resisted U.S. Army attempts to force them onto reservation land. The Nez Perce resistance held off five thousand U.S. military troops, headed by General Oliver O. Howard, for five months. On October 5, 1877, Chief Joseph surrendered to the U.S. forces, with each side having suffered approximately 250 casualties. The 1877 surrender took place near the Montana-Canada border. The Nez Perce were subsequently sent to the Indian Territory of Oklahoma, where many perished from malaria.

In the 1970's the Nez Perce Reservation in Idaho consisted of a total population of fifteen hundred to seventeen hundred. The reservation comprised 34,000 acres of tribal land and 53,000 acres of land for individual use. Many of the surviving Nez Perce have left the Idaho reservation to join the general U.S. populace. On the reservation, cultural traditions such as ceremonial dances and ceremonies of the Seven Drums Society are still observed. As mentioned above, the existing reservations containing Sahaptin peoples are somewhat syncretized, since many tribes were incorporated by force into the various reservations, not necessarily according to tribal distinctions.

—*Daniel L. Smith-Christopher*

See also Cayuse; Joseph the Younger; Looking Glass; Molala; Nez Perce War; Palouse; Tenino; Umatilla.

BIBLIOGRAPHY

Lavender, David S. *Let Me Be Free: The Nez Perce Tragedy.* New York: HarperCollins, 1992.

U.S. National Park Service. Division of Publications. *Nez Perce Country.* Washington, D.C.: U.S. Department of the Interior, 1983.

Nez Perce War

DATE: June 15-October 5, 1877

PLACE: Oregon, Idaho, and Montana

TRIBE AFFECTED: Nez Perce

SIGNIFICANCE: Chief Joseph, leader of the Wallamwatkins (Nez Perce tribe), led his people in retreat through Oregon, Idaho, and Montana almost 1,500 miles on one of the most remarkable and respected Indian war campaigns in U.S. history

During the nineteenth century the Nez Perce occupied various areas of the Northwest, including Washington, Idaho, and Oregon. There were five separate groups, each under the leadership of an autonomous chief. One group occupied Oregon territory in the Imnaha and Wallowa valleys and was under the leadership Old Chief Joseph. In 1855, Governor Isaac Stevens of the Oregon Territory signed a celebrated treaty with Old Chief Joseph and numerous other Nez Perce leaders, allowing the Indians ownership of all the land in the Imnaha and Wallowa valleys. The treaty was ratified by the United States Senate.

The treaty of 1855 proved short-lived, however, as the Civil War and discovery of gold at Orofino, Idaho, in 1860 led to an ever-increasing surge of immigration of white settlers into the valleys and territories claimed by the Nez Perce. Because of increasing tensions between the whites and Indians, in 1863 a new treaty was negotiated. The new terms excluded the Imnaha and Wallowa valleys as well as other vast areas of land that had been dedicated to the Indians in 1855. The revised treaty was signed by James Reuben and Chief Lawyer, but chiefs Old Joseph, White Bird, and Looking Glass refused to ratify it. Thus the Nez Perce became recognized as having "treaty Indians" and "non-treaty Indians."

In 1871, Old Chief Joseph died, leaving the leadership of his band (the Wallamwatkins) to Young Joseph (Chief Joseph). The continuing influx of white immigrants into the Nez Perce lands caused increasing problems between Indians and whites. In 1876, a commission was appointed to investigate complaints, and it was decided that the non-treaty Nez Perces had no standing and that all groups should go to designated reservations. In 1877, the U.S. Department of the Interior issued instructions to carry out the recommendations of the assigned commission. Preparing for the transition, a council was arranged to meet with Indian leaders and U.S. government officials on May 3, 1877. Chief Joseph and his brother, Alokut, represented the Nez Perce, while General Oliver O. Howard represented the U.S. government. The final understanding was that the non-treaty Indians would be on the designated reservations by June 14, 1877.

The Wallamwatkins Attack. On June 15, 1877, word was received at Fort Lapwai, Idaho, that the Wallamwatkins had attacked and killed several settlers around Mount Idaho,

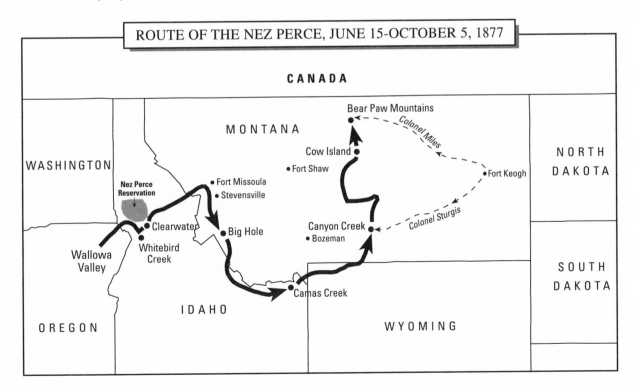

ROUTE OF THE NEZ PERCE, JUNE 15-OCTOBER 5, 1877

Idaho. U.S. Army troops were sent from Fort Lapwai under the command of Captain David Perry to counterattack. The Wallamwatkins, aware of the soldiers coming, moved their camp approximately 8 miles to Whitebird Creek. The next day, troops began pursuit into Whitebird Canyon and engaged in a terrifying encounter with the Wallamwatkins. The U.S. Army suffered resounding losses, losing thirty-four troops and numerous horses. The Nez Perce, numbering only seventy warriors, suffered only four wounded in the battle.

General Howard assembled troops at Fort Lapwai and hurried to reinforce the remaining troops at Mount Idaho. The battle was joined—Chief Joseph and his entire tribe (including women and children), totaling approximately four hundred, against the U.S. Army. By July 13, after numerous skirmishes with Captain Perry's and General Howard's troops, Chief Joseph led his people eastward toward the Lolo Trail in the Bitterroot Mountains and began a remarkable retreat march into Montana. Chief Joseph kept track of Howard's position and was able to stall and frustrate Howard's advancement. As a result, Chief Joseph led the Wallamwatkins through Lolo Trail and into the Missoula area. General Howard subsequently contacted Colonel John Gibbon at Fort Shaw, Montana, and instructed him to take up the pursuit. Gibbon was able to muster 146 men of the Seventh Infantry and thirty-four civilians.

Retreat and Surrender. Chief Joseph crossed the Continental Divide and camped his weary followers in the Big Hole Valley, unaware of Colonel Gibbon's pursuit and position. On August 9, Gibbon's troops made a surprise attack on Chief Joseph's camp and engaged in a long and difficult battle. Losses on both sides were substantial, but Chief Joseph was able to gather his warriors, recover lost ground, and recapture his large herd of ponies and make good his retreat.

By August 27, Chief Joseph had led the Wallamwatkins into Yellowstone Park, with General Howard and his troops in continuing pursuit. By September 6, Chief Joseph made his retreat through the northeast corner of Yellowstone Park. Continuing north, Chief Joseph led his people up through the Snowy Mountains and finally into the northern foothills of the Bear Paw Mountains, an easy day's ride to the Canadian border. Unknown to Chief Joseph, however, Colonel Nelson A. Miles, having been notified by General Howard, was in pursuit from Fort Keogh and was paralleling Chief Joseph's trail. On September 30, Colonel Miles's troops made a surprise attack on the Wallamwatkins' camp. The fighting was intense, the army losing fifty-three men and the Indians eighteen warriors. On the night of October 4, General Howard rode into Miles's camp and provided the reinforcements that would ensure a final surrender from Chief Joseph. On October 5, at 2:20 P.M., all firing ceased. At 4:00 P.M., Chief Joseph offered one of the most famous surrendering speeches ever documented. Turning to the interpreter, Chief Joseph said:

> Tell General Howard I know what is in his heart. What he told me before, I have in my heart. I am tired of fighting. Our chiefs are killed. Looking-Glass is dead. Tulhulhutsut is dead. The old men are all dead. It is the young men who say yes or no. He [Alokut] who led on the young men is dead. My people, some of them, have run away to the hills and have no blankets, no food; no one knows where they are—perhaps freezing to death. I want to have time to look for my children and see how many of them I can find. Maybe I shall find them among the dead. Hear me, my chiefs. I am tired; my heart is sick and sad. From where the sun now stands I will fight no more, forever.

Thus ended the Nez Perce War, one of the most remarkable and respected Indian war campaigns of U.S. history.

—*John L. Farbo*

See also Cayuse; Joseph the Younger; Looking Glass; Molala; Nez Perce; Palouse; White Bird.

BIBLIOGRAPHY

Adkison, Norman B. *Indian Braves and Battles with More Nez Perce Lore.* Grangeville: Idaho County Free Press, 1967.

_____. *Nez Perce Indian War and Original Stories.* Grangeville: Idaho County Free Press, 1966.

Beal, Merrill D. *I Will Fight No More Forever: Chief Joseph and the Nez Perce War.* Seattle: University of Washington Press, 1963.

Chalmers, Harvey, II. *The Last Stand of the Nez Perce.* New York: Twayne, 1962.

Fisher, Don C. *The Nez Perce War.* Thesis. Moscow: University of Idaho, Department of History, 1925.

Niantic: Tribe

CULTURE AREA: Northeast
LANGUAGE GROUP: Algonquian
PRIMARY LOCATION: Connecticut, Rhode Island

The Niantic, a branch of the Algonquian family, lived on the coasts of Rhode Island and Connecticut. Their name means "at a point of land on an estuary." Evidence suggests they had lived in the area for thousands of years. They lived in permanent villages and ate a diet of fish and seafood as well as maize, beans, and pumpkins. They cooked food in clay pots, stirring it with wooden utensils, and created beautiful woven fabrics, splint baskets, and leather goods. Their houses, called wigwams, were made on a bent and lashed pole framework; in later years they often included European furniture. During the sixteenth century, the tribe was divided into the Eastern Niantic and the Western Niantic by a series of Pequot attacks. The Western Niantic, who numbered about 600 in 1600, lived on the coast between the Connecticut River and Niantic Bay. This land was much desired by white settlers, who continually tried to take it. After their population was decimated by a series of epidemics in 1616-1619, the Western Niantic were all but wiped out by the Pequot War in 1637. Those who survived became subjects of the Mohegan. Since the nineteenth century, no one has claimed Western Niantic as his or her tribal identity. The Eastern Niantic merged with the Narragansett in the 1670's. Population counts after the merger treated the two tribes as one group.

See also Algonquian language family; Mohegan; Narragansett; Northeast; Pequot War.

Ninham, Daniel (c. 1710—Aug. 31, 1778, Kingsbridge, N.Y.): Tribal chief

TRIBAL AFFILIATION: Mahican

SIGNIFICANCE: Daniel Ninham sought the return of Mahican lands and fought on the colonial side during the American Revolution

Daniel Ninham was a leader of a Mahican band in Westenhuck, New York, who allied with Sir William Johnson and the British against the French in the last of several colonial wars in North America (1754-1763). He took part in the Battle of Lake George, September 8, 1755.

As the war with France neared its conclusion, Ninham traveled to England with other native leaders, principally Connecticut Mohegans, to seek return of lands they contended had been illegally taken by British colonists. The American Revolution intervened, and the legal actions filed by Ninham and others never were heard in court. Ninham joined the American Patriots during the Revolution and was killed fighting on their behalf at Kingsbridge, New York, August 31, 1778.

See also Mahican.

Ninigret (c. 1600—c. 1678, Wequapaug, R.I.): Tribal chief

ALSO KNOWN AS: Ninicraft, Nenekunat

TRIBAL AFFILIATION: Niantic

SIGNIFICANCE: Ninigret was sachem of the eastern branch of the Niantic of southern Connecticut; he skillfully avoided being drawn into the seventeenth century wars between the Indians and the English settlers

In the early 1630's, Ninigret was principal sachem of the eastern branch of the Niantics. The Eastern Niantics occupied the coastal region of western Rhode Island and were subject to the more numerous and powerful Narragansetts, to whom they paid tribute. Ninigret was notable for struggling to preserve his independence from the British while avoiding a war with them such as destroyed other New England tribes. He joined the British Mohegan-Narragansett attack on the Pequots in 1636-1637, but in the 1640's Ninigret repeatedly clashed with British authorities for his support of the Narragansetts in their war with the Mohegans. In 1653-1654, Niantic attacks on the Montauks of Long Island brought more disputes with colonial authorities, and a small British army invaded Niantic country to chastise Ninigret. He evaded contact by hiding in swamps with his people. During King Philip's War of 1675-1676, Ninigret avoided participation until the later stages of the conflict, when his Niantics assisted the British. In contrast, the Narragansetts had chosen to fight the British and suffered terrible losses. Regarded by the British as a schemer, Ninigret was a cunning survivor who recognized the reality of British power and reluctantly accommodated himself to it.

See also King Philip's War; Montauk Confederacy; Narragansett; Niantic; Pequot War; Sachem.

Nipissing: Tribe

CULTURE AREA: Northeast

LANGUAGE GROUP: Algonquian

PRIMARY LOCATION: Ontario

The Nipissing, a branch of the Algonquian family, were so named because the French found them in 1613 living on the shores of Lake Nipissing in Ontario, Canada. The name means "little-water people." From the first contact with French missionaries, the Nipissing were friendly with them. They accepted Christianity but without giving up their traditional shamanism. They had steady contact with British traders after 1610 but remained allies of the French through the French and Indian Wars. The Nipissing lived in permanent villages along the lake, traveling throughout the fall to gather food. They grew a few crops, but fished in southern waters and traded with Cree neighbors to the north. Chiefs were elected from a group of eligible males. The Nipissing had great skill as jugglers. Reliable population counts are unavailable. Their numbers were small through recorded history. Many were killed by Iroquois attackers in the middle of the seventeenth century, and at various times groups moved away and disappeared from record. In the late nineteenth century, the last known group of Nipissing were living with other Algonquians at Lake of Two Mountains in Quebec. When the church and its records burned in 1877, the last register of Nipissing families was destroyed. Probably Nipissing descendants are included among recent counts for other tribes, but no separate population figures for the Nipissing are recorded.

See also Algonquian language family; French and Indian Wars; Indian-white relations—French colonial.

Nipmuck: Tribe

CULTURE AREA: Northeast

LANGUAGE GROUP: Eastern Algonquian

PRIMARY LOCATION: Central Massachusetts

POPULATION SIZE: 376 (1990 U.S. Census)

The Nipmucks relied upon moose, deer, black bear, and numerous fur-bearing mammals for food and utilitarian by-products. Smaller animals, such as the hare, squirrel, weasel, and rabbit were trapped and snared, as were certain birds. Stream fishing and the gathering of roots, berries, and nuts, which stored well, supplemented the Nipmuck diet. Birchbark and willow were used extensively for containers, dwellings, and sundry other products. Winter travel was by snowshoe and toboggan. Permanent villages exercised control over an area's resources and territory, particularly its sugar groves.

The first European American contact was with the Pilgrims at Plymouth Rock. Though little is recorded, by 1674 the New England Mission had converted some Nipmucks to Christianity. In 1675, however, many Nipmucks fought against the colonists in King Philip's War, with many then fleeing to Canada or to tribes on the Hudson River. Their population was estimated to be five hundred in 1600 but had declined in 1910 to eighty-one, largely because of European American diseases, conflict with settlers, and low birthrates.

See also Algonquian language family; Indian-white relations—English colonial; King Philip's War.

Nisqually: Tribe

CULTURE AREA: Northwest Coast
LANGUAGE GROUP: Salishan
PRIMARY LOCATION: Washington
POPULATION SIZE: 447 (1990 U.S. Census)

The socially stratified Nisqually lived in permanent winter villages of split-planked rectangular houses. They were dependent upon both marine and land resources for food, practiced a definite yearly subsistence round of travel, and observed a strict division of labor.

The 1850 Donation Act of Oregon allowed settlers to acquire and settle on lands belonging to the Nisqually and others. The 1855 treaties of Point No Point, Point Elliott, and Medicine Creek reserved small tracts of land that eventually became reservations, including the Nisqually Reservation. Chief Leschi, who incited unrest among numerous groups, refused to accept the 1855 Medicine Creek Treaty. The U.S. Army occupied and eventually expropriated two-thirds of the Nisqually Reservation in 1917, forcing some inhabitants to relocate on other reservations. Other tribes lost valuable waterfront property to the expanding city of Tacoma. Many Nisqually live today on the Chehalis Reservation, along with some Clallam, Muckleshoot, Quinault, and Chehalis.

See also Chehalis; Clallam; Quinault; Salishan language family.

Nooksack: Tribe

CULTURE AREA: Northwest Coast
LANGUAGE GROUP: Salishan
PRIMARY LOCATION: Washington
POPULATION SIZE: 840 (1990 U.S. Census)

The Nooksack were a little-known tribe of the Central Coast Salish who once had close socioeconomic relations with the contiguous Upriver and Downriver Halkomelem. All the twenty permanent winter villages were river-oriented for travel and subsistence. Sea mammals were prized, along with eulachon, for oil. Land animals were hunted and trapped by men, whereas women gathered and collected roots, tubers, berries, fruits, and nuts.

The peoples of the Strait of Juan de Fuca were first contacted in 1787 by Charles Barkley, and in 1808 Simon Fraser of the North West Company charted the river which now bears his name. By 1811 land-based fur traders established themselves at the mouth of the Columbia, bringing considerable change to the Nooksack. By the 1870's and 1880's some Nooksack acquired homesteads in the Nooksack Valley, but considerable damage was done to salmon fishing—by 1900 there were at least seventy canneries at the mouth of the Columbia River.

See also Salishan language family.

Nootka: Tribe

CULTURE AREA: Northwest Coast
LANGUAGE GROUP: Wakashan
PRIMARY LOCATION: West coast of Vancouver Island
POPULATION SIZE: 4,325 (Statistics Canada, based on 1991 census)

The Nootka tribe may be an isolated representative of early Mongoloid hunters and fishers. The Nootka and the Nitinat subtribe are referred to as the "West Coast People." They have increasingly disliked appellations imposed by outsiders, however (Nootka is a white name), and since 1980 they have referred to themselves as "Nuu-chah-nulth."

At the first contact with Europeans in 1778, the Nootkans numbered about nine thousand to ten thousand and lived in twenty-five villages of different sizes along two hundred miles of coastline. The Nootka were a technologically capable people who were skilled hunters, fishers, and whalers. Land animals were a secondary food source. They amassed an abundance of food, which permitted lavish ceremonial feasts (convivial social gatherings) and potlatches. The potlatches allowed the host to distribute surplus wealth and gain honor status.

There was a highest-ranking chief for all the Nootka villages, a position obtained through titles and wealth. Maquinna and Wickanninish of the Clayoquet subdivision were two powerful chieftains. (Chiefs acted more as representatives of the various villages than as absolute rulers.)

Social and political life centered on the extended family, which lived together. The extended family cooperated to meet its needs and to amass wealth and status. Slaves were also kept. The family was presided over by a hereditary (patrilineal) chief. Although the extended family unit was autonomous, a number of families often wintered together, sometimes forming confederacies.

The spirit world was very much a part of Nootkan culture, and Nootkans often prayed for power to the Four Chiefs of Above, Horizon, Land, and Underseas. Two major ceremonies were the Wolf Ritual, to initiate a son or young relative, and the Doctoring Ritual, to help sick people.

A combination of disease, warfare, and integration into the white-controlled commercial economy caused a significant decline in population beginning in the late 1700's. A population low of 1,605 occurred in 1939, but numbers have gradually and steadily increased since then. The Nootkans' integration into the commercial economy capitalized on their native ways. They supplied furs, dogfish oil, seal pelts, and curios as well as becoming involved in commercial fishing and logging.

In 1871 the Nootkans became part of the Canadian Indian reserve system; missionary work began in 1875. By 1900 about 60 percent were at least nominally converted. During the 1960's and 1970's a pan-Nootkan or independence movement developed in order to establish a positive identity, control Nootkan affairs, and act as a counterpoint to assimilation into Canadian society. From the 1930's to 1958 the Nootkans belonged to the Native Brotherhood of British Columbia. In 1958 they formed their own organization, the West Coast Allied Tribes, later changed to the West Coast District Council, then to the Nuu-chah-nulth Tribal Council. A primary goal has been to obtain recognition of aboriginal land titles and to pursue land claims settlements.

See also Northwest Coast; Wakashan language family.

The Nootkas were accomplished hunters and fishers. (Library of Congress)

Northeast: Culture area

LANGUAGE GROUPS: Algonquian, Iroquoian, Siouan

TRIBES: Abenaki, Algonquin, Cayuga, Erie, Fox, Huron, Illinois, Kaskaskia, Kickapoo, Lenni Lenape, Mahican, Maliseet, Massachusett, Menominee, Miami, Micmac, Mohawk, Nanticoke, Narragansett, Neutral, Nottaway, Oneida, Onondaga, Ottawa, Pamlico, Passamaquoddy, Pennacook, Penobscot, Pequot, Petun, Piankashaw, Potawatomi, Sauk, Secotan, Seneca, Shawnee, Susquehannock, Tuscarora, Wampanoag, Wappinger, Winnebago

The northern boundary of the area known as the Northeast culture area is the southeastern margin of the boreal forest that stretches across Canada. The area includes the Great Lakes region and reaches (generally speaking) from the Atlantic Ocean in the east to the Mississippi River in the west. The boundary between the Northeast and Southeast culture areas is somewhat arbitrary, but the Northeast culture area is generally considered to extend to the Tidewater region of Virginia and inland through northern Tennessee. From prehistory, tribes and bands migrated throughout both Northeast and Southeast regions, and cultural influences of various groups upon one another were extensive. The societies of the Southeast tended to have a greater dependence on agriculture and a denser population, and they were socially and politically more complex. The one natural feature that was common to the entire Northeast area was the forest. The region was blanketed by extensive coniferous and deciduous forests, and trees provided the materials for tools, shelter, and modes of transportation (as in the well-known birchbark canoe).

Often commented upon by anthropologists are the marked Mesoamerican influences on Northeast cultures, some of which seem to date back to antiquity and all of which apparently were filtered through Southeast cultures. The Northeast cultural area seems to have evolved about three thousand years

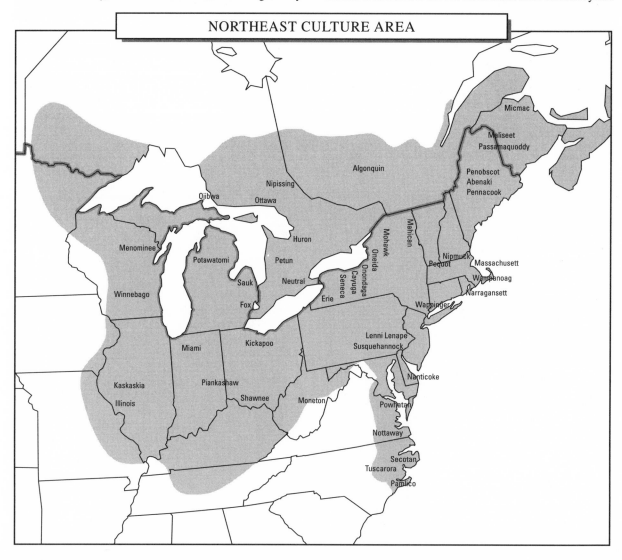

NORTHEAST CULTURE AREA

ago as a functionally integrated system interrelated with the natural environment. Its tribes gleaned much from other cultures without being overrun by them until the arrival of the European invaders in the sixteenth century.

At the time of the arrival of the Europeans, the coastal regions of the Northeast were occupied by Algonquian-speaking people, and the inland waterways were occupied by Iroquian-speaking people. The entire area was crisscrossed by the trails of a vast trading network. The Hurons, who occupied the region between Lake Ontario and Georgian Bay and were in contact with the people of the Subarctic, were the preeminent traders of the region. Huron was the language of trade. Storable foods were traded for furs, nuts, obsidian, shells, flints, and other items.

Three Northeast Subregions. Many scholars consider the Northeast culture area to consist of three major subregions: the coastal region, the St. Lawrence lowlands region, and the Great Lakes-riverine region. The coastal region included the area from the Atlantic Provinces of Canada to as far south as North Carolina. It was inhabited primarily by Eastern Algonquian speakers in a continuum along the coast, with a few Iroquoian-speaking bands in what is now coastal Virginia and North Carolina. Among coastal groups, the population grew denser, agriculture more important, and political organizations more complex as one went southward. These coastal Indians were the first to encounter the Europeans and the first to be decimated by the ravages of the diseases carried by whites. For the most part they had been wiped out or had been sent into forced migration by 1850, with the largest number surviving in Maine and the Maritime Provinces. Little of their culture was preserved or recorded by the religious refugees from England. In the years from 1615 to 1619, even before the Pilgrims arrived, disease carried by French and English adventurers and traders had killed an estimated two-thirds of the population of New England.

The St. Lawrence lowlands section included the St. Lawrence river area, southern Ontario, New York State, and the Susquehanna Valley. These were the homelands of Iroquoian-speaking peoples. ("Iroquoian" refers to speakers of the language group, whereas "Iroquois" refers to members of the League of the Iroquois—the Iroquois Confederacy—in most reference guides.) These tribes had similar patterns of horticulture, fishing, fortified villages, prisoner sacrifice, and spiritual rituals, and they had a highly codified matrilineal property system. Of the groups inhabiting the Eastern Woodlands (both Algonquian- and Iroquoian-speaking), those who were most agrarian were matrilineal, and those to the far north who subsisted as hunting bands were usually patrilineal.

The Great Lakes-riverine region was populated by Algonquian and Siouan-speaking groups who had limited contacts with whites until the late seventeenth century. Their politics were determined by pressure from the Iroquois League, whose warriors overran the lower Michigan peninsula in the 1600's and who established a hegemony over much of the region that lasted until after the American Revolution.

Cultural Similarities. There were many similarities between Iroquoian and Algonquian groups. Both were hunters and farmers, and both employed sachems to lead regional economic networks. Sachems came from elite families that collected and then distributed tribute in annual ceremonies of thanksgiving. The practice of living in seasonal camps took advantage of ripening food stocks in the north. Where a 160-day growing season existed, villages were stationary, and people grew corn as their staple. Where villages were stationary, more complex political systems evolved.

Most of the Indians south of the St. Lawrence River were village-dwelling people. Communal hunting of moose, deer, bear, and game birds supplemented agriculture based on corn, beans, and squash. Communal hunting techniques used fire, surrounds, and impounding techniques. Fish were also a significant food item; they were caught with traps, nets, hooks, spears, and poison. They could be taken through the ice in winter and, in the case of Atlantic salmon, caught on spawning runs. Wild plant foods, particularly berries, were so important that they were ceremonially gathered, as was maple sap. In the northern lake regions, wild rice was a staple.

The Algonquian tribes usually built oval-shaped or dome-shaped wigwams covered by mats or bark. Iroquoians, and Algonquians who had contact with the Iroquoians, lived in longhouses, usually about 20 feet wide and 50 to 100 feet long. As family units grew, the longhouses were extended.

Clothing consisted of animal skins, as did many parfleches, or carrying bags. Other containers were made from woven fiber or from clay. Necklaces, wristlets, earrings, and other items of ornamentation were made from hair, bone, native copper, shells, stones, and feathers.

Birchbark canoes were the primary mode of transportation of trade items. Wampum belts of shells and later beads described symbolically almost all dealings politically and ritually among and within tribes. The ritualized smoking of tobacco in ornately carved stone or clay pipes was common to all the tribes of the region.

Social organizations evolved from environmental necessity. Exploiting the environment in the north required small, autonomous, totemic, patrilineal bands. The other extreme was represented by the Iroquois tribes, who lived in fortified, stockaded villages, were matrilineal, and banded together into confederacies with very strong political and religious systems in which ultimate power was vested in the hands of the oldest "sensible" women of each clan. Some of the coastal Algonquians also organized into matrilineal clans.

Children were seldom physically punished. Iroquois men paid little attention to their own offspring; children were reared exclusively by women. At puberty, boys entered manhood through an initiation rite involving exile and fasting. Premarital and extramarital affairs were relatively common and carried no stigma. Marriages were arranged completely by clan mothers, and once marriage was consummated, divorce was very uncommon, because it would reflect poor judgment by the clan mothers. Murder within a clan was so uncommon that there were no rules governing its punishment.

Warfare between tribes was commonplace, but such activity resembled feuds more than organized wars. There was constant strife, even within language groups, until the fur trade and the economics of white society changed that forever. The Iroquois Confederacy, which may have been formed as a direct result of the fur trade, created the opportunity for the Five Nations of the Iroquois to establish a combined military force. In the mid-1600's, the Iroquois assembled an "army" of more than a thousand men and effectively eliminated the Huron, Erie, Petun (Tobacco), and Illinois from being factors in the overall scheme of the politics of the Northeast.

European Contact. Following European contact, life in the Northeast became very complicated. The existing fur trade intensified with the arrival of the French. The river systems that facilitated the fur trade created the basis of the relationship between whites and Indians. A growing European demand for furs transformed Indian political organizations. Most Northeast cultures were radically changed by the fur trade—in many cases even before any members of a tribe had even met a white person.

Geographical dislocations were common to every tribe and band. Tribal groups had three options: They could compromise with the invaders; they could adopt most of the outsiders' ways, including their religion; or they could violently reject the new cultures. As European encroachment advanced, some pantribal movements, such as those led by Tecumseh and Pontiac, evolved in an attempt to stop the whites. In other cases, refugees—for example, the Lenni Lenape—recombined to form new groups (in the case of the Lenni Lenape, the Delaware) and tried to make a stand while being pushed westward. Generally speaking, they were no match for the well-organized, commercially oriented, land-hungry Europeans.

—Glenn J. Schiffman

See also Algonquian language family; Architecture—Northeast; Arts and crafts—Northeast; Indian-white relations—Dutch colonial; Indian-white relations—English colonial; Indian-white relations—French colonial; Indian-white relations—Norse; Iroquoian language family; Iroquois Confederacy; King Philip's War; Longhouse; Longhouse religion; Midwinter Ceremony; Pequot War; Prehistory—Northeast.

BIBLIOGRAPHY

Ballantine, Betty, and David Hurst Thomas, eds. *The Native Americans: An Illustrated History.* Atlanta: Turner Publishing, 1993.

Newcomb, William W., Jr. *North American Indians: An Anthropological Perspective.* Pacific Palisades, Calif.: Goodyear, 1974.

Trigger, Bruce, ed. *Northeast.* Vol. 15 in *Handbook of North American Indians.* Washington, D.C.: Smithsonian Institution Press, 1978.

Northwest Coast: Culture area

LANGUAGE GROUPS: Athapaskan, Chinook, Penutian, Salish
TRIBES: Alsea, Bella Bella, Bella Coola, Chehalis, Chinook, Coast Salish, Coos, Eyak, Gitksan, Haida, Klamath, Klikitat, Kwakiutl, Nootka (Nuu-Chah-Nulth), Quileute, Quinault, Siuslaw, Takelma, Tillamook, Tlingit, Tsimshian, Umpqua

The Northwest Coast culture area extends from the modern regions of Yakutat Bay in southern Alaska south to Cape Mendocino in northern California. The temperate-zone rainforest ecology and abundant resources contributed much to the diverse cultures which developed in the area.

Natural History. Until about thirteen thousand years ago, much of the Northwest Coast area was covered with the ice of the Pleistocene Ice Age. When the ice began to melt, new vistas opened for the spread of plant, animal, and human populations. The once-white land was covered with a blanket of verdure so lush that one can hardly imagine it today.

There has been considerable debate regarding when humans first entered the area. Estimates range from about twelve thousand years ago to about fifty-five hundred years ago. Probably most arrived overland on foot, but quite possibly some came by boat as well. By the time of the first contact with Europeans there were more than 100,000 people populating the Northwest Coast area.

After the glaciers retreated but before human populations filled the environmental niches, the lushness of the land increased. Vegetation spread, and the animals followed; then came humans. Probably they came from Siberia over the so-called Bering Strait land bridge.

Cultural Geography. The diversity of physical types, languages, and cultures suggests multiple maritime origins. The coastal inhabitants appear unrelated to the Athapaskan stock said to have migrated overland from Eurasia, for example, and peoples north of the Columbia River are markedly different from those to the south. There is no consensus regarding the character of human penetration into the coastal ecosystem. Migratory groups appear to have settled gradually into their chosen coastal environments and developed into the cultures of the Northwest Coast culture area undisturbed over a period ranging from roughly twelve thousand to fifty-five hundred years ago.

Coastal cultures were originally river or river-mouth cultures, later beach cultures, and only finally (and only in part) seagoing cultures. They are said to have remained centered on the riverine and estuarine environments. Only some peoples took to sea. Among those who did not become maritime, such as the tribes south of the Columbia River, skills in canoe building were never as highly elaborated, nor was ceremonial life as complex, as among more northern groups.

Fishing and sea-mammal hunting were the most profitable activities. Harvesting maritime resources required tools that would allow hunters to use the available natural resources to the fullest extent, and most of the peoples of the coast developed such tools. Their lives moved with the rhythms of nature's cycles. Their needs were supplied by the forest and the sea. The materials needed for the construction of most of their material culture was readily available and at hand, yet they still engaged in widespread trade with other groups.

They used the moderate climate and wealth of resources well, creating bone fishhooks, harpoons, nets, and other hunting and gathering tools. They developed elaborate communities with ceremonial practices and intricate arts of a highly symbolic and abstract nature centuries before European peoples had laid the foundations of Western civilization. Their material culture was remarkable in its beauty, quality, and diversity.

Population density was influenced directly by the forest and the sea. Moreover, in richly provided areas, efficient food gathering and preservation created a large surplus of time that shaped community life and influenced the development of art and ceremonialism. The terrain was rough, a fact which discouraged farming and animal domestication. The fact that local stone was hard to work prevented the development of more advanced tools, and the absence of significant agricultural surpluses influenced trade patterns.

Village Life, Travel, and Trade. The Northwest Coast cultures lived peaceably for the most part, except for occasional slave raids or skirmishes over territorial boundaries. This condition led to the development of cultures with roomy, solid houses, seaworthy boats and canoes, elaborate art, intricate rituals and ceremonies, and a generally affluent and highly complex society. People lived in kinship groups, or clan units that were small and autonomous while being highly integrated into the overall cultural pattern of their area. Thus the village and the community it contained were of great significance in the social structure.

Peoples to the north were seagoing peoples and had an abundant surplus of resources. Peoples south of the Columbia River depended on the bays and the rivers for most of their livelihood; they had no need to look further. The sophistication of coastal peoples suggests that they had reached dynamic equilibrium with their environment and learned to maintain it long before Europeans came.

People of the Northwest Coast area probably arrived with their maritime adaptations intact and fully developed. Migration routes were coastal as well as interior. The Athapaskan-speaking peoples from Asia represent a later intrusion into a previously established cultural environment. There most likely were a number of basal cultures, or stable cultural traditions, in place by ten thousand years ago, and each culture was characterized by slightly different sets of tools and slightly different ways of life. Early cultural traditions gradually became more consistent throughout the area because of the increasing similarity of the postglacial environment.

Adaptation to Nature. Natural events such as glacial retreat, opening of new land and migration routes, changes in sea levels, stabilization of the climate, the consistent spread of plants and animals into available niches, and ongoing episodic volcanism throughout the inland ranges of the Cascades (from Northern California northward into Canada) had a profound influence on the evolving cultural systems along the coast. When sea levels changed, for example, there was a corresponding change in the technology of coastal cultures that gave rise to cultures more easily recognizable as the ancestors of those later subjected to ethnographic study. These cultures' status systems were based on wealth and craft. The diffusion of technological

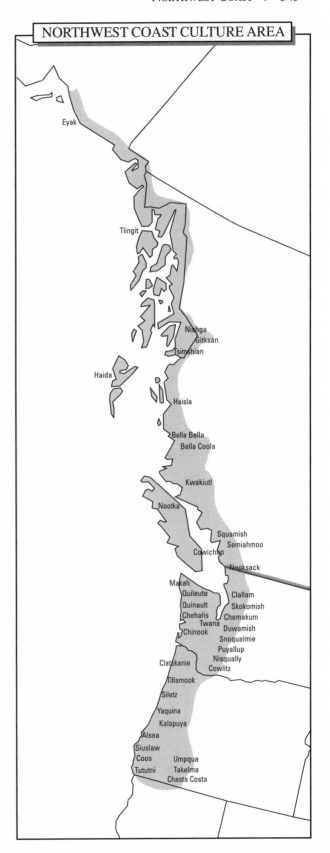

NORTHWEST COAST CULTURE AREA

innovations and new ideas, which led to even greater wealth among members of Northwest Coast culture area communities, was hastened by rapidly developing lines of trade; they were extensive and widespread, connecting distant groups.

Few generalizations regarding human origins are definitive. The Northwest Coast area has been habitable for more than forty to fifty thousand years and has probably been occupied continuously for the last seven thousand years at least. Stable cultural patterns probably have existed for more than five thousand years. The sources and processes of development of early culture on the coast are shrouded in mystery and myth. It is known that they had ceremonies, mythologies, rock art, and tooth pendants. Shamanic animism and the beliefs and practices associated with the power of guardian spirit entities were widespread. They smoked cultivated tobacco and used plants for healing rituals, in ceremonials associated with fertility, and in burials.

Status and Wealth. Wealth and status were interrelated in Northwest Coast cultures. Leaders had to be wealthy, a situation which led to ostentatious displays of rank and even to the ritualized destruction of wealth in the grand potlatches of the northern groups. Gift giving was a highly developed social practice. Some tribes, mostly to the south, appear to have practiced a less destructive form of potlatch in which wealth was displayed, then given away. In such cases the ceremony acted as a means of redistribution of wealth and an affirmation of status. Lineage granted hereditary family privileges and rights to those associated with certain family symbols, crests, or signs. The leadership system, then, was both a means of concentrating surpluses and of redistributing wealth among the general population.

Although the Northwest Coast is often regarded as a single culture area, this may or may not be the case. The great consistency among the material remains of early cultures in the forms of canoes, houses, clothing, basketry and weaving, carving in wood and stone, crafts, and technologies suggests a single areal culture. Yet it is clear that in spite of certain cultural consistencies (that may be attributed to the environment) coastal cultures were remarkably different from one another in important ways.

Some scholars therefore question the validity of the contention that this vast area is host to a single culture complex. The Salish-speaking peoples north of the Columbia River and the Penutian-speaking peoples to the south are not so alike as they might at first appear to be, and the ways of life of estuarine and riverine peoples are very different from those of seagoing maritime peoples.

Modern History. In the mid-1700's the Eurasian and European immigrants arrived: the Russians in 1741, the Spaniards in 1774, and the English in 1778. With these intrusions the prehistoric period came to an end and modern history began.

The fur trade emerged as a dominant influence, quickly drawing the indigenous communities into a growing world economy and giving them rapid access to luxury goods and metal-based technology. Yet social disintegration (as sources and concentrations of wealth changed), erosion of community identities in the face of decimating diseases, forced relocation to reservations, cultural decline because of the transformation of belief systems brought about by missionary activity, and loss of languages were widespread.

Colonization resulted in the loss of indigenous control over the environment and the eventual extinction of many smaller communities. Until European contact, Northwest Coast cultures were supported by a subsistence base distributed throughout a uniform, temperate, rain-forest environment. They were hunter-gatherers of the most advanced sort. In an environment of great abundance, diverse cultures developed that were highly civilized and comparable with civilizations elsewhere based upon agriculture and animal domestication. Their self-sufficient technologies were remarkably advanced.

This culture area contains the oldest and most variable evidence for flaked stone technological traditions in North America. It also contains the largest number of Native American languages and language families. Evidence suggests that many populations have lived at their present locations for long periods of time. Technological and linguistic diversity diffused rapidly as the historical period began, however, making it difficult to determine exactly how long cultures have been in residence.

—*Michael W. Simpson*

See also Architecture—Northwest Coast; Arts and crafts—Northwest Coast; Athapaskan language family; Penutian language family; Plank house; Potlatch; Prehistory—Northwest Coast; Salishan language family; Totem poles.

BIBLIOGRAPHY

Borden, Charles E. *Origins and Development of Early Northwest Coast Culture to About 3000 B.C.* Ottawa: National Museums of Canada, 1975. This is a complete archaeological survey of the data on the area.

Drucker, Phillip. *Indians of the Northwest Coast.* Garden City, N.Y.: Natural History Press, 1963. The author notes in this comprehensive survey that there is little physical data on where the first Northwest people originated and how they got to the Northwest.

Fladmark, Knut R. "The Feasibility of the Northwest as a Migration Route for Early Man." In *Early Man from a Circum-Pacific Perspective*, edited by Alan Bryan. University of Alberta Department of Anthropology Occasional Papers 1. Edmonton, Alberta: Archaeological Researchers International, 1978. Fladmark suggests there may be a variety of origins for the peoples who populated the area and suggests that the people of the Northwest are descendants of long-established Eskimo-Aleut culture area inhabitants.

Ruby, Robert H., and John A. Brown. *A Guide to the Indian Tribes of the Pacific Northwest.* Norman: University of Oklahoma Press, 1986. This book gives an excellent, updated listing of sources regarding the general history and current status of these tribes.

Waldman, Carl. *Atlas of the North American Indian.* New York: Facts on File, 1985. An excellent summary description, with maps, of the Northwest Coast culture area.

Northwest Ordinance

DATE: July 13, 1787

TRIBES AFFECTED: Those in Ohio, Indiana, Illinois, Michigan, Wisconsin

SIGNIFICANCE: Although it was considered the greatest achievement of the Confederation Congress because it provided terms for the creation of new states in the Old Northwest, the ordinance set a tragic precedent by denying Indian rights

By the Peace of Paris with Britain (1783), the United States acquired a vast inland empire bounded by the Appalachians, the Mississippi River, the Great Lakes, and the Gulf of Mexico. The task of disposing of this territory fell to the government as it was organized under the Articles of Confederation (1781-1789). Conflicting claims of states, settlers, land companies, and American Indians confused the issue. Lands south of the Ohio River were settled separately from those north of it. The Old Northwest, including the present-day states of Ohio, Indiana, Illinois, Michigan, and Wisconsin, was claimed by Virginia, Connecticut, and Massachusetts. Thomas Jefferson chaired a committee that in 1784 proposed to Congress the creation of a temporary government for the Northwest and the area's eventual division into sovereign states eligible to join the Confederation on terms equal to the original members. Though the plan was not enacted, it did provide a model for the Northwest Ordinance and facilitated the cession of western lands by Virginia (in 1784), Massachusetts (1784-1785), and Connecticut (1784-1786) to the national government.

If state claims were resolved, those of Native Americans were refused. Under British rule, by the Proclamation of 1763, the entire West had been set aside as Indian Country, starting at the Appalachian Divide. The pressure for white settlement of the region had been a contributing cause of the American Revolution, a lesson the Confederation had learned. As settlers from New England, Pennsylvania, and the South pressed toward the Ohio Country, Indian claims were extinguished. By the Treaty of Fort Stanwix (1784) the Iroquois, exhausted by war, surrendered their claims to western New York and Pennsylvania. The next year, major Ohio tribes relinquished their claims to most of the future state, with the exception of the southwest shores of Lake Erie. Formal concession came within a decade in the Treaty of Fort Greenville (1795), when, for a ten-thousand-dollar annuity, twelve tribes relinquished the southwest portion of the Old Northwest (Ohio and Indiana).

Utilizing Jefferson's plan, the Congress of the Confederation (1787), even as the Constitutional Convention was meeting, established the Northwest Ordinance, by which those lands would be organized as a territory, with a nationally appointed governor, secretary, and judges. It stated that when five thousand free white males resided there, a bicameral legislature was to be created. Eventually three to five states were to be formed (with a minimum of sixty thousand free white inhabitants needed for statehood), each to be admitted to the United States and to be equal in standing to the original states. Freedom of religion, the right to jury trial, public support of education, and the prohibition of slavery were to prevail. While this legislation is traditionally regarded as the greatest achievement of the Confederation Congress, it set a tragic precedent by riding roughshod over the rights of Native Americans.

See also Fort Greenville, Treaty of; Fort Stanwix, Treaty of; Proclamation of 1763.

Nottaway: Tribe

CULTURE AREA: Northeast

LANGUAGE GROUP: Iroquoian

PRIMARY LOCATION: Virginia

The Nottaway, a branch of the Iroquoian family, lived in southeastern Virginia on the Nottaway River. They called themselves *Cheroenhaka* but were known to the Algonquians as *Mangoac* and *Nadowa* ("adders," a common name for non-Algonquian neighbors). They lived in permanent villages and maintained little contact between villages. They lived mainly by growing crops but were also skilled hunters and gatherers. Corn was the most important crop, and women and girls seem to have done most of the field work. The Nottaway dialect was similar to that of the Tuscarora, the largest of the early Iroquoian tribes of the Virginia-North Carolina coastal plain. The Nottaway were not much affected at first by the expanding of the Jamestown colony in the seventeenth century. As trade grew after 1650, however, and as a major trade route passed through Nottaway lands, tensions increased. In the aftermath of Bacon's Rebellion in 1677, the Nottaway and their neighbors became subject to the dominance of the Virginia colonists. Through the next century they were pushed onto smaller and smaller allotments of land. They intermarried with free blacks and adopted European ways of life. In 1824 the Virginia legislature officially voted to terminate legal tribal status for the Nottaway. They tried for many years to maintain their identity and lasted longer than many of their neighbors, but intermarriage and geographical displacement made it impossible. William Lamb, the last person claiming Nottaway identity, died in 1963.

See also Bacon's Rebellion; Iroquoian language family; Northeast.

Oaxaca: Archaeological site
DATE: Since 1600 B.C.E.
LOCATION: Oaxaca, Mexico
CULTURES AFFECTED: Zapotec, Maya

The Valley of Oaxaca, in the highlands of southern Mexico, is one of the New World's most important centers of pre-Columbian civilization. The valley itself is Y-shaped, divided into three arms by the confluence of the Atoyac and Salado rivers. The lower portion of the valley is fertile, alluvial bottomland and remains a major area for agriculture production. Research undertaken since the late nineteenth century has revealed one of the longest sequences of indigenous cultural occupation in the Americas, beginning with early Archaic period hunter-gatherers and continuing to the thriving Zapotec communities of today.

One of the earliest sites in the valley is Guilá Naquitz, a rock shelter in the eastern arm of the valley, excavated in 1966 by archaeologist Kent Flannery. Stratified occupation levels date from 8750 to 6670 B.C.E. and represent seasonal use of the shelter by mobile bands of hunter-gatherers who consumed a variety of wild plant foods, including acorns, maguey hearts, mesquite seeds, and hackberries. Squash and beans may have been cultivated. Although no carbonized remains of maize were recovered, pollen from *Zea mays* was present in some levels.

By 1500 B.C.E., the earliest pottery-using farming village in the valley had been established at San José Mogote, also investigated by Flannery. Subsistence was based on maize supplemented by wild plants and game. Before 1150 B.C.E., it had become the largest of about two dozen Early Formative period villages in the valley. It was the first settlement with public architecture in the form of large, rectangular structures. Obsidian, conch shells, and stingray spines indicate long-distance exchange with cultures of central Mexico and the coast, and at least one workshop produced magnetite mirrors that were traded to contemporaneous Olmec sites such as San Lorenzo. San José Mogote remained the center of ceremonial activity in the valley until 500 B.C.E., when it was supplanted by Monte Albán. A carved Danzante (dancer) slab with a bloodied sacrificial victim placed at the threshold of a ceremonial structure suggests that the processes that led to the establishment of the hilltop center of Monte Albán may have had their beginning at San José Mogote.

Between 500 B.C.E. and 700 C.E., Monte Albán dominated the valley as a political and religious center, conducting long-

Ruins of Monte Albán in the Oaxaca Valley; the Monte Albán culture dominated the region between 500 B.C.E. and 700 C.E. (American Museum of Natural History)

distance relationships with Teotihuacán, in central Mexico, where there is evidence for a *barrio* (neighborhood) of residents from Oaxaca. The decline of Monte Albán may have been linked in some way to the collapse of the polity at Teotihuacán. Other factors included an increase in craft specialization and economic activity at sites away from the center, reducing Monte Albán's relative importance in political and exchange networks. From 700 to 1000 C.E., it experienced a population decline of about 25 percent, while centers on the valley floor such as Zaachila, Lambityeco, Jalieza, and Mitla increased in size. Monuments of this later phase include a number of genealogical registers, recording the royal marriages of Zapotec nobility. These indicate the importance of the establishment of kinship links between different polities, which played key roles in the reorganization of political alliances during the Postclassic period (1000 to 1500).

See also Maya; Mitla; Mixtec; Monte Albán; Zapotec.

Ocaneechi: Tribe

CULTURE AREA: Southeast
LANGUAGE GROUP: Siouan
PRIMARY LOCATION: Virginia, North Carolina

The small tribe of river-oriented Ocaneechi were horticulturalists about which little is known ethnographically. They had two chiefs, one who presided over warfare, and the other over matters concerning planting and hunting. Their so-called tribal symbol was a serpent. They are first recorded in 1670 as inhabiting a large island in the Roanoke River. Apparently, they later established and maintained close socioeconomic relations with the Tutelo and the Saponi, who shared the same language and who settled on two adjacent islands. In 1676, the Conestoga sought protection from the Ocaneechi against the English and Iroquois, but later the Conestoga attempted to dispose of their benefactors and were driven away. In time, after continual conflict with the Iroquois and Virginians, the Ocaneechi left their island and settled in North Carolina.

See also Tutelo.

Occom, Samson (c. 1723, New London, Conn.—Aug. 2, 1792, New Stockbridge, N.Y.): Missionary

TRIBAL AFFILIATION: Mohegan
SIGNIFICANCE: Samson Occom was one of the first American Indians educated by whites who successfully bridged both cultures as a missionary and teacher

Samson Occom was caught up in the religious enthusiasm of the "Great Awakening" when he was about sixteen. When he was twenty, his mother went to the Reverend Eleazor Wheelock, a prominent evangelical minister, and asked him to teach her son how to read.

Wheelock's success in teaching the highly motivated Occom led him to establish a school for Indians, Moor's Indian Charity School. Wheelock taught the basics of a secular and religious education. "Husbandry" (farming) was taught to boys, and girls were taught what today would be called home economics. Among other things, Wheelock taught Occom and his other students Greek, Latin, and Hebrew, which he believed were essential for future missionaries. (The Protestant emphasis on interpreting the Bible individually meant that students should be able to read the original Greek, Latin and Hebrew Biblical texts.)

Unable to attend college because of weak eyes, Occom became a teacher and minister to the Montauk tribe on the eastern tip of Long Island from 1749 to 1764. He was the town's minister, judge, teacher, and letter writer, and was expected to offer hospitality to visitors. He taught his students the alphabet, spelling, and the like. He received twenty pounds a year from the London Society for the Propagation of the Gospel for his work, less than what white missionaries received for similar work. He married Mary Fowler (a Montauk) in 1751.

Occom was ordained as a Presbyterian minister in 1759 by the Long Island Presbytery. Dr. Wheelock sent him on missions to the Oneida tribe in New York in 1761, 1762, and 1763. In 1764, he returned home to Mohegan, Connecticut, and in 1765 he accompanied the Reverend Nathaniel Whitaker to England to raise money for Wheelock's Indian school. In two years of preaching across Britain, Occom was able to raise twelve thousand pounds. Upon his return to America, Occom was unwilling to do missionary work among the Iroquois as Wheelock suggested, and was upset over Wheelock's use of the money raised for Indian students to found Dartmouth College in New Hampshire.

Occom severed his connection with Wheelock and became a poverty-stricken itinerant preacher to the New England tribes. His concern for protecting Indian lands helped cause a rift with his church. In 1773, he sought a land grant from the Oneida tribe to remove a selected group of New England Indians beyond the negative influence of whites. Although interrupted by the American Revolution, Occom was able to establish Brothertown in 1789, and pastored to his people for the remainder of his life. Occom's published works include *Sermon Preached at the Execution of Moses Paul, an Indian* (1772) and *A Choice Selection of Hymns* (1774).

See also Missions and missionaries; Mohegan.

Oconostota (c. 1710, eastern Tenn.—1783, Overhill Cherokee Territory): Tribal chief

TRIBAL AFFILIATION: Cherokee
SIGNIFICANCE: Oconostota helped to shape early Cherokee policy toward British and French colonists in what became the southeastern United States

Oconostota was born on the western side of the southern Appalachian Highlands. As a young warrior, he so distinguished himself that by 1736, in his mid-twenties, he was the war chief of the Cherokee. During the eighteenth century, a time of rivalry in North America between the British and the French, most Cherokee leaders favored ties to the British; Oconostota was the exception. When the smallpox epidemic of 1738 broke out, the French told the Cherokee that the British had planted the smallpox germ. Oconostota survived his bout with the disease, but for the rest of his life he blamed the British for his smallpox-pitted face.

Following the French and Indian War (1754-1763), Oconostota found it necessary to work for a mutually beneficial relationship with the British, including Cherokee neutrality during the American Revolution. Until his death in 1783, Oconostota tried to protect the rights of the Cherokee while maintaining peaceful relations with the new nation that was emerging from the American Revolution.

See also Cherokee; Cornstalk; Dragging Canoe; French and Indian Wars; Indian-white relations—English colonial; Indian-white relations—French colonial.

Ofo: Tribe

CULTURE AREA: Southeast
LANGUAGE GROUP: Siouan
PRIMARY LOCATION: Mississippi

Beginning in 1673, under pressure from the Iroquois, a Siouan tribe of eight villages moved in successive stages from the area of the upper Ohio River to land located on the Yazoo River in Mississippi. They were known as the Ofogoula (translated by some as "Dog People" and by others simply as "People"), Ofo (a contraction of Ofogoula), and Mosopelea. The first historical reference to the Ofo, in 1699, refers to a village of Ofogoulas among six river villages. In 1721, a mixed village of Ofogoulas and Curoas, consisting of approximately 250 persons, was reported.

In 1729, the Natchez Revolt against the French occurred; the Ofo refused to participate, moved south, and became allies of the French. In 1739, they joined the French in attacking the Chickasaw, and in 1764, they participated in a French attack on an English convoy on the Mississippi River. Many of the Ofo were killed. In 1784, a dozen or so were found with the Tunica Indians in a village on the Mississippi, eight miles north of Point Coupée. Following 1784, no mention is made of the Ofo in books. In 1908, the last surviving Ofo speaker was discovered. The woman, named Rosa Pierrette, had been taught the language by her grandmother, and all other remaining members of the Ofo tribe had died when she was young. She was interviewed, and she confirmed the name of the tribe and many of its cultural practices. She also provided a substantial amount of the Ofo language, enough to enable the publication in 1912 of an Ofo dictionary by the Smithsonian Institution.

See also Natchez Revolt; Siouan language family; Tunica; Tunica language.

Ojibwa: Tribe

CULTURE AREA: Northeast
LANGUAGE GROUP: Algonquian
PRIMARY LOCATION: Minnesota, Wisconsin, Michigan, upper Great Lakes area, southern Ontario
POPULATION SIZE: 103,826 in U.S. (1990 U.S. Census); 76,335 in Canada (Statistics Canada, based on 1991 census)

The Ojibwa, ancestors of today's Chippewa, Ojibwa, Mississauga, and Saulteaux, resided along the eastern shore of Georgian Bay, the north shore of Lake Huron, and west onto Michigan's Upper Peninsula before European contact. Changing residence with the seasons, they depended on hunting, fishing, and trading. The Ojibwas' basic sociopolitical units were small bands that traveled after game. No overall political organization united the bands. In the early 1600's, the Ojibwa encountered Samuel de Champlain, Jesuit missionaries, and *coureurs de bois* (French trappers).

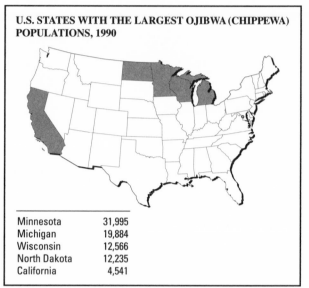

U.S. STATES WITH THE LARGEST OJIBWA (CHIPPEWA) POPULATIONS, 1990

Minnesota	31,995
Michigan	19,884
Wisconsin	12,566
North Dakota	12,235
California	4,541

Source: 1990 U.S. Census.

After 1650, the Ojibwa suffered setbacks from Iroquois raiders and their number declined substantially; however, they recovered before the century ended and pushed their way south, actively involved in the fur trade. Antoine Laumet de Lamothe Cadillac helped draw the Ojibwa south by establishing Detroit in 1701. One effect of the fur trade was growth in band populations and concentrations around trading posts; another was expansion of the band leader's authority and the evolution of leader into a hereditary position. The Ojibwa joined Pontiac in his war against the British in 1763.

In the late 1700's, Ojibwa began ceding land to the British and then to the Americans in the 1800's. Between the 1820's and 1860's, Michigan, Wisconsin, and Minnesota Ojibwa ceded much of their lands and were confined to small reservations; only a small number acquiesced to being removed to Kansas. Through the nineteenth century, non-Indians acquired and exhausted many of the natural resources upon which the Ojibwa traditionally depended. Between 1820 and 1840, some Ojibwa adjusted by becoming farmers, raising hay, wheat, oats, peas, Indian corn, and potatoes, and keeping livestock; others found wage opportunities in the lumber industries.

Ojibwas adapted in many ways to the changing world during the nineteenth century. They integrated Victorian fashions

Flat Mouth, an Ojibwa principal chief in the nineteenth century. (National Archives)

with traditional dress of buckskin breechcloth, leggings, and moccasins, sold native-made goods to non-Indians, and built log cabins to replace the dome-shaped wigwam covered with birchbark and cattail matting. Still, many continued to draw a living from what they gathered and continued to construct wooden utensils, birchbark containers, canoes, and cedar cradleboards.

Traditional Society. Status was earned in Ojibwa society through success as warriors, civil leaders, or shamans. Marriages were usually monogamous; polygyny was acceptable but rare. Individuals belonged to clans which were exogamous and patrilineal—children were born into their father's clan and could not marry another of the same clan. Clan rules remain important today. Children are highly valued, and child rearing was traditionally permissive. Fathers prepared sons, and mothers prepared daughters for adulthood. The most significant event in a child's life came at puberty, with boys making a vision quest for a guardian spirit. It was not expected, but girls could also have a vision at this phase. Kinship continues to be a strong binding force in Ojibwa society.

According to the Ojibwa religion, spirits reside in most things and places, and a supreme spirit presides over all. One can satisfy spirits with offerings to avoid suffering the consequences of offending them. Dreams are interpreted as revelations from the spirits. The Midewiwin, or Medicine Dance, existed before the Drum Dance and peyote cult were introduced around the beginning of the twentieth century.

Twentieth Century. The most significant change to occur in the twentieth century was the move to urban centers. The Depression struck the Ojibwa hard because they were already poor, but World War II offered economic opportunities as factories turned to war production, drawing Ojibwa away from their homes and into the cities. The trend continued under the federal government's relocation policies during the 1950's. During the 1960's and 1970's, many Ojibwas were involved in Indian activism and began to demand that the state and federal governments uphold the treaties they had signed. Many Ojibwa continue to be involved in gaining federal recognition in order to benefit from the promises made to their predecessors.
—*Sean O'Neill*

See also Activism; Algonquian language family; Beaver Wars; Indian-white relations—Canadian; Indian-white relations—French colonial; Midewiwin.

BIBLIOGRAPHY

Broker, Ignatia. *Night Flying Woman: An Ojibwa Narrative.* St. Paul: Minnesota Historical Society Press, 1983.

Clifton, James A. *People of the Three Fires: The Ottawa, Potawatomi, and Ojibwa of Michigan.* Grand Rapids, Mich.: Grand Rapids Inter-Tribal Council, 1986.

Schmalz, Peter S. *The Ojibwa of Southern Ontario.* Toronto: University of Toronto Press, 1991.

Okanagan: Tribe

CULTURE AREA: Plateau
LANGUAGE GROUP: Salishan
PRIMARY LOCATION: British Columbia, Washington State
POPULATION SIZE: 2,275 in Canada (Statistics Canada, based on 1991 census); smaller population in U.S.

Initially the Okanagan (also spelled "Okanogan" and "Okanagon") comprised two groups, the Northern Okanagan and Southern Okanagan (also known as the Sinkaietk). The Northern Okanagan lived near the Canadian boundary in the present province of British Columbia, and the Southern Okanagan inhabited the area around the Okanagan River, a tributary of the Columbia River, in north-central Washington.

The Southern Okanagan practiced the culture of the Plateau tribes, and their interaction with coastal tribes was minimal. The Okanagan followed a seasonal cycle. In the winter they lived in permanent camps, some in subterranean housing but most in a long mat lodge. A few lived in tipis. During the winter, they depended on the resources they had collected during the spring, summer, and fall, supplemented by whatever they could hunt or fish. Their principal food source was salmon, but deer were also important to their diet.

With the coming of spring, the gathering of food began to replenish the exhausted winter supply and the tribe became mobile, breaking up into different groups. One of the first activities was fishing for suckers, followed by steelhead trout. The most important fishing, however, took place in the summer salmon camps. Weirs were built to aid the capture of large catches. The salmon that were caught were either dried or frozen. All the available salmon were taken, and the old women of the camp would even pick up the dead salmon that had spawned and prepare them. Almost the entire salmon would be used, including the head.

Another food source was the variety of available roots and berries. Camps were established to gather the camas root, along with the numerous berries, including huckleberries, red or orange foam berries, and serviceberries. By fall, the Okanagan hunted deer, from which they used not only the meat but also the skins for clothing. Preparations were underway for winter camp by late fall.

Other aspects of Okanagan culture included a shaman and a dream cult. Sweatlodges were also used. Aboriginal culture persisted throughout the nineteenth century, and although the horse probably was introduced by the 1840's, it did not appear to have much effect on Okanagan culture. The Okanagan traded with the Hudson's Bay Company in the nineteenth century, which is probably how they acquired the horse.

Unlike many of the other Plateau tribes, the Okanagan did not enter into a treaty with the United States government until 1891—and this treaty was never ratified. In addition to the fur traders, their contacts with European Americans were through Roman Catholic missionaries, miners, and settlers. The Okanagan did not fight in any of the major Plateau wars with the whites, such as the Yakima War. They were unhappy, however, with the creation of the Moses Reservation in the 1860's; it was located on their land, but it only lasted until 1884. Upon termination of the reservation, many Okanagans remained in the area. Others lived in the area of the Colville

Reservation, which also included traditional Okanagan land. The Colville Reservation was first established in 1872 and became a home to the descendants of the Southern Okanagan, Colville, Sinkiuse, Senijextee, Nez Perce, Methow, Entiat, Nespelem, Sanpoil, Wenatchi, and Palouse. Its official governing body is the Business Council of the Colville Reservation.

Numerous claims have been filed by Salish and other Northwest tribes with the federal government for compensation regarding land and fishing rights. One of the claims dates back to the 1891 treaty, which was never ratified, in which the Okanagan were one of the tribes that agreed to cede 1.5 million acres for $1.5 million. An additional payment was awarded. Other claims concern lost fishing rights with the construction of dams, such as the Grand Coulee. The present-day economy derives revenue from timber and gambling.

See also Colville; Lake; Methow; Salishan language family; Sanpoil-Nespelem.

Okeepa

TRIBE AFFECTED: Mandan
SIGNIFICANCE: The Okeepa was a Mandan summer ceremony conducted to reestablish the tribe's ties with nature

The Okeepa was a ceremony conducted by the Mandans, a semi-nomadic tribe living in the northern Great Plains. It was a ritual held during the summer that was seen as a means to renew the life of the tribe and to reestablish the tribal relationship with nature. The specific purpose of the Okeepa was to appease the spirits of the waters, which Mandan legend claimed had once covered the earth in a flood. Tribal members took part in the ceremony by impersonating certain animal spirits, such as the snake or beaver. Other members were painted to represent day and night.

The main action, however, centered on two young men who dangled in the air, hung by ropes stuck into their flesh with pegs. After a certain period of time they were lowered to the ground. They then had to make their way to a masked warrior, who would proceed to cut off one or two of their fingers.

At the conclusion of this grueling experience, the two men ran a circle around the outside of the medicine lodge. Participants sometimes collapsed and had to be dragged. Any young man who excelled in withstanding the ceremony was considered a good candidate for future leadership positions.

See also Mandan; Plains; Sun Dance.

Oklahoma Indian Welfare Act

DATE: June 26, 1936
TRIBES AFFECTED: All in Oklahoma except those in Osage County
SIGNIFICANCE: This act allowed all Indian tribes, bands, or groups in Oklahoma to adopt a constitution allowing for self-government, allowed the secretary of the interior to purchase land to be held in trust for all Oklahoma Indians, and allowed small groups of Indians to form a local cooperative association and receive interest-free loans from the Revolving Loan Fund for Indians

A major reform of U.S. policy toward American Indians resulted in the Indian Reorganization Act (IRA, or Wheeler-Howard Act), enacted by Congress on June 18, 1934. With this act, further allotment of tribal lands to individual Indians was prohibited, purchase of additional lands for Indians by the secretary of the interior was authorized, and a fund (the Revolving Loan Fund for Indians) was established that could be used for tribal enterprises. The IRA allowed and encouraged the tribes or groups to adopt written constitutions allowing for self-government, gave Indians applying for positions in the Bureau of Indian Affairs preference over other applicants, and called for very strict conservation practices on Indian lands. Oklahoma, however, was excluded from the IRA because the IRA was essentially a system of reservation government, and it was deemed inappropriate for Oklahoma because, at the time of statehood, the Five Civilized Tribes had given up their autonomy.

In 1936, the benefits of the IRA were extended to Oklahoma by way of a separate statute, the Oklahoma Indian Welfare Act. This act authorized the secretary of the interior to purchase, at his discretion, good agricultural and grazing land, from within or without reservations, to hold in trust for the tribe, band, group, or individual Indian for whose benefit the land was acquired. Title to all lands was to be taken in the name of the United States and held by the United States. All land was exempt from any and all federal taxes, but the state of Oklahoma could levy and collect a gross production tax upon all oil and gas produced from the land. The secretary of the interior was responsible for overseeing the payment of these taxes to Oklahoma. Any tribe or band in the state of Oklahoma was given the right to organize for its common welfare and could adopt a constitution and bylaws; these had to follow the rules and regulations set forth by the secretary of the interior. Any ten or more Indians, as determined by the official tribe rolls, or Indian descendants of such enrolled members, in convenient proximity to each other, could be chartered as a local cooperative association for the following purposes: credit administration, production, marketing, consumers' protection, or land management. Funds from the Revolving Loan Fund for Indians could be used to provide interest-free loans to these groups.

See also Indian Reorganization Act; Indian Territory.

Old Briton (?, Wabash River area, northwestern Ind.— 1752, at Pickawillany, on the Miami River in Ohio): Tribal chief, trader

TRIBAL AFFILIATION: Miami (Piankashaw band)
SIGNIFICANCE: Old Briton attempted to change Miami trading partners and allies from the French to the English in the mid-eighteenth century

Frustrated by high prices and chronic shortages of French trade goods, Old Briton hoped to persuade his people to break ties with the French and open trade with the British. Having met British traders in his earlier travels along the lower Wabash and on the Ohio Rivers, he understood that political relations with the British would be advantageous. In the fall of 1747, after participating in a failed uprising against the French, Old Briton led his followers east and founded a new village, Pickawillany, on the Great Miami River in western Ohio. Old Briton sent a delegation to Pennsylvania, which signed a treaty of friendship and alliance and initiated the desired trading relationship. Despite repeated French efforts to persuade or intimidate Old Briton back into the old relationship, he diplomatically put them off. Pickawillany grew into a major western trading center, with Weas, Piankashaws, Kickapoos, and Mascoutens bringing their furs to the British. A small, ineffective French attack on Pickawillany in the summer of 1751 stimulated Old Briton to organize a general Indian war against the French, which included his execution of three French soldiers and mutilation of a fourth, who was then sent back to Canada.

Recognizing the threat Old Briton posed to their empire, the French enlisted Charles Langlade (Ottawa/French) in the spring of 1752 to raise a force of Ottawa, Ojibwa, and others to destroy Pickawillany. On June 21, just after most Pickawillany warriors had left to hunt, Langlade attacked. Caught by surprise, Old Briton was outnumbered ten to one. Wanting to make an example of Old Briton, Langlade had him executed, after which his body was boiled and his remains eaten by some of the attackers. Pickawillany was abandoned, but by the end of the decade the British had expelled the French in war and the Miami found themselves with no other trade partner but the British.

See also Indian-white relations—English colonial; Indian-white relations—French colonial; Miami.

Old Copper culture: Prehistoric tradition

DATE: c. 3000-700 B.C.E.
LOCATION: Wisconsin, Upper Peninsula of Michigan
CULTURE AFFECTED: Late Archaic

Approximately 3000 B.C.E., there appeared in the region from the Great Lakes to New York State and in the St. Lawrence River valley a culture known as Lake Forest Late Archaic. Within that cultural tradition, there was a subtradition known as Old Copper. In a few areas of the world, native outcroppings of relatively pure copper occur at or near the surface of the earth. One of those areas includes the Brule River basin of northeast Wisconsin, the Keweenaw Peninsula of Michigan, and part of the northern shore of Lake Superior and its Isle Royale.

Approximately 3000 B.C.E., natives of that area began to exploit these natural copper resources and a wide variety of western Lake Forest peoples continued to use those resources for more than two thousand years, and even to some extent until the arrival of white fur-traders in the area after 1650 C.E. The copper was used to make a wide variety of items. These included axe and adze blades, gouges, *ulus* (curved blade knives), wood-splitting wedges, and many types of awls. Fishhooks and gorges, and even gaffs for landing the catch, have also been found. Most common in the early period were the

socketed and tanged spearheads and arrow points and barbed harpoons of a hunting culture. Though made of a very different and usually superior material, these copper items bear a striking resemblance to the slate tools of the Lake Forest peoples. It is almost certain that the lifestyles of the groups were very similar.

The Old Copper peoples learned to quarry the relatively pure copper sheets and nuggets from under moderately thin layers of soil. They then heated the copper, just as stone was sometimes heated prior to chipping. The copper then would be hammered into the shapes desired. Since many of the recovered designs are quite delicate, the technical ability of the Old Copper metal workers must have been quite skillful. Finally, the material would be annealed—slowly cooled, probably in water to increase strength and reduce brittleness. Alternate heating and cooling, up to three or four times, renders copper quite useful.

The Old Copper culture exhibited one of the best evidences of transition from the Late Archaic period to the Early Woodland after 2000 B.C.E. Burial practices became much more elaborate, including a characteristic use of red ochre to cover the burial materials. This type of burial spread throughout the eastern United States, including into the celebrated Adena area of Ohio. Copper axes and adzes became common burial items, and thousands of copper beads indicate personal decoration was quite important. These copper items were spread throughout the eastern Woodlands areas by trade routes that dominated that society. When the copper items appeared outside the immediate Old Copper area, they were highly prized, and the appearance of copper burial items is one of the best indications of the social prominence of the person being buried.

After about 700 B.C.E., the amounts of readily available copper decreased and the Old Copper subculture disappeared. Some items, however, were still being made of copper when the French fur traders first reached the Lake Superior area in the 1650's.

See also Adena; Archaic; Prehistory—Northeast; Woodland.

Olmec: Tribe

CULTURE AREA: Mesoamerica
LANGUAGE GROUP: Olmecan
PRIMARY LOCATION: Southeastern Mexico

The Olmecs flourished between 1200 and 400 B.C.E. in the humid tropical lowlands of what is now the state of Veracruz in southeastern Mexico. The name "Olmec" was given arbitrarily to these ancient people by twentieth century archaeologists. It means "the people of rubber" in Nahuatl, the language of the Aztecs. The Olmecs were probably the first true civilization of ancient Mexico. Olmec culture spread throughout Mesoamerica, a region that includes southern Mexico and parts of Central America, and had great influence on later civilizations. Unrecognized before the middle of the twentieth century, the first evidence of Olmec culture was uncovered by José María Melgar in 1862. He found a gigantic carved stone head with features similar to those of Africans. It took nearly one hundred years, however, and many more discoveries of large and small artifacts, to convince archaeologists that this was a distinct and original culture.

While the large stone heads, measuring as much as 10 feet in height and weighing up to 20 tons, have sparked theories of African contact with prehistoric America, there is no consensus on their purpose or their meaning. Other, smaller statues depict individuals with different features, and the image most often found is that of a creature half jaguar and half human.

Although the land was fertile (the staple of the Olmec diet was maize), evidence suggests that the population was relatively small and not clustered into true cities. Archaeological remains show, instead, ceremonial centers, where conical-shaped pyramids and burial mounds were located. The Olmecs may have performed human sacrifices to a jaguar deity who was seen as a creation god. There is also evidence of a fire god as well as an early form of the Feathered Serpent deity that would play such an important role among later indigenous populations.

One of the most startling discoveries associated with the Olmecs was a system of mathematical symbols. Archaeologists had believed that the "long count" calendar, based on counting time from a base year, was developed by the Maya. In 1939, however, Matthew Stirling discovered a recorded date that was centuries earlier than the Maya, showing that the Olmecs had first developed this method of counting years. Using a bar for five, dots for ones, and a shell symbol for zero, the Olmecs had a numerical system that could go into the thousands. The Olmecs also produced an early form of hieroglyphic writing. One hundred and eighty-two symbols have been identified as having some form of specific meaning.

The spread of Olmec culture in art, religion, writing, and mathematics throughout coastal regions and into Central America has led to the belief that the Olmecs created the "mother civilization" of the region. Nevertheless, arguments persist as to whether the Olmecs conquered and controlled an empire or whether trade and other contacts spread their accomplishments.

See also Aztec; La Venta; Maya; Quetzalcóatl; Toltec; Tres Zapotes; Zapotec.

Omaha: Tribe

CULTURE AREA: Plains
LANGUAGE GROUP: Siouan
PRIMARY LOCATION: Nebraska, Iowa
POPULATION SIZE: 4,143 (1990 U.S. Census)

The Omaha moved from the eastern forests to the Missouri River between Iowa and Nebraska shortly before their first contact with European Americans. They became part-time buffalo (bison) hunters but clung to their Woodland agricultural practices as well. The Sioux and Pawnee were their most consistent enemies, and the Ponca were their closest relatives and allies. Their relationships with whites were often strained, but they were never at war with the colonial powers or with the

United States. They have recently reclaimed their most sacred tribal symbols from the museums in which they were placed in the late nineteenth century.

Early History and Traditional Lifestyle. The Omaha lived in the forests of eastern North America with four related tribes until around 1500, at which time the tribes moved west to the Mississippi and Missouri rivers. The Omaha became established on the Missouri near Omaha, Nebraska, probably pushing the Arikara north in the process.

They continued to grow corn, beans, squash, and other vegetables in the river's flood plain, but also moved into the Plains twice a year (spring and autumn) to hunt buffalo. Buffalo provided many of the tribe's needs: meat; hides for robes, clothing and tipi covers; shoulder blades for hoes; and more. The Omaha lived in earthlodges in their villages along the river, but in tipis while hunting buffalo. Dogs pulling travois carried their belongings in migrations across the Plains until the Omaha obtained horses in the middle of the eighteenth century.

The Omaha hunted over most of Nebraska. There they encountered Sioux or Pawnee hunting parties, with whom they often fought over hunting rights. Each of those tribes occasionally attacked the Omahas' earthlodge villages as well. The Ponca were usually allied with the Omaha against the Sioux and Pawnee. Occasionally, the Ponca joined the Sioux against the Omaha, or Pawnee and Omaha hunted together, reversing the more common relationships.

The social and spiritual life of the Omaha was more or less typical of Plains Indians. Men hunted, butchered, made and decorated their shields, bows and arrows, and fought to defend the tribe. Women cooked, preserved meat and other foods for future use, gardened, made and decorated clothes and tipi covers, and raised the tipi at a new campsite and took it down in preparation for a move. Both sexes participated in building the earthlodges.

To the Omaha, all aspects of nature were sacred and part of a vast network of natural interactions, with which they interacted through elaborate rituals and symbols. They did not develop the Sun Dance, which nearly every other Plains tribe practiced, but had other dances and ceremonies. A sacred pole and white buffalo robe were the tribe's most important spiritual symbols. Each of the two main divisions of the tribe, the earth people and sky people, had a sacred pipe.

The vision quest, in which a young man fasted in the wilderness hoping for a spiritual experience to give him special power, was a part of growing up for most Omaha boys. Men belonged to warrior societies, some of which were made up of men who had similar vision quest experiences. For most societies, however, eligibility depended on age, bravery, and service. At one time, Omaha chiefs were determined by hereditary lineages, but this changed to the more typical Plains system of choosing chiefs according to the criteria above.

Transition and Contemporary Life. The Omaha were never at war with the United States. They agreed to a series of treaties that eventually left them with a small reservation in Nebraska and Iowa. Their transition to the agricultural context

Oneida woman in Ontario standing beside a bark house; Iroquoian people used bark to construct dwellings, canoes, and carrying utensils. (National Museum of The American Indian, Smithsonian Institution)

of reservation life was probably easier than that of other Plains tribes, because they were part-time farmers before the accompanying restrictions were imposed. They share many of the problems of Indian tribes throughout the country, however—lack of education, poverty, and loss of native culture.

In the last half of the twentieth century, the Omaha have initiated several efforts to overcome these problems. They have regained possession of their sacred pole and sacred white buffalo robe, and have taken steps to preserve the Omaha language. They have sued the United States to recover a small portion of tribal land. Not every effort can be expected to succeed, but these and other efforts indicate the determination of the Omaha to maintain their culture and improve conditions for tribal members. —*Carl W. Hoagstrom*

See also Arts and crafts—Plains; La Flesche, Francis; La Flesche, Susan; La Flesche, Susette or Josette; Plains; Ponca; Siouan language family.

Oneida: Tribe

CULTURE AREA: Northeast
LANGUAGE GROUP: Iroquoian
PRIMARY LOCATION: New York State, Ontario, Wisconsin
POPULATION SIZE: 11,564 in U.S. (1990 U.S. Census); estimated 5,000 in Canada

One of the five (later six) tribes of the Iroquois Confederacy, the Oneidas were ancestrally located between the Onondagas to their west and the Mohawks to their east in what is now central New York State. Their language is very similar to other Iroquois languages; the name "Oneida" means "people of the standing stone." The Oneidas were at times overshadowed by the larger Onondaga and Mohawk tribes, and they attempted to rectify this imbalance at times in the Grand Council of the Confederacy when it met at Onondaga. The Oneidas held nine of the fifty seats in the Grand Council. Like all other Iroquois tribes, they adhered to a matrilineal clan system in which the matron of each clan appointed the sachem (chief) for each clan. The sachem participated in political activity at both the local and confederacy levels. The three Oneida clans are the Turtle, Bear, and Wolf clans.

Oneida society was traditionally matrilocal in that a marrying couple would live with the wife's family in her extended-family longhouse. A longhouse was made of poles or saplings as a frame, with the walls filled in with bark. These dwellings could be up to 70 feet long and could house up to thirty people or more. There were anywhere from ten to fifty longhouses in a village. Particularly after contact with Europeans, the villages were female-oriented places, as the men were often traveling for purposes of hunting, fishing, trading, and warfare. Women were the main breadwinners, growing and harvesting corn, beans, and squash, the staples of Iroquoian horticulture. The ceremonial cycle of Oneida (Iroquois) life made plain this orientation toward horticulture: the Maple Sugar Festival, the Green Corn Ceremony, the Strawberry Festival, the Harvest Festival, and the Midwinter Festival framed the religious year.

Increased contact with the French, Dutch, and English in the 1600's meant that Oneida society changed greatly. In addition to the escalation of warfare over the seventeenth and eighteenth centuries, disease epidemics took their toll on the Oneida people. They numbered about one thousand in 1677 but probably had much greater numbers before European contact. The patterns of warfare changed during the American Revolution when most of the Oneidas broke with the rest of the confederacy and sided with the Americans. Following this war, the Oneidas assumed that they would be able to retain their homeland, but they were increasingly marginalized by the U.S. government, which tried to convince them to move to Kansas. This was unsuccessful, but one faction of Oneidas did purchase a tract of land in Wisconsin and moved there in the 1820's. Others moved to Ontario and resided on an Oneida reserve on the Thames River near the Six Nations reserve, and still others moved to the Six Nations reserve itself. All the Oneidas—in Ontario, New York, and Wisconsin—have seen their landholdings dwindle at the hands of various governments and land speculators. The Ontario and New York Oneidas have remained more traditional than their Wisconsin counterparts. They still have matron-appointed sachemships and include some fluent Oneida speakers. Many of the traditional ceremonies, along with newer ones incorporated in the Handsome Lake religion (Longhouse religion), are still practiced. Oneidas living at the Six Nations reserve and on the Onondaga reservation in New York are minorities within these larger communities. The tiny remaining Oneida reservation in the ancestral homeland east of Syracuse, New York, is the site of the first tribal casino to open with the sanction of the New York state government, made possible partly because of a land claims case won by the Oneida tribe.

See also Beaver Wars; Cayuga; Handsome Lake; Indian-white relations—English colonial; Indian-white relations—French colonial; Iroquoian language family; Iroquois Confederacy; Longhouse; Longhouse religion; Mohawk; Onondaga; Seneca; Tuscarora.

Oneota: Prehistoric and protohistoric tradition

DATE: c. 800-1500
LOCATION: Upper Mississippi River valley
CULTURES AFFECTED: Early Iowa, Missouri, Oto, Winnebago; later Osage, Sioux

The Oneota are considered both a people and a cultural tradition. This tradition appears to have developed from the Late Woodland or Upper Mississippian tradition by times variously given as 400 to 800 C.E. The sites identified as emergent Oneota are located in Minnesota, Wisconsin, and Illinois, but later sites occur in Iowa, Missouri, North Dakota, Indiana, and the near corner of Michigan. The society was a mixture of hunter-gatherer and agricultural, with permanently established villages and houses. The houses, usually of wattle and daub construction with sod roofs, were single-family dwellings only 6- or 8-feet square in the early settlements; but some of the later ones featured longhouses as much as 90 feet in length. A late site near Cahokia, Illinois (a few miles from East St. Louis), had some twelve to fifteen hundred inhabitants and appears to have been a center for barter with other tribes. This was the exception, however; most villages had only one or two hundred residents, although they spread out to as much as a hundred acres in cultivated area.

The artifacts most often used to distinguish the Oneota tradition from others are their pottery vessels, which are smooth and globular with handles in pairs (when present), and with the upper half of the vessel decorated with line patterns of various sorts. Stone artifacts are found also: scrapers, drills, knives, and characteristic small, unnotched projectile points. Animal bones were used for needles, beads, fishhooks, and flint flakers, with scapulas of elk and bison serving as hoes. Some metal was used, mostly for personal ornaments.

The Oneota appear to have had extensive contact with surrounding Indian groups, including the trade already mentioned. At some time after 1400 or 1500 C.E., when written history in the European style commences, the account of the Oneota becomes that of the individual tribes in the Upper Mississippi area.

See also Cahokia; Prehistory—Plains; Woodland.

Onondaga: Tribe

CULTURE AREA: Northeast
LANGUAGE GROUP: Iroquoian
PRIMARY LOCATION: New York State, Ontario
POPULATION SIZE: 1,500 in U.S. (1990 U.S. Census); estimated 3,000 in Canada

In the Onondaga language, the name "Onondaga" means "people of the hill"; the main Onondaga village was on a hill southeast of present-day Syracuse, New York. The Onondaga tribe was the geographically central tribe of the Five (later Six) Nations of the Iroquois Confederacy. The capital of the confederacy was therefore at this main Onondaga village, and the Onondagas were the Keepers of the Council Fire of the confederacy. The main speaker of the council was always an Onondaga, as was the keeper of the council wampum. The Great Council of the Confederacy, which met each autumn and in emergency situations, was composed of fifty sachems (chiefs) from the five tribes. The Onondaga held fourteen of these hereditarily chosen sachemships, more than any other tribe. These rules were set down some time before European contact (estimates vary widely, from the 1300's to the 1500's) by the founders of the Iroquois League or Confederacy, Hiawatha and Deganawida.

The Onondaga tribe was organized into matrilineal clans: Wolf, Bear, Beaver, Turtle, Deer, Eagle, and Heron. Clan sachems were appointed by the clan matrons, the senior women of each clan. The Onondagas were also matrilocal, in that a marrying couple would live with the wife's family in an extended-family longhouse made of poles and bark. Each longhouse accommodated up to thirty people, and there could be from twenty to fifty longhouses in a village. The Onondaga population around 1600 was probably more than two thousand.

While men hunted for game and practiced warfare and trade at great distances, Onondaga women tended the fields adjacent to their villages, carrying on the main economic subsistence of the community. Corn, beans, and squash, along with sunflowers and tobacco, were the main crops grown by the women. The seasonal cycle of religious ceremonies reflected the importance of agriculture to the Onondagas: the Maple Sugar Festival, the Strawberry Festival, the Green Corn Ceremony, the Harvest Festival, and the Midwinter Ceremonies.

The Onondagas, along with the other Iroquois tribes, became involved in a spiral of warfare and imperialism in the seventeenth century which did not end until the war of the American Revolution. In the latter conflict, the vast majority of them, including the Onondagas, sided with the British and lost most of their ancestral lands across New York State. The Onondagas did manage to retain a reservation southeast of present-day Syracuse, but many Onondagas settled instead on the Six Nations reserve along the Grand River in what is now Ontario, Canada. Many who remained in what is now New York State were living at Buffalo Creek, a predominantly Seneca community. Eventually, most Onondagas at Buffalo Creek made their way back to the Onondaga reservation near Syracuse. The issue of rightful location of the seat of the Iroquois Confederacy became one of great contention among the Iroquois; the Grand River Onondagas claimed that the seat was at their Six Nations reserve, but the Buffalo Creek community also claimed the seat. The Buffalo Creek group acceded to the group at the Onondaga reservation, but a conflict still exists between the Onondagas (and all Iroquois) of the Grand River (Canadian) reserve and the Onondagas in their ancient homeland as to which council fire is the legitimate one.

The New York Onondagas still use the traditional method of deciding political leadership; the matrons of each clan appoint leaders. They are involved in ongoing negotiations with New York State and the federal government over sovereignty issues. The Canadian Onondagas are split into two governmental factions, traditional and elected leadership, and the Canadian government recognizes only the latter. The Onondaga language is still spoken by many older tribal members, and children learn it in school. Some adhere to Christian denominations, but at least a quarter of Onondaga people in both Ontario and New York practice the traditional Iroquois religion, the Longhouse religion, which is a mix of pre-contact belief systems and Christian ideas institutionalized by the prophet Handsome Lake in the early nineteenth century.

See also Beaver Wars; Cayuga; Fort Stanwix, Treaty of; Handsome Lake; Indian-white relations—English colonial; Indian-white relations—French colonial; Iroquoian language family; Iroquois Confederacy; Longhouse; Longhouse religion; Mohawk; Oneida; Seneca; Tuscarora.

Opechancanough (c. 1544, Va.—1644, Jamestown, Va.): Tribal chief

ALSO KNOWN AS: Mangopeomen, Massatamohtnock
TRIBAL AFFILIATION: Powhatan Confederacy

SIGNIFICANCE: Opechancanough was one of the earliest tribal leaders in the Southeast to plan and carry out a major offensive against European intruders

The limited available evidence suggests that Opechancanough, whose Algonquian name meant "he whose soul is white," was born about 1544 near the York River in Virginia. Although little is known about the first half of his life, some historians—based on largely circumstantial evidence—believe that Spanish explorers in the region may have taken him to Spain and Florida in the 1560s. If so, he may have returned when Spanish Jesuits attempted to establish a mission in Virginia in 1570.

A brother of Powhatan, chief of a powerful Tidewater Virginia confederacy of tribes, Opechancanough first appeared in English documents as chief of the Pamunkey tribe when Jamestown was established in 1607. In that capacity he confronted the English adventurer Captain John Smith on several occasions. Most notably, it was Opechancanough who captured Smith and took the Englishman to his brother's village where Smith claimed that Powhatan's daughter, Pocahontas, saved his life.

Shortly after Powhatan's death in 1618, Opechancanough became the great *werowance*, or chief, of the Powhatan Confederacy. Intent upon reversing his brother's accommodation to English encroachment on native lands, he developed a well-coordinated plan to exterminate the intruders.

Opechancanough's resolve was the product of many factors. He was alarmed by the rapid expansion of English settlements accompanying the tobacco boom in the colony's second decade of settlement, and the deadly impact of European diseases on his people. He also resented English efforts to assimilate the natives into their culture.

Opechancanough used the murder of Nemattanow as a pretext for his all-out assault. This man, a highly regarded warrior and religious prophet whom the English called "Jack of the Feathers," was killed by two settlers in March of 1622. While lulling the English into a false sense of security by permitting continued trade and promising that the sky would fall before he broke the peace, Opechancanough ordered an attack on March 22. The offensive claimed 347 English lives, almost a third of the population. In response, Virginia officials declared war on the natives, and a decade-long conflict resulted. The natives were driven deep into the Virginia interior.

From 1632 to 1644 there were sporadic skirmishes between Indians and whites as the English continued to expand their settlements. Still hopeful of at least slowing the encroachment, an aged, enfeebled, and nearly blind Opechancanough convinced most tribes to participate in one more assault in 1644. Although he had to be carried into battle, Opechancanough led his forces. While the attacks took more than four hundred English lives, the casualties were less devastating to the English colony because the total population had reached about eight thousand.

After the English settlers defeated the Powhatan Confederacy for a second time, a militia unit captured Opechancanough. He was murdered by a guard while in a Jamestown jail in 1644.

See also Indian-white relations—English colonial; Powhatan; Powhatan Confederacy; Powhatan Wars.

Opothleyaholo (c. 1798, Creek Nation, Ga.—1862, near Leroy Creek, Kans.): Tribal leader

ALSO KNOWN AS: Apotheyahola, Optothe Yoholo, Good Shouting Child

TRIBAL AFFILIATION: Creek

SIGNIFICANCE: Both in Georgia and after removal to Indian Territory, Opothleyaholo was a Creek tribal leader

As a leader of the traditional Creek warrior faction, the Red Sticks, Opothleyaholo fought with principal Creek leader William Weatherford against General Andrew Jackson in the Creek Wars of 1813-1814. Thereafter, Opothleyaholo was one of several chiefs opposing an illegal treaty ceding twenty-five million acres of Creek land, signed by William McIntosh, leader of the peace faction, the White Sticks.

In 1825-1826, Opothleyaholo led a Creek delegation to Washington, D.C., protesting removal. He signed the Treaty of Washington, ceding many, but not all, Creek lands. He signed a second treaty in Washington in 1832. Resisting removal to Indian Territory, in 1834-1835, Opothleyaholo attempted purchasing land in Mexico. The Mexican government, however, was uncooperative, and in 1836, he and his people were forcibly relocated to Indian Territory. There he became a head chief for temporarily reunited Creek factions, counseling peace with whites. He supported the Union during the Civil War, fleeing to Kansas after defeat by Confederate forces. Opothleyaholo died shortly thereafter.

See also Creek War; Indian Removal Act; Indian Territory; McIntosh, William; Menewa; Removal; Weapons.

Oral literatures

TRIBES AFFECTED: Pantribal

SIGNIFICANCE: With no written languages, American Indian peoples transmitted their ideas from one generation to the next through storytelling; the surviving legends link Indian history to the present

Among peoples who do not have a written language, cultural traditions and philosophies are transmitted orally. In traditional American Indian cultures, senior members of a tribe used storytelling to pass ideas, events, and value systems to the next generation. Oral storytelling differs greatly from written literature because stories are slightly varied with each telling. Storytellers have individual styles and preferences; they can exaggerate some aspects or eliminate ideas altogether. With each generation, stories are altered to fit the present situation.

Geographic Influence. Legends of American Indians relate closely to all elements of the natural environment. Tribes occupied a wide range of geographical landscapes, with some Indians living in desert conditions, others by the sea. Some tribes occupied wooded mountains where rivers and waterfalls were plentiful; others existed on dusty plateaus. In Indian tales, regardless of the environment, all parts of the natural landscape—pebbles, trees, mountains, rivers, shells—pulsate with life. Humans, animals, vegetation, and landforms are all interrelated.

The Supernatural. Indian stories are religious experiences that include taboo, ritual, and magic. Natural elements are often personified during the course of a storyline. Mountains, rocks, and rivers may be given human characteristics and feelings, while humans may be turned into fish, stars, or mountains. Just as quickly, these elements may return to their former states. Some characters are permanently assigned natural forms. For example, troublemakers may become mountain peaks as lessons for future rascals. Legends also set human lovers as stars in the sky, destined to chase each other for eternity. Indian tales are filled with an interweaving of supernatural and natural elements.

Story Structure. There is often a circular element to the progression of Indian legends and stories that is different from the linearity of European storylines. The time progression reflects the Indian belief that all reality is cyclical. The repetitive circular patterns allow listeners to hear subtle variations on themes, which promotes both the remembrance and the understanding of oral legends.

Those accustomed to European storylines have at times criticized Indian legends as chaotic or incomplete. They claim that recognizable beginnings and endings are missing. Indian stories are not intended to be evaluated by Western logic, however; oral stories are often told in chains, with one image or character triggering another story. The chain often reaches back in time. Many tales are not intended to be isolated from previous episodes; instead, these stories are parts of a progression. The knowledge of past legends may be needed to understand a particular story. Moreover, certain words may have meaning only if previous tales have been heard. For example, the word for "sun" may represent the name of a sun god who is present in a whole line of stories. Without knowledge of the full significance of the word "sun," listeners may misinterpret a particular story. Indian legends are not isolated stories for entertainment but are part of a lifetime collection which educates tribe members about religion, the supernatural, and living in harmony with nature and with other humans.

Many Indian tales center on celestial elements that are used to inspire appropriate behavior and to punish unacceptable actions and attitudes. They also attempt to explain the mysterious nature of the skies.

Sun and Moon. The sky held great significance for American Indians. They studied the stars carefully to determine when their crops should be planted and harvested. They followed the sun's placement in the sky as an indication of the seasons. This fascination with the heavens is reflected in Indian legends. The sun is seen as the great fertilizing agent of the universe. Although the Juchi, Cherokee, and Inuit regard the sun as female, most tribes give male attributes to the sun. In many tales, the sun makes love to mortal women who then give birth, not only to humans, but to animals. In a Brule Sioux

tale, the male sun removes an eye and throws it into the wind, where it becomes the moon, woman. The sun directs the moon maiden to walk along a bridge of lightening so that she can roam the earth. Man and woman then come together on Earth and through mutual understanding and caregiving join their bodies to people the earth.

In one Winnebago myth of the sun's creation, the orb is reduced to a small object that is snared by Little Brother. The reward for his great power in bringing light to his tribe is that humans would thereafter be chiefs over animals. The Inuit tell about a brother raping his sister. After the rape, the sister runs, lighting her way with a torch. Her brother, who carries a torch of his own, follows, but falls in the snow, where his torch turns from flames to embers. A large windstorm lifts the brother and sister into the sky, where he is turned into the moon and she into the sun. They are always far away from each other, with the sun coming out only after the moon is gone. The Cherokee give female qualities to the sun, which is stolen by Grandmother Spider and brought to her people along with fire. The Zuni tell about Coyote, the trickster, who steals the sun and moon from the kachinas (supernatural intermediaries). Coyote is greedy, wanting the box of light for his own. Because of his curiosity, Coyote disobeys the chief and opens the box to examine the light. The moon and sun escape into the sky, and cold comes to the world.

The Stars. The Plains tribes were primarily nomadic hunters and gatherers; they relied greatly on the stars to indicate direction, time, and the seasons. These Indians considered the celestial bodies supernatural beings and often told stories of various stars taking human form. The Blackfoot explain the origin of the North Star in this way: A young maiden looks longingly at the Morning Star and wishes that she could have that star for her husband. In time, the Morning Star appears on Earth as a handsome youth who takes the maiden to the house of his parents, Sun and Moon. The maiden is married to Morning Star and lives a life of ease in Sky Country; however, her curiosity and disobedience result in her son being turned into a star. This star, the North Star, never moves and is called the Fixed Star by the Blackfoot and the Star That Does Not Walk Around by the Omaha.

The seven stars of the Pleiades hold great significance for many cultures. This small cluster of stars helps define the calendar and signals coming events. The disappearance of the Pleiades tells the Tapirape Indians that the rainy season will soon end. The Zuni of New Mexico use the Pleiades to determine when planting should begin. The Cherokee of the Southeast give special significance to the Pleiades because there are seven stars in the group. Seven is a sacred number because it represents seven directions—north, south, east, west, up, down, and center.

Many Indian legends incorporate the Pleiades. The Onondaga of the Northeast tell of seven children who neglect their chores and dance throughout each day. After several warnings from the elders, these children become so lightheaded that they drift into the sky, never to return. The Shasta, from the forested lands of Northern California, tell how the greed and selfishness of Coyote, the trickster, lead him to kill Raccoon. As punishment, the children of Raccoon kill all Coyote's children, except for Littlest Coyote, who is not selfish. Raccoon's children and Littlest Coyote run away to Sky Country to be protected from the selfishness of Coyote. They become the Pleiades.

Earth. Many tribes have myths which explain the emergence of the earth. Many explanations describe a watery primordial environment from which mud is brought up to make the earth. Some tribes describe life in the interior of the world. These inhabitants dig their way up from the center of the world until the top layer, earth, is reached. Earth is that environment which is in light. Indians of the Northwest tell of entering a hole in the sky in order to emerge on the earth. From the California region and the Southwest come tales about the original world parents, Earth and Sky. Many myths have the creation of Earth eliminating the darkness of the universe.

The Cherokee describe an Earth suspended in delicate balance, which humans must maintain for survival. The earth floats on waters and is tied to the ceiling of the sky by four ropes connected to the sacred four directions. If the ropes break, the world will tumble, carrying all living things to death. The earth will then be like a submerged island, covered with water. This tale also incorporates the supernatural, for sorcerers and shamans are called upon to put the sun higher so that the earth will not be too hot for human survival.

The Hopi tell a tale about two goddesses who cause the waters of the world to recede eastward and westward until dry land appears. To bring light and warmth to this land, the sun removes his skin of gray fox and dons a yellow skin to brighten the sky. The two goddesses then create a little wren out of clay. Animals and humans are later brought to life, always in pairs. Humans feed mostly on rabbits and deer, which leads to many quarrels. In frustration, the goddesses leave to live in the middle of the ocean.

Humans. Human creation myths seek to answer mysteries about the human condition. Humans are generally created from supernatural beings, from natural elements, or from animals. In most tales, animals and plants precede the creation of humans.

A number of legends have the first woman of Earth impregnated by a sunbeam, a salmon, or the west wind. For some tribes, the first human is a child endowed with supernatural powers. The Sioux tell of Stone Boy, who brings sacred ceremonies and prayers to his tribe by building the first sweatlodge for purification. The Brule Sioux, however, say that the first human is an old woman who has sacred medicinal powers. Many legends have women as the first humans, for women are associated with fertility, conception, and pregnancy. In some stories, the first humans are twins, born of a supernatural god. In others the trickster, Coyote, is given credit for breathing life into humans. The deceitful side of humans is the result of having been created by Coyote.

The Modoc tell about Kumush, Old Man of the Ancients. He and his daughter descend into the underground, where spirits gather to sing and dance. Darkness permeates the underworld, and after a week, Kumush longs for light. When he returns to the upper world, he takes some underground spirits with him to people his world. To feed these people, he supplies fish and beasts, roots and berries. He then designates certain roles for the people: "Men shall fish and hunt and fight. Women shall get wood and water, gather berries and dig roots, and cook for their families."

In human creation myths, the earth and the universe are often seen as neverending circles within which humankind is just another animal. Because all elements of nature are related, animals are often responsible in whole or in part for the creation of humans. In a tale from the White River Sioux, a rabbit comes across a clot of blood and begins to kick it around as if it were a ball. The movement of the clot brings it to life in human form. At times, the processes and rhythms of nature bring life to humans. The Penobscot tell of a young man "born from the foam of the waves, foam quickened by the wind and warmed by the sun." The same legend tells of a girl born after "a drop of dew fell on a leaf and was warmed by the sun."

Some stories explain the different races. The Pima tell how Man Maker uses clay to mold human images and then places them in an oven. When he removes the various forms, they have different shapes and colors. He saves the forms that please him best; the others are sent to live in various places across the water. The Modoc explain that Kumush, Old Man of the Ancients, gathers bones in the underworld and selects certain ones to make Indians to reside in particular places. He makes the Shastas brave warriors, the Klamath easily frightened, and the Modoc the bravest of all.

Love. Indian love stories teach responsibility and commitment to loved ones. The characters are often given tests to demonstrate the strength of their commitments. In some tales, battles are fought between two men for the love of a young maiden. These contests are fought until death, a death in the name of love. Legends of love also weave the natural and supernatural together. In various stories, human lovers are transformed into stars; a whale takes a human wife; a man marries the moon; and a wife follows a butterfly man. These tales also include traditions that had significance in the courting process. The Keres Pueblo tell a story about men and women who try to live apart. The tale illustrates that women depend on men for survival. A legend of unselfishness comes from the Multnomah; it concerns a maiden who shows great love for her people by sacrificing her life to the spirits so that all those suffering from sickness will be cured. She jumps from a cliff as the moon rises over the trees. Today, her spirit, dressed in white, exists in the waters of Multnomah Falls.

Death. American Indians believe that accepting death is an affirmation of life. Crazy Horse claimed that being willing to die was a way of honoring the human spirit. Indian tales reveal not only human death but also the crumbling of cultures and nations. The end, however, makes way for the arrival of the new. The Caddo explain that people must die because the earth is too crowded. To ease the pain of losing loved ones, a medicine man sings songs that call the spirits of the dead to come and reside with those still living. The Haida tell of a great flood which takes the lives of many people. Survivors drift in the waters until they reach mountain peaks sticking out of the ocean. The tribes are dispersed in this way. The Wishram tell of an Indian hunter who kills more elk than is needed for food. In doing so, he also kills his guardian elk. Because his guardian spirit no longer exists, the young brave dies in the Lake of the Lost Spirits. From the Brule Sioux comes another story which teaches that humans must live in balance with nature. In the worlds before this world, people did not know how to act properly, so Creating Power used fire, earthquakes, and floods to destroy the previous worlds. He then remade the world and populated it with people of understanding and speech. He told the people that they must live in harmony with one another and with all living things.

All Indian legends teach the need for balance between living creatures and natural phenomena. When greed and egotism cause humans to treat nature or other people abusively, then the offenders are punished. By weaving natural and supernatural elements into every story, Indians pass on models of behavior that reflect harmony between physical and spiritual realms.

Oral storytelling gives importance to the elders in a tribe, for they are respected for their wisdom. They are the transmitters of traditions and history. Through their art, they preserve culture. —*Linda J. Meyers*

See also Ethnophilosophy and worldview; Oratory; Religion; Sacred narratives; Wampum.

BIBLIOGRAPHY

Bemister, Margaret. *Thirty Indian Legends of Canada*. Vancouver, British Columbia: J. J. Douglas, 1973. Most of these stories are taken from their original sources. A pronunciation guide to vocabulary is included.

Erdoes, Richard, and Alfonso Ortiz, eds. *American Indian Myths and Legends*. New York: Pantheon Books, 1984. This collection of 166 Indian legends covers a wide range of native people of North America. An appendix gives background on sixty-eight tribes from North America. A fine bibliography is included.

Kroeber, Theodora. *The Inland Whale*. Bloomington: Indiana University Press, 1959. This collection of nine California Indian legends is followed by a thorough discussion of each piece. A discussion is also offered about qualities of Indian stories and about the place of oral literature in the study of comparative literature.

Monroe, Jean Guard, and Ray A. Williamson, comps. *They Dance in the Sky*. Boston: Houghton Mifflin, 1987. This collection of star myths comes from North American Indians who lived all across the United States. The selections are arranged geographically. Included are a glossary and suggested further readings.

Ywahoo, Dhyani. *Voices of Our Ancestors*. Boston: Shambhala, 1987. This book does not include stories but is a discussion of the philosophy behind many Cherokee traditions. Ywahoo discusses oral teachings rather than oral stories.

Oratory

TRIBES AFFECTED: Pantribal

SIGNIFICANCE: In traditional American Indian cultures, which had no written languages, the ability to speak effectively was a respected trait—and a necessary one; oratorical skill is still highly valued today

The ability to speak powerfully and persuasively is a talent every culture admires. For Native Americans, oratory is an extremely important element of ceremonial and nonceremonial life. Before the invasion of North America by Europeans, most native peoples had no written language, so human experience was memorized and transmitted orally from one generation to the next. The information handed down included family and tribal histories, mythology, craft techniques, and the content and syntax of rituals and ceremonies. Many tribes honored articulate speakers with leadership, since oratory was seen, along with dreaming, as a spiritual power. Most tribes developed both understandings of what made oratory effective and formal rituals surrounding the practice of it.

Perhaps the most concise division of the types of Native American oratory comes from A. LaVonne Brown Ruoff's book *American Indian Literatures* (1990), in which the author suggests that Native American oratory may be ceremonial, nonceremonial, or a mixture of these two. Donald M. Bahr, in *Pima and Papago Ritual Oratory* (1975), uses a more complex system for categorizing such orations as ritual oratory, preaching, and songs and stories.

Ceremonial or ritual oratory occurs in sacred situations. These addresses may be directed toward the powers of nature or to the tribe itself, and may take the form of prayer or the tale of a hero's journey. Nonceremonial oratory, or preaching, takes place in public settings, such as at parties, political events, battle sites, and council meetings. In his essay "The Plains Indian as a Public Speaker," Theodore Balgooyen writes, "Public speaking was associated with nearly every kind of public ceremony and was an important means of settling political and legal questions. Every respected warrior was expected to speak on matters of policy if he had a strong opinion."

In daily practice, oratory took many forms. In the Southwest, tribal leaders often gave a sermon each morning from the top of a hut or mound. In rituals of mourning and celebration, leaders and warriors were often moved to eloquence as they expressed sorrow, hope, and thanksgiving for all that the Great Spirit had done. The most commonly collected examples of native oratory are speeches given at tribal councils and U.S. government forums in which Native Americans struggled for peace and for their rights. Children and adults learned history and geography from tribal storytellers, as well as tribal values and the original meanings behind customs and ceremonies.

The right to speak publicly, Ruoff notes, was generally restricted to men, but there have been numerous exceptions, including Chief Viola Jimulla (Yavapai), Sarah Winnemucca (Paiute), Celsa Apapas (Cupeño), Warcaziwin (Sioux), and Gertrude S. Bonnin (Sioux name: Zitkala Sa). Over the past several decades, particularly, the status of women as orators has grown significantly.

A variety of techniques can be identified in Native American oratory, whatever its context. One of the most common tropes is repetition. By repeating key words or phrases, the orator is able to emphasize certain themes and is able to make each speech more memorable for his or her listeners. For example, when Creek leader Tecumseh confronted Governor William Henry Harrison about his violation of various agreements, he frequently referred to Harrison as "brother." This was ironic, because Tecumseh was notifying Harrison that if he did not make amends with the Indians, they would declare war. By repeatedly calling his potential enemy "brother," Tecumseh suggested that his people wanted peace and he reinforced the idea that European Americans and Native Americans were equal.

Another technique which Bahr describes is the "there was/he did" technique. This device operates as a form of parallel construction, in which one section—the *there was* line—"states the existence of a thing," while the following section—the *he did* line—"tells what was done to it." Using this technique, an orator was able to construct long chains of events, thus forming a logical and descriptive narrative.

Other oratorical techniques used by Native Americans include the careful use of rhythm, metaphor, assonance, and alliteration. These techniques, which can help make speeches more easily understood and remembered, were common among all tribes, and they remain in use by Native American orators today.　　　　　　　—*Kenneth S. McAllister*

See also Kinship and social organization; Music and song; Oral literatures; Political organization and leadership; Wampum.

Oregon Trail

TRIBES AFFECTED: Chinook, Kalapuya, Molala, Umpqua, Wishram

SIGNIFICANCE: The Oregon Trail, stretching from Independence, Missouri, to Portland, Oregon, was one of the primary westward routes of settlers in the 1840's

The Oregon Trail was an overland migration that began in Independence, Missouri, and followed a path adjacent to or near the Platte, Snake, and Columbia rivers westward to Portland, Oregon. Families in canvas-covered Conestoga wagons, commonly called "prairie schooners," arrived in Independence every May from the early 1840's through the mid-1850's to begin a journey of five or six months on what became known as the Oregon Trail. After 1849, many wagons took the southern cutoff at Soda Springs (in the present state of Idaho) and headed for California and possible gold rather than the fertile bottomlands of the Willamette Valley of Oregon.

The influx of white settlers moving into Oregon country via the Oregon Trail set off a chain reaction of events that resulted in the signing of the Oregon Treaty of 1846, the naming of Oregon as a territory in 1848, and the dislocating of virtually every Indian tribe in Oregon, especially those on the western slopes of the Cascade Mountains and in the Willamette Valley. The rich bottomland and meadows of the Willamette Valley were especially coveted by Oregon Trail veterans who had emigrated from Kentucky, Illinois, Iowa, and Missouri for just such prime farmland. The Oregon Treaty of 1846 settled the boundary dispute between the United States and England: It extended the international boundary along latitude 49 degrees north to Puget Sound, thence to the Pacific Ocean through the Juan de Fuca Strait, leaving Vancouver Island to Canada. The

Drawing of the first wagon train on the Oregon Trail; it departed from St. Louis in April, 1830. (Library of Congress)

treaty was one of the notable compromises of the administration of President James Polk.

Absent in this decision was any articulated voice of the native peoples who had lived in the region for millennia. Even before the incursion of settlers into the Willamette Valley in the 1840's, there was a series of epidemics (perhaps propagated through contact with traders) in the 1830's that significantly depopulated the tribes of north-central Oregon. The double blow of epidemic followed by mass immigration of outside peoples in successive decades effectively decimated certain tribes and forced some tribes to merge with others. It was during this period, for example, that the Wishram were essentially amalgamated with the Chinook.

The most famous chronicler of the Oregon Trail remains Francis Parkman, whose text *The Oregon Trail* (1849) attempted to document the mass social migration across the continent. Parkman departed from St. Louis, not Independence, Missouri, but he helped to define the Oregon Trail and provided commentary on the people he observed.

See also Chinook; Molala; Sioux; Walla Walla Council; Wishram.

Ornaments

TRIBES AFFECTED: Pantribal

SIGNIFICANCE: In traditional Indian cultures, people decorated their bodies as well as objects such as garments, weapons, and pouches

Ornaments among North American native cultures were as diverse in type as the peoples that produced them. Decorations were added to possessions as well as to the human body, serving various purposes from helping in functional activities to beautifying an individual to visually delineating status, gender, or age.

Indigenous mineral and animal materials were often formed into ornaments. Eagle talons, bird feathers, sea otter and beaver teeth, molted puffin beaks, bone, and ivory are some examples of varied animal parts used as objects of enhancement. Precious stones and reworked silver, copper, lead, brass, and steel were made into jewelry, bells, tacks, hairplates, and buttons, and they were inlaid into functional objects. Archaeological remains have revealed that some ornaments were of specific rare materials, including circular shell gorgets (throat protectors) with incised figures from the Mississippian period; turquoise and shell jewelry and feather pendants from the Hohokam and Anasazi of the Southwest Desert cultures; and ivory clothing toggles from prehistoric Arctic sites.

Because of the portability and rarity of such objects, they were used as trade items and gifts among many native cultures. Coastal peoples traded shell jewelry for goods from inland tribes, while Mesoamerican Indians traded jade and turquoise for desired objects from northern peoples.

Many ornaments took the form of functional objects that went beyond their aesthetic role, such as the beaded pouches, painted bark bags (parfleche), and embroidered porcupine quill garments of the Plains Indians; California Pomo Indian baskets with feathers or beads tightly woven into or attached to the surface; or the snow goggles, fishing equipment, and engraved ivory pipes of the Inuit and Aleut. For example, Aleut men's bent-wood fishing visors were individually painted and lavishly adorned with colorful beads, carved ivory amulets, and sea lion whiskers. The form of the visor kept the sun out of a fisherman's eyes while the embellishments ensured a successful hunt by protecting the wearer and attracting the desired prey with the beauty of the object.

Ornamentation of a highly personal nature among some American Indians consisted of permanent body adornment in the forms of lip labrets made of bone and ivory; ear bobs and nose plugs of metal, ivory, shell, and precious stones; and tattoos. Objects and designs of this type, which are physically incorporated into a wearer's body, defined indelible status within the culture. Cultural affiliation and status were also evident in decoration applied to architecture and transportation as seen in the surface painting and/or carving on canoes, houses, and tipis.

See also Appliqué and ribbonwork; Beads and beadwork; Dress and adornment; Feathers and featherwork; Headdresses; Quillwork; Shells and shellwork.

Ortiz, Simon (b. May 27, 1941, Albuquerque, N.Mex.): Poet

TRIBAL AFFILIATION: Acoma Pueblo

SIGNIFICANCE: Ortiz is a respected and widely read American Indian poet

Ortiz spent his early years at Deetseyamah on Acoma Pueblo land. He is a member of the Eagle (Dyaamih hanoh) clan. He attended McCartys Day School in McCartys, New Mexico, St. Catherine's Indian School in Sante Fe, New Mexico, and Grants High School in Grants, New Mexico.

Following high school, he worked in uranium mines for Kerr-McGee, served in the U.S. Army, and was graduated from both the University of New Mexico (BA) and the University of Iowa (MFA). He has taught at Sinte Gleska College in South Dakota and at the University of New Mexico. Ortiz is the author of the books of poems *Going for the Rain* (1976), *A Good Journey* (1977), and *Fight Back: For the Sake of the People, for the Sake of the Land* (1980). He is also the author of a collection of short stories, *Fightin': New and Collected Stories* (1983), and edited a collection of native fiction, *Earth Power Coming* (1983). Ortiz' work reflects his Acoma Pueblo heritage; it has also been influenced by the social movements of the 1960's and 1970's.

See also Pueblo tribes, Western.

Osage: Tribe

CULTURE AREA: Plains

LANGUAGE GROUP: Siouan (Dhegiha)

PRIMARY LOCATION: Oklahoma

POPULATION SIZE: 9,527 (1990 U.S. Census)

The Osage are one of five tribes in the Dhegiha group of the Siouan linguistic family. Osage is a French corruption of the tribal name Wa-zha'zhe. At the time of first white contact, the Osage lived primarily in western Missouri. Tribal legend and archaeological evidence suggest, however, that the ancient Osage lived east of the Mississippi River.

Traditional Life. Among early Plains tribes (before the introduction of the horse), the Osage held high rank. Although they depended heavily on the buffalo, the Osage also developed a strong agricultural base; they relied on dogs as beasts of burden before the horse. Their villages were permanent. Their lodges were wood frames covered with woven mats or bark, and they ranged from 36 to 100 feet long. As buffalo grew scarce in the Mississippi Valley, bands were forced to extend hunting trips farther onto the Plains.

The Osage comprised two divisions (moieties): the Tzisho, or Sky People, and the Hunkah, or Land People. These moieties were then divided into twenty-one clans, with each person inheriting his or her father's clan. The chief of the Tzisho division was the peace chief, while the war chief came from the Hunkah. Since the early nineteenth century, there also existed three political groups: the Great Osage, the Little Osage, and the Arkansas Osage. In marriage, spouses were required to be from opposite moieties, and a man who married an oldest daughter also held marriage rights to his wife's younger sisters, a form of polygamy. The Osage believed in a supernatural life force, Wakonda, which they believed resided in all things. Shamans provided religious leadership, although there also existed a religious society to which both men and women belonged. Physically, the Osage have been a noticeably tall tribe; they often adorned themselves with tattoos.

History. The first recorded contact with the Osage was by French explorers Father Jacques Marquette and Louis Jolliet (1673). The French subsequently established a lucrative trade and a strong alliance with the Osage. Trade made the Osage a significant force among Plains tribes. The Osage recognized their strategic position in the Plains trade as middlemen and as gatekeepers to the region and were persistent in protecting that advantage. Trade rivalry existed within the tribe, however, and ultimately caused factionalism. In the mid-1790's, trader Auguste Chouteau established a post on the Arkansas River in Oklahoma and persuaded a large faction to locate there permanently, thus creating the Arkansas Band.

In 1808, the Osage ceded the northern half of Arkansas and most of Missouri to the United States, and the Great and Little Osage bands moved to the Neosho River in Kansas. This area became the center of tribal life. As the government removed eastern tribes to Indian Territory, however, clashes between the Osage and removed Cherokee over hunting rights to the region escalated into a long, bloody war. United States agent William Lovely finally convinced the Osage to cede the region to the Cherokee in 1817. Still, hostilities continued, including one of the bloodiest Indian battles in Oklahoma history, the battle of Claremore Mound.

By 1825, the Osage had ceded all their lands to the United States through treaties and were given a reservation (in present-day southern Kansas) in Indian Territory. During this

Bacon Rind, an Osage leader in the late nineteenth and early twentieth centuries; he was elected principal chief in 1909. (Library of Congress)

time, Protestant missionaries established among the Osage some of the first missions and schools in the region, though later they were replaced by Roman Catholic missionaries.

After the outbreak of the Civil War, Confederate commissioner Albert Pike was able to secure the allegiance of many Osage to the south, though many sided with the Union as well. This factionalism created tension among tribal members, already suffering from the ravages of white guerrilla raiders. After the war, the Union used the tribe's Confederate allegiance to secure large land cessions through Reconstruction treaties. Ultimately, the Osage were forced to sell all their lands to the government and use the proceeds to purchase a new reservation in the eastern end of the Cherokee Outlet (all of present-day Osage County, Oklahoma). The post-Civil War years were hard on the tribe, bringing a nearly 50 percent decline in the tribe's population because of poor medical aid and a scarcity of food and clothing. The buffalo were gone, and the land given the Osage was the poorest in Indian Territory for agriculture. The range-cattle industry of the 1880's, however, offered some economic relief for the tribe; they leased grazing rights to cattlemen. Some very lucrative oil and gas deposits were then discovered under the barren Osage lands. The royalties received from the leases on these resources catapulted the Osage from a privatious to an indulgent lifestyle and have since provided the financial foundation of the Osage Nation. Because of their shrewd leasing arrangements, the Osage have become one of the wealthiest of Indian nations on a per capita basis.

Contemporary Life. Osage interests are governed by an eight-member tribal council, along with the principal chief and assistant chief, with the ever-present supervision of the Bureau of Indian Affairs. The Osage Agency, located at Pawhuska, Oklahoma, is unlike other agencies in Oklahoma in that all expenses accrued are paid with tribal funds. One of the biggest issues the tribe has had to confront in the twentieth century has been tribal membership: The tribe's wealth has made citizenship in the nation an enticing relationship. Because of the wealth that oil brought to the tribe, the name Osage was once synonymous with profligate spending. Wealth also brought conflict, and many tribal members have been torn between modernity and traditional ways. Ultimately, the tribe realized the necessity of moderation, and in that light the oil industry has given the tribe economic independence and great advantages in educational and societal matters. Even with the wealth and modernity which have threatened to eradicate the traditional Osage ways, the tribe has retained interest in its culture, arts, crafts, and language.   —*S. Matthew Despain*

See also Buffalo; Pawhuska; Plains; Ranching; Siouan language family; Tallchief, Maria.

BIBLIOGRAPHY

Baird, W. David. *The Osage People*. Phoenix: Indian Tribal Series, 1972.

Din, Gilbert C., and Abraham P. Nasatir. *The Imperial Osages: Spanish-Indian Diplomacy in the Mississippi Valley*. Norman: University of Oklahoma Press, 1983.

Matthews, John Joseph. *Sundown*. Norman: University of Oklahoma Press, 1934.

_____. *Wah'Kon-Tah: The Osage and the White Man's Road*. 1932. Reprint. Norman: University of Oklahoma Press, 1981.

Rollings, Willard H. *The Osage: An Ethnohistorical Study of the Hegemony on the Prairie-Plains*. Columbia: University of Missouri Press, 1992.

Wilson, Terry P. *The Osage*. New York: Chelsea House, 1988.

_____. *The Underground Reservation: Osage Oil*. Lincoln: University of Nebraska Press, 1985.

Osceola

(c. 1804, at Tallassee on the Tallapoosa River near present-day Tuskegee, Ala.—Jan. 30, 1838, Fort Moultrie, Charleston, S.C.): Resistance leader

ALSO KNOWN AS: Assiola (Black Drink Singer), Tallassee Tustenuggee, Billy Powell

TRIBAL AFFILIATION: Creek, Seminole

SIGNIFICANCE: Allegedly a participant in the First Seminole War, Osceola became a leader of the Seminoles, who refused to be moved west of the Mississippi; he initiated the Second Seminole War

Osceola later insisted, and some historians maintain, that both his father (name unknown) and mother (Polly Copinger) were Creeks and that his mother later married an Englishman, William Powell. A 1991 study by Patricia R. Wickman, however, provides impressive evidence that Powell was indeed Osceola's father, that Copinger's grandfather (James McQueen) and father were white, and that the boy also had black ancestors, as did many children who were born in the Upper Creek town of Tallassee. Nevertheless, Osceola was considered to be an Upper Creek, like his mother.

Osceola's mother's uncle, Peter McQueen, was chief of the village where Osceola was born and became a leader of the Red Sticks during the Creek War of 1813-1814. As that conflict escalated, many Creeks fled from Alabama into Florida. Among the refugees were Osceola and his mother, who followed McQueen and became separated from Powell during the migration. The young Osceola was captured by Andrew Jackson's troops during his 1818 campaign in Florida, but he was released because of his age. Allegedly he fought against Jackson in the First Seminole War.

Osceola settled in central Florida after Jackson's campaign and, like many dislocated Creeks, became known as a Seminole. He was never a hereditary chief, nor was he apparently ever elected to such a post; however, in the controversy surrounding the signing of the treaties of Payne's Landing in 1832 and of Fort Gibson in 1833, both of which provided for the relocation of the Seminoles to the West, he emerged as a leader of those who opposed removal.

A heated clash with Wiley Thompson, the federal Indian agent for central Florida, made Osceola an outlaw. Abolitionists later wrote that Thompson aided two slave catchers to capture one of Osceola's wives, who was a mulatto, but there is no evidence for this tale. Instead, the conflict apparently originated when Thompson called a council at Fort King to confirm the earlier treaties. Most of the Seminoles who were present silently refused to sign the documents placed before them, but Osceola allegedly plunged a knife through the agreement. Again, no contemporary account supports this story.

Other confrontations in the summer of 1835 led Thompson to have Osceola imprisoned in shackles, but Osceola was released when he agreed to support removal. Rather than abide by his agreement with Thompson, Osceola organized Seminole resistance and killed Charley Emathla, a chief who had supported emigration. Osceola and his followers then attacked a baggage train during December, 1835. Later that same month, he killed Thompson, while allies ambushed a force of more than a hundred regulars and killed all but three of them. On New Year's Eve, 1835, a large party led by Osceola attacked another detachment of regulars and punished them severely in the First Battle of the Withlacoochee, where Osceola was wounded slightly in the hand or arm but escaped capture.

This began the Second Seminole War, which would last until 1842. Until his capture in 1837, Osceola was the primary target of army operations because the U.S. military recognized his importance as a leader in the resistance. Participants in the campaigns against him noted that many of his followers were black. They would have supported him instead of the hereditary chiefs, and his desire to protect them may have been part of his motivation for continuing to fight long after his health began to fail. His evasion of army columns and bold attacks made him something of a folk hero in the United States, but it also earned him the hatred of military leaders, especially after he liberated more than seven hundred Indians held in a detention camp in June, 1837.

In October, 1837, General Thomas S. Jesup, frustrated by Osceola, treacherously accepted his request for a parley under a flag of truce. The Seminole leader, who was then suffering from malaria, and more than eighty of his followers were captured at their camp near Fort Peyton in a flagrant violation of the truce. Despite the public outcry, he was taken to Fort Mellon at St. Augustine, where two of his wives and two children, as well as his half-sister and others, joined him. These two wives may have been the two sisters he had married in accordance with Creek custom, though there appear to have been others.

After several other Seminoles escaped, Osceola and his group were transferred on New Year's Eve, 1837, to Fort Moultrie at Charleston, South Carolina. There his health declined rapidly, and he died on January 30, 1838. Allegations vary as to the cause of his death, but most agree that his depression contributed to his rapid demise. Wickman says that quinsy, or tonsillitis complicated by an abscess, was the immediate cause of Osceola's death, and both malaria and recurring fevers were contributing factors in his declining health.

Osceola was buried outside Fort Moultrie on Sullivan Island with military honors, but before interment his head was removed by Frederick Weedon, the physician who had attended him during his fatal illness. It was displayed in a medical museum maintained by Valentine Mott of the Medical College of New York until the building was allegedly destroyed by fire in 1866.

The betrayal of Osceola destroyed any realistic hope of unity among the Seminoles. The war continued sporadically until 1842, when most of the surviving Seminoles moved West, as his family had after his death. Only a few remained in the swamps. The circumstances of Osceola's fight, capture, and death, which were often misrepresented, made him a folk hero to many. No fewer than twenty towns in the United States now bear his name, as do three counties, two townships, one borough, two lakes, two mountains, a state park, and a national forest.

—*Richard B. McCaslin*

See also Creek; Creek War; Seminole; Seminole Wars.

BIBLIOGRAPHY

Boyd, Mark F. "Asi-Yaholo or Osceola." *Florida Historical Quarterly* 30 (July, 1951): 249-305.

Covington, James W. *The Seminoles of Florida*. Gainesville: University Presses of Florida, 1993.

Goggin, John M. "Osceola: Portraits, Features, and Dress." *Florida Historical Quarterly* 33 (January-April, 1955): 161-192.

Hartley, William, and Ellen Hartley. *Osceola: The Unconquered Indian*. New York: Hawthorn Books, 1973.

Mahon, John K. *History of the Second Seminole War, 1835-1842*. Gainesville: University Presses of Florida, 1967.

Wickman, Patricia R. *Osceola's Legacy*. Tuscaloosa: University of Alabama Press, 1991.

Oshkosh (1795, Old King's Village on the Fox River near present-day Green Bay, Wis.—Aug. 20, 1858, Keshena, Wis.): Chief

ALSO KNOWN AS: Oshkusi, Oiscoss (His Hoof, His Nail, or the Brave)

TRIBAL AFFILIATION: Menominee

SIGNIFICANCE: Oshkosh was first appointed chief by federal agents during mediation of a land dispute; he helped to negotiate removal of the Menominee Indians

Oshkosh, descendant of chiefs, originally allied with the British during the War of 1812, fighting with Chief Tomah in the battle at Fort Mackinaw, Michigan, and at Fort Stephenson, Ohio. In 1827, he was appointed chief by U.S. agents Lewis Cass and Thomas McKenney as they mediated a border dispute between the Chippewa and the Menominee and a subsequent disagreement between the Menominees and a group of New York Iroquois, led by Eleazar Williams, who wished to settle on Menominee land.

Although originally appointed by white agents, Oshkosh retained leadership throughout his life. He aided the United States during the Black Hawk War of 1832 and afterward continued to ensure Menominee compliance with white authority. Menominee land claims were continuously eroded, and removal was completed when Wisconsin became a state in 1848 and Oshkosh signed the Treaty of Lake Powahekone ceding the last Menominee lands to the federal government. Oshkosh died in 1858 in a drunken brawl and was succeeded by his son. The town of Oshkosh, Wisconsin, is named for him.

See also Black Hawk War; Indian-white relations—U.S., 1775-1830; Menominee; Williams, Eleazar.

Otherday, John (1801, Swan Lake, Minn.—1871, Sisseton Sioux Reservation, S.Dak.): Army scout

ALSO KNOWN AS: Angpetu Tokecha, Other Day

TRIBAL AFFILIATION: Wahpeton Sioux

SIGNIFICANCE: As an army scout and protector of whites, Otherday was honored by the U.S. government

As a young man, Otherday was reputedly a heavy drinker and brawler, having killed other Sioux in arguments. After becoming a Christian, he married a white woman, adopted the name John, and settled on the Minnesota Sioux Reservation.

On several occasions, Otherday aided whites. After the Spirit Lake Uprising of 1857, he rescued white female captives and assisted in the search for Sioux raiders. During Little Crow's uprising of 1862-1863, he led white settlers to safety. In retaliation, Little Crow burned Otherday's home.

As a U.S. Army scout, Otherday worked for General Henry Hastings Sibley, aiding his search for Little Crow. In reward for his services, he was granted $2,500 by the U.S. government, which was presented during a ceremony in Washington, D.C. With his reward he purchased a ranch, which quickly failed. He thereafter returned to the Sioux reservation, where the U.S. government built him a house. He died in 1871, a victim of tuberculosis.

See also Inkpaduta; Little Crow; Minnesota Uprising.

Oto: Tribe

CULTURE AREA: Plains
LANGUAGE GROUP: Siouan
PRIMARY LOCATION: Oklahoma
POPULATION SIZE: 1,840 ("Otoe-Missouria," 1990 U.S. Census)

Oto (or Otoe) tradition indicates that these people lived at one time with the Missouri, Iowa, and Winnebago tribes somewhere in the upper Great Lakes region. Probably pushed by other tribes squeezed from the east, they began moving west and south, perhaps in the 1500's, leaving the Winnebago in the Green Bay, Wisconsin, area, and the Iowa people at the confluence of the Mississippi and Iowa rivers. The Oto and Missouri continued south along the Mississippi and west along the Missouri until reaching the confluence of the Missouri and Grand rivers. At this point there was a conflict between the two groups involving a romantic relationship between the Missouri chief's daughter and the Oto chief's son. Consequently, the Oto continued west along the Missouri while the Missouri people remained. This conflict explains the Oto tribal name, originating from the Chiwere word *wahtohtata*, meaning "lovers" or "lechers." (The Oto and Missouri shared the Chiwere language with the Iowa.)

In the late 1600's, the Otos lived in what is now the state of Iowa, on the Upper Iowa and the Blue Earth rivers, but they were not numerous. Their population at that point was probably about 800. For most of the eighteenth century, they lived further west, along the Platte River near its mouth at the Missouri River. The Otos benefited from trade with the French and later the Americans, but they were also devastated by disease and warfare brought by these outsiders. Their rivals in warfare were mainly the Pawnees, Mesquakies (Fox), and Sauks. The Pawnees at times dominated the Otos militarily.

By 1829, the Otos and Missouris had merged, both having suffered greatly, and having had their populations shrink, from smallpox and other diseases. The following decades were difficult, as they and other beleaguered tribes fought for scant food resources. By 1854, the Oto-Missouris (or Otoe-Missourias) had ceded all of their lands to the United States and moved to a reservation on the Big Blue River, near the Kansas and Nebraska territories. Eventually, one faction split off and moved to Indian Territory (Oklahoma) in 1880. A decade later the rest followed them. In 1907, the Oklahoma reservation was allotted to individual tribal members.

Oto culture of the prereservation era reflected an adaptation to a Plains environment from the eastern woodlands. While women cultivated corn, beans, squash, and melons in the bottomlands along the rivers, men spent much time hunting. Major buffalo hunts were carried on in the spring and fall, with deer, turkey, raccoon, and rabbit hunting occupying other times. While on hunting trips, the Otos stored their food in underground bell-shaped caches and used skin tipis for shelter. Their villages, however, were quite substantial. Depending on the population of a village, there were forty to seventy earth-lodges 30 to 40 feet in diameter. Each lodge had a heavy wooden framework filled in with brush and grass and covered with an outer layer of earth or clay. Villages were divided socially into ten clans, each clan representing several related extended households. Oto society was patrilineal (one belonged to one's father's clan), but the lodges and all other household property were owned by the women. Different clans were responsible for various seasonal celebrations or leadership for particular hunts, and clan chiefs, war chiefs, and spiritual leaders were hereditarily chosen. Curing societies and dance societies such as the Medicine Lodge and the Buffalo Doctors Lodge specialized in particular ceremonies necessary for communication with the spiritual world. Mourning practices were highly ritualized, sometimes involving the killing of a horse so that the deceased person could ride to the afterlife.

Although loss of their homeland and reservation has resulted in some acculturation, the Oto-Missouri tribe still has some tribally owned land in Oklahoma and holds ceremonies and traditional dances each year. Oto-Missouri children started in the 1970's learning their Chiwere language in school, with the aid of a published grammar of the Chiwere language.

See also Iowa; Missouri; Siouan language family; Winnebago.

Ottawa: Tribe

CULTURE AREA: Northeast
LANGUAGE GROUP: Algonquian
PRIMARY LOCATION: Michigan, Oklahoma (U.S.); Ontario, Canada
POPULATION SIZE: 7,522 in U.S. (1990 U.S. Census); estimated 3,500 in Canada

The Ottawa, members of the Algonquian language group, came from north of the Great Lakes with the Chippewa (Ojibwa) and Potawatomi; they formed the Council of Three Tribes. By the 1600's, the tribes had separated, with the Ottawa controlling the northern shore of Lake Huron and Manitoulin Island in the lake and the other two tribes settling farther south and west. "Ottawa" means "to trade" in Algonquian, and tribal members controlled commerce in furs, skins, corn, sunflower oil, tobacco, roots, and herbs among the Native American tribes in the northern Great Lakes region before the coming of Europeans. They were famous for the quality of their birchbark canoes and their abilities as businessmen.

The Ottawa were skilled hunters and fishermen, though in the harsh winter months they had to eat bark to survive. Women gathered blueberries and strawberries and tapped trees for maple syrup while the men hunted. Samuel de Champlain, the French explorer, made contact with the Ottawa in 1615, and he reported that they tattooed their bodies, painted their faces, pierced their noses, and had very long hair. They hunted mostly deer and small game with bows and arrows, and they wore no clothes in warm weather, although in the winter they put on buffalo robes. Jean Nicolet, a French trader, met the Ottawa in 1635 and exchanged guns and powder for furs. The Ottawa lived in small villages in bark- and skin-covered homes. They divided into four bands, named after the places they lived: the Kiskakon, the Outaouae Sinago, the Sable, and the Nassawaketon. Traditional Ottawa religion stressed belief in a spirit world governed by Manitou, the "Great Spirit."

Contact with the French eventually led to displacement and disaster for the Ottawa. In 1649 and again in 1660, the Iroquois from New York attacked in Michigan and southern Canada as they sought expansion of their trade empire. After this attack, the Ottawa retreated to the area of Green Bay, Wisconsin, where they remained until 1670 when, under French protection, they returned to the Lake Huron region. Ten years later, the Ottawa moved again, this time to Mackinaw Island and St. Ignace, Michigan, where they joined temporarily with the Huron and were converted to Christianity. A smaller band moved south to the southeastern shore of Lake Michigan where they remained until 1769, when they moved again after warring against the British.

A key event in Ottawa history took place in 1720 with the birth of the great chief Pontiac. Little is known of his early life. During the French and Indian War (1756-1763), Pontiac led the combined forces of Ottawa, Chippewa, and Potawatomi in the battle against British occupation of the Great Lakes region. When the French surrendered, he organized a "conspiracy" to continue the war against the British. Pontiac assembled a large force of Indians in a siege of Detroit, the main British outpost in the west, that lasted from May to December, 1763. Influenced by the "Delaware Prophet," a holy man who claimed direct contact with the Manitou, Pontiac called for a return to traditional Indian lifestyles and a rejection of white trade goods, except for guns. The siege ended, however, after traitors told the British of the Indians' plan of attack and a supply ship managed to reach Detroit with food and ammunition. Over two thousand settlers and Indians died during the "conspiracy," which the British blamed on the French. Pontiac escaped and went to Illinois, where he was killed in 1769 by a Peoria Indian, probably in the pay of the British.

In 1831, tribal leaders accepted lands in Kansas under provisions of the Indian Removal Act. Fifteen years later, however, this cession became more valuable to white farmers, and the Ottawa ceded them back to the United States in exchange for land in Indian Territory (Oklahoma). Only a few Ottawa moved to this new reservation, and many others returned to Michigan. By 1910, more than twenty-four hundred of the 2,717 members of the tribe resided in Michigan, and not on reservations. Of the Ottawa population of the early 1990's, more than half lived in Michigan, three thousand lived in Ontario, and fewer than five hundred lived on the Oklahoma reservation. Many made their livings as farmworkers, sawmill laborers, and fishing guides. The Ottawa of Ontario still spoke the tribe's language, though it had largely disappeared among American-born tribal members. —*Leslie V. Tischauser*

See also Algonquian language family; Huron; Northeast; Ojibwa; Pontiac's Conspiracy; Potawatomi.

Ouray (c. 1820, northern Mexico, in present-day southern Colo.—Aug. 24, 1880, Ignacio, Colo.): Tribal chief
ALSO KNOWN AS: Willie Ouray, Ure
TRIBAL AFFILIATION: Ute
SIGNIFICANCE: Ouray led central Colorado (Uncompaghre) Utes from the mid-1860's to 1880, convincing them to conciliate rather than fight with encroaching whites

Ouray was the son of a Ute-Apache union. His band ranged the mountains of central Colorado and hunted buffalo on the Plains east of the Rockies. Ouray spent his youth near Taos, New Mexico, as a shepherd; there he learned the Spanish language and culture, possibly as an Indian captive. He then rejoined his mother's Ute band, where he gained prominence as a warrior and hunter, and was useful as an interpreter.

Ouray was a minor signatory on the 1863 treaty ceding parts of southern Colorado to the United States, but was a leading chief of the Uncompaghre (central Colorado) Utes by the time an 1868 treaty was signed. In the 1870's, other Utes began to resent his influence, the preferential treatment he obtained from the U.S. government, and his autocratic and often tyrannical leadership. He successfully thwarted more than one plot by subchiefs, including his own brother-in-law, to kill him.

In 1873 Ouray cooperated in obtaining the necessary signatures to ratify a new agreement ceding more lands, for which he was given special concessions as well as a $1,000 annual salary, a home, and a 400-acre ranch at a new agency. Here, Ouray appeared to adopt the whites' lifestyle, wearing broadcloth suits, riding in a carriage, and living in a cabin with standard American furniture. Despite continued antagonism by some northern Colorado Utes who accused Ouray of betraying his people for a salary, he could not be dislodged from his band leadership or the U.S. government's insistence on using him as head chief for all Utes.

In 1879, Utes of northern Colorado attacked and besieged U.S. troops in what they believed was a defense of their reservation. They killed their unpopular agent and massacred agency workers. Ouray was instrumental in halting the attack and aiding the government in freeing white women who were taken prisoner. Whites used this incident to expel the Utes from Colorado. The Northern Utes were removed to Utah, and the U.S. government renegotiated the 1873 agreement with the Uncompaghre and Southern Utes. A three-fourths tribal ratification was required, and it was believed that only Ouray could obtain these signatures. After obtaining his own band's signatures, he traveled to the Southern Utes' agency at Ignacio, Colorado, to obtain the remainder. On the way he became sick, and he died on August 24, 1880. A negotiator bribed the Utes for the remaining signatures, and in 1881 Ouray's band was ultimately removed to Utah. Ouray had recognized the inevitability of the loss of Indian land to incoming whites, gaining as much as possible through peaceful means while he could and keeping his people relatively free of disastrous warfare.

See also Captain Jack; Colorow; Ute.

Ozette: Archaeological site

DATE: 100-1930
LOCATION: Olympic Peninsula, Washington
CULTURE AFFECTED: Makah

The Ozette site, located on the westernmost point of the Olympic Peninsula on the Pacific coast of Washington, represents the remains of a large, late prehistoric whaling village. Portions of the site that were buried by catastrophic mudslides have provided a large number of organic remains, preserved by their rapid burial and the site's waterlogged condition. Ozette has provided information that is invaluable for the reconstruction of ways of life on the Northwest Coast that predate the arrival of Europeans. The village is believed to have been occupied by ancestors of the Makah Indians, modern indigenous residents of the region who still occupied parts of Ozette as recently as the 1920's.

In 1970, a violent winter storm eroded sections of a mudbank at the site, exposing buried timbers and other wooden artifacts. These were brought to the attention of archaeologist Richard Daugherty, who undertook the excavation of five houses buried by a massive mudslide in the fifteenth century C.E. These large, boxlike structures, occupied at the time of their burial, had been constructed of cedar planks up to 1.5 feet wide that were laced to upright wooden posts with twisted branches. Roofs were made of planks that were lapped to make them watertight and held in place with logs and large stones. In some cases, whale bones were used to shore up walls and to divert water and mud away from houses.

Raised sleeping platforms were found along the inside walls of these buried houses. Near them were a wide variety of organic artifacts, including baskets, mats, woven cedar bark hats, carved wooden clubs, combs, boxes, and bowls. The large house size (about 65 by 35 feet) and the presence of multiple hearths within houses suggest that these dwellings were occupied by more than one family unit. In one structure, whaling harpoons and ceremonial gear were concentrated in one quarter of the house, indicating the presence of a family of high status.

Ozette is estimated to have had a maximum population of about eight hundred. The principal subsistence activities focused on the hunting of whales, fur seals, sea lions, porpoises, and other sea mammals. These were supplemented by the hunting of elk and deer; the collection of oysters, mussels, and clams; and fishing for halibut, cod, and salmon. Parts of large, oceangoing canoes, wooden paddles, harpoons, bone fishhooks, hook shanks, and barbed points for spearing fish are among the artifacts that were used for these activities. Whale bones in the earliest levels of the site, dating to the first centuries C.E., are testimony to a long tradition of whaling on the Northwest Coast.

The significance of this site lies principally in the excellent preservation of entire houses containing a wide variety of organic remains. These testify to the origins of the distinctive lifestyle of Northwest Coast tribes nearly two thousand years ago and its development over the centuries.

See also Arts and crafts—Northwest Coast; Makah; Prehistory—Northwest Coast; Whales and whaling.

Paints and painting

TRIBES AFFECTED: Pantribal

SIGNIFICANCE: Painting has been a primary American Indian art form for thousands of years and is used for social, historical, and decorative purposes

American Indian painting reaches back to the earliest known inhabitants of the Americas. Some of the earliest paintings are called pictographs, which simply means paintings or drawings on rock. These drawings and paintings were highly symbolic and stylized and can be seen even today in certain areas, especially the Southwest of the United States.

Before the coming of the Europeans, many different forms of painting were in existence. Painting was prevalent in the Plains and East in the form of painting on animal skins and tattooing, in the Northwest Coast on wooden poles and masks, and in the Southwest and Mexico on pottery, rock, and adobe walls. These different forms of painting had primarily religious, decorative, and historical purposes, with the emphasis on content rather than form.

Styles of painting varied among tribes and regions and were based on such factors as tribal experience and available materials. Designs were generally two-dimensional and geometric, or linear, showing simple frontal and profile figures and shapes or geometric patterns. Designs developed as a result of visionary experiences were painted on shields, tipis, and clothing and were believed to give protection. Symbolic painting,

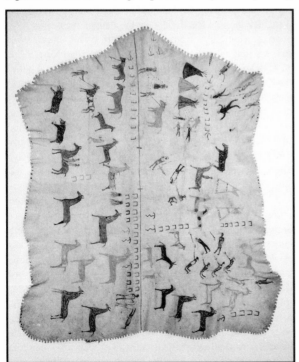

A nineteenth century elk skin robe painted to depict horses, tipis, and Indians fighting. The robe belonged to a Piegan (Blackfoot). (National Museum of the American Indian, Smithsonian Institution)

which was more stylized and abstracted than representational, was often used for ceremonial mural and sand painting, rock art, heraldics, pottery, masks, and body painting. Representational painting was commonly used for historical purposes such as the recording of events and for calendrical use.

The choice of medium was determined by what was available in the natural world in a given geographic area. Pigments were made from mineral, and sometimes vegetable, sources, with the most common colors being red, yellow, dark brown, and white. Paint colors sometimes symbolized the four cardinal points as well as the zenith and the nadir, with the specific colors for each point tribally determined. The colors themselves were believed to have special attributes or magical powers. By 1300 C.E., polychrome rather than monochrome paints were being used. Painting was done with a stylus made of bone or wood, with brushes made of animal hair, or simply with the fingers and hand.

Contemporary American Indian painting uses modern materials and reflects both the preservation and adaptation of traditional subject matter and styles. Since the late 1800's, painting has changed in purpose, reflecting European influence in materials, marketing, and attitude. The emphasis shifted to the individual artist from Indian painting as an ethnic or folk art, and artists began to sign their names to their work. As an art form, painting continues to be a primary means of expression for American Indians and is pursued as a profession by many Indian painters.

See also Art and artists, contemporary; Arts and crafts; Auchiah, James; Awa Tsireh; Dress and adornment; Hokeah, Jack; Petroglyphs; Pottery; Sand painting; Symbolism in art; Tattoos and tattooing.

Paiute, Northern: Tribe

CULTURE AREA: Great Basin

LANGUAGE GROUP: Uto-Aztecan

PRIMARY LOCATION: Nevada, California

POPULATION SIZE: 11,142 (total Paiute population, 1990 U.S. Census)

The Northern Paiute, or Paviotso, a branch of the Shoshonean division of the Uto-Aztecan language group, originally occupied the far western region of Nevada, the southeastern part of Oregon, and the far eastern fringes of central California. "Paviotso" is actually a derogatory Shoshone word meaning "root digger," so members of the tribe prefer to be called Paiute, which means "pure water." The Southern Paiute spoke the same language but inhabited the deserts of northern Arizona and western Utah and had little contact with their northern brothers.

Traditional Lifeways. The Northern Paiute fished, hunted deer, antelope, and bighorn sheep, and gathered piñon nuts. During harsh winters, the women dug plant roots to eat (the derivation of the name Paviotso). In winter, the Paiute lived in grass-covered, cone-shaped structures that had a smokehole at the top. In summer, they moved outside and lived in areas surrounded by trees to protect them from the hot winds. Usually no more than fifty persons, or three or four families, lived in each campsite, with the winter homes widely scattered. In the summer, women wore aprons of rabbit skins, but changed to buckskin dresses in the winter. Men wore rabbit skin shirts in the hot months and buckskin leggings when it started to get cold.

The eldest males usually made key decisions, though each village had a "headman" who enforced law and order. Paiute religion stressed belief in a world inhabited by many spirits. These spirits could be found almost everywhere in nature: in animals, plants, stones, water, the sun, moon, thunder, and stars. Individuals prayed to these spirits for help in hunting and food gathering. These supernatural powers gave orders that had to be followed, such as how to divide the remains of a hunted animal, or who to marry. Failure to follow these instructions could be punished by sickness, misfortune, or death. Contact with the spirits could be sought by anyone. Usually a seeker had to visit a dark and dangerous cave or spend the night on a remote mountaintop to get the spirit's attention, but if contact was made the seeker would receive great powers to heal sicknesses or become a successful hunter. If a Paiute obeyed the spirits, upon death his soul would be rewarded by being taken to another world filled with dancing, food, and gambling.

Post-contact Life. The Paiute acquired horses sometime in the early 1700's, although they did not make contact with whites until 1804, when a few Paiute hunters came upon the Lewis and Clark expedition exploring the Louisiana Purchase. In 1827, an expedition led by the famous explorer Jedediah Smith began trading furs for guns in western Nevada. In the 1830's and 1840's, thousands of white settlers poured through the region on their way to gold strikes in California and farms in Oregon. They brought chaos with them as their wagons, horses and cattle destroyed meager food supplies in the Great Basin. In response, Paiute bands attacked the wagon trains and killed dozens of migrants. Not until after the Civil War did U.S. Army forces "pacify" the territory by killing hundreds of Indians.

Government officials established a reservation in Oregon in 1874, but thousands of Paiutes refused to go. They did not want to become farmers, especially on land that was almost desert. Many Paiutes became ranch hands, cowboys, and sheepherders for area whites. Paiute women worked as housekeepers or servants. In 1887, a Paiute holy man named Wovoka ("the Cutter") had a vision which he described to Indians throughout the Great Basin and beyond: If Indians could dance for five nights and listen to the drums, the fish and wildlife would return, dead Indians would rise from their graves, and whites would disappear from the earth. This "Ghost Dance" movement had spread all the way to Wounded Knee, South Dakota, by the winter of 1890. It led to the last great massacre in Indian history, when army troops killed more than two hundred men, women, and children who were trying to dance whites out of the world.

In the 1930's, cattle ranching became the most important economic activity on the reservation. Paiutes either leased their land to whites or tried to raise their own herds. Paiute cowboys have a reputation for being excellent horsemen and dedicated workers. Most Paiutes do not live on the reservations in Nevada and Oregon, preferring to find jobs for themselves on the cattle and sheep ranches in the area.

—*Leslie V. Tischauser*

See also Ghost Dance; Great Basin; Paiute, Southern; Ranching; Uto-Aztecan language family; Wovoka.

Paiute, Southern: Tribe

Culture area: Southwest
Language group: Uto-Aztecan
Primary location: Northwestern Arizona, southern Nevada, southwestern Utah
Population size: 11,142 (total Paiute population, 1990 U.S. Census)

The Southern Paiutes belong to the Numic-speaking group of the Shoshonean branch of the Uto-Aztecan family. They call themselves *nuwu*, which literally means "human being." The Paiutes spread across the Great Basin into the northern portion of the southwestern United States around 1000 C.E., replacing prehistoric Pueblo-like peoples who had inhabited the region. Similarities in agricultural production and pottery making indicate that the Southern Paiutes must have learned much from the Pueblos they replaced. Defensive structures and artifacts dated at mid-twelfth century suggest that strife may have existed between the groups, causing the Pueblos to flee the region and allowing the Paiutes to expand their territory eastward. By the eighteenth century the Paiutes were living in a great crescentic region from southeastern Utah to northeastern Arizona to the deserts of Southern California and Nevada.

Aboriginal Paiute Culture. During their aboriginal period the Paiutes were primarily gatherers of wild plants, roots, berries, and seeds, supplemented by some hunting of rabbits, deer, mountain sheep, and some insects and lizards. Farming was severely limited and included only corn, beans, and squash. During this early period the Paiutes traded with nearby tribes including the Hopi, Havasupai, Walapai, and Mojave. There is evidence to suggest that these groups existed peaceably with one another.

It is doubtful that the Paiutes had any tribal/political organization binding them into one nation during aboriginal times. Shortages of food and water forced the dispersion of the Paiutes into small family groups. Occasionally, larger social groups came together to harvest piñon nuts or to hunt for rabbits; however, these groups remained together only until the task was completed, then dispersed again. Political or social leadership is evident in the form of praise given to a respected person, a good hunter, or a great dance leader. Religious and other cultural developments were severely limited among the Paiutes because they spent virtually all of their time searching for food and pursuing the other necessities for survival.

Their tools included bow and arrows, hunting nets, seed beaters, gathering baskets, flint knives, digging sticks, and flat grinding stones. Their clothes consisted of rabbit-skin robes, bark or hide aprons, and sandals or moccasins. Their dwellings were rudimentary, constructed mainly of grass, sticks, and mud. Every aspect of their development manifests of the Paiutes' marginal subsistence pattern.

European Contact. The Southern Paiutes, historically, were one of the last Indian groups to have sustained contact with whites. While other southwestern groups experienced early contact with the Spanish, the Paiutes' first contact was with the Dominguez-Escalante expedition of 1776. The Spanish explorers described the Paiutes as the lowliest of peoples, destitute and degraded. The Spanish had a number of significant effects upon the Paiute peoples. The spread of horses to neighboring tribes facilitated trade with such tribes as the Ute and Navajo. The most devastating effect was the beginning of slave trading in the Southwest. Small Paiute bands were prey to Ute and Navajo raiding parties in which they would steal children, especially young girls, and trade them to the Spanish for goods. In some instances, the Paiutes would trade their own children to the Utes for horses (which they would later kill and use for food) or other necessary goods. This slave trade led to a severe depopulation of the Paiutes but also led to their acquisition of material goods such as horses, guns, knives, tipis, kettles, and dogs. This trade persisted well into the nineteenth century, when the Mormons, under Brigham Young, caused it to end.

During the first half of the nineteenth century the Paiutes also came into contact with fur trappers and explorers because of their position along the Old Spanish Trail. Notable among these were Jedediah Smith, Peter Skene Ogden, James Ohio Pattie, and John C. Frémont. These men, too, were critical of Paiute culture and wrote degradingly of them as savages. Indian-white contacts intensified greatly when the Mormons began to settle in southern Utah in 1850. John D. Lee was the church's recorder and wrote extensively of the Paiute Indians. He seemed much less critical of their nature than were the Spaniards or the trappers. Relations between Paiutes and Mormons were generally peaceful and respectful. Although the Mormons subscribed to many of the stereotypes of Indians as lazy, thieving, and savage, because of their theological beliefs they also believed that they had the responsibility to teach the Paiutes to be civilized. The Mormons taught the Paiutes farming and other useful skills. Because of their ever-increasing contact with whites and their low immunity to European diseases, the Paiutes were struck heavily by measles and smallpox. A smallpox epidemic in which hundreds died was recorded in 1877.

Modern Movements and Civilization. In 1873 the Bureau of Indian Affairs sent a special commission, headed by John Wesley Powell, to Utah to suggest the removal of the Southern Paiutes away from the white settlements. They had recommended removal of the Paiutes to the Uintah reservation in northeastern Utah, but because of the Paiutes' animosity with the Utes it was decided to create the Moapa Reservation in Nevada. Many groups resisted and tried to subsist in their old ways, but the expansion of white farming and grazing made this impossible. The bureau's concern for Paiute welfare also expanded into issuing cattle to the Indians because they could not survive solely on farming. The Paiutes subsequently have become fine ranchers.

Other reservations, closer to their traditional lands, were later created by the bureau; among them were the Shivwits reserve in 1891, near Santa Clara, Utah, and the Kaibab reserve in northern Arizona, near Fredonia, in 1907. Many Paiutes, however, unaided by the federal government, were given assistance and protection by nearby Mormon settlements. Drastic changes were taking place among the Paiutes in different degrees depending on contact with whites. Some adopted white culture readily, while others resisted and became hostile. Many smaller family groups formed large bands for the first time in an effort to stop the white intrusion. The Kaibab, Moapa, and Shivwits were among the most notable of these newly formed bands.

Southern Paiute children began attending federal day schools in the 1890's, and some have attended colleges and universities in Arizona, Utah, New Mexico, and California. During the first half of the twentieth century the Paiutes simply existed and continued to be dependant on the charity of the Mormons and others around them; however, three pivotal events occurred that improved the circumstances of the Paiutes. In 1946 the Paiutes filed suit against the federal government for their lands that had been unlawfully taken. The issue was hotly debated, and finally, in 1970, the Paiutes were awarded a settlement, bringing needed money into the reservations. Second, in 1951, the Paiutes established their official constitution and bylaws "to improve our civilization." This allowed them to elect a tribal council and to have a more secure land base. Finally, in 1957, the Southern Paiutes were voluntarily terminated from federal control. In these reforms, the Kaibab band has been the most progressive.

Income-producing opportunities are scarce on the reservation. The tribal chairman is the only paid employee of the tribe, and the federal government employs only a few people for maintenance purposes. Most obtain part-time work at locally white-owned ranches. Most of the cultural traditions of the early periods are remembered only by a few older individuals, and the majority of the children do not hear their native language spoken at home. Nevertheless, the Paiutes' continued survival is a direct result of their successful attempt to join together their voices and fight for survival.

—Robert E. Fleming

See also Paiute, Northern; Southwest; Uto-Aztecan language family.

BIBLIOGRAPHY

Dutton, Bertha P. *The Rancheria, Ute, and Southern Paiute Peoples.* Englewood Cliffs, N.J.: Prentice Hall, 1975.

Euler, Robert C. *The Paiute People.* Phoenix: Indian Tribal Series, 1972.

Fowler, Catherine S., and Don D. Fowler. "Southern Paiutes and Western Shoshonis." *Utah Historical Quarterly* 39 (April, 1971): 95-113.

Kelly, Isabel Truesdell. *Southern Paiute Ethnography.* Salt Lake City: University of Utah Press, 1964.

Knack, Martha C. *Life Is with People: Household Organization of the Contemporary Southern Paiute Indians.* Socorro, N.Mex.: Ballena Press, 1980.

Manners, Robert A. *Southern Paiute and Chemehuevi: An Ethnohistorical Report.* Vol. 1 in *American Indian Ethnohistory: California and Basin-Plateau Indians.* New York: Garland, 1974.

Martineau, LeVan. *The Southern Paiutes: Legends, Lore, Language, and Lineage.* Las Vegas: KC Publications, 1992.

Palenque: Archaeological site

DATE: 514-784
LOCATION: Chiapas, Mexico
CULTURE AFFECTED: Maya

Palenque is the modern name given to the ruins of one of the most important metropolises of the ancient Maya civilization. Its original name is lost; the present toponym is derived from the nearby small modern town of Palenque in the southern Mexican state of Chiapas. Since the time of its discovery in 1773 by a Spanish missionary, Palenque has become one of the most studied areas of the ancient Maya civilization. Considered by some to be the most beautiful of all Maya centers, it lies in the drainage basin of the Usumacinta River, within the tropical rain-forest zone.

Dates from the Maya Long Count at Palenque, carved on stone panels and stuccoed surfaces of walls, indicate that the city thrived for some 270 years—from 514 to 784 C.E. It is hypothesized that Palenque led the other Maya cultural areas in artistic, intellectual, and architectural developments. The Palenque culture rose to its summit shortly before 700, but by 800 the city had been abandoned; it soon fell into ruin. This change was related to the great crisis that affected the entire central Maya area between 800 and 900 and ended with the disappearance of Classic Maya civilization.

The buildings of Palenque exhibit standard Classic Maya architecture such as corbeled vaults and decorative high roofs (roof combs or crest walls). Unlike other Maya cities, the structures at Palenque have comparatively thin walls and spacious bays and openings (in contrast to the massive walls and narrow rooms at Tikal, for example). Prominent at Palenque are two groups of eight buildings, divided by a small gully.

The largest building at Palenque is the palace. It is 300 feet long and 240 feet wide, and it sits on top of an artificial platform that rises more than 30 feet. A large number of galleries and rooms are situated around four courts. The sections of the palace were successively added between 602 and 783, and a unique four-story square tower, with an interior stairway, dominates the structure.

The temples of Palenque, named the Inscriptions, the Cross, the Sun, and the Foliated Cross, are all built atop step pyramids. The latter three are arranged around three sides of a plaza on the eastern end of the site. Excavations in 1952 revealed that the tomb of Palenque's greatest ruler, Pacal, was located under the pyramid supporting the Temple of the Inscriptions. Pacal ascended the throne at age twelve and died in 683 at the age of eighty.

The lid to his coffin was carved with a symbolic scene of death and resurrection. The ruler's face was covered with a now-famous mosaic jade mask, and he wore several ornaments of jade, pearl, conch shell, and pyrite. Stucco reliefs line the walls of the burial chamber, representing the nine gods of the underworld. Six skeletons lie outside the chamber and were probably servants who were sacrificed so that they could accompany their master to the afterlife. The staircase that led up to the temple was filled with rocks, and a fitted stone slab was put into the floor. Pacal's son and successor, Chan Bahlum ("Snake Jaguar"), constructed this large complex, along with the other smaller temples mentioned.

The Palenque artists excelled in stucco work. Painted figures of stucco relief found on buildings and monuments disclose a definite color code: The exposed skin of humans was red, while that of the gods was painted blue.

See also Chichén Itzá; Copan; Maya; Quetzalcóatl; Tikal; Uxmal.

Paleo-Indian: Prehistoric tradition

DATE: 10,000-7500 B.C.E.
LOCATION: North, Middle, and South America
CULTURES AFFECTED: Pancultural
SIGNIFICANCE: The Paleo-Indian tradition represents the earliest clear evidence of human occupation of the Americas by people hunting Ice Age animals, using distinctive fluted spear points

There is artifactual evidence of human occupation throughout the Americas by Paleo-Indians by 9500 B.C.E. They hunted large Pleistocene (Ice Age) animals. The Paleo-Indian fluted points were finely made spear points chipped on both sides, with a distinctive flute removed from the base on both sides. The fluted points were hafted to the end of a spear. Spears were thrown with the aid of a spear thrower, or "atlatl," which increased the throwing distance.

The Paleo-Indian period is divided into the Early Paleo-Indian period, consisting of the Clovis tradition (9500-9000 B.C.E.) and the Folsom tradition (9000-8000 B.C.E.), and the Late Paleo-Indian tradition. The Clovis tradition is named for the discovery site of Clovis, New Mexico, and their environmental adaptation focused on hunting Pleistocene mammoths and mastodons. The Folsom tradition, named for the Folsom site in New Mexico, emphasized the hunting of extinct bison, *Bison antiquus*. Clovis points are relatively large, with a flute that extends only part way from the base toward the point tip, whereas Folsom points are smaller and have a flute that extends almost to the point tip. Late Paleo-Indian points lack the distinctive flute of the earlier periods. The adaptation of the Late Paleo-Indian people was more regionally diversified, as reflected in their greater variety of point styles. The Paleo-Indian tradition is marked by fluted points as found at such sites as Clovis, Folsom, Lindenmeier, Olsen-Chubbuck, and Casper in the western United States; Debert, Bullbrook, Shoop, Parkhill,

Udora, and Sandy Ridge in the Northeast; Ladyville, Turrialba, and Los Tapiales in Middle America; and Monte Verde in South America.

The Paleo-Indians were descendants of hunting people who followed Pleistocene animals across the land bridge, Beringia, from Asia. At various times during the Pleistocene period when the glaciers advanced, the sea level was lowered, providing the opportunity for people to travel from Siberia to Alaska. During the late Pleistocene, Beringia consisted of a 1,000-kilometer (600-mile) land bridge between 75,000 and 40,000 B.C.E. and between about 23,000 and 12,000 B.C.E. Once in Alaska, early humans were blocked from southward travel by the Laurentide ice sheet to the east and the Cordilleran ice sheet to the west. The occurrence of Paleo-Indian artifacts in the continental United States by 9500 B.C.E. indicates that people were able to penetrate the ice barrier, either by a Pacific coast route or through the "ice-free corridor" between the ice sheets. With the extinction of more than thirty genera of animals at the end of the Pleistocene (associated with the climatic changes and, in some instances, perhaps related to Paleo-Indian hunting overkill), people changed their subsistence adaptations to emphasize hunting smaller animals and collecting wild plants throughout the Americas in what is termed the Archaic tradition.

See also Archaic; Beringia; Clovis; Folsom; Lehner; Plano; Prehistory.

Palouse: Tribe

CULTURE AREA: Plateau
LANGUAGE GROUP: Sahaptian
PRIMARY LOCATION: Washington State

Traditionally the Palouse lived along the lower Snake River and its tributaries, including the Palouse River. The Palouse are considered a Plateau tribe. They organized into three independent groups and lived in villages during the winter months in wooden houses.

Similar to other Columbia Basin Indians, their economy depended on salmon fishing in the Columbia River, gathering roots (such as the camas) and berries, and hunting. The area in which they lived was arid and flat, broken by steppes. Hunting increased in importance after the horse was introduced in the mid-1700's. The Palouse became excellent horsemen, and their economy expanded to include horse trading in the early nineteenth century. Their first European American contact was with the Lewis and Clark expedition in 1804, followed by fur traders exploring the area in the early 1800's. Friction with whites began almost immediately and persisted throughout Palouse history. Of any of the Plateau tribes, the Palouse were the most resistant to U.S. government plans to resettle them on reservations. In one of their initial contacts with fur traders, one of their members was found guilty of stealing from a Pacific Fur Company manager. For this crime the thief was executed, much to the horror of the Palouse and nearby Nez Perce. After the incident, the Palouse and Nez Perce kept their distance from the traders.

Further contact with white people was inevitable as white settlers sought to settle eastern Washington and Oregon. In 1855, Washington Territorial Governor Isaac Stevens held the Walla Walla Council to negotiate with tribes throughout the Columbia Plateau. Stevens wanted to confine the Indians to a limited area and open the region to homesteaders. During the treaty negotiations, the Palouse tribe was considered part of the Yakimas. The council was concluded with the Yakima Treaty. The treaty was signed by Kamiakin, who was chosen Yakima headman by Stevens; it included the Palouse as being one of the signatories who made up the Confederated Tribes of the Yakima Indian Reservation. Kamiakin claimed that he never signed the treaty. The Palouse also had their own representative, Koo-lat-toosa, again appointed by Stevens to act as chief.

Dissatisfied with the treaty, the Palouse joined in the Yakima War, led by Kamiakin, who was part Palouse. Despite defeat in 1856, the Palouse refused to move to the reservation and occupied their ancestral lands, located between the Nez Perce, Umatilla, and Yakima reservations. White settlers, however, wanted the land, and the Palouse population, which had dwindled to less than two hundred, still posed a threat. Some members of the tribe, remembering the Yakima War, did move to either the Yakima, Nez Perce, Warm Springs, or Umatilla reservations, while others remained off the reservation.

In 1863, problems ensued when gold was discovered in the Clearwater River on the Nez Perce reservation. Trying to stave off a gold rush, the government negotiated the Lapwai Treaty with the Nez Perce, in which the Nez Perce ceded more land. Although the nearby Palouse did not sign the treaty, the federal government insisted that they follow treaty provisions. Thus the Palouse were treated as a subtribe of the Nez Perce. Part of the Nez Perce (about one-third), however, did not abide by the treaty and lived off the reservation in the Wallowa Valley. By the 1870's, white settlers wanted these lands as well, and in 1877, the army ordered Nez Perce Chief Joseph and his tribe to return to the Nez Perce reservation. While moving to the reservation, hostilities occurred and several whites were killed. Chief Joseph and his band of eight hundred, which included a small number of Palouse, fled to Montana and tried to reach Canada. The army defeated them, however, and the remaining Nez Perce and Palouse were forced to move to Oklahoma Territory and finally to the Colville Reservation. Today the Palouse tribe has no official population figures; many Palouse Indians undoubtedly intermarried with surrounding tribes and have thus kept their ancestry alive.

See also Colville; Kamiakin; Nez Perce; Walla Walla Council; Yakima.

Pamlico: Tribe

CULTURE AREA: Southeast
LANGUAGE GROUP: Algonquian
PRIMARY LOCATION: Pamlico River, North Carolina

Though there are numerous references to this tribe, little is known about them. The Pamlico were horticulturalists whose subsistence base consisted essentially of maize, beans, squash, and a wide variety of cultivated foods, supplemented by men's hunting, trapping, and fishing. Women dug roots and gathered berries and nuts, some of which were dried for winter storage.

The first mention of the Pamlico was by the Raleigh colonists in 1585, who called them Pomouik. The population of the Pamlico was estimated to be nearly one thousand in 1600. The Pamlico suffered a devastating smallpox epidemic in 1696 that left only seventy-five survivors, who by 1710 were living in a single village. In 1711, the Pamlico participated in the Tuscarora War, at the end of which the Tuscarora, under treaty with the English, agreed to exterminate the remaining Pamlico. Those not killed were incorporated as slaves by the victorious Tuscarora.

See also Tuscarora.

Pan-Indianism

TRIBES AFFECTED: Pantribal

SIGNIFICANCE: American Indians have long attempted to balance tribal loyalties and affiliations with the possibilities and benefits afforded by intertribal unity; during the latter half of the twentieth century, pan-Indianism has become a hotly contested issue

Since the 1960's American Indians have become increasingly politicized and reform-minded. This mobilization has occurred along three lines: tribal, pantribal, and pan-Indian. Tribal activity currently focuses on organizations or actions by and for members of a specific tribe. This type of movement usually concentrates on the protection or expansion of a single tribe's rights or opportunities. Pantribalism occurs when two or more tribal entities unite in pursuit of a mutually beneficial goal. The Council of Energy Resource Tribes (CERT) is an example of such activity. Tribal and pantribal mobilizations are distinct from the pan-Indian movement, which promotes the universality of the Indian experience and emphasizes ethnic identification rather than tribal affiliations. According to Vine Deloria, Jr., a nationally recognized authority on Indian rights, in his work *The Nations Within: The Past and Future of American Indian Sovereignty* (1984), "the tribes are concerned with the substance of Indian life while the ethnics [pan-Indianists] look to the process."

Historical Background. The pan-Indian movement had its inception during the opening decades of the nineteenth century. The first definable pan-Indian action occurred during the War of 1812 at the instigation of the Shawnee chief, Tecumseh, and his brother, a revivalist religious leader named Tenskwatawa (the Shawnee Prophet). Urging the various tribes at the frontier to put aside their differences and to oppose the encroachment of the U.S. government, Tecumseh proclaimed in 1810, "The only way to stop the evil is for the red men to unite in claiming a common and equal right in the land, as it was at first and should be now—for it was never divided but belonged to all." The pan-Indian activity during the remainder of the nineteenth century focused on a combination of strategies and objectives guided largely by religious inspiration. The most notable of these mobilizations remains

the Ghost Dance revivals of the Great Plains fostered by the Paiute spiritual leader Wovoka.

At the beginning of the twentieth century, this movement acquired different direction and form. The focal point shifted from religious revival toward political and civil equity and more formal organization. In 1912, for example, a group of Indians drawn together by common experience founded the Society of American Indians. This group continues its commitment to collective action and its promotion of a variety of pan-Indian and pantribal activities. One such organization was the National Congress of American Indians, founded in 1944 by the Indian employees of the Bureau of Indian Affairs. Its primary purpose remains the lobbying for American Indian causes and rights.

Developments Since World War II. During the last half of the twentieth century, distinctions between pantribal and pan-Indian mobilizations became more pronounced. Government programs and policies aimed at termination of tribal status gave the movements greater impetus. The general atmosphere of protest and reform during the 1960's and early 1970's radicalized the behavior of Indian reformers. An early indicator of the growing schism and changes in tactics was the founding of the National Indian Youth Council in 1961. Frustrated by the "poetic" responses of the older, more established pan-Indian organizations, a group of younger, more radical leaders led by Clyde Warrior, a Ponca, and Melvin Thom, a Paiute, formed a new organization. They urged their audiences to come to grips with the continued paternalism of the federal government and its failure to correct dire social and economic conditions confronting Indians everywhere. Their cause, according to Thom, was "a Greater Indian America." This action also foreshadowed the development of the Red Power mobilizations of the 1970's and the constituency within which they would find their base. This movement attracted the interest of urban Indians whose identification was ethnic rather than tribal in nature.

Among the most important and visible organizations of the next generation of organizations was the American Indian Movement (AIM), founded in 1968 in Minneapolis by Dennis Banks, George Mitchell, and Clyde Bellecourt of the Chippewa (Ojibwa), and Russell Means, a Sioux. This group advocated a much broader range of tactics to accomplish their purpose. In addition to legal recourse, they employed protest demonstrations, sit-ins and occupations, and occasional violence to promote their causes. Two of the most memorable of these activities were the occupation of Alcatraz Island in 1969 and the violent stand-off at Wounded Knee in 1973. The founding of the International Indian Treaty Council and the Women of All Red Nations represents institutional outgrowths of the AIM mobilization.

During the 1970's and into the 1980's, this movement has also discovered some limitations, especially with regard to goal setting and continued competition with traditional tribal organizations. The strongest supporters of the pan-Indian mobilization remain urban Indians whose tribal affiliations have eroded. In large and often hostile cities, Indians of various tribes find it easier to identify with one another than with the larger communities that surround them. They acknowledge a common ethnic origin and welcome partnerships across tribal lines. This tendency places them at odds with many tribalists who are more traditional in their approach and perceive this blending as a dilution of their identities. Pan-Indianists have also realized that defining themselves, their ideals, and their objectives in the abstract is much simpler than developing specific plans of action. All but the broadest of their objectives involve groups too specific to be truly considered pan-Indian in nature. —*Martha I. Pallante*

See also Activism; American Indian Movement (AIM); Council of Energy Resource Tribes (CERT); Ghost Dance; National Congress of American Indians (NCAI); National Indian Youth Council (NIYC); Society of American Indians (SAI); Tecumseh; Tecumseh's Rebellion.

BIBLIOGRAPHY

Barsh, Russel Lawrence, and James Youngblood Henderson. *The Road: Indian Tribes and Political Liberty.* Berkeley: University of California Press, 1980.

Deloria, Vine, Jr., and Clifford M. Lytle. *The Nations Within: The Past and Future of American Indian Sovereignty.* New York: Pantheon Books, 1984.

Hertzberg, Hazel W. *The Search for an American Indian Identity: Modern Pan-Indian Movements.* Syracuse, N.Y.: Syracuse University Press, 1971.

Nagel, Joane. "The Political Mobilization of Native Americans." *Social Science Journal* 19 (July, 1982): 37-45.

O'Brien, Sharon. *American Indian Tribal Governments.* Norman: University of Oklahoma Press, 1989.

Olson, James Stuart. "Native Americans in Contemporary Society." In *The Ethnic Dimension in American History.* New York: St. Martin's Press, 1979.

Waldman, Carl. *Atlas of the North American Indian.* New York: Facts on File, 1985.

Papago. *See* **Tohono O'odham**

Parfleche

TRIBES AFFECTED: Plains tribes
SIGNIFICANCE: Widely used within and outside the Plains, parfleches were both practical devices for storing and transporting food and clothing and objects subject to sophisticated ornamentation

A parfleche is a rawhide storage container that was used primarily among Plains tribes to store dry meat, pemmican, or clothing. It was made of a single sheet of hide folded into an envelope, with leather laces passed through holes in flaps to keep it closed. Often parfleches were made in pairs. Variant types of rawhide containers formed into a box shape and often referred to as parfleches were manufactured by tribes who had contact with Southern Siouan groups. The Iowa, Oto, Ponca, and Santee (Sioux) cut pieces from a large hide and then bent, folded, and sewed them together in a box. The Sauk and Fox,

Kickapoo, and Menominee used a single piece of buffalo rawhide and folded and bent it into a box. Parfleches were widely diffused outside the Plains area partly through friendly visits during which gifts were exchanged and trade occurred.

Women manufactured parfleches and applied incised or painted designs to them. There were distinctive tribal variations in designs with symmetrical geometric designs consisting of straight lines, triangles, rectangles, and diamonds predominating, although the Blackfoot often integrated some curved lines. Patterns were sometimes incised. In this method the artist scraped away portions of the rawhide, leaving lighter and darker shading. Designs were also painted onto the rawhide, with colors derived from iron-containing clays that yielded yellow, brown, red, and black, with some green and blue. Parfleches were useful, compact storage containers that were well-adapted to the mobile Plains lifestyle; they also served decorative purposes and were often prominently displayed in the tipi and reflected the industriousness of the women.

See also Arts and crafts—Plains; Hides and hidework; Ornaments; Paints and painting.

Parker, Ely Samuel (c. 1828, near Pembroke, N.Y.— Aug. 31, 1895, Fairfield, Conn.): Tribal chief

ALSO KNOWN AS: Donehogawa, Hasanoanda (the Reader, or Coming to the Front)
TRIBAL AFFILIATION: Seneca
SIGNIFICANCE: Parker was a Seneca chief who became a member of Ulysses S. Grant's staff during the Civil War; he was the first Indian appointed commissioner of Indian affairs

Parker was born on the Tonawanda Seneca reservation in western New York. He was a member of the Wolf clan, in keeping with the Seneca and Iroquois custom of remaining in the clan of one's mother. Parker's mother was Elizabeth Parker (Gaontgwutwus). His father, William Parker (Jonoestowa), had a white mother but served as the chief of the Tonowanda Seneca. His maternal grandfather, Jimmy Johnson (Sosehawa), was high priest of the Six Nations of the Iroquois and a nephew of Red Jacket (Sagoyewatha), a noted Seneca leader.

Educated in a missionary school and two local academies, Parker was pressed into service at an early age as an emissary for Seneca leaders who were negotiating with the James K. Polk administration and United States Senate over land titles. These negotiations, and some related court cases, were eventually settled in favor of the Seneca. Parker also helped Lewis H. Morgan with his landmark study of the Iroquois, the first scientific work on the tribe. On September 19, 1851, Parker became a sachem. He assumed the title of Donehogawa, which signified the traditional role of keeper of the western door of the council house. At this time he was formally entrusted with keeping the silver medal given to Red Jacket by George Washington in 1792, though Parker had worn it previously.

After serving as an emissary for the Seneca, a role that he periodically repeated before the Civil War, Parker studied law,

Ely Samuel Parker served on Ulysses S. Grant's staff in the Civil War and was appointed commissioner of Indian affairs when Grant became president. (Library of Congress)

but was not admitted to the bar because he was not a United States citizen. In 1849, he joined a state engineering party. He learned this profession as he worked; there is no record of his attending Rensselaer Polytechnic Institute, as some sources assert. A few years later, he became an engineering officer for the state militia, and he was active in the Masons. He failed to obtain a promotion from the state, so he resigned and secured an appointment as a civil engineer with the federal government. He directed the construction of a customhouse and marine hospital at Galena, Illinois, from 1857 to 1859, then supervised several other federal projects in the area. It was at this time that he became acquainted with Ulysses S. Grant.

Parker lost his federal appointment in the scramble for offices after Abraham Lincoln's election. His attempt to obtain a commission in the Corps of Engineers at the outbreak of the Civil War proved fruitless, allegedly because of his race. He returned to the reservation in New York, where he farmed and unsuccessfully applied for citizenship, the lack of which he believed was preventing him from receiving a military commission. Although he did not become a citizen, on May 25, 1863, Parker was appointed an assistant adjutant general with the rank of captain on the staff of General John E. Smith, a former Galena jeweler who was in command of a division for Grant at Vicksburg. Traditionally, a sachem could not hold a military title, but this restriction was waived since Parker would not be fighting another tribe.

In September, 1863, he was transferred to Grant's staff as an assistant adjutant general. Grant became a lieutenant general and went east in the spring of 1864; he took Parker along, and in August, 1864, appointed him as his military secretary, with the rank of lieutenant colonel of volunteers. Parker earned a brevet as a colonel of volunteers before General Robert E. Lee surrendered in April, 1865, at Appomattox, where Parker had the honor of writing the final copy of the terms of surrender. Allegedly, Lee was momentarily taken aback by the swarthy appearance of Parker, but he recovered his composure and declared that it was nice to have a "real American" present for such a historic occasion. For his Civil War service, Parker was brevetted a brigadier general of volunteers in 1865, to date from April 9, the day that Lee capitulated.

Parker was one of several negotiators who met with Indians at Fort Smith, Arkansas, in September, 1865, and he was often asked to repeat this role immediately after the war. In July, 1866, when Grant became general-in-chief, Parker became his aide-de-camp. When the volunteers were mustered out, Grant secured the rank of lieutenant in the regular army for Parker, and this was quickly followed by brevets up to brigadier general. Grant took office as president in 1869 and appointed Parker as Commissioner of Indian Affairs, the first Indian to hold that office. Parker worked zealously to promote peaceful settlements of Indian problems within the "Quaker Peace Policy" adopted by Grant, which earned Parker some powerful enemies. In 1871, the House of Representatives tried him for defrauding the government. He was acquitted of all charges, but the experience prompted him to resign on August 1, 1871.

Although he remained very active in veterans' organizations, Parker never again worked for the federal government. He had married Minnie Orton Sackett, who was twenty years his junior, in 1867; after he resigned, they settled in Fairfield, Connecticut, where one of her close friends resided. Maude T. Parker (Ahweheeyo), their only child, was born at Fairfield in 1878. Parker invested in a variety of enterprises; various setbacks eliminated his fortune, though he retained his real estate. In 1876, he accepted an appointment as superintendent of buildings and supplies for the New York City Police Department. He held this post until his death on August 30, 1895, at the home of his wife's friend in Fairfield. Bright's disease killed him, but he also had diabetes and suffered several strokes.

Parker was buried initially in Fairfield, but in January, 1897, his body was removed to a plot at Forest Lawn Cemetery in Buffalo, where Red Jacket's remains had been interred in 1884 in a ceremony at which Parker spoke. Ironically, Parker's final resting place was within the shadow of a heroic statue of his illustrious ancestor, which had been commissioned after his own suggestion for a design commemorating the decline of the Iroquois Confederation was rejected. —*Richard B. McCaslin*

See also Indian-white relations—U.S., 1831-1870; Iroquois Confederacy; Red Jacket; Seneca.

BIBLIOGRAPHY

Armstrong, William H. *Warrior in Two Camps: Ely S. Parker, Union General and Seneca Chief.* Syracuse, N.Y.: Syracuse University Press, 1978.

Parker, Arthur C. *The Life of General Ely S. Parker, Last Grand Sachem of the Iroquois and General Grant's Military Secretary.* Buffalo, N.Y.: Buffalo Historical Society, 1919.

Yeuell, Donovan. "Ely Samuel Parker." In *Dictionary of American Biography.* Vol. 14, edited by Dumas Malone. New York: Charles Scribner's Sons, 1943.

Parker, Quanah

(c. 1845, near Cedar Lake, Tex.— Feb. 23, 1911, Fort Sill Reservation, near Lawton, Okla.): Tribal chief

ALSO KNOWN AS: Kwahnah (Sweet Odor)

TRIBAL AFFILIATION: Quohada Comanche

SIGNIFICANCE: Although a fierce warrior and battle leader, Quanah became an outspoken advocate of Indian assimilation and aided his people in the transition from freedom to reservation life

Quanah Parker was the son of a Nacona Comanche chief named Peta Nocona and a white woman named Cynthia Ann Parker. A mixed band of Comanches, Paiutes, and Kiowas captured Cynthia Ann (age nine at the time), her younger brother, and her older female cousin in 1836 during a raid on Parker's Fort in what is now east-central Texas. Cynthia Ann's brother and cousin escaped captivity within a few years, but a Comanche family adopted Cynthia Ann and reared her as a Comanche. At age seventeen or eighteen she married Peta Nocona and in due course gave birth to Quanah, another boy named Pecos, and a daughter named Topasannah (Prairie Flower).

Comanche chief Quanah Parker fought fiercely against confinement to reservations, but after 1875 he became an advocate of acceptance and assimilation. (Library of Congress)

In December, 1860, a Texas Ranger named Sul Ross (later a governor of the state) led a force of 120 men against a Comanche camp on the Pease River near the present Oklahoma-Texas border. In a running fight, the Rangers killed a number of Comanches and captured others—among them Cynthia Ann and her daughter. Quanah's father died at the hands of Sul Ross himself during the battle, and his brother died shortly afterward, leaving the fifteen-year-old boy without close relatives. He was adopted by the Quohada Comanches and quickly proved himself an able warrior.

The Quohadas were a nomadic people who hunted buffalo from Kansas into Mexico, but their primary territory was the Llano Estacado (Staked Plain), especially the area that is now the Texas panhandle. Although Texas records do not mention Quanah by name during the next decade, he almost certainly participated in some of the Comanche raids that resulted in many deaths and much property damage in the Southwest during the 1860's. Many of the young white men being in the Confederate army during the early part of the decade, the frontier became especially vulnerable to Comanche raids. During the 1860's, Quanah apparently distinguished himself in raids and became a subchief. The raids of the 1860's pushed back the frontier more than one hundred miles and left many hundreds of white settlers dead. In 1866, the federal government enacted legislation to deal with the "Indian problem," which resulted in the Medicine Lodge Treaty of October, 1867, which specifically targeted the Plains Indians and directly affected Quanah.

Representatives of the U.S. government met with leaders of the Arapahoes, Eastern Apaches, Cheyennes, Comanches, and Kiowas on Medicine Lodge Creek in southern Kansas on October 19, 1867. Many of the chiefs at the negotiations signed the treaty between October 21 and 27, agreeing to take their people to reservations in Oklahoma and Texas. Quanah Parker was not among those who signed the agreement. He and other Comanche subchiefs vowed they would never be confined to reservations, and led their bands to the Llano Estacado in the Texas panhandle. For the next seven years they raided incessantly throughout the Southwest. General William Tecumseh Sherman, army commander in the region, attempted to force the recalcitrant chiefs and their people to relocate to the reservation, but with little success. Quanah and other leaders managed to evade the army units put into the field against them. Colonel Ronald Slidell Mackenzie led many expeditions against the Comanche from 1868 to 1873, but usually failed to find his adversaries. Indians and whites committed many atrocities against each other during the raids and battles during this period.

On June 27, 1874, Quanah's band fought a hard battle at Adobe Walls in the Texas panhandle. Many of the Comanche bands had come under the influence of a medicine man named Isatai, who claimed to have spoken with the Great Spirit in heaven. The Great Spirit had told him that if the Indians did a Sun Dance they would be immune to bullets and would drive the whites from their lands. Quanah and Isatai were instrumental in organizing a large-scale attack on a group of buffalo hunters at Adobe Walls. The attack ultimately failed, and many Indians died despite Isatai's promises. After the battle, many of Quanah's allies agreed to go to the reservations after an ultimatum from the federal government. Only Quanah's band and a few others remained at large. The U.S. Army consequently launched a three-pronged campaign against the recalcitrant bands that eventually forced them onto the reservations.

On June 2, 1875, Quanah led his band into Fort Sill, Oklahoma, and surrendered to Mackenzie. Quanah, who had been the fiercest opponent of white settlement on the Texas plains, immediately became the most outspoken Comanche advocate of Indian assimilation into white culture. In time, he became the principal chief of the Comanche nation. From that position, he advocated Indian education in American-style schools and Indian technical education. Quanah became friends with many wealthy and influential white men, including Theodore Roosevelt, in whose inaugural parade he rode in 1905. He used his influence to fight for Indian rights for the remainder of his life.

Quanah later became a judge for Indians accused of crimes and a deputy sheriff. He also became a successful capitalist as a rancher and as an investor in the stock market. Ironically, he made considerable profits from railroad investments—strange for the man who had done much to retard the building of railroads in the Southwest. As recognition for his efforts in white-Indian relations, he became a favorite speaker at social gatherings throughout the Southwest and eventually had a Texas town named for him.

Quanah's popularity with many whites probably derived from the fact that he himself was half-white. After his surrender, Quanah became fascinated with his mother's people. He arranged to have her remains disinterred and buried on his reservation, with the intention of being buried beside her. He visited many of his mother's surviving relatives, including her brother, who had been captured with her. His unique white-Indian heritage, coupled with his positions of leadership in both cultures, allowed Quanah Parker to become a major force in reconciling the differences between the two cultures.

—*Paul Madden*

See also Adobe Walls, Battles of; Comanche; Medicine Lodge, Treaties of; Sun Dance; Texas Rangers.

BIBLIOGRAPHY

Carter, Robert G. *On the Border with Mackenzie*. Washington, D.C.: Enyon, 1935.

Jackson, Clyde L., and Grace Jackson. *Quanah Parker: Last Chief of the Comanches*. New York: Exposition Press, 1963.

Richardson, Rupert N. *The Comanche Barrier to South Plains Settlement*. Glendale, Calif.: Arthur H. Clark, 1933.

Tilghman, Zoe A. *Quanah: The Eagle of the Comanches*. Oklahoma City: Harlow, 1938.

Wallace, Ernest, and E. Adamson Hoebel. *The Comanches: Lords of the South Plains*. Norman: University of Oklahoma Press, 1952.

Passaconaway (c. 1568—c. 1665): Chief

ALSO KNOWN AS: Bear Cub

TRIBAL AFFILIATION: Pennacook

SIGNIFICANCE: Passaconaway was the principal Indian leader in southern New England during early English colonization

The leader of the powerful Pennacook Federation during the beginning of the European settlement of New England, Passaconaway was born and lived most of his life at Pennacook, near the site of present-day Concord, New Hampshire.

During the early colonization, Passaconaway was the principal chief of a number of Pennacook bands in the area that the colonials called southern New England. His influence spread westward to the fringes of Mohawk Country and southward toward the expanding British settlements. Passaconaway fought British encroachment, and his warriors made occasional small-scale attacks. In 1642, colonial troops moved on his village. Passaconaway was not there at the time, but his wife and son were taken prisoner. He negotiated their release and in 1644 pledged a cessation of hostilities. The son, Wannalancet, was principal chief after Passaconaway.

Passaconaway's later life is obscure. He died in the mid-1660's, probably 1665 or 1666.

See also Indian-white relations—English colonial; Pennacook.

Passamaquoddy: Tribe

CULTURE AREA: Northeast

LANGUAGE GROUP: Algonquian

PRIMARY LOCATION: Maine

POPULATION SIZE: 2,398 (1990 U.S. Census)

The Passamaquoddy tribe has many similarities to the Abenaki tribes of Maine, New Hampshire, Vermont, and southern Quebec. All these tribes referred to themselves as Wabanaki.

The first contact with Europeans occurred in the late 1400's, when English, Scandinavian, Spanish, and French fishermen discovered the great quantities of cod along the Maine coast. Giovanni de Verrazano left the first written descriptions of the Maine natives in 1524. Both the English and the French tried to colonize the area, and the contact with new people brought devastating epidemics of smallpox and other diseases to the natives.

Fur trading changed the traditional life by introducing guns, alcohol, and new religions. Many Native Americans converted to Catholicism and were sympathetic toward the French and supported the colonists during the American Revolution. The Passamaquoddy tribe was one of three Maine groups who remained in their original land, although for economic reasons they ceded more than a million acres of it to Massachusetts by treaty in 1794.

The Passamaquoddy followed the traditional lifestyle of the Abenaki. They had summer fishing villages and moved to northern hunting territory in the fall and late winter months. Winter clothing included skin leggings and a long cloak of beaver fur with sleeves tied on separately, with fur-lined moccasins or boots and tapered snow shoes. Traditional utensils and lightweight canoes were made from waterproof, durable, white birchbark. Ash provided the material for splint baskets, later an important item in trade. Beads made of quahog shell were woven into decorative items of clothing and also used for currency and in treaty negotiations.

It was not until 1980 that the Passamaquoddy and their Maine neighbors, the Penobscot, were recognized as a tribe by the federal government and became eligible to receive health and welfare services. The Maine Indian Claims Settlement Act in 1980 established an $81.5 million fund for the tribes which has been used to repurchase 300,000 acres of land, to work toward economic independence through such businesses as a blueberry farm, and to preserve culture with school education and a radio station.

See also Abenaki; Algonquian language family; Diseases, post-contact; Penobscot.

Patayan: Prehistoric tradition

DATE: c. 500-1600

LOCATION: Western Arizona, southeastern California, northern Baja California

CULTURES AFFECTED: Havasupai, Mojave, Yuman language groups

Patayan, as a designation for the ancestors of the Yuman-speaking peoples of the Colorado River Basin from the Grand Canyon to the Gulf of California, along with the surrounding upland areas, first appeared in the 1930's, when a familiar division of prehistoric Southwest cultures emerged: Anasazi, Hohokam, Mogollon, and Patayan. Since the 1950's, there has been support for an overall designation of Hakataya, with Patayan to be restricted to the upland regions of Arizona and Laquish to be used for the lower Colorado Basin area. Some scholars, however, continue to use Patayan as an overall designation.

The key to understanding the Patayan is their extremely dry and rugged country, which receives less than ten inches of rain a year. The terrain is rocky with sparse vegetation. It was the most difficult terrain of any of the southwestern cultures, and one of the most difficult in America for a hunting, gathering and marginally farming people.

Culturally, the Patayan had certain common traits, including a predominance of hunting and gathering. There is considerable evidence that the Patayan peoples, particularly in their Patayan I phase (up to 1100 C.E.), remained almost as nomadic as their desert culture ancestors or their Great Basin cultural relatives to the north. They used stone-lined roasting pits for food preparation, sealed vessels for food storage, percussion-flaked choppers, mortars and pestles (which are found in great numbers), and circular rock shelters of a type of construction known as jacal (but not pueblo-like apartment structures). They almost all cremated their dead, though some burials are known. One of the most identifiable characteristics was the use of ceramics that were finished by paddle and anvil technique, and were of varying colors resulting from uncontrolled firing, with no further decoration. The most typical was a buffware jar with tapered chimney neck and a rounded Colorado shoulder. Only the northeastern area near the Grand Canyon showed any gray coloration from anoxic firing of the clay, which was common among other southwestern cultures.

Certainly the most possibilities for economic advances were found in the lower Colorado River basin, where inundation (flooding) irrigation was used to produce a much stronger agricultural base. The tidal bores of the river regularly caused problems, however. Because the Gulf of California is a long narrow body of water, a combination of high tides and southern winds could drive a twenty-foot high wall of water up the river almost to the Grand Canyon before modern breakwaters prevented the problem. Though the roar, similar to a locomotive, gave ample warning to evacuate to the hills, crops, homes and cultural items often were washed away.

Linguistic evidence indicates that the modern Yuman-speaking peoples of the Colorado basin are direct descendants of the Patayan. Along with the Pueblo to the east, the Patayan-Yuman represent one of the longest-term sequences of one people in one area in the United States.

See also Acorns; Hohokam; Mogollon; Prehistory—Southwest; Yuman language family.

Patents

TRIBES AFFECTED: Pantribal
SIGNIFICANCE: Thousands of American Indians lost their land as federal protection was removed and they were left to fend for themselves

Under provisions of the General Allotment Act of 1887 (the Dawes Act), Indians could become American citizens after living on land granted them by the federal government for twenty-five years. Until that time elapsed the land would be held in trust by the government, but then the Indian owner could do whatever he wanted with it. Government officials hoped Indians would use this time to learn about farming, but since few Indians actually became farmers they were allowed to lease their property to others beginning in 1891. At least some income could be gained from leasing. In 1906 Congress added an amendment further expanding Indian control of their lands by giving the secretary of the interior power to release Native Americans from the twenty-five-year time period for full citizenship rights but only if they showed that they were "competent" to handle their own affairs. Bureau of Indian Affairs agents would judge competency.

In 1913 Commissioner of Indian Affairs Cato Sells used this power to launch a "New Policy" aimed at ending Indian dependency on the government and speeding the process of assimilation into American society. Under the New Policy, all adults one-half or less Indian would be automatically considered competent, as would all Native American students, aged twenty-one or over, who had diplomas from government schools. This meant that nearly all restrictions on selling land would be removed but also that local property taxes would have to be paid. The results were disastrous, as more than twenty-one thousand Indians were released from federal pro-

tection between 1917 and 1921 under the patent system but lost their land for failure to pay state taxes. Others sold their land to whites at outrageously low prices because money was more useful to them than land. The Bureau of Indian Affairs, under a new commissioner, called a halt to this program in 1921.

See also Allotment system; Civil rights and citizenship; General Allotment Act; Indian Citizenship Act.

Patwin: Tribe
CULTURE AREA: California
LANGUAGE GROUP: Wintun (Penutian)
PRIMARY LOCATION: From Suisun Bay to Little Snow Creek, California

The patrilineal Patwin were divided by territory into Hill and River Patwin, whose villages were always located on streams. A single village constituted a tribelet. They had a diversified subsistence base that included fishing, hunting, trapping, gathering, and collecting. Though they had four types of structures, all were earth-covered and semi-subterranean, with either circular or elliptical ground plans; each housed several families. Their sweathouses were also subterranean. They had numerous rites of intensification, but rituals of particular importance were the Kuksu and Hesi cult systems. The Kuksu cult, in all its ritual complexity, may in fact have originated among the Patwin.

Prior to 1800, there were numerous Spanish missionary accounts and vital statistics concerning the Patwin. After coming into contact with European Americans, they became serfs and a valuable labor force to Mexicans. Several Indian leaders arose in opposition, forming alliances with other Indian groups. The Patwin suffered greatly from epidemics and conflict with settlers, miners, and the military; eventually they were forced onto reservations. The decline in Patwin population and ethnographic identity continued into the twentieth century, and by 1972 the Bureau of Indian Affairs could locate only eleven people who claimed Patwin ancestry.

See also California; Kuksu rituals and society.

Paviotso. *See* **Paiute, Northern**

Pavonia Massacre
DATE: February 26, 1643
PLACE: Pavonia, New Amsterdam (modern New Jersey)
TRIBES AFFECTED: Hackensack, Wecquaesgeek
SIGNIFICANCE: This massacre, perpetrated by European settlers on peaceful Indian tribes, led to brutal retaliation by the Indians and the eventual destruction of Pavonia

Pavonia, a Dutch settlement located in the current Staten Island and Bayonne-Jersey City region, was the terminus of a trail used by Indians to move trading goods. A use tax imposed in 1639 and other incidents so outraged the Hackensack that in 1642 they killed two settlers. In 1643, a number of Wecquaesgeek Indians fled in terror from Mohawk raids—some to Pavonia, near the Hackensack, seeking Dutch protection.

Following a carefully laid-out plot, 80 soldiers launched a brutal surprise attack on the Indian camp shortly after midnight on February 26 to revenge the killing of the settlers. Between 80 and 120 Indians were killed and about 30 prisoners taken. In retaliation for this massacre, regional tribes intermittently terrorized the Dutch over the next decade.

See also Indian-white relations—Dutch colonial; Peach Wars.

Pawhuska (c. 1760, Little Osage River in central Mo.—Aug. 25, 1825, present-day Vernon County, Mo.): Chief
TRIBAL AFFILIATION: Osage
SIGNIFICANCE: Pawhuska participated in 1808, 1818, and 1825 treaties ceding Osage land in Missouri and Arkansas

Pawhuska is thought to have been born in a Great Osage tribal village located on the Little Osage River in what is now Truman Reservoir in central Missouri. Pawhuska was a tribal leader when Zebulon Pike established Camp Independence in Osage territory in 1806. He later agreed to ceding all Osage lands in Missouri at the Treaty of Fort Clark in 1808.

The name Pawhuska, which means "white hair," was derived from an incident in which Pawhuska captured the French General St. Clair's wig during a skirmish. From that point on, Pawhuska wore the wig as a medicine symbol. While a young man, he managed to displace the Osage hereditary chief, Tawagahe. Pawhuska retained power through the help of white traders such as Pierre Chouteau. Later, through alliances with other tribal leaders such as Cashesegra, and continued white influence, Pawhuska signed all pivotal nineteenth century treaties ceding Osage land rights.

Pawhuska regarded white traders highly and allowed them to live among the Osage when the need arose. When the United States acquired Osage territory, his advice and counsel was sought by President Thomas Jefferson. As a result of Pawhuska's close relationship with the Chouteau trading family, the Osage, during the War of 1812, remained loyal to the United States.

Pawhuska was instrumental in the establishment and continued development of several religious missions to the Osage. He was buried in Osage style in a large tomb on Blue Mound, Vernon County, Missouri.

See also Indian-white relations—U.S., 1775-1830; Osage.

Pawnee: Tribe
CULTURE AREA: Plains
LANGUAGE GROUP: Caddoan
PRIMARY LOCATION: Oklahoma
POPULATION SIZE: 2,892 (1990 U.S. Census)

Early accounts indicate that the Skidi Pawnees, as early as 1600, first came into what would become known as Nebraska from the south. Their previous home was a "place where sugarcane grew," possibly in the lower Mississippi Valley. It was not until the eighteenth century that other Pawnees entered the Nebraska region to join the Skidi. The Pawnees' northernmost extension was into South Dakota.

By about the 1760's, a situation that would dominate Pawnee existence for a full century began: warfare with Siouan tribes over hunting in many of the same areas. Many experts believe that, had it not been for their continual struggles against the Sioux, the Pawnees would not have had a single name describing them as "one." Their tradition usually emphasizes separate exploits by key groups: the Skidis, Chauis, Kitkehahkis, and Pitahauerats. Common cultural elements, however, mark the Pawnees. Well-known religious symbols included the star deities—the Morning and Evening Stars—whose daughter was betrothed to the son of Sun and Moon, called "Closed Man." This couple was instructed by four gods whose special knowledge (in lodge building and ceremonies) was passed on to all Pawnee tribes.

In 1749-1750, French traders arranged a peace between the main Plains tribes, allowing them to penetrate Pawnee territory. Wider trade relations increased Pawnee access to guns, at least until the "French and Indian War" (between the English and French) ended with France's defeat in 1763. Thereafter, the Pawnees lost their dominance in Kansas and reconcentrated farther north along the Platte River in Nebraska. After the late 1760's, three tribes (the Grand Pawnees, the Kitkehahkis, and the Pitahauerats) began attacking their Skidi predecessors in this area. By the time the expedition of Meriwether Lewis and William Clark followed the Platte River (in 1804), they found that the Skidis had become increasingly subordinate to the Grand Pawnees.

Inevitably, the entire area inhabited by the Pawnees and Sioux attracted the attention of American military outposts (specifically at Fort Atkinson, near Omaha). In 1825 the Pawnees signed a fateful treaty promising safety for settlers along the Santa Fe Trail in return for (undefined) "benefits and acts of kindness" from the U.S. government. When what were assumed to be Pawnee raids continued, chances of more forceful intervention by Washington policy makers mounted.

Escalation grew from the government's post-1830 decision to relocate eastern tribes into the vast open areas west of the Missouri. Before long, newly relocated tribes such as the Delawares and Shawnees clashed with the Pawnees over hunting grounds. Warfare was "settled" only temporarily by the signing, in 1833, of a treaty giving up Pawnee claims to territories south of the Platte. By the 1833 treaty, the Pawnees received paltry payment ($1,600) and were promised a twelve-year annuity of goods and cash plus "advantages" (such as agricultural instruction and the construction of mill sites) for agreeing to settle in the North Platte Loup Fork area. Soon afterward, missionaries and traders arrived in the area to settle Fort William (later Fort Laramie). American officials intended to bring Oglala Sioux elements from the Black Hills into this "neutral" zone—a move that inevitably heightened hostilities with the Pawnees along the North Platte.

After this turning point, Pawnee prospects for an independent existence declined steadily. Increasingly they found that they could not survive without the government annuity promised (but not always given) in 1833. Worse still, the

Alex Mathews, Pawnee tribal chairman, at the opening ceremony of an intertribal meeting with president Bill Clinton in April of 1994. (AP/Wide World Photos)

Pawnees suffered defeats dealt them by the Great Sioux between 1842 and 1846 and were driven to refuges south of the Platte. There they became so destitute that they sold the best land they occupied for the construction of Fort Kearney.

It was not until four years after the Kansas-Nebraska Act of 1854 that a special Pawnee treaty was ratified by Congress. This treaty determined that the Pawnees were to return north to resettle Loup Fork as a Pawnee Indian reservation with government aid. As late as 1865, President Abraham Lincoln's Pawnee Agent, Benjamin Lushbaugh, tried to obtain congressional money to help resolve pressures affecting Pawnee security. A so-called great peace treaty of 1868, however, apparently only helped their Sioux enemies to obtain guns and press toward Loup Fork.

Rather than continue to commit Indian Agency funds to help Pawnees on Loup Fork, policy makers decided to move them again—this time to undeveloped Indian territory farther west. By 1874 the movement to a new reservation had begun. The area reserved was west of the Arkansas River in what became Oklahoma. Although some two thousand Pawnees were relocated in the 1870's, by the 1890's there were only about eight hundred left. In the meantime, their agency had been combined with that of the Ponca and Oto tribes.

The sad state of Pawnee marginality was to continue until, under the Roosevelt Administration in 1932, special attention was given to their case. In the June, 1936, Oklahoma Indian Welfare Act, they were allowed to elect their own tribal council. It was not until 1957, however, that Pawnees gained effective rights to use lands on their reservation as they saw fit. Receipt of federal partial payment for lands taken away from them nearly a century earlier came in 1964. Four years later, actual ownership of their reservation lands was turned over. From the middle of the 1970's the Pawnees began to register gains, partially as a result of the Indian Self-Determination Act of 1975, partly because of the dynamic leadership of Council Chairman Thomas Chapman.   —*Byron D. Cannon*

See also Caddoan language family; Oklahoma Indian Welfare Act; Oto; Plains, Pomo; Sioux.

Paxton Riots

DATE: December 14 and 27, 1763
PLACE: Conestoga, Lancaster (Pennsylvania)
TRIBES AFFECTED: Conestoga, Lenni Lenape
SIGNIFICANCE: The Paxton Riots, a series of attacks by frontier settlers on innocent Conestoga Indians in Pennsylvania, were motivated by fear of Indian attacks and frustration with Pennsylvania politics

On December 14, 1763, Matthew Smith led fifty-seven armed and mounted men from Paxton to Conestoga "manor" fifty miles away. Conestoga manor was home to the Conestoga

Eighteenth century depiction of the "Paxton boys" murdering Conestoga Indians in Lancaster, Pennsylvania, in 1763. (Library of Congress)

Indians, who had lived peacefully with colonists for nearly a century. The Conestogas survived by selling handicrafts, begging, and subsistence farming. They had remained at peace with their neighbors during the past summer despite the outbreak of "Pontiac's Rebellion." Smith and his "Paxton Boys" were riding to Conestoga because they were frustrated. They were convinced that the Conestoga were spies for the enemy Indians who attacked the frontier with seeming impunity. Once at Conestoga, the Paxton boys killed three men, two women, and a child. Fourteen Indians escaped, and the Pennsylvania government took the survivors into protective custody. Two weeks later fifty Paxton Boys swept into Lancaster, Pennsylvania, and stormed the Conestogas who had taken shelter in the Lancaster jail. There the Conestogas were, in the words of Benjamin Franklin, "inhumanely murdered! In cold Blood!"

The Paxton massacres took place against the backdrop of Pontiac's Rebellion. By December, 1763, the "rebelling" Indians had killed or captured nearly two thousand colonists. Officials reported that the Indians had driven the frontierspeople eastward nearly 50 miles since the war began. John Penn, William Penn's great-nephew and the current governor of Pennsylvania, issued a proclamation for the arrest of the Paxton boys when he learned of the attack. Although the citizens of the western counties knew who participated in the murders, no one stepped forward with information.

Not content with these attacks, Smith and his followers threatened to attack Philadelphia. Moravians had sent 125 Christian Delawares eastward, where these pacifists were now housed at Province Island for their protection. Smith and his followers marched on Philadelphia, where only the timely intervention of Benjamin Franklin prevented more bloodshed, this time between colonists.

Although Smith and his followers directed their anger at the Indians, it was apparent that political antagonisms were also part of the equation. In their "Remonstrance" to the government they wondered why eastern counties denied their western counterparts equal representation in the colonial assembly. In this protest against political oppression, they also exhibited the religious tensions that underlay Pennsylvania politics.

Quakers dominated the assembly. Given their religious convictions, the Pennsylvania assembly had refused to sanction the military buildup frontiersmen believed necessary to protect themselves from the Indians. The frontiersmen, many of whom were Scots-Irish Presbyterians, believed the Quakers refused military help because they were overly parsimonious and not sufficiently religious. Many of Smith's followers were influenced by the end of the Great Awakening and the recent arrival of new immigrants. These Presbyterians wished to challenge the Quaker stranglehold on Pennsylvania politics and end Pennsylvania's official policy of pacifism toward the western Indians. In the end, the Paxton massacre produced a political stalemate in Pennsylvania politics that not even Lord Dunmore's War (which began as a Pennsylvania-Virginia dispute) could break.

See also Indian-white relations—English colonial; Lenni Lenape; Lord Dunmore's War; Pontiac's Conspiracy.

Peach Wars

DATE: 1655-1664
PLACE: Hudson River valley, New York
TRIBES AFFECTED: Esophus, Lenni Lenape
SIGNIFICANCE: This conflict is regarded as the most significant confrontation between the Dutch and the Indians; the end of the conflict also marked the end of Dutch rule

Dutch traders depended upon the Indian tribes of the Hudson and Niagara regions for their livelihood. With the development of frontier trading posts in 1620, the Dutch established a permanent presence in the wilderness. Governor-general William Kieft began an extensive campaign to intimidate and subjugate Indian tribes after he took office in 1639. In 1655, a Dutch farmer killed a Delaware woman for picking peaches in his orchard. Her tribe quickly retaliated, and ambushes occurred throughout the Hudson Valley, even at New Amsterdam.

Fighting was particularly fierce on the northern reaches of the Hudson, at the settlement of Wiltwyck. The new governor-general, Peter Stuyvesant, arrived with a militia that forced the attacking Esophus tribe into negotiation. The Dutch, however, murdered the Indian delegation. Retaliatory raids resulted in eight Dutch casualties, and warfare continued for five years.

In 1660, Stuyvesant embarked on a new policy: taking Indians as hostages to ensure peace. The Esophus, however, refused all Dutch peace offers until Stuyvesant ordered the hostages sold into slavery. In 1664, after the Mohawks agreed to help the Dutch defeat the Esophus, the English captured New Netherland, ending both the Peach Wars and Dutch rule.

See also Indian-white relations—Dutch colonial; Iroquois Confederacy; Lenni Lenape.

Pemmican

TRIBES AFFECTED: Pantribal
SIGNIFICANCE: A winter food, pemmican was used throughout the climates of North America where winter resources were limited

Pemmican is a winter food. The word *pemikan* is of Cree origin, from *pimii*, meaning grease or fat. The usage of pemmican was universal throughout the temperate climates of North America where winter resources are limited.

Pemmican was prepared by North American indigenous peoples from a variety of ingredients. The primary ingredient was strips of dried lean meat (or fish). The type of meat used varied from one locale to another—elk and venison in the woodlands, buffalo on the Plains, and salmon on the Northwest Coast. The meat was ground or pounded into a powder. It was sometimes mixed with ground seeds or nuts of various kinds, depending on availability.

The dry ingredients are moistened slightly and then combined with fresh berries or other fruit and animal fat. The specific ingredients vary depending upon locale and availability. When the mixture is thoroughly combined and of the correct consistency, it is shaped into cakes by hand. The cakes are then set aside to dry. They are stored for later use as a winter food, to supplement the diet, or as emergency rations when other foods are not available.

Pemmican is a nutritious and palatable food. It combines proteins, carbohydrates and sugars, and animal fat in such a way as to fulfill minimum energy requirements in winter. It stores well and can be used by village dwellers as well as hunters and travelers on expeditions.

See also Food preparation and cooking; Subsistence.

Peña, Tonita (June 10, 1893, San Ildefonso Pueblo, N.Mex.—Sept., 1949, Cochiti Pueblo?, N.Mex.): Painter

ALSO KNOWN AS: Quah Ah (Little Bead or Pink Shell)
TRIBAL AFFILIATION: San Ildefonso, Cochiti
SIGNIFICANCE: The influential Peña painted scenes of traditional dances and women's work

At San Ildefonso Day School, between 1899 and 1905, Tonita Peña was encouraged by teacher Esther B. Hoyt to use crayons to depict dances. Later, archaeologist Edgar Hewett kept her supplied with good paper and watercolors and was her patron until his death. In 1905 Tonita was moved to Cochiti Pueblo to be reared by her aunt. While she was attending Saint Catherine's Indian School in Santa Fe, the elders of Cochiti arranged her marriage at age fourteen. Two years and two children later, her husband died. Peña returned to St. Catherine's after a second arranged marriage (to Felipe Herrera, by whom she had another child, Joe H. Herrera) and she resumed painting. After the death of her second husband, she married a third time, in 1922, and bore five children. In addition to mothering, housekeeping, cooking, dancing, farming, tending one hundred fowl, hogs, and a flower garden in the pueblo, she painted by kerosene lamp. She taught pottery at local Indian schools and collaborated on murals for the Works Progress Administration. She painted scenes of women's work and pueblo dances on paper, wood, masonite, and canvas, using watercolors, casein, pen and colored ink, and oils. Painters Joe H. Herrera (her son) and Pablita Velarde cite her influence on their careers. Upon her death, all of her possessions, including paintings, were burned.

See also Art and artists, contemporary; Arts and crafts—Southwest; Paints and painting; Pueblo tribes, Eastern.

Pennacook: Tribe

CULTURE AREA: Northeast
LANGUAGE GROUP: Algonquian
PRIMARY LOCATION: New Hampshire

The Pennacook are part of the western branch of the Abenaki family. Their name means "bottom of the hill," and they encompass a number of Algonquian-speaking bands, seventeen tribes of which were united as the Pennacook Confederacy by their best-known leader, Passaconaway, in the early seventeenth century. In 1614, there may have been as many as twelve thousand people in thirty villages along the Merrimack River.

In 1675, their chief, Wanalancet, led the Pennacook deep into the woods to avoid becoming involved in King Philip's War. In 1689, the last chief of the Pennacook, Kankamagus (also known as John Hawkins), under threat of Mohawk attack, led the tribe north. Many tribespeople joined French mission villages in Canada (such as St. Francis), where their tribal identity was lost. Metallak, said to be the last of the Pennacook, returned to the United States and died in New Hampshire in 1848.

In the summer, family groups lived together in sturdy bark-covered, domed, rectangular longhouses with separate fires for each family. As many as sixty people lived in a house. In hunting seasons, smaller groups lived in conical moveable wigwams.

Religious beliefs and traditions, handed down by oral tradition to those who now identify themselves as descendants of the Pennacook and other New Hampshire Abenaki, had led to conflicts between state officials and the 2,134 Native Americans (1990 census figure) living in New Hampshire. Burial sites are protected by federal law. Early Abenaki custom, however, was to bury the dead in unmarked sites near their homes; thus, all former homesites are considered sacred burial sites. The state has generally not recognized these claims. There is no reservation land in New Hampshire.

See also Abenaki; Algonquian language family; Indian-white relations—English colonial; Indian-white relations—French colonial; Northeast; Passaconaway.

Penobscot: Tribe

CULTURE AREA: Northeast
LANGUAGE GROUP: Algonquian
PRIMARY LOCATION: Maine
POPULATION SIZE: 2,173 (1990 U.S. Census)

The Penobscot, of the eastern branch of the Abenaki family, whose name means "the rocky place," live along the river and the bay that bear their name on the Maine coast.

Tradition says that prophesies foretold the coming of white men who would bring a time of trouble because of their desire for the land. Unlike some other Abenaki groups that gave up their New England homelands and migrated north under pressure from white settlers, the Penobscot remained in their original area. During the American Revolution, the Penobscot helped turn back the British, and Chief Joseph Orono was rewarded with a visit to Boston and Newport, Rhode Island.

Their traditional lifestyle began to die out in the early 1800's, as overhunting and increased lumbering diminished the profitable fur trade and traditional game hunting. The Great Miramicki Fire in 1825 destroyed much of the Maine woodland; disease also took its toll on the tribe. Under economic and political pressure, the Penobscot sold much of their land. The last lifetime chief was Joseph Atteau, chosen in 1858, who is mentioned as a guide by Henry David Thoreau in his book *The Maine Woods* (1864).

By the beginning of the twentieth century, many of the

Penobscot lived in poverty and isolation on an island in the river near Old Town. The state granted Indians voting privileges only in 1954—the last state to do so. In 1965, Maine became the first state to establish a Department of Indian Affairs, and in 1980 a long legal battle resulted in the Maine Indian Claims Settlement Act, which allocated $81.5 million to the Penobscot and two other Maine tribes. The money has been used to purchase land, improve housing and schools, and build a factory and a gambling casino to provide employment. About a quarter of the population lives on reservation land, where the schools teach traditional arts and language.

See also Abenaki; Algonquian language family.

Penutian language family

CULTURE AREA: Northwest Coast

TRIBES AFFECTED: Alsea, Cayuse, Chinook, Coos, Costanoan, Klamath, Maidu, Miwok, Modoc, Molala, Nez Perce, Takelma, Tsimshian, Wasco, Yokuts, other Northwest Coast and California tribes

The Penutian language family is large enough that many scholars call it a language phylum—a unit including a number of language families; it is sometimes referred to as Macro-Penutian. Penutian is composed of several families, subfamilies, branches, and dialects and is spoken by many Northwest Coast culture area peoples, primarily those living in Oregon, especially along the coast. According to John Powell (1891), isolates of the language system may be spoken to the south by some Californian peoples (Costanoan, Maidu, Miwok, Wintun, and Yokuts), and possibly as far south as Guatemala among the Maya.

Eastward and inland, the speakers of Athapaskan and Siouan languages dominated. North of the Columbia River, speakers of the Salishan languages were in the majority. Regional trade languages such as Chinook jargon also developed across the Columbia Plateau in response to the need for commerce between diverse groups of unrelated stock. At the time of first contact with whites in the early 1800's, tribal informants used Chinook jargon to communicate with the explorers.

Penutian language families are thought to include Chinookan, Takelman, Alsean, and Kusan. Oregon and Coastal Oregon Penutian includes Yakonan as well. Chinookan branches include Upper and Lower Chinookan and the Cathlamet, Multnomah, and Kiksht dialects.

The Takelman family includes the subfamilies of Takelma and Kalapuyan and the Tualatin-Yamhill, Central Kalapuyan and Yoncalla branches. The Alsean family includes the Alsea and Yaquina subfamilies. There is a Siuslaw language isolate that includes the Siuslaw and Lower Umpqua dialects of Yakonan, which are also related to the Kusan language family and its branch isolates of Miluk and Hanis.

These languages and their more distant inland relatives, especially Klamat-Sahaptian (Cayuse, Klikitat, Molala, Nez Perce, Palouse, Umatilla, Walla Walla, and Yakima), are spoken as far north as the Columbia River basin and inland into the territories of the Yakima, Wasco, and Nez Perce tribes.

The people who spoke Penutian languages were the southernmost peoples to practice head-flattening. They did not have totemic clan systems. They usually lived in small settlements along streams, rivers, and bays with blood relations, and they usually married outside their own immediate group. Their myths and traditional culture show evidence of substantial contact with Californian peoples to the south and, to a lesser degree, with Salishan peoples to the north.

Some evidence suggests that speakers of these languages may have migrated into the Northwest Coast culture area from central America or southern Mexico and may have originally come into the Americas from the South Pacific rather than across the Bering land bridge.

Other evidence, however, suggests that Penutian speakers migrated into the coastal areas and river basins from the north. Tribal stories suggest that the peoples who spoke Penutian languages were created in, and have always resided in, the territories they occupy today. Thus the origins of the language phylum are still uncertain, but collected texts give evidence of its origins in the sea. It is rich in myths, legends, and stories reflective of the maritime, estuarine, and riverine environments its speakers occupied, and which their descendants still occupy today.

The first major work in the study of these languages was done by Powell in the late nineteenth century. Leo Frachtenberg, in the texts he collected (1913, 1914), compared the Miluk and Hanis dialects of the Kusan family and in later work included vocabularies and a listing of formative elements. Melville Jacobs, in his work of 1939 and 1940, made recordings of, and commentaries on, the vocabularies, structure, and contents of many of the Alsean and Siuslaw isolates as well as Kusan dialects.

Penutian languages have some features in common with Plateau, Californian, and Subarctic language families, but they have other elements which make them unique among the languages of the world and specific to the coastal cultures of Oregon. Most of the languages in the Penutian phylum are considered to be extinct; there are no longer any living native speakers of coastal Oregon languages in this phylum, although some attempts at revival have been made, and some second-language speakers continue working to maintain what remains of them.

Related languages, spoken among the Columbia Basin peoples, are still in use today, although for the most part they exist as artifacts, testimony to a way of life forever departed from the lands of the Northwest. It must be noted that living descendants of the tribes which spoke, or which may still speak, these languages often dispute the assumed relationships between languages and cultures supposed to be true by the classification systems of the dominant American culture.

—*Michael W. Simpson*

See also Alsea; Chinook; Coos language; Klamath; Language families; Modoc; Nez Perce; Northwest Coast; Tsimshian.

Peoria. *See* Illinois

Pequot: Tribe

CULTURE AREA: Northeast
LANGUAGE GROUP: Algonquian
PRIMARY LOCATION: Connecticut
POPULATION SIZE: 536 (1990 U.S. Census)

In the early seventeenth century, the Pequot, probably numbering about thirteen thousand persons, occupied a territory on the lower Thames River in present-day Connecticut. The Pequot were a horticultural people, subsisting chiefly on corn, beans, and squash raised by the women. Men hunted to supplement these foods, and both sexes harvested the rich resources of fish and shellfish available nearby. There were two large, fortified villages with about seventy wigwams each, several smaller, unfortified ones, and a number of scattered hamlets. Sassacus, who became chief sachem in 1634, lived in the principal village, Weinshauks, in present-day Groton. The chief sachem, chosen from a chiefly lineage or family, exercised a limited, traditional authority through persuasion and influence rather than through direct power. Each subsidiary village had one or more local sachems. There were said to be twenty-six lesser sachems under Sassacus. This no doubt included those of conquered, tributary peoples. Considered the most warlike tribe in southern New England, the Pequot had forced a number of small tribes in the valley of the lower Connecticut and on Long Island to become their tributaries.

In 1633, a smallpox epidemic ravaged the region, reducing Pequot numbers to about three thousand. The severe population loss among the tribes of the lower Connecticut River encouraged English settlers from Plymouth and Massachusetts Bay colonies to move into the area, disrupting native political arrangements. This, along with trade rivalries and attribution to the Pequot of the murder of several English traders, precipitated the Pequot War of 1636-1637. Crushed in that war, many of the one thousand to fifteen hundred Pequot survivors were divided among the colonists' Indian allies. Others found a haven with distant tribes, and for some years the Pequot were forbidden to have an independent existence. In time, several small villages were permitted to reconstitute themselves. Their descendants today, largely assimilated and no longer speaking the Pequot language, occupy two small reservations: Mashantucket, in Ledyard, and Paucatuck (or Lantern Hill), at North Stonington, Connecticut.

See also Algonquian language family; Indian-white relations—English colonial; Pequot War; Sachem; Sassacus; Uncas.

Pequot War

DATE: 1636-1637
PLACE: Connecticut
TRIBES AFFECTED: Mohegan, Narragansett, Niantic, Pequot
SIGNIFICANCE: The Puritans' war of extermination against the Pequot Indians culminated the fierce competition for control of the prosperous Connecticut River valley, establishing Puritan dominance in New England and hastening further English settlement

In the 1620's and early 1630's an uneasy truce existed between the aggressive Pequots, who had recently migrated from the Hudson River valley, and the powerful Narragansetts, who until the Pequots' arrival had dominated the region. The Pequots had recently won the competition for control of the weaker tribes of the Connecticut River valley, thus entitling them to tribute from each tribe. Furthermore, the Pequots functioned as intermediaries between their tributary tribes and the Dutch, who maintained trading ships off the Connecticut coast.

Early Hostilities. Pequot dominance, however, was short lived, and by the 1630's it was already eroding because of conflicts between rival tribes and between Indians and whites. In 1632 their tenuous peace with the Narragansetts collapsed when the Narragansetts aided the Mohegans, rival Pequots who had earlier separated from the tribe and were encroaching on Pequot territory.

Pequot control was weakened further in 1632 when the Dutch, anxious to secure the region against English expansion, established the outpost House of Hope near present-day Hartford. House of Hope facilitated direct Dutch trade with area tribes, thereby eliminating the Pequot's trade monopoly. Angered by Dutch encroachment, the Pequot attacked and killed some Indians gathering to trade at the settlement. Retaliating, the Dutch slew the Pequot's religious leader and chief, Tatotem, resulting in additional demoralization and defections from the tribe.

At the close of 1632, the Pequots thus were without Indian or white allies. Moreover, the tribe was weakened by a devastating smallpox epidemic which had little effect on the Dutch or English. Increasingly desperate, the Pequots in 1634 entered into a treaty with Massachusetts Bay through which they hoped to secure Puritan aid against the Narragansetts. As the price for this arrangement, Massachusetts Bay exacted a huge tribute from the Pequots, who initially complied. The Bay Colony, however, having in the meantime discovered the Long Island source of the region's finest wampum (from a tribe which paid large tributes to the Pequots), was determined to gain mastery over the region. To this end, they deviously added a provision to the treaty to which the Pequots could not adhere; that is, the Pequots were to relinquish the murderers of a white trader, John Stone, although the Bay Colony was aware that scant evidence linked the Pequots to the murder.

Response to Endecott's Expedition. The issue of Stone's murder lay dormant for two years, to be resurrected only after the murder of another English trader, John Oldham. In this instance, too, the Pequots were innocent, for Oldham had been executed by the Narragansetts. Nevertheless, on August 25, 1636, ostensibly to avenge Stone's and Oldham's murders, John Endecott led an expedition to Block Island charged with killing all the male Indians and plundering the village. Both Narragansetts and Pequots were to be punished by Endecott despite Pequot innocence of either murder. Endecott, having discovered only a few Indians at the settlement, satisfied his responsibilities by burning the Indian village and crops.

A 1638 engraving of the 1637 defeat of the Pequots at Fort Mystic, their fortified village. The engraving appeared in Newes from America *in London.* (Library of Congress)

Afterwards the Pequots, increasingly concerned by white duplicities, solicited a pan-Indian alliance aimed at the expulsion of the European settlers. Influenced by religious leader Roger Williams, a friend of the Narragansett grand sachem Canonicus, the Narragansetts refused, and the Pequots proceeded alone.

In April, 1637, they laid siege to the English Fort Saybrook. The siege lasted nine months, until the Pequots were drawn off to aid Indians near Wethersfield. There, white settlers had broken their purchase agreement with the local Indians and driven them from their homes. Seeking vengeance, the Pequots killed nine settlers while they worked their fields and made hostages of two young females.

White Encroachment. While hostilities mounted between the Puritans and the Pequots, the situation was further complicated by movement of Puritan settlers into the region. Encouraged by the depopulation following a smallpox epidemic, which they believed had been sent by God to aid them in their mission, the settlers violated treaties by purchasing land from individual Indians. By 1636 the migrating Puritans had established three new towns.

Several divisions existed within the Puritan settlements that jeopardized their religious "errand into the wilderness." Waves of immigrants, first of all, increased pressure for new lands. Furthermore, tensions were raised by internal religious crises that resulted in the Bay Colony's expulsion of Roger Williams and Anne Hutchinson. Meanwhile, the Pequots, whom the colonists increasingly associated with Satan, served a cause by uniting the colonists in a holy war.

Fort Mystic. Hostilities peaked in 1637 with a predawn military strike on the Pequot village, Fort Mystic. Surrounding the fortified settlement, Puritan soldiers burned wigwams and shot fleeing Indians. Indian casualties, primarily women and children, ranged somewhere between four hundred and one thousand; only two of the well-armed white soldiers were slain. Appalled by the brutality of this massacre, the Narragansetts largely abandoned their Puritan allies, but the killing continued after the assault on Fort Mystic. Indeed, for several weeks Puritans routed all remaining Pequots from the surrounding forests and villages. Pequot women and children lured from hiding were sold into the West Indian slave trade, and all others were put to death.

Motivated by land hunger and their desire to control the source of wampum, and heartened by the smallpox epidemic of 1634, Puritans resolved their internal division, joining to rid the area of the once-powerful Pequots. By decimating the Pequots, the Puritans removed the barriers for their own expansion throughout New England.   —*Mary E. Virginia*

See also Canonicus; Indian-white relations—Dutch colonial; Indian-white relations—English colonial; Mohegan; Narragansett; Niantic; Pequot; Saybrook, Battle of.

BIBLIOGRAPHY
Bourne, Russell. *The Red King's Rebellion: Racial Politics in New England, 1675-1678*. New York: Atheneum, 1990.

Jennings, Francis. *The Invasion of America: Indians, Colonialism, and the Cant of Conquest*. New York: W. W. Norton, 1975.

Salisbury, Neal. *Manitou and Providence: Indians, Europeans, and the Making of New England, 1500-1643*. New York: Oxford University Press, 1982.

Segal, Charles M., and David C. Stinebeck. *Puritans, Indians, and Manifest Destiny*. New York: G. P. Putnam's Sons, 1977.

Vaughan, Alden T. *New England Frontier: Puritans and Indians, 1620-1675*. Boston: Little, Brown, 1965.

Petalésharo (c. 1797—c. 1833): Tribal chief

TRIBAL AFFILIATION: Pawnee
SIGNIFICANCE: Petalésharo ended the use of human sacrifice in the Pawnee Morning Star Ceremony

"Petalésharo" seems to have functioned as a title, as well as a personal name, during the early eighteenth century among the Pawnee; several outstanding warriors used the name, and it is sometimes difficult to attribute biographical details to one individual.

The best-known person to claim the title distinguished himself not only as a warrior but also as humanitarian. He aggressively curtailed the Pawnee use of human sacrifice in certain rituals. Until his time, the Pawnees would raid another tribe for a girl about thirteen years old, treat her well for a year, then sacrifice her in the Morning Star Ceremony. During one such ceremony in the late 1820's, Petalésharo is said to have protested by rescuing a young woman from sacrifice. Petalésharo cut the bonds that held the woman to a sacrificial cross, carried her to a horse to escape, then fed and protected the woman before taking her home.

During the fall and winter of 1821, Petalésharo toured the urban areas of the Northeast, including Washington, D.C., where he spoke at a conference attended by President James Monroe and Secretary of War John Calhoun. He also attended a New Year's reception at the White House. He probably died during a smallpox epidemic around 1833.

See also Morning Star Ceremony; Pawnee.

Petroglyphs

TRIBES AFFECTED: Pantribal
SIGNIFICANCE: Indian designs carved on rock represent a rich legacy of Native American culture, expressing myth, history, and ethnic identity

Petroglyphs are designs that have been pecked, abraded, or incised into a rock's surface, frequently by direct percussion with a hammer stone or indirect percussion with a chisel. These are different from pictographs, which are images painted on rock surfaces. There are petroglyphs that have also been painted, but this is rare.

Petroglyphs are found throughout the continental United States, Alaska, and Hawaii. Some of the densest concentrations in the entire world occur in California, the Southwest, the Great Basin, and the Columbia Plateau. The content of petroglyphs includes images of animals, humans, plants, cultural items, and geometric designs. They are portrayed in an array of styles, from realistic to curvilinear or rectilinear abstract.

Ever since English settlers of the Massachusetts Colony first noticed petroglyphs at Dighton Rock in the 1600's, a persistent question has been, "Who made them?" A number of fanciful explanations have been put forward through the years; they have been attributed to Egyptians, Phoenicians, Iberians, and many other Old World groups, and even to extraterrestrials. None of this is supported by the evidence, which has firmly established that Native Americans were the makers.

This is known partly because living Indian traditions regarding petroglyphs still exist today. Petroglyphs do not involve a hieroglyphic system or even a pictorial version of a sign language system. No one can walk up to a cliff face and "read" petroglyphs like a book. Contemporary traditions, then, give valuable insight into another common question, "Why were they made?"

The evidence shows they were made for a wide variety of cultural purposes. The Hopi identify images at the Willow Springs site near Tuba City, Arizona, as clan symbols made by members on journeys from their mesa villages to sacred salt deposits. In Northern California, so-called "baby rocks" of the Pomo and "rain rocks" of the Hupa, Karok, and Tolowa reflect a concern with human fertility and world renewal. Rites of passage for Interior Salish youth included portraying dream quest visions on the rocks, while nearby, petroglyphs were seen carved at Fort Rupert on the Northwest Coast in the context of a Hamatsa ritual.

Even where passing time and memory have erased cultural links, purpose is sometimes evident. For example, spiral petroglyphs on Fajada Butte carved by the Anasazi of Chaco Canyon have been shown to be astronomical calendars, recording the movement of the sun and moon. Evidence belies a common claim that this art is idle "doodling" or prehistoric graffiti. Exceptions occur, but the vast majority of it reflects a purposeful, patterned expression of the makers' values, priorities, and worldview.

A Nez Perce petroglyph representing Tsagiglalal, a guardian spirit. (Library of Congress)

The most difficult question to answer is, "When were the petroglyphs made?" Relative and absolute dating methods have shown some to be recent, while others date back to the time of the first people in the Americas. The richness of such a legacy for all people should lead to its preservation and protection. A growing awareness of this fact was symbolized by the inauguration of Petroglyph National Monument near Albuquerque in 1990, the first national monument in America to be dedicated to a purely cultural resource.

See also Anasazi; Chaco Canyon; Codices; Dating methods; Hamatsa; Symbolism in art.

Petun: Tribe

CULTURE AREA: Northeast
LANGUAGE GROUP: Iroquoian
PRIMARY LOCATION: South of Georgian Bay

Located just west of the Hurons, the Petun Nation (also known as the Tobacco tribe) were very closely related culturally and linguistically to the Hurons, particularly the Attignaouantan band. *Tionontati* was the name for them in the Attignaouantan language, meaning "people of the place where the hills are." The other distinctive geographic feature of the Petun region was its microclimate, which made possible the cultivation of highly specialized varieties of tobacco. The neighboring Hurons were not able to grow tobacco in this fashion; therefore, the Petun people had an economic advantage.

The basis of the Petun economy, however, was rooted in corn, beans, and squash grown by the women of the tribe. Men hunted and fished to complement these products, and fruit was gathered for variety. In all other ways, including village habitation, matrilineal and matrilocal longhouse dwelling, dress, and spiritual practices, the Petun seem to have been highly similar to the Huron peoples. In one respect they differed slightly, in that they divided their tribe into two groups, the Deer and the Wolves.

Population figures for the Petun tribe are difficult to discern, since the French often grouped them together with the Hurons. They may have numbered as many as eight thousand before contact with these Europeans. The French Jesuits set up missions to the Tobacco people in the 1630's, and smallpox epidemics reduced the population, probably to about three thousand. The Petun people were caught in the Huron-Iroquois rivalry, and after the Iroquois destroyed Huronia in 1649-1651, some Huron survivors took refuge among the Petuns, only to come under attack again when the Iroquois subsequently turned their wrath on the Petun nation. The few surviving Petuns and Hurons who were not adopted into Iroquois families traveled further north and west after 1652. A few of them later journeyed to the St. Lawrence Valley with Jesuits, but others remained in the Michigan-Wisconsin area and eventually, by about 1870, acquired lands in Indian Territory, now Oklahoma. In the twentieth century, the Wyandot tribe of Oklahoma included some people who were partly of Petun ancestry, but their ancestors were absorbed into the Huron-Wyandot group and are not distinguishable from them.

See also Beaver Wars; Erie; Huron; Indian-white relations—French colonial; Iroquoian language family; Iroquois Confederacy; Neutral.

Peyote and peyote religion

TRIBES AFFECTED: Pantribal
SIGNIFICANCE: Since the late nineteenth century, peyote has played a central part in an American Indian religious movement; peyote is viewed as a spiritual teacher, and its use forms a part of a long, complex ceremony

To the American Indians who practice peyotism, peyote is considered a spiritual being. This is a concept which defies accurate definition in Western terms. Indians describe peyote iconically and refer to it as "medicine"; it is used as a sacrament. The ritualistic use of peyote in a religious setting to communicate with and be instructed by "spirit" is accepted as a way to "return to the source."

Peyote itself comes from a type of cactus with the scientific name *Lophophora williamsii*, a small, spineless cactus with a rounded top. The parts of the cactus that contain peyote are referred to as "buttons." A peyote button contains more than fifty alkaloids, one of which, mescaline, induces a state of consciousness that can be likened to a healing or religious experience. There is no evidence that peyote is addictive or harmful.

Peyote Religion. The religion, often called peyotism or the Peyote Cult, is at the center of a pan-Indian movement. The religion has doctrine, an ethical code, unique rituals, and origin legends. Fire, water, the medicine, the eagle, and a drum are the central symbols. Precise rituals involve long, extensive prayer meetings and require knowledge of many songs with repetitive, chanted musical bridges. The peyote religion, referred to formally as the Native American Church of North America (NAC), is pan-Indian, both geographically and tribally. It appeared suddenly after 1880 and spread rapidly.

The origin of the peyote religion as practiced in North America is unknown. James Slotkin (*The Peyote Religion*, 1956) describes twenty-nine different traditions of origin. The ritual of the modern Native American Church is very different from the pre-Columbian and Mexican Indian use of peyote. Peyote reveals itself to the Indian people as a transformer which is integratable and renewing. After 1880, tribal religious traditions, devastated by the relentless encroachments of European Americans, opened to the inevitability of profound change. The church origin legends reflect the devastation suffered by the old ways and depict the need for transformation in the Indian psyche.

Origin legends and doctrinal formulations are of secondary importance to Indians, who are more concerned with original religious experiences. If there is doctrine, it can be said that God put humankind on Earth for a purpose, and it is up to humans to learn that purpose directly from God on "the peyote road" via the mediation of peyote, prayer, and focus or awareness. People should then fulfill that purpose via a moderate lifestyle, outlined by Slotkin as "care of one's health and welfare, care of family, brotherhood, self-reliance, and by belief in the power of peyote to 'teach one how to live.' "

Church Ritual. Church members describe their religion and ritual as uniquely Indian. Some standards seem to have developed, leading to various forms referred to as Kiowa-Apache, Southern Plains, and Oklahoma Fireplace. A number of elements, however, are consistent at every meeting since James Mooney's description of a peyote ceremony in 1892. At all the fireplaces the door opens east, and the roadman, or church leader, sits opposite the door. The meeting (as the church services are called) opens with the placing of the Chief Peyote on the altar and closes with the Chief's removal. The most common form for the altar is a crescent or "half moon," shape. There are five officers, or roadcrew, who have various formal functions in the ceremony: roadman, drummer, cedarman, fireman, and dawn woman. Each one at some point during the meeting will offer a "prayer smoke"—each will roll tobacco in a corn husk and pray with this smoke communicant.

All movement during the meeting is clockwise. The drum is a water drum made from a six-quart metal pot into which are placed water and four coals from the fire. The vessel is then covered with a hide, usually deerskin, and tied with a long rope which wraps around seven stones pocketed in the hide so that the rope makes a seven-pointed star, seen as the morning star, around the bottom of the vessel. The fireman, aside from keeping a ritually constructed fire going through the night, maintains a poker or burning stick from which all "prayer smokes" are lit. Other ritual paraphernalia invariably found at meetings are a bone whistle, gourd rattles, a beaded staff, sage, feather fans, and corn husks and tobacco used in making the hand-rolled prayer smokes. There are always four stages to each meeting: opening, midnight, morning, and closing ceremonies. Particular songs are sung in conjunction with these stages no matter which tribe or fireplace is holding the ceremony, because these particular songs were given through the origin story. Four foods—meat, berries, corn, and water—are also always a part of the ceremony.

Some details of the four stages vary with each roadman. The reason is that peyote teaches a roadman his way; this is a mark of the church's and the religion's vitality. These variations come from prayer, searching, and the medicine. A roadman's ceremony is called his Fireplace.

The ritual is only sketched here; it is extremely complex, more complex than Christian ceremonies. Meetings usually last a minimum of twelve hours, and the roadman is in control of all of it and aware of the psychological state of every member of the meeting throughout. The ceremony often has aspects of a long, soul-searching journey through the night for each of the participants. It is understood to be a prayer meeting from beginning to end. Church members come to a sacred area, concentrate on its transcendental center or source, and sit with their peers in community to receive healing and instruction.

—*Glenn J. Schiffman*

See also Native American Church; Pan-Indianism; Religion.

BIBLIOGRAPHY

LaBarre, Weston. *The Peyote Cult.* 1938. Reprint. Hamden, Conn.: Shoestring Press, 1964.

Laney, John H. *On the Symbolism of the Native American Church of North America.* Zurich, Switzerland: C. G. Jung Institute, 1970.

Shonle, Ruth. "Peyote, the Giver of Visions." *American Anthropologist* 40 (1932): 698-715.

Slotkin, James. *The Peyote Religion.* Glencoe, Ill.: Free Press, 1956.

Pima: Tribe

CULTURE AREA: Southwest
LANGUAGE GROUP: Piman (Uto-Aztecan)
PRIMARY LOCATION: South-central Arizona
POPULATION SIZE: 14,431 (1990 U.S. Census)

Although direct evidence is inconclusive, many scholars believe that the Pimas (or Akimel O'odham) are descended from the prehistoric Hohokam people of the Southwest. The Pimas developed extensive canals and dams for their farmlands, and they were considered the best farmers of all Arizona tribes. The missionary Eusebio Kino in 1687 introduced new crops, including barley and wheat, to the Pimas and supplied them with cattle and sheep. A century later, in 1793, the Pimas numbered about four thousand and resided in seven villages near the Gila River. They grew cotton, corn, melons, and pumpkins, and they traded their spun and woven cotton cloth to the Mexicans to the south.

In the 1840's the Maricopa tribe, seeking to avoid hostilities with other tribes, took refuge among the Pima and have remained with them ever since. The Pimas came under United States jurisdiction in 1853, when the Gadsden Purchase ended Mexican rule. The United States introduced the reservation system in the 1870's. In 1990, Pima and Maricopa tribes continued to occupy the Gila River and Salt River reservations of 427,807 acres near Phoenix, Arizona.

The Gila River Farmers Association was organized in the 1930's to deal with federal government water issues. The Indian Reorganization Act of 1934 led the Pimas to exercise powers of self-government. The Gila River Pima community established a seventeen-member tribal council as its central governing body and voted for a governor and lieutenant governor every three years. A tribal constitution, adopted in 1960, dictates procedures for the election of these officers. The council members, from seven political districts based on population, are elected to serve staggered terms. The council meets twice a month. The standing committees include committees on economic development, natural resources, government and management, health and social issues, and education.

The majority of Pimas live and work in their reservation communities in schools, government agencies, a tribal hospital, and stores.

See also Hohokam; Indian Reorganization Act; Pima uprisings; Southwest; Tohono O'odham.

Pima uprisings

DATE: 1695, 1751
PLACE: Southern Arizona, northwestern Mexico
TRIBE AFFECTED: Upper Pima
SIGNIFICANCE: These uprisings, instigated by Spanish mistreatment and possibly by personal ambition, caused significant death and destruction and undermined the formerly cordial relations between the Spanish and Indians

By the late 1600's the Spanish Jesuits had established a successful system of missions and maintained cordial relations with the Upper Pimas. In Tubutama, however, in 1694 the Spanish unjustly and summarily executed three Pimas for alleged horse stealing and forcibly silenced Pima leaders who were openly critical of the Spaniards and their methods. Christianized Opata Indians who oversaw running the mission herds and lands at Tubutama alienated the Pimas with attitudes of condescension and superiority.

In 1695 an uprising occurred by a disaffected faction of Pimas at Tubutama. Three Opata were killed. Moving southwest and enlisting some allies, they destroyed the presidio at Altar and killed the missionary at Caborca.

The Spanish retaliated immediately. They killed a few women and children and destroyed fields at Caborca as a lesson but were not able to find the instigators of the uprising. The aid of peaceful Pima leaders who were not part of the uprising was enlisted to identify the instigators. The first one identified was instantly beheaded. This set off a frenzy among the Spanish, who killed nearly fifty Pimas, including several peaceful ones.

As soon as the Spanish left, enraged Pimas organized and destroyed Tubutama, Caborca, and churches at Imuris and San Ignacio. Again, Spanish forces, this time aided by friendly Pimas, retaliated by killing a few Pimas and burning their crops, but they were again unable to engage the instigators. A number of Pima headmen who realized they could not oppose the Spanish arranged to surrender the instigators to the Spanish soldiers, who then left. The damage was done, however; much of Pima territory was destroyed. The Pimas were divided into pro- and anti-Spanish factions. Anger and distrust of the Spaniards smoldered among many Pimas.

A second Pima uprising occurred in 1751. The uprising was instigated by Luis Oacpicagigua, who had formerly served the Spanish so well that he was made captain-general of the Pimas. Oacpicagigua claimed that he revolted against the cruelty and oppression of Spanish military and missionary rule and was trying to end their domination over his people. The Spanish claimed that he desired to be chief of all the Pimas. This uprising was isolated rather than general. It began at Saric, near Tubuand. Oacpicagigua and some Western Pimas killed eighteen Spaniards invited to his house, attacked Tubutama, and killed two missionaries at Caborca and Senoita. After the deaths of more than a hundred Spaniards and more than forty Pimas and a loss of support, Oacpicagigua ceased hostilities and was imprisoned.

The Jesuit missions never recovered from this uprising by the time of their expulsion in 1767. Several missions remained in operation but with successively declining success and influence. By the beginning of the nineteenth century, the Pimas had pretty much returned to their former way of life.

See also Indian-white relations—Spanish colonial; Pima.

Pine Ridge shootout

DATE: June 25-26, 1975
PLACE: Pine Ridge Reservation, South Dakota
TRIBE AFFECTED: Oglala Sioux
SIGNIFICANCE: The Pine Ridge shootout was a turning point for the American Indian Movement (AIM) in their relations with the Bureau of Indian Affairs (BIA)

In 1973, members and supporters of the American Indian Movement (AIM) occupied the town of Wounded Knee, South Dakota, on the Pine Ridge Reservation. The activists were demonstrating against what they considered to be autocratic and sometimes corrupt practices of the Oglala Sioux tribal political leaders, especially Richard Wilson, the tribal chairman. Wilson, an aggressive opponent of AIM, along with local Bureau of Indian Affairs (BIA) officials, requested federal support in removing the activists. The occupation evolved into a state of siege lasting seventy-one days and leaving two native people dead. AIM leaders were indicted, but the case was dismissed after a federal judge accused the Federal Bureau of Investigation (FBI) of gross misconduct.

Discontent and strong opposition to the Pine Ridge Reservation tribal government and the chairman continued. On June 25, 1975, violence erupted again when a BIA policeman killed a young Oglala man. The following day, in an exchange of gunfire, two FBI agents were slain outside a house about fifteen miles from the town of Pine Ridge. Although the occupants of the house fled, two Oglala men were ultimately apprehended and charged with the murders; they were acquitted. Leonard Peltier, another suspect, was arrested in Canada, extradited to the United States, and sent to prison after a controversial trial in which he was sentenced to two consecutive life terms. Since Peltier's imprisonment, Indian rights activists have lobbied for his release and he is considered to be a political prisoner by Amnesty International. Other victims of the 1975 violence included Leonard Crow Dog, an Oglala medicine man and spiritual leader of the movement who was arrested at his home on the neighboring Rosebud Reservation, and AIM supporter Anna Mae Aquash, a Micmac Indian woman, believed by the FBI to be a witness to the killing of the two agents. Aquash was found murdered in 1976.

See also Activism; Alcatraz Island occupation; American Indian Movement (AIM); Wounded Knee occupation.

Pipestone Quarries: Archaeological site

DATE: Seventeenth century
LOCATION: Southwest Minnesota
CULTURES AFFECTED: Plains, including Blackfoot, Crow, Iowa, Mandan, Oto, Pawnee, Ponca, Sioux

The quarries, located in southwest Minnesota, were being worked in the seventeenth century with metal tools acquired from European traders. From the beginning, the area was considered a sacred place where peoples from various tribes could quarry stone in peace. The quarry contains a soft pink or red stone called catlinite, named for George Catlin, who visited the quarries in the 1830's. (He sent a sample for analysis to a friend in Boston who then named it for Catlin.) The catlinite, or pipestone, was formed when clay was pressed between layers of sand deposited when the area was an inland sea; pressure and chemical reactions then created thin layers of pipestone sandwiches between thicker layers of quartzite. The layers of quartzite must be removed to obtain the pipestone, which gets its pink or red color from traces of iron.

The earliest diggers were the Iowa and Oto. By the 1700's, the Dakota Sioux had acquired a monopoly, trading pipestone extensively throughout North America. The stone, prized for its color and softness, was ideal for carving ceremonial pipes, including calumets, called "peace pipes" by Europeans. Pipes were so valuable that a finely carved pipe could bring a horse in exchange. By 1851, the Dakota, through treaties, had lost rights to the quarries. Until 1926, the Yankton Sioux struggled to maintain control, losing title through a Supreme Court ruling. In 1937, an act of Congress created the Pipestone National Monument. All native peoples were granted access to the quarries. By the early 1950's, pipe carving and work in the quarries had all but ceased. The revival of tribal traditions and arts has led to a resurgence of carving, however, and the quarries are again actively used.

A variety of legends surrounds the site, each attesting its sacredness. In one account, an Omaha Indian woman followed a sacred white bison whose hooves turned the rocks red. In another, borrowed by Henry Wadsworth Longfellow for *The Song of Hiawatha*, the Great Spirit (Kitchi Manitou), in the form of a bird, calls the people together. Drawing out a piece of red stone, He fashions a pipe and begins to smoke. He tells the people that the red rock is their flesh and is to be used only for making ceremonial pipes. Yet another legend traces the quarries' origins to a time when people from many tribes were fleeing a flood. Unable to escape, all perished but a single young woman. The bodies of the dead became the pipestone. The communal origins of the site meant that all peoples were free to use it in peace.

Today an interpretive center housing displays of carvings and quarrying techniques is on the site and open to public view.

See also Arts and crafts—Plains; Calumets and pipe bags; Tobacco.

Pit house

TRIBES AFFECTED: Southwest tribes
SIGNIFICANCE: Pit houses are among the earliest types of structures known to have been built in the Americas
Pit houses (or pithouses) are the earliest recognizable form of architecture adopted by semi-sedentary cultures in the southwestern United States and northern Mexico. Pit houses appear with the Hohokam culture in Arizona as early as 300 B.C.E.,

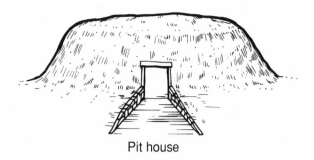

Pit house

and with the Anasazi Basketmaker culture of southwestern Colorado by 200 C.E. Associated with the introduction of domesticated crops and pottery, pit houses remained the principal architectural form until approximately 700, when they were replaced by masonry and/or adobe Pueblo-style architecture.

Pit houses consisted of excavated earthen pits, between 2 and 5 feet deep and 10 and 25 feet in diameter, usually lined with adobe or stone slabs. The pit was covered with a domed log roof topped with thatch and earth or adobe. Early varieties were round in plan; they were entered through a lateral doorway at the east end and contained a small smoke hole in the roof above a central fire pit. In later versions, plans were generally square, the lateral entrance decreased in size, sometimes becoming a mere air vent, and the smoke hole was enlarged to become the primary means of entrance via a ladder. Primarily single-family dwellings, pit houses could be found as isolated units or grouped into village clusters of a hundred or more, though rarely were they organized into formal village plans. Later versions may have combined domestic and ritual functions, since many examples contain ceremonial features such as the *sipapu*, symbolizing the mythological hole of emergence (according to Hopi mythology), and surrounding benches, features commonly associated with later Pueblo kivas. Pit house prototypes associated with Archaic hunter-gatherers have been found in Canada and eastern Siberia.

Beginning around 700, pit houses apparently evolved into two distinctly different and more specialized forms: the square, aboveground Pueblo style room-blocks which served primarily utilitarian functions, and the round subterranean kivas, which served more religious or esoteric functions.

See also Architecture—Southwest; Basketmaker; Earthlodge; Hohokam; Kivas; Pueblo; Snaketown.

Pitchlynn, Peter Perkins (Jan. 30, 1806, in present-day Miss.—1881, in present-day Okla.): Tribal chief and statesman
ALSO KNOWN AS: Hatchootucknee
TRIBAL AFFILIATION: Choctaw
SIGNIFICANCE: As leader and representative of the Choctaw Nation, Pitchlynn worked for his people's rights in tribal consolidation, relocation, government reimbursement, and involvement in the Civil War

Peter Pitchlynn was the son of John Pitchlynn, a Choctaw interpreter for the United States. The Choctaw tribe had fairly readily accepted whites, and as the younger Pitchlynn grew up, interaction with them was quite commonplace. He was educated at Nashville University and returned to the Choctaw Nation where he headed, in 1824, the lighthorse force. Members of this force served as judges, juries, and sheriffs, riding across the Choctaw lands settling difficulties between parties and individuals. The United States provided a permanent annuity for this organization, beginning in 1825.

After the Choctaws adopted a constitution in 1860, Pitchlynn was elected to the central executive position, or principal chief, and served in that capacity from 1864 to 1866. Pitchlynn had argued, unsuccessfully, for Choctaw neutrality during the Civil War, but as principal chief he was able to sign an armistice ending Choctaw involvement in the war as a member of the Confederacy.

Pitchlynn also handled matters involving the so-called Net Proceeds, United States government money paid to the Choctaw Nation from sales of ceded Choctaw land. These funds, appropriated in 1859, were almost totally lost or dissipated during the confusion surrounding the Civil War. The fact that the Choctaw had joined the Confederacy, against the counsel of Pitchlynn, lost them their claim to much of the money.

He also served at the Fort Smith Council, which required the Choctaws to either abolish slavery and accept the freedmen into the tribe as equals or provide other appropriate provisions for them. Pitchlynn served as a delegate in Washington, and while there he fought against the forced consolidation of Choctaws with neighboring tribes, and against the removal of the Choctaws to the Oklahoma Territory.

See also Choctaw; Removal; Southeast.

Plains: Culture area

LANGUAGE GROUPS: Algonquian, Athapaskan, Caddoan, Kiowa-Tanoan, Siouan, Uto-Aztecan

TRIBES: Apache of Oklahoma, Arapaho, Arikara, Assiniboine, Atsina, Blackfoot (Blood, Piegan, Siksika), Caddo, Cheyenne, Comanche, Crow, Hidatsa, Iowa, Kansa (Kaw), Kiowa, Mandan, Missouri, Omaha, Osage, Oto, Pawnee, Ponca, Quapaw, Sarsi, Sioux (Santee, Teton, Yankton), Tonkawa, Waco, Wichita

The Plains culture area extended from southern Canada to southern Texas and from the foothills of the Rocky Mountains to the Mississippi River. It included short-grass plains in the west, tall-grass prairie in the east, and mixed tall and short grasses in between. Many tribes from different regions and cultures moved into the area, but all adopted the basic Plains culture based on hunting bison (buffalo). Aspects of the parent cultures were apparent in Plains Indian culture, but they were modified by the Plains environment and by cultural exchange with other tribes to produce the unique Plains culture.

Regional Prehistory. According to the most popular theory, the earliest Indians in the Plains area were descendants of Asiatic peoples who traveled from Siberia to Alaska over the Bering Strait land bridge some twelve thousand years ago. At the time, glaciers covered much of Eurasia and North America. The water in the great ice sheets was taken from the oceans, lowering sea level and exposing a 1,000-mile-wide land connection between parts of Siberia and Alaska that were not glaciated.

As the glaciers melted, a corridor of unglaciated land was opened to more southerly parts of North America. The prehistoric Indians (or Paleo-Indians) moved through that corridor, eventually reaching the tip of South America. The first North Americans hunted mammoths and other large mammals, but the populations that occupied the Plains area went through several cultural and economic transitions before the historic Indian tribes entered the Plains. The relationship between the Plains tribes occupying the area at the time of European contact and the prehistoric Indians is obscure.

Most versions of the origins of modern tribes suggest that they moved into the grasslands from the Eastern Woodlands (the Sioux, Cheyenne, and Arapaho from the Northeast culture area and the Pawnee and Wichita from the Southeast) and the Southwest (Comanche and Kiowa). Subdivisions of tribes from other culture areas also used the Plains, and their cultures were molded to some extent by the Plains. The Ute and Shoshone of the Great Basin, Nez Perce of the plateau, and Cree from the Subarctic are examples.

Before Horses. Whatever their origins, the Plains Indians became nomadic buffalo hunters when they moved into the grasslands. Buffalo meat supplied food, some of which was smoked and dried for sustenance between hunts. Buffalo hides supplied robes, rawhide, and leather for other items of clothing and the cover for tipis. The Indians also hunted deer, pronghorn antelope, and other big game and used the meat and hides in similar ways. They gathered fruit, seeds, roots, and other vegetable foods as well. All these resources were important, but the buffalo was central to Plains Indian survival and culture.

The buffalo culture was firmly established before the Plains tribes obtained horses. Four main techniques were used to kill the buffalo: They were surrounded and killed with arrows and lances, driven over cliffs, driven into enclosures and killed there, and nearly surrounded by fire and killed as they fled the flames through the opening. These techniques were sometimes combined—for example, fire could be used to drive bison over a cliff.

The Indians followed the herds on foot using dogs, often pulling travois, to carry their possessions. The tipi, easily erected and taken down, lent itself to regular movement. The men hunted and waged war. The women cooked, preserved, sewed, collected plant foods, and put up and took down the tipi. Some tribes (Omaha and Ponca, for example) used tipis only during the buffalo hunts in early summer and in autumn. They lived in earthen lodges near the Missouri River during the rest of the year. There they planted gardens of corn, beans, and squash. The Pawnee, who lived south of the Platte River, practiced a similar schedule. The western Plains tribes (Ara-

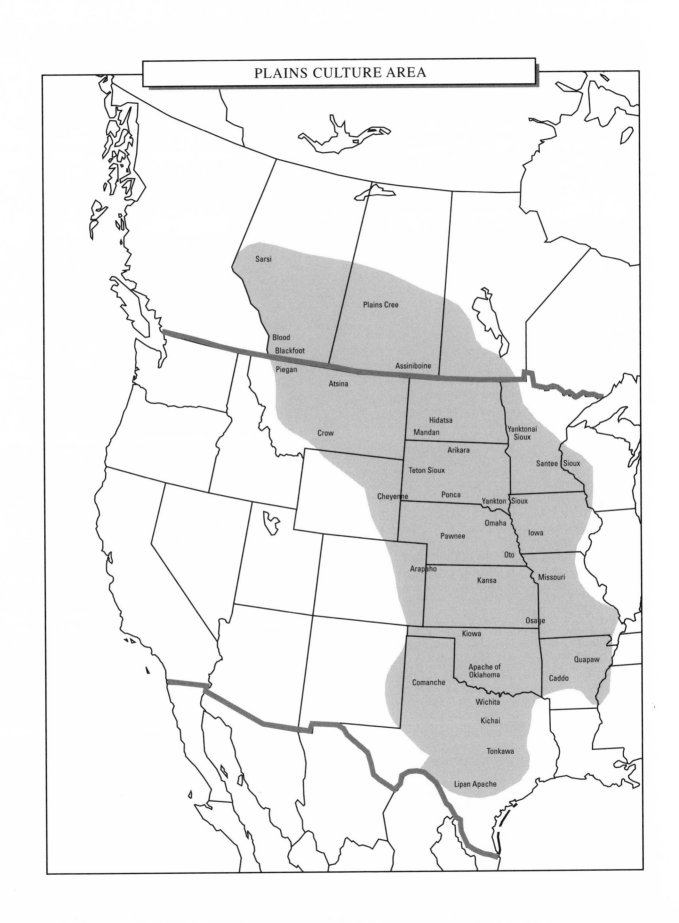

PLAINS CULTURE AREA

Sarsi

Plains Cree

Blood
Blackfoot

Piegan

Assiniboine

Atsina

Crow

Hidatsa
Mandan

Yanktonai
Sioux

Arikara

Santee Sioux

Teton Sioux

Cheyenne

Ponca

Yankton Sioux

Omaha

Iowa

Pawnee

Oto

Arapaho

Missouri

Kansa

Osage

Kiowa

Quapaw

Apache of
Oklahoma

Caddo

Comanche

Wichita

Kichai

Tonkawa

Lipan Apache

paho, Cheyenne, and Teton Sioux) lived in tipis year round, came together in large groups for the hunting season and for ceremonies, and scattered in extended family groups to the protected valleys of the foothills of the Rocky Mountains for winter. In winter they continued to hunt but depended on food preserved from the summer buffalo hunts for much of their sustenance.

Religion, Status, and Art. The spiritual life of Plains Indians was closely integrated with secular life. They held elaborate ceremonies, such as the Sun Dance, when the tribe was together for the buffalo hunt. Most tribes had a sacred symbol, often a medicine pipe. The term "medicine" in this context is probably better translated "power," as the Indians believed the pipe to be a symbol of the power which assured their success in hunting, warfare, and other endeavors. Several such symbols were kept in a medicine bundle. The circle (wheel) was of great importance to the Plains Indians as a symbol of the unity and continuity of all aspects of nature.

Many individuals also kept a personal medicine bundle. The symbolic contents of these bundles were often obtained during a vision quest, in which a young man (occasionally a young woman) fasted alone in a wilderness area hoping to receive a vision from which he obtained his medicine (power), indicating his particular abilities and often giving direction to his life. His medicine bundle would then be made up, using symbols of his medicine.

Games, hunting, warfare, and choice of leaders were spiritual endeavors in Plains Indian culture. Games such as shinny (something like field hockey) were parts of certain religious ceremonies. Supernatural signs were sought to determine whether a raid or hunt should proceed. Daring deeds such as touching a live enemy ("counting coup") ranked above killing an enemy in determining the respect due a warrior. Leadership positions were obtained by performing such deeds, demonstrating skill in hunting, and practicing generosity. Advancement through the male societies (lodges), which played important roles in tribal organization, depended on a man's bravery and his ability to provide for—and willingness to share with—the tribe. Most Plains tribes chose their chiefs based on these characteristics. Some tribes had hereditary chiefs, but to maintain a following the chief had to demonstrate these qualities.

Some Plains Indian art forms were spiritually symbolic and some were not. Pictographic art, usually produced by men, often depicted feats performed in hunting and warfare. The patterns used in much of the decorative art were based on straight lines, triangles, and diamonds, and their meaning was known only to the artist. Porcupine quills and later beads were extensively used for decoration. Any of these may have been produced simply for their beauty and symmetry, but it is likely that many such works also held spiritual meaning for their creator. Circles used in artworks probably were symbolic of the unity of nature.

Impact of Horses. The horse, introduced in historic times by the Spanish, fit beautifully into Plains Indian life. Buffalo hunting became easier and often involved a new technique in which individual bison were chased and brought down with bows and arrows. The travois was enlarged and fitted to the horse, so moves could be made more rapidly. Warfare could be carried out over greater distances, with greater speed and daring. Even when armed only with bows and arrows, Indians on horseback were skilled and fearless fighters, as the United States Army learned in the Plains Indian wars. Rifles, obtained from European Americans to the east, made them even more formidable. Their conquerors ranked them among the greatest mounted warriors in history.

The wars were primarily fought as a result of repeated encroachment by European Americans on Indian land, and they came to a close so quickly primarily because of diseases (especially smallpox) and the near extinction of buffalo, not because of superior skill and strategy on the part of the invading armies. The most intense phase of the Plains wars began with the Sand Creek Massacre of Cheyenne and Arapaho (1864). This period included the Fetterman fight and Bozeman Trail war with the Sioux; the Red River war with the Comanches, Kiowa, and Cheyenne; and the battle with the Sioux and Cheyenne on the Little Bighorn River. It finally ended with the massacre of Sioux at Wounded Knee Creek in South Dakota (1890). The greater numbers and advanced technology of the whites left little doubt as to the outcome. Against these odds, the Plains Indians left an indelible mark on American history and the history of warfare.

Most elements of Plains Indian culture were not unique to those Indians but were shared with surrounding culture areas, especially the Woodland Indians to the east. The specific combination of characteristics, however, was found in no other group. With few exceptions, and with abundant variation, this combination was shared by all the tribes in the Plains. Symbolic of independent life lived in harmony with nature, Plains culture is the American Indian culture most familiar to the rest of the world.   —*Carl W. Hoagstrom*

See also Architecture—Plains; Arts and crafts—Plains; Buffalo; Caddoan language family; Horses; Prehistory—Plains; Siouan language family; Tipi.

BIBLIOGRAPHY

Andrist, Ralph K. *The Long Death: The Last Days of the Plains Indians*. New York: Macmillan, 1964. An excellent outline of the Plains Indian wars. Even-handedly puts Indian behavior and response to government initiatives into a cultural context. Maps, illustrations, index, and bibliography.

Bancroft-Hunt, Norman, and Werner Forman. *The Indians of the Great Plains*. Norman: University of Oklahoma Press, 1981. A well-written, extensively illustrated (with photographs) outline of Plains Indian culture. Index and brief bibliography.

Hoover, Herbert T. *The Yankton Sioux*. New York: Chelsea House, 1988. This is one volume in an excellent series of short books called Indians of North America (series editor, Frank W. Porter III). Other books in the series include *The Arapaho*, *The Cheyenne*, *The Comanche*, *The Crow*, *The Hidatsa*, *The Kiowa*, *The Osage*, and *The Quapaws*. Other topics, such as women, archaeology, and federal Indian policy, have their own books as well. All have illustrations, index, and brief bibliography.

Lowie, Robert H. *Indians of the Plains*. New York: McGraw-Hill, 1954. Reprint. Lincoln: University of Nebraska Press, 1982. Excellent introduction. Covers prehistory, history, and most aspects of culture. Maps, tables, illustrations, index, and a short bibliography. The preface (1982) gives additional information and references.

Sturtevant, William C., gen. ed. *Handbook of North American Indians*. 9 vols. in publication. Washington, D.C.: Smithsonian Institution Press, 1978-1990. This series is the best source on North American Indians available, with some volumes, including *Plains*, still to be published. Volumes on culture areas surrounding the Plains contain information of interest. Illustrations, extensive bibliographies, indexes.

Thomas, Davis, and Karin Ronnefeldt, eds. *People of the First Man*. New York: E. P. Dutton, 1976. An annotated abbreviation of the German aristocrat Maximilian's notes on Indians along the Missouri River in 1833-1834. Reprints of artwork by Karl Bodmer, the Swiss artist who accompanied him, are included. Maps; index.

Plank house

TRIBES AFFECTED: Auinault, Bella Coola, Chehalis, Chinook, Coast Salish, Coos, Haida, Hupa, Karok, Klamath, Klikitat, Kwakiutl, Nootka, Takelma, Tillamook, Wivot, Yurok
SIGNIFICANCE: Large plank houses were widely used in the Northwest Coast culture area, where there were abundant forests to supply the material

Plank houses of the Northwest were usually built of white cedar. An oblong or rectangular area was cleared and the earth removed. The area could be from 10 to 30 feet long or more, from 6 to 20 feet wide, and 1 to 3 feet deep. Vertical posts were sunk into the ground, or log walls were built around the shallow pit and were capped with wooden beams.

Cured logs of cedar were split into planks with stone hammers and wedges. The planks were from 1 to 3 feet in width, and could be up to 60 feet long. Planks were usually at least several inches thick. The size of the planks was determined by

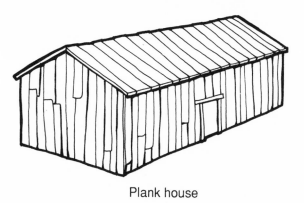

Plank house

the type of structure to be built. Planks were then attached to the vertical posts using cords braided of roots or vines. The structure was sealed with a mixture of pitch and charcoal or other substances which made it waterproof and windproof.

The roofs of plank houses could be either single or double pitch. A hole was made in the roof to allow smoke to exit and air to circulate. Doors were cut into either end.

Large longhouses with elaborate carvings on the posts and beams were common north of the Puget Sound and Columbia River areas. Several families could occupy each house. Common hearths were established in the center, with living areas to each side partitioned off by mats, skins, or other means, which allowed some privacy. The size and style of plank houses tend to become smaller and simpler the further south the tribal group.

See also Architecture—Northwest Coast; Longhouse; Northwest Coast.

Plano: Prehistoric tradition

DATE: 8000-5000 B.C.E.
LOCATION: Plains
CULTURE AFFECTED: Plano

The Plano tradition, dating 8000 and 5000 B.C.E., represents the last period of the hunting of now-extinct large Pleistocene mammals, especially giant bison, in North America. It is preceded by the Clovis (9500 to 9000 B.C.E.) and the Folsom (9000 to 8200 B.C.E.) periods, although Folsom and Plano are usually discussed together. Sites of this tradition are found over a wide area of North America, ranging from Alaska to Texas.

While Clovis peoples hunted mammoth, Folsom/Plano subsistence was oriented toward the pursuit of the now-extinct giant longhorn bison (*Bison antiquus* and *Bison occidentalis*) and later the modern *Bison bison*. Folsom/Plano cultures are known from occasional campsites and a large number of kill sites marked by beds of bison bone with stone artifacts. Tool technology was characterized by a wide variety of projectile point and knife styles used for killing and butchering. Folsom points, marked by a broad channel scar that runs most of the length of the point, belong to the fluted-point tradition that begins with Clovis. Plano cultures are associated with several unfluted styles, among them Plainview/Firstview, Eden, Scottsbluff, Claypool, Milnesand, Agate Basin, San Jon, and Angostura.

Plano Lifeways. The Folsom/Plano peoples ranged across the Great Plains in small, nomadic groups that followed seasonal rounds conditioned by the migration of bison herds. On these migrations, they took advantage of several sources for fine-grained, knappable stone. This material was used to manufacture points, knives, scrapers, and other tools, many of which required a high degree of skill in pressure flaking. Bison hunting, although likely to have included single-animal kills, was made very productive through the employment of mass-kill techniques. These included driving animals over cliffs or into natural traps, such as ditches and arroyos, box canyons, stream channels, and crescent-shaped sand dunes, and then killing them with spears. Such hunting would have required extensive knowledge of bison behavior as well as intensive investments of energy in tracking and stalking. These techniques would have required the participation of more than a single family and would have provided enough meat and hides for several bands. Animal resources such as skins, meat, bone, and marrow were efficiently utilized, often with very little waste.

Plano Archaeological Sites. Plano campsites tend to be situated on knolls or hills from which watering holes and bison herds could be observed. Lindenmeier is the largest known camp associated with the Folsom culture. It was located on the banks of a marshy lake in northeastern Colorado, now buried under sediments. Excavations revealed remains of hearths with broken tools and discarded bones that have been dated to approximately 9000 B.C.E. Bison bones were the most numerous, but bones of wolf, coyote, fox, hare, rabbit, turtle, deer, and antelope were also present. The large collection of stone tools included more than 250 Folsom points. The site appears to have been occupied by at least two different groups, based on differences in the size of projectile points and the fact that some were made of obsidian from a source in New Mexico, whereas others were made of material from Wyoming. The wide range of raw materials utilized by Folsom/Plano peoples suggests that they were covering vast distances in cyclical migrations.

The Olsen-Chubbuck site, in eastern Colorado near the Kansas state line, provides an example of a large-scale bison kill. At around 8200 B.C.E., almost two hundred bison (*Bison occidentalis*) were trapped when they were stampeded down a steep hillside into a narrow arroyo. The age of the animals, which included calves, yearlings, and bison of both sexes, suggests that the kill took place in the spring. The composition of piles of bones indicates that the animals were butchered in a consistent pattern, beginning with skinning and removal of hump meat and proceeding from the front to the hindquarters of the animals. Among the tools used were Firstview (Plainview) points, knives, scrapers, and cobbles to break bones for the extraction of marrow. Some of the chert used to make tools came from sources in Texas, supporting models for the seasonal migrations of Folsom/Plano peoples across a wide geographical range.

The Casper site in central Wyoming provides evidence for the slaughter of a small herd of bison around 6000 B.C.E. The animals were driven into the central concavity of a parabolic sand dune, where they were killed and butchered. The predominance of young animals in this bone bed suggests a degree of selectivity in the size of animals taken. Butchering was done efficiently, with deliberate stacking of bones. At the Hawken site in the Bighorn Basin of northeastern Wyoming, bison were killed when small herds were driven upstream into an increasingly narrow, steep-sided arroyo until they were wedged against one another and trapped at its box canyon terminus, where they were killed by hunters with spears. The

Horner site, also in northeastern Wyoming, has evidence of two bison kills spaced approximately a thousand years apart. Bison may have been corralled with drive lines; excavator George Frison suggests the practice of frozen caching of partially butchered carcasses for utilization at different times.

Plano Technology. In general, Folsom/Plano populations practiced a more sophisticated use of natural resources than did their predecessors. They covered much greater geographical ranges, probably moving with seasonal migrations of bison herds, and took advantage of several different sources of lithic materials. In addition to improvements in stone tool manufacture, there were significant technological advances in the ways that animals were slaughtered, butchered, and utilized. The wide variety of projectile point styles suggests the gradual emergence of distinct cultural groups whose identities became strengthened through periodic episodes of cooperative hunting.

The Plano tradition comes to an end with the decline of populations of giant bison, probably precipitated by climatic changes that reduced the size and range of their modern descendants for several thousand years. Patterns that evolved from Plano, however, continued for thousands of years. The hunting of bison remained one of the most important strategies for survival in the Plains until the destruction of large herds by European settlers in the nineteenth century.   —*John Hoopes*

See also Buffalo; Clovis; Folsom; Hunting and gathering; Prehistory—Plains; Projectile points.

BIBLIOGRAPHY

Frison, George C., ed. *The Casper Site: A Hell Gap Bison Kill on the High Plains.* New York: Academic Press, 1974.

_____. *Prehistoric Hunters of the High Plains.* New York: Academic Press, 1978.

Frison, George C., and Lawrence D. Todd, eds. *The Horner Site: The Type Site of the Cody Cultural Complex.* Orlando, Fla.: Academic Press, 1987.

Irwin, H. T., and H. M. Wormington. "Paleo-Indian Tool Types in the Great Plains." *American Antiquity* 365 (1970): 24-34.

Wheat, Joe Ben. "The Olsen-Chubbuck Site: A Paleo-Indian Bison Kill." Vol. 37 in *American Antiquity*. Washington, D.C.: Society for American Archaeology, 1972.

Wilmsen, Edwin N. *Lindenmeier: A Pleistocene Hunting Society.* New York: Harper & Row, 1974.

Plateau: Culture area

LANGUAGE GROUPS: Penutian, Sahaptin, Salishan

TRIBES: Coeur d'Alene, Colville, Flathead, Kalispel, Klamath, Klikitat, Kutenai, Lake, Lillooet, Methow, Mical, Modoc, Molala, Nez Perce, Okanagan, Palouse, Sanpoil, Shuswap, Spokane, Tenino, Thompson, Tyigh, Umatilla, Walla Walla, Wanapam, Wauyukma, Wenatchi, Yakima

The intermontane, semi-arid Plateau culture area consists of the low-elevation Columbia River basin of generally low, local relief, bounded on the west by the Cascade Mountains, on the east by the Rocky Mountains, to the north by the Fraser River, and somewhat to the south by the Blue Mountains. The most unique internal feature of the Plateau area is the numerous flood-scoured Scabland channels that are characterized by basalt cliffs, buttes, rock shelters, and thousands of small basins containing small lakes and seasonal wetlands. The Plateau was once viewed by anthropologists as a "transitional area" because of cultural influences from the Plains and the Northwest Coast. Archaeological evidence establishes an early and successful continuous inhabitation of eleven thousand years. The greatest influences on the Plateau cultures during the protohistorical period (1700-1805) were the adoption of the horse and prophetic religious revival.

The major shared cultural features of the Plateau were relatively simple political organization with leadership through consensus of opinion, riverine settlement patterns, reliance upon aquatic foods, a complex fishing technology, mutual cross-utilization of subsistence resources, extension of kin ties through systematic intermarriage, institutionalized trade, vision quest of a tutelary spirit, and an emphasis on democratic and peaceful relations. The introduction of the horse had a complex effect upon peoples of the eastern Plateau, particularly the Flathead and Nez Perce, who adopted many Plains traits in sociopolitical organization. The most devastating effects were created by numerous European American epidemics that greatly reduced aboriginal population.

Language. There were two major language families: In the southernmost Plateau was Sahaptin (Dalles, Klikitat, Nez Perce, Palouse, Umatilla, Walla Walla, Wanapum, and Warm Springs), and to the north was Salish (Columbia, Kalispel, Lillooet, Okanagan-Colville, Thompson, and Shuswap). Other dialects were Wasco-Wishram, Carrier, Chilcotin, and Kutenai. Chinook (Kiksht) was a lingua franca (trade language) along the Columbia and Spokane rivers. There was no sign language except what was learned from the Plains. Many dialects were mutually intelligible, and most people were multilingual because of trade, intermarriage between different ethnic groups, and sustained polyadic relationships necessitated by differential resources.

Technology and Subsistence. Implements of hunting were often the same ones used for warfare, and men made their own implements and tools for hunting and fishing. Though various woods and cordate were gathered locally, lithic (stone) material for knives and projectile points often was traded. Men made mortars, pestles, pipes, beads, fishing weights, axes, and cutting tools. A woman's most important tools were a fire-hardened digging stick and those implements associated with tanning and sewing deer and elk hides. During the year women collected and stored great quantities of thinly split lengths of spruce, cedar, pine roots, and willow that were carefully stored for making baskets.

Though house types within the Plateau varied, the principal winter structure was, in the late prehistoric period, a tule mat-covered double apsidal pole-constructed lodge that housed one or more extended families who shared a cooking fire. The floor was covered with old tule mats, skins, bear grass, or white sage. Tules were important multipurpose plants

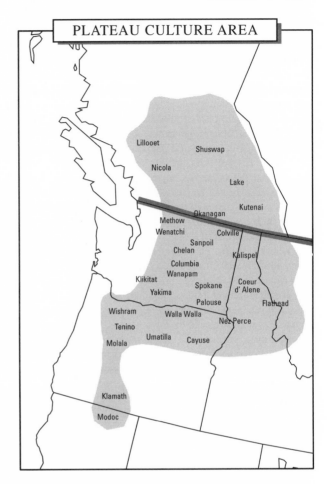

PLATEAU CULTURE AREA

for making mats, bundle boats, hats, and rain capes. Firewood and kindling were stored in an outside mat-roofed shed. Spring, summer, and fall structures were usually temporary and were built primarily for privacy and inclement weather.

As foragers, Plateau people lived for three to four months in permanent riverine winter villages in areas of low elevation, sometimes supplementing their stored animal and plant foods with occasional forays for land mammals and ice fishing. Winter villages had permanent semisubterranean storage pits, earth ovens, sweathouses, and family menstrual huts. Winter was a time of leisure when people repaired and manufactured predation technology, visited, and listened to elders telling often long accounts of creation and individual exploits. Acclaimed storytellers enjoyed high status. It was not unusual for shamans to conduct power duels in the winter.

Subsistence orientation was hunting, gathering, and fishing, regulated by season and a well-defined annual subsistence round. The southern Plateau diet consisted of approximately 40 percent plant food, 50 percent salmon, and 10 percent land mammals. The percentages varied according to a group's location, particularly in the northern Plateau. These activities commenced in early spring when groups would dismantle their winter houses and move to higher elevations to establish temporary camps to exploit traditional resource sites. Men would gather in great numbers in the spring to exploit fish stations mutually, using weirs, traps, harpoons, and spears, sometimes fishing until fall to harvest salmon and other fish. Food was preserved by drying and then cached in tree platforms and storage pits.

Women would visit traditional root fields in late spring to dig bitterroot, camus, numerous species of *Lomatium*, and other roots, which were dried and transported in great number to winter storage areas. In July and August, people would gather and pick numerous berry crops, particularly huckleberries. In late summer and early fall, groups would gain elevation—men to hunt deer and elk and women to gather medicines, hemp, and punk wood. After a killing frost the women cut and gathered tules.

Social Systems. The main feature of Plateau sociopolitical organization was village autonomy. There existed what may be called chiefs, however, men who influenced decisions of consensual opinion through judgment, knowledge, and example and who retained office through generosity, skillful decisions, oratory skills, and the possession of religious power. A chief's main responsibility was to maintain tranquility by resolving differences of opinion and making final arbitration. This office, sometimes hereditary, was never based on the assumption of accrued wealth or material possessions. A composite band could have two or three petty chiefs. Salmon chiefs, shamans, and war leaders, all of whom had special religious powers, were apparent during specific occasions.

There was gender equality, and a bilateral kinship system existed. Marriage was commonly monogamous, but polygamy, particularly polygyny, occurred. A main concern was to extend one's kinship ties through marriage. Social control was maintained by threats of sorcery, gossip, high division of labor, myth, public opinion, public whipping, and resident rules.

Pregnant women observed strict dietary and behavioral taboos and were expected to work industriously during their confinement; violations were explanations for congenital defects or later aberrant behavior in the child. Women were delivered, if possible, in isolated delivery huts by their mothers, who would ritually dispose of the placentas and make the required prophylactic devices to protect the new child. A berdache or shaman could assist in a difficult delivery. Infanticide and abortions were considered moral transgressions. Naming usually occurred at birth, and an infant was often named for a deceased kinsperson.

Adolescent children were indulged by kinspeople, but prior to puberty rites children embarked upon rigorous physical training in preparation for adulthood. Grandparents spent inordinate time with grandchildren, and a child's first exposure to adult activities was frequently supervised by a concerned grandparent who also made prototype toys of adult activities. The most dramatic change in the individual's life was the puberty ceremony; for a girl it was her first confinement to the menstrual hut, and for a boy, his vision quest for a tutelary spirit.

Marriage, after a period of courtship, was usually arranged by both families with a feast. Though a man could later take a second wife, usually a widow who demonstrated certain skills, particularly hide processing, the cowives did not share the same dwelling. Divorce was with mutual consent, usually for reasons of laziness or adultery.

Upon death the individual was immediately removed from the structure, washed, and buried, usually with grave goods. Special rituals and taboos were followed to ensure the incorporation of the soul in an afterlife and to prevent the occurrence of lingering ghosts. The surviving widow or widower observed strict taboos for one year, at which time a feast was held to give away certain possessions of the deceased. A newborn was never named after a deceased sibling for fear of recurrence of death.

Belief Systems. Though there were group differences in the complex Plateau animistic mythical charter, the main concern was one's daily intimate relationship with the supernatural, which if violated could cause personal failure, illness, and even death. Complex notions of how order was brought from chaos during the origins of humankind were based essentially on the supernatural world, theriomorphic forces, and natural forces which controlled humans and animals. Shamans were religious practitioners (male or female) who had acquired their power in a variety of ways, particularly through dreaming, a vision quest, recurring events, special signs, and unique experiences.

Plateau peoples had various elaborate rites of intensification, usually during midwinter, when sacred communal efforts were strictly followed to ensure world renewal, personal well-being, return of migratory animals, and a renewal of one's power. Shamans were effective as curers, employing medicaments, legerdemain, ventriloquism, massage, sucking, and acupressure. They sought to rid a patient of sorcery-induced spirit or object illness or soul loss; they also heard confessions of moral transgressions. All of these, it was believed, could eventually kill a patient if not attended to. Shamans were capable of transformation, and they publicly demonstrated their power's flight from their body by enduring painful proofs of ordeal.
                                                                    —*John Alan Ross*

See also Architecture—Plateau; Arts and crafts—Plateau; Hunting and gathering; Penutian language family; Prehistory—Plateau; Salishan language family; Tule.

BIBLIOGRAPHY

Hunn, Eugene S. "The Plateau Culture Area." In *Native North Americans: An Ethnohistorical Approach*. Edited by Daniel L. Boxberger. Dubuque, Iowa: Kendall/Hunt, 1990.

Kroeber, Alfred L. *Cultural and Natural Areas of Native North America*. Publications in American Archaeology and Ethnology 38. Berkeley: University of California Press, 1939.

Ray, Verne F. "Cultural Element Distributions: The Plateau." *Anthropological Records* 8 (1942): 99-257.

————. *Cultural Relations in the Plateau of Northwestern America*. Los Angeles: Southwest Museum, 1939.

Ross, John A. "Aboriginal Peoples of the Plateau." In *Northern Columbia Plateau Landscapes*, edited by Michael Folsom. Cheney: Eastern Washington University Press, 1984.

Spencer, Robert F. "Plateau." In *The Native Americans*, edited by Robert F. Spencer, Jesse D. Jennings, et al. New York: Harper & Row, 1965.

Walker, Deward E. *Mutual Cross Utilization of Economic Resources in the Plateau: An Example from the Aboriginal Nez Perce Fishing Practices*. Laboratory of Anthropology Report of Investigations 41. Pullman: Washington State University, 1967.

Plenty Coups (c. 1849, near Billings, Mont.—c. May 3, 1932, Pryor, Mont.): Tribal chief

ALSO KNOWN AS: Aleekchea'ahoosh (Many Achievements)

TRIBAL AFFILIATION: Crow

SIGNIFICANCE: Plenty Coups allied the Crows with the U.S. Army against other Indian tribes

Plenty Coups, whose Crow name means "Many Achievements," was the principal chief of the Crows during the latter stages of the Plains wars. He spearheaded the Crows' decision to cooperate with the U.S. Army in its pursuit of the Cheyennes, Sioux, Arapahoes, and other "hostiles." Plenty Coups's Crows provided scouts for George Armstrong Custer in his 1876 defeat at Little Bighorn.

Crow leader Plenty Coups urged his people to side with the U.S. military against other Plains tribes. (Library of Congress)

Plenty Coups was groomed for chieftainship from an early age, and uncommon attention was paid to him as a child by the Crows. When Plenty Coups was nine years old, one of his brothers was killed by the Sioux, creating a lifelong enmity.

After Little Bighorn, the Crows under Plenty Coups continued to support the U.S. Army as it drove the Cheyennes and Sioux into subjugation. Crow warriors aided in the pursuit of Sitting Bull into Canada, the hounding of the Northern Cheyennes, and the surrender of Crazy Horse. Plenty Coups urged his people to become farmers and ranchers, and he abandoned his tipi for a log farmhouse. Plenty Coups also opened a general store so that the Crows could buy trade goods at fair prices.

Plenty Coups traveled to Washington, D.C., several times after 1880 to assure trade and aid for the Crows. He was noted for his sagacity in business dealings. During World War I, Plenty Coups encouraged young Crow men to leave the enforced idleness and alcoholism of the reservation and join the U.S. Army. After the war, in 1921, he was chosen to represent all American Indians at the dedication of the Tomb of the Unknown Soldier in Arlington, Virginia. In 1928, his health failing, Plenty Coups willed his personal real estate, about 200 acres, to the U.S. government for the future use of the Crow people. Plenty Coups died May 3, 1932. The Crow council at the time so revered him that its members refused to name another principal chief in his place.

See also Crow; Indian-white relations—U.S., 1871-1933; Little Bighorn, Battle of the.

Pocahontas (c. 1596, near West Point, Va.—Mar. 21, 1617, Gravesend, England): Daughter of tribal chief

ALSO KNOWN AS: Matoaka

TRIBAL AFFILIATION: Powhatan Confederacy, Algonquin

SIGNIFICANCE: Pocahontas confronted cultural barriers between the Powhatan and English settlers; while she came to symbolize for white Americans the possibility of cultural unity, for many Native Americans she symbolizes the loss of traditional cultures

Pocahontas, also called Matoaka, was the daughter of Powhatan, chief of the Powhatans of what is today the tidewater region of Virginia. The Powhatan Confederacy, as it has traditionally been known by historians, was a group of approximately thirty Algonquian-speaking tribes organized in large part by Powhatan in the last years of the sixteenth century. Pocahontas was born at Werowocomoco, north of what would become Jamestown along the York River, which was home to her father and the center of Powhatan culture.

The most memorable extant story of Pocahontas' early life is contained in Captain John Smith's 1624 work *The Generall Historie of Virginia, New-England and the Summer Isles*. Here, Smith reported that in 1608 Pocahontas saved his life as he was about to be killed on the orders of her father. As numerous Powhatans were ostensibly preparing to kill Smith, Pocahontas, "when no intreaty could prevail, got his head in her armes, and laid her owne upon his to save him from

Pocahontas, the daughter of Powhatan, married English colonist John Rolfe in 1614. (Library of Congress)

death." This apparent act of salvation led to a brief peace between the struggling colonists and Powhatan. Pocahontas brought food to the English at Jamestown through the starvation winters of 1608 and 1609, and she persuaded her father to assist the settlers also.

Pocahontas was kidnapped in 1613 by Captain Samuel Argall and taken to Jamestown and then to Henrico; she was held hostage for English prisoners of the Powhatan. While among the English colonists, she converted to Christianity and was baptized, taking the name Lady Rebecca. In 1614, Chief Powhatan and Virginia governor Sir Thomas Dale agreed to the marriage of Pocahontas to the English settler John Rolfe; the peace agreement between Powhatan and the English settlers that followed can in part be attributed to the marriage. The couple's son, Thomas, was born the following year.

In 1616, Governor Dale saw in the young Pocahontas an advertising opportunity for the Virginia Company, and Pocahontas—together with several other Powhatans—was compelled to sail with her husband and son for England, arriving in Plymouth on June 3. She was warmly received at court and throughout English society. While in England, she also became reacquainted with John Smith, who had returned there in 1609. Preparing to return to her native land in 1617, she contracted smallpox and died at Gravesend on March 21. John Rolfe also died in England, in 1622. Their son Thomas eventually returned to Virginia after receiving his education in England, and he became a prominent citizen in the colonies.

Since the beginning of the nineteenth century, when the United States began looking to the past to assess its history and culture, Pocahontas has held a central position in colonial mythology. Beginning in the early nineteenth century, writers

looked upon the John Smith salvation episode as a romantic symbol of the birth of the nation; the episode was the centerpiece of numerous of the "Indian plays" so popular in the first half of the nineteenth century. The portraits to be found here bolstered the stereotyped image of the "noble savage" that one finds so frequently in European American literature of the day. The standard American histories since 1800 have likewise all included the salvation tale.

The story of Smith's salvation by Pocahontas has been disputed since the mid-nineteenth century, when Charles Deane and Henry Adams suggested that Smith invented the whole episode. Leo Lemay argues convincingly in favor of the tale's veracity, however; Lemay carefully adjudicates the controversy, determining that the evidence lies heavily in favor of Smith and against his doubters. A larger question has emerged in the light of ethnographic scholarship: Did Smith misconstrue (or pretend to misconstrue) the event he witnessed? Studies have suggested that ritual salvations of the sort Smith describes were fairly commonplace events among the Algonquian-speaking peoples, and several similar tales survive, including at least one which Smith himself quite likely would have read. Though Smith believed that Powhatan was fattening him up for sacrifice, in fact the event that he made famous was likely to have been part of a ritual of adoption into Powhatan culture, in which Pocahontas played the role of Smith's sponsor. Smith himself tells us that two days later Powhatan approached him to say that he was now regarded as one of the Powhatans.

This question of interpretation—perhaps more troublesome than the question of the tale's veracity—will probably intrigue scholars for some time to come. The event, which has often been taken by white interpreters as a symbol of the blessing of the colonial settlement of America, in this more recent reckoning comes to symbolize instead the failure of European Americans to comprehend the cultures they encountered in the New World. Wishing to uncover forgiveness among the very populations that had been so devastated by European Americans, nineteenth century writers seized upon the romantic tale of Pocahontas-as-savior.

Along with other mytho-historical Native American figures such as Squanto and Sacagawea, Pocahontas came to symbolize for European Americans the innocence of the land as well as the possibility of a union of white and Native American ideologies. (European Americans ignored the fact that any such union would most likely take place on the terms of whites and at the expense of Native American culture.) Pocahontas' apparent salvation of Smith, her conversion to Christianity, and her marriage to a prominent white citizen all contribute to her central status in the mythology of early European contact with Native Americans.   —*Jeff Abernathy*

See also Algonquian language family; Powhatan; Powhatan Wars.

BIBLIOGRAPHY

Lemay, Leo. *Did Pocahontas Save Captain John Smith?* Athens: University of Georgia Press, 1992.

Mossiker, Frances. *Pocahontas: The Life and the Legend.* New York: Alfred A. Knopf, 1976.

Rountree, Helen C. *Pocahontas's People: The Powhatan Indians of Virginia Through Four Centuries.* Norman: University of Oklahoma Press, 1990.

Smith, John. *The Generall Historie of Virginia, New-England, and the Summer Isles.* London: J. D[awson] and J. H[aviland] for Michael Sparkes, 1624.

Young, Phillip. "The Mother of Us All: Pocahontas Reconsidered." *Kenyon Review* 24 (1962): 391-415.

Pochteca

DATE: 1364-1520's

TRIBE AFFECTED: Aztec

SIGNIFICANCE: The pochteca were a specialized group of long-distance traders commissioned by the Aztec ruler to obtain luxury items

The pochteca were an elite group of Aztec traders who traveled from the capital of Tenochtitlán in central Mexico to various places in Mesoamerica to obtain luxury goods and resources for the Aztec nobility. Jaguar pelts, chocolate, and feathers were listed by the Spanish chronicler Bernardino de Sahagun as being among the trade goods acquired by the pochteca. Although the pochteca were highly ranked in Aztec society, they hid their wealth and disguised themselves as poor traders. Transportation involved human porters carrying goods on tumplines, since there were no draft animals domesticated in Mesoamerica.

Often referred to as "trader-spies," the pochteca traded with rulers of other regions on behalf of the Aztec king and subsequently participated in military campaigns to conquer and incorporate new lands into the Aztec empire. On the philosophy that it is cheaper to exact tribute than to trade, the Aztecs conquered the Soconusco area of the Pacific coastal area of Chiapas, Mexico, to exact chocolate as tribute. Aztec trade enclaves may have existed on the gulfs of Mexico and Honduras, where Maya traders met with the Aztec pochteca. Archaeological evidence indicates extensive trade between the Aztec, Maya, and others in the Late Postclassic Period prior to the arrival of the Spanish in 1521.

See also Aztalan; Tenochtitlán.

Pokagon, Leopold (c. 1775, near Bertrand, Mich.—July 8, 1841, Cass County, Mich.): Orator

ALSO KNOWN AS: Pocagin

TRIBAL AFFILIATION: Potawatomi, Ojibwa (Chippewa)

SIGNIFICANCE: Leopold Pokagon was a forceful advocate of peace and a convert to Catholicism

Leopold (Leo) Pokagon sold the site of Chicago to whites in 1832 as part of the Treaty of Tippecanoe. A Chippewa who was captured and reared by Potawatomis in what is now Michigan, Pokagon—like many of his people—was converted to Catholicism by Jesuits as a young man. Once he became a chief, he requested a Jesuit to live in his village along the St. Joseph River, where Michigan borders Indiana. Stephen Badin, a Jesuit, soon took up residence there.

The place and date of Leo Pokagon's birth are not known exactly, but he was probably born about 1775 near Bertrand, Michigan. As the civil chief of his tribe, Pokagon worked to keep his people out of Tecumseh's uprising and the War of 1812—even as Topenebee, the tribe's war chief, advised taking a much more aggressive stance toward the invading whites. Twenty years later, Pokagon also rebuffed Black Hawk's urgings to ally for war, as Topenebee allied with the Sauk and Fox leader. Despite his alliance with white settlers, Pokagon was forced to relocate his village to Dowagiac, Michigan. Remarkably, even after whites had seized much of the land that had belonged to his people near southern Lake Michigan, Pokagon continued friendly relations with them. Pokagon was known as a forceful advocate of peace and an orator of rare abilities. Jesuit letters of the time indicate that Pokagon himself called the people to prayer. He died in 1841 in Cass County, Michigan.

See also Black Hawk War; Ojibwa; Pokagon, Simon; Potawatomi; Tecumseh's Rebellion.

Pokagon, Simon (c. 1830, St. Joseph Valley, Mich.—Jan. 28, 1899, near Hartford, Mich.): Tribal chief, writer

TRIBAL AFFILIATION: Potawatomi

SIGNIFICANCE: Pokagon was widely regarded as the best-educated Indian of his generation; his writings on Indian culture were published in many magazines

Simon Pokagon was a son of Leopold Pokagon, who had sold the site of Chicago to whites in 1832. His father died when Simon was ten years old; Leopold was succeeded in the chieftainship of his band by his son Paul, who died; another son, Francis, then became chief, until his death. The younger brother Simon then inherited the office of chief.

Pokagon, who was born in St. Joseph Valley, Michigan, spoke only Potawatomi until age fourteen but later studied English at Notre Dame University and Latin and Greek at Oberlin College. Pokagon mastered five languages and became an accomplished writer and organist. He was sometimes called the best-educated American Indian of his time.

Pokagon also used his education to advantage when meeting with presidents Abraham Lincoln and Ulysses S. Grant on behalf of the Potawatomis. He spoke at the Chicago World Exposition (1893) and composed poetry and several articles on Native American customs and beliefs. He also wrote an autobiographical romance in the Potawatomi language and later translated it into English: *O-Gi-Maw-Kwe Mit-I-Gwa-Ki (Queen of the Woods)*. The book was published in 1899, the year Pokagon died near Hartford, Michigan. A monument to Simon Pokagon and his father Leopold has been erected in Chicago's Jackson Park.

See also Potawatomi.

Political organization and leadership

TRIBES AFFECTED: Pantribal

SIGNIFICANCE: While Native American tribes and nations employed several modes of governance, counselor democracy was widespread; traditional modes of government survive today, alongside structures created and supported by the U.S. and Canadian governments

Across North America, indigenous nations and tribes evolved varied methods of ordering their political affairs. European colonists arriving in eastern North America encountered variations of a confederacy model, usually operating by methods of consensus that were unfamiliar to people who had been living in hierarchical societies governed by queens, princes, and kings. The best known of these consensual governments was the Iroquois Confederacy, which occupied a prominent position in the diplomacy of the early colonies. Although the consensus model seems to have been the one most often used across the continent, some native peoples maintained societies that were strikingly different. For example, the Northwest Coast peoples paid great attention to political hierarchy and economic status within their communities.

Eastern Confederacies. All along the Atlantic seaboard, Indian nations had formed confederacies by the time they encountered European immigrants, from the Seminoles (Michel-Guillaume-Jean de Crèvecoeur called them "a federated republic") to the Cherokees and Choctaws to the Iroquois and the Hurons, as well as the Pennacook federation of New England, among many others. The Illinois Confederacy, the "Three Fires" of the Chippewa, Ottawa, and Potawatomi, the Wapenaki Confederacy, the Powhatan Confederacies, and the tripartite Miami were other examples. These systems had evolved to coordinate governance across geographic distances that seemed huge to European eyes at the time and to permit maximum freedom to nations within confederations and to individuals within nations.

Iroquois Confederacy. The Iroquois system was the best known to the colonists, in large part because of the *Haudenosaunee*'s pivotal position in diplomacy not only between the English and French but also among other native confederacies. Called the Iroquois by the French and the Five (later Six) Nations by the English, the Haudenosaunee (the word is Iroquois for "people of the longhouse") controlled the only relatively level land pass between the English colonies along the coast and the French settlements in the Saint Lawrence Valley.

Cadwallader Colden, who, in the words of Robert Waite, was regarded as "the best-informed man in the New World on the affairs of the British-American colonies," provided the first systematic study of the Six Nations in 1727 and augmented it in 1747. In his *History of the Five Nations Depending on the Province of New York in America*, Colden, an adopted Mohawk, compared the Iroquois to the Romans because of their skills at oratory, warfare, and diplomacy, as well as the republican nature of their government: "When Life and Liberty came in competition, indeed, I think our Indians have outdone the Romans in this particular."

Describing the Iroquois form of government extensively, Colden wrote that it "has continued so long that the Christians know nothing of the original of it." "Each Nation is an Absolute Republick by its self, governed in all Publick affairs of War and Peace by the Sachems of Old Men, whose Authority and Power is gained by and consists wholly in the opinions of the rest of the Nation in their Wisdom and Integrity," Colden wrote; "They never execute their Resolutions by Compulsion or Force Upon any of their People." Colden wrote that "The Five Nations have such absolute Notions of Liberty that they allow no Kind of Superiority of one over another."

The Iroquois Confederacy was formed by the Huron prophet Deganawida (called "the Peacemaker" in oral discourse). Deganawida enlisted the aid of a speaker, Aiowantha (also called Hiawatha), to spread his vision of a united Haudenosaunee confederacy because he stuttered so badly he could hardly speak. The oral history attributes the Peacemaker's stuttering to a double row of teeth. The confederacy originally included the Mohawks, Oneidas, Onondagas, Cayugas, and Senecas. The sixth nation, the Tuscaroras, migrated into Iroquois country in the early eighteenth century.

Peace among the formerly antagonistic nations was procured and maintained through the Haudenosaunee's Great Law of Peace (*Kaianerekowa*), a complex system of checks and balances between nations and sexes. Rights, duties, and qualifications of sachems were explicitly outlined in the Iroquois Great Law. Clan mothers could remove (or impeach) a sachem who was found guilty of any of a number of abuses of office, from missing meetings to murder. A sachem guilty of murder not only lost his title but also deprived his entire family of its right to representation. The women relatives holding the rights to the office were "buried," and the title was transferred to a sister family.

The Great Law stipulated that sachems' skins must be seven spans thick to withstand the criticism of their constituents. The law pointed out that sachems should take pains not to become angry when people scrutinized their conduct in governmental affairs.

European and European American shapers of thought from Benjamin Franklin to Friedrich Engels expressed astonishment at how the Iroquois and other Native American groups maintained social cohesion and resolved interpersonal conflict without lawyers, jails, and edicts. Instead of formal instruments of authority, the Iroquois governed behavior by instilling a sense of pride and connectedness to the group through common rituals. Ostracism and shame were the punishments for transgressions until people had atoned for their actions and demonstrated that they had undergone a purification process.

Huron Confederacy. The system of the Hurons was remarkably similar to that of their neighbors, the Iroquois. According to Bruce G. Trigger's *Children of the Aataentsic: A History of the Huron People* (1976), the Hurons' polity, like that of the Iroquois, was rooted in family structure. Leaders of the various clans used public opinion and consensus to shape decisions. Issues "were usually decided upon by majority vote . . . [and] discussed until a general consensus was reached." People would not be expected to be bound by a decision to which they had not given their conscious consent.

As with the Iroquois, the clans—Porcupine, Snake, Deer, Beaver, Hawk, Turtle, Bear, and Wolf—created familial affinity across the boundaries of the four confederated Huron nations. Members of each clan could trace their ancestry to a common origin through the female line. In each village, clan members elected a civil chief and a war chief. The titles were carried through the female family line but bestowed on men, again resembling the Iroquois approach. While the titles were hereditary in that sense, they did not pass from head to head of a particular family as in most European monarchies. When the time came to choose a leader, members of each clan segment in a particular village had a choice of several candidates, among whom, according to Trigger, personal qualities counted most heavily: "intelligence, oratorical ability, reputation for generosity and, above all, performance as a warrior."

The four Huron nations held a central council, which, according to Trigger, probably consisted of all the village chiefs, representing all the clans. The central council dealt with issues that affected all four nations, such as trade with Europeans and treaty negotiations.

Cherokee Consensus. The Cherokee, who called themselves *Ani-Yunwiya* ("the real people" or "the principal people"), were organized in settlements scattered in fertile bottomlands among the craggy peaks of the Great Smokey Mountains. The Cherokees took public opinion so seriously that they usually split their villages when they became too large to permit each adult a voice in council. In the early eighteenth century, the Cherokee Nation comprised sixty villages in five regions, with each village controlling its own affairs. Villages sent delegates to a national council only in times of national emergency. The villages averaged three hundred to four hundred persons each; at about five hundred people, a village usually split in two.

In Cherokee society, each adult was regarded as an equal in matters of politics. Leadership titles were few and informal. When Europeans sought "kings" or "chiefs" with whom to negotiate treaties, they usually did not understand that whomever they were speaking with could not compel allegiance or obedience of others.

As among the Iroquois, each Cherokee was a member of a matrilineal clan: Wolf, Deer, Bird, Blue, Red Paint, Wild Potato, or Twisters. The clans formed an intervillage kinship system which linked them in peaceful coexistence. As in many other confederacies, a clan system among the Cherokees bound the individual villages. The clan system cemented the confederacy, giving it a strength and enduring quality that prevented a high degree of local autonomy from degenerating into anarchy.

Cree Governance. Among the Crees, a subarctic people who inhabited the southern reaches of Hudson Bay in present-day Ontario and Quebec, there was no central political organization, as among the Iroquois and Hurons to the south. Even the individual bands or hunting parties had little or no organized political structure. Such a lack of structure is sometimes called "atomistic" by scholars.

Instead of formal council, Cree bands informally selected a wise elderly man, usually the head of a family, as a source of advice. He exercised informal, limited influence. As with the sachems of the more organized farming and hunting peoples to the south, these informal leaders usually did not relish the exercise of power, probably because most of the people who sought their advice resented any attempt to dictate. According to John J. Honigmann, who studied the Cree social structure, "Too great evidence of power is resented and feared by those whom it affects."

Cree life was marked only rarely by multifamily celebrations or rituals. Social life and social control were usually functions of the extended family. Outside the family, a Cree might appear ambivalent or reticent, usually out of respect for others' autonomy. People who transgressed social norms of interpersonal behavior became targets of gossip or sorcery (a technique for social control that was used widely across the continent). Although their society was family based, the Crees recognized no clan or other kinship system between different bands. The society thus did not have the interconnections between settlements offered by the clans of the Iroquois, Hurons, and Cherokees.

Western Apache. Apache society was centered on groups of two to six matrilocal extended families, a unit sometimes called a *gota*. Members of the gota lived together, and members of the different households cooperated in the pursuit of game and the raising of crops. A gota was usually led by a headman who assumed his status over several years by general consensus of the extended families in the gota. The headman in some cases inherited the title of "true chief." He would not retain the position, however, unless he displayed leadership. If no qualified headman was raised through inheritance, a consensus would form in favor of another leader who would be informally "elected" by members of the gota. Headmen were invariably male, but women exercised influence as political advisers. Their kinship lineages maintained the Apaches' matrilineal society.

A headman could wield considerable influence but only if the people in the extended families he led were willing to follow his advice regarding how to hunt, the techniques of agriculture, and who should work with whom. He also coordinated labor for hunting and foraging, advised parties engaged in disputes, and was sought for advice regarding who should marry whom. As a chief aged, he was charged not only with maintaining exemplary behavior but also with identifying young men who might become leaders in the future. He was expected to tutor younger men in the responsibilities of leadership. A chief was also charged with aiding the poor by coordinating distribution of donations from more affluent members of the gota. If two or more gotas engaged in conflict, their headmen were charged with resolving the dispute.

Each Apache was a member not only of a gota but also of one of sixty-two matrilineal clans which overlapped the individual settlements. Members of a clan (and, in some cases, of others identified as being close to it) helped one another in survival tasks and usually did not intermarry. Unlike the Iroquois and Hurons, however, the Apaches did not maintain a formal political structure beyond the local level except for the interpersonal networks of clans.

Mandan and Cheyenne. Political organization among the Mandans (who occupied present-day North and South Dakota) was restricted to the village level, with no central governance. The Mandans' village governance system included elements of representative democracy but also recognized some degree of rank and economic status, which was often determined by a family's ownership of sacred medicine bundles that were vital to tribal rituals. The owners of such bundles often built their lodges closest to the ceremonial center of a given village. Most Mandan villages were quite similar, with closely packed family lodges clustered around the central plaza, which was usually at least 100 feet across. Men selected from lodges which held sacred bundles comprised a council. These men selected two from their number, one of whom displayed special talents at organizing war parties. The other leading chief's talent lay in his peaceful disposition and his ability to broker disputes, dispense wisdom, stage feasts and rituals, and greet diplomatic envoys.

The Cheyennes maintained a powerful central government which united the various Cheyenne bands as well as family-based affinities. At the head of this organization was the Council of Forty-four, on which civil chiefs served ten-year terms. The Cheyenne system closely resembled the Sioux "Seven Fires" confederacy, although the Sioux were not as tightly organized.

Six Cheyenne military societies served as police as well as organizers of war parties. These voluntary organizations were open to all men in the nation and were similar to the police societies of the Lakota. All these societies grew out of the horse culture of the Plains. As a civil function, the military societies often carried out the council's orders. As the periods of peace dwindled with the onset of the European American invasion, the police societies evolved into war societies which took over much of the authority of the Council of Forty-four. Cheyenne myth says that the Council of Forty-four was started by a woman, but its members were male. New chiefs were chosen by the council itself to replace those who left at the end of their terms.

Classes, Castes, and Slavery. The Nootka peoples of the Northwest Coast, who occupied the west coast of Vancouver Island in present-day British Columbia and the extreme northwest coast of Washington State, departed from the general reliance on a consensus model of government. This departure was not slight: Their system was entirely different. It was status-driven, caste-bound, and, compared to those of many native peoples, very aggressive, even among peoples who shared cultures very similar to their own. From the Chickliset in the north to the Makah in the south, the Nootkan peoples took sturdy whaling canoes to sea; in times of war, which occurred with a frequency and intensity that usually surpassed most native peoples in North America, the canoes could be used for raiding and for capturing slaves from neighboring native nations.

Nootkan peoples recognized three classes that seemed as imperishable as the red cedar from which they constructed their lodges: nobility, commoners, and slaves. The nobility comprised chiefs and their closest relatives; the eldest son was the family head. He, his family, and a few associates lived in the rear righthand corner of the house, abutted by people of lower status. These people were said to be "under the arm" of the chief. The next highest ranking chief, usually a younger brother of the head chief, invariably occupied the rear lefthand corner of the house, with his family. He, too, had a number of people "under the arm." The other two corners were occupied by lesser chiefs' families. The space between the corners, along the walls, was used by commoners' families, and a few very junior-ranking members of the nobility. They were called "tenants"; the nobility in the corners reserved the right to ownership of the house.

Commoners could move from one house to another at will, and since they often performed arduous but necessary skilled labor (such as carpentry or whaling), chiefs competed to retain the best workers. The most successful chiefs were affectionate and generous toward the common families who chose to live in their lodges. Slaves had no designated lodgings or rights; they were captured in raids of other peoples along the coast and were sometimes traded for other slaves or for goods. A noble in one village could be captured and sold into slavery in another. The captive's relatives might then mount a counter-raid to free him.

The speakers and war chiefs of a village usually were reared from youth through inheritance among the children who had a small quantum of royal blood. They tended to be administrative officers who carried out the will of the chiefs. Although most war chiefs were selected by the high chiefs from their families, one of the few ways in which a Nootka commoner family could advance in the village class structure was to have its eldest son receive such an office. Once a common family had been elevated in this way, the title of war chief remained with it as a right of inheritance.

Unlike some of the more democratic native peoples elsewhere on the continent, the Nootka did not have an elaborate kinship system. The existence of clans tends to create affinity structures independent of class structures, and the Nootka defined themselves, above all, by rank. Notions of status also seemed to be the major method of controlling interpersonal conflict. Should a verbal disagreement explode into a fistfight, members of each participant's family would urge him to cease or risk bringing shame on them. The two combatants might then relapse into a vigorous verbal battle, throwing the worst imaginable insults at each other, as relatives continued to pacify them: "Don't think about him anymore. It's not right to fight. You have a good name. Don't bring it down. Don't think about it—just let it go." In some cases, people who engaged in fisticuffs might be upbraided before the community and abjectly humiliated at public occasions. Outside of this, the Nootkas, unlike the Cheyenne, Huron, Mandan, and Iroquois, had no formal methods of social control within their communities. The Nootkas' use of sorcery was infrequent and mild compared to that of peoples who were less class conscious.

Colonial Governance. From the beginnings of contact with Europeans, Native Americans faced the imposition of governmental systems by colonial authorities. During the years of subjugation, much native governance on reservations was conducted in a summary fashion by the United States military. In the later nineteenth century, the Bureau of Indian Affairs (BIA) was created to conduct reservation governance as a civilian agency. In 1934, with the passage of the Indian Reorganization Act (IRA), native reservation-based governments recognized by the Bureau of Indian Affairs were granted very limited autonomy through elective councils.

Even with limited twentieth century self-government, Native Americans in the United States still operate within a legal system that in the 1830's began defining Native Americans as "wards of the state." This legal characterization continued to shape BIA policy throughout the twentieth century, as Native Americans asserted their rights to act on their own behalf. The definition of wardship often conflicts with the rights of citizens, extended to American Indians as a whole in 1924.

Today, many traditional forms of governance survive on native lands throughout North America. They often operate with very little outside publicity on reservations that also have BIA-recognized "elective" governments, which some Native Americans boycott as vestiges of colonialism.

—*Bruce E. Johansen*

See also Bureau of Indian Affairs (BIA); Clans; Ethnophilosophy and worldview; Indian Reorganization Act; Iroquois Confederacy; Sachem; Social control, traditional; Societies, non-kin-based; Sovereignty.

BIBLIOGRAPHY

Bowers, Alfred W. *Mandan Social and Ceremonial Organization*. Chicago: University of Chicago Press, 1950. Provides an overview of Mandan social structure and organization.

Cohen, Felix S. "Americanizing the White Man." *The American Scholar* 21, no. 2 (Spring, 1952): 177-191. An early article describing ways in which Native American concept of governance helped shape the thoughts of American society generally. For details regarding the use of Iroquoian and other Native American precedents in the evolution of democratic thought, see Donald A. Grinde and Bruce E. Johansen's *Exemplar of Liberty* (Los Angeles: UCLA American Indian Studies Center, 1991).

Corkran, David H. *The Cherokee Frontier: Conflict and Survival, 1740-62*. Norman: University of Oklahoma Press, 1962. Traces the evolution of Cherokee social structure during the early contact period.

Drucker, Philip. *Cultures of the North Pacific Coast*. San Francisco: Chandler, 1965. Surveys of Northwest Coast tribes' lifeways, including political organization.

Grinnell, George Bird. *The Cheyenne Indians: Their History and Ways of Life*. 2 vols. 1923. Reprint. Lincoln: University of Nebraska Press, 1972. A comprehensive guide to Cheyenne political society.

McKee, Jesse O., and Jon A. Schlenker. *The Choctaws: Cultural Evolution of a Native American Tribe*. Jackson: University Press of Mississippi, 1980. Describes the development of Choctaw society and political organization.

Reid, John Phillip. *A Better Kind of Hatchet: Law, Trade, and Diplomacy in the Cherokee Nation During the Early Years of European Contact*. University Park: Pennsylvania State University Press, 1976. Evaluates the effect of colonization on Cherokee social structure, including governance. See also Reid's *A Law of the Blood: The Primitive Law of the Cherokee Nation* (New York: New York University Press, 1970).

Trigger, Bruce G. *Children of the Aataentsic: A History of the Huron People to 1660*. Montreal: McGill-Queen's University Press, 1976. The authoritative work on Huron social structure, governance, and other aspects of Huron culture.

Wallace, Paul A. W. *The White Roots of Peace*. Philadelphia: University of Pennsylvania Press, 1946. Describes the origin epic of the Iroquois League.

Pomo: Tribe

CULTURE AREA: California
LANGUAGE GROUP: Hokan
PRIMARY LOCATION: Clear Lake, Northern California
POPULATION SIZE: 4,766 (1990 U.S. Census)

The Pomo Indians are one of the many California native groups who shared traits with a wide variety of hunter-gatherer tribes in the California area. In 1770, the number of Pomo was estimated at 8,000, which had dropped to 1,143 by the 1930 census. Pomo Indian traditional areas include Cleone Duncan's Point and inland as far as the Clear Lake (Stony Creek) area, north of the San Francisco Bay.

California Indians generally are not to be understood as "tribes," but rather as small "tribal groups" of a hundred persons at most. These groups, usually not permanent, surrounded a centrally recognized permanent village. The Pomo shared many common cultural traits with other village communities up and down the California coast as far south as the beginnings of the great Mexican tribal groups, where the appearance of pottery and other traditionally Mexican native arts in the region of Southern California signals a mixing of cultures on a spectrum approaching the great civilization centers of central and southern Mexico.

Pomo people are most noted for their distribution of shells as a kind of currency exchange. They also developed basketry to perhaps the highest art form among all the California tribal groupings, incorporating styles and designs that mark Pomo artistry in a manner that is clear even to those not widely familiar with California basketry. Because of their residency near Clear Lake, the Pomo also developed canoes, the use of the single-blade paddle, and the use of balsa rafts.

As with other California tribal groupings, shamanism was practiced among the Pomo as a healing and supernatural art. Pomo ceremonial life is also noted for the use of sweatlodges, heated by direct fire rather than by steam (steam was absent throughout California tribal use of sweatlodges). Of particular interest with regard to Pomo religion is the Maru Cult, a religious ceremony of ritual and dancing that is a direct descendant of the influence of the Ghost Dance of 1870 on the Pomo people. The Maru Cult rituals are still observed among many modern Pomo members.

In terms of family life, the Pomo practiced the purchase of brides as an essential aspect of matrimony. There was no recognized "chief" in Pomo tradition, but rather a leadership of recognized male leaders of the settlements.

See also Hokan language family; Maru Cult.

BIBLIOGRAPHY

Brown, Vinson, and Douglas Andrews. *The Pomo Indians of California and Their Neighbors.* Heraldsburg, Calif.: Naturegraph, 1969.

Kroeber, Alfred. "The Indians of California." In *The North American Indians: A Sourcebook*, edited by Roger Owen, James Deetz, and Anthony Fisher. New York: Macmillan, 1967.

Meighan, Clement W., and Francis Riddel. *The Maru Cult of the Pomo Indians: A California Ghost Dance Survival.* Southwest Museum Papers 23. Los Angeles: Southwest Museum, 1972.

Ponca: Tribe

CULTURE AREA: Plains
LANGUAGE GROUP: Siouan
PRIMARY LOCATION: Nebraska, Oklahoma
POPULATION SIZE: 2,913 (1990 U.S. Census)

The Ponca were Plains Indians who retained aspects of the culture of the woodlands from which they entered the Plains. Their closest relatives and associates were the Omaha; their relationships with the Sioux and Pawnee were always stormy. They were generally friendly with European Americans. Their chief Standing Bear forced a court ruling extending the personal liberties guaranteed by the Constitution to Indians.

Early History and Traditional Lifestyle. Sometime between 1200 and 1500, the Ponca entered the Plains from the Ohio River valley. They eventually settled along the Niobrara River in northeast Nebraska, where they lived in earthlodges and farmed the river's floodplain as they had in the eastern woodlands. In spring and early summer, and again in autumn, they moved into the Plains, where they lived in tipis and hunted buffalo (bison) as Plains Indians. The Ponca obtained horses in the mid-1700's and extended their hunting range beyond the Black Hills of South Dakota.

Ponca society and religion were much like those of other Plains Indians. Men hunted and waged war; women cooked, gardened, and made clothes and tipi covers. The women also took down the tipi before moving and put it up after the move. Unlike many Plains tribes, chief positions were hereditary. As with other Plains tribes, however, the chief had to demonstrate bravery and generosity to maintain a following. Ponca spiritual life included a sacred pipe, tribal medicine bundle, individual medicine bundles, vision quests, warrior societies, and Sun Dances.

The Ponca were always a small tribe and often united with the neighboring Omaha to defend themselves against the Sioux and Pawnee. Occasionally they joined the Sioux in disputes with the Pawnee or Omaha. Most of their conflicts occurred with the Sioux, who attacked them on their hunting grounds and in their villages. They were never at war with the United States.

Transition and Contemporary Life. The Ponca position on the Missouri assured them early contact with white explorers and traders. Meriwether Lewis and William Clark spent time with them on their trip to explore the Louisiana Purchase, as did Prince Maximilian zu Wied and Karl Bodmer on their trip up the Missouri. They traded early and extensively with European Americans. The Ponca were hospitable to their visitors and were respected by the explorers and traders.

Despite their friendly attitude toward the invading European Americans, the Ponca were treated no better than other American Indians. In 1858 they were assigned to a reservation within their traditional homeland, but in 1868 the same land was given to the Sioux. Responding to the resultant conflict between the tribes, the government determined to move the Ponca to Indian Territory (Oklahoma), a move the Indians attempted to resist.

In 1877, the Ponca tribe, under Chief White Eagle was forcibly moved. Many died on the trip, and more died in the first years in Oklahoma. In 1879, Chief Standing Bear, determined to bury his dead son in Nebraska, suggested that the tribe return to the Niobrara. Most Poncas, including White Eagle, believed that they would only be forced back to Oklahoma and chose to stay. Nevertheless, Standing Bear and several others moved north, reaching the Omaha reservation near Omaha, Nebraska, where they were arrested by the United States Army.

An editor of an Omaha newspaper, Thomas H. Tibbles, aroused public sentiment with his accounts of the situation. Two lawyers sued the government on behalf of Standing Bear's right to go where he pleased. The government argued that Indians had no such rights. The judge ruled against the government, and government appeals (eventually to the Supreme Court) were dismissed. The ruling gave Indians the same personal liberties as white Americans. Application of the law was not that simple, but Standing Bear had forced a first legal step in the direction of Indian equality.

The Northern Ponca were eventually given a small reservation, but the General Allotment Act (Dawes Act) of 1887 gave allotments of reservation property to individual Indians and allowed the "extra" land to be sold to whites. The loss of their tribal land base was devastating to both Ponca subdivisions, but both survived because of their determination to do so. For example, when the government withdrew tribal recognition from the Northern Ponca in 1962, the Ponca returned to the courts of law. Tribal status was restored in 1990. The Ponca continue to struggle with poverty and undereducation, but their continued existence as a tribe attests their character and determination.

—Carl W. Hoagstrom

See also Omaha; Plains; Prehistory—Plains; Siouan language family; Standing Bear.

Pontiac (c. 1720, along the Maumee River, northern Ohio— Apr. 20, 1769, Cahokia, Ill.): Chief

ALSO KNOWN AS: Obwandiyag

TRIBAL AFFILIATION: Ottawa

SIGNIFICANCE: In 1763, in the wake of the French defeat during the French and Indian War, Pontiac envisioned a pan-Indian confederation to drive the British from Indian land

Pontiac was born in present-day northern Ohio, the son of an Ottawa father and a Chippewa (Ojibwa) mother. According to Ottawa custom, which allowed polygamy, presumably he married on several occasions, though only one wife, Kantuckeegan, and their two sons, Otussa and Shegenaba, have been identified. Pontiac, a large, imposing warrior, was esteemed for his strategic skills as well as for his intelligence and eloquence. By 1755, he had become an Ottawa war chief.

The four colonial wars culminating in the French and Indian War (1754-1763) had pitted the French and their Indian allies against the British. Although the British had occasionally courted Indian alliance, Indians had disdained them, preferring the French, who practiced fair trade, provided lavish

Ottawa leader Pontiac organized pan-Indian resistance to British colonists in the 1760's. (Library of Congress)

tribute, and established few permanent settlements on Indian land. The English scorned Indian culture, but the French were historically more tolerant, frequently marrying Indians and being welcomed into tribes.

The Ottawas, like most of their Great Lakes neighbors, were primarily fur traders who shared a congenial and mutually beneficial relationship with the French. During the French and Indian War, Pontiac fought with the French, helping to defeat General Edward Braddock and his British troops at Fort Duquesne (later Fort Pitt), modern-day Pittsburgh.

French defeat in 1763 proved disastrous for frontier Indian tribes, whose fate was suddenly thrust into British hands. Westward settlement was unimpeded with the removal of the French, and Indians faced new threats from migrating settlers. Furthermore, the British, through an unsympathetic commander-in-chief, Lord Jeffrey Amherst, alienated Indians by abandoning the French policy of bestowing gifts; Amherst viewed the practice as extravagant. The Indians, meantime, had grown dependent on European tools and weapons; French gunpowder had enabled them to supply vast quantities of fur as well as meat for their tribes. Indians faced genuine hardship when the British refused them supplies of gunpowder. In addition, Amherst, who during the war had fostered Indian addiction to alcohol, afterward prohibited its sale.

In 1763, Pontiac, hoping to seize the initiative during the postwar confusion and possibly encouraged by promises of French aid, planned an offensive strike to drive the British from the frontier. In the meantime, another leader, known as the Delaware Prophet, was formulating his own plans for a unification of Indian tribes. Claiming to be the recipient of visions from the spirit world, the Prophet denounced European technology and alcohol and proposed a return to traditional Indian customs. Like Pontiac, the Prophet envisioned a pan-Indian alliance; unlike Pontiac, he was an advocate of peaceful methods.

On April 27, 1763, Pontiac convened a general war council during which he finalized his war plans. In a single massive assault, he intended to capture British forts ranging across the frontier. To that end, he delivered a general call to arms in the form of red wampum, to which several tribes responded, including the Chippewas, Delawares, Hurons, Illinois, Kickapoos, Miamis, Mingoes, Potawatomis, Senecas, and Shawnees. On May 8, Pontiac and three hundred warriors entered Fort Detroit, concealing weapons and ready for an offensive strike. Realizing his plans had been revealed to the fort commander, Major Henry Gladwin, Pontiac withheld his battle signal. The next day, however, he and his men laid siege to the fort and continued it successfully for six months. During that time, nine other British forts were captured by Indians, and the British suffered more than two thousand casualties.

Fearing collapse of their frontier defense, the British mustered their strength and successfully counterattacked. By late 1763, the Indian resistance was weakening. Protracted warfare was inimical to Indians, who were accustomed to short strikes, and French support had failed to materialize. As the winter drew near, warriors became concerned about providing food, as the long disruption of their hunting and fishing threatened hardship for their families. Moreover, at Fort Pitt, soldiers under the command of Captain Simeon Ecuyer precipitated a devastating epidemic by distributing blankets infected with smallpox, a disease for which Indians had little resistance.

In late autumn, Pontiac ended his siege of Fort Detroit. Independent tribes remained hostile, however, engaging in battle throughout 1764. By July, 1765, Pontiac tentatively agreed to peace, formalizing his agreement in a treaty signed at Oswego in 1766 and thereby earning British pardon. Afterward he returned to his village along the Maumee River. His peace treaty angered many Indians, however, who were reluctant to end hostilities. Consequently, Pontiac, his family, and a small group of supporters were driven from their village.

In April, 1769, Pontiac traveled to a trading post at Cahokia, Illinois. There he was murdered by a Peoria Indian named Black Dog, whom the British may have paid to assassinate the great leader in an effort to curb future rebellions. Pontiac's murder precipitated a war among the Indians, as several tribes united against the Illinois Indians to avenge his death.

Prior to the American Revolution, Pontiac and his pan-Indian alliance provided the greatest native threat to British expansion in the New World. Several more Indian leaders over the coming century attempted rebellion, including Little Turtle in 1790-1794 and Tecumseh in 1809-1811, sustaining a tradition of Indian rebellions beginning in the early seventeenth century and lasting until the Battle of Wounded Knee in 1890.

—Mary E. Virginia

See also French and Indian Wars; Indian-white relations—English colonial; Indian-white relations—French colonial; Ottawa; Paxton Riots; Pontiac's Conspiracy; Proclamation of 1763.

BIBLIOGRAPHY

Leach, Douglas E. *Arms for Empire: A Military History of the British Colonies in North America, 1607-1763*. New York: Macmillan, 1973.

_____. "Colonial Indian Wars." In *History of Indian-White Relations*, edited by Wilcomb E. Washburn. Vol. 4 in *Handbook of North American Indians*. Washington, D.C.: Smithsonian Institution Press, 1988.

Parkham, Francis. *The Conspiracy of Pontiac and the Indian War After the Conquest of Canada*. 2 vols. 7th rev. ed. Boston: Little, Brown, 1874.

Peckham, Howard H. *Pontiac and the Indian Uprising*. Princeton, N.J.: Princeton University Press, 1947.

Sosin, Jack M. *Whitehall and the Wilderness: The Middle West in British Colonial Policy, 1760-1775*. Lincoln: University of Nebraska Press, 1961.

Pontiac's Conspiracy

DATE: 1763-1764
PLACE: Old Northwest (Great Lakes region)

TRIBES AFFECTED: Old Northwest tribes, principally Chippewa, Huron (Wyandot), Lenni Lenape, Menominee, Miami, Ottawa, Potawatomi, Sauk, Shawnee
SIGNIFICANCE: This uprising resulted in the defeat of British troops and influenced British policy to restrain white westward expansion

The defeat of the French in the French and Indian War left the Indians of the Old Northwest without protection from intrusion of white traders and settlers upon their lands. The British commander-in-chief in America, Jeffrey Amherst, refused to continue the French practice of giving Indians provisions and arms for hunting. Indians now had to travel long distances to deliver their furs and were also at a disadvantage as to the prices they received. Overall, the British exhibited a contemptuous attitude toward the Indians. The Delaware Prophet launched a revivalist religious movement, calling upon the Indians to rid themselves of the corrupt influences of the whites and to resist the intrusion of the settlers' frontier. Upon the scene appeared a charismatic Ottawa chief, Pontiac, who envisioned a united stand by Native Americans, north and south.

Having previously failed to capture Fort Detroit by tricking the garrison into unpreparedness, Pontiac opened hostilities on May 9, 1763, by killing settlers near the fort. Pontiac's main contribution to the general Indian uprising that ensued was to lay siege to Fort Detroit (lasting six months) with warriors of his own tribe and those of the Chippewas and Potawatomis. Throughout the war, the Indians had logistical assistance from French traders.

With virtually all the tribes of the Old Northwest joining in the rebellion, British posts west of Niagara and Fort Pitt, except Detroit, fell to the Indians. A relief party under Lieutenant Abraham Cuyler, traveling by water from Niagara to Detroit, landed at Point Pelee, 25 miles from Detroit, and was ambushed by Indians on May 28. The attack resulted in the loss of fifty-one of the ninety-six men.

The siege of Detroit was not complete, since the water communication between that fort and Niagara was never severed. On occasion, reinforcements reached Detroit. With his garrison strengthened, Major Henry Gladwin, commandant at Detroit, sent Captain James Dalyell to make a sortie outside the fort; at what became known as "Bloody Run," Dalyell fought Pontiac's Indians on July 31, which resulted in Dalyell being killed along with sixty-six other British casualties. The forts that the British lost (in most instances with many of the garrison soldiers being killed) were Fort Sandusky on Lake Erie, May 16; Fort St. Joseph (Niles, Michigan), May 25; Fort Miami (Fort Wayne, Indiana), May 27; Fort Ouiatenon (Lafayette, Indiana), June 1; Fort Michilimackinac (on the straits between Lakes Huron and Michigan), June 2; Fort Edward Augustus (Green Bay, Wisconsin), abandoned in June; Fort Venango (Franklin, Pennsylvania), June 16; Fort Le Boeuf (Waterford, Pennsylvania), June 18; and Fort Presque Isle (Erie, Pennsylvania), June 20. Indians swept through the Monongahela Valley, attacking Fort Ligonier and laying siege to Fort Pitt. One atrocity involved the "Paxton boys," a group of whites under Lazarus Stewart, who descended on peaceful Indians who had settled at Conestoga, in Lancaster County, Pennsylvania, on December 14 and 27, 1763, killing twenty-two Indians.

By fall, 1763, many bands of Indians were making peace. Pontiac discovered that his support had substantially dwindled; he lifted the siege of Detroit on October 30, 1763. At the battle of Bushy Run, August 5-6, 1763, Colonel Henry Bouquet, with troops conducting a relief train of supplies for Fort Pitt, defeated a force of Delawares (Lenni Lenapes), Shawnees, Senecas, and Hurons, though one-fourth of his detachment were casualties. Pontiac again attempted to renew the conflict, even soliciting support from Choctaws and other southern Indians. Two British expeditions in late summer, 1764, though not engaging the enemy in battle, ensured the British victory; Colonel John Bradstreet, with twelve hundred men, went from Niagara to Detroit, and Colonel Bouquet, with a force of fifteen hundred, went from Fort Pitt to the Muskingum River. Bradstreet, however, was duped into a false peace, and briefly Delawares and Shawnees engaged in further hostilities.

On April 18, 1765, Pontiac met with an agent sent by the new British commander, General Thomas Gage, and accepted a pension from the British government, an event which aroused enmity and jealousy from other Indian leaders. At Fort Oswego (in New York) on July 24, 1766, an official peace was concluded between Pontiac and Sir William Johnson, the British superintendent of northern Indian affairs. Pontiac lived up to his pledge of loyalty to the British. Pontiac's War forced the British government to assume a more realistic approach to western Indian affairs, resulting in both curtailing westward settlement and more strictly managing the Indian trade.

See also Delaware Prophet; Ottawa; Paxton Riots; Pontiac; Potawatomi; Proclamation of 1763.

Poospatuck: Tribe

CULTURE AREA: Northeast
LANGUAGE GROUP: Algonquian
PRIMARY LOCATION: Long Island, New York
POPULATION SIZE: 264 (1990 U.S. Census)

The Poospatuck, also called *Uncachogue*, were one of thirteen tribes occupying Long Island, New York, in the seventeenth century. They, along with other Algonquian tribes, had lived in the area for thousands of years. The thirteen tribes made up the Montauk Confederacy, which controlled all of Long Island except the far western end. The chief of the Montauk tribe was considered—by both American Indians and Europeans—the head of all the thirteen tribes. Many scholars, in fact, consider the Montauk Confederacy one tribe and view the thirteen smaller units as clans.

The Poospatuck lived on the eastern half of the island's south shore. They lived in permanent villages and ate a diet of fish and seafood as well as maize, beans, and pumpkins. Food was cooked in clay pots and stirred with wooden utensils. The Poospatuck created beautiful woven fabrics and leather goods. In the early seventeenth century, the Pequots conquered the Montauk Confederacy. After the Pequots were nearly wiped out in 1637, the Narragansett began to attack the Montauk, forcing them to seek refuge with whites. In 1666, the Poospatuck were granted a reservation on the Forge River. They tried to maintain their traditional life even as their numbers dwindled. The tribe's last chief, the sachem Elizabeth Joe, died in 1832, but the Poospatuck reservation is still intact and recognized by New York State.

See also Algonquian language family; Montauk Confederacy; Northeast; Pequot; Sachem.

Popé (?, San Juan Pueblo—1690): Tribal leader, medicine man

TRIBAL AFFILIATION: San Juan Pueblo
SIGNIFICANCE: Popé inspired and led the Pueblo Revolt against Spanish colonists in New Mexico in 1680

Little is known of the early life of Popé, a medicine man of the San Juan Pueblo in seventeenth century New Mexico. As an older man, Popé became an ardent opponent of the Spanish regime. The Spanish, whose colony was established in 1598, became more oppressive as more settlers arrived. Franciscan missionaries forced the Pueblos to abandon their own religion in favor of Christianity, while *encomenderos* exploited Pueblo labor. In the 1670's, drought and famine brought Pueblo resentment and desperation to a peak. In 1675, signs of unrest prompted Governor Juan Francisco Trevino to punish the Pueblos by arresting and flogging forty-seven Pueblo medicine men, including Popé. Popé then moved from San Juan to Taos, where he began to organize a general revolt against the Spanish.

Popé had brilliant organizational and leadership skills. He preached a millenarian message in which he promised that the ancient gods would return, bearing gifts of prosperity, as soon as the Christians and their gods were dead. Popé offered land and liberation from Spanish slavery for warriors who would fight the Spanish. Spreading his message through the Pueblos, Popé engineered a coordinated attack on the Spanish, beginning on August 10, 1680. Franciscans living in the Pueblos were massacred, and Santa Fe was beseiged. By August 20, the surviving Spanish and a group of loyal Indians fled south to El Paso.

As the leader of the Pueblos, Popé urged the destruction of all vestiges of Christianity and promised the return of prosperity as soon as the Pueblos revived their own ancient religion. Drought, internal dissension, and attack from neighboring tribes continued to disrupt Pueblo life. Popé's influence waned, and he died in 1690. The Spaniards returned to reconquer New Mexico between 1692 and 1694, though they never subjected the Pueblo to such harsh exploitation as they had before the revolt of 1680.

See also Indian-white relations—Spanish colonial; Pueblo (Popé's) Revolt; Pueblo tribes, Eastern.

Popovi Da (April 10, 1923, San Ildefonso Pueblo, N.Mex.—Oct. 17, 1971, Santa Fe, N.Mex.): Potter

ALSO KNOWN AS: Antonio Martínez

TRIBAL AFFILIATION: San Ildefonso Pueblo (Tewa)

SIGNIFICANCE: Popovi Da, son of María and Julian Martínez, continued the pottery renaissance that they had begun at San Ildefonso, adding many significant contributions of his own

In 1948, Popovi Da (Red Fox) legally changed his name from Antonio Martínez to his Tewa name and opened a studio of Indian art at San Ildefonso, where he sold outstanding examples of Indian arts, including his mother's pottery. By 1950, he was helping with the decorating of his mother María's pottery, and by 1956 his experiments with polychrome ware had resulted in the revival of a style that had been seldom seen since the mid-1920's. Popovi, who had studied at the Institute of American Indian Art in Santa Fe in the early 1930's, had developed an innovative approach to design and technique and was now winning awards for his work at the Gallup Ceremonial and elsewhere.

From 1961 to 1964, he developed two new pottery types: sienna ware and black-and-sienna ware. Both types involved a complicated two-firing process. One of the most beautiful new finishes Popovi created was the gunmetal ware, fired in the same way as the black ware but in a hotter fire for a longer period of time. Popovi was also the first contemporary Pueblo potter to set turquoise stones into his pottery.

Popovi Da was a religious, community, and business leader as well as an outstanding artist. He served several terms as governor of San Ildefonso, was chairman of the All-Pueblo Council, and was a member of the New Mexico Arts Commission.

See also Arts and crafts—Southwest; Martínez, Julián; Martínez, María Antonía; Pottery.

Porter, Pleasant (Sept. 26, 1840, Clarkesville, Ala.—Sept. 3, 1907, Okla.): Chief, educator

ALSO KNOWN AS: Crazy Bear, Talof Harjo

TRIBAL AFFILIATION: Creek

SIGNIFICANCE: As a principal chief, Pleasant Porter sought acculturation and accommodation with whites

The grandson of a Creek chief, Tulope Tustunugee, Pleasant Porter also had black ancestry. Born in Alabama, he moved to Indian Territory, where he became a respected leader. During the Civil War, along with most Creeks, he supported the Confederacy, becoming a lieutenant in the Confederate Second Creek Regiment. He was wounded in battle.

After the war, he was active in tribal politics, a leader of a faction of mixed-blood Creeks who supported an imposed constitutional government and acculturation to white customs. He served as a prominent member of the Council of the Creek Nation, and in that capacity he traveled on several occasions to Washington, D.C. For nearly twenty years after the Civil War, Porter was also Creek school superintendent, establishing an exemplary Creek educational system.

In 1889, Porter supported the Dawes Commission in ceding Creek lands to the United States for white settlers. In 1902, he ceded all Creek lands in support of the allotment policy by which individual tribal members would receive private allotments. He was principal chief when Indian Territory became Oklahoma in 1907. He died of a stroke in the same year.

See also Allotment system; Creek; General Allotment Act; Indian Territory.

Posey, Alexander Lawrence (Aug. 3, 1873, near Eufaula, Creek Nation, present-day Okla.—May 27, 1908, Oktahutchee River): Journalist

TRIBAL AFFILIATION: Creek (Tuskegee)

SIGNIFICANCE: Posey's Fus Fixico letters combined political satire, local color, and dialect humor in the tradition of Mark Twain

Alexander Posey grew up in a large rural Oklahoma family, speaking Creek as his first language but educated in English at the Creek national public school and at Bacone Indian University. He was the first American Indian owner/editor of a daily newspaper; he published the weekly *Indian Journal* of Eufaula, Oklahoma. He was active in Creek politics and helped prepare the census of Creek Indians for the Dawes Act (General Allotment Act) allotments. Posey accepted the Dawes Act but sympathized with traditionalists who foresaw the damage that allotment would do to Creek life. His life was cut short in 1908 when he drowned near Eufaula. He was survived by his wife, Minnie Harris Posey (Lowena), and his children, Wynema Torrans and Yohola Irving.

In the "Fus Fixico" letters, Posey's major contribution to American literature, fictional characters reflect on the pressing issues of allotment and Creek independence. Posey was reluctant to editorialize, so he created the personas of Hotgun, Fus Fixico, Chinubbie Harjo, Tookpafka Micco, Kono Harjo, and Wolf Warrior, who became voices of skepticism, tradition, advocacy, or resistance as Posey sought to educate his readers about the changes being imposed upon the Creek people. The letters transcend local concerns and exhibit an economy of style and superb rendering of dialect in their trenchant political commentary.

See also Allotment system; Creek; Journalism; Political organization and leadership.

Potawatomi: Tribe

CULTURE AREA: Northeast

LANGUAGE GROUP: Algonquian

PRIMARY LOCATION: Oklahoma, Wisconsin

POPULATION SIZE: 16,763 in U.S. (1990 U.S. Census); 85 in Canada (Statistics Canada, bsed on 1992 census)

The Potawatomi, a tribe of the Algonquian language group, originally came from north of Lake Superior. About 1500 C.E., they migrated south to the eastern shore of Lake Michigan, where they built a dozen villages along the St. Joseph River.

Traditional Lifeways. The Potawatomi hunted deer, elk, buffalo, and small game, fished, and gathered berries and nuts.

They also planted and harvested corn and squash. Women worked the crops while the men hunted. The Potawatomi moved their villages every ten to twelve years, when the soil became exhausted. The name of the tribe resulted from a misunderstanding by Jean Nicolet, the French fur trapper and explorer who first made contact with the Potawatomi in 1634. He asked his Huron guide, "Who are these people?" The guide misunderstood and answered, "They are making fire," which sounded like "pota wa tomi" to the Frenchman. They actually called themselves "Neshnabek," meaning "the true people," but the other name stuck.

Traditional Potawatomi religion stressed the power of Wiske, the Master of All Life. Wiske had a twin brother, Chipiyapos, the Destroyer, but the gods looked so much alike people could tell the difference between them only with great difficulty. Potawatomi children began being taught about the difference between good and evil at age twelve, when they went on "vision quests" in the wilderness. Here they walked alone, naked, and without food or drink, praying and meditating. If they were purified by their suffering, a guardian spirit (*manitou*) would appear to them and lead them to safety. The manitou would protect the youth for the rest of his life.

Post-contact Life. In 1641, the first Catholic missionaries appeared and set up a mission at St. Joseph, Michigan, though they met with little success in converting Indians to Christianity. In the 1650's, the Iroquois of New York attacked all other tribes in Ohio, Michigan, and Indiana, seeking to expand their control of the fur trade. They defeated the Potawatomi, and the "true people" ended up in northern Wisconsin, along Green Bay.

From their new homeland, the Potawatomi became involved again in the fur trade, mainly with the French. Many French traders married Indian women, but the Potawatomi considered children of mixed marriages (call Brules—burned ones—by the natives and Metis—mixed people—by the French) aliens, and refused to let them live in their villages. Full-bloods lived in clans, which included the living, the dead, and the not-yet-born family members.

In the French and Indian Wars (1754-1763), the Potawatomi attacked British forces as far east as New York and Virginia. In 1755, they acquired horses for the first time, and the horse quickly replaced birchbark canoes as their major mode of transportation. In 1763, Potawatomi warriors joined in Pontiac's war against the British, but the Ottawa chief's rebellion failed and he signed a humiliating peace treaty.

In 1794, the American army defeated another Potawatomi force at the Battle of Fallen Timbers, and the Indians gave up a large amount of land in Ohio and Indiana. In 1807, the "true people" joined Tecumseh in his war to unite all Indians and expel whites from their old homelands, but this fight also ended in failure. As the fur trade declined, tribal leaders found the sale of land to whites at very low prices one method of avoiding absolute poverty. In 1831, under the terms of the Indian Removal Act, the Potawatomi agreed to resettle in Kansas, though only about a half of the tribe's twenty-seven

hundred members actually moved. The others remained in the East and came under state authority, chiefly in Michigan and, later, Wisconsin.

After the Civil War, the "strolling Potawatomis" of northern Wisconsin, so called because they were landless and frequently moved from place to place, moved onto the Menominee reservation. Here they became involved with the Strange Woman religion led by a Dakota who claimed she had had a vision of Christ, who would soon return and restore his people to power and respect. If her followers would beat a giant drum and dance steadily for four days, the whites would fall dead to the earth. This "Dream Dance" is still performed four times a year, but mainly as a tourist attraction. In the twentieth century, the Potawatomi received their own reservation in Wisconsin, and they worked as migrant agricultural workers and basketmakers. The result was increasing poverty and despair. Only the legalization of bingo on tribal land offered any opportunity for economic growth; otherwise jobs and opportunity proved very scarce.
—*Leslie V. Tischauser*

See also Algonquian language family; Northeast.

Potlatch

TRIBES AFFECTED: Bella Coola, Chehalis, Chinook, Coos, Haida, Hupa, Karok, Klamath, Klikitat, Kwakiutl, Nootka, Quinault, Salish (Coast), Takelma, Tillamook, Tlingit, Tsimshian, Wivot, Yurok

SIGNIFICANCE: Widely practiced throughout the Northwest, the potlatch involved feasting and gift-giving, and it helped ensure or lift the status of the person giving it

The word "potlatch" is from the Chinook language, although it originated in the Nootka language as *patshatl*, which means "gift," or "giving." A potlatch is a ceremonial winter feast. The details of organizing and carrying out the event vary from one areal group to another. Preparation could take months or even years. Each guest invited was fed, housed, entertained, and often given many valuable gifts for the duration of the event, which could last from a few days to a few weeks, depending on the status of the hosts and size of their community.

Invitations were sent out in the form of elaborate beaten copper plates of various shapes representing deities, ancestors, or clan symbols. These "coppers" could be from 1 to 3 feet wide and up to 4 feet in height. They were very thin and intricately engraved with stylized designs. They were sometimes referred to as the "bones of the dead" because they might depict a deceased relative. On occasion they were broken up and given out to a number of members of a given family or clan and then presented and reassembled upon arrival at the host village.

Dancing, storytelling, group activities, and other (often elaborate) entertainment, including mourning the dead, commemoration of deceased relatives and friends, speeches, and the exchange of gratuities occurred. These would honor the host and ensure the host's importance. Initiations into secret societies, tattooing, piercing of body parts for adornment, and other ceremonial and ritual activities also took place. All those

A potlatch photographed in Alaska circa 1900. (Museum of New Mexico)

in attendance would then be obligated to the host in one way or another, thus assuring that the host would improve or maintain high social position and status.

Some potlatches were of the grand sort. At the end of these enormous festivities, the host would destroy (by burning) great quantities of goods in addition to those already given away. Toward the southern reaches of the Northwest Coast culture area, the potlatches were less dramatic and consisted only of gift giving and an elaborate display of wealth by the host.

After colonization, missionaries eventually managed to have the potlatch prohibited (it was prohibited from 1884 to 1951), as it appeared to them to be unnecessarily destructive and to impoverish many lower-status members of the community. In spite of this incorrect perception, and the prohibition based on it, the practice continues to this day, although in a somewhat modified form, again depending on the nature of the local culture.

See also Chinook; Feasts; Kwakiutl; Northwest Coast.

Pottery

Tribes affected: Pantribal

Significance: A variety of pottery-making techniques were used to make vessels for cooking and carrying as well as items used for ceremonial purposes

Pottery is made of clay. Such wares as bowls, plates, storage containers, animal effigies, smoking pipes, and beads are made by using a wide variety of methods, materials, tools, finishing processes, and firing methods.

The earliest evidence of the crafting and use of pottery in the United States has been found in the Southeast culture area. Types of clay, methods of building, and firing procedures vary enormously from tribe to tribe. The making and use of pottery is nearly universal in temperate climates where it is needed for daily use. In wetter or colder climates, pottery may be absent or used only rarely. Other types of objects, such as baskets in the Northwest and animal skins or stone in the Arctic and elsewhere, were used for cooking and storing.

Materials. Clay is composed of aluminum and silicon in the form of aluminum silicate or of calcium and carbon in the form of calcium carbonate. The presence of hydrated trace minerals in clay, such as magnesium, manganese and iron, gives the respective gray and white types of pure clay their various colors, most notably red, yellow, black, green, and blue.

Erosion, earthquakes, landslides, and water movement are some of the natural processes that both reveal and mix the elements into the various types of clay used in the making of pottery. Clay is usually found along streams, rivers, and lakes. Pure clay must be mixed with fine particles of sand, ground-up

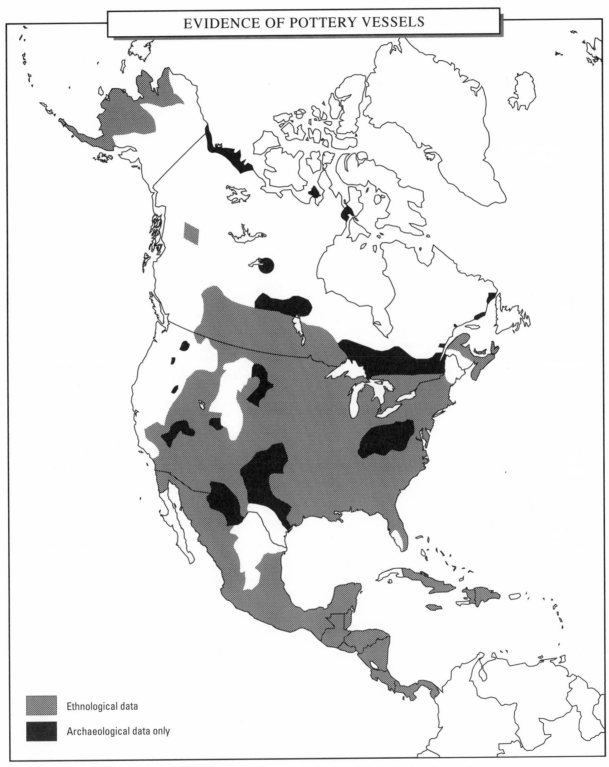

EVIDENCE OF POTTERY VESSELS

Ethnological data

Archaeological data only

Source: After Driver, Harold E., and William C. Massey, *Comparative Studies of North American Indians*, 1957.

pottery, ashes, or other substances which will ensure slow even shrinkage of pots as they dry and are fired. The larger the pot to be built, the more of this "grog" the potter must use to ensure the integrity of the walls of the piece.

Pottery clay is gathered, cleaned, processed, and stored, either wet or dry, for future use. It is collected with respect for Mother Earth, with songs, prayers, and offerings of sacred plants; permission is asked and thanks given for its use. The clay is worked by hand to the proper consistency to remove air bubbles and foreign material that could cause cracks if not removed. It is then wedged or pounded with a wooden paddle into a uniform mass.

Process and Craft. Pottery is formed using many different methods and tools. It is made by pinching, from slabs, by coiling, or in wooden molds. Tools such as wooden sticks and paddles, bone implements, and stones were used to shape, incise designs, mold, or finish the clay. A variety of brushes and paints (vegetable- and mineral-based) were used to add color and symbolic meaning to the surfaces of pots.

Pottery is slowly dried, and in the drying process it may be incised with a variety of abstract designs, decorated, or painted, and then perhaps rubbed with a stone, bone, or other smooth implement ("burnished") to a glassy finish. Some potters paint a thin layer of clay of another color—called "slip"—over the pot to add depth and color to the design.

Firing Pottery. After the pottery is thoroughly dried, it is ready to be fired. Many methods and materials are used in the firing process. Some tribes use a shallow open pit, some a walled enclosure made of dung, wood, bark, or clay, and others more complex methods involving an earthen mound. Fuels include grass, hard and soft woods, barks, and animal dung. Firing times can be anywhere from several hours to three days.

The pottery which results can be red, black, yellow, or multicolored depending on whether the firing process involves oxidation or reduction. The longer and hotter the fire, the harder and longer-lasting the pottery. Temperatures can vary from 900 to 1300 degrees Fahrenheit at the peak of the firing. When the ashes cool and the pots are removed, they are gently cleaned with a piece of cloth or hide and rubbed with fat to make them shine. Some pottery was made impervious to water by a smoking process that impregnated the inner walls of the pot with oily carbon compounds derived from pine pitch, corn cobs, or other substances.

Traditional pottery was porous "bisqueware" and therefore was not usually put into direct contact with either water or fire unless especially made for those purposes. Pots used for cooking were often filled with water and heated stones placed therein to bring the water to a boil.

Pots usually only lasted a few months if put to daily use. The broken and cracked pieces or shards were often placed in a dump a short distance outside of villages—leaving modern investigators a wealth of artifacts to puzzle over and analyze.

Cultural History. During the early colonial period, the use of pottery began to be displaced by the introduction of glass, iron, and copper wares. In many cases the traditional building and firing methods were nearly lost as new materials and technology took over where tradition left off. As tribes were exterminated, consolidated, or removed to reservations there was loss or fusion of the old ways.

Modern American Indian pottery retains many of the traditional qualities, and most of the classic beauty, of works produced in prehistoric times. Individual potters from a variety of tribes have become well-known artists in their own right, selling their work for hundreds or thousands of dollars per item.

Modern pottery is often fired twice, in gas-fired kilns, the second time at much higher temperatures, a process that makes it impervious and as hard as glass or stone. Earthenware, stoneware, and even porcelain are produced by native artisans across the land. Intricate and innovative methods of carving, painting, and glazing are used today to preserve ancient and traditional designs and forms, while new techniques and designs are used to create beautiful fine arts.

There are many books and films on the subject available today, but these will never replace the knowledge that still can be gained from elders, through the oral tradition, who know the craft and subtleties of the art and are willing to teach it to the next generation. —*Michael W. Simpson*

See also Arts and crafts—Southeast; Food preparation and cooking; Martínez, Julián; Martínez, María Antonía; Paints and painting; Popovi Da.

BIBLIOGRAPHY

Bushnell, G. S. H., and Adrian Digby. *Ancient American Pottery*. London: Faber & Faber, 1955.

Quimby, Ian M., ed. *Ceramics in America*. Charlottesville: University Press of Virginia, 1980.

Savage, George. *Pottery Through the Ages*. Harmondsworth, Middlesex, England: Penguin Books, 1959.

Simpson, Michael W. *Making Native American Pottery*. Happy Camp, Calif.: Naturegraph Press, 1991.

Poundmaker (1842-1886): Tribal leader and spokesman

ALSO KNOWN AS: Opeteca Hanawaywin

TRIBAL AFFILIATION: Cree

SIGNIFICANCE: Poundmaker fought in the Second Riel Rebellion

Poundmaker, whose followers included Plains Cree and some Assiniboines, fought with Louis Riel and other Metis in the Second Riel Rebellion. Poundmaker had initially urged peace, but his young warriors pushed him into raids on settlements and a brief (but successful) battle with three hundred soldiers.

Riel had become a Metis spokesman by 1870 (Metis people are of mixed French and Indian descent); he joined with other Indians to block surveyors from entering the Red River Country. Riel and his allies, including Poundmaker's people, prevented a newly assigned governor from taking up residence in the area; they also seized Fort Garry, a Hudson's Bay Company outpost near St. Boniface. After that, the Metis and their allies established a provisional government. Two attempts to recapture the fort failed as the Metis sent a delegation to Ottawa to argue their case for independence.

Poundmaker pledged to assist Riel and his followers to the end. The uprising was short-lived: The newly constructed railroad allowed the Canadian government to transport a large number of troops into the area in a short time. Riel's second rebellion was crushed in a few days, and Poundmaker was arrested and sent to prison.

Riel was tried for sedition and hanged on November 16, 1885. Afterward he became a martyr and folk hero to many Metis and French Canadians. Poundmaker died the next year.

See also Cree; Indian-white relations—Canadian; Riel Rebellions.

Poverty Point: Archaeological site

DATE: 1700-800 B.C.E.

LOCATION: Near Epps, West Carroll Parish, northeastern Louisiana

CULTURE AFFECTED: Woodland

The Poverty Point site is noted both for its impressively sized earthen mound and for its antiquity. It was once renowned as the earliest mound site in Louisiana (dating to 1700-800 B.C.E.), but now it is apparent that some other mounds predate it. So far, however, the volume of the Poverty Point earthen architecture exceeds that of its antecedents.

Poverty Point covers more than a square mile near Epps, in northeastern Louisiana. The extent of the site was not recognized until the 1950's, when the true nature of the earthen modifications was noted on aerial photographs. Poverty Point contains six parallel earthen ridges that arch around a meandering bend of Bayou Macon, forming a semicircle. The ridges are unequally subdivided by several aisleways, which radiate from the center of the site to its perimeter. The site contains two earthen mounds and additional features. Mound A (sometimes described as a bird effigy mound) rises to 70 feet and is located on the western, or outer, margin of the concentric ridges. The 21-foot Mound B is located northwest of the ridges and may have a later date of construction.

Poverty Point is characterized by a distinctive array of artifacts (manufactured objects). People at this site made tiny stone tools (microliths), stone bowls, stone beads and ornaments, and ceramic cooking balls (termed Poverty Point objects), which were used to heat earthen ovens. Many other types of tools used for hunting, food preparation, and other activities have also been found at the site. Poverty Point dates to a time in Louisiana when people were not commonly using ceramics, so only a few fragments of ceramic vessels have been found.

Many of the Poverty Point artifacts were manufactured from exotic materials, some of them from as far afield as the Great Lakes area. Poverty Point was at the terminus of a vast trading network. Researchers are still uncertain of the mechanism which powered this exchange system. Possibly traders of goods, who may have also offered such intangibles as religious knowledge or politically advantageous information,

traveled across the country. Alternatively, perhaps objects were exchanged from one neighboring community to another and achieved a wide distribution through time.

There is also debate concerning the size of the site's population, its social organization, and the people's subsistence. One hypothesis suggests that the site was constructed quickly by a highly organized chiefdom-level society with a large population. An alternative view hypothesizes that the site grew slowly and may have been fully occupied only for limited periods of time, perhaps serving a seasonal function such as a market location or a religious center. The limited subsistence data available uphold the importance of fishing, hunting, and gathering, possibly supplemented by squash cultivation.

See also Dating methods; Effigy mounds; Mounds and mound builders; Prehistory—Southeast.

Powhatan (c. 1550, Powhatan, near Richmond, Va.—Apr., 1618, Powhatan, Va.): Chief

ALSO KNOWN AS: Wahunsonacock

TRIBAL AFFILIATION: Powhatan Confederacy

SIGNIFICANCE: Leader of a powerful confederacy, Powhatan chose to pursue a policy of accommodation with early British settlers in Virginia

Powhatan was most likely born near present-day Richmond, Virginia, around 1550. Named Wahunsonacock, he took the name of the confederacy created by his father upon his parent's death in the mid-1570's.

An imposing figure—Captain John Smith described him as well proportioned and tall—Powhatan spent the three decades prior to the arrival of the British in Virginia expanding his confederacy. As high priest and king, Powhatan ruled absolutely. Expanding his power largely through intimidation, Powhatan would willingly order the destruction of a village that resisted his control. By 1607, there were twenty-eight tribes with nearly nine thousand people living in about two hundred villages in the confederacy along Chesapeake Bay.

It is not entirely clear why this powerful leader did not simply annihilate the few British who settled Jamestown. Instead, he made several peaceful overtures to them. Occasionally, he supplied food when the settlers faced critical shortages. After his brother, Opechancanough, had captured Captain John Smith, he chose not to execute the British leader.

Powhatan permitted Pocahontas, his favorite daughter, whom Smith claimed interceded to save his life, to visit the British settlement several times in 1608 and 1609. Her presence made it easier for the British to trade with the confederacy. She advised Smith which tribes to avoid, and she helped the British negotiate for food.

Perhaps Powhatan believed that the British could serve as an ally in his attempt to consolidate his control in the region. Their weapons impressed him, and Powhatan admired the courageous and resourceful John Smith. By early 1609, however, Powhatan realized the threat the British presented to his people. In a meeting with Smith, Powhatan explained that initially he had believed that the British had come only to

Powhatan was the leader of a powerful confederacy at the time English colonists first arrived in Virginia. (Library of Congress)

trade, but that now it was clear that their ultimate intent was to possess the land.

Powhatan's response to this reality was to move his home deeper into the interior and to permit his warriors to engage in more intense fighting with the British. Although not continuous, the warfare intensified between 1609 and 1614. Pocahontas became one of the victims of the conflict when the British captured and held her hostage in 1613. Powhatan refused to meet their demands for a release of British prisoners and food, and he made no effort to free his favorite daughter. While a hostage, Pocahontas converted to the Anglican Church and married a planter, John Rolfe. Again, Powhatan did not protest, and he even sent a brother to attend the wedding.

Powhatan may not have wished to endanger his daughter with continued warfare, or he may have decided that recent battles had so weakened his confederacy that he could no longer successfully confront the British. It is likely that Powhatan was sincere when he told an Englishman in 1614 that he was now an old man who simply wanted to live out his life in peace. He got his wish. Until his death in April, 1618, there was little conflict between Indians and whites in Virginia.

See also Indian-white relations—English colonial; Opechancanough; Pocahontas; Powhatan Confederacy; Powhatan Wars.

Powhatan Confederacy

Tribes affected: Chickahominy, Gingaskin, Mattaponi, Nansemond, Nottoway, Pamunkey, Patawomeck (Potomac), Rappahannock, Weyanoke, Wiccocomicos, about twenty others

Culture area: Southeast
Language group: Algonquian
Primary location: Virginia

The American Indians who encountered the first permanent English colonists at Jamestown, Virginia, in 1607 were Powhatans. The name can be a source of confusion because it has at least four related but distinct meanings. First, it is applied collectively to those early seventeenth century Virginia tribes that acknowledged the leadership of a paramount chief. After 1607 this chief was generally called Powhatan by the English (though his personal name was Wahunsonacock). Powhatan was also the name of the chief's native village at the falls of the James River. (The term literally meant "at the falls.") Finally, the name is applied to the Algonquian dialects spoken by Powhatan's subjects.

The Powhatan tribes lived in eastern Virginia, between the Potomac River and the south bank of the James River. There were approximately thirty tribes or groups that acknowledged Powhatan's supremacy. Some of these (such as the Mattaponi, Pamunkey, and Rappahannock) survived into later centuries; most of the others (such as the Patawomecks, Weyanokes, and Wiccocomicos) did not.

Traditional Lifestyle. By the time of contact with the English, the Powhatans had evolved a settled way of life based on a mixed economy of agriculture and foraging. Powhatan tribes lived in villages located on the many creeks and rivers that fed into Chesapeake Bay. The men hunted and foraged for food, while the women were responsible for planting and harvesting corn and vegetables. The sexes enjoyed greater equality than existed in contemporary European society. Powhatan society was relatively stratified, with recognized ruling families in each village, as well as priests and military leaders, all ranking above the commoners. The political organization that had evolved by the time of contact was relatively elaborate. Each group had its own chief (or *weroance*), though all swore allegiance to Powhatan. Individual village chiefs were the lowest tier of authority. Though often styled a confederacy, Powhatan's polity is more accurately termed a paramount chiefdom because it was based on the subordination of its member tribes rather than their voluntary association. Powhatan was not an absolute ruler, however, and his power was greater over some tribes than others.

Contact with the English. Powhatan's life was changed forever by the arrival of the English in Virginia in 1607. While Indian assistance in the form of food and knowledge was essential to the colony's survival, a clash of cultures almost immediately ensued, and conflict became the dominant pattern. Wars were fought with the English in 1610-1613 under Powhatan's leadership and in 1622-1632 and 1644-1646 under Opechancanough, Powhatan's younger brother and successor as paramount chief. The second of the wars began with a surprise uprising that killed a quarter of Virginia's white population. Opechancanough was killed during the last of the wars, and thereafter the paramount chiefdom disintegrated.

An attempt was made, with English encouragement, to resurrect it in the 1670's under Cockacoeske, queen of the Pamunkeys. By this time, however, the Powhatan tribes that survived preferred dealing with the English on an individual basis. In 1677, treaties were made with the colony of Virginia in which several of the tribes accepted reservations. The Powhatans were clearly a civilization in decline. The combination of wars and European diseases had reduced their numbers from twelve thousand in 1607 to one thousand in 1700. Over time the Indians became increasingly acculturated. By the mid-eighteenth century, the Powhatan language had died out.

Modern Struggles. Despite a decimated population and social disorganization, the Virginia tribes that survived managed to maintain a strong sense of Indian identity. During the nineteenth and early twentieth centuries, they faced an uphill struggle to preserve it. To many white Virginians, the descendants of the Powhatans did not seem very "Indian": They spoke English, farmed, and dressed like other Virginians. Moreover, many had intermarried—with blacks as well as whites—in an era of increasing racial consciousness. The Gingaskin and Nottaway tribes (the latter a non-Algonquian group) agreed to termination in the early nineteenth century, and their reservation lands were divided among themselves. The Pamunkeys and Mattaponis hung onto their reservation lands, though at times with difficulty. The nonreservation tribes (such as the Rappahannocks, Nansemonds, and Chickahominies) had more problems maintaining separate identities and were not recognized by the state government as Indians. (Since the treaties governing Virginia's Indians were made long before American independence, the Virginia tribes never entered into a formal relationship with the United States government and lacked federal recognition as Indians.)

Probably the greatest difficulties for Virginia's Indians came during the era of racial segregation, when state authorities sought to treat Indians as they treated African Americans. Indians resisted, however, often wearing their straight hair long to display their physical distinctiveness. During World Wars I and II, reservation Indians were able to establish their claim to Indian status and thus served in white, rather than black, units.

The twentieth century witnessed a revival among Virginia tribes of Powhatan ancestry. The Pamunkey and Mattaponi continue to maintain their reservations, and nonreservation groups organized and sought formal recognition from the state. By 1990, five such groups had obtained state recognition: the Upper Mattaponi, the United Rappahanock, the Nansemond, the Chickahominy, and the Eastern Chickahominy. Organized legally as corporations, the nonreservation tribes adopted democratic governments that elected councils and chiefs. The reservation tribes by this time also had elected governments, though they limited participation in them to male reservation residents. —*William C. Lowe*

See also African American-American Indian relations; Algonquian language family; Indian-white relations—English colonial; Mattaponi; Nottaway; Opechancanough.

BIBLIOGRAPHY

Craven, Wesley Frank. *Red, White, and Black*. Charlottesville: University Press of Virginia, 1971.

Paredes, J. Anthony, ed. *Indians of the Southeastern United States in the Late Twentieth Century*. Tuscaloosa: University of Alabama Press, 1992.

Rountree, Helen C. *Pocahontas's People: The Powhatan Indians of Virginia Through Four Centuries*. Norman: University of Oklahoma Press, 1990.

_____., ed. *Powhatan Foreign Relations, 1500-1722*. Charlottesville: University Press of Virginia, 1993.

_____. *The Powhatan Indians of Virginia: Their Traditional Culture*. Norman: University of Oklahoma Press, 1989.

Williams, Walter L., ed. *Southeastern Indians Since the Removal Era*. Athens: University of Georgia Press, 1979.

Powhatan Wars

DATE: 1622-1646
PLACE: Virginia
TRIBES AFFECTED: Powhatan Confederacy
SIGNIFICANCE: Led by Opechancanough, the Powhatan Confederacy unsuccessfully attempted to drive English settlers from Virginia

The Powhatan tribes of the Chesapeake Bay region of Virginia had been at peace with the English settlers during the eight years prior to the outbreak of the Powhatan Wars. Powhatan, the chief of this confederacy of about nine thousand, had engaged the English in intermittent warfare from the time of their settlement of Jamestown in 1607. The combination of serious losses of warriors in those conflicts and the 1614 marriage of his daughter Pocahontas to English planter John Rolfe persuaded Powhatan to avoid further hostilities.

Upon Powhatan's death in 1618, his brother Opechancanough continued his policy of accommodation. Yet Opechancanough was alarmed at the continued expansion of English settlement on Powhatan land, and he resented the English efforts to assimilate his people into their culture. Consequently, he patiently planned a colony-wide uprising in the hope of driving the English from Virginia.

While often professing to the English his hopes for continued peace, Opechancanough negotiated with the almost thirty tribes in the Powhatan Confederacy to join in his proposed campaign. When the English murdered a highly regarded warrior and prophet named Nemattanow in early March, 1622, on suspicion of killing a white trader, Opechancanough realized that his enemies had presented him with an incident to rally his forces. In two weeks of visits with confederacy tribes, Opechancanough persuaded them to attack simultaneously on March 22.

The devastating strike claimed 347 lives, almost a third of the English population in Virginia. More would have died had not a Pamunkey servant informed his master, who, in turn, warned the main settlements in and around Jamestown, allowing them to prepare for the attack. In response, the English launched a vigorous counterattack, including military expeditions, the destruction of crops, and the burning of villages.

This struggle, which took more native lives than English, continued for a decade and ended with a truce in 1632.

Opechancanough ended the truce a dozen years later. Feeble and nearly blind—according to the English sources he was one hundred years old—the Powhatan leader once again persuaded confederation tribes to participate in a coordinated attack on English settlements. Beginning on April 18, 1644, the attack claimed nearly five hundred lives but proved less devastating to the English than the 1622 foray because there were now about eight thousand settlers in Virginia.

The fighting, which lasted for two years, effectively concluded with the English capture of Opechancanough. He was taken to Jamestown, where a guard killed him two weeks later. In October, 1646, the colonial assembly made peace with Opechancanough's successor, Necotowance. The treaty provided for a clear boundary between the two peoples, roughly along the York River. Neither side was to enter the other's territory without the colonial governor's permission.

The English victories in the Powhatan Wars virtually ended native opposition to English expansion in Virginia. The combination of two decades of warfare and disease took a heavy toll not only on the Powhatan Confederacy but also on all Virginia tribes. By 1670, there were only about seven hundred warriors in a total population of barely three thousand. Since the English population had grown to more than forty thousand, further resistance was futile.

See also Indian-white relations—English colonial; Opechancanough; Pocahontas; Powhatan; Powhatan Confederacy.

Pow-wows and contemporary celebrations

Tribes affected: Pantribal

Significance: American Indians, historically as well as currently, have placed great emphasis on ceremony and celebration, which often have religious significance and almost always involve music and dancing

Ancient and traditional tribal ceremonies are still held on reservations and other places in many areas of North America. In some cases they remain a serious and integral part of contemporary life; in others, they represent rather a means of remaining in touch with ancient cultural traditions. In still other cases, they may be performed primarily for tourists. In addition to those gatherings and events unique to individual contemporary tribes, many intertribal gatherings are held each year. Pow-wows generally include food, music, and dancing, as well as events such as dance competitions, and are often open for all to attend.

Religious Beliefs. Since so much of tribal ceremony is related to religious beliefs, it is essential to consider the current state of American Indians' religious beliefs and practices. The original inhabitants of North America had as diverse a culture as that of the Europeans or Asians, but there were certain beliefs that were nearly universal. There was a strong tie to the earth. Few Indian tribes considered the possibility that people could "own" land; on the contrary, they belonged to the land. There was a reverence for all life. Spirits lived in trees, in animals, in the sky, and the waterways.

In modern times a great many Indians have adopted Christianity, but with the exception of totally urbanized Indians who have no connection with their origins, there is always a mixture of the new and the old. In some of the more traditional tribal cultures, for example, when a person dies, two funerals will be held: one Christian, one tribal. As a general rule, non-Indians are excluded from the tribal rituals.

Song and Dance. Tribal ceremonies are intimately tied to singing and dancing. Both of these tend to be highly ritualized, often repeating cycles of songs and dances in specific sequence; a hundred or more individual dances and chants may be tied to a specific ceremony. The forms of all these songs and dances, like the religious beliefs they represent, are many and varied among the various Indian cultures, but they are largely concerned with the earth and the spirits that represent and control aspects of the land, sky, and water.

There are ceremonies and accompanying songs for hunters to gain control of animal spirits. There are elaborate rituals, songs, and dances involved in initiation into puberty and into priestly societies, as well as relating to births and deaths. There are rituals to encourage rain in desert areas and to appease the water gods in times of flooding, all with their elaborate dance steps and chanting cycles.

Potlatch and Pow-wow. Finally, some Indian ceremonies are not religious or are only tangentially religious in their intention. The Northwest potlatch, for example, is basically a party, sometimes planned years in advance, given with the intent of increasing the host's status among the tribe and surrounding tribes. A person of stature will call a potlatch, invite the people he wants (or needs) to impress, and give out a large number of gifts, thereby increasing his standing in the group.

"Pow-wow" is an English rendering of an old Algonquian word originally referring to the shamans widely termed "medicine men." It was later applied to the practice of religious ceremonies and then further broadened so that it means little more than a big gathering of people for a celebration. There are many such gatherings—to celebrate births, deaths, marriages, initiation ceremonies, changes of season, and many other aspects of life.

Generally, these gatherings are joyful, filled with singing, dancing, and feasting, and sometimes have religious significance. In many cases, Christianity has been worked into these ceremonies. Christmas, for example, is often celebrated with virtually the same ceremonies once used to celebrate the winter solstice.

Current Practice. The best place for non-Indians to see traditional Indian ceremonies may be the West, especially the Southwest. This is the area with the greatest number of Indian reservations, and the demonstration of tribal cultures has become a commercial enterprise. In the Northwest, especially in Alaska and in northwestern Canada, the old tribal traditions still exist, relatively untouched by white culture. Unfortunately, these areas tend to be difficult to reach; sometimes there are no roads, and the only alternatives for travel are bush planes and dogsleds.

—Marc Goldstein

Two girls waiting for their turns to dance at the Taos Pueblo Buffalo Pasture Pow-wow. (Elaine Querry)

See also Dances and dancing; Feasts; Music and song; Pan-Indianism; Potlatch; Religion; Rites of passage.

BIBLIOGRAPHY

Bancroft-Hunt, Norman. *People of the Totem.* New York: G. P. Putnam's Sons, 1979

Hudson, Charles. *The Southeastern Indians.* Knoxville: University of Tennessee Press, 1976.

Reichard, Gladys A. *Navaho Religion: A Study of Symbolism.* 2 vols. Princeton, N.J.: Princeton University Press, 1950.

Spencer, Robert F., Jesse D. Jennings, et al. *The Native Americans.* New York: Harper & Row, 1977.

Wissler, Clark. *Indians of the United States.* Garden City, N.Y.: Doubleday, 1966.

Praying Indians

TRIBE AFFECTED: Northeast Algonquian (Massachusetts)

SIGNIFICANCE: Seventeenth century Puritan missionaries urged Indian converts to Christianity to establish their own communities away from the influence of other, non-Christian Indians

John Eliot was a Puritan missionary involved with preaching to and converting Indians in the earliest British colonies in the "New World." Eliot himself was of a scholarly orientation, having learned the Algonquian dialect of the people he was working with to such an extent that he translated the entire Bible into their language.

Scholars debate the impact that Puritan missionaries had on the Algonquian tribes of the Northeast. Some suggest that the conversions were the creative and self-preserving response of a people who realized that their old lifestyle was gone forever, while others see it as the violent imposition of a foreign lifestyle on Native American tribes who were weakened by waves of disease that accompanied early European contact on the coasts of Canada and the United States.

However their conversions are now understood, as a number of Indians became converts, they were resettled in villages and towns to be separated from those of their tribes who did not convert to Christianity. The idea was to separate them from their cultural influences in order to train them more easily in the ways of "Christianity and civilization." In the Puritan mindset, work and productivity were measures of spiritual maturity, and thus the "civilizing" influence was explicitly seen as part of the message of Christianity.

In her analysis of the "praying Indian town" phenomenon, Elise Brenner stated that these praying towns were, in actuality, strongly akin to reservations. Furthermore, the goal of settling otherwise nomadic peoples made them easier to control and inculturate. As Brenner states, "Christian Indians . . . were part of the European long-term plan of establishing total colonial authority in New England."

Eliot experimented with a number of different styles of governance in his attempt to transform the "praying Indians" into proper European converts. For example, he borrowed a "Mosaic" code of governance taken from his interpretation of the Book of Exodus, which imposed "leaders of ten," over

whom were "leaders of fifty," who answered to "leaders of one hundred," with a court composed of "leaders of a thousand."

A full integration into European American society was never the goal of the praying town system. There was constant suspicion among the English settlers themselves, and funds were typically raised among Christians in England whose image of the work in the colonies was colored by the reports of missionary fundraisers. When it was seen that these praying Indians might be armed as a buffer between the European settlers and the hostile tribes further west, however, settler interest increased.

Recent scholarship has focused on the manner in which praying Indian towns were as much new expressions of Indian society and cultural values as they were a system imposed by European settlers. In fact, there was considerable self-governance and authority among the Indian converts, and many aspects of traditional society and creativity were maintained within the context of the newly proclaimed Christian faith. Indigenous expressions of Christianity, such as the continued use of native terminology to refer to God, were not unusual in these villages, although the use of native terms and concepts raised the suspicions of some missionaries who believed such "syncretism" to be unacceptable. Eliot himself was not above using whatever similarities he saw between native traditions and Christian conceptions.

When compared with more violent contacts between Europeans and Native Americans, the praying town phenomenon had certain humane features, and Eliot was certainly more informed of native language and culture than most settlers. Ultimately, however, the separation of Native Americans from their fellow tribal members must be seen as being part of the systematic destruction of native life that has occurred in American history.

See also Indian-white relations—English colonial; Massachusett; Missions and missionaries.

BIBLIOGRAPHY

Brenner, Elise. "To Pray or to Be Prey: Strategies for Cultural Autonomy of Massachusetts Praying Town Indians." *Ethnohistory* 27, no. 2 (1980): 135-152.

Eliot, John. *A Late and Further Manifestation of the Progress of the Gospel Amongst Indians in New-England.* London: J. Allen, 1655.

Jennings, Francis. "Goals and Functions of Puritan Missions to the Indians." *Ethnohistory* 18, no. 3 (1971): 197-212.

Salisbury, Neal. "Red Puritans: The 'Praying Indians' of Massachusetts Bay and John Eliot." *William and Mary Quarterly* 31, no. 1 (1974): 27-54.

Vaughan, Alden T. *New England Frontier: Puritans and Indians, 1620-1675.* Boston: Little, Brown, 1965.

Prehistory—Arctic

DATE: c. 10,000 B.C.E.-c. 1800 C.E.

LOCATION: Bering Strait land bridge (Beringia), northern Alaska, northern Canada, the Canadian Archipelago, Greenland

CULTURES AFFECTED: Aleut, Eskimo (Inuit)

The Arctic ordinarily is defined as the circumpolar region lying north of the treeline where the warmest temperature is below 10 degrees centigrade; it only roughly approximates the Arctic Circle. In the Western Hemisphere, the prehistoric Arctic culture area included the Bering Strait land bridge (Beringia), northern Alaska and northern Canada, the Canadian Archipelago, and most of Greenland. Next to the Antarctic, it was the last of the global niches in which humans made those adaptations essential to their survival, a process that had begun by 10,000 B.C.E.

Serious archaeological research into the Western Hemisphere Arctic began in the 1920's with the work of Knud Rasmussen, Kaj Birket-Smith, and Terkel Mathiassen. It bared the outlines of a whale-hunting Eskimo culture named Thule, the origins of which lay in Alaska, where a Paleo-Arctic tradition dated to 10,000 B.C.E. In 1925, archaeologist Diamond Jenness unearthed evidence of a hitherto unknown Arctic culture, since called Dorset, that predated the Thule tradition. A rapid extension of Arctic research after 1945 by Helge Larsen, Jorgen Meldgaard, J. Louis Giddings, William Taylor, and Elmer Harp, Jr., among others, broadened knowledge of Thule and Dorset cultures. They and other researchers also provided evidence of a pre-Dorset culture that spread across the northern, central, and eastern Arctic during postglacial warming periods and discovered an Arctic Small Tool tradition as well. By the 1990's, the Arctic prehistoric cultural sequence—as defined by archaeological findings—proceeded from Paleo-Arctic (10,000 B.C.E.-6000 B.C.E.), to the Arctic Small Tool tradition (4200 B.C.E.-3100 B.C.E.), to pre-Dorset (4500 B.C.E.-c.1300 B.C.E.) to Dorset (700 B.C.E.-1000 C.E.), to Thule (100-c.1800). Note that there are gaps as well as periods during which traditions overlap. These historically related traditions underlay more recent Aleut and Eskimo cultures and undoubtedly had still more ancient origins in Asia.

See also Aleut; Arctic; Beringia; Dorset; Inuit; Thule.

Prehistory—California

DATE: c. 8000 B.C.E.-c. 1600 C.E.
LOCATION: California and northernmost Baja California
CULTURES AFFECTED: Achumawi, Atsugewi, Cahuilla, Chemehuevi, Chumash, Costanoan, Cupeño, Diegueño, Esselen, Fernandeño, Gabrielino, Hupa, Juaneño, Kamia, Karok, Luiseño, Maidu, Mattole, Miwok, Patwin, Pomo, Quechan, Salinan, Serrano, Shasta, Tolowa, Tubatulabal, Wailaki, Wappo, Wintun, Wiyot, Yahi, Yokuts, Yuki, Yurok

The prehistory and ethnology of California's Indian societies significantly contribute to understanding the hunting-gathering cultures in rich and varied environments. Although archaeological findings that are conjectural (and controversial) have placed Paleo-Indian cultures in California as early as 50,000 B.C.E., hard evidence confirms their existence there by 8000 B.C.E. Such evidence consists of Clovis points—fluted stone projectile points used in big-game hunting—discovered throughout present-day California in at least eleven archaeological sites, among them Borax Lake, Lake Mojave, Tulare

Lake, China Lake, Pinto Basin, Tiefort Basin, and Ebbetts Pass. In addition to Clovis points, other artifacts have been found at many of these digs, including hammer stones; cutting, scraping, chopping, and engraving tools; other projectile points; awls; charms; shell beads; and atlatl (throwing) hooks. At sites in central and Northern California, such artifacts have been located amid the remains of mammoths, giant bison, camels, horses, deer, elk, seal, small land animals, fish, and birds. Cemeteries with human remains in the Sacramento Valley attest the sedentary occupations and lengthy settlements that characterized a number of diverse and complex prehistory communities. Overall, these California communities have been grouped by archaeologists and ethnographers into four broad cultural provinces that roughly coincide with California's major environmental features: Northwest Pacific, Central-trans-Sierran, Southern Coastal, and Southern Desert. Archaeologists estimate the population of prehistoric California at between 300,000 and 350,000 people, comprising nearly five hundred distinct communities and ethnic groups.

See also Arts and crafts—California; California; Clovis; Hunting and gathering; Projectile points.

Prehistory—Great Basin

DATE: c. 9500 B.C.E.-c. 1800 C.E.
LOCATION: Central and southern Oregon, eastern California, Nevada, Utah
CULTURES AFFECTED: Bannock, Gosiute, Kawaiisu, Mono, Paiute, Shoshone, Ute, Walapai, Washoe

In the Great Basin, which included portions of present-day central and southern Oregon, eastern California, Nevada, and much of Utah, prehistoric Native Americans confronted the most rigorous environment they encountered anywhere. The region's prehistorical importance, therefore, stems from archaeological evidence that indicates the adaptations made by the ancestors of more than a dozen major tribes to this difficult environment. Archaeological discoveries at Tule Springs, Nevada, suggest that parts of the Great Basin may have been occupied by Pleistocene peoples by 26,000 B.C.E., while other findings in south-central Oregon suggest human occupancy by 11,200 B.C.E. These dates are highly controversial, however; uncontroverted evidence places earliest human occupancy of the region at between 9500 B.C.E. and 9000 B.C.E., particularly evidence of the presence of Clovis people, whom archaeologists now believe to have been widespread in the Great Basin as well as the rest of the West by those dates.

Major archaeological discoveries, among a number confirming this, are located at the C. W. Harris site in San Diego, California; Gypsum Cave and Fallon, Nevada; Fort Rock Cave, Oregon; Death Valley, Owens Lake, and Tulare Lake, California; and Danger Cave, Deadman, Promontory, and Black Rock caves in Utah. Throughout most of the Great Basin, early peoples formed small nomadic groups that foraged for lake plants and animals. In environmentally favored sections of the Basin, village life developed and lasted for several millennia. Contacts among regional groups appear to have been frequent, and trade was sophisticated. Artifacts from throughout the Great Basin include a rich variety of projectile points, knives, scrapers, milling stones, coiled basketry, cloths, moccasins, jars, and appliqued pottery.

See also Arts and crafts—Great Basin; Clovis; Danger Cave; Great Basin; Hunting and gathering.

Prehistory—Northeast

DATE: c. 9000 B.C.E.-c. 1600 C.E.

LOCATION: Connecticut, Delaware, Illinois, Indiana, Kentucky, Maine, Massachusetts, Michigan, New Hampshire, New Jersey, New York, Ohio, Pennsylvania, Rhode Island, Vermont, West Virginia, Wisconsin (United States); New Brunswick, Nova Scotia, southern Ontario, southern Quebec (Canada)

CULTURES AFFECTED: Abenaki, Adena, Algonquin, Erie, Fox, Hopewell, Huron, Illinois, Iroquois, Kickapoo, Lenni Lenape, Mahican, Maliseet, Massachusett, Menominee, Miami, Micmac, Mohawk, Nanticoke, Narragansett, Neutral, Old Copper, Ottawa, Owasca, Passamaquoddy, Pequot, Petun, Potawatomi, Sauk, Shawnee, Susquehannock, Tuscarora, Wampanoag, Winnebago, Woodland

The Northeast Woodlands region was the heartland of the forebears of the Algonquian linguistic family. Evidence suggests that Iroquoian speakers have also lived there for thousands of years.

Paleo-Eastern Woodlanders used stone tools and foraged for small game and seasonal plants. Grit-tempered, cord-marked pottery dates from 2500 B.C.E., and fiber-tempered pottery appeared at about 500 B.C.E. Evidence suggests the Adena cultural influence from about 1000 B.C.E. and then Hopewell mound cultural influences from the beginning of the millennium entered the Northeast. After 500 C.E., the region was the recipient of migrations from Caddoan-speaking or Siouan-speaking people of the Mississippian mound cultures. The most important influence on the area two thousand years ago was the agricultural culture associated with Iroquoian-speaking people, who emerged from an archaeological complex called Owasco. It was the Owasco who began to create tribal units and to cultivate crops, returning to agricultural sites year after year simply because certain crops grew well in certain soils and zones.

Native seeds such as squash and bottle gourds have been gathered and planted by paleo-Indians of the Northeast Woodlands for four thousand years. Local economies based on the slash-and-burn agriculture of many native crops had evolved by about 100 C.E. It was only around 800 C.E. that maize (corn) was introduced, probably from the Southwest. It may have been the introduction of corn throughout the continent that lessened the religious influence of the mound-building culture called Hopewell. The cultivation of corn and corn's concomitant mythologies loosened the religious hold Hopewell thought had on the Northeast.

The Northeast Woodlands have long had cultural interchanges with other areas, and this area was the focus of migratory movement from the Great Lakes, the Ohio River valley, and the Eastern shore routes for thousands of years, setting the stage for the arrival of Europeans in the 1600's.

See also Adena; Arts and crafts—Northeast; Corn; Hopewell; Indian-white relations—Norse; Mounds and mound builders; Northeast; Old Copper culture.

BIBLIOGRAPHY

Jennings, Jesse D. *Prehistory of North America*. New York: McGraw-Hill, 1968.

Newcomb, William. *North American Indians: An Anthropological Perspective*. Pacific Palisades, Calif.: Goodyear, 1974.

Prehistory—Northwest Coast

DATE: c. 9500 B.C.E.-c. 1800 C.E.

LOCATION: From Yakutat Bay in southern Alaska to Cape Mendocino in Northern California

CULTURES AFFECTED: Bella Coola, Chehalis, Chinook, Coast Salish, Coos, Haida, Hupa, Karok, Klamath, Klikitat, Kwakiutl, Nootka, Quinault, Takelma, Tillamook, Tlingit, Tsimshian, Wiyot, Yurok

The Northwest Coast culture area extends from the modern regions of Yakutat Bay in southern Alaska south to Cape Mendocino in Northern California. It has a rugged coastline with many deep inlets. In the northern half, mountains rise several thousand feet directly from the edge of salt water. There are numerous small islands offshore, but there are few beaches or low-level areas convenient for village sites.

Natural History. Climatic conditions along this coastal strip are characterized by even temperatures and heavy rainfall (up to one hundred inches a year in many places). The abundant rainfall and moderate temperature of the region produce a distinctive and dense vegetation. Forests extend from the Pacific shoreline to near the highest ridges of the major river drainage systems, such as the Columbia, Fraser, and Skeena rivers.

As one goes southward, the terrain changes from towering mountains of raw, naked rock cut by deep canyons gouged out by glacial flow and watercourse turbulence to, around upper Puget Sound and along the Oregon and northwestern California coasts, steep but rounded coastal hills and estuaries resulting from the buildup of sand bars formed at the river mouths.

In prehuman times, wildlife and game of all sorts were unimaginably plentiful. In fact, the extreme abundance of natural resources in this culture area later gave rise to a high degree of civilization without the emergence of agriculture. Maritime, estuarine, and riverine resources were the mainstays that provided an ample foundation for the building of prehistoric human cultures.

The sea and the forests, even today, are the most important providers of sustenance. Fishing and sea mammal hunting required an intricate extraction technology that allowed the first human hunter-gatherers, after their arrival thousands of years ago, to harvest and use the available natural resources to the fullest extent. This required each community to develop the complex tools and skills necessary to ensure their individual success among the many diverse communities that eventually developed in, and occupied, the region.

Archaeological History. Archaeological research has been undertaken in this culture area since the late 1800's. Sites such as those discovered at Port Hammond, Marpole, Vancouver, Yakutat, Graham Island, and the more recent Montague Harbor have revealed numerous peoples, languages, and communities of great biological and cultural diversity.

This culture area is thought to have been inhabited initially by maritime peoples, with highly developed Stone Age technology, and mobile cultures, who could have come from many directions. Athapaskan, Salish, and Penutian speakers were subdivided into more than a hundred communities and dialects, spread from one end of the area to the other, which have provided modern researchers with a wealth of artifacts and information.

Northwest Coast studies entered a new phase with the 1970 discovery of water-saturated "wet" sites, where immersion of material remains below the water table and the lack of oxygen prevents vegetal decay. Sites at Ozette and Prince Rupert are particularly notable for the sophisticated methods of study used in both field and laboratory work.

Radiocarbon dating and other scientific techniques indicate constant occupation of this culture area since at least ten thousand years ago. Localized tribal creation stories suggest that peoples have always existed in their lands. If prehistoric peoples did indeed migrate into the area, linguistic and genetic distribution suggests that they could have come from such diverse places as Siberia (traveling across the Bering Strait land bridge), northeastern China (traversing the exposed continental shelf), or even from Polynesia (boating across the South Pacific) to Mexico or Central America, then as far northward along the coastline as the Columbia River basin.

Various basal cultures have been defined by their remains through a wide variety of descriptive means. Early boreal and protowestern cultures, microblade and pebble tool traditions, and stemmed point and fluted point traditions are all names commonly used to describe these early prehistoric cultures. It is generally thought that the diversity of peoples can best be explained through a combination of migration, diffusion, and adaptation.

—Michael W. Simpson

See also Architecture—Northwest Coast; Arts and crafts—Northwest Coast; Beringia; Dating methods; Northwest Coast; Ozette.

BIBLIOGRAPHY

Borden, Charles E. *Origins and Development of Early Northwest Coast Culture to About 3000 B.C.* Ottawa: National Museums of Canada, 1975.

Cressman, Luther S. *The Sandal and the Cave: The Indians of Oregon.* Corvallis: Oregon State University Press, 1981.

Drucker, Phillip. *Indians of the Northwest Coast.* Garden City, N.Y.: Natural History Press, 1963.

_____. "Sources of Northwest Coast Culture," In *New Interpretations of Aboriginal American Culture History.* Seventy-fifth anniversary volume of the Anthropological Society of Washington. Seattle: Anthropological Society of Washington, 1955.

Fladmark, Knut R. "The Feasibility of the Northwest as a Migration Route for Early Man." In *Early Man from a Circum-Pacific Perspective,* edited by Alan Bryan. University of Alberta Department of Anthropology Occasional Papers 1. Edmonton, Alberta: Archaeological Researchers International, 1978.

_____. "The Patterns of the Culture." In *Indians of the North Pacific Coast,* edited by Tom McFeat. Seattle: University of Washington Press, 1966.

Prehistory—Plains

DATE: c. 9500 B.C.E.-c. 1800 C.E.

LOCATION: Western Canada and United States

CULTURES AFFECTED: Apache of Oklahoma, Arapaho, Arikara, Assiniboine, Atsina, Blackfoot, Caddo, Cheyenne, Comanche, Crow, Hidatsa, Iowa, Kansa (Kaw), Kiowa, Mandan, Missouri, Omaha, Osage, Oto, Pawnee, Ponca, Quapaw, Sarsi, Sioux, Tonkawa, Waco, Wichita

The prehistory of the Great Plains begins with evidence of nomadic Paleo-Indian bands at around 9500 to 9000 B.C.E. These groups arrived before the end of the Pleistocene epoch and took advantage of herds of large mammals, such as mammoth, giant bison, camels, and horses, that have since become extinct (the horse was not reintroduced until the sixteenth century). It ends with the proto-historic period, when Spanish and other European explorers contacted agricultural village peoples and mobile bison hunting groups in the sixteenth through nineteenth centuries.

The earliest Paleo-Indian populations utilized large, bifacial, fluted Clovis points for hunting mammoth. They captured the animals by chasing them into natural traps, such as stream heads or lakes, where females and immature animals were the most likely to be killed. Artifacts such as bifacial scrapers, choppers, worked flakes, and a variety of bone tools were used for butchering and processing hides. Sites of this period, known mainly from the southern and western Plains, include both kill sites and quarries for stone. Examples include Miami (Texas), Blackwater Draw Number 1 (New Mexico), Dent (Colorado), Domebo (Oklahoma), and Colby (Wyoming). No campsites, burials, or remains of dwellings have been discovered for this period.

Around 9000 B.C.E. Clovis points were replaced by unfluted points known as Plainview, shorter fluted points known as Folsom, and other successive styles such as Firstview, Midland, Agate Basin, Hell Gap, Albert, and Cody. The Hell Gap (Wyoming) site provides a long record for bison hunters in the form of a series of temporary campsites that are chronologically transitional between Clovis and Folsom. The hunting of large herds of bison was a Plains tradition for thousands of years, and Folsom culture was based on the nomadic hunting of the giant precursors to modern buffalo, such as *Bison antiquus* and *Bison occidentalis*. These animals were stalked in small groups or killed in large numbers by stampeding herds off cliffs, into ditches, or into traps. Large hunts, which provided abundant supplies of meat, may have required the cooperative efforts of several bands working together. At Olsen-Chubbuck, a site in eastern Colorado, almost two hundred bison were killed and slaughtered. Bones indicate systematic butchering and selective use of choice animal parts. Several sites, such as Lindenmeier (Texas), suggest regular use by nomadic groups from year to year.

The Paleo-Indian way of life, based on large-game hunting, was transformed around 6000 B.C.E. by the end of the Pleistocene and the extinction of species such as *Bison antiquus*. Projectile point styles such as Agate Basin were followed by styles of the Plano tradition, such as Scottsbluff, Milnesand, Portales, and Eden. These were utilized by the last of the big-game hunters until around 5000 B.C.E.

Archaic Period. Between around 5000 and 2500 B.C.E., both human and animal populations in the Plains regions were affected by a period of warmer and drier climates known as the Altithermal period. During this period, reduction of grasslands and water sources resulted in smaller, more highly dispersed human groups. The archaeological evidence of this period is scarce compared with that for earlier and later periods. Sites of this period consist mostly of temporary campsites. When bison were hunted, they belonged to the smaller, modern species *Bison bison*. There is evidence for local experimentation with fiber-tempered pottery in the central Plains around 3000 B.C.E., but this technology does not become important until a much later time.

Among the sites that have provided an understanding of this tradition is Mummy Cave (Wyoming), where thirty-eight distinct cultural levels bore evidence of a hunting and gathering lifestyle oriented to mountain resources between 7300 B.C.E. and 1580 C.E. By 2500 B.C.E., people living in the cave used milling stones, tubular bone pipes, coiled basketry, and fiber cordage. Sites from between 2500 B.C.E. and about 100 C.E. suggest a continuation of the pattern of small groups of nomadic foragers. These groups moved across the landscape in conjunction with the seasonal availability of plant and animal resources, collecting seeds, roots, nuts, and berries when they were in season and doing occasional hunting of bison.

Woodland Period. The Woodland tradition in the Plains begins with the widespread use of pottery. During the Early Woodland period, the eastern Plains were inhabited by semisedentary villages of incipient agriculturalists. The year-round occupation of settlements resulted from a combination of increasing sedentism by earlier peoples and the colonization of portions of the central Plains by village cultures from farther east via fertile river valleys.

Although there is no evidence for maize farming until around 500 C.E., by 250 B.C.E. Plains peoples were experimenting with sunflower, chenopodium, squash, and marsh elder. Ceramic styles of eastern Kansas and western Missouri suggest participation in the larger "Hopewell Interaction Sphere," through which maize may have been introduced during the latter part of this period.

In the vicinity of Kansas City, Hopewellian villages approached 4 hectares (10 acres) in area. Among the new features associated with them were earth-covered burial mounds with stone chambers, usually built on the tops of bluffs. Houses were more substantial, sometimes marked with oblong patterns of postholes. The pottery of this period includes cord-marked and rocker-stamped wares with shapes and decorations similar to Early Woodland styles of the eastern United States. Other Hopewell markers include platform pipes. Maize and beans were cultivated, and large-stemmed or corner-notched projectile points were used for hunting deer and bison.

Burial mounds of the late Plains Woodland and early Plains Village periods are found throughout the eastern Dakotas and in southern Manitoba. Frequently grouped, these were usually situated on bluffs overlooking lakes and valleys. Their forms consisted of low, circular and oblong shapes as well as long, linear embankments. Burials with pottery vessels were placed in timber-covered pits below or within mounds.

In the northwestern and southern Plains, there was a persistence of mobile Archaic patterns. A number of sites indicate the continued practice of communal bison hunts. It is likely that bison hunters were in contact with village farmers, exchanging meat, hides, and other products for cultivated foods.

Plains Village Period. The Late Woodland, beginning around 900 C.E., is marked by an increased reliance on the cultivation of maize in alluvial river valleys. In eastern Kansas there is evidence that suggests contact with Mississippian cultures (probably via canoe along the Missouri River) and the possible existence of trading colonies. Plains Village cultures may have been trading buffalo meat and hides with their neighbors to the east. Among the most characteristic bone artifacts of Plains Village culture is the bison scapula hoe. Ceramics of this period were typically cord-roughened. Some pottery from sites of this period in the vicinity of Kansas City display "sunburst" motifs and other designs reminiscent of the Mississippian culture at the large temple mound village at Cahokia, Illinois.

There was a wide variability in cultures of the Plains at this time. In the central Plains, the best-documented cultures are the Upper Republican, Nebraska, Smoky Hill, and Pomona. Characteristic house types included rectangular earth lodges with four central posts supporting timber roofs covered with soil. Earth lodge villages ranged in size from about fifty to one hundred people. Along the middle Missouri River in the Dakotas, villages of as many as three hundred people were surrounded by ditches and palisades.

Maize was one of the principal cultigens of the Plains Village tradition. A characteristic agricultural implement of this period was the bison scapula hoe. Hunting of bison, deer, and antelope was undertaken with bows and arrows tipped with small, triangular, side-notched points. Fishing in rivers was done with bone hooks and harpoons. Animal products such as hides and bones were intensively utilized by Plains Village peoples. Sites have yielded a wide variety of bone implements, including needles, pins, punches, and flaking tools. Shell ornaments were common. In the Upper Republican and Nebraska phases, fine stone and ceramic pipes, occasionally decorated with human or animal effigies, were among the most important ceremonial items.

Large villages in the east were clearly affected by the contact with complex societies of the eastern Missouri and central Mississippi valleys. In the northwestern and southern Plains, however, ancient patterns of mobile foraging and bison hunting still continued. Nomadic bison hunters traded with both the Plains Village peoples to the east and the Pueblo peoples of northern New Mexico and southern Colorado.

Between 1400 and 1500 C.E., a culture known as the Lower Loup phase appeared along the banks of the Loup and Platte rivers in eastern Nebraska. Their earthlodge villages were substantially larger than earlier settlements, sometimes covering an area of 100 acres, and were often fortified. In central Kansas, the contemporaneous Great Bend culture was characterized by large agricultural villages that were occupied at the time of the first European incursions, as evidenced by fragments of Spanish armor. In the Middle Missouri region, the proto-historic period is represented by villages with circular house foundations that were probably occupied by the agricultural ancestors of the historic Mandan, Hidatsa, and Arikara peoples. In the far western and northwestern Plains, the mobile bison hunting pattern that had begun at least ten thousand years earlier persisted into the nineteenth century, but it was aided by the introduction of the horse. The historic heirs to this tradition, whose ancestors may never have participated in agricultural Plains Village patterns, are tribes such as the Blackfoot, Arapaho, and Assiniboine.

The first Spanish to arrive in the Great Plains included Francisco Vásquez de Coronado, who in 1541 traveled north in search of a kingdom known to him as "Gran Quivira." Reaching central Kansas, he was disappointed to discover settled Great Bend villages with little gold. Nevertheless, it is clear that the indigenous peoples of the Plains share a rich and ancient cultural history. *—John Hoopes*

See also Archaic; Architecture—Plains; Arts and crafts—Plains; Buffalo; Clovis; Corn; Earthlodge; Folsom; Hunting and gathering; Paleo-Indian; Pipestone Quarries; Plains; Woodland.

BIBLIOGRAPHY

Adair, Mary J. *Prehistoric Agriculture in the Central Plains.* University of Kansas Publications in Anthropology 16. Lawrence: University Press of Kansas, 1988.

Bamforth, Douglas B. *Ecology and Human Organization on the Great Plains.* New York: Plenum Press, 1988.

Frison, George C. *Prehistoric Hunters of the High Plains.* 2d ed. San Diego: Academic Press, 1991.

Wedel, Waldo C. *Central Plains Prehistory: Holocene Environments and Culture Change in the Republican River Basin.* Lincoln: University of Nebraska Press, 1986.

_____. "The Prehistoric Plains." In *Ancient North Americans,* edited by Jesse D. Jennings. San Francisco: W. H. Freeman, 1983.

Prehistory—Plateau

DATE: c. 9500 B.C.E.-c. 1800 C.E.
LOCATION: British Columbia, eastern Oregon, Idaho, Washington
CULTURES AFFECTED: Plateau tribes, including Coeur d'Alene, Flathead, Nez Perce, Spokane, Yakima

The Plateau culture area is enclosed between the Cascade mountain range to the west and the even higher northern Rockies to the east. The area is very dry; it is closely related to the Great Basin, but its dryness is tempered somewhat by its more northerly location (and therefore cooler temperatures) and the presence of two major river systems, the Columbia and the Fraser.

Alone among all the major regions of the United States, the Plateau does not show any evidence of the fluted Clovis points. Instead, at Lind Coulee in southeastern Washington, non-fluted spear points dated to 9500 B.C.E. have been found. This possibly indicates the hunting of a variety of Ice Age and modern large animals.

Around 9000 B.C.E., life changed at The Dalles in Oregon (a Columbia River site) with the advent of salmon fishing, which would continue to be a major part of the Plateau diet until this century. Salmon may have supplied as much as half of the food, because it could be dried and stored for long periods. Other items used included birds, mussels, rabbits, beaver, and numerous types of roots and bulbs. This would indicate that the western Archaic form of life, known as the Desert culture farther south, could have begun in this region. Scholars disagree about the similarity of the cultures of the Plateau and the Great Basin. Some have seen very little difference, based on similar tools, moccasins, and folklore. Others feel that the availability of salmon created a much more sedentary lifestyle for the Plateau tribes.

By 5000 B.C.E., Plateau peoples were making grinding stones and living in pit houses, and by 4000 B.C.E., pit house villages existed in the Snake River Valley of Idaho. Well-made, leaf-shaped points were being used to hunt deer, elk, and pronghorn antelope to supplement the river's resources.

Contact with the outside led to changes. Algonquian-speaking peoples appeared about 1000 B.C.E., and with them came the use of ground-stone tools including mauls, pestles, atlatl weights, fish gorges, and tubular pipes, as well as animal sculptures. Contact with the northwestern coastal cultures along the Columbia and Fraser river valleys led to the final culture phase, called Piqunin. After 1300 C.E., Plateau peoples lived in villages of five to ten earthlodges in the sheltered canyons of the rivers, which often were ten degrees warmer than the surrounding winter countryside. Here they hunted deer and fished for salmon, which they preserved by drying. In the spring and fall, they set up temporary camps in the smaller canyons and uplands to collect canas and kous roots, along with berries, and to hunt larger game.

Plateau peoples were some of the last to come into direct contact with Europeans, with first known encounters being with the Alexander Mackenzie expedition of 1793, along the

Fraser River, and the Lewis and Clark expedition, when it reached the Columbia River and its tributaries in 1805.

See also Archaic; Architecture—Plateau; Arts and crafts—Plateau; Desert culture; Hunting and gathering; Plateau; Prehistory—Great Basin.

Prehistory—Southeast

Date: c. 9500 B.C.E.-c. 1600 C.E.

Location: Southeastern North America

Cultures affected: Alabama, Atakapa, Biloxi, Caddo, Calusa, Catawba, Cherokee, Chickasaw, Chitimacha, Choctaw, Coushatta, Creek, Hasinai, Hitchiti, Mobile, Natchez, Pensacola, Seminole, Timucua, Tuskegee, Yamasee

The prehistory of the Southeast may be divided into five basic periods: Paleo-Indian, Archaic, Early and Middle Woodland, Mississippian, and Later Woodland Tribal.

The first known inhabitants of the Southeastern region were Clovis culture Paleo-Indians who arrived about 9500 B.C.E. following the herd of mammoths. They were efficient hunters, and by 9000 B.C.E., aided by a warming climate, they had killed all the mammoths. They were replaced by the bighorn bison specialists known as Folsom. Adopting the atlatl (or spearthrower), they moved in smaller bands but still in a nomadic manner. Local variations of nomadic big-game hunters, including the Cumberland, harvested a variety of large animals until approximately 8000 B.C.E. One of the oldest Indian skeletons was found at Little Salt Spring in southern Florida, dated at 9000 B.C.E.

At approximately 8000 B.C.E., a transition was made to the Archaic culture. For 6,500 years, or more than half of the entire period of human occupation, the Archaic peoples dominated the Southeast. Spread over eons of time and a large region, there were many variations of the culture. All showed a mastery of hunting and gathering and effective adaptation to life in the river and stream bottoms of a wet area. They hunted white-tailed deer, buffalo, rabbit, squirrel, and ducks and other birds. They became the first fishers of the area, specializing in catfish in many areas. They also gathered the abundant wild plant matter. From the first, they wandered less, and by 4500 B.C.E. they had settled down to centralized movement based on two homes: one on the stream and one nearby in the hill country. This brought about a population explosion. By 2500 B.C.E., pottery had reached the Savannah River area, from where it slowly spread throughout the Southeast. In 1700 B.C.E., the Poverty Point culture appeared in northern Louisiana; it probably consisted of migrants from Mexico. They brought elaborate villages, small-scale agriculture, and jade-working.

Combined with influences from the north, Poverty Point led to the Early Woodland phase. The most noticeable factor in Early Woodland is the appearance of a cult of the dead, with its burial mounds filled with grave goods. By 1 C.E., improved agriculture had led to the much more elaborate Middle Woodland, with hundreds of oval and circular burial mounds. Their grave goods included copper from Lake Superior, obsidian

from the Rockies, and soapstone from Minnesota, indicating both a long-range trading system and excellent craftsmanship. After 400 C.E., Middle Woodland declined from overpopulation, too much violence, local goods competing with the imported, and perhaps other causes.

About 800 C.E., the climactic Mississippian culture emerged to dominate most of the Southeast, except Virginia and Florida, until 1600. Based on an elaborate maize, beans, and squash agriculture (with fields often running for miles along river bottoms), they developed city-states such as Moundville, Alabama; Mound Bottom, Tennessee; Etowah and Okmulgee, Georgia; and Natchez, Mississippi; all of which were centered on mound towns. Mound towns were temple mounds on which were built religious and governmental centers and possibly homes for the prominent. They were a highly stratified society led by priest-rulers and a nobility. After 1200, the Southern Death Cult imported from Mexico dominated religion. Art reached its pre-white climax in pottery, statuary, and shell-work.

The Mississippians dominated the Southeast when Hernando De Soto traveled the region from 1539-1543, but they had disappeared from everywhere but Natchez by the early 1600's. European diseases are often blamed for their downfall, but it is also known that Moundville split up from overpopulation. The Mississippians were replaced by the Cherokee, Choctaw, Creek, and Chickasaw, as well as many other tribes, by the time of white entry in the early 1600's.

See also Archaic; Architecture—Southeast; Arts and crafts—Southeast; Etowah; Key Marco; Mississippian; Mounds and mound builders; Moundville; Paleo-Indian; Poverty Point; Southeast; Southern Cult; Spiro; Woodland.

Prehistory—Southwest

Date: c. 10,000 B.C.E.-c. 1540 C.E.

Location: New Mexico, Arizona, southern Utah, southern Colorado

Cultures affected: Anasazi, Hohokam, Mogollon

Archaeologists have determined that the first people in the Southwest were nomadic hunting and gathering peoples who drifted into the region in small groups in the late Pleistocene period. These people, known in archaeological literature as the Cochise, had minimal tools and equipment, although some of their stone implements were expertly flaked into beautiful spear points and knives. There are several different groups of these "early man points," which are identified by the localities where they were first discovered: Folsom, Sandia, and Clovis.

Near the pueblo of Santa Ana, evidence has been found of a semipermanent camping ground dating back to the Cochise. Apparently, game was abundant in this area and water was available from several springs. Artifacts found here include a number of stone tools such as knives, scrapers, drills, choppers, points, and grinding implements. These grinding tools, which indicate that the Cochise supplemented their meat diet with seeds and wild grains, consisted of a large, irregular stone with a shallow, concave area in which seeds or grains were placed and a smaller, rounded stone with which the grinding was done. These crude grinding stones ultimately developed into the metate-mano combination which allowed the later agriculturists in the region to prepare corn.

Development of Agriculture. Over a period of centuries, the Cochise evolved from a nomadic society into several different cultures that were primarily agricultural and sedentary. The major stimulus for this change was the introduction of corn into the region. Corn had been grown in Mexico since about 7000 B.C.E., and over time new genetic strains more resistant to cold and drought were developed, which made it a viable crop for the Southwest. By about 300 B.C.E., the Cochise had settled down to farming and village life, and by circa 300 C.E., three major agricultural groups had materialized: Hohokam, Mogollon, and Anasazi. All three of these cultures depended on the "sacred triad" of corn, beans, and squash for their subsistence. They practiced simple farming methods, with the digging and planting stick as their principal tool. Agriculture and an accompanying interest in the weather eventually led the three cultures to the development of religious and ceremonial practices by which they hoped to influence nature in their favor.

With the possible exception of the Hohokam, who appeared in southern Arizona along the Gila River in the third century B.C.E., the agriculturalists of the Southwest were indigenous. It was a situation of a people adopting new ideas and developing a new way of life rather than of migrants coming into the area with a new, ready-made culture. Many scholars believe that the Hohokam came from Mexico, although no geographical area of origin has been identified. If, on the other hand, the Hohokam evolved from the Cochise, as did the Mogollon and Anasazi, it is certain that they were an important conduit for influences from the cultures in Mexico to come into the Southwest.

Of the three prehistoric groups, the Mogollon in the mountains of southern New Mexico were the first to cultivate corn and first to have the bow and arrow, probably having acquired both from cultures in Mexico. The Mogollon were never a cohesive society, perhaps because of the rugged terrain along the Little Colorado River where they lived. Their culture consisted of scattered groups of small villages which, while sharing certain basic traits, were characterized nevertheless by many regional differences.

The Hohokam are generally divided into two main groups: the Desert and the Riverine. The Desert Hohokam, the smaller

Pueblo Bonito ruins at Chaco Canyon, New Mexico. Chaco Canyon was inhabited by the Anasazi, and it has been estimated that two thousand to four thousand people once lived in the area. (Museum of New Mexico)

group, did not settle near streams and so were less successful agriculturally. The Riverine Hohokam built villages along rivers and developed an extensive irrigation system consisting of many miles of canals constructed with rudimentary hand tools. The building of these canals, each of which served several villages, required a high degree of social and political organization as well as effective intercommunity cooperation.

The Anasazi, who lived in the high plateau country of the Four Corners area, apparently acquired corn from the Mogollon. Their first farming methods were extremely crude compared to the other two cultures, but they were such a vigorous, dynamic, and creative people that they soon surpassed their neighbors to the south and were farming the mesa tops as well as the valleys, using irrigation systems of their own design.

Housing. Early in their development, all three prehistoric cultures constructed permanent dwellings known as pit houses. Generally, this was simply a shallow pit dug into the ground, lined with rocks or logs to prevent the sides from collapsing inward, and then covered with a roof made of slim branches and twigs with several inches of mud on top.

The Mogollon pit house was circular, with a single center post to support a conical roof and a short, sloping ramp on one side which served as an entryway. A hole in the center of the roof provided a vent for the fire pit.

The Hohokam pit house was a rectangular hole about 30 feet long with an entire structure built inside it, using the "wattle-and-daub" method, which consisted of small posts set into the ground a few inches apart, interlaced with brush and packed with mud. It was topped by a double-pitched roof and entered by a sloping ramp on one side.

Although the earliest Anasazi lived in caves, by circa 500 C.E. they had developed a circular pit house, about 5 feet deep and up to 25 feet in diameter. The structure had a flat roof, with entry by ladder through the smoke hole. By circa 700, the Anasazi had developed stone architecture and were building aboveground pueblos. As their culture spread through the Southwest, they gradually absorbed most of the other two groups.

Crafts. One of the benefits that results from social organization and specialization is leisure time that can be devoted to the development of arts and crafts. As the Mogollon, Hohokam, and Anasazi began to make utilitarian objects such as pottery, baskets, sandals, robes, and mats, they decorated them according to their own rapidly developing aesthetic tastes. From the beginning, all three groups made jewelry from shells, bone, and minerals such as turquoise. A careful study of all these things reveals the emergence of a rich artistic tradition which was related to other aspects of these prehistoric cultures and which constitutes the artistic heritage of the modern Puebloan artist.

—LouAnn Faris Culley

See also Anasazi; Architecture—Southwest; Arts and crafts—Southwest; Canyon de Chelly; Chaco Canyon; Clovis; Corn; Desert culture; Hohokam; Mesa Verde; Mogollon; Pit house; Pottery; Southwest.

BIBLIOGRAPHY

Amsden, Charles A. *Prehistoric Southwesterners from Basketmaker to Pueblo*. Los Angeles: Southwest Museum, 1949.

Cordell, Linda S. *Prehistory of the Southwest*. Orlando, Fla.: Academic Press, 1984.

Cummings, Byron. *The First Inhabitants of Arizona and the Southwest*. Tucson, Ariz.: Cummings Publication Council, 1953.

Gummerman, George J., ed. *Exploring the Hohokam: Prehistoric Desert Peoples of the American Southwest*. Dragoon, Ariz.: Amerind Foundation, 1991.

Muench, David. *Anasazi, Ancient People of the Rock*. Palo Alto, Calif.: American West, 1975.

Noble, David G., ed. *The Hohokam: Ancient People of the Desert*. Santa Fe, N.Mex.: School of American Research Press, 1991.

Prehistory—Subarctic

DATE: c. 25,000 B.C.E.-c. 1700 C.E.
LOCATION: Alaska, Canada, Greenland
CULTURES AFFECTED: Aleut, Athapaskan, Eskimo (Inuit), Haida, Tlingit, Tsimshian

Determination of the lifeways and approximate dates of prehistoric cultures can be accomplished only through examination of archaeological sites and artifacts. Precisely dating the prehistory of the Subarctic is impossible. Considering the fact that many of the languages spoken in this area are related to those spoken in Siberia, however, it is generally considered that early Subarctic dwellers entered North America over the land bridge that connected Siberia and Alaska, where the Bering Strait is now located, during the last Ice Age. There were at least two separate migrations, and probably three, during a period between 25,000 and 10,000 years ago.

The earliest migration probably involved the Athapaskans, as their language group is by far the most widespread and has apparently changed the most over time. The Athapaskan languages spoken in Alaska and Subarctic Canada are related to the Navajo and Apache languages of the American Southwest. Eskimo groups, on the other hand, have languages so similar that a native of Alaska can easily communicate with one of Greenland. A third group, completely unrelated to the other two, is the Northwest Coast Indians.

In a real sense, the prehistory of the Subarctic extends as late as the late nineteenth century, when whites were first attracted into Alaska and Yukon by the gold rush. Unfortunately, the cultures in the region were changed by the impact of white culture before they were thoroughly studied. Some of the more remote regions were never seen by white people until the mid-twentieth century, when air travel made it easier to visit any place on earth. Before this time, transport was primarily by boat in the summer and dog sled in the winter.

Prehistoric Eskimos and Aleuts lived in igloos, made of packed snow. The Athapaskans lived in log cabins quite similar to those built by others much farther south. There were a great number of tribal rituals, some of which are still practiced, but details are difficult to determine, because in most instances outsiders are barred from these rituals; moreover, they are held in native languages that few outsiders understand.

See also Architecture—Subarctic; Arts and crafts—Subarctic; Athapaskan language family; Beringia; Dorset; Subarctic.

Proclamation of 1763

DATE: October 7, 1763
PLACE: Colonial North America
TRIBES AFFECTED: Tribes of the Northeast and Southeast
SIGNIFICANCE: The Proclamation of 1763, issued by the British crown, attempted to draw a line between American Indian lands and the American colonists; ultimately it added to the discontent the colonists felt toward English rule

British officials hoped that this decree would end the problems associated with colonial western expansion, a problem exacerbated when Britain drove France from the interior of North America at the conclusion of the American phase of the Seven Years' War. With the Proclamation of 1763, officials hoped to resolve Anglo-Indian misunderstandings dating back more than a decade.

John Pownall was the primary author of the Proclamation of 1763. At the time, Pownall was undersecretary to the Board of Trade. In drafting his proposal, he relied on a series of letters he had received from his brother, Thomas. Thomas Pownall had originally gone to New York as secretary to Sir Charles Hardy in 1755. When Hardy died later that year, Thomas Pownall found himself without a job. He became the "eyes and ears" of the Duke of Halifax, newly arrived British commander. In this unofficial capacity, he attended the Albany Congress of 1754 and met the major figures in Anglo-Indian affairs: William Shirley, William Johnson, John Lydius, and George Croghan.

As an edict, the proclamation attempted to do three things. First, it forbade colonial governments from surveying and issuing patents for lands lying beyond the headwaters of any river feeding the Atlantic Ocean. Imperial officials hoped that the proclamation would end the colonists' constant attempts to gain western lands. Officials wanted to slow the pace of western expansion because they thought western settlers were the most difficult colonists to control. Indeed, royal officials blamed these frontiersmen for the outbreak of Pontiac's Rebellion. Second, the decree prevented private individuals from purchasing Indian lands. Third, the proclamation organized four new British colonies: the island of Grenada, Quebec, East Florida, and West Florida. By outlining these three areas, imperial officials formally defined the "Indian country" for the first time.

Once it was implemented, the crown expected the British military and Indian superintendents to enforce the measure. Even though both military and Indian department officials supported the plan, the proclamation was much easier to write than implement. The difficulty with implementation concerned what colonial governments and land companies such as the Ohio Company of Virginia had already done. Virginia had already promised this western land to veterans of the Seven Years' War, and the Ohio Company patent lay in the region now closed to settlement. The Proclamation of 1763 shows clearly how colonial objectives and imperial policy were in conflict.

The proclamation also contained a clause that undermined the hopes of imperial officials from the beginning. When issued, the proclamation included an exception to the acquisition of western lands. Retiring military personnel could secure between 50 and 5,000 acres, depending upon their rank. This exception fueled colonial discontent with the edict. Equally important, any Indian group could still sell land to speculators in the future. In 1763, no one considered this flaw fatal because London officials considered the Proclamation of 1763 a temporary expedient. This temporary line would allow Indian agents to negotiate a more lasting settlement. Other events and issues undermined the hopes of officials in drawing this boundary, however, so the promise implied in the Proclamation of 1763 was never realized.

See also French and Indian Wars; Indian-white relations—English colonial; Pontiac's Conspiracy.

Projectile points

TRIBES AFFECTED: Pantribal
SIGNIFICANCE: Projectile points tipped spears, arrows, and other tools for thousands of years in prehistoric North America

Projectile points are thin, symmetrical artifacts with bases thinned for mounting on shafts. The name is somewhat misleading, since many of these items were never used on projectiles (such as javelins or arrows), but rather were the points for thrusting spears; some clearly were used as knives and similar tools. Most points were made of flaked stone, though some were made of ground stone (especially slate) or bone. The width of the base of a point indicates the type of weapon on which it may have been used, since its basal width must approximate the width of the shaft on which it was mounted, and thick shafts could not be used for arrows. A few types of points had cylindrical bases and presumably were mounted in

Scandia   Clovis   Folsom

Projectile points typical of three prehistoric cultural traditions.

sockets at the tips of their shafts. Recognizing that the characteristics of projectile points vary greatly over time and among tribes, archaeologists have expended considerable energy in studying them, and the dates of manufacture for point types in North American now are largely known.

See also Bows, arrows, and quivers; Clovis; Folsom; Lances and spears; Weapons.

Puberty and initiation rites

Tribes affected: Pantribal

Significance: Puberty and initiation rites represented the important transition from childhood to adulthood in the Indian life cycle

American Indian cultures contained special ceremonies and tribal guidelines marking one or more stages of the life cycle—birth, puberty, reproduction, and death. Puberty, especially for girls, held great importance as it represented the formal end of childhood and the availability to marry. (Some tribes, such as the Blackfoot and Arapaho, however, had no special ceremonies for puberty.)

Because of close living quarters, children grew up aware of sexual relations. Puberty often altered familial relations, as brothers and sisters were no longer permitted to be by themselves without supervision. In addition, postpuberty children would often sleep separated from their parents. These changes were celebrated, as puberty and initiation rites represented the movement of the tribes' children to adulthood. Common community events marking this life change included gift giving, feasts, and musical celebrations.

Becoming a Woman. Almost every tribe put strict limitations on the behavior of menstruating women. Because of a strong belief in the spiritual nature of blood, women were isolated during this time to avoid contamination of food, weapons, and other essential elements of Indian life. During her first menstruation, an Indian girl was isolated from the community and instructed on these taboos. A special tribal ceremony commemorating the girl's new adult status often accompanied this isolation.

The Navajo puberty ceremony for girls, *Kinaaldá*, was one of the most elaborate rituals in Indian culture. The ceremony, which took place as close to the first menstruation as possible, lasted four days and ended with a community celebration. A specific order of events was followed, including a symbolic molding of the body to resemble the Changing Woman (the first mother), which prepared the girl for motherhood. Another event involved three daily runs toward the east—at dawn, noon, and sunset—to strengthen the body. Each day, corn was ground in preparation for a community celebration on the final day. Immediately prior to this celebration, the young girl was bathed and dressed in new clothing to represent her new status. The Apache also conducted a puberty ceremony similar to the Kinaaldá.

Other tribes marked the first menstruation with a variety of ceremonies. Among the Hopi, when a girl "came of age" she moved to a bed distant from her parents and was instructed on

the religious secrets of the culture. Sioux girls, upon their first menstruation, added an eagle plume to their hair; this symbolized their new status as adult women. A special ceremony was also held in the girl's honor. The father of a Cheyenne girl called out the news of his daughter's menstruation. She would then be painted red and sent to a special lodge for the duration of her menstruation. When the girl emerged from the lodge, she walked through smoke to purify her body.

Becoming a Man. Few tribes celebrated formal ceremonies for their male children. Young boys started their quest for adult status at a young age with increased responsibilities such as caring for warriors on the hunt and using larger bows. In many cases, taking care of the tribes' horses represented the first "adult" rite. When a boy's voice changed, parental authority passed from his mother to his father and he received advanced instruction on the arts of hunting and war. Some tribes had ceremonial dances, such as the Sioux Sun Dance, which acted as a test of endurance for young warriors. Physical toughening served as a measure of status in the Apache path to manhood.

Hunting also served as an initiation rite for boys, who were trained since early childhood for the hunt. The first large kill was a gift to the needy people of the group and represented a proud moment for the boy's family. Cheyenne boys received adult status for a successful hunt or war record.

Male puberty also included a strong spiritual element. Vision quests, common among the Plains Indians, often took place for the first time during puberty and represented not only a religious rite but also an initiation rite. Young boys first visited the sweatlodge to breathe the "breath of life" created when water was poured on hot stones. The youth was then left with no clothing or food in a secluded area for four days and nights. Facing the elements as well as hunger and loneliness, the youth's bravery and courage was tested while he waited for a vision (dream). This vision would then be interpreted by tribal elders and used to give the boy his adult name and, in some cases, his occupation. The Lakota vision quest, *Hanblapi*, was also undertaken by the tribes' girls.

Another major element in male puberty was the initiation into a sodality. Similar to a modern fraternity and often strongly tied to religion, a sodality represented a social as well as educational passage into adult life. Among the Pueblo and Hopi, youths between the ages of ten and twelve were initiated into a sodality called the Kachina Cult. Boys moved into a sacred building called a kiva, where they were freed from parental supervision and trained in the tribes' religious beliefs. The process almost always included physical beatings to impress the seriousness of tribal and religious responsibilities. Algonquians separated their boys from their families for nine months some time between the age of ten and fifteen for their introduction to religion.

Reservation Rites. After Indians were forced onto reservations, tribal rites and ceremonies were limited because of the U.S. government's restrictions on assembly (caused by fear that assembly would lead to war parties and rebellion). Events

An Apache girl, Little Cornflower (center), is sprinkled with pollen as part of her coming-of-age ceremony. (AP/Wide World Photos)

such as the Kinaaldá were scheduled once a year and lost many of the ancient taboos. In addition, the separation of brothers and sisters virtually ended once Indian children were enrolled in public schools. Reservation life did not completely remove the importance of puberty, however, and tribes, determined to carry on ancient rituals, found ways to maintain tradition in a modern world. —*Jennifer Davis*

See also Children; Gender relations and roles; Kachinas; Masks; Names and naming; Rites of passage; Sweatlodges and sweatbaths; Visions and vision quests.

BIBLIOGRAPHY

Driver, Harold E. *Indians of North America*. 1961. Reprint. Chicago: University of Chicago Press, 1969.

Frisbie, Charlotte Johnson. *Kinaalda: A Study of the Navaho Girl's Puberty Ceremony*. Middletown, Conn.: Wesleyan University Press, 1967.

Gill, Sam D. *Dictionary of Native American Mythology*. Santa Barbara, Calif.: ABC-Clio, 1992.

Lowie, Robert H. *Indians of the Plains*. New York: McGraw-Hill, 1954.

White, Jon Manchip. *Everyday Life of the North American Indian*. New York: Holmes and Meier, 1979.

Public Law 280

DATE: August 15, 1953

TRIBES AFFECTED: Pantribal

SIGNIFICANCE: This law limited tribal sovereignty by allowing courts in some states to have jurisdiction over Indian reservations

During the early 1950's, federal Indian policy returned to the goal of promoting the assimilation of Indians into American society. Tribes were considered to be major barriers to this end, and a number of policies were developed to reduce their influence. One of these measures was Public Law 280, which sought to place tribal Indians under the jurisdiction of the laws of the states in which they resided. This marked a significant change in the legal status of Native Americans, for while Indians had long been subject to federal law, they had usually been considered to be subject to their own tribal courts when on reservations. Like other measures of the 1950's, Public Law 280 sought to undermine those aspects of Indians' legal status that set them apart from other Americans.

Passed by Congress in August, 1953, Public Law 280 authorized state courts to assume civil and criminal jurisdiction of all Indian lands in the states of California, Minnesota, Nebraska, Oregon, and Wisconsin. (Three reservations were excluded by name in the act.) Furthermore, other states were allowed to extend jurisdiction over reservations if they desired by making the necessary changes in their laws or constitutions. A few limits were placed on state powers: States could not levy property taxes on reservations or exercise jurisdiction with regard to Indian water rights. By 1968 nine additional states had extended jurisdiction over Indian lands within their borders.

Public Law 280 was very unpopular with American Indians, who saw it as a drastic limitation on the tribal right of self-government that had been enacted without their consent. (President Dwight D. Eisenhower had objected to the lack of a provision for tribal consent but had signed the act when Congress refused to amend it.)

Indian resentment of the act helped to persuade Congress to amend its provisions in the changed atmosphere of later years. The American Indian Civil Rights Act of 1968 included provisions (known collectively as the Indian Bill of Rights) that were intended to safeguard Native American rights. One section altered Public Law 280 to require Indian consent before future extensions of state jurisdiction. States were also allowed to return jurisdiction to tribes. Public Law 280 was further limited in its impact by the Indian Child Welfare Act (1978), which gave tribal courts exclusive jurisdiction over child custody cases on reservations.

Though initially regarded as a major threat to tribal self-government, modification of Public Law 280 lessened its potential for restricting tribal authority. Some states found that they preferred to avoid the expense involved in extending legal jurisdiction, while some tribes found it useful to ask the states to provide law and order. By the late twentieth century, the law was being used in a somewhat more cooperative manner that took Indian opinions into account.

See also American Indian Civil Rights Act; Civil rights and citizenship; Courts, tribal; Sovereignty; Termination policy.

Pueblo

TRIBES AFFECTED: Pueblo tribes (prehistoric to modern)

SIGNIFICANCE: The Anasazi, the most creative and enduring of the prehistoric cultures of the Southwest, were the first to acquire the architectural and engineering skills needed to build aboveground pueblos, establishing a tradition that survives today

At the beginning of the Pueblo period, around 700 C.E., the Anasazi pit house evolved in two different directions: It came up above the ground to become a house, and it sank deeper into the ground to be formalized as a kiva. Building on mesa tops and in valleys at sites such as Chaco Canyon, Mesa Verde, and Kayenta, the Anasazi chose communal dwellings over individual houses. They constructed slightly curved rows of single-story contiguous rooms, using a method known as "jacal." Walls were built using posts set a few inches apart, with adobe packed into the spaces between. Then, around the base of each wall, stone slabs were set in place with adobe mortar. Roofs consisted of slender cross-poles interlaced with brush and twigs and topped with a layer of mud several inches thick. The rooms, each housing an entire family, faced to the inside of the curve, with several kivas in the center.

Gradually, the Anasazi dispensed with the wooden framework and developed a crude masonry technique using large, unshaped rocks laid in irregular rows and packed with adobe, which often made up more than half the wall. As they refined their masonry techniques, the Anasazi began to shape sandstone into building blocks by using stone tools that were not much harder than the sandstone itself.

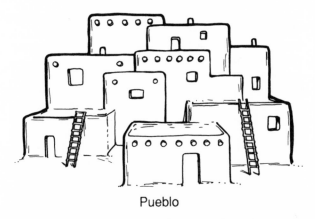

Pueblo

As construction techniques improved, the size and complexity of the pueblos increased, finally resulting in the great cities of the Classic Pueblo period. The largest of these, Pueblo Bonito in Chaco Canyon, housed a probable population in excess of one thousand people in its more than eight hundred rooms, which rose to four and five stories and covered some 3 acres of ground. Pueblo Bonito was arranged in a horseshoe pattern around a central plaza, with each row of rooms rising one story at a time toward the rear. A row of single-story rooms across the front enclosed the plaza, which contained the ceremonial kivas. As they had done since Developmental Pueblo times, the women of the pueblo used the rooftops for cooking and other household chores.

Under Anasazi influence, the Mogollon and Hohokam peoples began to build surface pueblos, as did the later Sinagua and Salado. As the Anasazi moved away from the northern plateaus around 1300 C.E., they migrated to three main areas: the Rio Grande Valley and Zuni in New Mexico, and the Hopi Mesas in Arizona. The cultures that developed in these areas in the fourteenth and fifteenth centuries are ancestral to the Pueblo cultures that exist there now. Although construction of these pueblos varied with time and place, in general the Anasazi traditions of communal living have prevailed, with pueblos consisting of large numbers of rooms, built of masonry or adobe, arranged around a central plaza containing several ceremonial kivas.

See also Adobe; Anasazi; Architecture—Southwest; Chaco Canyon; Cliff dwellings; Hogan; Kivas; Mesa Verde; Pit house; Pueblo tribes, Eastern; Pueblo tribes, Western.

Pueblo (Popé's) Revolt

DATE: 1680
PLACE: New Mexico
TRIBES AFFECTED: Eastern Pueblo tribes
SIGNIFICANCE: Though its results were short-lived, the 1680 Pueblo Revolt was one of the few successful indigenous uprisings against European colonizers

Sedentary horticulturalists living in autonomous villages distributed along the Rio Grande and its tributaries, the New Mexican Pueblos endured throughout the seventeenth century an intense Spanish colonization effort that subjected them to onerous social, economic, and especially religious obligations and restrictions. In addition, epidemics, droughts, and numerous Navajo and Apache raids increased the Pueblos' pressures, reducing a population of more than thirty thousand to about seventeen thousand by 1680, still far outnumbering the non-Indian population of thirty-five hundred.

In this climate, Popé, a medicine man of San Juan Pueblo, emerged as the instigator of a general Pueblo revolt. Planning in Taos, Popé enlisted the aid of other native leaders, as well as a number of mixed-bloods, convincing them that a rejection of the Spanish and Christianity would bring prosperity and the return of the kachinas, the ancestral spirits who brought rain and good health. Those still unconvinced were forced into cooperation with threats of reprisals. Dispatched from Taos, native messengers carried knotted yucca cords to the other pueblos, a calendrical device to synchronize the uprising.

On August 10, 1680, the Pueblos struck, isolating the scattered Spanish settlements and killing in a few hours over four hundred settlers and twenty-one priests. The survivors gathered in Santa Fe with Governor Antonio de Otermín and endured a nine-day siege before breaking free to escape to the south, joining other refugees at El Paso del Norte. Meanwhile, Popé ordered the Pueblo peoples to go to the river and wash off the taint of Christian baptism, to put aside wives acquired in Christian ceremony, and to destroy all vestiges of the Spanish occupation.

Within the year, the Pueblo alliance began to fracture as village autonomy reasserted itself. Further droughts, pestilence, and increased nomadic Indian raids also contributed to factionalism and internecine warfare, belying Popé's millenarian promises. Between 1692 and 1696, Governor Don Diego de Vargas, completed the reoccupation of New Mexico and the recolonization of the Pueblo peoples.

See also Indian-white relations—Spanish colonial; Missions and missionaries; Popé; Pueblo tribes, Eastern.

Pueblo tribes, Eastern

TRIBES AFFECTED: Cochiti, Hano, Isleta, Jemez, Nambe, Pecos, Picuris, Pojoaque, San Felipe, San Ildefonso, San Juan, Sandia, Santa Ana, Santa Clara, Santo Domingo, Taos, Tesuque, Tigua, Zia
CULTURE AREA: Southwest
LANGUAGE GROUPS: Keresan, Tanoan
PRIMARY LOCATION: Hopi First Mesa, Rio Grande Valley
POPULATION SIZE: 24,055 (1990 U.S. Census)

The Puebloans say that they have occupied the Southwest from "time immemorial"; indeed, archaeological investigation has proved that they are descended from the prehistoric Anasazi, "the Ancient Ones." As the Anasazi abandoned their great population centers at Mesa Verde, Chaco Canyon, and Kayenta around the year 1300, they migrated into three main areas, one of which was the Rio Grande Valley in New Mexico. There they built new settlements, which were still occu-

U.S. STATES WITH THE LARGEST PUEBLO POPULATIONS, 1990

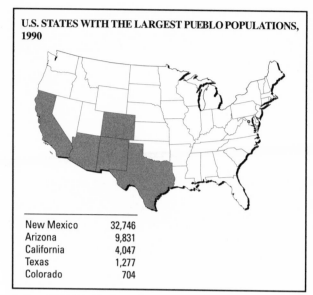

New Mexico	32,746
Arizona	9,831
California	4,047
Texas	1,277
Colorado	704

Source: 1990 U.S. Census.

pied at the time of the Spanish entry into the Southwest around 1540; most of these continued to be occupied into the twentieth century.

The indigenous peoples whom the Spaniards encountered were, for the most part, agriculturists with a sedentary, settled lifestyle. They lived in villages consisting of terraced, flat-roofed, communal dwellings of stone and adobe built around a central plaza. The Spaniards called these villages "pueblos" and their occupants "Pueblo Indians," as distinguished from the nomadic Apache. With more than 25 percent of their yearly food supply provided by their own crops, the Puebloans had been able to develop a stable and organized way of life, with ample time to devote to art and religion.

Contact with the Spanish. The Spaniards came into the Southwest looking for gold but, finding none, settled for declaring it a missionary domain for the Franciscans. They divided the area into districts, each of which was assigned to a Catholic priest. All the pueblos were given Spanish saint names, and the Puebloans were forced to swear allegiance and vassalage to the Spanish crown and the Church. Some Puebloans were driven from their homes so that the Spanish soldiers, priests, and settlers could be housed.

Spanish oppression became more and more unbearable until finally, in 1680, the Puebloans revolted, driving the conquerors back to El Paso del Norte. In 1692, however, General Don Diego de Vargas led his armies back into the territory, successfully recapturing it.

The Mexican Revolution of 1821 put an end to Spanish rule in the Southwest, but little changed for the Puebloans except that they were now designated citizens of the Mexican Republic. In 1846, war broke out between the United States and Mexico, ending in 1848 with the Treaty of Guadalupe Hidalgo, which ceded New Mexico and upper California to the United States. The treaty also obligated the United States to recognize Indian rights previously established under Spanish and Mexican rule. In 1849, the Bureau of Indian Affairs sent the first Indian agent to the New Mexico Territory. In the Gadsden Purchase of 1853, the United States acquired more land in the Southwest from Mexico; in 1861, parts of the New Mexico Territory were designated as the Territories of Arizona and Colorado. For decades afterward, titles to Indian lands in these new territories were in question. Most of the pueblos had no documents confirming their Spanish land grants, and land-hungry settlers coming into the area took what they wanted. Beginning in 1856, federal government surveys were made and were later confirmed by the Supreme Court, with the result that many Puebloans were given official title to their lands in 1864. When both New Mexico and Arizona joined the Union in 1912, the Indians became United States citizens but were not granted citizenship by either state until 1948.

Tiwa-Speaking Pueblos. The Tanoan language, one of the two major language groups of the Eastern Pueblos, contains three subfamilies or dialects: Tiwa, Tewa, and Towa. The northern Tiwa are the pueblos of Taos and Picuris, while the southern Tiwa are located to the north and south of Albuquerque in the pueblos of Sandia and Isleta. A fifth Tiwa group, the Tigua, lives at El Paso, Texas.

Taos Pueblo, the northernmost of all those in the Rio Grande Valley, was built around 1700 after the original pueblo, dating several hundred years earlier, was destroyed by fire in the 1690's. The pueblo consists of two communal structures, Hlauuma (North House) and Hlaukwima (South House), which are located on either side of Taos Creek. The first Spanish contact was made by Pedro de Alvarado in 1540, followed by Juan de Oñate in 1598, who named the pueblo "San Miguel." The Spaniards built two churches in the pueblo, one in the early seventeenth century and one in the early eighteenth century, both of which were subsequently destroyed (the present church dates from 1847). In 1639, harsh Spanish rule forced the people of Taos to flee to the north, where they built a new pueblo in what is now Scott County, Kansas. Two years later, however, the Spaniards forced them to return to Taos. Their two-year residency among the Plains Indians influenced the dress, the customs, and even the physical makeup of the people of Taos, and for many years Taos was a trading center for the Ute, Apache, and Comanche.

The original pueblo of Picuris dates from around 1250 and was named San Lorenzo by the Spaniards, who built a mission there in 1621. Like Taos, Picuris had its problems with Spanish authority; the governor of Picuris was one of the leaders of the Pueblo Revolt, and after the Spanish reconquest in 1692, the people of Picuris escaped to western Kansas, where they lived until 1706. At that time, weakened by disease and warfare, they returned to their pueblo.

The pueblo of Sandia dates from about 1300. The Spaniards built a mission there in the early seventeenth century (San Francisco), but it was destroyed in the Pueblo Revolt. After the Spaniards destroyed Sandia Pueblo in their attempts at reconquest, the people of Sandia took refuge with the Hopi, building

Musicians and singers of the Santa Clara pueblo perform at a celebration. (AP/Wide World Photos)

Taos pueblo, photographed by Ansel Adams in 1941. (National Archives)

the village of Payupki on the Second Mesa. In 1742, about five hundred people returned to Sandia and built a new pueblo on the site of the old one.

Isleta, with its 210,445 acres, is the largest of all Rio Grande pueblos in terms of area. In the 1600's, many people from other Tiwa villages came to Isleta to escape Apache raids. At the time of the Pueblo Revolt, Isleta's population numbered about two thousand people, many of whom were forced to accompany the Spaniards as they fled south to El Paso del Norte. Their descendants, the Tiguas, still live at Ysleta del Sur, about twelve miles south of El Paso, where they built a pueblo arranged around a rectangular plaza. As several schol-

ars have established, the northern Puebloans virtually disowned the Tiguas because they did not fight the Spaniards in the Pueblo Revolt. As a consequence, the Tiguas have never been allowed to join the Pueblo Conference, although Texas recognized their tribal status by creating the Tigua Indian Reservation in 1967.

Tewa-Speaking Pueblos. There are seven Tewa pueblos: San Juan, Santa Clara, San Ildefonso, Nambe, Tesuque, and Pojoaque in the Rio Grande Valley, and Hano in Hopi country. The pueblo of San Juan is the largest of the Tewa-speaking pueblos and has been continuously inhabited since 1300. Juan de Oñate designated San Juan as his first capital in 1598 but appropriated the pueblo of Yunqueyunque the following year, sending its inhabitants to live in San Juan. In 1675, when Spanish repression of Pueblo religion reached the point where forty-seven Pueblo leaders were convicted of witchcraft and whipped, Popé, a San Juan medicine man, was among them. It was he who later planned and led the Pueblo Revolt.

The pueblos of Santa Clara and San Ildefonso date from the early fourteenth century. The Spaniards built missions in both pueblos; both were destroyed in the Pueblo Revolt. As the Spaniards attempted to reconquer the area, people from both pueblos took refuge atop nearby Black Mesa but surrendered after a nine-month siege. Most of the Santa Clarans abandoned their pueblo again around 1696 and moved west to the Hopi villages, where they built the pueblo of Hano on First Mesa. By 1702, the Spaniards had repopulated San Ildefonso with other Tewa-speaking people, but the pueblo continued to have serious troubles throughout the eighteenth century: A small-pox epidemic decimated half the population, Spanish repression of Puebloan religion continued, and many witchcraft trials occurred at the pueblo.

The pueblos of Tesuque, Nambe, and Pojoaque, which all date from around 1300, also took part in the Pueblo Revolt after destroying the Spanish mission in each. They joined the other Tewas at Black Mesa but, by the early 1700's, had returned to their own pueblos. While Tesuque has continued to follow the traditional Puebloan way of life, both Nambe and Pojoaque have more or less ceased to exist as Pueblo communities. Only the kiva at Nambe distinguishes it from any other rural Rio Grande village.

Jemez Pueblo. The only Towa-speaking pueblo still in existence is Jemez, located on the Rio Jemez in the Jemez Mountains west of Santa Fe. Hostile toward the Spanish from the outset, the Jemez fostered two rebellions against them even before the Pueblo Revolt of 1680. After the reconquest, the Jemez, retreating to a mesa-top fortress, continued to raid the Spaniards but were defeated in the late 1690's. Those who escaped Spanish retribution took refuge with the Hopi and the Navajo. By 1703, most of the people had returned to the Jemez Valley and rebuilt their pueblo. In 1838, when Pecos Pueblo, another Towa-speaking village in the Galisteo Basin, was abandoned, its seventeen residents moved to Jemez Pueblo. Pecos, like all the other Tanoans, originated early in the fourteenth century and had continued as an important center until the early nineteenth century.

The Keresan-Speaking Pueblos. The five extant Keresan-speaking pueblos in the Rio Grande Valley are Cochiti, Santo Domingo, San Felipe, Santa Ana, and Zia. All the original pueblos dated from the late thirteenth or early fourteenth century; in the late sixteenth century, all were visited by the Spaniards, who built missions in each pueblo in the seventeenth century. All the Keres took part in the Pueblo Revolt and in resisting Spanish reconquest in the 1690's. When Zia Pueblo was attacked and destroyed, six hundred people were killed, and the others were sold into slavery. Some who escaped fled to Jemez but were induced to return a few years later to rebuild at Zia. The Santo Domingans resisted reconquest by destroying their pueblo in 1692 and joining forces with Jemez Pueblo. When attacked by the Spaniards there in 1694, many fled to Hopi while others, accompanied by some refugees from Cochiti, moved into Acoma territory, where they built the new pueblo of Laguna. Later, some Santo Domingans returned to rebuild on the original site of their own pueblo. All the eastern Keres pueblos are still occupied, with the exception of Santa Ana. A lack of agricultural land and water for irrigation forced most of the people to move to a farming community near Bernalillo, with only a few caretakers remaining in the pueblo. In the late eighteenth and early nineteenth centuries, Cochiti Pueblo served as a refuge for Spanish and Mexican settlers from Apache and Navajo raids.

Pueblo Culture. Pueblo society is communal, with emphasis placed upon the welfare of the entire group, as opposed to that of any one individual. As many scholars have observed, the Puebloans had two highly desirable culture-forming assets: time and space. With time to think matters through carefully and space to see things clearly, they developed a culture that allowed them to enjoy the pleasures of each day to the fullest, without pressure for constant and immediate change. When change was called for, they reflected carefully, discussed it as a group, and then decided on a course of action.

The Puebloans had no written language; they maintained their culture orally, passing down knowledge from one generation to the next, often narrating it through ritual dances and other ceremonies. They have a great reverence for tradition and for truth and would never change or embellish their history for any reason, political or otherwise. As events have had an impact on Pueblo life through the centuries, they have been included in the history; thus, the Spaniards appear in the ritual stories today. The Puebloans, who always relate their history "from the beginning," share a similar creation belief in which humankind originated in the center of the earth, finally emerging onto the surface through a ceremonial opening known as the *sipapu*. As they came up into the light, they were divided into different groups that spoke different dialects, and they were sent to make their homes in different regions.

Religion is integrated with all other aspects of Pueblo life; it influences art, crafts, all industries, and the social structure. The fundamental belief underlying the Pueblo religion is that a person must live so that he or she is always in harmony with nature, with nature's basic rhythm. Other facets of existence have significance only in terms of how they relate to this principal belief. There are ceremonies and rites that are appropriate to each of the seasons—planting, growing, harvesting, and hunting. Many of the motifs that appear in their art are derived from their ceremonial beliefs, and even such mundane activities as the gathering of salt and clay are accompanied by special prayers. Lack of success in any endeavor is not blamed on the spirits but on the person who failed to observe the rituals properly.

The various pueblos have developed some similarities in their social and cultural patterns as they have interacted with one another through the centuries, yet each one is a closely united and distinct entity. Their ceremonials, for example, are similar, but important variations exist.

In each pueblo, authority is divided between religious and secular leaders, and the distinction between the two is carefully maintained. The slate of secular officers that resulted from a decree issued by the Spanish king in 1620 is still in effect: a governor, two lieutenant governors, a sheriff, and the *fiscales*, positions derived from the office of prosecutor. These officials serve for one year at all but four pueblos, where they serve for two years. The Spanish presented the first secular officers with metal-topped canes inscribed with the Spanish cross as emblems of their authority. When Mexican rule began in 1821, the system was maintained, and the officers were given new canes with silver tops as additional badges of office. Then, in 1863, Abraham Lincoln rewarded the Puebloans for their neutrality during the Civil War by giving silver-crowned ebony canes inscribed with his signature to all the secular officials, who now had three emblems of office. These canes are still displayed on important ceremonial occasions in most of the pueblos, along with the silver medals decorated with profiles of Lincoln and President Dwight D. Eisenhower made to commemorate the "Republican Centennial, 1863-1960" and the small cherrywood canes with white bronze tops presented to the Puebloans in 1980 in celebration of the Tricentennial of the Pueblo Revolt of 1680.

Division into Moieties. Another major cultural characteristic of the Rio Grande Pueblos is their division into dual ceremonial groups known as moieties. For example, in the pueblos of Cochiti, Jemez, Sandia, San Felipe, Santa Ana, Santo Domingo and Zia, the moieties are divided into the Turquoise and the Squash. At San Juan, Santa Clara, San Ildefonso, Nambe, Pojoaque, Tesuque, and Hano, they are Winter People and Summer People, and at Taos Pueblo they are North and South. A moiety can also be a political division; many pueblos alternate the position of governor annually between the two moieties. A moiety is often mistaken for a clan by outsiders who do not realize that in Pueblo tradition a clan is a group of related persons who trace their matrilineal descent from a common ancestor.

In the dual system of the Tanoan Pueblos, each moiety has its own priest, or *cacique*—a term of Caribbean origin which was first used by the Spaniards to designate Pueblo religious leaders and was eventually adopted by the Puebloans themselves. In the Tanoan dichotomy, the caciques, who hold office for life, are an important part of the hierarchical form of government of each pueblo. The Keres Pueblos have a somewhat more complicated social structure involving clans, kiva groups, and medicine societies as well as moieties. In these pueblos, a single cacique is responsible for the spiritual well-being of all the people and also appoints those who hold secular offices.

While adhering to their own traditional beliefs, many Puebloans also practice Catholicism; they find no inconsistencies in this, since they are able to keep the two religions separate.

Each pueblo still observes the ancient ceremonies and rites, encouraging its young people to participate fully.

Puebloans in the latter half of the twentieth century found themselves plagued by the same economic problems that beset many people in the United States as a whole—such as inadequate land resources, dwindling revenues from agriculture, unemployment, lack of adequate funding for education and health care—but they must also contend with increasing pressures from the non-Indian world. In spite of this, they continue to retain most of their native culture, being bound together by love of tradition, by common languages, and by their strong religious beliefs.   —*LouAnn Faris Culley*

See also Cacique; Gadsden Purchase, Guadalupe Hidalgo, Treaty of; Indian-white relations—Spanish colonial; Popé; Pueblo; Pueblo (Popé's) Revolt; Pueblo tribes, Western; Southwest.

Bibliography

Baldwin, Gordon C. *Indians of the Southwest.* New York: Capricorn Books, 1970. After an excellent introduction to the prehistoric ancestors of the Puebloans, the author details the relationship between natives and the Spanish, Mexicans, and Anglo-Americans who invaded their lands. Illustrated with black-and-white photographs of the land and the people.

Dutton, Bertha P. *The Pueblos: Indians of the American Southwest.* Englewood Cliffs, N.J.: Prentice Hall, 1976. A brief general history of each of the Puebloan groups, with an explanation of the mythology, religion, secret societies, and cults that play such an important role in Indian life.

Sando, Joe S. *The Pueblo Indians.* San Francisco: Indian Historian Press, 1976. The author, himself a Puebloan from Jemez, has written the traditional Pueblo history as the Pueblo Indians themselves know it, pointing out all the ways in which their viewpoint differs from the formalized narratives, dominated by European ideology, found in most history texts.

Tanner, Clara Lee. *Southwest Indian Craft Arts.* Tucson: University of Arizona Press, 1968. A discussion of Southwest Indian arts, which includes detailed information about materials, techniques, forms, styles, designs, and design elements. An in-depth exploration of intertribal contacts; Spanish, Mexican, and Anglo-American influences; and commercialization, which have all affected the styles, designs, and functions of each of the art forms.

Underhill, Ruth. *Pueblo Crafts.* Washington, D.C.: U.S. Bureau of Indian Affairs, 1944. Reprint. Palmer Lake, Colo.: Filter Press, 1979. An extremely detailed account of the materials and techniques which produced the arts and crafts of the Southwest Pueblos, from the ancient period to modern times. Illustrated throughout with diagrams and photographs.

Wormington, H. M. *Prehistoric Indians of the Southwest.* Denver, Colo.: Denver Museum of Natural History, 1970. A very readable account of the prehistoric cultures in the Southwest, intended for the layperson rather than the scientist. Illustrated throughout with helpful maps, diagrams, and photographs.

RR AMERICAN INDIANS

LIST OF ENTRIES BY CATEGORY

ARCHAEOLOGICAL SITES

Awatovi
Aztalan
Bat Cave
Cahokia
Canyon de Chelly
Chaco Canyon
Chichén Itzá
Copan
Cuello
Danger Cave
El Tajín
Emerald Mound
Etowah
Key Marco
Koster
La Venta
Lehner
Mesa Verde
Middens
Midland
Mitla
Monte Albán
Oaxaca
Ozette
Palenque
Poverty Point
San Lorenzo
Snaketown
Spiro
Tenochtitlán
Teotihuacán
Tikal
Tres Zapotes
Tula
Uxmal
Veracruz
Yaxchilan

ART AND ARCHITECTURE

Adobe
Appliqué and ribbonwork
Architecture—Arctic
Architecture—California
Architecture—Great Basin
Architecture—Northeast
Architecture—Northwest
    Coast
Architecture—Plains
Architecture—Plateau
Architecture—Southeast
Architecture—Southwest
Architecture—Subarctic
Art and artists, contemporary
Arts and crafts—Arctic
Arts and crafts—California
Arts and crafts—Great Basin
Arts and crafts—Northeast
Arts and crafts—Northwest
    Coast
Arts and crafts—Plains
Arts and crafts—Plateau
Arts and crafts—Southeast
Arts and crafts—Southwest
Arts and crafts—Subarctic
Beads and beadwork
Chickee
Earthlodge
Grass house
Hogan
Igloo
Lean-to
Longhouse
Mosaic and inlay
Paints and painting
Petroglyphs
Pit house
Plank house
Pueblo
Quillwork
Sculpture
Shells and shellwork
Symbolism in art
Tipi
Totem poles
Turquoise
Wattle and daub
Wickiup
Wigwam

BELIEFS AND RELIGION

Bundles, sacred
Corn Woman
Ethnophilosophy and
    worldview
Guardian spirits
Kachinas
Kivas
Kuksu rituals and society
Longhouse religion
Manibozho
Maru Cult
Medicine bundles
Medicine wheels
Mother Earth
Native American Church
Peyote and peyote religion
Praying Indians
Quetzalcóatl
Religion
Religious specialists
Sacred narratives
Sacred, the
Sand painting
Shaker Church
Totems
Tricksters
Visions and vision quests
Windigo
Witchcraft and sorcery

CEREMONIES, DANCES, AND FESTIVALS

Bladder Festival
Booger Dance
Buffalo Dance
Chantways
Dances and dancing
Death and mortuary
    customs
Deer Dance
False Face Ceremony
Feast of the Dead
Feasts
Ghost Dance
Gourd Dance
Grass Dance
Green Corn Dance
Hako
Hamatsa
Husk Face Society
Midewiwin
Midwinter Ceremony
Morning Star Ceremony
Okeepa
Potlatch
Pow-wows and contemporary
    celebrations
Puberty and initiation rites
Rite of Consolation
Rites of passage
Shaking Tent Ceremony
Shalako
Snake Dance
Spirit Dancing
Stomp Dance
Sun Dance
Tobacco Society and Dance
White Deerskin Dance

CONTEMPORARY LIFE AND ISSUES

Activism
African American—American
    Indian Relations
Alcoholism
American Indian studies
    programs and archives
Amerind
Art and artists, contemporary
Certificate of Degree of
    Indian Blood
Civil rights and citizenship
Councils, tribal
Courts, tribal
Diseases, post-contact
Education, post-contact
Employment and
    unemployment
Federally recognized tribes
Gambling
Guns
Indian police and judges
Land claims
Medicine and modes of
    curing, post-contact
Pan-Indianism
Pow-wows and contemporary
    celebrations
Ranching
Relocation
Reservation system of the
    United States
Reserve system of Canada
Resources
Stereotypes

Suicide
Tribe
Urban Indians

Voting rights—Canada
Voting rights—United States
Water and water rights

White Paper of Canada
Winnebago Uprising
Wolf Mountains, Battle of
Wounded Knee Massacre

Wounded Knee occupation
Yakima War
Yamasee War

CULTURE AREAS

Arctic
California
Great Basin
Northeast
Northwest Coast

Plains
Plateau
Southeast
Southwest
Subarctic

DRESS AND ADORNMENT

Beads and beadwork
Dress and adornment
Feathers and featherwork
Headdresses
Moccasins

Ornaments
Quillwork
Shells and shellwork
War bonnets

HISTORICAL EVENTS

Acoma, Battle of
Adobe Walls, Battles of
Alcatraz Island occupation
Apache Wars
Articles of Agreement
Bacon's Rebellion
Bannock War
Bear River Campaign
Beaver Wars
Black Hawk War
Bozeman Trail wars
Cayuse War
Cherokee Tobacco case
Cherokee War
Creek War
Declaration of First Nations
Fallen Timbers, Battle of
Fifteen Principles
Fort Mims, Battle of
French and Indian Wars
Gadsden Purchase
Kickapoo Resistance
Kickapoo uprisings
King Philip's War
Little Bighorn, Battle of the
Lone Wolf v. Hitchcock
Long Walk
Longest Walk
Lord Dunmore's War
Manhattan
Meech Lake Accord
Meriam Report
Minnesota Uprising
Modoc War

Natchez Revolt
Navajo War
Nez Perce War
Northwest Ordinance
Pavonia Massacre
Paxton Riots
Peach Wars
Pequot War
Pima uprisings
Pine Ridge shootout
Pontiac's Conspiracy
Powhatan Wars
Proclamation of 1763
Public Law 280
Pueblo (Popé's) Revolt
Red River War
Riel Rebellions
Rosebud Creek, Battle of
Sand Creek Massacre
Saybrook, Battle of
Seminole Wars
Sioux uprisings
Snake War
Tecumseh's Rebellion
Termination policy
Texas Rangers
Thames, Battle of the
Tippecanoe, Battle of
Trail of Broken Treaties
Trail of Tears
Wabash, Battle of the
Wagon Box Battle
Walla Walla Council
Washita River, Battle of the

INDIAN-WHITE RELATIONS

American Indian
Captivity and captivity
  narratives
Indian
Indian Territory
Indian-white relations—
  Canadian
Indian-white relations—
  Dutch colonial
Indian-white relations—
  English colonial
Indian-white relations—
  French colonial
Indian-white relations—
  Norse
Indian-white relations—
  Russian colonial
Indian-white relations—
  Spanish colonial
Indian-white relations—
  Swedish colonial

Indian-white relations—
  U.S., 1775-1830
Indian-white relations—
  U.S., 1831-1870
Indian-white relations—
  U.S., 1871-1933
Indian-white relations—
  U.S., 1934-1995
Journalism
Keetoowah Society
Missions and missionaries
Native American
Oregon Trail
Patents
Railroads
Removal
Santa Fe Trail
Sovereignty
Trading posts
Wild west shows

LANGUAGES

Algonquian language family
Atakapa language family
Athapaskan language family
Beothuk language
Caddoan language family
Chitimacha language
Coos language
Eskimo-Aleut language
  family
Hokan language family
Iroquoian language family
Karankawa language
Keresan language family
Kiowa-Tanoan language
  family
Kutenai language

Language families
Muskogean language family
Na-Dene language family
Penutian language family
Salishan language family
Sign language
Siouan language family
Syllabaries
Timucua language
Tonkawa language
Tunica language
Uto-Aztecan language family
Wakashan language family
Yakonan language family
Yuman language family
Zuni language

LEGISLATION

Alaska Native Claims
  Settlement Act
American Indian Civil
  Rights Act
American Indian Religious
  Freedom Act

Burke Act
General Allotment Act
Indian Act of 1876 (Canada)
Indian Act of 1951 (Canada)
Indian Act of 1989 (Canada)
Indian Child Welfare Act

PREHISTORIC CULTURE

TRADITIONAL LIFEWAYS

Iowa
Iroquois Confederacy
Juaneño
Kalapuya
Kalispel
Kamia
Kansa
Karankawa
Karok
Kaska
Kawaiisu
Kichai
Kickapoo
Kiowa
Klamath
Klikitat
Koyukon
Kutchin
Kutenai
Kwakiutl
Lake
Lenni Lenape
Lillooet
Luiseño
Lumbee
Lummi
Mahican
Maidu
Makah
Maliseet
Manahoac
Mandan
Massachusett
Mattaponi
Mattole
Maya
Menominee
Methow
Metis
Miami
Micmac
Missouri
Miwok
Mixtec
Mobile
Modoc
Mohawk
Mohegan
Mojave

Molala
Moneton
Montagnais
Montauk Confederacy
Mountain
Muckleshoot
Multnomah
Nabedache
Nanticoke
Narragansett
Naskapi
Natchez
Nauset
Navajo
Neutral
Nez Perce
Niantic
Nipissing
Nipmuck
Nisqually
Nooksack
Nootka
Nottaway
Ocaneechi
Ofo
Ojibwa
Okanagan
Olmec
Omaha
Oneida
Onondaga
Osage
Oto
Ottawa
Paiute, Northern
Paiute, Southern
Palouse
Pamlico
Passamaquoddy
Patwin
Pawnee
Pennacook
Penobscot
Pequot
Petun
Pima
Pomo
Ponca
Poospatuck

Potawatomi
Powhatan Confederacy
Pueblo tribes, Eastern
Pueblo tribes, Western
Puyallup
Quapaw
Quechan
Quileute
Quinault
Salinan
Salish
Samish
Sanpoil-Nespelem
Sarsi
Sauk
Sekani
Semiahmoo
Seminole
Seneca
Seri
Serrano
Shasta
Shawnee
Shinnecock
Shoshone
Shuswap
Siletz
Sioux
Siuslaw
Skagit
Slave
Snohomish
Snoqualmie
Sooke
Spokane
Squamish
Suquamish
Susquehannock
Swallah
Tahltan
Tanaina
Tanana
Tenino
Thompson
Tillamook
Timucua
Tiou
Tlingit
Tohome

Tohono O'odham
Tolowa
Toltec
Tonkawa
Tsetsaut
Tsimshian
Tubatulabal
Tunica
Tuscarora
Tuskegee
Tutchone
Tutelo
Tututni
Twana
Tyigh
Umatilla
Umpqua
Ute
Waccamaw
Waco
Walapai
Walla Walla
Wampanoag
Wanapam
Wappinger
Wappo
Wasco
Washoe
Wenatchi
Wichita
Winnebago
Wintun
Wishram
Wiyot
Yahi
Yakima
Yamasee
Yana
Yaqui
Yaquina
Yavapai
Yazoo
Yellowknife
Yokuts
Yuchi
Yuki
Yurok
Zapotec